English Dictionaries 800–170

The Topical Tradition

Publisher's Acknowledgement

This book was originally commissioned for publication in the former series *Oxford Studies in Lexicography and Lexicology* under the series editorship of Richard W. Bailey, Noel Osselton, and Gabriele Stein, whose role in the conception and development of this book the publisher most gratefully acknowledges.

English Dictionaries 800–1700

The Topical Tradition

WERNER HÜLLEN

CLARENDON PRESS · OXFORD

OXFORD
UNIVERSITY PRESS

Great Clarendon Street, Oxford OX2 6DP

Oxford University Press is a department of the University of Oxford.
It furthers the University's objective of excellence in research, scholarship,
and education by publishing worldwide in

Oxford New York

Auckland Cape Town Dar es Salaam Hong Kong Karachi
Kuala Lumpur Madrid Melbourne Mexico City Nairobi
New Delhi Shanghai Taipei Toronto

With offices in

Argentina Austria Brazil Chile Czech Republic France Greece
Guatemala Hungary Italy Poland Portugal Singapore
South Korea Switzerland Thailand Turkey Ukraine Vietnam

Oxford is a registered trade mark of Oxford University Press
in the UK and certain other countries

Published in the United States
by Oxford University Press Inc., New York

British Library Cataloguing in Publication Data
Data available

Library of Congress Cataloging-in-Publication Data
Data available

Typeset by Cambrian Typesetters, Frimley, Surrey
Printed in Great Britain
on acid-free paper by
Biddles Ltd.
King's Lynn, Norfolk

ISBN 0-19-823796-0   978-0-823796-9
ISBN 0-19-929104-7 (Pbk.)   978-0-19-929104-5 (Pbk.)

1 3 5 7 9 10 8 6 4 2

To my wife, Marei,

and to our family, Bettina, Christopher, and Charlotte,
with Teresa and Tabea

ALICE. *N'avez-vous pas déjà oublié ce que je vous ai enseigné?*
KATHERINE. *Non, je réciterai à vous promptement: d'hand, de fingres, the mails,—*
ALICE. *De nails, madame.*
KATHERINE. *De nails, de arm, de ilbow.*
ALICE. *Sauf votre honneur, d'elbow.*
KATHERINE. *Ainsi dis-je; d'elbow, de nick, et de sin. Comment appelez-vous le pied et la robe?*
ALICE. *De foot, madame; et de coun.*

William Shakespeare, *Henry V,* III, iv, 37–46

Encyclopaedia *est scientiarum omnium systema, methodice conditum, et velutum* **Orbem redactum.**
Encyclopaedia *is the system of all sciences, based on method and laid out like the world itself.*

Johannes Amos Comenius, *Lexicon Reale Pansophicum,*
in: *Consultatio catholica* tom. II, col. 953

Contents

Figures

Tables

Preface

In 1989 I published my monograph on the Royal Society (Hüllen 1989), the last chapter of which, dealing with John Wilkins' universal language scheme, was entitled 'In search of the onomasiological alphabet' ('*Suche nach dem onomasiologischen Alphabet*'). It was then that I became interested in the phenomenon of the non-alphabetical arrangement of words, and since then I have been researching what I now call the topical (or onomasiological) tradition. The present book is the result of this work.

As is natural with a project lasting almost ten years, I presented provisional results and findings when called upon to read papers at conferences and to contribute to collected volumes and journals (see Bibliography). I acknowledge with thanks the permission given by publishers to use some of this material. As a rule, I do not give references to these papers in my book, unless there is a special reason for doing so.

As is also natural with a project lasting almost ten years, I discussed my topics, my queries, and my findings with many colleagues, with the students in my seminars between 1989 and 1993 (when I resigned from my teaching obligations), and with the members of the Henry Sweet Society, whose annual meetings I attended fairly regularly. Much of their advice and knowledge has gone into my deliberations. I cannot do otherwise than to thank all who helped me generously.

There are some colleagues, however, who deserve more than this. The late Vivien Law of Cambridge shared with me her knowledge of post-classical linguistics and medieval glosses. David Cram of Oxford made available to me his as yet unpublished check-list of nomenclators and classified vocabularies (Cram 1991b). Moreover, he read and commented on Chapter 8 of the book. Gabriele Stein (The Hon. Lady Quirk) of Heidelberg read a first version of the whole book and stimulated countless improvements. Jana Přívratská, of Prague, to whom I owe my introduction to the complex world of Comenian thought, read Chapter 10 of the book and, together with Vladimír Přívratsky, pointed out some of its original shortcomings. Finally, Richard Brunt of Essen went through this non-native author's English text with untiring attention and gave it its last linguistic touch. I thank them all for their generosity. It goes without saying that all shortcomings and blemishes of the book remain my own.

Most of my research work was done in several of the great European libraries. I wish to thank the German Research Association (*Deutsche Forschungsgemeinschaft*) for providing a travel grant which allowed me to carry out long-term work at the British Library, and I thank the research department of the Herzog August Bibliothek in Wolfenbüttel for a grant covering a three months' stay at this wonderful place for academic studies.

A book like the present one emerges slowly out of the masses of excerpts and notes produced and accumulated, copied and arranged over the years. It appears inevitable that, in the course of time, mistakes and errors should creep in. The use of a computer during the last five years of my work has done much to make at least note copying error proof. In order to render my quotations and statements verifiable for readers I have added the shelf-marks of the books I used. I have tried conscientiously to eradicate all inconsistencies, even when in the last phases of the actual writing of the text I no longer had a chance to go back to the sources in cases of doubt. I must ask my readers for indulgence towards what I have to say.

The manuscript was completed at the end of May 1998, the revision at the end of April 2005.

W. H.

Acknowledgements

The author would like to thank the following library and publishers for permission to use printed material:

Bayerische Staatsbibliothek, Munich, for *Inkunabel BSB Inc. c. a. 4° (Adam von Rotweil, Introito e porta)*.

John Benjamins, Amsterdam, for W. Hüllen, 'A close reading of William Caxton's "Dialogues . . . to lerne Shortly frenssh and englyssh"', in A. Jucker (ed.), *Historical pragmatics. Pragmatic developments in the history of English* (Amsterdam: Benjamins, 1995), 99–124.

Ecole Normale Supérieur de Fontenay/Saint-Cloud, for W. Hüllen, 'Women and their world in Withals' dictionary of 1553', in *Histoire Epistémologie Langage*, vol. 16, fasc. II, 1994, 191–212.

Nakladatelství Av Čr Academia, Prague, for pictures taken from Johannes Amos Comenius, *Opera Omnia*, vol. 17.

Gunter Narr Verlag, Tübingen, for W. Hüllen, 'Die semantische Komponente der Universalsprache von John Wilkins', in U. Hoinkes (ed.), *Panorama der Lexikalischen Semantik. Thematische Festschrift aus Anlaß ds 60. Geburtstags von Horst Geckeler* (Tübingen: Narr, 1995), 329–46.

Max Niemeyer Verlag, Tübingen, for W. Hüllen, 'Von Kopf bis Fuß. Das Vokabular zur Bezeichnung des menschlichen Körpers in zwei onomasiologischen Wörterbüchern des 16. und 17. Jahrhunderts', in W. Hüllen (ed.), *The World in a list of words* (Tübingen: Niemeyer, 1994), 105–22.

University of Exeter Press, Exeter, for W. Hüllen, 'In the beginning was the gloss', in G. James (ed.), *Lexicographers and Their Works* (Exeter: University of Exeter Press, 1989), 100–16.

University of Tampere, for W. Hüllen in cooperation with R. Haas, 'Adrianus Junius on the order of his *Nomenclator*', in H. Tommola *et al.*, *EURALEX '92 Proceedings I–II. Papers submitted to the Fifth International Euralex Congress on Lexicography in Tampere, August 4–9 1992*. [= Studia translatologica Ser. A. Vol. 2] (Tampere: Tampere University Press, 1992), II, 581–600.

Note on the text

Quotations reproduce the original texts as accurately as possible. All long 'S's have been changed into short ones. Where book titles or parts of texts were originally capitalized, the capitalization has only been retained in the first letter of each word. Varying sizes of fonts, decorative letters, ornaments, quotations, etc. on title pages have been ignored. Ends of lines have not been indicated.

All quotations of *foreign*-language text have been italicized. In this respect, Old English, Middle English, and Early Modern English have been treated as 'foreign'. This is why italics in original, mainly Early Modern English, texts could not be retained. There are only a few exceptions to this rule, and they are specifically pointed out.

Round brackets () are part of the quoted text. Square brackets [] indicate that I (W. H.) have changed the original either by explaining otherwise unintelligible references, or by expanding abbreviations. Exclamation marks in square brackets [!] have only been used if otherwise an error in reproduction, rather than in the original, could have been assumed. Errors and irregularities in the originals are not marked.

Whenever a letter in the original was illegible, a question mark has been inserted instead, even if a sensible solution for the reading problem was easily to be found. **Bold face** has sometimes been added to allow the reader a better overview of the quoted text. It is in no case part of the original.

The appendix contains a number of supplementary tables. Readers are not required to study them in order to understand the book, although they may find them helpful.

Abbreviations

BL	British Library, London
BSB	Bayerische Staatsbibliothek, Munich
DNB	Dictionary of National Biography
GöL	University Library, Göttingen
NL Praha	National Library, Prague
OED	The Oxford English Dictionary
PC	private copy
s.d.	*sine dato* (without year of publication)
s.l.	*sine loco* (without place of publication)
s.n.	*sine nomine* (without name of publisher)
STC	Short Title Catalogue
WF	Herzog August Bibliothek Wolfenbüttel

A. Opening the Topic

1

The onomasiological approach

1.1 Lexicographical practice and theory
1.2 Linguistic and encyclopaedic knowledge
1.3 Alphabetical order and topical order
1.4 The forgotten debate on onomasiology
1.5 The onomasiological dictionary as text

1.1 Lexicographical practice and theory

The history of science is, above all, the history of ideas. Ideas are the result of experience and reflection. Since they have been preserved and handed down to us in (manuscripts and) books, the history of science is always also a history of books. Moreover, depending on the specific nature of each scientific discipline, its history is additionally marked by relevant facts.[1] The history of physics, for example, is a history of documented ideas plus a history of experiments, including a history of tools and technical devices; the history of geography is a history of documented ideas plus a history of travelling experience, including a history of vehicles. The history of lexicography, being part of the history of linguistics, is marked by being dependent on a certain type of intellectual activity which demands a certain way of handling language, namely language teaching and learning (in the broadest sense).

There never was *lexicography* without word-lists and/or dictionaries,[2] but there were for a long time (and still are) word-lists and/or dictionaries without lexicography. Thus, lexicography has its *raison d'être* in a language-bound technique which preceded it in time and which may even today exist in its own right.

---

[1] For a more elaborate treatment of these interdependencies see Hüllen 1996a or 2002, 16–28, and 2005.

[2] It is with dictionaries as with elephants: everybody recognizes them at once, although it is quite difficult to define them according to genus, species, etc. I assume that every reader of this book knows what a dictionary is. See note 6. My discussion is limited to those aspects that lead to and explain the onomasiological approach. For a 'definition' of the term *dictionary* see Green 1997, 20–4.

Roughly speaking, this technique consisted and consists of listing words[3] in a certain order. Such word-lists[4] were and are of different sizes, varying from clusters of glosses, which merely fill part of an ordinary book page, to comprehensive many-volume works. In the past, they were often parts of books, for example, of grammars or dialogue books, now they are almost always a genre of their own. We cannot rule out the possibility that, under certain cultural circumstances, this listing of words was done orally. For example, before (and even a considerable time after) printing was invented, that is, during the centuries when the *ars memorativa* ruled intellectual life, it was common to memorize lists of words in a strict order which would today be laid down in a dictionary (Carruthers 1990, 16–45). Word-lists of liturgical litanies, which are meant for oral declamation, also have a certain affinity to secular word-lists. As a rule, however, word-lists attract our attention only in their written form. Their order is determined by the purpose(s) for which the words were listed. For languages which developed a writing system of letters, the alphabet was and is the most powerful order of this kind.

If we call *dictionary making* 'lexicographical practice' or 'lexicographical technique', we can call *lexicography* a theory which describes, pervades, and guides this practice. It is a subdiscipline of linguistics and shares basic assumptions about language with other subdisciplines of linguistics, in particular with phonetics and phonology, morphology, syntax, and lexical semantics. Although for many centuries lexicography in this sense did not exist, the compiling of word-lists and, in particular, the making of dictionaries were guided by principles which, when put into words, would have assumed the status of theoretical, that is, lexicographical, statements. To them belong such essential assumptions as 'words are self-contained semantic entities of a language' or 'words as names identify objects in the world'.[5] We may speak of a crypto-form of lexicography at the beginning and in the early centuries of lexicographical practice. It may often have worked unconsciously; sometimes we find traces of it in the prefaces of dictionaries. In particular during the nineteenth and twentieth centuries, it has developed into the analytical, fully grown, hypothesis-driven science we have today.[6] But even now-

---

[3] This general statement rules out dictionaries which list quotations, proverbs, routine formulae, or otherwise marked sentences as a particular dictionary type, although most of what follows also applies to them. It does, however, not rule out the listing of phrases (NP, VP, AdjP, AdvP, PP) or of embedded clauses after complementizers. They are entries of (head-)words with their special grammatical properties.

[4] I differentiate between *word* and *lexeme*, between *headword* and *lemma*. *Lexeme* and *lemma* are used in a more linguistically technical sense, in particular in connection with some lexicographical observation or procedure, *word* and *headword* in a more common sense.

[5] See Chapter 11, 439–42. For these early stages of lexicographical practice and their general neglect in theory see the introductions to Stein 1985 and 1997.

[6] See the annoted bibliography of Zgusta 1988. For comprehensive treatment see Householder and Saporta 1962; Zgusta 1971; Hausmann, Reichmann, Wiegand, and Zgusta 1989–91. For a more concise treatment see Landau 1984 and Béjoint 1994. Various collected volumes are given in Reichl 1993, 100–2. Moreover, there are journals, like *Dictionaries. Journal of the Dictionary Society of North America* (Terre Haute, IN), the *International Journal of Lexicography* (Oxford University Press), yearbooks, and

adays lexicographical practice can produce dictionaries without employing the corpus of knowledge which lexicography has accumulated in the meantime. Although linguists may choose to frown upon them, such freelance products can serve their purposes quite well and lexicographers cannot help but incorporate them into their deliberations *post festum*.

Generally speaking, lexicography is today regarded as the theoretical discipline that guides contemporary lexicographical practice. In this capacity it exploits three main sources: (i) linguistics in all those branches that determine what information about words is worth mentioning in a dictionary; (ii) research on the needs of dictionary users, determining the aims of dictionaries as a basis for ascertaining what they should be like in order to meet these needs; (iii) the history of lexicographical practice and its accompanying theory, which show the abundance of knowledge and of experience that has been collected in this field over the centuries.[7]

A fourth source will be mentioned later.

The most obvious purpose of dictionaries was and still is to explain what in one or several given language(s) is unfamiliar to common users and would otherwise remain unintelligible to them. This can pertain to foreign languages *in toto*, but also to foreign elements in one's own language such as old words, dialect words, words difficult to semanticize, words in an uncommon style, etc. Historically, this explains the early predominance in Europe of bilingual, that is, Latin and vernacular, dictionaries. They were followed by the bi-variety dictionary. This means that early (and indeed most of present-day) dictionaries served bilingualism, either inter- or intralingually. More generally speaking, it is the purpose of dictionaries to provide linguistic knowledge of any kind for the sake of correct and successful performance (of which there are many kinds). In pursuing this aim, dictionaries rely on one of the most essential properties of natural languages, namely, not only to refer to material and to mental reality on the object level but also to refer to themselves on a metalevel. Lexicographical technique is one very special way of explaining language with the help of language, as also happens, in a different way, in almost any conversation or written text.[8] This explanatory function can target all properties of words. The way in which this is done determines the so-called microstructure (see below) of dictionary entries. Best known are perhaps syntactic categorization, such as word-classes or subcategorization, and semantic glosses, usually done by definition, paraphrase, or quotation. But, depending on the complexity of the microstructure, spelling,

book series, like *Lexicographica. International Annual for Lexicography . . ., Lexicographica Series major* (both Tübingen: Niemeyer), as well as the proceedings of regular conferences, for example of the Euralex group. In general, I refrain from referring to publications which are mentioned in Zgusta 1988, unless there are compelling reasons to do so (e.g. historical impact, quotation).

  [7] Sources (i) and, in particular, (iii) will be discussed in this book, whereas source (ii) however will be almost totally ignored. For general information see Béjoint 1994.
  [8] See de Beaugrande and Dressler 1981, *passim*.

pronunciation, stylistic marking, idiomatic usage, and other properties may be mentioned as well. Explanation of the unfamiliar, as the general purpose of dictionaries, even bridges the otherwise important dichotomy between bi- or multilingual dictionaries on the one hand and monolingual ones[9] on the other. In achieving this aim, they are of equal status, although the degree of foreignness is much higher in the first than in the second dictionary type.

Explaining foreign languages or areas of native languages which remain foreign, that is, unintelligible, to the common speaker and writer has given the dictionary for most of its history a mediating position for language use. As a rule, dictionaries have no ends in themselves, neither scholarly nor practical. They serve language-in-performance by providing linguistic[10] knowledge (see below). Only late in the history of the genre, that is, in the nineteenth century, were dictionaries compiled with the primary aim of documenting the total vocabulary of a national language. The ambitious works well known by the names of James Murray in Britain, the brothers Grimm in Germany, Paul Robert in France, and that of other lexicographers in almost every major European[11] language have, in the meantime, all outgrown their beginnings and are at present gigantic undertakings administered by whole teams of experts. But they are still a special dictionary type. They are meant as an aid for language users on a broad national scale, more than in their everyday performance.[12] Dictionaries outside the documentary type were and still are regularly compiled to facilitate the solution of communicative problems in practice.

On the one hand, this gives dictionaries a somewhat subordinate status. On the other, it makes them an integral part of culture. Language performance is the process by which almost all cultural activities proceed. The features of these activities determine the features of the language used and they, in turn, determine the features of dictionaries. The reverse is also true: the features of a language, as they appear in dictionaries, determine the features of cultural activities. The accepted

---

[9] Monolingual dictionaries for learning a foreign language are a recent development in lexicography, which however do not pose principally different problems. They rest on the assumption that, fairly early in the process of learning, learners reach a state of knowledge in which the foreign language can be made intelligible to them by the foreign language itself.

[10] Linguistic knowledge is everybody's knowledge pertaining to one language, several languages, or language in general. It is not knowledge in the sense of (scholarly) linguistics, though this can be part of linguistic knowledge as well. I do not assume a difference in principle between common linguistic knowledge and expert linguistic knowledge. They just differ in their degree of analysity and formality. Most of all, this applies to the faulty distinction between so-called linguistic and so-called communicative competence. See also below.

[11] As the scope of this book is limited to English dictionaries and to the European tradition they are embedded in, I am speaking only of European languages. It goes without saying that the languages of other continents have their own lexicographical traditions and that they are all worthy of scholarly attention. See also Chapter 2.

[12] The examples given by names of authors refer to dictionaries of total (national) languages. There are also documentary dictionaries of limited areas of vocabulary like the terminology of some academic disciplines, slang, etc. Of course, documentary dictionaries can be used as works of reference, that is, as other dictionaries are used. Concise editions, such as exist of the *OED* or of *Larousse*, were certainly planned to encourage this.

value of Homer's epics gave rise to dictionaries of poetic language. The wide use of Latin during the Middle Ages made Latin dictionaries necessary, just as the growing awareness of vernaculars stimulated the mass of bilingual and multilingual dictionaries after the Latin period.[13] Science and technology led to scientific and technological dictionaries. Intellectuals, travellers, merchants, noblemen and politicians, the military—they all had and have their own linguistic needs and, consequently, their own dictionaries. Once extant, all these dictionaries have their repercussions on the very activities that brought them forth. Dictionaries are like webs which spiders produce and by which they provide, form, and delimit their own ways of living.[14]

This is why the history of lexicographical practice and theory as one of the three sources of present-day lexicography is also part of the general history of ideas, and the historiography of lexicography is not just subservient to dictionary making, past and present. It is a particularly promising access to researching our intellectual history in so far as it is bound to language. We may even say that, in the course of the centuries, a dictionary culture of its own has emerged in most European languages as part of general culture and is just as worthy of research as the latter. Like all culture, it is made up of ideas. But in this case, ideas are ultimately incorporated into the universally adopted technique of listing words.

1.2 Linguistic and encyclopaedic knowledge

Linguistic knowledge can attain different degrees of abstraction, from local rules which are needed to overcome sources of trouble in performance to global rules which are valid for the generative mechanism of a whole linguistic system. In their entries, dictionaries provide this knowledge in application, that is, on a rather low level of abstraction, although, in order to do this, they employ highly abstract knowledge which the dictionary user must understand or at least be able to work with. For example, word-classes, syntactic categorization, the subcategorization of verbs, semantic networks, or register marking constitute such abstract linguistic knowledge. It depends largely on the language users themselves how much of this abstract linguistic knowledge they understand.[15] The ultimate intention of dictionary use, however, is quite limited.

Thus, dictionaries employ and, at the same time, create on various levels linguistic knowledge to help users to overcome difficulties in their language performance. But for this very purpose they also need and use encyclopaedic knowledge.

---

[13] See Chapter 9.

[14] This is a metaphor which Humboldt used for language generally. See *Werke* 1968 (1906), vol. 5, 387–8.

[15] I do not use *langue* and *parole* for this differentiation because I do not think that the terms are valid. I do not use the dichotomy *competence* vs. *performance* either, for the same reason. The word *performance*, as I use it, lies outside the Chomskyan model.

Clarifying the meanings of the words of a foreign language and also, in a different way, of a native language is probably the oldest, certainly one of the most important and the most popular, purposes that dictionaries have. For many people, this is the only reason for using one. For the average dictionary user it is probably important whether dictionaries gloss their headwords in the same language or in a different language, that is, by translation. But, lexicographically speaking, the difference between monolingual and bi- or multilingual dictionaries is not so great as it may appear, because they use the same techniques of semanticizing, with or without translation. Depending on the microstructure of entries, either the clarification of a lexeme is done by using it in a syntagma in the form of a definition or a paraphrase or a sample sentence, which frequently is a quotation or an utterance taken from a corpus. In this case the assumption is that the sense of the syntagma will help to narrow down and finally identify the meaning of one of its own lexemes. Or it is done by the juxtaposition of a synonym, a hyponym or hyperonym, the negative form of an antonym, or another type of lexeme which bears a fixed semantic relation to the lemma. In this case the assumption is that the relationships of meanings within a fairly closed set of lexemes help (again) to narrow down and finally identify the meaning of one of its members. Of course, the techniques can be combined. Experience, however, shows that these ways of semanticizing, and possible others like illustration or using, for example chemical, formulae, always employ more knowledge than is indicated in the explanatory lexemes themselves. This is universal background knowledge, which in fact is indispensable for any kind of semantic explanation, also outside dictionaries. Individuals gather it from everyday experience, of which language education and professional training are a part. If we understand the term *encyclopaedia* to signify a corpus of knowledge which is universal, including items from the very general to the highly specific, and which is rather loosely, that is, according to expert standards not scientifically,[16] ordered, it makes sense to call this general background knowledge *encyclopaedic*.

The meanings which are denoted by a lexeme are part of our linguistic knowledge. The semantic presuppositions which we must know in order to understand the linguistic knowledge as meaningful are our encyclopaedic knowledge. There are almost no words in a natural language which could be grasped without the background of such encyclopaedic knowledge.[17]

---

[16] This definition does not agree with *encyclopaedia* as used, for example, in the sixteenth and seventeenth centuries, although there are overlapping areas of meaning. At that time the word was a name for general scientific thought which integrated most of the disciplines which we are today accustomed to think of as sciences with a modular independence, in particular in method. See contributions in 'Encyclopédies et civilisations. Encyclopedias and civilizations. Enciclopedias y civilizationes', *Cahiers d'Histoire Mondiale, Journal of World History, Cuadernos de Historia Mundial* 1966 (Commission internationale . . . 1966). See also Chapter 11.

[17] An exception may be numerals, which could be said to have only linguistic meanings. But, for example, the notions 'low number', 'normal number', 'high number' are also part of the meanings of numerals, and they can only be identified by comparison with a world in which certain objects are

It is very difficult, and a cause of endless debates, to clearly differentiate between the two.[18] Among other reasons, this is so because for any item of encyclopaedic knowledge the language, usually, provides a lexeme. So every piece of encyclopaedic knowledge can be turned into linguistic knowledge. This is indeed done as soon as encyclopaedic knowledge is made explicit in language. But then it needs different items of encyclopaedic knowledge itself in order to be understood. It depends on the context whether an item of knowledge is linguistic or encyclopaedic. Note the following example:

Academic is used . . . to describe work done in schools, colleges, and universities, especially work that involves studying and reasoning rather than practical or technical skills. (*Collins Cobuild English Language Dictionary*.)

This definition implies encyclopaedic knowledge about the British system of educational institutions with its inherent ranking (schools, colleges, universities). It also implies encyclopaedic knowledge about the dichotomy theoretical vs. practical work in modern societies, which educational institutions try to match. Theory goes together with books ('studying') and brain work ('reasoning'), which both have their own kind of social status; practice goes together with arts and crafts and the special abilities in handling them ('skill'), which again have their own kind of social status. All these meanings are not contained in the denotation of *academic*, but they are necessary for it to be understood. In order to show this and give them a name, we have turned encyclopaedic knowledge into linguistic knowledge.

If encyclopaedic knowledge is the background to every kind of linguistic knowledge, dictionaries will convey the latter only if they also provide the former.[19]

It is in the nature of encyclopaedic knowledge that it can be provided in widely differing quantities, but perhaps never totally. Lexicographically, we can imagine a scale with two extremes. At the one end are dictionaries which merely presuppose a minimum of encyclopaedic knowledge, trusting that users will add whatever is necessary of their own accord. At the other end are dictionaries whose authors focus equally on encyclopaedic and on linguistic knowledge. These latter dictionaries mark the borderline between dictionaries and encyclopaedias, which *in concreto*, however, it is very difficult to draw.

In fact, since the eighteenth century the history of dictionaries in all widely used languages has included the *encyclopaedic dictionary*, which by using definitions,

rare, common, numerous, etc., which certainly depends on encyclopaedic knowledge: 'The car costs (only) one thousand pounds'; 'He has a collection of (as many as) one thousand dictionaries in his library'.

[18] See Cruse 1986, and for a distinction between a minimalist, an intermediate, and a maximalist position in defining encyclopaedic knowledge, Cruse 1988. See also Béjoint 1994, 18–23.

[19] The general habit of listing proper names, geographical or historical names, etc. in appendices but not in the main body of the dictionary has its systematic justification perhaps in the fact that in these cases a distinction between linguistic and encyclopaedic meanings can hardly be made.

pictures, charts, logical stemmata, etc. unfolds the basic stock of knowledge necessary to understand word-meanings. Such dictionaries are not only helpful for
people seeking linguistic information but also for the general education of all.
Encyclopaedic dictionaries shade into encyclopaedias proper which are meant to
present the sum total of the knowledge of their time[20] and which have only this in
common with dictionaries: that their articles are attached to headwords arranged
alphabetically. The European Enlightenment with its cult of education for everybody initiated the period of encyclopaedias which is still with us and whose
national masterpieces, for example in Britain, France, and Germany are well
known. But even at the beginning of Northern European culture we find Isidore of
Seville's (*c.*560–636) *Etymologiae*, a listing of items worthy of being known at the
time, arranged non-alphabetically (except book X on man) according to headwords. They treat the liberal arts (books I–III), medicine (IV), law (V), theology
(VI–VIII), languages and social groups (IX), natural sciences (XI–XIV), and what
could be called *civilization* (XV–XX).[21]

The common definition is that dictionaries explain language, whereas encyclopaedias explain subject-matter. It is a perfectly valid one but difficult to
handle concretely, because subject-matter can only be expressed in language, and
it is a legacy of European thinking that the knowledge of subject-matter is broken
down into units which can be tagged with a (head-)word functioning as a general
term. Encyclopaedias are content-oriented books which use the techniques of
language-oriented dictionaries.

All lexicographical debates on the dichotomy encyclopaedic dictionary vs.
language dictionary agree that no exact dividing line can be drawn. As a rule, a
general affinity between the two is noticed (e.g. Béjoint 1994, 31). It is the weight that
is given to details which distinguishes the two. Encyclopaedic dictionaries are more
interested in factual information, which includes a preponderance of nouns with
precise meanings, of special language, and even proper names. Language dictionaries are more interested in communication about factual information, which
includes a strong interest in adjectives and verbs and, in particular, in lexemes which
carry an abundance of different, frequently imprecise, meanings. Encyclopaedic
dictionaries are not really interested in grammatical information and they are not
meant to provide it. Therefore they tend to neglect structure words, whereas
language dictionaries almost always treat them with particular care.[22]

All dictionaries, not only the encyclopaedic type, contain encyclopaedic knowledge more or less openly. Of course, it is scattered throughout the alphabetical

---

[20]   This statement is also valid for encyclopaedias covering only a limited area of knowledge such
as, for example, horse breeding, linguistics, or health care. By definition, they try to be exhaustive
within their limits.

[21]   See Chapter 11, 435–9.

[22]   There is an extensive discussion of this problem in Hupka 1989, 24–39, 146–8. For representatives of lexicography who stress the common properties of the two dictionary types rather than their
differences see, among others, Quirk 1982.

entries. It gives the dictionary as a whole a backgrounding semantic world-view which may be difficult to filter out and to understand as a cohesive network of meanings. Alphabetical dictionaries mirror the encyclopaedic knowledge, that is, the culture, of their time in the way in which a shattered looking-glass mirrors the surrounding world. It is, nevertheless, the fourth source from which lexicography takes its ideas for a treatment of dictionaries, present-day and historical.

1.3 Alphabetical order and topical order

For languages with a writing system of letters, the most common *macrostructure* of dictionaries is the one according to the alphabet. It has its disadvantages. For example, it separates words which morphologically and semantically belong together. *Creatine* is placed between *create* and *creation, credenza* between *credential* and *credibility*. But it has the great advantage that an order of headwords is possible which allows no exception. This is an almost indispensable prerequisite of usability.

As basic as the vertical alphabetical order of macrostructure is the linear order of *microstructure*. The microstructures vary considerably, but they have in common that the unfamiliar word, the *explanandum*, is in the leftmost position, whereas all kinds of familiar, explaining words, *explanantia*, follow to the right. In linear arrangement, the lemma is complemented by one or several explanation(s) like phonetic transcription, translation, synonym, definition, etc. As, in European culture, reading like writing moves from left to right, this arrangement guarantees that the dictionary user is led from the unfamiliar to the familiar, which, as stated earlier, is the overall purpose of dictionaries.

Although this seems the only sensible thing to do, the linear arrangement places a heavy burden on dictionary users. It presupposes that they know at least from the spelling what they do not know in other respects, namely, phonetically, semantically, stylistically, etc. If this is not the case, alphabetical dictionaries of the *explanandum–explanantia* type are of no value, at least in principle.

In fact, this arrangement has served and still serves one special type of linguistic performer and dictionary user. It is the translators of a foreign-language text who find a word before their eyes or hear it spoken in their ears but do not understand it. In terms of communication theory we can say that alphabetical dictionaries serve the needs of a receiver of a linguistic message. As always in the lexicographical context, *foreign* is to be understood in the narrow sense of a non-native language, but also in the wider sense of, for example, a hard word in one's own language which needs explanation.[23]

---

[23] *Translator* has the same expanded meaning, that is, translation operates interlingually as well as intralingually. In Hüllen 1990a I showed that the beginnings of English monolingual lexicography in so-called *hard word dictionaries* treated English as if it were two languages, an easy (native) and a hard (foreign) one.

Historically speaking, reading a text in a foreign (in fact the Latin) language was indeed the first default situation which urgently needed repair. Monks were studying such codices and needed translation aids. This set going the production of glossaries and then dictionaries which semanticized a Latin lexeme with a vernacular one.[24] This type, in turn, stimulated the entire development of dictionary production in Europe, which was, consequently, geared to the necessities of a translatory, that is receptive, handling of foreign languages.[25]

For the so-called productive handling of a foreign language or foreign elements of one's own language, that is, for writing a text or preparing a speech, the dictionary which moves from the unfamiliar to the familiar element is of no use, at least not in its original simple form. With the elaboration of dictionary types and the augmentation of entries, this first inbuilt deficiency has been at least partly rectified today. Among these developments we count, above all, the fact that bilingual dictionaries were doubled, because dictionaries that juxtapose a foreign language with a native one (e.g. Latin–English or French–English) have regularly been complemented by dictionaries that juxtapose a native language with a foreign one (English–Latin or English–French). As a result, users can start with the known lexeme of their own language and then look up the foreign one. However, this solution has its price (not only in the monetary sense). As almost every word of a natural language is polysemous, starting from the native-language lexeme leads right away into the undergrowth of synonyms and multiple meanings which demands double and triple checking across the two languages. With their enormous and often unreadable complexity, present-day dictionary entries pay tribute to this problem and sometimes cause as many errors as they solve.

There are other dictionary types which combine alphabetical order with some other kind of arrangement. In them headwords are given according to the alphabet, complemented by synonyms, antonyms, or other lexemes with clear semantic relations to these keywords. Whatever their order is, it is not alphabetical.[26] Synonyms may be explained by the differences between their meanings, or they may be simply enumerated cumulatively. Besides synonyms, the lexemes of a semantic domain can find their place under such headwords. This arrangement follows the assumption that people in search of unknown words have some general or vague notion of what they are looking for and can start from this. The alphabetical order leads them easily to well-known lexemes which function as signposts to those unknown lexemes which the dictionary user, when producing a text, needs. In fact, having some general or vague notion relies heavily on encyclopaedic knowledge, which, consequently, is the basis for using such dictionaries of synonyms to an even greater extent than alphabetical ones. Even more

---

[24]   See Chapter 3.

[25]   I use the terms *receptive* and *productive* in their common and traditional meanings. They should not be understood as distinct psychological terms.

[26]   See, below, the discussion on pragmatics. There are some exceptions to this rule. Names of the genera of trees can, for example, be given alphabetically under the headword *tree*.

radical is an arrangement which does away with the alphabet altogether and orders the entries of a dictionary *in toto* according to the presumed encyclopaedic knowledge of its users. It is the *topical* (*thematic* or *conceptual* or *ideographical* or *onomasiological*) dictionary.[27] Their authors assume that people preparing a text productively know *what* to say (if only vaguely), but they do not know *how* to say it. They need a dictionary which helps them find words expressive of the contents which they have in their minds. This reverses the linear order of dictionaries, their microstructure, and makes the alphabetical vertical order, their macrostructure, useless.

In a topical dictionary the left-hand position is given to the familiar word, the *explanantium*, which is juxtaposed by unfamiliar ones, *explananda*, in the right-hand position. This means that headwords (or keywords[28]) are used to express familiar meanings, either in the native language of the dictionary user or in a foreign language. They are general terms, prototypical names of classes of objects, tags for semantic domains,[29] formal expressions which allow concretizations, nodes in semantic networks, etc.—in short, anything that can stand for one other or many other (or a group/class of) lexicalized meanings. Of course, even such keywords and headwords can only appear in the shape of lexemes. However, they must not be misunderstood as the lexemes of a language, they must be taken as formal linguistic means representing a meaning. In some cases, they are supposed to stand for meanings which are language independent, that is, which can be expressed in any language of the world, or for meanings which are typical of a large number of languages, for example the Indo-European group. It depends on the training of dictionary users whether they grasp the distinction between the language-specific form and the language-independent meaning of the lexeme in the leftmost position.[30] Even if untrained users do not, they will still find the dictionary useful when they move from an easily understood lexeme with a

---

[27] For topical dictionaries, the term *thesaurus* has been made popular by *Roget's Thesaurus*. In principle, there are no lexicographical differences between a topical dictionary and a thesaurus. *Onomasiological* is the more scientific term and refers to the linguistic background compared to the rather general term *topical*. The same relation applies between *semasiological* compared to *alphabetical*. McArthur 1986a uses the term *thematic dictionary*. See also below.

[28] The difference between *headwords* and *keywords* is one of semantic range. Keywords tag large numbers of lexemes belonging to one semantic domain, headwords introduce semantically more narrow entries. With reference to dictionaries of synonyms, the term *keyword* will in most cases be appropriate, with reference to other alphabetical and non-alphabetical dictionaries the term is *headword*. Admittedly, there are cases where it is difficult to draw a clear line between the two.

[29] *Semantic domains* are groups of lexemes whose affinity in meanings is occasioned by the natural co-occurence of referents and senses (things and concepts) in real-life situations. They may belong to all word-classes. The term is similar to, but not identical with, *word-field*, in which, as a rule, lexemes belong to one word-class. See also below.

[30] Strictly speaking, topical dictionaries have no headwords but *head-forms* as linguistic dummies for their meanings. Admittedly, a highly developed linguistic awareness is needed to keep this difference in mind when using a topical dictionary. Hence the humorous criticism that in order to work with such dictionaries you must be so highly educated that you do not need to consult a dictionary at all.

general meaning in the left-hand position to more specialized lexemes hitherto unknown in the right-hand one. Sometimes the headword is replaced by a picture or some other kind of visualization. The lexemes, the *explananda*, in the right-hand position, understood to be in juxtaposition to the linguistic forms, the *explanantia*, in the left-hand position, are of the same kinds as found in the right-hand position of alphabetical dictionaries. They are synonyms, given with distinctive definitions or cumulatively, antonyms, hyponyms and hyperonyms, definitions, paraphrases, quotations, etc. Practice shows that topical dictionaries, almost exclusively, concentrate on semantic glossings and neglect other linguistic information.

The question remains of what takes the place of the alphabet, that is, what the macrostructure of topical dictionaries is like. As a rule, a systematic arrangement of topics is selected which is derived in a popularized form from some scientific system, or a semantic classification which can be expected to be generally understood. Unavoidably, the order of a topical dictionary is dependent on a certain philosophical understanding of the world, although it must remain commonly intelligble. This is why such dictionaries are liable to religious, ideological, political, scientific, or otherwise predetermined world-views. Their macrostructure is semantic, in opposition to the formalism of the alphabet, and its semantic substance is filled with encyclopaedic knowledge. Whereas in the alphabetical dictionary this knowledge is scattered in the background, it occupies the foreground in topical dictionaries and is, moreover, systematized.

Note, for example, the following overview (from the *Longman Lexicon of Contemporary English*):

A	Life and Living Things
B	The Body; Its Functions and Welfare
C	People and the Family
D	Buildings, Houses, the Home, Clothes, Belongings, and Personal Care
E	Food, Drink, and Farming
F	Feelings, Emotions, Attitudes, and Sensations
G	Thought and Communication, Language and Grammar
H	Substances, Materials, Objects, and Equipment
I	Arts and Crafts, Science and Technology, Industry and Education
J	Numbers, Measurement, Money, and Commerce
K	Entertainment, Sports, and Games
L	Space and Time
M	Movement, Location, Travel and Transport
N	General and Abstract Terms

These fourteen chapters are subdivided into 128 subchapters.

Topically determined chapters of this kind constitute semantic areas with many words which have adjacent meanings. Stable relations as defined in structural semantics, such as opposition, contrast, hyponymy, hierarchical structure, or part-whole, and formalized differences as expressed by semantic markers occur again and again. However, these formal devices are used according to practical feasibility. There is no dictionary in existence which organizes its vocabulary entirely according to abstract semantic relations or to the system of semantic markers. The encyclopaedic order is essentially different from such strictly hierarchical systems (Hüllen 1989, 204–5).

All this means that topical dictionaries are organized according to the semantic structure of a whole language, which, however, depends on the structure of reality as language users believe they understand it at a given time.

Of course, it requires some routine for dictionary users to handle such systems. Some ingenious typographical devices like indenting or bracketing have been introduced to help. The most elaborate help is, of course, an additional alphabetical register which indicates the (sub)chapter where a lexeme can be found.[31]

Topical dictionaries help users in finding words or the synonyms and antonyms of words or stylistic variants. They provide the basic vocabulary within a semantic domain, or within cognitive frames which may be parts of larger cognitive schemata. As many semantically related words are presented side by side, they can augment the power of expression and also the sense of logic of their users. Certainly, they help in spreading encyclopaedic knowledge. Whereas alphabetical dictionaries use this kind of knowledge only as a tool for defining linguistic knowledge, topical dictionaries make it their organizing principle and, thus, give encyclopaedic knowledge a much higher rank. Quite often, the authors of these dictionaries seem to be enchanted by the inherent systematicity of their semantic organization and are lured into a perfection and exhaustiveness which overshoots lexicographical purposes. Here, again, the borderline between a dictionary and an encyclopaedia is reached.

The alphabetical dictionary of synonyms, mentioned above, halts, as it were, halfway between the alphabetical and the topical. It combines a formal, that is alphabetical, macrostructure with a semantic microstructure. This semantic microstructure is a calque of the semantic macrostructure of topical dictionaries.

The most important consequence of these deliberations is that the topical dictionary, which, historically speaking, precedes the alphabetical one (McArthur 1986a), deviates, as mentioned above, from the *explanandum–explanantia* pattern which mirrors the general function of dictionaries, namely, explaining what is unfamiliar in a language. It does not equate an unknown linguistic form with a known one, rather it turns general (or vague) encyclopaedic knowledge into concrete (or more precise) linguistic knowledge. It presupposes language-bound encyclopaedic knowledge and, for the sake of language use, upgrades it into a linguistic one. Speaking in terms of communication theory we may say that topical dictionaries serve the needs of a sender of a linguistic message.

---

[31] See, however, below.

1.4 The forgotten debate on onomasiology

Scholarly attention was devoted to the difference between alphabetical and topical dictionaries in a long-drawn-out debate during the first half of the twentieth
century, in which German, French, and Swiss linguists were perhaps more actively
engaged than British. German linguists who devoted themselves to their own
language or to the Romance languages were more numerous among them than
Anglicists. However, it was an English publication, namely *Roget's Thesaurus*, first
published in 1852, which stimulated the debate more than others. At that time, the
term *semasiological* for the alphabetical dictionary and *onomasiological* for the
topical type came into use.[32] In French, the words *analogue* and *idéologique* were
(and still are) preferred. In the countries of the former Eastern bloc linguists
spoke (and still speak) of *thematic* dictionaries (Burkhanov 1995).[33] The terms
indicate that not external criteria like the arrangement of entries but a certain attitude towards the relation between meaning and form in language determine the
non-alphabetical type of dictionaries. In fact, it is the assumed priority of meaning over form (*Bedeutung* as expressed in *onoma* or *idea* as expressed in
idéologique, contrary to *sign* as expressed in *sema*) which provides the essential
criterion.

The immediate cause of the debate lay in the criticism which linguists around
the turn of the century levelled against the older generation, the so-called
Neogrammarians (*Junggrammatiker*). It focused on this criticism and, at the same
time, centred on problems which had been well known for a long time and which,
for example, Gottfried Wilhelm Leibniz (1646–1716) had already described in his
'*Unvorgreifliche Gedanken*' (produced 1696–7) with unsurpassable precision:

*Ehe ich den Punct des Reichthums der Sprache beschließe, so will ich erwähnen, daß die Worte
oder die Benennung aller Dinge und Verrichtungen auf zweyerley Weise in ein Register zu
bringen, nach dem Alphabet und nach der Natur. / Die erste Weise ist der Lexicorum oder
Deutungs-Bücher, und am meisten gebräuchlich. Die andere Weise ist der Nomenclatoren,
oder Nam-Bücher, und geht nach den Classen, Sorten der Dinge ... Die Deutungs-Bücher
dienen eigentlich, wenn man wissen will, was ein vorgegebenes Wort bedeute, und die Nam-
Bücher, wie eine vorgegebene Sache zu nennen. Jene gehen von dem Worte zur Sache, diese von
der Sache zum Wort.*[34]   (1966, I, 475–6.)

---

[32]   Christian K. Reisig used the term *Semasiologie, semasiologisch* for the first time in his lectures
on Latin philology in 1825 (Davies 1998, 311–14). A. Zauner used the term *Onomasiologie, onomasiolo-
gisch* for the first time in his paper on the names of parts of the human body in Romance languages in
Romanische Forschungen in 1903.

[33]   See the relevant entries ('analogical', 'ideographic', 'onomasiological', 'semasiological', 'thematic',
'systematical', etc.), in Burkhanov 1998.

[34]   'Before I close the topic "wealth of language", let me mention that the words or names of all
things and actions [can] be brought into a list in two different ways, according to the alphabet and
according to nature. The first way is that of dictionaries or explaining books, and the most popular.
The other way is that of nomenclators or naming books, and follows the classes and kinds of things.

For Leibniz, the pairing of *matter* ('content', 'message') and *word* ('form') obviously posed no problems. He does not provide examples of dictionaries 'according to the alphabet'. But for those 'according to nature' he refers to the great examples of the sixteenth and seventeenth centuries, for example to Stephanus Doletus (Étienne Dolet, 1509–46), Hadrianus Junius (1511–75), Nicodemus Frischlin (1547–90), and Francesco Alunno (Francesco del Bailo, 1485–1556).

There are also statements which show that the ideas which Leibniz expresses in this paragraph were well known in England at that time. Note, for example the debate on universal languages:

> Here again I was at a stand what method of many that offered themselves to follow, whether: 1. the Alphabetical order of the words, or 2. if I should distribute them under certaine commone Heads as Junius in his *Nomenclature* and Comenius in his *Janua Ling[uarum]*.[35]

Moreover note the way in which John Wilkins explains the difference between his 'Philosophical Tables' and the alphabetical dictionary appended to his *Essay* (1668): 'The Design of the Philosophical Tables is to enumerate and describe all kinds of *Things* and *Notions*: And the Design of this Dictionary, is to reckon up and explain all kinds of *words*, or *names* of things.'[36]

In the twentieth-century debate, the pairing of *matter* and *word* was in obvious need of reformulation, because the Neogrammarians had, in the eyes of their followers, reduced language to sound structures and morphological paradigms. This was the price they had paid for their widely acknowledged merits, the formal presentation of interrelationships within the family of Indo-European languages, and the ordering of language change with the help of laws of sound. Both merits had given two linguistic subdisciplines of long standing a new scientific start, namely language comparison and etymology (Malkiel 1993). In addition, a perfection of methods used in the editing of old texts developed which had been hitherto unknown.

The new linguists claimed for historical linguistics what we would today call *semantics*, in particular the *referential function*. Rudolf Mehringer (1909) gave this movement the name *Wörter und Sachen* ('words and matter'), which was adopted for an influential journal after his seminal paper. He explained that the findings of archaeology and ethnology were an essential precondition for all historical linguistics. Without them no statements about language change or the etymology of words could be made. According to Mehringer, language is dependent on

... The explaining books help if somebody wants to know what is the meaning of a given word, the naming books [help with] what to call a given thing. The former go from the word to the thing, the latter from the thing to the word.' (My translation, W. H. This translation, like all *ad hoc* translations in this book, is meant to convey only the meaning of the original text and may, consequently, contain un-idiomatic English.)

[35] Dalgarno 'The autobiographical treatise' (2001, 354). I thank David Cram and Jaap Maat for drawing my attention to this text. See also Chapter 8, 247–50.

[36] Wilkins 1668: 'An Advertisement to the Reader', n.p. See also Chapter 8.

culture and, consequently, historical linguistics is dependent on cultural history. Moreover, the similarities between the Indo-European languages were not to be understood as merely morphological and sound based, but as a network of facts and ideas.[37]

What Mehringer claimed for historical linguistics, Titkin (1910) claimed for synchronic linguistics when he demanded that the lexicographer should question, for example, the bell founder in order to ensure the correctness of the relevant entries for bells in a dictionary. Thus, the onomasiological principle, that of the primacy of matter, of pre-linguistic meaning, over words, was claimed for linguistic work in general. It was pointed out that former analyses had unwittingly relied on it. Such had been the case, for example, in Delbrück's research on the Indo-European names for family relationships (1889), which presupposed these relationships before giving names to them, and in Dietz's research on the development of Romance vocabulary from Latin (1875), which had indeed been arranged in topical word-lists. Many scholarly activities in the fields of word geography, dialectology, stylistics, and language change came into being and became the core of philology at the beginning of the new century. The methods of field-work laid down for language atlases also derived linguistic insights from presupposed factual knowledge.

This discussion in the first half of the twentieth century has been excellently covered by the Swiss linguist Bruno Quadri (1952). He interprets the change from *Wörter und Sachen* to *Wörter und Ideen* as an extension of the onomasiological principle from the primacy of the objective to the primacy of the mental world. It is to be found in the early Saussure reception in which the structure of a language (*langue*) was understood very much in the same way in which Humboldt had defined the dependence of language on culture. Leo Weisgerber (1927) and Jost Trier (1931) developed their concepts of the word-field (*Wortfeld*)[38] and of language as a mediating semiotic system (*sprachliche Zwischenwelt*). Stephen Ullmann mentioned its 'outstanding importance' as a Neo-Humboldtian school of linguistics (Ullmann 1962, 250). Less known but worth discussing are the deliberations on

---

[37]   See also Mehringer 1912, 22: '*Mit vielen anderen sind wir überzeugt, daß Sprachwissenschaft nur ein Teil der Kulturwissenschaft ist, daß die Sprachgeschichte zur Worterklärung der Sachgeschichte bedarf, sowie[!] die Sachgeschichte, wenigstens für die ältesten Zeiten, der Sprachgeschichte nicht entraten kann. Wir glauben, daß in der Vereinigung von Sprachwissenschaft und Sachwissenschaft die Zukunft der Kulturgeschichte liegt.*' 'With many others we are convinced that linguistics is only part of the cultural sciences, that the history of language is in need of the history of things in order to explain the meanings of words, in the same way in which the history of things cannot do without the history of language, at least for ancient times. We believe that the future of cultural history lies in the union of linguistics and the cultural sciences.' (My translation, W. H.) The linguistic movement and its cover-term gained quite an international reputation. There is, for example, an entry *Wörter und Sachen* in the *OED* (Supplement). Unfortunately, the important German journal succumbed to political pressure after 1933, and was no longer edited by Rudolf Mehringer but by Walter Wüst.

[38]   In fact, G. Ipsen coined the term. It gained considerable, although rather vague, international popularity, perhaps more than any other German linguistic term of the first half of the twentieth century. For the history of the term and its various meanings see Herbermann 1996. For the most recent analysis and definitions see Lutzeier 1981 and 1993.

conceptual nuclei (*Begriffskerne*) as mental correlates of words by Karl Jaberg (1937). The conceptual nuclei are conceived as language independent and serving to explain the word-store of languages, not the other way round. As regards real objects, however, Jaberg also subscribed to the opinion that things shed more light on language than language does on things.

The onomasiological debate, as reported by Quadri, was not exclusively devoted to lexicography. We could perhaps call it *semiotic*, because it pertained to the epistemological access to semantics. But there was always a close proximity to lexicography. It linked up with an existing debate on the dictionary of synonyms. It led towards the dichotomous question concerning the 'alphabetical or scientific' dictionary (Baldinger 1952, 1956, 1960*a*, 1960*b*, Tollenaere 1960*a* and 1960*b*). The question was raised against the theoretical background that a dictionary *in toto* should mirror the semantic structure of a language *in toto*. An alphabetical dictionary cannot do this, but an onomasiological dictionary was supposed to be able to do so by definition. *Roget's Thesaurus* of 1852 was the unloved model. As early as 1885, Carl Abel had published a German translation of the categorial system which structured Roget's *Thesaurus*. This was part of an essay devoted to the possibilities of how to elucidate the 'spirit of a language' (Abel 1885, 243–82). For later linguists, the English work as a whole was admired, but its practical, or, according to these linguists, unscientific intentions were criticized. A high point in this discussion was Rudolf Hallig and Walther von Wartburg's (1952) system of concepts (*Begriffssystem, Système raisonné des concepts*)[39] which was meant as a foundation for onomasiological dictionaries of all languages. They did not want it to be seen in the wake of Roget. An abbreviated overview of the system reads thus:

A. *L'UNIVERS*
I. *Le ciel et l'atmosphere*
II. *La terre*
III. *Les plantes*
IV. *Les animaux*
B. *L'HOMME*
I. *L'homme, être physique*
II. *L'âme et l'intellect*
III. *L'homme, être social*
IV. *L'organisation sociale*
C. *L'HOMME ET L'UNIVERS*
I. *L'a priori*
II. *La science et la technique*

In their introduction, the two authors gave their system an elaborate theoretical underpinning, in which they defined the relations between reality, concepts, and language with the help of the phenomenological philosophy of their time. This

---

[39] The book was written in German and French.

vast undertaking was presented at the Congess of Linguists in London in 1952, where a whole section was devoted to onomasiology.[40]

But this was a Pyrrhic victory (Hüllen 1990*b*).[41] The structuralist paradigm with its dominance in phonology and syntax began to gain ground in Western linguistics. From *c*.1950, it supplanted semantics and with it onomasiology for at least two decades. This is certainly true for theoretical work in lexicography, perhaps not so for the practical world where the cultivation of topical dictionaries was continued because the market demanded it. For example, the elaborate introduction by Hallig and von Wartburg obviously remained unread. True, the terms *semasiological* and *onomasiological* did not vanish from the language of lexicographers, but since that time they have no longer been understood as concerning the history of linguistic ideas, neither of the earlier centuries for which Leibniz had spoken nor of the early twentieth century, when the discussion had started anew.[42] In the seminal publication of conference papers by Householder and Saporta (1962), for example, 'the semantic (analogical, ideological) dictionary' is mentioned only in a few sentences in Yakov Malkiel's contribution (1962, 17–18), and these do not contain much more than references to the works of Roget, Boissière, and Casares. The term *onomasiological* is not used, although the 'Wörter-and-Sachen school of etymology' is referred to (1962, 20). Ladislav Zgusta's *Manual of lexicography* (1971), for many years the standard reference handbook of the discipline, concedes that arrangements of entries different from the alphabetical 'such as, e.g., arrangement by semantic connections, or by the derivation of the words, have great advantages for different purposes', only to conclude, however, that 'for general purposes, alphabetical order is optimal' (1971, 282, see also 198). Landau (1993) makes just a few historical remarks. The present state of affairs is perhaps not as rigorously exclusive as that, but still rather blind to the peculiarities and in particular to the long tradition of semantically arranged dictionaries. In his historical overview, Green (1997, 39–54) mentions the 'various types: some alphabetical, some based on the appearance of the glossed words in the text under consideration, some by semantic field and so on' (1997, 43). But he does not attach any importance or further considerations to this observation. The most comprehensive treatment at present of lexicography (Hausmann *et al.* 1989–91) contains only a few articles (by Hausmann, Marello, and Reichmann, all

---

[40] F. Mezger's report in the anonymously published proceedings shows the tremendous importance and expectations that were attached to these dictionaries. 'These dictionaries map out the realm of expression, the spiritual world of a linguistic community at a given period. By comparing the different conceptual systems as embodied in the different systems of linguistic experience, we create an instrument which will make it possible to write the history of ideas, the change of values, the growth of institutions, the spiritual welding together of the Western nations.' (Anonymous 1956, 85.)

[41] In fact, the discussion on semasiology and onomasiology has never ceased. For German linguists see, for example, Heger 1964, Wiegand 1969–70, and the entry *Onomasiologie* in Lewandowski 1976, vol. 2, 484–5. For English and American linguists see McArthur 1986*a* and 1986*b*, and Kipfer 1986. The term has, however, only a four-line entry in David Crystal's *A First Dictionary of Linguistics and Phonetics* of 1980. See also Zgusta 1988, *x* (preface).

[42] For a more elaborate treatment of the early debate on onomasiology see Hüllen 1990*b* and 1997.

1990) in which the terms *semasiological* and *onomasiological* are discussed as indicating features of dictionaries with various purposes. But it appears as if two more or less parallel types of dictionaries are outlined, of which dictionary users choose one according to taste. Or worse, it appears as if the history of lexicography were in fact the history of alphabetization of word-lists, with authors who chose a different order being influenced by 'apparent lethargy' and 'innate conservatism' (Green 1997, 56).

In German linguistics the discussion on semasiology and onomasiology shifted from lexicography to lexicology, that is, from the applied theory of dictionary making to the pure theory of structural semantics. H. E. Wiegand (1969–70), for example, discusses the two terms as indicative of two ways to analyse the lexis of a language. The one starts from an abstract concept (*Begriff*) and aims at finding (all) the lexicalized meanings that can be subsumed under it. The other starts from an individual lexicalized meaning and, by analysing its semantic structure (according to semes, lexical markers, etc.) and that of similar lexicalized meanings, aims to arrive at the abstract concept to which they belong. It is the author's opinion that both procedures work together, that the onomasiological way down is always complemented by the semasiological way up.[43]

Alphabetical dictionaries have conquered the market. This fact will not change in the near future.[44] One consequence of this is that they have also conquered the attention of scholars. Yet, it seems high time that non-alphabetical dictionaries should at least regain their history. This is not to revive the onomasiology debate of the early twentieth century, which is now obsolete because it has been overtaken by new theories of the linguistic sign and in particular of semantics. Moreover, it suffers from unsolved epistemological problems. It is rather to give a name to the deep-rooted differences between non-alphabetical and alphabetical dictionaries, which are hardly recognized, and to make people fully understand a dictionary type which has marked European lexicographical tradition perhaps not as intensively but as continuously as the alphabetical dictionary. With reference to history, only few scholars (e.g. Béjoint 1994, 15) seem to have been aware of the importance of onomasiological works so far. Among them are DeWitt T. Starnes and Gertrude Noyes with their treatment of what they call 'Medieval and Renaissance Vocabularies' (1946, 197–211). The new edition of their seminal book with an introduction by Gabriele Stein (1991*a*) was a historiographical deed also from this point of view. More recent and actually closer than anybody else to the treatment of onomasiology in the present book is Claude Buridant (1986), except that his overview is limited to the Middle Ages and to the French and German tradition. This pertains to his general appreciation of dictionaries as a source of present-day knowledge of cultural history, of onomasiological dictionaries in

---

[43] This short summary cannot do justice to this massive paper with its highly abstract and terminologically elaborate treatment of the problem. See also Heger 1964.

[44] See, however, Burkhanov 1994.

particular,[45] and of the function of the onomasiological principle in works as different from dictionaries in their arrangement and purposes as, for example, dialogues. Finally, Tom McArthur (1986*a* and 1986*b*), himself the author of an onomasiological dictionary, gives an outline of what he calls 'thematic lexicography'. Consequently, both publications pertain largely to the selection of works for the purpose of analysis in this book, but not for the linguistic method applied.

The task remains to be undertaken of making people aware that there has been and there still is a particular tradition running through European intellectual history which, in its unbroken permanence, allows comparisons with such fully recognized traditions as those of grammar or rhetoric. To call it 'a sideline of mainstream lexicography' (Green 1997, 177) is to apply a purely quantitative yardstick to historiography.

1.5 The onomasiological dictionary as text

A general guideline for the method which will be employed in undertaking this task is the assumption that onomasiological dictionaries, at least up to 1700, that is, during the period considered in this book,[46] are texts in the full semiotic sense of this term. As texts they form a unit which is constituted by hierarchically ordered subunits. It seems feasible to introduce three levels of hierarchical organization on which are located (i) the *dictionary entry* on the *microlevel*, (ii) the *section* on the *mesolevel*, and (iii) the *dictionary as a whole* on the *macrolevel*. In fact, individual onomasiological dictionaries may have their own structures with several levels between the microlevel of entries and the macrolevel, as subsequent analyses will show.

According to Charles Morris (1938), the cohesion of a text is achieved by three structural systems which are determined by the nature of the linguistic sign. These are the *semantic*, the *syntactic*, and the *pragmatic*. Semantic features determine reference and meaning (or sense), syntactic features determine intersignal relations, and pragmatic features determine variations which depend on the basic needs of communication in a given situation. All three systems of features create together the network of signs which makes a language unit cohesive.

Users of language, authors as well as receivers of a text, create an awareness of *coherence* in their mental representations which depends on the understanding of the three kinds of features mentioned. The awareness of coherence depends on the understanding of linguistic *cohesion*, but does not merely mirror it. In particular, receivers add all their own linguistic experience to the signs of cohesion and may create a text in their minds which deviates from the intentions of the

---

[45] '*Le groupement onomasiologique est d'une importance particulière pour la lexicographie médiévale; son but est pédagogique: il s'agit de faciliter le travail de la memoire*' (Buridant 1986, 15). He also acknowledges its special dimension *touchant à l'encyclopédie* (1986, 14).

[46] See Chapter 11.

author.[47] Semantic, syntactic, and pragmatic features are to be found on all three levels of a text and must be sought there. But there are levels which offer a particularly visible platform for each of them. For semantic features this is the text as a whole, its macrostructure, for syntactic features this is the sentence, its microstructure, and for pragmatic features this is a range of various units between the two. If this is so and if onomasiological dictionaries are texts in the full semiotic sense of the word, general deliberations about textuality can be applied to them just as they can be applied to texts in their usual linguistic *Gestalt*.

Above all, the system of semantic features is established by the general text topic[48] (Lyons 1977, van Dijk 1980, Brown and Yule 1983). It gradually accumulates in the linear arrangement of the text, although there is a preconceived topical concept which selects this process of accumulation. The topic is often epitomized in a phrase, for example the title, but it can be too complex for this method. This gives certain satellite-like texts, like tables of contents, overviews, or abstracts, their importance.

Within their own quantitative limits, onomasiological word-lists and dictionaries follow a universalist tendency. They give a picture of reality, and in the way in which they do this they establish a global text topic. They do this on the macrolevel of the dictionary which emerges out of the interplay of the other, hierarchically lower, levels. These are the so-called *sections*, that is, the semantically related groups of entries, and the entries themselves. Sections may but need not have their own subtitles. The best epitome of the global topic of an onomasiological dictionary is the overview of sections, which thus gains great importance for understanding it as a whole.

The system of syntactic features pertains to the individual sentence. As texts consist of several, frequently of masses of, sentences, there is a repetitive moment in them. In spite of the possibilities of syntactic variation, relatively few structures occur again and again. This repetition is the machinery that keeps the process of accumulating the global topic going.

There are also anaphoric, cataphoric, and other interconnections between sentences. However, their binding power does not extend very far and cannot replace the principle of repetitiveness of syntactic structures in texts.

What the sentences are for a text, the entries are for the onomasiological dictionary. It is by their repetition that the global topic is gradually accumulated. Compared to sentences in spoken or written texts of the general kind, the variation within the structures of entries is only poorly developed. Contrary to the

---

[47] Note the difference from Halliday and Hasan 1976, who introduced these terms. There is no doubt about the seminal importance of their book. But the strict differentiation between semantic and syntactic text signals cannot be maintained. Moreover, there are texts with dense signals of cohesion which nevertheless fail to establish coherence in the mind of the reader/listener, and there are also texts with very slack signals of cohesion which do the opposite. See Bublitz 1996.

[48] The terms *discourse topic* and *text topic* are used synonymously. I prefer *text topic* in order to avoid associations to spoken language in the term *discourse*.

former, strict homogeneity, not stylistic variation, is the ideal. Anaphoric and cataphoric relations between entries are to be found, and (as analyses will show) they are not exceptional. Mostly they consist of the identity relation between consecutive entries in cases where a first entry is glossed, for example with a translation, a second entry however with an anaphoric *idem (est)*. In cases where several entries are bracketed and complemented with one gloss, in order to show their synonymous character, we have anaphoric and cataphoric references occurring together between the members of one group of lexemes (Stein 1997, 257–60).

The system of pragmatic features uses the potential of semantic and syntactic characteristics in order to establish regularities which pertain less to structure than to a norm. They express communicative needs which emerge from the individuality of communicators when confronted with special contexts of situation. On the one hand, such needs depend on very general principles of language use such as logic, precision, sincerity, and politeness, as expounded, for example, in Grice's maxims (Grice 1975). On the other hand, they depend on the very concrete circumstances in which a text is performed.

The pragmatic features of onomasiological dictionaries are to be found in the arrangement of entries on the mesolevel of sections.[49] They introduce very general principles, such as progress from the general to the specific (or from the specific to the general, but not an arbitrary sequence), prototypicality (Rosch 1973, Taylor 1989), the practical progress of some human action, the rhythm of biological life, etc. Lexemes denoting the parts of a ship may be arranged in the sequence in which these parts are built in the shipyard. Lexemes denoting dishes may be given in the sequence of a huge meal. Lexemes denoting the parts of the human body are almost always arranged in an order which was obviously felt to be the natural one, that is, from head to foot. Each dictionary has such pragmatic norms of its own.[50]

Textuality (as cohesion) is deliberately constructed by the author of a text and also of an onomasiological dictionary. It must be reconstructed (as coherence) by receivers if they endeavour to decode the text as a linguistic unity. The question is whether the users of an onomasiological dictionary do this. Or will they not, rather, look for a local piece of information *within* this text and not observe the whole?

The analyses that follow will show that the early onomasiological glossaries and the subsequent onomasiological dictionaries, eventually known as *nomenclators*, were given an encyclopaedic and didactic function. They were meant to provide new words as the carriers of new knowledge. These functions were fused. This means that the order in which the new words and their meanings were arranged acted as the principle for teaching and learning. Whereas the alphabetical glossary and dictionary stated equations between word-meanings, the onomasiological

---

[49] Béjoint 1994, 11–14 and *passim* uses the terms *macrostructure* and *microstructure* in a sense different from mine. He does not ground them in text linguistics. Consequently, there is no mention of pragmatic features and the mesolevel of their realization.

[50] See, in particular, Chapters 6 and 7.

glossary and dictionary transported word-meanings in a global semantic context. This means that they were deliberately used as a text.

Of course, there was hardly any theorizing about this. Yet there are a few significant sources. For example, Stephanus Doletus, the most eminent member of the famous French family well known for its scholarship (Green 1997, 53–4), prefaced his *Commentariorum Linguae Latinae tomus primus / secundus* (Doletus 1536–8) by pointing out the advantages of the topical over the alphabetical arrangement. His main argument is that in the topical arrangement users of his Latin glossary learn not only words but also matter.

Horvm Commentariorum id meum primum institutum fuit, ut autor essem noui Dictionariorum conscribendorum ordinis, quem nec Graecus quisquam, nec Latinus sibi uendicare posset. Qui ordo est . . . ut non seriam alphabeticam sequamur (quod uulgus Grammaticorum facit) sed res rebus attexamur, & dictiones significatione cognatas, inter se copulemus. In quo non solum dictionum ipsarum significationes potes compraehendere, sed rerum etiam naturam. (*4)[51]*

Another example is Nathaniel Duez (1609–?1670), a translator of Comenius's *Janua linguarum* (1661—see Loonen 1994) and editor of a nomenclator in French, (Low-)German, Italian, and Latin (Duez 1652).[52] In spite of the selection and sequence of languages, Latin certainly has the leading part. This is suggested by the Latin title and by the address to readers in the same language. One passage from this address shows the concept for teaching vocabulary typical for the onomasiological tradition:

Est autem haec Nomenclatura eo directa, ut perquam commode familiaribus colloquis adjungi poßit. Siquidem vocabulorum copia, multiplexque varietas, Linguarum studiosis non minus necessaria est, quam colorum diversitas pictoribus: quorum illi citra controversiam optimi, qui variis coloribus apposite industrieque digestis, res omnes ad vivum repraesentant. Quid aliud autem elegans sermo, variarum dictionum convenienti mixtura & digestione politus, quam rerum quarumlibet viva effigies, propriis coloribus eleganter depicta?[53]

Finally, Huldreich Schober's dictionary of 1684 (Schober 1684)[54] can be mentioned. Again in the preface (written by the well-known Humanist Johannes

---

[51] BL fol. 69. g.12. 'It is the first intention of these comments that I am the author of dictionaries written according to a new order which no Greek and no Latin [author] can claim for himself. This order is that we do not follow the alphabetical sequence (which the great number of grammarians does), but that we complement things with things, and that we connect known words by their meaning[s]. By which you can not only understand the meanings of the words themselves, but also the nature of things.' (My translation, W. H.)

[52] BL 1568/2977 (also WF Kb 31).

[53] 'It is, however, this nomenclator which can be formed in such a way that it can properly be joined to familiar colloquies. Because the set of words and [their] multiple variety is no less necessary for the students of languages than the diversity of colours [is] for pictures: of which, doubtless, they [= the pictures] are the best which, by adequate and careful arrangement of various colours, represent all things according to life. What else, after all, is refined speech—a mixture of various harmonious words and polished by distribution, by the lively image of whatever things, depicted elegantly by the proper colours?' (My translation, W. H.)

[54] WF Kb 75. The author, Huldreich Schober, is not mentioned in the title of the book.

Sturmius (1507–89)) the idea is expressed that the dictionary conveys all the words necessary in sections that coincide with the domains of reality in which the language to be learned is used:

Nihil videatur in corpore hominis, nihil in pecudibus, nihil sit in culina, in cella vinaria, in cella frumentaria: ad coenam quotidianam nihil afferatur: nihil in hortis conspiciatur herbarum, fructicum, arborum, nihil in scholis sit usurpatum, nihil in bibliotheca: nihil in templis frequentarum: nihil in coelo sensus quotidie hominum moveat: quod Pueri, quoad ejus fieri poterit, non queant latino nomine nominare.   (I, 2)[55]

There are also statements of this kind to be found outside dictionaries.[56] More important, there are school statutes extant which prove that the onomasiological principle of dictionaries was observed in daily practice. Note, for example, the 'Bangor Friar School Statutes' of 1568:

Item. They shall begin with words that concern the head reciting orderly as nigh as they can every part and number of the body and every particular of the same, after that they shall teach the names of sickness, diseases, virtues, vices, fishes, fowls, birds, beasts, herbs, shrubs, trees, and so forth . . .   (Watson 1968, 384)

To an even more elaborate list of classes of names, the Rivington Grammar School Statutes of 1566 add the advice: 'and cause them to write every word that belongs to one thing, together in order' (Watson 1968, 384). Before printed dictionaries were used extensively, we must indeed assume that memorizing long word-lists was one of the most important procedures of language learning.[57] Memory was the central agency of intellectual activity. This means that older onomasiological word-lists and dictionaries have certainly to be understood as textbooks for language teaching, and mostly as textbooks to be memorized *in toto*. In the sixteenth and seventeenth centuries they grew into full-sized books with 10,000 or even 20,000 entries, because the whole of Humanist scholarship found a place in them. Of course, this created limits on their usability as texts. But even then many theories of language learning made it clear that *nomenclators*, as onomasiological dictionaries were then called, were still looked upon as textbooks, even if not as textbooks to be learned by heart.[58] The critical point was

---

[55]   'Nothing should be seen in the human body, nothing in cattle [= animals], nothing should be in the kitchen, in the wine cellar, in the granary; nothing should be brought for the daily meal, in the garden nothing should be seen of herbs, fruits, [and] trees; nothing should be made use of in schools, nothing in libraries, nothing in temples, frequently visited, nothing should daily move the senses of men in the sky; what pupils are not able to denominate with a Latin name, as it can be done of them.' (My translation, W. H.)

[56]   There are quite a number of tracts on teaching which establish this principle on didactic grounds. So do John Brinsley in his dialogue *Ludus literarius or, the Grammar School* (1612) and Obediah Walker in *Of Education, especially of young gentleman* (1673). Comenius constructed a comprehensive didactic theory from these ideas, which gained Europe-wide recognition. See, in particular, Chapters 6 and 10.

[57]   See Chapter 3. In fact this pertains to all kinds of learning, for example as part of the training of orators, of lawyers, etc.

[58]   See Chapter 9.

reached when onomasiological dictionaries came to be accompanied by alphabetical dictionaries. This opened the way for using them only in order to find local information and without recognition of their overall textual structure. Although onomasiological dictionaries did not lose their textual cohesion, their incoherent use was now made possible.

It is an irony of the history of dictionaries that, because of subsequent technical developments, the textual qualities of onomasiological dictionaries became more and more cohesive, until they reached a state of perfection in our day which seems unsurpassable. Admittedly, however, access to these onomasiological dictionaries is now sought via the shorter route of an alphabetical index rather than via the semantic relativities of entries.

For this reason, besides other more practical considerations, the analyses that follow are limited to onomasiological dictionaries which appeared before 1700. Those appearing later demand a different treatment.[59]

[59] See Chapter 11.

2

On establishing a tradition

2.1 General

It is the aim of this book to establish a tradition.

The lexeme *tradition* is explained in the *Oxford English Dictionary* (definition 5b) as follows:

A long established and generally accepted custom or method of procedure, having almost the force of a law; an immemorial usage; the body (or any one) of the experiences and usages of any branch or school of art or literature, handed down by predecessors and generally followed. [. . . A]n embodiment of an old established custom or institution, a 'relic'.

In the field of linguistics, theoretical as well as applied, there are several such 'established custom[s] or institution[s]', the most noteworthy of which is probably grammatography, the description of analogous structures of any language for the sake of teaching and improving its use according to certain criteria. Indeed, in Europe we have used in grammatography a stable, that is, a traditional, terminology since Dionysius Thrax (?170–?90 BC) (Law and Sluiter 1995). Another tradition of this kind has been rhetoric since the days of Cicero (106–43 BC) and Quintilian (?35–?100) (Plett 1995); a third is what would today be called *semiotics*, meaning the explanation of the nature and the functions of various kinds of signs, notably the linguistic ones, as has been done since Aristotle (384/3–322 BC) and St Augustine (354–430) (Deely 1982, Posner, Robering, and Sebeok 1997).

The three examples show, however, that traditions are not only 'long established and generally accepted', and 'handed down by predecessors'. If they want to,
successors who bow to the law of their elders nevertheless find an opportunity to
mix tradition with innovation. The history of grammatography, of rhetoric, and
of semiotics frequently presents a tradition of terms rather than one of concepts.
The reverse is also true. Latecomers in history frequently use innovative terms in
order to give a new and attractive garb to traditional concepts. Both these converse
developments make use of the fact that historical texts, which are the proof of the
origins or early stages of a tradition, are always ambiguous and open to an almost
infinite variety of interpretations.

The levels of awareness with which all this is performed differ considerably.
There are traditions which are consciously and deliberately preserved in order to
keep old knowledge and old techniques alive. There are traditions which are
instrumentalized for all kinds of purposes but not taken seriously in their own
right, and there are conventions which are merely carried on without people
knowing what they are doing. It may even be the case that the last mentioned attitude is the most frequent one. Tradition becomes 'the body . . . of the experiences
and usages of any branch or school of art or literature', it becomes general knowledge whose dependence on earlier historiographers and historical authors has
been forgotten and remains in the dark (Hüllen 1996a, 115, no. 17 and 2005, 11).
Anybody can be a good present-day grammarian without any knowledge of the
origins and history of grammatical concepts and terminology. Of course, they run
the risk of repeating what other linguists have said before. (This trap seems to be
particularly wide open today.) The fact of 'handing down' a tradition from predecessors to successors may therefore be objectively true although it did not subjec-
tively happen. Traditions are diachronically what cultures are synchronically,
namely, a vast web of intricate and complex mental or practical usages that have
grown over time and which people have internalized without knowing the exact
connections and dependencies.

This is also why it is possible for a tradition to be carried on through centuries
but hardly ever to be reflected upon. It runs of its own accord, as it were. In our
opinion this is the case with topical word-lists and dictionaries, which are given
the linguistic name *onomasiological*.[1]

The ranges of traditions vary enormously. Theoretically, they reach from the
few cultural domains of this world which are delimited by the great world reli-
gions to the habits of thinking and acting that an individual has developed for
herself or himself or inside a family. Between these two extremes there is an infinite variety of possible ranges of the validity of a tradition. The three examples
from linguistics that were quoted have, of course, been alive in the whole, cultur-
ally so-called, Western world.

There is also the observation that traditions originate and are kept alive in such

---

[1] See Chapter 1.

different parts of the world as have with certainty not had any contact with each other. This suggests the idea that there are universals, limited by the equally universal constraints of reality, which determine the possibilities available to mankind of making use of experiences with the intention of serving its own good. In the case of linguistics this means that there are universal features of languages and the use that mankind makes of them. That languages, for example, have analogous structures is part of their essence. This determines grammatography in the whole world in a certain way which goes beyond the common traits which we find, for example, in the grammatography of the languages of the Indo-European group. Topical word-lists and dictionaries also seem to be a relevant case in point, not however rhetoric which is tied closely to the Greek and Latin tradition.

2.2 Historical cases

Topical word-lists are to be found in many parts of the Asian and European world and in varying centuries. Obviously the knowledge of such lists regularly formed a stage in the education of children. This pertained to their training in reading, but also to the acquisition of general knowledge. Lists were ordered according to the number of syllables, topical classes, or the alphabet (where applicable). They contained the names of gods and heroes, of kings, generals, towns, rivers. Thus they could be used for teaching the pupils mythology, history, and geography (Debut 1983, Green 1997, 39–54). Most likely, they were dictated, copied, and learned by heart (see below). They had great importance in the cultures of the Near East, Egypt, and Greece. But we also find such lists in China and in India.

The following are historical cases sketched out for the sake of illustration (and not more). They appear in temporal order, rather in the manner of scenes in a chronicle play.

2.2.1 Egyptian word-lists

The Egyptian word-list culture mirrors the intensive scribal training which, besides reading and writing, also comprised solving mathematical and geometrical problems (Johnson 1994). There are word-lists arranged by subject-matter, but also word-lists arranged by assonance, that is, pseudo-alphabetically. The bulk of the latter word-lists appeared late, after 323 BC when Alexander the Great had conquered Egypt and the country came under Greek and Roman influence. Prior to that date all word-lists were organized by subject-matter and written in hieratic script. This means that, though far apart in time, neither type of word-list was taken for granted but was the result of considered choice.

The relevant texts from the Middle Kingdom (*c.*2040–1650 BC) are onomastica rather than glossaries, that is, lists of entities rather than lists of words. They were compiled 'as much to give instruction in the natures and sources of the things brought to the king by way of tribute as to fulfil the mere function of spelling exercises' (Gardiner 1947, vol. I, 4). The natural species of animals appear in them and likewise the objects of human habitat and life. They also convey an impression of the geographical conditions of Egyptian life. The *Rammasseum Onomasticon* of the thirteenth to fourteenth dynasty has sections on 'plants and liquids', 'wickerwork, minerals and seed', 'birds', 'fishes', 'birds' (again), 'quadrupeds', and the names of southern Egyptian fortresses (Gardiner 1947, vol. I, 7–23). The later *Onomasticon of Amenopĕ*, of the twenty-first or twenty-second dynasty, that is, immediately following the reign of Rameses II (1290–1224 BC)[2], of which eight manuscripts—papyri and ostraca—are extant, has nine sections with 610 entries, namely:

I. Introductory heading, II. Sky, water, earth, III. Persons, court, offices, occupations, IV. Classes, tribes, and types of human being, V. The towns of Egypt, VI. Buildings, their parts, and types of land, VII. Agricultural land, cereals and their products, VIII. Beverages, IX. Parts of an ox and kinds of meat.   (Gardiner 1947, vol. I, 37)

These sections allow an unsurpassed insight into the areas of Egyptian wisdom and the inner mechanism of Egyptian life, among other domains the Pharaonic court with its numerous offices (see Table A.1).[3]

2.2.2 Chinese word-lists

Erya, the first Chinese lexicographical work from the third century BC, contains, among other things, glosses in a topical ordering, namely kinship terms, architectural terms, utensils and tools, musical instruments, astronomical, calendrical, and meteorological terms, geographical and geological names (hills, mountains, rivers), and items related to them like grasses, herbs and vegetables, trees and bushes, insects, spiders, and reptiles, fish, wild and domestic animals, poultry (Malmqvist 1994, 5). These glosses were taken from classical texts. There is also *Fagyan*, China's earliest dialect vocabulary, attributed to Yang Xiong (53 BC–AD 18), whose current version has 658 entries in thirteen sections, of which some are devoted to word-classes but others contain words in a topical order, like clothing (sect. 4), utensils, furniture, and farming implements (sect. 5), wild and domestic animals (sect. 8), waggons, boats, and weapons (sect. 9), and insects (sect. 11). However the choice of these sections was made, they are expressive of the underlying idea that words can usefully be arranged according to an order taken from everyday life. This idea suggested itself the more, because the writing system was not alphabetical.[4] The purpose of these compilations was scribal training and interdialectal translation, i.e. practical.

---

[2] According to another counting 1279–1213 BC.

[3] I give the glosses from Alan H. Gardiner's autographed text (1947, vol. I, 13*–59*) which also contains the hieratic signs and sometimes extensive comments.

[4] This precluded, of course, an arrangement according to letters but not one according to other formal devices like the number and sequence of strokes necessary to write a logograph.

2.2.3 The Ameracósha of Sanskrit

'The celebrated *Ameracósha*, or *Vocabulary of Sanscrit* by Amera Sinha, is, by the unanimous suffrage of the learned, the best guide to the acceptations of nouns in Sanscrit.' (Sinha 1808, 1.)[5] It also goes under the title *Tricánda* ('three books') or *Abhid'hána* ('nouns'). Its author flourished in the sixth century AD or even two centuries earlier[6] and culled his words from texts which were already old then. Etymologies and derivations follow the rules set up by the much older Pānnini (*fl.* fourth century BC). The entries with the lemmata and their semantic explanations are metrically patterned, generally an entry and a stanza being coextensive, which means that they were meant to be learned by heart. This is in accordance with the generally known fact that Sanskrit was a holy and élite language which had to be learned in schools. These word-lists, of which the *Ameracósha* is the oldest extant, were tools for composing religious poetry.

It is historiographically significant that the structural, or morphological, nature of Sanskrit has attracted so much more attention in linguistics than this important onomasiological dictionary, which Wilhelm von Humboldt counted among the outstanding examples of '*[n]ach Kategorien geordnete[r] Wörterbücher*' ('dictionaries ordered according to categories').[7] Even very modern treatments of *Sanskrit* or *Indian Linguistics* (Deshpande 1992, Cardona 1994) speak only of the grammatical nature of the language. The importance which the analysis of Sanskrit had for the concept of the Indo-European language family, in fact a very Eurocentric importance, accounts for this one-sidedness which still prevails today.

The dictionary[8] is divided into three books, each book into chapters, and many chapters into sections. In book I, chap. I in seven sections deals with 'Heaven', 'Sky', 'Time', 'Intellect (emotions, senses)', 'Speech', 'Sound', and 'Music'. Chapter II in three sections deals with 'Internal regions' ('Serpents'), 'Hell', and 'Water'. In book II, chaps I–III deal with 'Earth', 'Towns', and 'Mountains'. Chapter IV, divided into five sections, deals with 'Forests', 'Trees', 'Plants (mostly medical)', 'Useful plants', and 'Drugs'. Chapter V deals with 'Lions' and other animals, chap. VI in three sections with 'Man', 'Health', and 'Dress', and chaps VII–X with the so-called 'tribes' of human society. The arrangement of topics, although broadly comparable with other lists, is even more idiosyncratic than appears here on the less general level of their entries. The last four chapters break the whole of society down into four 'tribes', namely priests, military men, professions and husbandmen, and finally, mixed 'classes'. Each 'tribe' is connected with its activities like religious life, government and warfare, agriculture and commerce, and finally,

---

[5] Henry Thomas Colebrook (1765–1837), the editor, was one of the pioneers of Sanskrit scholarship, publishing a grammar as early as 1805. His dictionary is one of the earliest firsthand sources for Sanskrit in Europe.

[6] See Pinault 1996, who uses the spelling 'Amarakósha'.

[7] *Werke* 1968 (1906), vol. 5, 437; see also Hüllen 1990*b*.

[8] I quote the descriptive terms used in the Colebrook edition.

'artisans, jugglers, dancers, musicians, hunters, servants, barbarians, dogs, hogs', etc.

Whereas books I and II contain nouns only, book III lists adjectives separated into those pertaining to persons and to things and miscellaneous, and homonymous words. There then follow grammatical paradigms. 'The *Amarakósha* is an erudite encyclopedia rather than a dict[ionary] of the European type' (Pinault 1996, 22)—a characterization which shows its author's opinion of what a dictionary of the European type is.

2.2.4 *Graeco-Coptic* scalae

The old Egyptian onomastic tradition remained influential after the country fell under the influence of Greek, then of Roman culture and also, with the use of the Coptic language, after Christianization and Arabization. Graeco-Coptic *scalae*, or topical word-lists, appeared in the early Middle Ages besides Graeco-Arabic, Graeco-Copto-Arabic or Copto-Arabic ones (Sidarus 1978). The thirteenth and fourteenth centuries saw an outbreak of this tradition, obviously stimulated by the disappearance of Coptic as a vernacular and the concomitant philological attempts to save it, at least on a literary level. Different types of glossaries appeared, such as are also known from other traditions, namely, the text-bound glossary (e.g. the *Scala ecclesiastica*, following the New Testament, of Yūhannā 'l-Samannūdi, *fl.* 1235–57), the alphabetical glossary (e.g. the *Scalae rimatae* of Ibn al-'Assāl and Ibn al-Rāhib), and the best known of them, the classified vocabulary in the old Pharaonic mode (e.g. the *Scala magna* of Abū 'l-Barakāt ibn Kabar, d. 1324). Experts attribute to it a great importance for Arabic–Coptic lexicography and a deep-rooted dependence on older onomastica. Note the following overview of the *Scala magna* as drawn up in descriptive terms by Adel Sidarus (1990*a* and 1990*b*, 13):

[Monde supérieur]

I/1	*Dieu (biblique, chrétien, philosophique)*
I/2	*Hiérarchies célestes (bibliques et chrétiennes)*
I/3	*Cosmos astral (ciel, astres, étoiles)*
I/4	*Phénomènes atmosphériques, éléments géophysiques (. . .)*

[Sphère humaine]

II/5	*Homme physique: sens, opérations psychologiques, âges, corps humain*
II/6	*Langues, nations religions; famille*
II/7	*Qualificatifs moraux et sociaux (positifs et negatifs)*
II/8	*Opérations physiologiques et psychologiques, actions intellectuelles et morales*
II/9	*État/Société: Hiérarchies civiles et militaires; professions; armes et vêtements des puissants*
II/10	*Vêtements et outils relatifs aux arts et métiers*
II/11	*Maladies, infirmités, états d'âme*

[Monde inférieur]

III/12	*(faune): Mammifères (sauvages, domestiques); III/13 Oiseaux; III/14 Poissons et espèces aquatiques; III/15 Reptiles et insectes*
IV/16	*(flore): Arbres, fruits, fleurs; IV/17 Drogues, parfums, épices; IV/18 Grains, céréales, oléagéneuses (. . .)*
IV/19	*(minéraux) Métaux et pierres précieuses; IV/20 Couleurs et teintures*
VI/21	*Géographie et toponymie (égyptienne et autre; mers et fleuves; varia)*
VI/22	*Église (édifice, varia liturgica, ordres ecclésiastiques, etc.)*
VIII/23–X/30	*Appendices lexicographiques variés.*[9]

2.2.5 Arabic–Syriac word-lists

There was also an early medieval onomasiological tradition in the Arabic–Syriac area. The oldest word-list still extant is *al-Garīb al-muṣannaf* ('lexical particulars in systematic order') of Abū 'Ubaid al-Qāsim ibn Sallām (*c*.770–838) whose topical arrangement was very influential (Weninger 1994). It contains the language of Arabic Bedouins, pre-Islamic poetry, and proverbs. Another work of the genre is *Fiqh al-luga* ('essential knowledge of language') of Abū Manṣūr 'Abd al-Malik aṭ-Ta'ālibī (*c*.961–1038) with sections on clothes, arms, tools, voices, sounds, animals, diseases, and kinds of death. The arrangement in oppositions is unique: for example, the first and the last of something, things long and short, broad and narrow, above and below, small and big; plenty and scarcity, things dehydrated and fresh, hard and soft. This arrangement follows inherent features of things rather than any hierarchical classification. The best known of these onomasiological dictionaries is, however, 'the book of the translator for teaching in the language of the Syriac' of Elias bar Šīnāyā (Elias of Nisibis, *c*.975–1040) with the Arabic title *Kitāb at-Targūmān fī ta'līm lugat as-Suryān* (Weninger 1994). As the title makes clear, the book has practical aims. It was an aid for writing letters and for preaching. It will also have been used as a text-book for Arab-speaking people who learned Syriac. The first twenty-nine lessons present nouns, verbs, and particles; some lessons are ordered alphabetically, but most of them follow the onomasiological principle. This means that the author selected a variety of linguistic arrangements for what he wanted to achieve. The onomasiological principle is unique in Syriac (not in Arabic) lexicography.

Each of the thirty lessons (*ta'ālīm*) is divided into several thematic paragraphs (*fuṣūl*). Stephan Weninger (1994, 57) gives the following overview: God (lesson 1), humans (lessons 2–10), human environment (lessons 11–14), and animals (lessons 15–18), human and animal voices and sounds (lesson 19). There then follows the inanimate world (lessons 20–24). Lessons 25–29 have odd topics like, for example, colours (lesson 27) and verbs (alphabetically). Thematic paragraphs, for example of lesson 2 pertaining to the human body, are: 1. Words for man and the elements men consist of (fire, air, etc.), 2. General parts (body, liquids, etc.), 3. General

---

[9] See also Sidarus 1990c.

organs like bones, skin, etc., 4. Special parts of the body and hypernyms for organs like the respiratory organs and procreational organs, 5–10. Parts of the body from head to foot, then inner organs, procreative organs, excreta.

2.3 Onomasiology, an autonomous tradition

The historical cases mentioned have been painted with a broad brush, almost in the way in which a backdrop is painted on a stage. This was in fact the intention. It has been shown that, with great temporal and spatial distance to each other, there are lexicographical works with fairly close affinities. These pertain (i) to the technique of culling lexemes (mostly) from texts and arranging them in long lists, (ii) to the arrangement of these lexemes in a number of semantic domains, and (iii) to the use of these lists for either practical or encyclopaedic purposes or a combination of both. Naturally, we know only such word-lists as were written down in a pre-dictionary form, that is, as glossaries, or as dictionaries. But they will also have existed within oral linguistic practice. The arrangement of lexemes shows obvious parallels, mainly because of the recurring topics universe, mankind, nature, society, artificial objects, and language. Within these topics it varies widely in ways which, clearly discernible to the later historiographer, are culture dependent. The practical use of these works pertains to language teaching and learning, in particular foreign languages, including foreign dialects. Furthermore, it pertains to scribal training. The encyclopaedic use aims at making people aware of the world around them, again in a culture-dependent way, and conveying knowledge to them with the help of name-giving lexemes. The historical examples given in section 2.2 show the structural homogeneity and also the culture-dependent differences mentioned.

Experts often take great pains to prove traditional connections within and between these culture-dependent onomasiological works. Thus, for example, a Pharaonic–Christian–Muslim, or Egyptian–Coptic–Arabic, tradition is reconstructed in the case of the relevant onomastica and *scalae*; as is the influence of Greek linguistics, for example via the *Onomastikon* of Julius Pollux (*c.*170 AD), in the case of Syriac works. On a lower level of historical importance, family connections between, for example, vocabularies of the sixteenth and seventeenth centuries are uncovered, showing the paths which certain lexemes collected therein have followed, perhaps crossing linguistic boundaries, like dialects, or boundaries of objective culture, like homes or travel equipment. Lexicographic analyses are, thus, made a tool of historical lexicology and dialect geography. Such research is of high philological value, and yet it leaves essential questions open. Most importantly, it cannot explain any cases where direct or indirect contact is unprovable and in all likelihood impossible. Even if it can be shown beyond doubt who met whom or who knew which book or who was educated in which tradition (e.g. Green 1997, 47), the gain in knowledge still remains on the surface because it does not elucidate which reasons made an author follow a tradition or deviate from it or even reject it.

Vis-à-vis an almost omnipresent phenomenon like that of topical dictionaries it seems justifiable to speak of an *autonomous tradition*. The term applies to a 'custom or body of behaviour' which comes into being at different places and at different times, without provable contact, simply because the nature of the phenomenon makes it natural to behave in this way. The 'body of experiences and usages' that develops out of this shows a remarkable stability across time and space, which is exactly what we call *traditional*. Calling this tradition *autonomous* does not preclude concrete influences that pass from one author to another or from one national convention to the next. In these cases it is often the general autonomy of the tradition, observable almost anywhere and at all times, that stimulates an author to accept a more narrowly delimited and specialized tradition from his or her predecessor. The cases of provable influence and dependency would be much smaller in number, if there were no autonomous tradition *per se*. And even if this should not be so in concrete cases, the handing down of a tradition by many people, in many places, and at many times adds up to a network of influences and dependencies which enters the general knowledge of dictionary writers and users and appears to them in its own self-contained mode.

An autonomous tradition poses its own problems of historiographical investigation. Vivien Law (1990) proposed four potential methods of research: (i) The *sources-and-influence method* which focuses on the historical network of events, persons, and texts and seeks to identify a chain of influences between them. (ii) The *nexus-of-ideas method* which focuses on the evolution of concepts as a self-induced process in which person-authors play the role of performing agents only within certain limits which guarantee that the nexus is meaningful in itself. Michel Foucault is its great protagonist. (iii) The *projective method* in which the historiographers determine the themes as a result of their own present-day interests and in which the reconstructive element of historiography is particularly strong. Chomsky's famous look back on Cartesian linguistics is a notorious case in question. (iv) The *historiography-of-consciousness method* which treats texts with all their historical qualities as complex signals of underlying habits of thought and *mentalités* (Law 1990, 67–9). In an obvious attempt to do justice to the potentials and merits of all four, Vivien Law nevertheless sides with the fourth method.

It requires (and deserves) an elaborate discussion to determine the merits and shortcomings of these four methods,[10] in particular the special nodes of the complex 'body of experience and usages' from which they start and which they prefer in their treatments. The sources-and-influence method (i) relies mainly on historical facts as they happen in space and time and regards them as the natural mechanism that keeps the development of ideas going. The nexus-of-ideas method (ii) relies more on the propositions of historical texts which, taken together, fall into a coherent configuration of meaningful statements, paying less

---

[10] See my own, more general, contribution to this discussion in Hüllen 1996a or 2002, 16–28, and 2005.

attention to the life-conditions of authors which produce these texts. This means that the two methods do not actually preclude each other, though their authors have widely differing opinions about what is important in historiographical work. Researchers who reject the projective method (iii) must still acknowledge that the present-day interests and conditions of historiography influence any reconstruction of the past, that history is always looked at through the eyes of historiography. This should at least lead to a critical awareness of historiographical methods. The historiography-of-consciousness method (iv), finally, looks at the nexus of ideas as an indication of one or several mental state(s) which are more general and more comprehensive than the domain investigated and thus allow insights of a wider, though also more conjectural, validity. Again these methods do not preclude each other although their authors have different opinions about the important areas of historiography.

In the case of the onomasiological tradition, the point of departure for historiographical research in recent linguistics and the interests of present-day lexicographical thinking have already been shown.[11] Beyond the general interest in the history of linguistic ideas, this justifies the attempt to establish a tradition in a field where so far it has been almost totally overlooked (and answers the demands of the projective method (iii) in a special way). This justification is corroborated by the astonishing nexus of ideas, extending across many centuries, to be shown in the plethora of historical works available. This will be the main purpose of the present book (thus employing more than others the nexus-of-ideas method (ii)). The network of factual sources and influences, that is, the substratum in reality which carries the coherent configuration of ideas, will only be mentioned in a confirmatory manner (which means a certain neglect of the sources-and-influence method (i)). It is hoped to make the nexus of linguistic ideas understandable as significant for more general mental states and attitudes, for example of a philosophical kind, although this aim (agreeing with the historiography-of-consciousness method (iv)) can only be approached with a good portion of modesty.[12] The history of lexicography, as far as it will be re-created here with the means of historiography, is not to be understood as a continuum, as a thread running through the centuries, but as a sequence of (groups of) works of which each in its individuality uses an old tradition in an innovative way.

Establishing a tradition means making common features visible which have hardly been noticed so far. It means securing historical phenomena which can then be subjected to other investigations. As these phenomena are to be found in glossaries, dictionaries, and related text-genres, these are the direct objects of

---

[11] See Chapter 1, 16–22.

[12] In McArthur 1986*b* much of the material to be analysed in the present book is treated as phases and documents of a general history of the collecting, storing, retrieving, and conveying of human knowledge. The author's aim is less linguistically oriented, but lies rather in the area of cultural history. The special merit of the book is, of course, to have focused for the first time on such phenomena as, from my linguistic point of view, are called the *onomasiological principle* or *tradition*.

description and analysis. This is why some of the following chapters are reports on books in the narrow sense: on their appearance, their print, the history of their publication. These books are the concrete objects in which, on the level of historical facts, the concepts and arguments appear which constitute the onomasiological tradition. They are marked as a genre by the three features already mentioned above: (i) the technique of collecting lexemes in long lists, (ii) the arrangement of these lexemes in a number of semantic domains, and (iii) the use of these lists for either practical purposes like language teaching or theoretical purposes like conveying encyclopaedic knowledge, or a combination of both. Our search through history will also encounter works marked by the latter two features but not the first one. They are either dialogues or treatises which employ the onomasiological principle but are not onomasiological glossaries or dictionaries in the narrow sense.

Finally, the presence of the three essential features requires that the concept of onomasiology is the focus of attention, not the vocabulary as such. Lexemes are linguistically characterized by the registers to which they belong, that is, when they were used and where, in which medium mainly, in which contexts, on which stylistic levels, etc. Moreover, their historical path through texts (e.g. early dictionaries) and their appearance in other texts (e.g. later dictionaries) is of historiographical interest. Important and interesting as relevant findings of this kind are, they do not contribute much to the nexus of linguistic ideas which onomasiological dictionaries and related text-genres show. Rather, they enrich our knowledge on the factual level of sources and influence. For practical reasons, the wish to establish a so far covert tradition made it necessary to decide for the one and against the other method (without excluding the latter altogether). It goes without saying that, the onomasiological tradition once being established, it would be good to add as many analyses of the vocabulary of existing onomasiological dictionaries as possible.[13]

It also goes without saying that a tradition can hardly ever be presented historiographically in an exhaustive way. This has various causes. If anything, onomasiology is a European phenomenon using and deploying many languages. As is the common case with dictionaries, the later stand on the shoulders of the earlier ones and there are many cross-relations because of adaptations. Older attempts at establishing exhaustive bibliographies for all languages, including the non-European ones (Marsden 1796, Vater 1815), have, most likely, been given up. The last ones were Collison (1955), Zaunmüller (1958), and Zischka (1959).[14] The 619 international dictionary bibliographies listed in Cop (1990) show the incredible number of titles which an attempt at collecting a bibliography of all dictionaries

---

[13]   See Chapter 1, 24–7.

[14]   But see van Hoof 1994, which is formally a *petite histoire*, substantially however an extremely well-ordered bibliography of dictionaries from the beginnings with Varro (116–27 BC) till today, with reference to the old languages and to Dutch, English, French, and German. Occasionally, mention is made also of extra-European languages as well as of Spanish and Italian.

for all languages would have to cope with. Recent bibliographies on a national scale are Alston (mainly vols. ii, iii, v, and x, 1974) for English, Claes (1977) for German, Lindemann (1994) for French, and Niederehe (1995) for Spanish.[15] A special case is Stankiewicz (1984) because it is devoted to all Slavic languages. This makes it impossible to treat the historical development of onomasiological dictionaries only in one and certainly in several or even in many countries exhaustively.

All the works mentioned and analysed in the present book are therefore thought of as examples. The properties to be described pertain to the dictionaries analysed but also to others not mentioned. Many of the works not mentioned are known to researchers. The ones mentioned were selected because of their own convincing nature and their historical impact or both. Occasionally more accidental findings during the many years of research have been included.

We can be sure that there is a plethora of onomasiological works still to be discovered in the archives and libraries of this world.

---

[15] Additional information can be obtained from the catalogues of collections. See, for example, Fuller 1942, Learmouth and Macwilliam 1986, and O'Neill 1988.

B. The English Tradition of Onomasiology

3

Hermeneumata, Latin–English glosses, and *nominales*

3.1 The classical base

Glosses and compilations of glosses, that is, glossaries, are the result of comments on texts in order to make them intelligible. Intelligibility is hampered most by words which are old and which have fallen into disuse, or which are only understood in particular regions. Intelligibility is also hampered by homonyms—formally identical words with several meanings. Glosses explain such rare words to language users who are not accustomed to them, and they decide which of two (or more) meanings apply in a given text. Explaining words with the help of words presupposes synonymity in natural languages, that is, the fact that meanings and senses can be expressed in more than one way. The awareness of this fact stands at the beginning of classical, and this means of European, thinking about language (Schmitter 1991). *Glossography* is, thus, part of reception theory and of *explication de texte* (Hunt 1991, vol. I, 3). As with lexicography in general, there is no glossography without glosses, although there has been a production of glosses and glossaries for a long time without glossographic reflections. It is the historiographers who must endeavour to supply them with their hindsight.

There is evidence of plenty of glossaries in the Hellenistic and the Roman period, 'but there is frustratingly little that survives in anything like its original form' (Hunt 1991, vol. I, 4). In the context of the *physei–thesei* issue as discussed in *Kratylos*, lists of synonyms were culled in order to explain their meanings. They became influential for the Greek technique of defining terms and the rational combination of words (Dornseiff 1933, 30–1). From the fourth century BC, lists of lexemes were compiled in order to explain rare words from Homer and the old comedies. Early work in natural history led to collections of names (*onomastica*) for plants, animals, winds, months, etc. as they were used in different regions, or dialects, of the country. A high point of these activities was the *Glottai* of Aristophanes of Byzantium (*c.*275–180 BC), head of the library of Alexandria. Only a short time afterwards, Julius Pollux (Polydeukes, *fl.* second century AD) produced his famous onomasticon which provided a wealth of expressions in Attic style for public speech.

In Republican Rome, glossators turned to commenting on individual authors like Plautus (*c.*254–184 BC), Ennius (239–170 BC), or Lucilius (*c.*180–103 BC). However, glosses became abstracted from their sources and contexts, were borrowed and reborrowed, became mixed and slowly developed into independent commentaries written in so-called glossary Latin, a register of its own which did not mirror actual language use any more.

These developments tended to detach glossaries and onomastica from texts which needed explanation, and to make them a means of collecting encyclopaedic knowledge with the help of names of objects. Behind this was certainly the drive of many ancient cultures, to adhere, at least for some time, to the magical identification of words and referents (Ullmann 1967, 40–1). This is why lists of words can represent the world, and the compilation of such lists can have the aim of incorporating all the knowledge of the world that exists at a given moment, and also the best ways of speaking about it. In this case, glossators do not solely serve the *explication de texte* any more. They become supportive of the *production de texte*. This accounts for the conceptual proximity of Roman encyclopaedias like those of Martianus Capella (*fl.* fifth century AD), Cassiodor (490–585), and Isidore of Seville (*c.*560–636), and glossaries. The technique of listing words according to the semantic information which these words give, also accounts for the meaningful arrangement of entries that would become canonical for such word-lists and the later onomasiological dictionaries which grew out of them. Julius Pollux's onomasticon, for example, had the following order:[1]

1. Gods, places of cults, images, altars, temples, edification and destruction, priests, prophets and prophecy, pious and impious people, kings, colours, merchants, artisans, ships, houses, weather, soldiery, horses and horsemanship, domestic animals, agriculture, plough, carts, bees.
2. People, age groups, birth, parts of the body.

[1] According to Dornseiff 1933, 33. My translation, W. H.

3. Sex, family relationship, marriage, children, friends, masters, slaves, bankers, money, stay in the countryside, travel, mourning, joy, disease, buying and selling.
4. Grammar, rhetoric, philosophers, sophists, poets, music and musical instruments, dance, theatre, astronomy, medicine and diseases.
5. Hunting, dogs, game, jewellery, courage, fear, pharmacy, prayer, glory.
6. Symposia, wine, dishes, ointments, conversation, flatterers.
7. Market, buying and selling, traders, goods, clothes, money, artisans, tools.
8. Court, judges, trials, punishments, sycophants.
9. Town and countryside, public buildings, coins, games of children and adults.
10. Containers, toilets, washing bowls, tables, cooking pots, pots for ointments, ladies' toiletry, tools to be used by ephebes.

In its domains of topics and in its arrangement, this onomasticon foreshadows many glossaries and onomasiological dictionaries to come. So does its technique of close as well as loose associations between words, including pockets of an obviously disordered arrangement.

In particular, Isidore's *Etymologiae sive Origines* (Isidore of Seville 1911) combined linguistic (semantic, grammatical, etymological), with factual information and were, for centuries, received in their hybrid position between two book-genres. At first sight, the collection appears to be a glossary because it consists of words explained. However, on closer inspection it appears to be an encyclopaedia because its entries are sentences, that is, texts, and not lexemes. In the sixth century—at the beginning of Western European culture north of the Alps—Isidore's *Etymologiae* were the most influential work to start the onomasiological tradition.[2]

3.2 *Hermeneumata*

3.2.1 *General*

The *Hermeneumata Pseudodositheanea*, so called because in the Codex Sangallensis 902 they occur together with the Latin texts by the Greek grammarian Dositheus (fourth to fifth century AD) and were for some time attributed to him, are Greek–Latin schoolbooks which, judging from the number of copies still extant, must have been quite popular in Western Europe between the third century and the late seventh century. Originally, they served the learning needs of people like administrators, traders, or soldiers who had some official function in either the Latin-speaking or the Greek-speaking part of the Empire. After that they became part of the greater glossaries coming into existence in the eighth and the following centuries, for example, of the *Leiden Glossary* (*c.*800).[3] They remained in use as Latin schoolbooks, because learning Greek had already fallen

---

[2] See overview in Table A. 22.
[3] The fact that many of the *Hermeneumata* copies which have come down to us are younger than the glossary copies (Derolez 1992, 20) does not preclude their historical precedence as text-types, although it shows how difficult it is to reconstruct the paths of reception as they actually were.

into disuse in the Carolingian era. But as late as 1495 Conrad Celtes (1459–1508) obviously used one copy for his own Greek textbook.

The *Hermeneumata* have been preserved in seven different versions (Dionisotti 1982, 87; Debut 1984), which were collected in Goetz's monumental *Corpus Glossariorvm* (*Corpus* 1882–1923, vol. III, 1892). The versions show obvious proximity and overlappings, although it is not possible to combine them into a coherent stemma. Apart from lexemes and phrases occurring in several versions and allowing groupings among those which are nearer to each other than others, their most obvious proximity lies in the four recurring elements which constitute them: (i) an alphabetical word-list, consisting mostly of verbs, occasionally with paradigms of conjugation; (ii) a topical word-list, called *capitula*, covering various domains of reality; (iii) a colloquy between learner and teacher; and (iv) some classical texts for reading. Almost no version has these four elements in full length. Rather, they constitute the traditional parts of the text-genre. They are hardly the traces of the hand of one unknown first author. Likewise the words in the lists belong in part to the stock of lexemes traditionally to be found in schoolbooks and are not indicative of one common instigator. The generally accepted hypothesis is that the original Greek texts were brought to the West by successive generations of teachers. Here they served the legendary Greek schoolmasters in Roman households as teaching material for quite elementary teaching, which obviously focused on Greek as a living and contemporary language (the *koiné*), not as the language of the classical authors. When used for teaching and learning Greek, these originally monolingual textbooks gradually became bilingual. Then, rather late, they were additionally used for the teaching of Latin to Greek native speakers. Obviously, no traditional method for the teaching of classical Greek developed. This may have been one of the reasons for the fact that the knowledge of Greek deteriorated so quickly and drastically after the end of the Roman Empire. Although stemming from the East, the *Hermeneumata* as schoolbooks were obviously mostly produced in the West. All the texts that have been preserved originated here, only one papyrus copy testifying to the existence of the *Hermeneumata* in the East.

It is certainly noteworthy that 'the idea of a dictionary by topics seems to travel from East to West, beginning in cuneiform and fetching up ... in Seville' (Dionisotti 1982, 91).[4] There are other works which corroborate this statement or which, at least, show that extra-European cultures indeed knew this technique of handling language for their own purposes at the same time as it developed under European conditions. The Graeco-Coptic vocabularies, for example, seem to be quite comparable with the *Hermeneumata* (Sidarus 1990*a* and 1990*b*). They are school texts, that is, abecedaries and syllabaries, topical word-lists, text glossaries, and alphabetical vocabularies (Sidarus 1978). Among other methods of teaching a foreign language, they served translation. The appearance of the celebrated *scala*

---

4 For this and the following statements see Chapter 2.

magna and other *scalae* in the high Middle Ages can only be understood with this background in mind.[5]

In Roman culture, which is more directly responsible for early cultural development north of the Alps, topical word-lists were made instrumental to foreign language teaching and learning from the third century on. Almost all the versions of the *Hermeneumata* have introductions which are as conventional in their reiteration of thoughts as the textbooks themselves. They stress the didactic function of the word-lists and of the conversations. This means that the lists were meant to be learned by heart and were not for reference, and that the colloquies were meant to provide the vocabulary of everyday life and not of literature. This is corroborated by the fact that even the conversations and the reading texts are arranged in lists of one or two words, as if they consisted of syntagmatically independent lexemes. Often the Greek words are in the left-hand column and the Latin words in the right-hand one, but there are cases where this order is reversed.[6] It is important that the classification of words mirrors the general knowledge about the world which was available at the time. '*Couvrant tous les domaines de la vie et de l'activité, [le vocabulaire thématique] permettait à l'apprenti latiniste ou helléniste de posséder tous les éléments susceptibles d'alimenter une conversation courante. La pédagogie était la même, qu'il sâgit d'enfants ou d'adultes;*' (Debut 1984, 74).

The *Hermeneumata Leidensia* (Cod. Leiden Voss. gr. Q.7. sec. X, ff. 3–39, *Corpus 1882–1923*, vol. III, 1892, 3–72), for example, contain the following lists of semantically related word entries (Greek lexemes omitted):

deorum nomina—dearum nomina—de caelo—de aedibus templis—de diebus festis—de spectaculis—de uentis—de membris—de natura—de escis—de potione—de secunda mensa—de oleribus—de piscibus—de auibus—de quadrupedibus—de serpentibus—de habitatione—de ciuitatibus—de suppelectile—de ueste—de coloribus—de aureis—de argenteis— de aereis—de ferro—de fictilibus—de pellibus—de studiis—de artificibus—de arboribus—de agricultura—de militia—de magistratibus—de cognatione—de nauigatione—de medicina— de signis xii.

The first seven of these *capitula*, by their titles as well as by their entries, show the Roman cosmogony, including everyday lexemes for the weather in *de caelo* and *de ventis*. *De membris* brings natural history into the picture with man occupying the first place in the arrangement, annexed with *de natura*, which gives characteristic features of human beings, bodily and mental. The following four chapters, however, show that in fact *Romanus*, that is, man in the Roman world, was behind the entries of *de membris*, because they lead back to Roman lifestyle which man would be subject to. It is with *de piscibus* that nature, finally, comes into its own. Humans as natural beings having already been dealt with, fish, birds, quadrupeds, and reptiles are the classical divisions for the animate world. A division according to elements

---

  [5] See Chapter 2, 33–4.
  [6] For a detailed analysis of the various parts of the *Hermeneumata* texts, including extensive quotations, see Debut 1984.

runs through this classification. The following five chapters, ranging from housing to clothes, apply to the man-made objects which are necessary for living, as opposed to the natural ones. That the following four pertain to metals, which could have just as well been located right after the chapters on the living world, makes sense, however, in the light of the following four chapters which contain entries on human vocational activities. Obviously, the metals are taken to be the material of such. Very much the same idea surfaces in the vicinity of *de arboribus* and *de agricultura*. Trees are a requisite of agriculture, certainly for the Romans. The next five chapters belong to life in a human society alone. The final *de signis xii*, the zodiac, leads back to a cosmological aspect with which the whole list had commenced.

This order of *capitula* shows rough divisions which will reappear in many glossaries and dictionaries to come in later centuries. They are the distinction between cosmos and man, the kingdoms of nature, the difference between the natural and the artificial, human society with its typical institutions and occupations. They foreshadow the great systems of *ordo* which would give cause for many philosophical and scientific reflections. In the centuries to come we also will meet the fact again and again that this order, without losing essential parts, is kaleidoscopically rearranged according to the special aspects which mark a historical era.[7]

Note as an example of entries under one heading, the words contained in *de studiis*:

orator—grammaticus—declamatio—sententia quae reis datur—enarratio—lectio—fabula—disputatio—auditorium—auditores—nomen—appellativum—quantitas—species—forma—casus—tempus—seimplex—similitudo—numerus—uerbum—coniunctio—singulare—anceps—signum—librum—uolumen—uersum—dictatum—paginae—grecum—latinum—rectum—translatio—causa—iudicium—terminum—dispositio—locus—memoria—gustum—auditus—praeceptor—magister—discipuli—condiscipuli—doctrina—eruditio—disciplina—mendatio—correptio—elementa—membra—buxum—titulus.

Almost the whole of European intellectual tradition seems to appear in this (and other) chapter(s) of this late-classical schoolbook.

The arrangement of the *capitula* of the *Hermeneumata Vaticana* (Cod. Vat. 6925, saec.X, ff. 67–78, *Corpus* 1882–1923, vol. III, 1892, 421–38) is a good example for showing the overlappings between the various texts and, at the same time, the importance of the general cultural context. Note:

Incipit liber I.—Itaque ergo supercaelestibus aedibus regiis stat illa sole sacra et divina sanctae et inviolatae trinitatis natura . . .—De caelo—De superaetheriis—De terra—De arboribus—De silvestribus—De floribus—De oleribus—De bestiis—De iumentis—De armentis—De pecudibus—De porcis—De reptilibus—De aquis—De avibus—De piscibus.

The words subsumed under each heading show clearly that the list is pagan in origin and has later been reworked in order to adapt it to Christian ideas. In

---

[7] See Chapter 11.

particular, the many names of gods and goddesses in the second chapter were replaced by forty-nine epithets of the Holy Trinity. Moreover, the entries were changed in order to conform to the narrative of Genesis. Yet there are classical ideas discernible, if dimly, in the background of the eighteen chapters. This applies to the cosmological concepts of chapters 3 and 4 as well as to the role that the four elements play for the classification of objects of reality. Assuming that memorizing a list of words like this was part of foreign language learning, this includes the fact that a generally accepted order of lexemes was also supposed to be essential. This is why the adaptation of Christian ideas was perhaps not simply an act of authoritarian conformity, but was meant to enhance learnability.

3.2.2 Capitula *and* ars memorativa

When speaking of ancient and medieval culture, we, as a rule, hardly ever realize that it depended almost entirely on oral communication. The very fact that writing was possible and that manuscripts and codices were produced, exchanged within the country, and kept in libraries, certainly does not mean that the intellectual life of that time was mediated by writing, perhaps even in the way in which it is done today. Authors such as Aristotle (384–322 BC), Cicero (106–43 BC) or Quintilian (35–95), just like Albert the Great (*c.*1206–80) or Thomas Aquinas (*c.*1227–74), would have done most of their research, their teaching, and conversing without any written material, solely relying on their memory. Roman orators and Christian preachers, politicians, and lawyers, and, of course, authors and bards of the classical and medieval epics performed by heart. Although intellectuals had the opportunity to write their ideas down and circulate them among their friends, all work on the spot depended on oral performance and its basis, memory. No wonder the art of memorizing itself was supposed to be of the utmost importance, and being able to learn long texts or long lists of words by heart counted as a special gift. Many of the great personalities such as Aristotle, Cicero, or Caesar (102–44 BC) are said to have excelled at it. The notorious training of orators in Athens and Rome was, of course, a necessity under such circumstances. A written culture is not made by the fact that writing is possible at all, it depends on the functions which are attributed to the written or printed word. Moreover, written material must be easily accessible to (almost) everybody. In the seventeenth century, this made the introduction of paper almost as important for the general development of the printed media as the invention of the press. Therefore learning relied on the spoken word for a long time, even after printed material became available (Eisenstein 1983).[8] Between then and our present time there is the difference that classical and 'medieval culture [were] fundamentally

[8] Johannes Trithemius (Johannes Heidenberg or Zeller, 1462–1516), the famous abbot of Sponheim, even asked his scribes to copy printed books the traditional way because parchment would have a much longer lifespan than paper. See Eisenstein 1983, 10–11.

memorial, to the same profound degree that modern culture in the West is documentary' (Carruthers 1990, 8). All this is the background to the extraordinary
importance of *ars memorativa*.

Essentially, *ars memorativa* is a set of rules teaching people to transfer notions
and words, which they wish to store in their memories and retrieve in a given
order, to visual images arranged in some spatial pattern. Its start is the story told
by Cicero in *De Oratore* of the poet Simonides (fifth century BC) who escaped the
collapse of a roof under which people were assembled during a feast and who was
able to report on the victims because he remembered their faces in the order in
which they had been sitting around the table. All through the Middle Ages and
the Renaissance this anecdote was told in the way in which it appeared in
Rhetorica ad Herennium.[9] '[Its] section of Memory is our oldest surviving treatment of the subject. Based on visual images and "backgrounds", the mnemotech-
nical system which it presents exerted an influence traceable to modern times.'
And 'it is our only complete representative of the system it teaches' (Caplan 1970,
12 and 24).

The nucleus of *ars memorativa* is: If you wish to store knowledge of any sort in
your mind, organize it in a spatial arrangement. Select places for this arrangement
from your experience, like the order of sitting around a table, the sequence of
rooms in a house, the row of sculptures in a temple. Make each place, each *topos*,
a stimulus for possible retrieval by combining it with an image which somehow
points to the item of knowledge, to its shape, colour, sound, function, or something else. If there are no real places to select, imagine fictitious ones like spacious
buildings, gardens, voyages. Besides their associative power, images should have a
stimulating character that arouses emotions, like faces or human figures, but also
abstract schemata. They should impress themselves on memory because of their
beauty or their monstrosity. They stand for objects, but also for notions and
concepts, solely and in concatenation, that is, also for propositions. There arose a
long controversy whether texts could be remembered verbatim with the help of
this method, that is, by replacing each word or even each letter with an image.
Most authors, for example Quintilian but not Cicero, decided not to use *ars
memorativa* in this way because it would actually burden the powers of memory
more than help them.

Ars memorativa became an integral part of intellectual life in classical Rome
and in the Middle Ages.[10] Memory is the central place for any intellectual activity
and has to be understood in a much broader sense than today. It is integrated into
antique philosophy, for example in Aristotle's statement that every item of knowledge is stored as a notion in the memory, or in Plato's concept of *anamnesis*, that

---

[9] Collection of Ciceronian texts from around 700, first printed in 1470, thereafter frequently
edited, also under the title *Rhetorica nova*, and very influential. Cajus Herennius, the dedicatee, was an
otherwise unknown Roman. See Nüßlein 1994, 328–30.
[10] The following sketchy remarks are based on the enormously rich material in Yates 1966 and
Carruthers 1990. See also Caplan 1970.

is, (in modern terms) a retrieval procedure. It is, of course, integrated into classical rhetoric where memory figures as one of the five essential stages of preparing oratory. Best known of the classical sources is, probably, St Augustine's (Aurelius Augustinus, 354–430) theory of memory in his *Confessiones* (written *c*.397; book 10, chaps. VI–XXVII), where in passages almost unmatched in their literary quality the author speaks of the camps and storehouses, the caverns and halls of his memory in which every single experience of a human life is accumulated in order to be available for the love of God.

The faculty of recollection is also integrated into the medieval system of virtues, namely as prudence which uses the memory of past experience to guide future actions. At that time, a tremendous extension of memory training took place which was no longer confined to memorization techniques, even in their philosophical embedding. It now covered the visual representation in the mind of the whole universe, heaven, and hell, just like the virtues and vices. A system of allegorical figures, signs, and charts was developed which, in spatial representation, stood for the universe in its Christian understanding. Much of the medieval and Renaissance visual arts used, kept, and elaborated this system.[11]

The Renaissance, finally, filled the comprehensive schemata with new symbols and figures, for example from the Cabbalistic and the Hermetic tradition. They acquired a talismanic life of their own. They no longer served the visual representation of reality but disclosed new, hitherto hidden knowledge to those that had the spiritual awareness to understand it.

This history of *ars memorativa*, inevitably vague and sketchy, can nevertheless make people of the twentieth century become aware of a long tradition concerning the working and functions of memory, oscillating between a dry mnemonic device for learning something by heart and philosophical ideas about men's power of cognition and the universe. It must also have affected early techniques of language learning.

The general dominance of spoken language to be memorized over written language also prevailed in schools. Teachers taught by word of mouth, learners repeated what the teachers said. If at all, it was the teacher who was in possession of a book, which he would use over and over again. Certainly not every pupil had one, either, although the invention of printing made a larger supply available. Some schools even had libraries of their own (Orme 1973, 125–7). Possibly, teachers dictated grammatical rules or topical word-lists and learners noted them down on little tablets of wax or slate. But these texts were written down solely for memorization and were then erased.

It should not be forgotten that Latin as a language to be learned at school was not as dead as it is for today's learners, although its usability could never compete with that of vernaculars. The well-known *vulgaria* (English sentences which the pupils had to render into *latins*) show the teacher's attempt to introduce everyday

---

[11] See Volkmann 1929 with many illustrations.

events and experiences of a boy's life into the Latin classroom, thus stimulating the learner's interest and making Latin appear as a lively means of communication (Orme 1973, 98–100). The same could be effected by the semantic cohesion of word-lists, with their often everyday and down-to-earth vocabulary.[12]

According to whatever we know about the intellectual climate of the classical and early medieval eras, learning meant learning by heart and, thus, learning a language meant learning lists of words, of probably considerable length, by heart.[13] Grammar obviously consisted mainly of defining word-classes in the dialogical manner of Donatus (*fl.* fourth century AD) and then also of learning the definitions by heart. Next, learners had to run through morphological paradigms and to parse sentences.

The *capitula* of the *Hermeneumata* provided such word-lists in a certain accepted order. Admittedly, this was not a spatial arrangement in the narrow sense, but an arrangement which was judged to be philosophically meaningful. And this meaningfulness must have been looked upon as a warrant of success in learning. However, this order had a built-in spatial component, as can be seen, for example, from the *capitula* of the *Hermeneumata Vaticana* which have been quoted earlier. 'Above' and 'below' are clearly separated. The grouping of plants and animals, as it is done there, is also a grouping according to the places where the plants and animals can be found. *Ordo* in the philosophical sense was always very much an arrangement according to *topoi*. Learning, that is, memorization, was supposed to occur within this order of the universe. This is a learning theory in the robes of classical and medieval knowledge, which will remain influential through many centuries.[14]

The *Hermeneumata* started the tradition of topical word-lists in the Middle Ages. In the course of the following centuries, these topical word-lists, the backbone of the onomasiological tradition, would, of course, not be limited to strictly didactic purposes, although these remained to be perhaps more important than others.

3.2.3 The colloquies

The colloquies provided teachers and learners with the foreign language as used in everyday life. They introduced an element of natural language performance into the classroom. They have been called '*extrêmement original*' (Debut 1984, 84). This pertains in particular to their value as sources of our knowledge of cultural history. '*Ces textes, pleins de vie, avec leurs dialogues pris sur le vif et leurs détails concrets, nous donnent vraiment l'impression de partager la vie des bambins, d'assister à des*

---

[12] Orme 1973 does not treat topical word-lists at all.

[13] See Chapter 1, 26–7.

[14] It should be pointed out that all of St Augustine's metaphors for the human memory use spatial images and that all functions of memory are described by him as moving and re-moving objects within space.

procès, de faire le marché, d'aller aux thermes ou de faire de somptueux repas.' (Debut 1984, 84.)

From our present point of view, the colloquies of the *Hermeneumata* do indeed not contain much natural conversation or any features of oral language at all. Nor are there turns of speech as they actually occur between the partners of a conversation, that is, in this case, teachers and learners. Moreover, these colloquies seem not to have been spoken but dictated and written down. Note the preface to the *Hermeneumata Vaticana*:

Conversatio, usus cotodianus, debet dari omnibus pueris et puellis, quoniam necessaria sunt minoribus et maioribus, propter antiquam consuetudinem et disciplinam. Sic incipiam scribere, ab exordio lucis usque ad vesperum.[15]

With respect to the linguistic features of orality, the intention of including oral performance in foreign language teaching must perhaps stand for the deed. However, these colloquies were so much recognized and acknowledged that, in fact, the *Hermeneumata* became the first historical example of a genre of foreign-language teaching texts which would be imitated in the following centuries, as *Aelfric's Colloquy*[16] proves. They developed strongly in the fourteenth century and then became an established type of textbook for three hundred years and more.[17]

From the point of view of contents, all colloquies are conducted along similar lines. Roughly speaking, they are determined by the course of activities during one day. 'Getting up', 'At School', 'Lunch', 'Preparations for Dinner', 'At the Baths', 'After the Party', 'Bedtime', 'In the Forum' is a typical sequence of scenes (at the end slightly anomalous).[18] These scenes, which are not always plausible, are delimited according to time and space.

It is certainly noteworthy that many sentences of such colloquies read as if they were contextualized word-lists. So, in fact, they are a side branch of the onomasiological tradition. There are long series with enumerated words which stand in paradigmatic relation to each other and, semantically speaking, belong to one domain. The scenes and activities that evolve out of the narratives, serve quite

---

[15]   Greek version omitted. '[The] conversation, practised daily, must be given to all boys and girls, because they are necessary for beginners as well as for advanced, because of the old custom and way of teaching. Start writing in this way, from morning to evening.' (My translation, W. H.) The mention of 'beginners' and 'advanced' refers to the two variants of Donatus' grammar. The readers of *Donatus minor* were more occupied with learning inflectional morphology, but the readers of *Donatus maior* studied questions of syntax.

[16]   See Chapter 4.

[17]   See Chapter 4. I am leaving aside the important influence of the methods of argumentation by a guided dialogue in the tradition of Socrates and Plato, which certainly gave the strongest impetus to this kind of teaching. But dialogues in the context of foreign-language learning have a different, non-philosophical function.

[18]   The example is taken from Dionisotti 1982, from the text arranged by Conrad Celtes following a classical source. The following quotations are also taken from there. Dionisotti gives a commentary and comparisons with other colloquies.

naturally to demarcate these domains. Note the following extracts of the Latin text of the *Hermeneumata Vaticana:*[19]

[Within 'Getting up']: *Hoc primum facio (primum feci), deposui dormitoria, et sumpsi linteum, amictulum, pallium, fasciam, tunicam, et reliqua indumenta. . . . Hinc postea procedo de domo in publicum, in auditorium, in pontem, in vicum, in forum, cum meo puero capsario, aut paedagogo, aut condiscipulo. . . . Deinde regredior ad domum patris. Eo salutare parentes, patrem et matrem et avum et aviam, fratrem et sororem et omnes cognatos, avunculum et amicos, nutricem et nutritorem, maiorem domus, omnes collibertos, ostiarium, domesticum, vicinos, omnes amicos, incolam, insularium, eunuchum.*[20]

There are many utterances of this sort. They prove that, in this case, words are not meaningful constituents of a syntagma, but that the sentences are constructed in such a way that the words as names for related objects can be collected in them. The paradigmatic relationship of lexemes is made visible in the syntagmatic. This is the onomasiological principle in only a slight disguise.

3.3 A typological view of Old English glosses

The beginnings of English lexicography, and indeed of the lexicography of other European languages, lie in glosses, which have been preserved in quite considerable numbers from the eighth century onwards. As is well known,[21] such glosses are scribblings, sometimes only scratched with a dry point (Merritt 1945, Page 1979, Derolez 1992, 39), between the lines or in the margins of Latin codices, giving explanations with reference to a word or a phrase of the text which had obviously been found difficult to understand by its reader(s). They were fixed by somebody for his own benefit, and perhaps for the benefit of his fellow readers, who would presumably have the same difficulties with the Latin tongue and read the same codex. Besides being used as study aids, they will also have served as teaching aids, as a word difficult to understand is also a word difficult to teach. Thus, glosses

---

[19]   See also Chapter 4, 78–9.

[20]   'I do (have done) this first, have laid down [my] night-[shirt], taken [my] linen [shirt], coat, cloak, wrap-over [a bandage to be worn round the belly or round the legs or round the head], tunic, and the other clothes. From here, later, I proceed from the house to the public storehouse, the school, the bridge, the street, the market-place, with the servant for boy[s] or the servant for children, or with my fellow-pupils . . . Then I go back to my father's house. I go [in order to] greet [my] parents, father and mother and grandfather and grandmother, brother and sister and all relatives, [maternal] uncle and friends, [the] wet nurse and attendant, [the head] butler, all who are free as myself, [the] porter, friend of the house, [the] neighbours, all friends, [the] inhabitant [in the country], [the] one [confined] to an island, [the] eunuch.' (My translation, W. H.)

[21]   Anglo-Saxon glossography is, of course, a wide and complicated field of research which cannot and need not be shown here in all its aspects and its academic history. Recent concise introductions are the article 'Glossen, Glossare' in *Lexikon des Mittelalters* (1989) which includes paragraphs on Middle Latin (Lapidge), German (Schmitt), the Romance languages (Gier), English (Gneuss 1989, 1513–14), and the Slavonic languages (Hannick), and also Derolez 1992. Our present interest is limited to showing how the ideas and techniques of onomasiology and topical word-lists were taken over from older traditions and shaped in a culture-specific way.

allow insight into 'the realities of medieval literacy and education' (Hunt 1991, vol. I, vii). These realities were, among others, determined by the fact that in one monastery there would, as a rule, be only one copy, one manuscript or codex, of a classical text which served as teaching material and which was in continual use, sometimes over several generations. This explains why glosses are often written by different hands and at different times and obviously following different principles.

The special attraction of glosses is that they allow a glimpse into the medieval classroom, at least as far as translation work was done there. Although this is true in general, we must be warned against too direct expectations. In her recent survey on the nature of Latin glossaries, A. C. Dionisotti (1996, 222) warns against assuming 'we knew a whole lot about the activities of monastery teachers between the fifth and the seventh centuries' and continues: 'actually we know next to nothing, but it would be a safe bet that they did not spend much time combing the margins of the pagan classics'. This is the reason for a number of inconsistencies. There are many coinciding glosses in different copies of the same text proving that they must have a common origin and must have travelled with the text, possibly from the Continent to the British Isles. Consequently, they cannot be the reflection of an individual monk wrestling with the Latin difficulties of this manuscript. Moreover, the glossing of a text is often very unsystematic. This indicates careless copying of glosses together with the texts (Lapidge 1982). Nevertheless, these scribblings between lines or in margins or somewhere in the empty space on the page signal that texts, whenever and wherever, were in the hands of people who had their difficulties with them. Thus, they give us semantic and grammatical information about the linguistic performance of the time (Derolez 1992, 35).[22]

Glosses are either Latin, Old (or, later, Middle) English, Anglo-Norman, Old French, or in rare cases Greek synonyms of the vocabulary of the text, and/or comments of an encyclopaedic nature or applying to grammar. Synonyms and comments are sometimes given in two or even three languages. English (and indeed European)[23] glossography has been a field of ongoing historiographical research for more than one hundred and fifty years, lying at the crossroads of linguistics, philology, palaeography, and codicology.[24] The primary stimulus of this work was the intention of nineteenth-century philologists to print and publish the manuscripts available, establish unambiguous readings, determine

---

[22] There are also glosses on prosody.

[23] For an edition and recent treatments of German glosses see Steinmeyer and Sievers 1879–1922, Schwarz 1977, Sonderegger 1987, and Sanders 1992, each with additional references. See also the relevant contributions on the history of the lexicography of various European languages in Hausmann *et al.* 1989–91, vol. 2, arts 181–219 (1990).

[24] See introductory remarks to the most important editions of glossaries: Wright and Wülcker 1884 (a re-edition of Wright 1857 and 1873), Sweet 1885, Hessels 1890 and 1906, Napier 1900, Oliphant 1966, and others. For more recent treatments, including ample bibliographical information on editions and analytical literature, see Gneuss 1996, 11–13, 86–8; Hunt 1991, vol. I, 3–55 and *passim*, and Derolez 1992. For recent lexicographical treatment see Stein 1985.

where, that is, in which dialect, and when they came into being and, because of obvious overlappings, what the genealogical relations were amongst them. Our own treatment does not add anything to the philological achievements of this research, but looks at glosses as given sources embedded in the intellectual history of their own time[25] and tradition, and reflects on them as tokens of the history of the concept of onomasiology. The scarcity of information which we have of the early medieval centuries makes these reflections more hypothetical than historiographical in the descriptive sense.

Besides the Old English texts, glosses are the most important sources of our present knowledge of the early phases of the English language and the culture of which it was part. The juxtaposition of Old English with other European languages is a particularly helpful device for establishing word meanings. There is a historical irony in the fact that nowadays we can learn about Old English because in its own time it was useful for people in teaching and learning, for example, Latin.

Intellectual work in the early Middle Ages would typically consist of reading Latin texts in order to extract traditional, that is, Greek and Roman, knowledge from them. They were the carriers of almost all the information that monks, the intellectuals of the period, were concerned with. This meant that a fair command of Latin was presupposed. Therefore, self-instruction and the teaching and learning of Latin, most of all to and by novices, became very important tasks. Intellectual work could not proceed unless the monasteries educated their members in this respect. In all likelihood, every novice master had his own teaching method and would try to write his own teaching texts. Consequently, glossing and the use of glosses was at the heart of the intellectual life and took on a large share of the work which we nowadays call the reception of classical culture in Europe. It was a phenomenon *sui generis* (Derolez 1992, 12) with many special aspects and far-reaching consequences. We find it at the centre of Anglo-Saxon cultural development, with Aldhelm (*c.*640–709) and in Canterbury at the time of Theodore (602–90).With the different kinds of potential uses of glosses in mind, a typology[26] can be created which has the function of an ordering schema. It will show in which way the topical glossary, which continues the classical onomasiological tradition and which is our concern, evolves out of the conditions, needs, and intentions of reading Latin texts.

The first type of gloss (i) is the *text-dependent* gloss. It was intended to be an explanation of a (piece of) text. Its explanatory power is highly context sensitive, the attention of the scribe focusing on the text in front of him. It appears either in

---

[25]   For earlier deliberations of this kind see Sweet 1885 and Lindsay [1921].

[26]   A typological view is independent of chronology. However, some temporal order of the origin of various types of glosses and glossaries will be mirrored in it. The processes of the copying, writing and rewriting, arranging and rearranging of glossaries etc. can, however, not appear. The idea of a typology of glosses is not new (see Murray 1900, in particular 50–1), but it has not been made the starting-point of onomasiology so far. A possible exception to this is Buridant 1986. See also Derolez 1992, 20–1, Law 1994 and Sauer 1999. My typology differs from theirs because of the special concern behind it.

occasional glosses or in full interlinear versions, which come near to translations. If meant for teaching purposes, the gloss was and still is situation sensitive in a way which is very difficult to understand from historiographical hindsight.

The limited, text-bound usability of glosses changed as soon as some of them were collected as *glossae collectae* and put together into longer and longer lists of lemmata with their explanations. Nobody would have done this if there had not been a need for it. Such glosses constitute the second type (ii), which stands between individual glosses and a glossary. It could still be used for one source text only. Working with *glossae collectae* could, however, be more convenient than with individual glosses, because in various texts at least some of the difficult words would recur frequently and the list would save glossing them each time if explanations worked out for one case could be applied to others. This resulted in a loss of text sensitivity of glosses which, in turn, meant an increase in usability. This is true for glossaries where the source texts are still mentioned as headings of batches of lemmata; it remains true even when the source texts are no longer given but were presumably recognizable to their users from the arrangement of lemmata.

The third type (iii) is the *alphabetical* glossary. Although we can quite often trace sources even for alphabetically arranged glosses, they no longer serve explanatory purposes for these alone, but extend their usability to any book. It does not matter that alphabetical glossaries show their origins in context-bound glosses by the fact that they frequently list their lexemes in inflected forms, that is, exactly as they appeared in a sentence of a given text. Neither does it make a typological difference whether the A-order, AB-order, or in fact, the A...n-order is observed. These are grades of formal perfection.

The sequence of the three types marks a gradual disintegration of the link between text or teaching situation and glossary. The fourth type (iv), the *topical* glossary, is very different from the first three. It exists either as collections of lemmata belonging to a (relatively) homogeneous semantic domain, such as names of parts of the body, of plants, precious stones, or instruments, or as collections of lemmata belonging to several factual domains in reality and leading to corresponding semantic domains of lexemes which, however, show a certain homogeneity on a higher level. Their order can be alphabetical or non-alphabetical. Topical glossaries sometimes exist as batches (nests) within other glossaries, for example *glossae collectae*. The variants of topical glossaries will become sub-typologically more lucid, if we hypothesize various intentions of the scribes for them.

(a) A scribe may read a (passage of a) text with topically related words which need explanation. The topical glossary is, then, in fact nothing but a limited text-dependent glossary.

(b) A scribe may read a (passage of a) text with topically related words which he finds important as a (quasi-)systematic source of information. Culling them from the source(s) is, thus, done not just for explanation's sake but for the documentation and storage of information. The motive behind such word-lists could, for example, be to collect as much knowledge as possible for medical purposes when the scribe wrote down names of the parts of the human body or of herbs.

(c)   A scribe may extract topically related terms from a source text and arrange them alphabetically. In this case, the lemmata follow an external arrangement whose general usefulness for the purpose of reference as well as information retrieval is obvious. It leads to extended usability and shows that glossaries also acquired a function in the development of medieval culture and scientific thinking, over and above their function as study and teaching aids.

(d)   Finally, a scribe may arrange topically related terms from source texts in a systematic way, where the sequence of lemmata represents some kind of unity binding together all (or most of) the entries. The simplest example of this is when, for example, the names of the parts of the human body start from the head and move in an orderly fashion down to the feet, and when, in addition, they clearly distinguish between the visible members and the invisible organs of the body. This is the onomasiological word-list proper.

Obviously, topical (nests of) glossaries can serve the same purposes as general glossaries if used for the comprehension or for the teaching of specialized texts. The subtypes ((a) to (d)) are marked by the same gradual disintegration of the link between text or teaching situation and glossary. In this case, however, the loss of text dependency is counterbalanced by a gain in information. Thus, glossaries move into a typological position where they serve to represent and transmit the specialized knowledge of the time in lists of words. In those early centuries of European culture, people had no other way of enriching, for example, their botanical knowledge than equating new (or even well-known) plants with new Latin names.

The systematic topical glossary (type (iv), subtype (d)) is actually a borderline case of glossography. It has a clear tendency to represent knowledge of the world in a comprehensive way. It arranges batches of semantically related lexemes, each of which could constitute a topical glossary in its own right, in such a way that their sequence becomes meaningful on its own. Guidelines for this arrangement may either be works of the encyclopaedic tradition or the result of experience which was supposed to recognize some natural order of reality.

Besides the different intentions in writing different types of glossaries, there seems to have been a different understanding of language incorporated in them. Naturally, it concerns only the status of words.

The linguistic background of the first and second types (text-dependent glosses and *glossae collectae*) seems to remain in a pre-paradigmatic[27] state. Words

---

[27]   I am using the term in a loose sense, of course stimulated by Thomas S. Kuhn in choosing it, but not agreeing with his theory.

function semantically as context-dependent units which, however, have a recognizable morphological independence. The latter is revealed in the inflectional systems of Latin which played such an important role in grammatical education. Thus, semantic dependency and morphological independence work together to establish the word as a linguistic unit to be taken for granted. This is also true for the assumption of its interlingual translatability.

In the third type (alphabetical glossary) even more insight into the independent morphological state of words is shown by their formal arrangement, which presupposes some phonetic analysis. In addition, it proves the early influence of alphabetical script on language awareness. In the fourth type (topical glossary), the word is more and more, that is, from subtypes (a) to (d), understood to be the name of a thing. Historically, this could be called a referential paradigm in linguistic thinking. Word meaning is now understood to be determined by objects of reality or of the mind. While meaning in the previous types of glossaries was determined by translation and paraphrase, that is, by exclusively linguistic means, it is now determined by reference.[28]

Examples of text-dependent glosses (type (i)) are, of course, numerous. They appear in many text editions. Most of all, they apply to the psalter, canticles, and hymns. Aldhelm (*c.*640–709) is probably the most glossed author, followed by Prudentius (348–?410). Other names are St Augustine, Bede (672–735), Boethius (480–524), Gregory the Great (*c.*540–604), Isidore, Jerome (*c.*340–420), Priscian, Prosper (*c.*390–465), and the two Testaments (Napier 1990, xi–xxiii; Merritt 1945, xii–xviii).[29] Nouns and adjectives are often given in oblique cases, verbs in different tenses, which shows the textual dependency of entries. From the level of glossing we can guess whether the glossator had a good command of the language or was more or less ignorant. Obviously, Latin–Latin glosses betray a higher competence in Latin than Latin–Old English glosses do.

The *Leiden Glossary* (MS Leyden Voss. Lat. Q. 69, written *c.*800 in St Gallen, ed. Hessels 1906)[30] is a case of a non-alphabetical collection (type (ii)). Its 255 Latin (sometimes Greek)–Latin and Latin–Old English (sometimes also Old High German) glosses are broken down into forty-eight chapters according to the source texts which are given as headings. Its sources, besides smaller ones, are the Bible, the Rule of St Benedict, Rufinus' (*c.*340–410) translation of Eusebius' (*c.*260–340) *Ecclesiastica Historia*, Isidore, Gregory, and various hagiographical works. Sweet (1885, 6 and 10) comments: 'L[eiden] cannot, in fact, be strictly regarded as a single glossary, but rather as a collection of smaller glossaries, not yet digested into a single whole . . . These non-alphabetical glossaries were probably at first intended only to serve the purpose of a running commentary and glossary to each text, and the plan for utilizing them for *general* reference was an afterthought.'

---

[28] See Chapter 11.

[29] Wilson 1958 gives an excellent overview of the manuscripts which medieval libraries in Britain would stock. This is, at the same time, an overview of potential sources of glosses.

[30] See Ker 1957, Appendix No. 18; for a description in detail see Hessels 1906, ix–xli.

However, some chapters of the *Leiden Glossary* give us the opportunity to follow the path from *glossae collectae* to a topical glossary. Chapter XLI, for example, contains six entries from various *canones concilii*, ten entries with names for precious stones from *Apocalypse* XII, 19, and five more entries from Sulpicius Severus' (*c*.363–425) lives of the saints. The whole is headed '*Item de nominibus diuersis*'. The interesting case is that of the glosses on precious stones. They are disconnected from other Bible glosses and placed as a nest between two topically unrelated groups. These facts, as well as the neutral heading, point towards a potentially new interest in glossing, namely, collecting names for precious stones irrespective of the source text from which the glossator culled them and also irrespective of their linguistic difficulties. We can assume that he knew the source, but did not care to mention it. This points to type (iv), subtype (b), that is, relatively closed topical batches in a glossary.

Chapter XLIV is headed '*Item alia; de caelo*', referring back to chap. XLIII which is called '*Item de diuersis nominibus*'. In fact, its entries are taken from Isidore's *De natura rerum*. They stem from the same semantic domain because of the topic specialization of the source. This points to type (iv), subtype (a), that is text-dependent topical glosses.

A similar case is that of chap. XLV, '*Verba de multis*'. It contains items from the grammars of Phocas (a late Roman grammarian of unknown dates), very much, though not in every case, following the sequence of Phocas' word-lists. This results in batches of names of animals (glosses 51–79) which already occur in the grammar. Again we are referred to type (iv), subtype (a). Finally, in chap. XLVIII, there are groups of names of birds (glosses 51–70), fish (glosses 9–12 and 71–5) and other animals (glosses 76–80), swine (glosses 91–4), and vegetables (glosses 96–101). Its source is supposed to be one of the *Hermeneumata*, with the Greek entries dropped, Latin glosses retained, and Old English glosses added. Remaining Greek words and misreadings point to this technique. The word-lists in this schoolbook, whose source copy may have come from Ireland where monks knew Greek and would give Irish interpretations, which however were lost because they were not understood, were arranged in similar groups, so the Old English glossator could simultaneously follow his linguistic needs and his encyclopaedic curiosity. Note Lindsay's hypothetical, but quite plausible attempt at an explanation:

So we need not call up the picture of some compiler laboriously searching through the pages of every abstruse book in Benedict Bishop's library and culling from one author the name of some out-of-the-way plant, from another author some botanical term equally remote. How much more natural that he got them all without effort from the plant-name section of a Hermeneumata MS!   (Lindsay n.d. [1921], 9.)

In some chapters, the *Leiden Glossary* also exemplifies an intermediate state between text arrangement and alphabetical arrangement. Chapter IV, taken from Rufinus' translation of Eusebius' *Ecclesiastica Historia*, follows the text, whereas chapter V, taken from the same source, is alphabetized.

The *Corpus Glossary* (MS Corpus Christi College, Cambridge, 144, written in Canterbury in the second half of the ninth century, ed. Hessels 1890 and Lindsay [1921])[31] is one of the many alphabetical glossaries (type (iii)), that have come down to us. Its original manuscript stems from the beginning of the eighth century. It consists of two parts, a list of Hebrew and Greek names taken from St Jerome's *Liber de nominibus Hebraicis* and, to a small extent, from a treatise *De Graecis nominibus* ascribed to Eucherius, bishop of Lyons,[32] and a much longer list of words and glosses compiled from various sources. The first list is in alphabetical sequence in the A order, the second list is in alphabetical sequence in the AB order. The Latin entries are glossed by Latin and/or Old English words. There are over 2,000 glosses in Old English. As with all alphabetical glossaries, the *Corpus* has been assembled from earlier ones. In trying to trace the glosses back to their sources, we must assume intermediate stages. Note Hessel's old but still valid explanation:

By 'sources' we need not necessarily understand 'authors'; for the words of glossaries like that of the Corpus MS., which is already alphabetically arranged according to the first letters of each word, must have been collected in earlier glossaries according to the first letter of each word. The latter, in their turn, were no doubt compiled from the so-called class-glossaries, in which glosses had been copied from various authors or interlinear glosses, in the order in which they followed each other in the texts, or arranged under subjects. So that the glosses, before they were copied into the Corpus MS, must have already passed through at least two or three stages in other MSS.   (Hessels 1890, xvi.)

The *Durham Glossary of Plants* (MS Durham Hunter 100, ed. von Lindheim 1941)[33] can serve as an illustrious example of a topical glossary, alphabetically arranged (type (iv), subtype (c)). The manuscript was written between 1100 and 1135; its source, however, seems to have also originated in the *Hermeneumata* tradition, which means that its roots ultimately go back to the third century. The glosses are Greek/Latin–Old English, with only one (No. 208) still being trilingual. The glossary has 342 entries of Latin herb names in alphabetical sequence. Its contents are, of course, of great significance for the botanical and pharmacological knowledge of its time, as all glossaries of plant names are. Lexicographically speaking, it is only its strict alphabetization which is noteworthy.

It must be remembered that our definitions of types and subtypes of glosses/glossaries have the function of an ordering schema. They hardly do justice to any glossary as an individual text which originated in a certain situation and was written by an author with special intentions in mind. Typicality means that accidental features of glossaries are overlooked and that they are valued for their accordance with types, not for their many other characteristics. In particular, the linguistic quality of glossing remains unexamined. Questions like the following are perfectly justified.

---

[31]   See Ker 1957, No. 36. This is a fuller version of the glosses in the Épinal–Erfurt manuscript. See the edition by Bischoff *et al.* 1988.

[32]   Dates not known.   [33]   See Ker 1957, No. 110.

How commonly are vernacular and Latin glosses intermingled by the same glossator? To what extent are vernacular glosses provided as an adjunct to Latin glosses or do they occur independently of the provision of glosses in Latin? Do the Latin and vernacular glosses 'double' each other or do they highlight different aspects of the lemma? How far is the resort of the vernacular occasioned less by the rarity of the lemma than by the lack of obvious Latin synonyms?   (Hunt 1991, vol. I, 17.)

These and many other questions remain to be asked and answered if we want to research glosses and glossaries thoroughly, a topic which, however, is outside our present concern. Yet it is our concern to detect glosses and glossaries as the beginnings of lexicography, as types of dictionaries which would develop via many intermediate stages in later centuries. Types (i) and (ii), just like subtypes (a) and (b) of type (iv) have all the time led a rather unofficial life as teachers' and learners' notes, either interlinear or marginal in texts or in note-books and containing help for either general or specialized foreign language. They are in private use even today. Type (iii) initiated the general alphabetical dictionary of at least two languages, type (iv) the specialized dictionary either in alphabetical (subtype (c)) or in topical fashion (subtype (d)). The borderline case of the latter type, the universal topical glossary, was to become of prototypical importance for the development of onomasiological dictionaries.[34]

3.4 Aelfric's Glossary

The most noteworthy example of an Old English universal topical glossary (type (iv), subtype (d)), representing the beginnings of English onomasiological lexicography, is the one attached to Aelfric's (*c.*955–1020) grammar.[35]

Teaching and learning Latin meant teaching and learning, besides vocabulary, the grammar. It is well known how much concentration on this second focus of classical heritage dominated medieval intellectual activities, eventually equating Latin grammar with universal grammar and universal (Latin) grammar with general structures of cognition (e.g. Bursill-Hall 1971). During the medieval centuries a didactic interest in Latin as a foreign language broadened into a highly abstract epistemological treatment of the relationship between language and thought.

Following Dionysius Thrax (*fl. c.*100 BC, Law and Sluiter 1995), the leading figures of Latin grammar were Varro (116–27), Donatus, and Priscian. The insular grammarians can be grouped according to the ways in which they followed these

---

[34] Even the later dictionary according to word-classes is foreshadowed in the Anglo-Saxon period. In his grammar, Aelfric gives many lexemes, for example of nouns following the -o declension etc. These lists of examples read like glossaries *en miniature.*

[35] See Ker 1957: Nos. 17, 71, 154A, 158, 227, 362, 384, 398, and 406, besides some minor manuscripts. For lexicographical treatment under the heading, 'The London Vocabulary', see Stein 1985, 32–43.

models. In particular, *Donatus minor* influenced a group of grammarians who concentrated on inflection, *Donatus maior* another group of grammarians who included questions of syntax (Law 1982). There is unanimity among historiographers that Aelfric's grammar takes precedence among all of them. It is called the most important linguistic document of the so-called third period, that is, the tenth and eleventh centuries, which, with the leading figure of King Alfred (848–?900), saw the development of a new linguistic culture, after the cultural stagnation of the preceding century (Gneuss 1996).

Aelfric is not just a grammarian, but also an influential writer of homilies (Dubois 1943 (1972); Reinsma 1987). His grammar probably dates from 993–5 (Hunt 1991), when he was a member of the Abbey of Cerne in Dorset, becoming Abbot of Eynsham in 1005. Both posts would have involved him in teaching Latin as a foreign language to novices. Aelfric's sources are Donatus, minor and major, and part of Priscian's *Institutiones grammaticae*, as well as commentaries on and excerpts from both authors. All definitions are given in Old English (or in Latin plus Old English), a method which made Aelfric the originator of a consistent terminology in the vernacular. Thus, the book which was meant to spread a knowledge of Latin marks an important step in the elaboration of Old English. The number of manuscripts that have come down to us testifies to its great success. Gneuss (1996, 11) assumes that there was no English library in the eleventh century which did not possess one or several copies of it.[36] This success stabilized the teaching of grammar until the Norman Conquest. Most of all, this meant a focus on inflectional paradigms and relative neglect of what would today be termed syntax. This method of linguistic description of Latin would remain dominant almost until the nineteenth century, even spilling over into the grammars of English, although from the seventeenth century on many grammarians claimed to free themselves from the fetters of Latin grammatography.

Aelfric's *Grammar* consists of the grammar proper, of which fifteen manuscripts have survived, and the so-called *Glossary* (Zupitza and Gneuss 1966)[37] which is appended to seven of them. Four manuscripts have added the *Colloquy* (Wright and Wülcker 1884 (1968) which is supposed to be the work of Aelfric's disciple called Aelfric Bata (*fl.* eleventh century) who worked at Canterbury.[38]

Typically, the glossary consists of entries containing a Latin lemma and its Old English gloss. Mostly, the lemma is one lexeme, but there are lemmata consisting of two or three synonymous lexemes linked with *or*. Similarly, the gloss is mostly one Old English lexeme, but can also be several synonyms linked with *or* or a

[36]   Ker 1957 refers to twelve manuscripts, most of them in the BL, the Bodleian Library, Cambridge University Library, Corpus Christi College in Cambridge, St John's College in Oxford and Worcester Cathedral Library. The one in St John's College is called '[t]he only complete copy and probably the earliest' (Ker 1957, No. 436).

[37]   The *Glossary* was also edited in Wright and Wülcker 1884, cols 304–37, here called 'Anglo-Saxon Vocabulary. 11th century'.

[38]   The *Colloquy* will be dealt with in Chapter 4, 79–81.

phrase. There are three cases where explanations are appended to the lemma: *deus omnipotens*, *unicornis*, and *griffes*. Note the standard forms of entries in Table A.2. An overview like that given in the table shows the following semantic macrostructure[39] of the glossary:

1.   God, heaven, earth, mankind
2.1 Parts of the human body,
2.2 church offices,
2.3 family relationships,
2.4 state offices including crafts and instruments as well as tools,
2.5 negative features of human character,
2.6 intellectual work,
2.7 diseases, afflictions, merits,
2.8 weather, universe
3.   Birds
4.   Fish
5.   Wild animals
6.   Herbs
7.   Trees
8.1 Buildings (churches, monasteries), materials and objects used there,
8.2 war, castles, arms, valuable materials,
8.3 various,
8.4 human vices.[40]

Obviously, there are homogeneous and rather mixed sections. The former pertain to natural history, that is, the universe as a whole and nature (1, 3–7), the latter to the world of humans (mainly 2 and 8). However, on closer inspection the mixed sections betray plausible internal associations. Sections 2.1–2.4 can, for example, be subsumed under the heading *membra* if given a wide, rather philosophical meaning: church, society, and state as organisms. Sections 2.5–2.8 can, accordingly, be read as extensions of these different conceptions of organism with members. Admittedly, it seems difficult to find a common denominator for 8.1 and 8.2–8.4, unless we choose the opposition between the holy world of churches and monasteries and the unholy world of wars to be the link.

There is also order recognizable within sections which is not marked in writing/printing. Within the section devoted to *nomina avium*, for example, we find names for big birds, small birds, poultry, (again) small birds, and insects[41] all in distinct groups. Similar groups are to be found within *nomina ferarum*, though here, as in other cases, the grouping is not very strict.

[39]   From the point of view of the history of human knowledge this overview (in slightly different form) is mentioned in McArthur 1986*b*, 75.

[40]   The headings of the sections were chosen according to the semantic affinity of entries. This does not preclude the fact that there are single entries which do not fit or which defy grouping altogether. Generally speaking, such odd entries tend to appear in small clusters at the ends of sections.

[41]   To place insects among birds is common practice almost to the end of the seventeenth century.

Apart from the *Glossary*'s being the earliest specimen of its kind,[42] several features of *Aelfric's Glossary* seem particularly noteworthy. First, there is an obvious universalism, a tendency to cover the whole world with words. This surfaces in the first section with its lemmata on God and the universe, in the other sections about nature and the world of men, and finally even in the coda sentence ('*Wê ne magan swâþêah ealle naman âwrîtan nê furþon geþencan.*'), whose obvious resignation betrays a sense of obligation that the author should actually have assembled all possible words. Second, there is Aelfric's dependence on classical encyclopaedic literature which had already been known to the intellectuals of the Old English period since before the ninth century (Gneuss 1996, 8–11). His main and 'predictable' (Hunt 1991, vol. I, 100) debt is to Isidore. A close comparison between Aelfric's entries and Isidore's terms explained would probably prove that his books I–X remain neglected, that XI–XIV are the source for Aelfric's sections 1 and 3 to 7, and that the remaining books XV–XX provided at least some material for sections 2 and 8. As a whole, however, Aelfric's intentions were certainly different from Isidore's, as a comparison of the headings and the sequence of his twenty books of *Etymologiae sive Origines* shows.[43]

Moreover, Isidore's way of defining words and placing them into small contexts marks an important difference between him and Aelfric, who is 'only' a bilingual lexicographer. Whatever Aelfric's debt to Isidore and others is,[44] his originality was to cull words from certain sources and arrange them in a meaningful sequence. This represents the difference between an encyclopaedia and a glossary. Third, Aelfric's glossary is appended to an influential grammar. Obviously it was meant to be part of a schoolbook. The author must have thought of these two texts as essential parts of teaching and learning Latin. The later *Colloquy* was probably exercising material for both of them.

It testifies to the importance of Aelfric's grammar and glossary and, even more important, to the general acceptance of the linguistic and pedagogical presuppositions incorporated in them that the glossary also appears in Cornish, that is, in quite a different language spoken in a country with its own intellectual, namely Celtic, traditions (Stein 1985, 35–6). The translation uses the same Latin lexemes and, thus, the same body of knowledge; it uses the same arrangement and, thus, the same teaching method. Note the first batch of entries in their Cornish rendering:[45]

[42] For manuscripts, editions, and analytical literature see Zupitza and Gneuss 1966, Lazzari and Mucciante 1984, Hunt 1991, and Gneuss 1996. Lazzari and Mucciante give an exhaustive concordance of the lemmata of the *Glossary* compared to the other major Old English glossaries.

[43] See Chapter 11 and Table 7.22.

[44] There are also striking parallels between Aelfric's sections and those of Julius Pollux, whom Aelfric certainly did not know. This fact simply stresses the power of anonymous tradition.

[45] I quote entries according to Zeuss and Ebel 1871, 1065–6. I have changed the distribution of Roman and italicized fonts to harmonize the print with the extracts from the Anglo-Saxon version of Aelfric (see Table A.2). In their volume which gives samples from the various branches of Celtic, Zeuss and Ebel comment extensively on every single lexeme. I thank David Cram for valuable help in this matter.

Deus omnipotens, duy chefuidoc. *Celum,* nef. *Angelus,* ail. *Archangelus,* archail. *Stella,* steren. *Sol,* heuul. *Luna,* luir. *Firmamentum,* firmament. *Cursus,* redegua. *Mundus l. cosmus,* enbit. *Tellus,* tir. *Teram,* doer. *Humus,* gueret. *Mare,* mor. *Peagus,* mor difeid. *Occeanum,* mor tot. *Homo,* den. *Mas l. masculus,* gurruid. *Femina,* benenrid. *Sexus,* antromet.

Aelfric certainly did not know the rules of rhetoric with their stress on memory. Yet, even without these theoretical foundations, the combination of a grammar with a universal word-list can be seen as a means for what we would today call productive foreign-language teaching. Memorizing word-lists in order to be able to construct sentences according to the grammatical rules will also have been an essential part of a lesson. As explained above, this was a consequence of the fact that 'lessons were given by word of mouth, as boys could not in those times be accommodated with books' (Wright and Wülcker 1884, 'Original introduction', in reprint 1968, v). The arrangement of the glossary must then have appeared useful to the author for this way of teaching, that is, the order of traditional encyclopaedias must have been judged as being supportive of learning by heart. Isidore's small monolingual texts of explanation were replaced by a didactic order of bilingual entries. This order, in combination with the universalism mentioned, was a theoretical as well as a practical achievement. It followed insights into the world which we would nowadays call *scientific,* and it was at the same time what we would nowadays call *pedagogical.* It is this combination of the highly theoretical and the highly practical which marks *Aelfric's Glossary* most and gives it its outstanding position at the historical beginnings of post-classsical topical word-lists. The texts of classical authors and grammars were the means of understanding the foreign language receptively. Word-lists and grammars were the means of using the foreign language productively. Translation combined both ways of teaching and learning in order to ensure correct semanticization.[46]

All this means that word-lists were seen as a rudimentary form of coherent texts. It is not astonishing that, later, they would indeed be transformed into such. The wordbooks of the twelfth and thirteenth centuries can be looked at as contextualized glossaries.[47]

3.5 Later glossaries and *nominales* and the *Mayer Nominale*

3.5.1 *Topics covered*

Teaching and learning Latin remained a basic and highly important task in the intellectual life of England (and indeed of all other European countries) until, from the early sixteenth century on, people's linguistic attention started to focus on their own vernacular—and well beyond this dateline. During this long period,

---

[46] For conversation in the foreign-language classroom see Chapter 4.
[47] See Chapter 4.

word-lists in Latin and the vernacular were important tools for teaching and learning the classical language.

In a bird's-eye view of the centuries, that is, till printing started to change the technique of fixing vocabulary, Latin–Old/Middle English glossaries and vocabularies[48] give evidence of the continuous effort to collect all information about the world which was available, and to incorporate it into lists of words. Among them, the so-called *nominales* play an outstanding role. They are marked by a preponderance of nouns. However, there were also bilingual *verbales* and *adiectivales* in existence (Stein 1985, 56–9; 1997, 130 and 145–6). All of them are examples of an early tendency to collect words according to word-classes. In the minds of authors the awareness of the referential relation between reality and lexeme obviously mingled with the awareness of grammatical structures which, at that time, centred on the word-classes and their inflectional paradigms. *Nominales*, which often include adjectives, are predominantly a mirror of people's awareness of the world around them. This is why they testify to the validity of the onomasiological principle. It would, however, be worth while devoting research to the question of whether *verbales* mirror people's awareness of their actions and emotions in a similar way.[49]

A comparison of the longer glossaries, collected by Wright and Wülcker (1884), can lead to an overview of the various fields of topics which were regularly represented by words.

First, the parts of the human organism become an indispensable topic. Names of these parts are given from head to foot with very little variance in order. Compared to the rest of the body, the parts of the face are named in the greatest detail. Names of the palpable and visible parts of the body far outnumber those of the inner organs. In a rudimentary way, the *nomina de membra corporis* reveal the biological and also the medical knowledge as tradition presented it up to that time.[50] In the fifteenth century, this domain became important enough to be placed at the beginning of *nominales*.

Second, nature is a domain in every glossary and *nominale*, though in different degrees of detail. Words for animals and plants always outnumber words for inorganic materials. Among animals, the names of birds and fish mostly appear in their own chapters, and also *animals* meaning mammals and quadrupeds. Sometimes a division between domestic and wild animals is indicated, but even if this is not so, domestic animals are in the majority, apart from a few exotic beasts like lions and bears. As a rule, the sequence of names goes from large to small, *nomina vermium*, which includes insects, sometimes forming a group of their

---

[48]   This term is used by Wright and Wülcker 1884 in their influential, though by now outdated, collection.

[49]   See Chapter 4, 89–93, with its treatment of a *nominale sive verbale* following the treatise of Bibbesworth.

[50]   Note also the medical knowledge in a glossary of the names of plants with the division into *Chaudes herbes, Freides herbes*, etc. (Wright and Wülcker 1884, cols 554–9).

own. Among plants, almost exclusively herbs and trees, including their fruit if edible, are named. This points to usability by humans as an important criterion of selection.

Of inorganic materials, metals are mentioned, though seldom. Nature in its cosmic dimensions, as in the opening entries of *Aelfric's Glossary*, and the four classical elements in the function of an ordering system for all kinds of natural phenomena, which will quite regularly appear in the dictionaries of the sixteenth and later centuries, are still missing.

Third, human society as a domain of reality in its own right is given more and more entries. In particular, this pertains to three areas, (i) to the hierarchy of offices in the church, frequently including objects which their members use during their duties, or garments they wear in office, (ii) to the hierarchy of offices in the state from the emperor to the nightwatchman in a town, and (iii) to the great variety of arts and crafts whose activities dominated life in the towns. Whereas words pertaining to nature are more orientated towards rural life, words pertaining to offices and crafts evoke life in towns. Of course, arts and crafts have no hierarchical order in the strict sense,[51] but are arranged more loosely according to who does what, or which material is worked with. Area (iv) of human society is consanguinity, which is given in genealogical order.

Fourth, houses and their interiors constitute a domain which is linked to nature and to society in various ways. The names of this domain, unlike those of nature, apply to artificial objects. As an extension of society the house contains names of objects and activities which are a corollary to the ways of life that people lead in society. Houses are presented in terms of their rooms, most of all, their halls, kitchens, and bedrooms. Words referring to these rooms include what could be called extended fields: furniture and household utensils with reference to halls, food, cooking utensils, and dishes with reference to kitchens, and places of rest as well as garments and clothes with reference to bedrooms.

Glossaries and *nominales* are neither natural taxonomies nor scientific inventories. They are word-lists written by their authors with special intentions, which may vary from case to case. Apart from their individual traits, however, they reflect the world around these authors in a more general way than that of an individual person.

3.5.2 *The* Mayer Nominale

One of the richest and most informative *nominale* is the *Mayer Nominale* from the fifteenth century, so called after its owner who was a schoolmaster in Liverpool (Wright and Wülcker 1884, cols 673–744, Stein 1985, 53–65). It is classified into seven *capitula* with many more subtitles. It lists Latin lemmata, that is, nouns which are accompanied by *Hic, Hec, Hoc* in the place of an article, glossed by

---

[51] But see Chapter 4, 133.

Middle English lemmata accompanied by *a*, *A^{ce}*, *A^{cce}*, meaning 'Anglice'. Occasionally, there is a Latin gloss in the form of a paraphrasing sentence. A few additional Latin remarks also occur. Some entries consist of several synonyms instead of a lemma. Some glosses consist of phrases instead of lexemes. Some lexemes are given in the nominative and the genitive.

The following overview is given in order to show how much *world* is incorporated in this and other world-lists and which general structures of order apply. This means that these remarks show the need for and the possible rewards of a word-for-word analysis rather than give it.[52]

DE VOCABULIS AD SINGULA MEMBRA HUMANI CORPORIS SPECTANTIBUS

The first entry is *Hoc principium, inicium, exordium, primordium, origo*, all glossed 'A begynnyng'. There follow 180 entries on the human body. By and large, the sequence is the usual one from head to foot, but it is not very strict. For example, *Hic stomacus* 'a stomake' comes between *Hoc epiglotum* 'a thotegole' and *Hoc brachium* 'a narme';[53] the sequence *fingernail, joint, body, skin, back* is not very convincing either. In particular, the names of inner organs frequently deviate in their sequence from a top-to-bottom arrangement. There is no strict differentiation between the tangible and the (normally) intangible parts, but the location of the elements of the latter are, by and large, correct. Towards the end, we find a series of entries giving more abstract terms on a scientific level, for example for the fluids of the body and the five senses. The final entries are: *Hec anima* 'a salle', *Hic spiritus* 'a spret', *Hec mens* 'a mynde', *Hic sensus* 'a wyte', *Hoc factum* 'a dyde', *Hec vita* 'A^{ce} lyfe', *Hec conversacio idem est.*

CAPITULUM 2. NOMINA DIGNITATUM CLERICORUM

The chapter consists of sixty-eight entries giving names of offices of the church from the pope to the novice. Included are words like *magister, scriptor, iudex,* etc., which in this context prove the proximity of intellectual activities to the church. Teaching Latin is also an intellectual activity. The last entry is *Hic latinista* 'a Latynmaker'. Of special historical interest is perhaps the glossed lemma *Hic archisinagogus, i. princeps sinagogie.*

CAPITULUM 3. NOMINA RERUM PERTINENCIUM CLERICO

The chapter consists of twenty-five entries all of which are semantically connected with the work of a scribe.

---

[52] Such remarks have obvious spatial limitations, so countless details and exceptions to statements cannot be pointed out. This is why the numbers of entries/lemmata are often given only approximately. Clusters of semantically related lemmata are very often interrupted by unrelated entries. These cases are disregarded.

[53] Wrong agglutination is frequent in the glosses.

CAPITULUM 4. NOMINA DIGNITATUM LAICORUM

The chapter consists of fifty-six entries belonging to various domains. The hierarchy of dignitaries from emperor to mayor makes a well-ordered sequence. There then follow words pertaining to the ages of men, their position in a town, military ranks, servant work in a household, and some lexemes which preclude grouping, including such interesting ones as *Hic Romanus* 'a Romayn', *Hic Iudeus* 'a Jew', and *Hic Saracenus* 'a Sarzyn'. Also noteworthy is the entry *Hic, hec homo/Hic mas* 'a man', because of its unusual differentiation of gender.[54]

CAPITULUM 5. NOMINA ARTIFICIUM

The chapter consists of 160 entries of which as many as 135 are names of artisans, including beggars, and a few instruments which they use. As in almost all chapters, the first four are more general Latin words with the glosses 'byer, seller, merchant, mercer'. The last twenty-one entries preclude grouping. They include such contextually odd equations as *Hic, hec comes*, 'A^{cce} a felow', *Hic tantillus* 'a dwarf', and *Hic texillaris* 'a spy in batylle'. Complementing *comes*, there is again the unusual differentiation in gender. This last group proves the general observation that sections of lexemes with a rather strict order have often what could be called a shaggy end.

CAPITULUM 6. NOMINA CONSANGUINITATIS ET AFFINITATIS

The chapter consists of sixty-six entries, beginning with great-great-grandparents, three generations in the past, and proceeding to grandparents and parents with their children and their children's offspring, thus, three generations in the present and future. There then follow step-relatives and parentless children, after that the in-law relations derived from husband and wife. Noteworthy perhaps is *Hic postimus*, 'he that is born aftyr the deth of hys fadyre', a rather special case of a family position which, however, appears in almost all comparable lists. Perhaps there were legal reasons for having this Latin word which did not find an English synonym.

CAPITULUM 7. NOMINA DIGNITATUM MULIERUM

The chapter consists of twenty-nine entries. It is a parallel to chapter 4. After the diverse ranks of gentlewomen follow some unconnected entries like *midwife*, *abess* or *nun*.

NOMINA ARTIFICIUM MULIERUM

The chapter consists of eighteen entries giving the names of arts and crafts exercised by women. It is a parallel to chapter 5.[55]

---

[54] It is interesting to note which lemmata are glossed in Latin and to reflect why this may be so. Note: *Hic ramex, locus genitalium* (perhaps for pedagogic reasons), *Hic primpilius, qui fert pila ad prelia* (perhaps because there was no English translation available for the author).

[55] From now on the numbers for chapters, like the word *chapter* itself, are omitted in the original.

NOMINA IUGULATARUM MULIERUM

The chapter consists of nine entries with the names of feminine players of musical instruments and of dancers. A similar group for men is yet to come. Giving these words is not unusual in glossaries, but their being put together in one section is.

NOMINA REPREHENSIBILIUM UIRORUM

The chapter consists of thirty-six entries. Among others, typical masculine vices are gluttony, adultery, usury, murder (of parents). Bizarre in this context is the entry *Hic bilinguis, qui habet binas linguas* (obviously a professional liar), perhaps amusing is *Hic zelotopus* 'a kukwald' with the additional explanation: *Hunc dico zelotopum cui non sua sufficit uxor.*

NOMINA REPREHENSIBILIUM MULIERUM

The chapter consists of eleven entries, which centre around *Hec adulteria* 'a spowsbrekere'. Breaking down human vices into those committed by men and those committed by women is not unusual.

NOMINA RERUM PERTINENCIUM UXORI

The chapter consists of thirty-one entries which all belong to spinning and the spinning-wheel. Again, listing these words is not unusual, but their being put together in one section is.

NOMINA IUGULATORUM

The chapter consists of twenty entries with names of players of musical instruments, this time men, dancers, and some other jugglers. It is a parallel to the earlier chapter which listed such names for women.

NOMINA OPERARIORUM

This chapter consists of fourteen entries which are obviously added to the long list of the chapter with *nomina artificium.*

NOMINA ANIMALIUM DOMESTICORUM

The chapter consists of sixty-nine entries giving names for the equine, bovine, suilline, caprine, asinine, canine, and feline classes of animals. The sequence can perhaps be called *prototypical* in the psychological sense (Rosch 1973; Taylor 1989). Inserted between *mula* and *canis* are the astonishing entries *Hic camelus* 'a camylle', *Hec camela, uxor ejus, Hic dromedarius* 'a dromedary', and *Hic dromedus* 'a dromund', the names of animals which the author most likely never saw, but may have read of, for example in the Bible.

NOMINA FERARUM

The chapter consists of forty-five entries. The list starts with exotic animals like lion, leopard, elephant, and unicorn, again animals which the author would not know from personal experience. It goes on with animals living in the woods of England (and comparable regions), including the wolf, ordered from large (*Hic cervus* 'a hart') to small (*Hic mus, -ris* 'A^cce a mows'). There then follows an unconnected group of lemmata which the author obviously was eager to explain, for example, *Hic tigris, -ris vel -dis, velox animal* or *Hic gamelion, animal varii coloris et sola aere vivit* 'a buttyrfle', and some others. Internal grouping as in this and the preceding chapter makes, as it were, the thoughts of the author visible with his wish not only to break down the *nominale* into chapters with their own headings but also to give these chapters a coherent logic.

NOMINA VOLATILIUM DOMESTICORUM

The chapter consists of twelve entries with the names of poultry, ending with the peacock and the swan.

NOMINA VOLATILIUM INCOMESTILIUM

The chapter consists of sixty-seven entries with the names of birds. Similar to the lists of *nomina ferarum*, they are arranged from the exotic and large and not known by sight to the indigenous and small and well known. The bat counts as a bird. The last six entries are devoted to fowling.

PARTES ANIMALIUM BRUTORUM

The chapter consists of thirty-one entries with the names of peculiarities of the animal body like horns, feathers, wool.

NOMINA PISCIUM

The chapter consists of forty-nine entries. Its order is different from the preceding chapters on animals, because edible and inedible fish are within one section. Moreover, the difference between sea mammals, fish, and shellfish imposes an order of its own. The opening entry is simply *Hic piscis* 'a fyche'. There are then four entries on *whale, dolphin*, etc. with a following long sequence of edible and catchable fish, led by the most popular one *Hoc allec* 'a herynge'. It lists as many as twenty-five different kinds. The astonishing *Hec sirena* 'a mermaydyn' is followed by fourteen entries on shellfish, conches, etc.

NOMINA VERMIUM ET MUSCARUM

The chapter consists of sixty-one entries pertaining to serpents, frogs, insects, snails. There is an unusually large number of Latin glosses and mythological explanations, like *serpens cum tribus capitibus* and *serpens habens faciem hominis*. Of course, the author did not see the difference between mythological and other explanations, as many of them came from books, and not from experience. There is a rough ordering into serpents, frogs, worms, and insects, of which six pertain to bees. But they are not set apart as useful insects in contrast to all the others.

NOMINA MORBORUM ET INFIRMORUM VIRORUM

The chapter consists of forty-eight entries. The first fourteen give the names of diseases which affect the skin, from *Hec lepra* 'a mesylry' to *nodositas manuum*. There then follow cough and asthma and non-connected entries, including the most general *Hic febris* 'the fevere', which was taken to be *the* sign of being sick, and *Hoc vulnus* 'a wonde'. After that we have diseases of women, including menstruation (counted among the diseases, in this case) but also *Hec exstisis* 'a swoynyng', and finally blindness, deafness, and some others.

NOMINA INFIRMORUM

The chapter consists of thirty entries which all have adjectives as lemmata. The list seems not to be geared to the preceding list of nouns, although it overlaps with it.

NOMINA ARBORUM ARABILIUM ET FLORUM

The chapter consists of 101 entries. Their rough order is: plants used for preparing dishes, either as vegetables or for seasoning; flowers; fragrant herbs.[56] It should perhaps be mentioned that, as in many other places, we find here the comment on a homonym attached to *Hec hinnula* 'a scalyone' (an onion without a bulb with a long neck): *Fantulus est filius, sed fantula crescit in ortis.*

DE NOMINIBUS SPECIERUM

The chapter consists of forty-nine entries all of which, except for the two general initial ones, give names of spices well known for use and of measures for weighing them. At the end there are entries with the names of raisins, figs, and almonds, being well-known, but certainly exotic kinds of fruit which, even at that time, were not spices in the narrow sense. We are astonished to find *Hoc butumen* 'terre' and *Hec pix, -cis* 'pyk' between them.

NOMINA ARBORUM ET EARUM FRUCTUUM

The chapter consists of 126 entries which can be broken down into four groups. The first gives the names of trees, their fruit, and place of growth, mostly in clusters of three, as for example: *Hec pomus* 'a nappyltre', *Hoc pomum* 'a nappylle', *Hoc pometum, locus ubi crescunt.* All of the trees are indigenous. The second group gives the names for trees which are not fruit-trees in the typical and popular sense though they have fruits, like beeches or poplars. Here, as for the cedar or box, the names of the fruit and the place of growth are frequently missing. The examples show that non-indigenous trees are also mentioned. The third group gives the names of kinds of growth, like wood, bush, or briar, the fourth, finally, gives the names of the parts of trees, for example bark or branch.

---

[56] The vocabulary for plants has been so thoroughly researched that further analytical remarks seem superfluous. See Bierbaumer 1979 and Sauer 1992.

HEE SUNT PARTES FRUCTUUM

This chapter contains eight entries which are a follow-up to the last group of the preceding chapter, that is, parts of trees.

NOMINA DOMORUM ET RERUM ECCLESIATICARUM

The chapter consists of 134 entries. The first thirteen give the names of architectural parts of *Hoc monasterium* 'a mynster', the following fifty-nine give the names of books and other objects used in services. This includes the entry *Hec bibliotheca* 'a bybulle', with the comment: *Bibliotheca mea servat meam bibliothecam.*

Furthermore, there are twenty entries with the names of the garments of priests, and another twenty with the names of surrounding places like cloister and churchyard, including *candle*. Finally, there are seven entries for the crypt, the dormitory, and the cell. All this suggests a coherence of its own: the church as a building, objects for liturgy, the garments to be worn by the priest during service, a procession around the church as part of the service (this is why candles are mentioned here), a return to the other rooms, finally the cell—this sequence almost presents some liturgy performed by a priest. As is frequent, the very last of these entries, *Hoc centorium/Hoc tabernaculum* 'a tabernakylle', seems misplaced. The series of church-related entries is, finally, rounded off by entries on houses, from the *domus regis* to *hoc oppidum*, possibly the town in which the church as a building and a place of worship is situated.

NOMINA DOMO PERTINENCIA

The chapter consists of 218 entries. This means it is the longest of all. Unlike the following chapter its lemmata denote only objects and animals kept and used inside a house. This is obviously a large farmhouse which includes a mill, a fact which gives the chapter a quite heterogeneous character. It starts with a cluster of lemmata pertaining to a room with *Hoc lavatorium* 'a lavyre'. But then, with the exception of various entries on clothes, food, and cooking utensils scattered throughout the chapter, all the others speak of the house as a place of work, not a place to live in. First, there are words for objects inside a storeroom (*Hoc selarium* 'a selere'), among them vessels for drinking and for keeping drinks. The subsequent clusters of between six and twelve entries each are devoted to clothes, equipment for working in the fields, various containers and dishes, milling, and baking, to be followed by a very heterogeneous group (sixteen entries) which leads to a cluster of about twenty lemmata with the names of different species of grain. Note that they are not given as plant names, that is, as a part of natural history, but as the names of objects which are to be found in a farmhouse. There then follow twelve entries with the names of agricultural equipment and a cluster of about forty-five entries pertaining to stables, tools, carts, and, in particular, horses. Finally, there are about forty unsystematic entries, of which many pertain to containers. The chapter closes with fourteen entries on building a wall.

JAM DE EDIFICIIS DOMORUM

The chapter consists of 124 entries. As a counterpart to the preceding chapter, this time houses are presented as architectural objects. The opening entries are again very general, as in *Hoc edificium* 'a bygyng'. Besides these, roughly the first half (fifty-four entries) is concerned with the rooms of a house, with different types of houses as they can be found in the architectural ensemble, for example, of a big estate, and finally with houses typical of a village or town. These three groups are by and large, but not strictly, separated into clusters. Examples of the first are *Hoc pretorium* 'a moythalle' or *Hoc refectorium* 'a fermory', of the second *Hec fabrica* 'a forge' or *Hoc columbare* 'dowfhows', and of the third *Hec fornix, -icis* 'a bordyl-hows' or *Hec apoteca* 'a spycerschoppe'. The second half is concerned with parts of houses as architectural objects, like walls, roofs, doors, and with the materials they are made of, like mortar, stone, and plaster.

NOMINA VESTIMENTORUM

The chapter consists of fifty-nine entries, all of which pertain to human clothes. More general entries are followed by those pertaining to coats and cloaks, to parts of these like *Hec manica* 'a slefe' and *Hoc pannideusium* 'a boton', and finally to accessories like *Hoc pendulum* 'a pendand' and *Hoc capicium* 'a hod'. As is obvious, the lemmata are restricted to a certain type of clothes, namely that worn in public.[57] No distinction between men and women is made.

[NO HEADING]

This chapter has no heading. It consists of seventy-five entries arranged in coherent clusters which, however, are only loosely interconnected. The first pertains to wind, frost, ice, and the sea. There then follow entries with lemmata on day, night, some holidays of the church, and the seasons. They give way to a cluster of words with geographical names like the ones for earth, hill, or field. Finally, the chapter returns to a cluster of lemmata for ships and objects connected with it. With the exception of the third cluster, this chapter seems to be concerned with sailing and its dependence on weather conditions.

NOMINA LUDORUM

The chapter consists of twenty-five entries. Apart from the inevitable general lemmata, the first twelve give the names of games with balls and dice, the following give the names of musical instruments.

DE VITE ET MATERIIS IPSIUS

The chapter consists of sixteen entries pertaining to vines and grapes. Of them, as many as twelve have Latin glosses.

---

[57] Note (again) that the *nominale* was used as a schoolbook.

DE CIBUS GENERALIBUS

The chapter consists of eleven entries on meat (victuals), and meals.

DE PANIBUS ET PARTIBUS EORUM

The chapter consists of seventeen entries on bread, loaves, and pieces of loaves.

DE SPECIEBUS LIGUMINIS

The chapter consists of twenty-one entries on vegetables, various dishes, and ingredients for dishes like honey and oil.

DE CIBUS GENERALIBUS

The chapter consists of thirty-three entries. Most of them pertain to various meat dishes.

DE LECTIS ET ORNAMENTIS EORUM

The chapter consists of forty-four entries with lemmata for beds and parts of beds like canvas and mattress and, at the end, tapestry, pillows, and cushions. Twenty-five of the forty-four entries are glossed only in Latin.

3.5.3 *Concluding remarks on the* Mayer Nominale

The almost 2,000 entries of the *Mayer Nominale* create a panaroma of the world which seems almost replete with concrete objects of all kinds, natural and artificial. We can make out three large sections. One large section is man within the orders of his societal life. It is certainly not accidental that the chapters on the body and on arts and crafts are among the three with the largest numbers of entries. That the world of women is presented in its own chapters is a special feature of this *nominale* which should not be taken for granted. The other large section of this panorama is nature as portrayed in the descriptions of natural history and/or as an object of human experience. In many cases, experience also means usefulness for human life. The two chapters on diseases seem to be misplaced and could easily find a better slot, for example after the two chapters with *nomina reprehensibilium*. The third section of the panorama is houses as the man-made world and what is done in them—living, working, preparing food, dressing and sleeping. It is not without significance that the chapter on the interiors of houses is the longest of all. However, not all divisions of the *nominale* are convincing. *Nomina operariorum* are obviously an afterthought to *Nomina artificium*. The chapter on the parts of fruits might just as easily have been included in the preceding chapter. Finally, the five chapters on food at the end of the *nominale* might have been combined into one. Such comments, futile as they are *vis-à-vis* a historical text, nevertheless help to show the system that lies closely beneath the surface, as it were, and that organizes the word-list very much in the same way as later encyclopaedias will do.

The *Mayer Nominale* presents a world in which the so-called productive arts, as they had been developed by medieval society, play an important role. It is not the world of ideas and abstract hierarchies which we usually think of when speaking about the Middle Ages, it is the world of manual labour, of hand-made objects, and of the skills employed for improving conditions of life. After all, monastic rules, for example, looked on piety and learning, but also on labour and practical skills, as a positive means of salvation (Whitney 1990, 13 and *passim*).

However, the panaroma of the world is not to be mistaken for a panorama of experience. There are many names of animals or plants which were outside the observations of the author and, just as importantly, of the reader, that is, the teachers and the learners of Latin. There is no difference between mythological and positive meanings, except that the former are mostly glossed in Latin. At the time of the *Mayer Nominale*, knowledge came from books, not from experience, and this included the unicorn and the griffin. Moreover, many of the items that might have come from experience were, actually, beyond the reach of those who used the *nominale*. The interiors of monasteries, estates, or large houses were certainly not familiar to ordinary teachers (monks), and ordinary learners (novices). This *nominale,* just like other word-lists, contains the store of potential information available at the time, but certainly not actually available to everybody.[58] And yet this standard of general information was supposed to be the obviously best means for teaching and learning a foreign language.

With the *Mayer Nominale* onomasiological glossaries have already gone a long way towards the encyclopaedia.

---

[58]   See Chapter 4, 137–9.

4

Colloquies, wordbooks, and dialogues for teaching and learning foreign languages

4.1 Colloquies and wordbooks for learning Latin

The colloquies[1] of the various *Hermeneumata* were the first instance of a hybrid text-genre between a conversation and a glossary. At least in parts, they are contextualized word-lists with semantically related lexemes. As didactic dialogues, they suffer from what we would today call an inversion of functions. Considering the fact that the teacher ought to provide most of the foreign language in the classroom, we

---

[1] The differentiation between (i) colloquies, (ii) wordbooks, and (iii) dialogues is meant to express the differences between (i) the *Hermeneumata* in their dialogical parts and the Old English *Aelfric's Colloquy*, (ii) the treatises of Adam of Petit Pont, Alexander Nequam, John of Garland, and *Femina*, and (iii) the various versions of *Manière* and Caxton's *Dialogues*.

find that his share in speaking is actually very small. He asks rather short questions, but the learners give answers of considerable length, that is, they do not learn, they already know. In fact, these texts do not mirror classroom reality, as later dialogues will, but 'are exercises in the vocabulary and idiom of everyday life, including dialogue, of course, but only as a component, not as their overall form' (Dionisotti 1982, 93). And this component can be very small indeed, for example, consisting only of '*ave, domine, avete; bene tibi sit*' (Dionisotti 1982, 98, line 16). Note, for a fairly extensive example, a passage from the *Hermeneumata Einsidlensia* (cod. Einsid. 19 (124), *Corpus* 1882–1923, vol. III, 1892, 223–79), which contains a longer dialogue than other texts with more turns of speech:

[P]oposci aquam ad faciem, lauo primo manus, deinde faciem, laui, extersi, deposui albam paenulam, processi de cubiculo cum paedagogo salutare patrem et matrem, ambos salutaui et deosculatus sum et sic descendi de domo. eo salutare omnes amicos, et dominus procedens obuiauit amico suo et dixit: salue, Caie, et tenuit eum et resalutauit eum dicens: est te uidere? quid agis? omnia recte. quomodo habes? gratulor tibi sicut mihi iudicium. ad quem? ad quaestorem? non ibi. sed ubi? ad proconsulem? nec ibi, sed ad magistratus ex subscriptione praesidiis prouinciae. quale autem est ipsum negotium? non ualde magnum. es enim pecuniarum, ut totum scias. (226–7.)[2]

Aelfric's Colloquy (BL Cotton Tiberius A. iii, f. 11, ed. Wright 1857, Stevenson and Lindsay 1929, Garmonsway 1953, Napier 1900, glosses only)[3] is another example of this hybrid genre.[4] It belongs to Aelfric's grammar and glossary, although it obviously was not written by Aelfric, but by his disciple Aelfric Bata, who taught in Canterbury. It provides material for exercises in connection with the *Grammar* and the *Glossary*.

The *Colloquy* consists of a conversation between a master and a group of young learners, probably monks, wanting to learn Latin. The Latin text is continually glossed with an Old English version. As in the *Hermeneumata*, the teacher only asks short and stimulating questions, whereas the learners provide plenty of linguistic material in their answers. Many of these answers are in fact vocabularies in disguise, that is, contextualized word-lists, similar to the arrangement of the *Hermeneumata*. Note for example:

Magister: Quid sciunt isti tui socii? / hwæt cunnon þas þine geferan?. Discipulus: Alii sunt aratores, alii opiliones, quidam bubulci, quidam etiam uenatores, alii piscatores, alii aucupes,

---

[2] 'I ask for water [to wash my] face, I first wash my hands, then my face, I have washed, wiped [= rubbed myself dry], laid down my white shirt, come out of my bedroom with the servant [for children] [in order] to greet my father and mother, I have saluted them both and I am kissed and so I have left the house. I go [in order] to greet all my friends, and the master, stepping forward, has come to meet his friend and said "Hallo, Cajus", and has touched him and greeted him again, saying: "[How is it that] I see you? What are you doing? [= Where are you going?]". "Everything all right. How are you?" "I congratulate you following my judgment [= for what I see]. To whom? To the officer of the treasury?" "Not there." "But where?" "To the proconsul?" "Not there either but to the magistrate because of the register [= taxes] for the support of the provinces." "Of what kind, however, is your negotiation?" "Not very much. It is namely because of money; so you know all [now]." ' (My translation, W. H.)   [3] See Quinn and Quinn 1990, H 004. See also Ker 1957, No. 362.
     [4] Edition used: Wright and Wülcker 1884, cols 89–103.

*quidam mercatores, quidam sutores, quidam salinatores, quidam pistores loci. / sume synt
yrþlincgas sume scephyrdas, sume oxanhyrdas, sume eac swylce huntan sume fisceras sume
fugeleras sume cypmenn sume scewryrhtan sealteras bæceras.*   (90.)[5]

This list of mostly agricultural labourers determines the subsequent dialogue,
because in the following conversation one representative of each kind of labour to
be done in farming characterizes his own activities. This occurs in the sequence
which was given in the answer quoted and presents several occasions for an accumulation of words belonging to one domain. Note:

*Arator: . . . exeo diliculo, minando boues ad campum, et iungo eos ad aratrum; non est tam
aspera hiemps ut audeam latere domi, pro timore domini mei; sed iunctis bobis, et confir-
mato uomere et cultro aratro, omni die debeo arare integrum agrum, aut plus. / ic ga ut on
dægræd þywende oxon to felda and iugie hig to syl nys hyt swa stearc winter þæt ic durre
lutian æt ham for ege hlafordes mines ac geiukodan oxan and gefæstnodon sceare and cultre
mit þære syl ælce dæg ic sceal erian fulne æcer oþþe mare.*   (90.)[6]

There are many details of historical knowledge about everyday life incorporated
in these exchanges, which sometimes uncovers hidden societal conditions, for
example with reference to the work to be done in the fields '*quia non sum liber*'.
Knowledge about everyday life covers plants, fruit, and animals used, for example,
as food. There are also many details of biological knowledge hidden in these
answers. Note, for example:

*Magister: Quales pisces capis? / hwilce fixas gefehst þu? Piscator: Anguillas, et lucios, menas, et
capitones, tructos, et murenas, et qualescunque in amne natant saliu. / ælas and hacodas,
mynas and æleputan sceotan and lampredan and swa wylce swa on wætere swymma þsprote.
. . . Magister: Quid capis in mari? / hwæt fehst þu in sæ? Piscator: Alleceds et isicios, delfinos
et sturias, ostreas et cancros, musculas, forniculi, neptigalli, platesia, et platissa, et polipodes, et
similia. / hærincgas and leaxas mereswyn and stirian ostran and crabban muslan pinewinclan
sæcoccaas fage and floc and lopystrian and fela swylces.*   (94.)[7]

The statements of labourers and artisans on their own activities end in an argument about which of them is the most useful. In this controversy, farming with all
its activities is contrasted to all the other crafts.

---

[5] 'Master: What [are] these your friends do[ing]? Pupil: Some are ploughmen, some shepherds,
certain ones are ox-drivers, others are also hunters, some are merchants, other shoemakers, some are
in the salt-works, some in the mills.' (My translation, W. H.)

[6] 'Ploughman: . . . I like going out driving oxen to the field and harness them to the plough; there
is no winter cold enough that I dare remain at home, out of fear of my master; and with the harnessed
oxen and fixed [plough-]shares and sharp plough I must plough all day long the whole acre, or more.'
(My translation, W. H.)

[7] 'Master: What fish do you catch? Fisherman: Eels and haddock, whitefish, eel-pout, trout, and
muraena, and every kind swimming in a salty river. Master: What do you catch in the sea? Fisherman:
Jelly-fish and mashed fish, dolphin and sturgeon, oysters and crab, mussels, small mussels, sea-cocks
[I can verify neither the Latin nor the Old English lexeme in the relevant reference works.], plaice and
sole and lobster and similar [fish].'

In comparison to the colloquies of the *Hermeneumata*, the topic of the conversations has changed from the activities of Roman urban life to those of the early medieval agricultural life of Britain. This new orientation will be found in many later sources. However, *Aelfric's Colloquy* ends with the description of all the duties and activities of a whole day, which in this case pertain to monastic life. Hence, it finally takes up as a topic what was the organizing principle typical for the *Hermeneumata*.

The twelfth and the thirteenth centuries saw the origin of Latin wordbooks[8] which, typologically speaking, have a similar position between glossaries, that is, word-lists, as schoolbooks and dialogues with the same function. These wordbooks exploit the fact that the arrangement of topical word-lists is *universalist*, that they have an inherent tendency to create a meaning beyond the sum of individual entries. They may also be regarded as contextualized word-lists, though slightly different from the colloquies mentioned so far. As such they are a natural extension of glossaries.

The three best known examples are the treatises of Adam of Petit Pont, Alexander Nequam,[9] and John of Garland (Green 1997, 60–6). All of them are Latin texts with Latin, Anglo-Norman, Old French, Old English, or Middle English glosses. They serve the teaching of Latin vocabulary to boys whose mother tongue was either English or Norman French. They also give some grammatical instruction. All three treatises originated in Paris. The fact that they were glossed is less interesting for our chain of thought than their textual structure.[10] Each of them can be taken as a sample of a slightly different subtype of the contextualized glossary.

Adam of Petit Pont (*fl.* 1132 to before 1159)[11] was born and died in England, but spent much of his life in the school of the Petit Pont in Paris. Besides other treatises, he published *De utensilibus* of which fifteen manuscripts have survived. This points to the popularity of his schoolbook, which indeed shows glosses by many generations of teachers. It must have been written in the 1140s or early 1150s. Its purpose was to teach boys Latin words pertaining to objects of everyday life. In an introduction, the aim of the book is given in the following way:

Materia (huius libri) sunt nomina utensilium. Intentio auctoris est colligere sub compendio nomina utensilium et rerum usitatissimarum que multis etiam eruditis ignota erant. . . . Utilitas est nominum et rerum cognitio et partium expositio. (Hunt 1991, vol. I, 168.)[12]

Nominum et rerum cognitio is a definition of *utilitas* which hovers between the linguistic and the encyclopaedic. However, as will become obvious, the intention

---

8   Term according to Hunt 1991, vol. I, chap. IV.
9   I use this spelling after Hunt 1991.
10   This is why I do not give the glosses in my quotations.
11   See Hunt 1991, vol. I, 165–6, vol. II, 37–62, for text and glosses and for biographical facts, manuscripts, editions, and historiographical literature. Another early edition is Wright 1857.
12   'The contents (of this book) are the names of tools. The intention of the author is, for the [general] benefit, to collect the names of tools and most useful things which are unknown [even] to the learned. . . . The usefulness [of all this] is the knowledge of things and the explanation of their parts.' (My translation, W. H.)

of conveying knowledge is different from the intention in earlier glossaries. It is fairly practical and refers to problems of practical life.

The special feature of this rather short treatise is its almost perfect textuality. This means *De utensilibus* has a discernible speaker and an addressee and it also has a coherent meaning, that is, a story. A person called Adam gives a report to his teacher Anselm, who used to criticize his Latin style. This report contains observations made during a stay on a country estate. He does this both to show his improved style and so that Anselm, who has bought a country estate himself, can take Adam's report as a guide for his own plans. The text is indeed stylistically extravagant, containing many obscure and unusual words. The intention of the text as a whole is given at the beginning and at the end, forming a frame around the report proper, which contains the names of as many details as it seems possible to mention. It starts with the approach to the buildings, describing fields, pastures, and outer works. Adam moves on to the great hall, where he as a visitor is met by people who used to know him before his departure. They have supper during which Adam enquires about some persons present. This gives an occasion for inserting direct speech. There then follow entertainment, a tour of the building, including the library, the chapel, the stables, the wine-pressing area and the kitchen, which is given a detailed description. Finally, the weaving-room is depicted with details about instruments, cloths, etc.

The text is written in the first person singular of the writer and includes the direct speech of the other speakers, marked with the *inquit* formulae in the usual way. It has a natural sequence of topics, based on a natural sequence of movements. And yet its covert but plainly discernible intention is to convey Latin vocabulary in meaningful contexts. Its most obvious syntactic form is the statement which includes the enumeration of long series of names for objects. Linguistically speaking, this is the listing of the items of a semantic domain. There is an obvious preponderance of nouns, so the semantic domain almost turns into a word-field.[13] Note the following extract which can stand for the structure and the style of the whole treatise:

In popina deinde verucula et crates . . . , ollas, patellas, cacbos, . . . , lebetas, sartagines, sed et mulgaria, . . . , et pelves, simphones. In angulo vero quodam erat girgillus (et) funis cum situla et utres in puteum dimittebantur. Iuxta quem stabat hinc telon, quod Hispani ciconiam vocant, et pirgus in quo coquebantur opacaorum genera. . . . Inde ferreus harpax. In alio etiam angulo nefrendes cum succula in arula latitantes intuiti (sumus). Post hec promtuaria introivimus. (Hunt 1991, vol. I, 174–5.)[14]

Some paragraphs of *De utensilibus* are obviously indebted to Isidore.

---

[13]   See Chapter 1, 18.

[14]   'In the tavern, [there] then were spits and wicker-baskets . . ., jars, dishes, cooking-pots, . . ., kettles, frying-pans, but also milk-pails . . . and basins, vessels. In some [= the] right corner was a roller and a rope with baskets and bottles to be lowered into the well. Opposite which stood this spit which the Spanish call *stork*, and a mug in which kinds of oil-baked cakes . . . are cooked. On that side [there was also] the hook of iron. In another corner we see toothless [= baby] animals with a suckling pig lying on a small plate. After that we entered the store-room.' (My translation, W. H.)

The step from a glossary with semantically related entries to a treatise like this is only natural if fully structured texts are regarded as the better material for foreign-language teaching. This, however, is not to be taken for granted. It shows the way in which the teaching and learning of Latin moved away from classical studies and natural history towards more common and practical language use.

Alexander Nequam (1157–1217) was 'one of the most versatile and prolific English scholars' (Hunt 1991, vol. I, 177) of the time.[15] He was born in St Albans, studied in Paris at the same school of Petit Pont as Adam, but went back to England in the 1180s, staying in Dunstable, St Albans, Oxford, and finally, after 1213, was abbot in Cirencester. His published work as a poet, scientist, and theologian surpasses the quite modest treatise *De utensilibus*, which must have been written between 1175 and 1185. The over thirty manuscripts extant often appear together with the similar treatises of Adam of Petit Pont and John of Garland. All three must have enjoyed a similar popularity. Their books were classbooks for boys who started to learn Latin. Alexander Nequam gives roughly the same intention for his work as Adam: '*Utilitas est ut perlecto libello sciamus nomina et significationes nominum utensilium*' (Hunt 1991, vol. I, 178).[16] Again *nomina et significationes*, words and subject-matter, are mentioned together.

In its textual coherence, Nequam's treatise is less convincing than Adam's, because he has no communicative frame, no plot, and no natural conversation with direct speech. He indeed gives lists of words embedded in syntactical patterns. Semantically, the words are confined to the names of domestic utensils, implements, and appliances. Their arrangement is not really systematic, but sequenced in a way for which hardly any logical reason can be found. The topics which Alexander Nequam includes (Watson 1968, 381) show his dependence on Adam of Petit Pont. Again, the list contains almost exclusively nouns. The most important topics are:

—kitchens and work there, like slicing vegetables and preparing fish, pots and pans
—storerooms and what is stored there
—equipment of travellers on foot and on horseback
—sleeping quarters
—clothes and pertinent instruments like thimbles
—food, sauces, wine, spices
—the construction of castles and machines for their defence
—granary and domestic birds

---

[15] See Hunt 1991, vol. I, 177–89, vol. II, 65–122, for texts and glosses, for biographical facts, manuscripts, editions and historical literature. Another early edition is Wright 1857. The authoritative biography of Nequam is Hunt 1984 (ed. Gibson). It includes a full bibliography of all manuscripts, editions, re-editions, etc.

[16] 'Usefulness is when by reading the little book we know the names and meanings of names of [the] tools.' (My translation, W. H.)

—stables
—weaving, including deliberations on the life to come
—carters and their vehicles
—construction of a hall
—rural life and farming.

There is a caesura here because the topics turn away from ordinary living quarters in the country. Now come: ships and their fittings,[17] a scriptorium and the instruments used there, including instruments of jewellers and ecclesiastical objects. Note the part on the kitchen:

In quoquina sit mensula, super quam olus apte minuatur et lecticula et pise et pultes et fabe frece et fabe silique et fabe ex(s)ilique et milium et cepe et huismodi legumina, que resecari possunt. Item sint ibi olle, tripodes, securis, mortarium, pilus, contus, uncus, cacabus, aenum, patella, sartago, craticula, urceoli, discus, scutella, parapsis, salsarium, artavi, quibus pisce(s) excenterari possunt.   (Hunt 1991, vol. I, 181.) [18]

The extract shows that Nequam's technique of listing words inside syntactical patterns is rather clumsy compared with Adam's. His treatise is, indeed, almost entirely names of things embedded in syntactical statements. Together with Adam of Petit Pont and also with John of Garland (see below) he shared Isidore's fondness for concrete details about everyday tools and artefacts, about buildings, clothing, weapons, navigation, household goods, and farm utensils. Although he does not theorize about this, he will also have shared the classical idea that non-banausic arts are those in which objects are produced out of materials by the application of rational rules with the help of tools. It was Isidore who had introduced this Aristotelian definition to post-classical culture which was less inimical towards technology and manual labour than we are inclined to think (Whitney 1990, 77–8 and *passim*).

Most of the words are ancient and come from classical poets. Some lines are very close to lines from Horace, Lucian, and Juvenal. All this points to the fact that Alexander of Nequam aimed at introducing young boys to the Latin which they would have to read in the coming years (Hunt 1984, 33). That almost every other Latin word is rendered into simpler Latin, French, or English certainly shows that the author did not think much of the linguistic knowledge of those teachers who would use his book (Watson 1968, 381).

---

[17] This part is famous for mentioning, for the first time outside China, the magnetic needle as a nautical instrument.

[18] 'In the kitchen [there] should be [= is] a little table on which cabbage is easily cut and lentils and peas and grits and ground beans and beans with husks and without husks and millet and onions and vegetables of the kind which can be cut. [There] should also be jars, tripods, [an] axe, mortar, pestle, pike, hook, cooking-pot, bronze vessel, dish, frying-pan, little wicker-basket, pitcher, plate, little flat dish, dessert dish, salt-cellar, fish-knife by which fish can be disembowelled.' (My translation, W. H.) Thirty-six lexemes from this passage are glossed in French: for example, *coquina*: quisine, *mensula*: table, *olus*: cholet, *minuatur*: mincé, *lenticule*: lentils, *pise*: peys, *pultes*: grueus, *fabe*: feve, *frese*: frisé, *silique*: en coys, *esilique*: sanc coys, etc.

The third relevant treatise, John of Garland's *Dictionarius*, was written in Paris in 1220.[19] The dates of the author's life are unknown. He studied in Oxford and Paris and later became the so-called master of grammar at Toulouse University. Besides his linguistic works he published on alchemy and mineralogy. The *Dictionarius* acquired a Europe-wide reputation. It is different from Adam's and Nequam's works because it consists of eighty-three numbered paragraphs, which consist of sentences giving statements on and often definitions of objects, animals, activities, etc. These statements are frequently based on the author's personal experience in Paris and Toulouse, when he mentions these towns or his neighbours there. Note the following examples:

14. Willelmus, vicinus noster, habet in foro ista vendenda ante se: acus et acuaria, saponem et specula et rasoria, cotes et pericudia vel fusillos.

35. Coquinarii vertunt et cocunt verubus colurnis anseres et columbas, altilia, sed frequenter vendunt carnes crudas simplicibus mancipiis scolarium cum salsamentis at alliatis male distemperatis. Quibus invident carnifices in macellis suis, vendentes carnes grossas bovinas et ovinas et porcinas, aliquando lepra percussas. (Hunt 1991, vol. I, 197, 198.)[20]

Actually, the *Dictionarius* approaches a dictionary in sentences, as would become popular later in William Bathe's *Janua linguarum*[21] which paved the way for Comenius' dictionary of the same name and which eventually conquered the schools in all of Europe.

The main topics of the *Dictionarius* are:

1	Introduction
2–7	parts of the body
8–54	tradesmen, their equipment and wares in Paris (in between 49 Toulouse, arms and defensive weapons)
55	domestic objects
56–7	possessions of a clerk
59	garments[22]
60–3	liturgical books, vestments, objects
64	table

---

[19] See Hunt 1991, vol. I, 191–203, vol. II, 125–56, for texts and glosses, manuscripts, editions, and historical literature. Many of John of Garland's works have remained unedited so far. See also Watson 1968, 381–3. He draws a straight line from Nequam and Garland to Bathe and Comenius and from them to James Hamilton (1769–1829) and François Gouin (1831–96) (see Howatt 1984), the reformers of foreign-language teaching methodology in the eighteenth and nineteenth centuries. Although this looks somewhat audacious it shows the correct idea of a long tradition that stands behind these relatively recent innovators.

[20] '14. William, our neighbour, has before him in the market the following goods for sale: needles and needle-makers' products, soap and mirrors and knives, whetstones and little spindles.' 35. 'The cooks turn around and cook on spits of hazel-wood geese and pigeons, fat poultry, but often they sell raw meat, because of the small means of the students, with brine and [moreover] with garlic badly spoilt. Because of which the butchers in their food-market stalls look envious, sellers of fat meat of cattle and sheep and pigs, sometimes ruined by sickness.' (My translation, W. H.)

[21] See Chapter 10, 377–82.   [22] No. 58 is missing.

65–9	women's occupations (spinning, carding, etc.)
70–3	animals (birds, fish, animals on a farm)
75–8	plants (herbs, flora in France, trees)
79	'my hall'
80–1	ships, shipwreck
82	musical instruments and monsters of hell
83–4	heaven, Last Judgement.

Of course, as a schoolbook the *Dictionarius* shares the practical outlook of the two preceding treatises. However, there is a remarkable shift in interest. 'Parts of the human body' in the first place and 'Last Judgement' in the last give the *Dictionarius* a quasi-theological framework which will reappear in many dictionaries and colloquies of the following centuries. Chapters on plants and animals show a revival of interest in natural history, whereas the elaborate chapters on crafts and trades introduce a topic which, though not unknown to earlier glossaries, marks a new attention to the reality of non-academic activities. This entails a shift of focus from rural to urban life and, consequently, from the well-to-do in the country, who live on estates and in castles, to the manufacturing and trading people in the towns (Lambley 1920, 5–25). All this mirrors the shift of topical interest in teaching and learning Latin as a foreign language. This shift will become much more intensive in its application to a vernacular as a foreign language like French. Although Latin was not dead in the sense that it is in the twentieth century, it was limited in its use to special domains of communication and had to be learned accordingly, that is, using methods different from those for the teaching and learning of French (or Dutch or German, etc.)

Later in the sixteenth century, it became the ambition of the Humanists to teach Latin (and to a certain extent also Greek) for academic but also for common communication. One method of doing this was conversations in class, frequently but not always between learner and teacher. The most famous cases are Erasmus of Rotterdam's *Colloquia familiaria*, which appeared for the first time in 1518, and Ludovicus Vives' *Linguae Latinae exercitatio*, published in its first edition in 1539. But there were numerous other Continental authors.[23] Erasmus (Caravolas 1994, 235–44) and Vives (Caravolas 1994, 266–83, 346–9) were present on the Continent with a plethora of editions of their textbook dialogues, and thus dominated the teaching of Latin there. They were also present in England. Erasmus, whose dialogues slowly turned away from the purely didactic purposes and became more and more literary, was highly esteemed as a Humanist and a theological writer and, as a consequence of this, was translated into English. But, in spite of occasional accumulations of semantically related words, these dialogues rarely employ the onomasiological principle. From the historiographical point of view, they arouse interest in two other respects. They often teach the art of conversing by

[23] Bömer 1897 contains biographical sketches, extensive bibliographies, summaries, and extracts of dialogues of not fewer than seventeen Continental authors.

giving structurally delimited text units, for example by offering various possibilities of initiating or ending conversations, of agreeing or disagreeing with a partner, etc. Such teaching methods are in high esteem even today, where they find support in conversational analysis. And they are, of course, an inexhaustible source of information on everyday culture, especially that of universities.

4.2 Wordbooks and dialogues for learning French

Of course, interest in learning French increased tremendously after 1066, though only in narrow circles and for special communicative functions (Lambley 1920, Kibbee 1991). At least in the official domains of communication, England became trilingual. Wherever Latin gave way, not English but French succeeded it, most notoriously in the law and court procedures. But there was never a possibility (or danger) of its taking over as a general means of communication. 'To postulate . . . the general retention of French as a vernacular in England a century and a half after the Battle of Hastings (i.e. about five or even six generations) is to fly in the face of common linguistic experience and historical evidence' (Rothwell 1976, 449.). Intermarriage between native speakers of Norman French and of English must have in many cases created a situation of uncertain bilingualism. This is why French had to be *taught*; at least for most people it could not simply be acquired in their families or in the streets. However, for quite a number of people knowledge of French was important. As a foreign language, French was more prestigious than any other language in Europe, and besides all the feudal connections that existed between England and France (certainly till the loss of Normandy in 1204) there developed a lively wool and wine trade between England and Flanders from the middle of the thirteenth century which made a command of French (and Low Dutch or Flemish) important. The early dialogues seem to be geared to practical and commercial interests, but feudal interests are revealed by the fact that these books, even more so the grammars and textbooks of the early sixteenth century, were frequently commissioned by members of the nobility (Stein 1997, 56).

Besides the court and commerce, it was the unity of the English and French Protestants which gave the teaching of French an additional support. It passed its first test when English Protestants fled to France and became acquainted there with the French language during the time of Queen Mary (particularly in the years 1551–8). After the Edict of Nantes (1598) easy contacts between the members of the relevant churches were possible in France, and after its revocation (1685) it passed its second test when French Hugenots could flee to England. Many earned their living in London as teachers of their mother tongue (Watson 1909, 395–442).

In the two centuries to come, and indeed well beyond that, teaching French in England gave rise to six types of manuals—orthographical treatises, grammars, model letters, *nominales*, wordbooks, and dialogues, of which grammars, wordbooks, and books of conversation are certainly the most important (Rothwell

1968, 37). Only the last three mentioned text-genres have a natural affinity to the phenomena and problems of onomasiology. However, even grammars sometimes disclose the fact that onomasiological thinking is active beneath the surface of structural analyses and descriptions.

John Palsgrave's French grammar, *Lesclarcissement de la langue francoyse*, of 1530, for example, is one of the most comprehensive and erudite undertakings of its kind in the sixteenth century. It is a detailed grammar for English native speakers learning French, with extensive word-lists, and is also famous for its contrastive point of view (Stein 1997, Swiggers 1997). In its third book, the author discusses '*the first accident of substantiues*', that is, gender as indicated by the definite article (fols. i^v–iii^r). In doing so, he forms groups of lexemes whose members belong to one gender. Note, for example:

First / all proper names / all names of dignite / office / and craftes / and also names of kynred or cognation spirituall / belongyng onely to men / be of the masculyn gendre: and the same names belo[n]gyng onely to women / be of the feminym gendre . . . .
Item the names of all maner trees / whider they beare frute or nat / be of the masculyn gendre . . . .
Item all names of frutes be of the femyne gendre . . . .
Item all suche substantiues / whose signification serueth to men onely / and fourmeth of them another substantyue belongyng onely to women / be of suche ge[n]der as their signification requireth . . . . And in like wise all names of any craftes men endyng in ier *be of the masculyn gendre / and all that be fourmed of them ending in* iere, *bycause they signifie theyr wiues / or women exercisyng the same crafte / be of the femym gendre . . . .*
Item all the names of the monethes and the four seasons of the yere / be of the masculyn gendre . . . .
Item all names of cyties be of the feminyne gendre.   (book three, fol. ii ^r–v)

Ranks and offices, trees and fruits, characterizations of men and women, male and female animals, months and seasons, large and small rivers, feasts, and finally parts of speech are all of them semantic domains which form typical sections in onomasiological works. Described and mentioned in a grammar, they remind us of the fact that some structural (grammatical) categories, for example *masculine* and *feminine*, are of a semantic nature and are part of the groundwork of onomasiology as well as of grammar (morphology).

In the following pages, only wordbooks and dialogues of the thirteenth to the seventeenth centuries will be dealt with as onomasiological text-genres in their own right, *nominales* having already been extensively discussed.[24] This reflects the greater influence on the onomasiological tradition of wordbooks and dialogues, as compared to grammars. In our treatment, William Caxton's *Dialogues* with their scholastic realism are given a chapter section of their own (see below) because of their character as an early culmination of the onomasiological tradition in the garb of foreign-language teaching methodology.

---

[24]   See Chapter 3.

Towards the end of the thirteenth century, and not later than 1280 (Koch 1934, 33), probably between 1240 and 1250 (Rothwell 1982) Walter of Bibbesworth[25] (*fl.* between ?1270 and ?1283) published a rhymed narrative, '*Tretiz de Langage*'.[26] He was a country gentleman living in Hertfordshire and Essex. In one version his treatise has 846 rhymed verses, in another 1134. It was modelled on the treatises in Latin with vernacular glosses by Adam of Petit Pont, Alexander Nequam, and John of Garland. However, 'its purpose was to teach French to the children of the English nobility and gentry' (Wright and Wülcker 1968, ix). It consisted of a French text with occasional English interlinear glosses. The author says in his text that a basic knowledge of French is presupposed. So the treatise is obviously not meant for children, as a schoolbook proper, but for teachers of French, whether Bibbesworth's patroness Dyonise de Mountechensi, whom he mentions in the prologue, or a professional teacher (Rothwell 1968, 37–9). The French used reflects the tradition of the insular variety as it had developed out of the Norman French that came to England after 1066 (Stein 1997, 97). It contains a collection of words and phrases of a very practical character, beginning with the nursing and feeding of a new-born child, followed by a description of objects which are important for the child's upbringing together with actions to be performed in daily country life, domestic arrangements, and a sumptuous feast (Lambley 1920, 14). The logical thread between these topics is the practicalities of country life. They fall quite naturally into various objective domains with their corresponding lexis. As always, a wealth of information on cultural history is contained in the text. The extant manuscripts and in particular the dialects present in the glosses prove that the treatise was very successful all over England for about one hundred years (Koch 1934, Rothwell 1982, 284–93).

For the evaluation of the onomasiological character of the treatise it is important to know that a *Nominale sive Verbale in Gallicis cum expositione eiusdem in Anglicis* (Skeat 1906) is in existence which uses the vocabulary of the older treatise, though in a different arrangement, and adds an English line-for-line gloss to the French text. According to the editor (Skeat 1906, 2) the manuscript was written about 1340. The words are introduced, for example in the sequence in which the relevant objects are needed for building a house, and embedded in simple sentences. Note:[27]

Qu veut edifier sur estage   *Primes deit a son escient*
Wo-so wole house   *At his wytyngge*
Couient qil soit riche et sage   *Sercher bon fundement*
Riche and wys   *Serche a gode grounde*

---

[25] Also spelled Walter of/de Biblesworth.

[26] Editions by Wright (Bibbesworth 1857), Owen (Bibbesworth 1929), and Rothwell (Bibbesworth 1990). A philological comment on the lexis is given by Schellenberg 1933, a minute comparison between editions and manuscripts by Rothwell 1982.

[27] Quotation from the Skeat 1906 edition, lines 428–47. I disregard Skeat's italicizations with which he indicates emendations to the text.

Leuer deit mure et messere	*Cumble heez et cheueroun*
Wal and gonele	*Roof firstre and sparre*
De sablon chaux et de piere	*Treefs et guenchisons*
With sonde lim and ston	*Bemes and ribresenes*
Amont cochera pur feare	*Clowes kyulyls et guenchons*
meson	*Nayles pynnes and lathes*
[line missing]	. . . .

One of the derivatives of Bibbesworth and of the *Nominale sive verbale* is a text of 1415 called *Femina* (Kibbee 1991, 75–8), preserved in 'a unique MS. in the library of Trinity College, Cambridge'.[28] The title signifies an idea behind the book which would nowadays be called *psychological*: Note the first sentence: '*Lyber iste vocatur femina quia sicut femina docet infantem loqui maternam sic docet iste liber Iuvenes rhetorice loqui gallicum prout infra patebit*'.[29] It contains rhymed couplets in French followed by their English translations. Thus, the principle of a complete translation is established, different from the occasional glossings of earlier texts. This part is followed by an alphabetical glossary of French words in three columns, of which the first column gives their spelling, the second their pronunciation, and the third their meanings in English. The first two columns show that, contrary to Bibbesworth's wordbook, the Continental variety of French was now taught, in particular that of Paris and Picardy (Stein 1997, 192). The text was written by a Norman scribe. There are dialect words in the French text, and the English translations are frequently incorrect.

The subjects of *Femina* are predominantly the same as in Bibbesworth and the *Nominale sive verbale*, though in an order differing from both of them. They are given in Latin headings. For a comparison of subjects between the *Treatise*, the *Nominale sive verbale*, and *Femina* see Table A.3.

The Latin headings show that the contents of *Femina* are similar to those which we know, namely, the human body, animals and plants in the country, crafts and trades, houses. They are indeed centred around the upbringing of a child. The first two chapters with their names of animals when congregated in groups and of their voices, taken from the *Nominale sive verbale*, but not from Bibbesworth, are even today typical beginnings of children's books. The third chapter explains the two main tasks of babies—learning to crawl, toddle, and walk and learning to speak not only their own language but also French. The headings of the following sections speak for themselves. The general aim is to make the child fit for life in the country. The introduction of lexemes denoting the voices of animals, in particular birds, and their assembling in herds and flocks respectively certainly serves the preparation of hunting, the noble countryman's main pleasure. '*De diversitate nominum*' and the following give a fairy tale of a knight dressed entirely

---

[28]   Subtitle of the edition by Wright 1909.
[29]   'This book is called *Femina* because as a woman teaches the child of the mother [how] to speak so this book teaches young people in the rhetorical way [how] to speak French as it is visible below.' (My translation, W. H.)

in red. The two last sections are concerned with general questions of manners for eating and upbringing.

The thematic concentration on the upbringing of a child is paralleled by a style which is obviously meant to express the tone in which a mother addresses her baby. The first lines are telling, even if somewhat conventionally stiff:

Beau enfaunt pur apprendre
En franceis deuej bien entendre
ffayre chyld for to lerne
In frensh je schal wel vnderstande
Coment vous parlerej bealment
Et deuaunt lej sagj naturalment
How je schal speke fayre
And afore þyee wyjemen kyndely.   (1.1–8.)

The sixth chapter, which gives the names for plants in the fields, for example, starts with a small introductory remark which has even more of the quality of a mother's voice:

Ore aloms as prees & champs
Pur norrer nostre enfauntej
Now go we to mede and feld
ffor to norshe oure chyldren.   (27.22–28.1.)

Something similar is to be read at the beginning of the eleventh chapter, which deals with the names for herbs and trees:

Le iour deuient beau & cler
Aloms en auste pur iuer
þe day by comeþ fayr & cleer
Go we in somer to pleye
En verger ou sount lej floures
Dount issent lej doulcej odourus
In erber wher ben þyje flourus
Wher of gon out þyje swete odourus
Erbej auxci pur medicine
Et lour nouns ieo voile deuine
Erbej al so for medicine
And here namej y wylle deuine.   (49.16–50.1.)

Such remarks establish a clear relation between a speaker and a (or several) listener(s) and, moreover, structure the text. They most frequently delimit topically coherent passages, and in the cases quoted they mark their beginnings. Sometimes such lines also have a closing function. Note, for example, the ending of the chapter on seeds, which deals with flax, spinning, etc.:

Tantost lej tromej ele vaudrat
Ore ay vous di quant apent

A noñ hyre tromej she wyndeþ vppe
Now y haue y seyd how muche longeþ.   (37.2–5.)

The main body of text consists of statements which introduce certain words in the manner of definitions or of assertions. This structure in particular connects *Femina* with the onomasiological tradition. Thus, the main purpose of the text is to introduce and semanticize word meanings. Typically, this is done in topical clusters. Note, for example, the chapter on animal voices (Middle English verses only):

Man spekeþ bere brayeþ
þᵗ out of mesure hyt affrayeþ
Lyon Romyþ Cran graulyþ
Kow loweþ hasyl bloweþ
Hors neyeþ / larke syngeþ
Coluere Iurrut & cok syngeþ
Kat meweþ addere cissit or fliet proprie
Asse rugeþ swan reflieþ   (6.14–15, 18–19, 22–3, 7.2–3.)

A sequence of such statements moves *Femina* into the vicinity of dictionaries made up of sentences such as John of Garland had already written and as Comenius would later do. There are other contexts where the sequence of statements results in a coherent description or narrative. Note, for example, the chapter '*De arte pistoris*' (Middle English verses only):

When jour korn ys wel y þrosse
After y wynwyd & wel y grounde
By þᵉ grindynge comeþ mele
And þen bred nyxjt on morwe
Also of corñ comeþ flour
By þᵉ buntynge of þᵉ bakere
And by þᵉ buntere ys deceueret
þe flour and bran þᵗ ys so clere.   (31.7–8, 11–12, 15–16.)

It is obvious that the syntactical structure of the language is richer and more varied here. It is, however, also obvious that the richer the syntax, or the more complex the message, the further away the text moves from the onomasiological origin and approaches a text containing general admonitions.

Besides what could be called realistic passages, couplets are inserted which treat grammatical gender and give rules for the pronunciation of French words, in particular of homographs and homophones.

The early fifteenth century also sees the appearance of a new type of conversation book, which will constitute a genre of its own (Kaltz 1995) in the centuries to come and which in many respects prefigures its first culmination point, Caxton. It is the *Manière de Langage*, 'intended for the use of travellers, merchants, and others desiring a conversational and practical rather than a thorough and grammatical knowledge of French' (Lambley 1920, 35). There are three versions, which go under the generalizing title of *Manière* (Baker 1989), the earliest dating from 1396 (Meyer 1903). Three years later appeared *Un petit livre pour enseignier les enfantz de leur entreparler comun francois*, which employs very much the same means of teaching as the *Manière*, geared however to the needs of children. Finally, *Dialogues* was composed late in 1415, precisely datable because of its references to the battle of Agincourt (Kibbee 1991, 81–2). It is quite realistic, mainly because a voyage is imagined, with dialogues (Gessler 1934, 9–42). In contrast to the dialogues in *La Manière*, the voyage is one through Britain (not France), with persons conversing in the 'sweet French' of Paris (Stein 1997, 101). As we will later find in Caxton, the conversations start with a religious invocation, but are followed by an enumeration of the parts of the human body. The various types of greetings are then added. There are dialogues between a host and his guest, between the master and his servant. These schemes will appear in many later books of the kind. A little drama is even created when the guest unexpectedly recognizes a friend in the hostel. The dialogues are dramatic and direct, sometimes developing into pure lists of words. However, this does not happen too often, indeed less frequently than will be found in Caxton's *Dialogues*. There are short narrative texts between the direct speech, which create natural scenes of communication and even some action. After a conversation during a meal we read, for example: '*Après vient le signeur et se monte à chival, et s'en vait chivalcher sur son chemyn; et quant il venra à boute de la ville, il demandera . . . à un pute veile ou à un aultre ainsi*' (Gessler 1934, 52), and then another dialogue follows. These dialogues are less didactic than others, because they show a human touch and are not loaded with word-lists. '*Ils sont plus courts et offrent moins d'intérêt pour la lexicographie, parce qu'ils sont moins riches en listes de poissons, de comestibles divers, d'objets d'habillement ou d'ameublement*' (Meyer 1903, 47).

From the versions of *Manière* and their progressive development into Caxton's *Dialogues* it is obvious that the dialogical procedure is useful for guaranteeing a fairly natural communicative situation such as also prevails in the normal contact between a sender and a receiver. This is what makes it valuable for foreign-language teaching which aims at practical competence. The dialogical procedure also guarantees semantically coherent contents with clear delimitations, which makes teaching and learning semantically meaningful and overcomes its formal character. Moreover, many linguistic rules like anaphora, cataphora, pronominalization, which are basic for textuality, but difficult to formalize, come into play quite naturally.

4.3 Caxton's *Dialogues in French and English*

4.3.1 *The original and its derivatives*

'Monarchs and magnates apart, William Caxton (*c*.1420–1491) is today probably the best-known and most widely honored Englishman of his century. All of

Caxton's fame depends on the activities of the last two decades of his life' (Needham 1986, 15). His was the first printing shop in England, in which he carried out an extremely varied programme. These activities resulted in the incredible output of eighty printed books within fourteen years. Indeed, William Caxton's fame appears to rest much more on the fact *that* he printed books in English than on *what* he printed.

In 1483 he issued a book without any title which has become known as *Dialogues in French and English* or *Vocabulary in French and English* according to its designation in diverse academic papers and editions (by Bradley [Caxton 1900], Gessler 1931, Oates and Harmer 1964). Needham (1986, Appendix B) lists all pertinent entries in the STC and similar censuses. In their introductions, Gessler (1931) and Oates and Harmer (1964) trace Caxton's book back to its origins and describe the manuscripts as well as their passage through the centuries.

Behind Caxton's book is the original work called *Livre des Mestiers* which must have originated around 1340 in Bruges and which has not survived. It was a manual of conversations in French and Flemish, obviously written by a schoolmaster using the linguistic varieties of northern Picardy, more precisely of Hainault, and of Bruges. The only transcription still extant, which is now kept at the Bibliothèque Nationale in Paris and whose identity with the original cannot be guaranteed, was printed for the first time by Michelant (1875). The topography of its dialogues is without any doubt the topography of Bruges, as can be seen from a map of the town drawn in 1562 by Marc Gheeraerdts: '*en effet, tous les noms qu'il cite étaient connus à Bruges ou le sont encore*' (Gessler 1931, 14). Besides the transcription used by Michelant, there is an adaptation from about 1420 in which the Flemish part of the original was replaced by a Dutch version in the dialect spoken between Limburg and the German border. The only example, entitled *Gesprächsbüchlein*, can now be found in Cologne (municipal archives). It was published by Hoffmann von Fallersleben in 1854. There must have been another adaptation, of which no copy has been preserved and which became the source of Caxton's French–English version of 1483 as well as of a French–Dutch version in the dialect of Antwerp published by Roland Vanden Dorp shortly before 1501. All published versions have been reprinted by Gessler who also worked out the filiation (1931, 47) by scrupulous comparisons.

The age of the lost prototype has been established on linguistic as well as on general historical grounds and on the basis of political geography as it appears in the dialogues and as we know it from the records of political history (Grierson 1957). Scholars are fairly unanimous on this score. There is less common agreement about the date of the French–English version and even about its author-translator. Grierson (1957) concludes on numismatic grounds that it must have been written in 1465–6. As Caxton lived in Bruges as a mercer between 1446 and 1476, it is, however, difficult to find reasons why he should have done the translating precisely within these two years. Blake (1965) argues that it was not Caxton at all who translated it, because the admittedly many mistakes of the English part are different in kind from the mistakes he made when translating *The History of Reynard the Fox* in 1481, and for this book Caxton's authorship of the translation is beyond doubt. If this is correct, the English translation of the French–Flemish dialogues could have been written in 1465–6 by somebody else, perhaps by a mercer of Caxton's acquaintance, and handed over to him much later, when he printed it in his own shop, not so much out of interest in the translation but as a matter of business. All this sounds quite artificial. Oates and Harmer (1964) accept the theory of Caxton being the translator when he lived in Bruges.

There is consensus among scholars that the translation deviates frequently from its source. Oates and Harmer even call it 'grossly inaccurate' (1964, XXVIII). Sometimes the semantic correspondence between French and English is lacking, sometimes the English is incomprehensible. It is irregular in a way which is regarded as typical of Caxton when he was translating, and it is obviously influenced by Flemish. As Caxton would, consciously or unconsciously, quite frequently be subject to interference from the Flemish language in his translations, this is another argument for his translatorship (Oates and Harmer 1964, XXVI).

Much philological work has been devoted to the *Livre des Mestiers* and its derivates. Interesting as the findings are in every single case, it seems irrelevant *vis-à-vis* the fact that the original manual of conversation in two languages, written in Bruges around the middle of the fourteenth century, obviously exercised no little influence on the people of that time. In the region of its origin, there must have been a lively interest in foreign-language teaching and learning. French and Flemish, Dutch in various dialects, German as spoken in the western part of the lower Rhineland, and, via trade connections, English were in competition with each other. The *Livre* may have met this interest quite well.

Caxton's *Dialogues* are taken here as an example of foreign-language teaching at the end of the Middle Ages. As such, it stands in a long tradition of texts devoted to that goal, and perpetuates old techniques. Most of all, they are determined by the onomasiological tradition. But as is usually the case with a particularly successful link in a traditional chain, it must also have added, or at least supported, new ideas and new techniques.

To make the old and the new visible, the *Dialogues* will be subjected to a linguistic analysis. The guidelines for this are the rules of text analysis as worked out by Sinclair and Coulthard (1975) and elaborated with reference to dialogue in the foreign-language classroom by Lörscher (1983). However, since the text under analysis is not oral performance with all its intricate pragmatic signs, but, if at all, oral performance streamlined, as it were, and turned into print, the Sinclair and Coulthard and the Lörscher models of analysis can be stripped down to a few basic ideas and terms. Their essential linguistic assumptions are the following: A teaching text like the *Dialogues* conforms to the general definition of *text* in so far as it is a large unit consisting of smaller subunits whose central obligatory part is a so-called *nucleus*. There are optional boundaries either preceding or succeeding the nucleus or both. Their function is the opening and closing of such speech as constitutes the central part. Before and after the teaching text, we find a frame introducing and rounding off the whole, together with so-called *pre-units* and *post-units* which are rather loosely connected with the main body of the text. All these textual differentiations can be kept apart on the basis of their diverging functions.

4.3.2   A close reading

Caxton's *Dialogues* can be broken down into the following linear sequence of units:

   (1) invocation of the Holy Trinity;
   (2) formulae for greetings;
   (3) objects: house and furniture;
   (4) objects: food;
   (5) objects: commerce and trade;
   (6) offices, social ranks;
   (7) proper names together with professions, trades, and crafts;
   (8) pilgrimage;
   (9) counting, money;
  (10) a final religious invocation.

As will be shown later, these units have fairly clear boundary markers, but the strongest criterion for their delimitation is the onomasiological principle, that is, their semantic cohesion, which discloses itself right away. This is even stronger than the table of contents which is given at the beginning for the benefit of the learner: 'For to fynde all by ordre / That whiche men wylle lerne' (1.3–4).[30]

FORMULAE AND RULES OF BEHAVIOUR

The first subunit after the invocation, (2), contains rules of behaviour, of what to do and what to say when meeting people in the street.[31] There then follow routine formulae for the opening and closing parts of conversations which give an interesting insight into the oral speech conventions of that time. More interestingly,

---

[30] Bradley's reprint of 1900 has become the most frequently quoted one, in spite of severe criticism. See Oates and Harmer 1964, XXXV: 'Bradley's text is very faulty and, according to Gessler ("Introduction", 36–9), diverges unwittingly from Caxton's text exactly 162 times. Gessler himself has diverged from it rather more often, but wittingly (ibid., 24 n.I.42).' As the facsimile edition is very difficult to read and the Gessler edition is difficult to come by, I will stick to quoting from Bradley. I only give the English utterances, and not their juxtaposed French versions.

[31] The following analysis should be checked against Tables A.4 and A.5. The terms *subunit, unit, boundary*, etc. are used in the sense defined above. For better orientation, the numbers of the tentative groups in linear sequence, as given above, are placed after the first mention of a subgroup, etc., because our analysis will follow their textual functions, but not their linear sequence. Numbers after quotations refer to pages and lines in the Bradley reprint.

these routine formulae are at least partly arranged in the sequence of a natural conversation with people greeting each other, enquiring after each other's health, their whereabouts in the recent past, mutual compliments, saying good-bye, etc. As the voice of the teacher giving introductory rules for proper linguistic behaviour is clearly recognizable, the subsequent conversations can also be understood as spoken by him in both parts, that is, the teacher performs a short role-play, thus illustrating his rules of behaviour given at the beginning.

Something similar happens in the subunit dealing with items of food (4). To begin with, there are somewhat moralizing rules on how married people should talk to each other, how they should talk to their children and to their servants. These are followed by a dialogue (10.7–11.15) in which a fictitious landlord orders a servant to buy food, providing an opportunity to use the vocabulary of various sorts of meat. Again, we have role-play with both parts of the dialogue spoken by one person, obviously the teacher, in order to illustrate at least some of the rules he has previously told the learner to observe.

An outstanding instance of this method is to be found in the following subunit (5), which deals with trade and commerce. The learner is first told where to go in order to buy cloth in different colours (14.25–15.4). Then we find a long conversation full of addresses, question and answer sequences, adjacency pairs, all of which deserve analysis in their own right using the method of conversational analysis. We find here routine formulae, instances of the co-operation principle, etc. (15.5–19.16). The conversation centres around the price, the yardstick to be used, the currency available, and, finally, other places and markets for different kinds of business. This lively exchange of speech is, again, obviously produced by one person, the teacher. One proof of this is that the parts of direct speech are introduced by an author-voice which, in so doing, refers to other parts of the book: 'So *may ye beginne / By suche gretyng / As it is in the first chapitre*' (15.2–4) or *Ye shall ansuere / Also as it is wreton els where* (19.17–18). The conversation itself is quite lively and deictically correct. It is dramatic in the technical sense of the theory of drama.

A last instance of fictitious dialogue is to be found in the subunit containing exchanges with reference to a pilgrimage (8). Rather extensive religious admonitions by the teacher merge into a conversation obviously conducted during a pilgrimage to Boulogne. It deals with asking the way, looking for accommodation, and the departure of a ship.

WORD-LISTS

Besides the technique of giving rules for acting and then staging a fictitious conversation in a role-play, the subunits on house and furniture (3), food (4), commerce and trade (5), and finally on offices and social ranks (6) contain long lists of semantically related words which are scantily embedded in syntactical structures whose only function is obviously to couch them somehow in speech. This is where the onomasiological principle shows most clearly through the disguise of additional teaching techniques. This principle can be very clearly illustrated by examples, of which the subunit on house and furniture gives a wide choice. After a description of how a house should be built, a long list of furniture and household goods is introduced by *'Now must you have beddes'* (6.33), enumerating all the things a bedroom should be furnished with, followed by a list of vessels introduced by *'Yf ye haue wherof* [i.e. bedroom furniture], */ Doo that ye haue / Werkes of tynne'* (7.14–16). Next comes a list of plates and cutlery introduced by *'Now must ye haue'* (7.29). Sometimes, lists of names of things are not only introduced but also concluded by remarks that place them in a context. For example:

Cuppes of silver,
Cuppes gylte,
Couppes of goold,
Cuppes with feet;
Thise things set ye
In your whutche or cheste;
Your jewellis in your forcier
That they be not stolen.   (8.15–22.)

Finally, some rather long lists of names of objects are interspersed by remarks which establish a loose but clearly discernible semantic cohesion over many lines. There is, for example, the introductory line *'The names of trees'* (13.10), followed by fifteen such names. Then the linking lines *'Vnder thise trees / Ben herbes suete smellyng'* (13.16–17) lead to eight more names, followed by:

In wodes ben the verdures,
Brembles, bremble beries,
Ther is founden ofte
In gardyns on the mottes.
Within the medewis is the grasse
Whereof men make heye;
So ben ther thistles and nettles;
Yet ben in the gardynes.   (13.22–9.)

This leads to nineteen more names of garden plants.

In the subunit devoted to house and furniture, the syntactic embeddings of word lists are comparatively elaborate and even have a background of common social experience, as is revealed in the remark on the jewels which are said to be stolen. In other subunits (e.g. 4), introductory or concluding remarks as boundaries are much briefer, for example, *'Of fruit shall ye here named'*, with fourteen names following (13.3–9) or *'The names of trees'*, with fifteen following (13.10–15).

It would be no trouble at all to sift the learning vocabulary out of these presentations and to arrange it in lexical domains, as indeed the text already does. Naturally, the choice of words is of tremendous interest for the historiographer of general cultural development. By and large, this choice agrees with the many topical word-lists that have come down to us and which the author or the translator could easily consult. Houses and furniture, plants, animals and food, objects of trade, oils and paints, finally grain and metals belong to the usual store of *nominales* and other word-lists. The teacher obviously started from given word-lists, wherever he found them or however he collected them himself. He then integrated them into his teaching by creating a minimal context which presupposes some knowledge of the world in which and for which the teaching is done.

BOUNDARY REMARKS

The boundaries around subunits and, within them, even around smaller sub-subunits, serve a function which is obviously different from giving rules for behaviour, staging role-plays, and delivering syntactically embedded word-lists. They explain beforehand what the teacher is going to do. If we think of the three functions which mark the teaching of a foreign language in the narrow sense, we can say that it is the function of such boundary remarks between teaching subunits to organize the teaching itself. Learners are obviously told what they have to expect, and in doing this the teacher imposes a clear order on his own activities.

The subunit on house and furniture (3), for example, is introduced by '*Now standeth me for to speke / Of othir thynges necessarie*' (6.16–17). It closes with the line: '*Here endeth the thirde chapitre*' (9.10). The greater number of such remarks are short and matter-of-fact, such as '*Yet I haue not named the metals / Whiche folowe*' (21.19–21) or simply '*Thise ben marchandises*' (21.30). Others are longer and more personal, such as '*For that I am not / Spycier ne apotecarie / I can not name / All maneres of spyces; / But I shall name a partie*' (19.33–6). But they all have the same function: they announce the beginning or end of a teaching phase and are thus not part of the teaching itself but of its internal organization.

NAMES AND MANNERS OF ADDRESS

Quantitatively speaking, the subunit on proper names together with professions, trades, and crafts (7) is of course most noteworthy. But it also seems remarkable in its way of presenting the foreign language. The names are introduced in alphabetical order and are made a pivot for various examples of everyday speech by which the bearer of the name is addressed. In spite of differing names, some of the speeches are connected with each other. The general context is the departure on a journey and having dinner at an inn. In a few cases, the bearer of the name is not addressed directly, in the second person singular, but information is given about him in the third person singular. We must assume that this information is addressed directly to the learner of the foreign language with the aim of rendering the ensuing dialogue intelligible. The following example mixes both procedures:

Agnes our maid
Can well name
All the grete festes
And the termes of the yere.
'Damyselle, name them.'
'I shall not, so god helpe me!
Agace shall name them'.   (28.5–11.)

And then Agace indeed does.

Following this, we have the many characterizations of professions, trades, and crafts which give a singular overview of the activities of people in a town like Bruges in the fifteenth century. Each is tied to a proper name. They follow each other alphabetically in an unbroken line from the beginning of the long subunit. Unlike the addresses to the persons whose proper names are given, the characterizations of professions, trades, and crafts are directed by the speaker, the teacher, towards the learner, and refer to the bearer of a name and his or her doings. For example:

David the bridelmaker
Is a good werkman
For to make sadles,
Bridles, and spores,
And that thereto belongeth.   (33.21–5.)

The number of details mentioned differs considerably. Thus, the speaker needs only four lines for *Colard the fuller* (32.9–12), but 36 lines for *Geruays the scrivener* (36.35–37.30). Occasionally, personal incidents and pieces of information are mentioned which betray the fact that the speaker is talking of persons of his acquaintance. Even here, the tendency to slip into a dialogue is at work. It already showed in the example of Agnes and Agace. Of the following example, the first six lines are descriptive, the last four, however, belong to a dialogue between the speaker as customer and Gabriel the linen-weaver as shopowner:

Gabriel the lynweuar   *Is it ended?*
Weueth my lynnencloth   *Ye, sith thursday*
Of threde of flaxe   *Hit is wouen*
And of touwe.   *For to doo white.*   (38.9–18)
My lacketh woef
And of warpe

All these texts are highly informative and a great store of knowledge for social historiography. Note, for example, the part on *'George the booke sellar'* who buys books *'Be they stolen or enprinted'*, that is, produced in the printing shop, *'Or othir-wyse pourchased'*. Among the books are *'Oures of our lady'* (prayerbooks for Angelus), and psalters, *'doctrinals'*, *'Donettis, partis, accidents'* (Donatus's grammar and other grammar schoolbooks), *'catons'* (copies of Cato's *Distycha*), *'Bookes of physike*, and *'kalenders'* (38.31–39.9), in total the whole range of religious, didactic, and scientific books that could be found in a bookshop (Lindemann 1994, 34).

Sometimes vignettes of impressionistic charm are produced. Apart from the naturalness of speech and of the fictitious dialogues, they give plenty of opportunities to mention words which semantically belong to one domain.

THE TEACHING TEXT ITSELF

Finally, mention must be made of the frame around everything described and explained so far—the teaching text *in toto*. At the beginning (1), after the overview of the chapters, we have an invocation of the Holy Trinity followed by a self-appraisal of the book, *'By the whiche men shall mowe / Reasonably vnderstande / Frenssh and englissh'* (3.22–4). Moreover, the usefulness of knowing foreign languages for successful business is pointed out. At the end (10), we have an invocation of the Holy Ghost, again with a self-appraisal of the book, this time pointing out that it facilitates learning French and English *shortly*. This frame binds the whole text together. In addition, there are quite a number of cross-references which serve the same function.

Summing up, we can say that, apart from the table of contents, there are five functionally distinguishable kinds of speech in Caxton's *Dialogues*: first, framing utterances situating the whole text, second, boundary utterances opening and rounding off subunits, third, informing utterances on what to do with the foreign language, fourth, teaching utterances of two kinds, either descriptive vocabulary containing long lists of semantically related words in syntactic embeddings, or such vocabulary in connection with direct addresses to imaginary people, and fifth, fictitious dialogues which serve as illustrations for language use. The utterances of the third, fourth, and fifth types form the nuclei of the subunits. A full subunit consists of an opening boundary, a nucleus, and a closing boundary. However, the closing boundary is obviously optional. It is quite frequently missing (see Tables A.4 and A.5). There are two cases in subunits 6 and 7 where two nuclei follow each other without a boundary. This is why they have not been counted as separate sub-subunits.[32]

The pre-unit, that is, the table of contents, has its clear function, which is even stated in its opening boundary. The post-unit is a kind of appendix which does not conform to the otherwise lucid structure of the whole text.

4.3.3 Performance in the classroom

It is not difficult to imagine this printed text as actually spoken in class. The teacher explains what he is going to do and how the language to be learned should be used. He teaches its vocabulary, he addresses imagined people whose occupations he supposes to be well known to his learners, and he stages role-plays in

---

[32]   The table of contents is different in this case. I give linguistic criteria priority.

dialogues. As far as the teacher is concerned, all important functional elements of foreign-language teaching in a classroom are present. The linguistic analysis of present-day classroom discourse, as carried out by Sinclair and Coulthard (1975) and by Lörscher (1983), yielded quite similarly structured dialogues. This is the great surprise of this analysis of an old text with the help of a modern analytical technique. Of course, we cannot know whether Caxton's *Dialogues* are real lessons orally performed and then turned into print, or whether they are just imagined lessons. Some anaphoric remarks point to the latter possibility. Here the author of the book refers to a previous chapter, where a performing teacher would speak of 'what he said before'. But even so, the *Dialogues* are characterized by what could be called their scholastic realism, which contains many features of orality, even if we admit that many pragmatic signals would be omitted and stylistic shifts would probably be effected by turning the imagined dialogues into performed speech. But there is no reason to assume that such shifts were particularly drastic.

Unfortunately, we have no trace of the learners' performance in Caxton's *Dialogues*. If it is right to see them as a mirror of classroom reality, it seems plausible to assume that the actual teaching was done by the teacher presenting the text as we have it and by the learners repeating and/or translating it, either in chorus or individually, with the intention of learning it by heart. Even if the learners' part was done in writing, the intention would still be to learn the dialogues by heart. For the book, the same procedure has to be envisaged. The reader-learner, who would act as his own teacher, would have to pronounce the texts and translate them, thus turning into a twofold speaker-learner. We must not forget that everything said/printed in the *Dialogues* is done in the two languages, utterances facing each other as a sign of their assumed translatory equivalence. Framing and boundary utterances are possibly to be exempted from repetition. Nothing is discernible about the teaching of grammar and of pronunciation. Both would become topics of textbook writers on French only in the first third of the sixteenth century (Stein 1997, 45–9, 60–78). While the latter may have been done by presentation (teacher) and imitation (learner), the former may perhaps have been dropped altogether, thus relying on a method which would equate learning with practice and teaching with presenting linguistic material in a way which would facilitate this practice.

If the reading and explanation of Caxton, as unfolded so far, is plausible, the title *Dialogues in French and English* turns out to be at least as inaccurate as the title *Vocabulary in French and English*. The whole book is in fact a monologue with role-play dialogues inserted. On the other hand, it seems understandable that the fictitious dialogical part should have been so impressive for the first editor. It is indeed *the* outstanding feature of the book. And, again, it seems understandable that the vocabulary part should have been so impressive, for example, for the editor of the French–Dutch version, because the text often reads like a contextualized word-list.

4.3.4 Caxton and the new medium

The march from the *Hermeneumata* to Caxton, through several centuries of foreign-language teaching, as far as the texts allow us to conjecture on what actually happened, is meant to show that two principles, among others, were at work throughout the centuries, namely, semantic cohesion of vocabulary, which often takes on the form of narrative, and dialogue. The former is easily recognizable in all the texts mentioned and it is also easy to assess its didactic function. The latter however, though present from the beginning, integrates only reluctantly and with some difficulties into a normal teaching procedure. It is with *La Manière* and with Caxton that we obtain a first fairly clear view of how fictitious dialogues were used in class as a teaching procedure.

The question arises of why teaching texts which employ natural dialogues seem to originate at the beginning of the fifteenth century. There may be two answers. Either earlier teaching was different or it was not different but its oral performance was not thought fit to be written down. If it was different it may very well be that new ideas about natural, that is, practical, teaching came into being because the learners demanded them. The goal of teaching French in England may have changed towards the realistic and the practical during the fifteenth century. As regards Caxton's book, a happy coincidence seems to have prevailed. As was explained, out of a regional linguistic situation around Bruges and in Flanders a whole family of books for foreign-language teaching originated, which Caxton (or somebody else) adapted to those English needs as had already surfaced in earlier texts (*Femina* and *Manière*) and had been made available to many learners in print. Anybody who cared (and had the money to buy a book) could now read what teachers would say in class by role-playing what native speakers would say in the streets or at the market. Caxton (or the technique of the *Dialogues*, which he printed) 'extended language learning beyond the classroom, creating a new ideal of the pedagogical text, the manual that replaced the master, an ideal which extended the learning of French to a new clientele' (Kibbee 1991, 94).

The early fifteenth century was not a time when the printing of oral speech could be considered a normal thing. It needed a man with linguistic ambition, enthusiasm for printing, and an interest in spreading a knowledge of useful foreign languages. This is the set of conditions that probably caused William Caxton to become involved. He had a lifelong interest in translations and became England's first printer after learning the art on the Continent. Moreover, he had spent thirty years in a country with a (for him) foreign language. As governor of the Mercers' Company, which held a royal charter and controlled the wool trade with the Low Countries, he knew about the importance of learning foreign languages. However, in order to be successful as a printer Caxton needed a public whose members were interested and literate enough to read printed texts and who shared so much common knowledge that they could understand them (Giesecke 1980). This was not too difficult in the case of literature and theology. But it must have been difficult in the case of foreign-language teaching and learning. Perhaps Caxton found such people among the Mercers' Company, whose members resided in London as well as in Bruges. Such companies would establish a system of communication among their members, which might include foreign language teaching. In the special case of the Mercers' Company there is no known proof of this. Still, the *Zeitgeist* of the fifteenth century would support this assumption. At that time, literacy, which had up to then been a privilege of the clergy, of administrators, who were often clerical, and of lawyers, was also adopted by merchants, craftsmen, and artisans (Orme 1973, 48–9). Besides the usual grammar schools with their Latin curriculum, studies in trade and business were set up, which not only included accounting and the drafting of contracts but also the teaching and learning of French as a foreign language (Orme 1973, 68–79). Significantly, in 1459 a merchant named Simon Eyre bequeathed the huge sum of £2,000 for the establishment of a school under the auspices of the Drapers' Company in London.

It is quite plausible that Caxton's teaching texts were meant for the teachers of mercers and for the mercers themselves in Bruges and in London and were specially geared to their needs. This is supported by the choice of vocabulary and the method of characterizing professional activities. Typically, word-lists for the parts of the human body, which are almost indispensable in similar texts before and after Caxton, are absent here, because they were obviously more suitable for children learning a foreign language than for grown-ups in their function as tradesmen.

Against this general background, the question of who translated the *Dialogues* loses its importance, although its answer remains biographically interesting. The important thing is that William Caxton recognized their potential as teaching and learning texts outside Bruges. A knowledge of similar enterprises in the *Femina* and *Manière* dialogues may have been helpful. Even if we accept that such productions as the *Dialogues* were needed to keep Caxton's press going (Blake 1969, 65–6), we need not assume that his decision to print them was made without careful deliberation. Too many details suggest that he knew what he was doing. Caxton's historical role seems to lie in the fact that he printed the right text at the right time.

For overviews of Caxton's *Dialogues* according to the lines of interpretation developed here, see Tables A.4 and A.5.

4.4   Didactic dialogues of the sixteenth and seventeenth centuries

4.4.1 General

According to Kaltz (1995), didactic material, besides grammars, typically exists in various text-genres, namely alphabetical and topical dictionaries, dialogues in the nature of the *Manière de langage*, and texts for reading and writing, among them model letters, proverbs, and prayers. We should perhaps add phonetic treatises (Stein 1997, 60–8) which deal exclusively with the correspondences and differences between pronunciation and spelling, unless we choose to look at them as a part of grammars. All these text-genres were often integrated[33] into one book. It is possible to set up a typology of textbooks for teaching foreign languages according to which of these genres are present in a particular edition (Lindemann 1994, 21).[34]

On a larger scale, the production of printed didactic material for the teaching and learning of foreign languages commenced after printing had been invented and made use of for practical purposes. The first topical dictionaries[35] for learning non-classical (vernacular) languages appeared on the Continent in the last third of the fifteenth century. Towards the end of the fifteenth century and in the sixteenth century, interest in this kind of book increased rapidly. More and more languages were covered, with books listing words of up to eight languages in parallel. However, on the Continent the interest in learning English by means of these books seems to have been as marginal as the interest in England in learning European languages other than Dutch and French, because English appears rather late and in relatively few of the multilingual dictionaries mentioned.[36]

Among the textbook-genres, glossaries or dictionaries and dialogues are the ones which make the onomasiological principle, in one form or the other, the agent of foreign-language teaching and learning. Both forms frequently occur together. On the Continent, two books had a seminal effect, (i) *Introito e porta*, which appeared for the first time in 1477 and instigated a many-branched filiation during the sixteenth and seventeenth centuries and even later with its word-lists arranged in topically organized chapters;[37] and (ii) Noel de Berlaimont's vocabulary in French and Flemish, which appeared for the first time in 1530 and, with its dialogues and alphabetical word-lists, also instigated a many-branched filiation for more than 170 years (see below). These long-lived Continental titles, which are almost two types of textbook in their own right, mirror the slowly growing interest on the Continent in English, if only as an interest in one European language among many others.

One bibliographical source (Lindemann 1994, 22–31) lists the titles of sixty-two relevant integrated textbooks, including Caxton, between 1483 and 1600. Of them sixteen contain topical word-lists and dialogues, that is, they employ the

---

[33] I use *integrated book* as a technical term for books which contain several or all of the genres mentioned.

[34] Lindemann's categories are: (1) alphabetical word-list, (2) topical word-list, (3) dialogues, (4) grammatical morphology, (5) pronunciation, and (6) letters (Lindemann 1994, 21).

[35] For quite a time, these dictionaries were very limited in the number of their entries, so it would be justifiable to refer to them as glossaries. For the sake of clarity, I refer to them as dictionaries when they appear as bound books with their own titles, and as glossaries when they are part of an integrated book with various kinds of text-genres for foreign-language learning. The term *word-list* appears, if not used as an abstract covering term, as a synonym for *glossary*.

[36] See Chapter 9.   [37] See Chapter 9.

onomasiological principle in two ways. Twenty-four titles contain one or the other, twenty-two dialogues only, and two a topical word-list only.

Among the sixteen titles with both genres these seven were produced in England: *Here is a good boke . . .* (London, c.1500); Giles du Wes: *An introductorie for to lerne to rede, to pronounce, and to speake French trewly . . .* (London, 1532); *A very necessarye boke bothe in Englishe & in Frenche wherin you mayst learne to speake & wryte Frenche truly in a litle space . . .* (London, 1550); Claudius Holyband: *The Frenche Littleton* (London, 1566), *The French School-maister . . .* (London, 1573), *A plaine pathway to the French tongue . . .* (London, 1575); James Bellot: *The French grammer: or An Introduction orderly and methodically . . . teachinge the French tongue . . .* (London, 1578).[38] Most of them saw more than one edition and were quite influential. Du Wes's book became the leading French text-book for about twenty years (Stein 1997, 49) till Holyband's took over and was popular even in the following century (Watson 1909, 425–7). His *French Littleton* was re-edited in 1578, 1581, 1583, 1591, 1593, 1597, 1602, 1607, 1609, 1625, and 1630. His *French School-maister* was re-edited in 1582, 1602, 1606, 1609, 1612, 1615, 1623, 1628, 1632, 1636, 1641, 1649, 1655, and 1660.[39]

Grammars and dictionaries have been treated historiographically for a long time. As regards dialogues in the wake of *Manière*, however, this analytical work is still in its infancy (e.g. Kaltz 1995). This is why some of them will be singled out here, although this cannot really fill the gap in research. The choice of dialogues is limited to two editions of the Berlaimont type, that is, dialogues in the multi-lingual tradition of the Continent which heavily influenced the English tradition, and some didactic dialogues of the seventeenth century with English as one of their languages, which were printed in England and, thus, form part of its ono-masiological tradition.[40] One guideline for selecting the titles to be presented here was to show the extraordinary variety of those textbooks, which becomes obvious as soon as you look at them closely.

4.4.2 *Noel de Berlaimont's* Colloquia et Dictionariolum

Of the author[41] nothing else is known except the fact that he was a schoolmaster from Antwerp. The first edition of his vocabulary appeared in 1530, but almost

---

[38] Jacques Bellot is also the author of *Familar dialogues, for the instruction of the[m], that be desirous to learne to speake English . . . . Dialogues familiers . . .* (London, 1578). This book is note-worthy in that it contains a special phonetic script for English and French.

[39] According to the BL Catalogue. Lindemann (1994, 23) also mentions John Palsgrave: *Lesclarcissement* (London, 1530) in this group; this however is erroneous as all lists in this comprehen-sive French grammar are by alphabet. But see above.

[40] The following choice of titles cannot be anything but subjective. For the European tradition on the Continent see Chapters 9 and 10. In order to distinguish the *Manière de langage* type of books from older colloquies, I retain the term *dialogue*, although the books of the sixteenth and seventeenth centuries mostly speak of *colloquia*. *Conversation* is used as a synonym for 'dialogue'.

[41] There are different ways of spelling the name (Berlaymont, Barlaimont, Barlamont, Berlemont, etc.). For the following compare Verdeyen 1925–1935, vol. I, XCI.

certainly there were earlier ones.[42] Between 1530 and 1703 there appeared more than one hundred editions expanding the original bilingual book into books which list up to eight languages. The long life of this publication mirrors the development of vernacular language teaching and, thus, book-history becomes an essential part of historiography. It includes not only the place and time of appearance but also the exact title, details of printing, and other arrangements. The first full book title extant is that of 1536. It reads:

Noel van Berlainmont scoolmeester Tantwerpen. Vocabulare van nyens gheordineert. Ende wederom gecorrigeert om lichtelic francois to leeren lezen scriven ende sprecen dwelc gestelt is meestendeel bi personagien.
Vocabulaire de nouveau ordonne & de rechief recorrige pour aprendre legierement a bien lire escripre & parler francois & Flameng lequel est mis tout la plus part par personnaiges.
Dese vocabularen vintmen te coope Tantwerpen tot Willem Vorstman Inden gulden Enhoren: Int jaer M.D. xxxvi. 4°.

The titles of the following editions vary enormously. The Dutch and French titles use *Vocabulaer / Vocabulaire* for both parts—the dialogues and the alphabetical word-lists; the Latin titles, which dominate in the multilingual editions, use *Colloquia* and *Dictionari(ol)um*. This latter version became almost a trade mark, in particular for those editions which no longer mentioned the author.

Including the first known edition of 1530, there were twenty-five bilingual ones.[43] As many titles disclose, the books aim at Dutch-speaking[44] people who wish to learn French. The French word for 'Dutch' is *Flameng*, the Dutch word is *Duytsch*. The bilingual edition of 1577 is the first to mention that both languages can be learnt via the other, that is, it addresses Dutch as well as French speakers. All bilingual editions, and indeed most of the later ones, were printed in the Dutch-speaking area (Amsterdam, Antwerp, Rotterdam, Ypres). The 1587 edition, printed in Cologne, uses *Teutsch* for the first time, which is rendered in French as *Haut-Alleman*. It addresses all readers who intend to learn either of the two (or both the?) languages. This means that *Duytsch* refers to what is today called *Niederdeutsch* including *Niederländisch/Flämisch* and *Teutsch* refers to *Hochdeutsch* or *Oberdeutsch*. The name *Teutsch* or *Deutsch* appears in the subsequent editions which were printed either in Cologne (1588, 1593, 1615) or in Strasbourg (1616, 1621). As Low Dutch and High Dutch were counted as two independent languages, which linguistically speaking they indeed were (and still are), this means that from 1587 onwards two different bilingual editions, a Low Dutch–French one and a High Dutch–French one, were in existence.

---

[42]   The most recent bibliography and historiographical commentary is Lindemann 1994, in particular 34–57. Earlier treatments are mentioned here and referred to. My own remarks are based, if not on personal inspection, on Verdeyen 1925–1935, because it contains the most exhaustive and precise list of book titles. See also Lindemann 1994, 34–42, 604–11, and the introduction and commentary to the editions by Rizza *et al.* 1996 and Waentig 2003. For editions which include Spanish see Niederehe 1995.
[43]   I exclude editions which are reported to have existed but which are no longer extant.
[44]   *Dutch* in the present meaning of the word; but see below.

The French–Latin edition of 1576 was the third in the group of bilingual ones, probably making use of a successful Dutch–French textbook for the teaching of Latin.

The bilingual editions regularly placed the (Low/High) Dutch version first in the title. This means that, in spite of different statements about the potential use of the book, the tendency was to move from Dutch to French, that is the book was aimed at Dutch-speaking learners of French.

The editions of 1615 and 1619 (Cologne), 1616, 1621, and 1634 (Strasburg), and 1631 and 1643 (Frankfurt) use *Berlaimont* as a name of the book-genre, eventually mixing it up with *parliament*. Note: *Parlement oder Gemeine Gespräch Deutsch und Frantzösisch* (Strasburg, 1634) and *Das new Parlament* (Frankfurt, 1643).

The first title of the 1576 bilingual edition is Latin.

There are twenty-three editions[45] in four languages. They cover all the Romance languages, including Latin. There are various arrangements: (i) three editions contain Dutch plus French, Latin, and Spanish (1551, 1556) or Dutch plus French, Spanish, and Latin (1647); (ii) thirteen editions contain Dutch plus French, Spanish, and Italian (1556, 1558, 1568(2),[46] 1569, 1573, 1580, 1596, 1600, 1608, 1624(2), 1635); and (iii) six editions contain Latin plus High Dutch, French, and Italian (1591, 1593(4), 1607) or Latin plus French, German, and Italian (1617).

Low Dutch (present-day *Dutch*) is identified by *Duytsch* (*Duyts*), *Flemisch*, *Belgick*, and *Vlaemsch*, which indicates the various dialects appearing. The Latin equivalent is *lingua Teutonica, Belgica, Flandrica*. German (High Dutch) is called *lingua Germanica*. Editions with versions in *lingua Germanica* were printed in Geneva and Basle, but also in Liège and Antwerp; all the others, which have Latin first titles, were printed in the Dutch-speaking region. This shows how the book wandered through Europe, but also how Dutch editors and/or printers were eager to cover not only their immediate vicinity. It remains to be investigated to what extent the various names for *Dutch* are simply synonyms or signify various Dutch dialects.[47]

The real innovation in these editions is, of course, the inclusion of Latin. But it is not really astonishing, once the editors and/or printers had gone beyond the two languages Dutch and French. The dialogue books of the Berlaimont type are significant for the wish to teach and learn a foreign language in a practical way and for practical purposes. But in the spirit of Humanism it was the wish to do exactly the same with Latin, that is, to change it from an academic to a common means of communication. Obviously, the books still envisage the Dutch-speaking users, because their language is given first, in the leftmost position. It is only the editions with German that place Latin first, probably exploiting Latin as the best-known foreign language anywhere. In addition, all these editions have Latin titles,

---

[45] I ignore three editions for various accidental reasons.
[46] This indicates that there were two (or in other cases, more) editions in one year.
[47] For the various names of languages see also Blamires 1990 and Rizza *et al.* 1996, V–X.

whereas of the others one has a Dutch title, four have Latin titles, four French, and six Spanish ones.[48] This shows the different groups of clients who were addressed.

A special case is Italian. In the sixteenth century it was one of the most important languages in Continental Europe,[49] but not so in the Netherlands. This is why Italian was included in the multilingual versions but was not chosen as a title. There are enough regional and cultural reasons to prove that German and French, the two adjacent languages, and Spanish, for political reasons, were more at the focus of the interest of Dutch-speaking people.

The eighteen editions with six languages can be broken down into one group which includes English and one which excludes it. Besides two extraordinary cases (discussed below), the appearance of English is the great innovation of the 1576 and of later editions (Stein 1989a).

In addition to the names for Dutch and German which we already know, *Neerduyts* and *Hoogduyts* and also *Niderlandisch* are now introduced. With one exception (1611), all three of the Romance languages are represented. Otherwise, there is great variety in the selection and arrangement of languages. In the editions that include English (see also Alston 1974, vol. II, nos 25–68) the order of languages is as follows:

(i) Dutch–English–German–French–Spanish–Italian (1576);
(ii) Dutch–English–Latin–French–Spanish–Italian (1579, 1583);
(iii) Latin–Dutch–French–Spanish–Italian–English (1584);
(iv) Latin–French–German–Spanish–Italian–English (1608, 1614, 1622(2), 1649, 1651, 1671);
(v) Latin–German–Dutch–French–Spanish–English (1611).

These arrangements allow the following comments to be made.

The first (the leftmost) language is that of the population directly addressed at the place of publication. The second language from the left is the most important foreign one. The editions of (i) and (ii) were published in Antwerp, with the most prominent foreign language being English. Furthermore, the languages are grouped according to their linguistic relatedness. In cases where Latin is the leftmost language, we take this work to address learners in any area who know this language. At the time of Humanism, it may be recalled, Latin had a special modernistic appeal. If Latin is the leftmost language, it is the second language from the left that is the national source language, and the third from the left is the most prominent foreign language. In (iii) these languages are Dutch and French; the place of publication is Antwerp. In (iv) they are French and German; the places of publication are Geneva, Strasbourg, and Cologne. The order (Latin)–French–German is new. In (v) the languages are German and Dutch ('Belgick'); the place of publication is Leipzig. This order is new, too.

---

[48] *Title* here means the linguistic title version that is placed first.
[49] See Chapter 9.

However, not only the first and second but also the last (the rightmost) position is significant. A textbook with six languages could not be used simply by reading from left to the right, although European readers would certainly always start with the left-hand column. The book must also have been meant to be used by column hopping or by jumping from the leftmost column to the rightmost one. It is easy to see that English, if not placed in the second position from the left, was always placed in the rightmost one. This means that in any case its position showed that it was of great importance.

The group of editions with six languages excluding English shows the following arrangements:

(vi) Dutch–Latin–German–French–Spanish–Italian (1583);
(vii) Latin–German–Dutch–French–Spanish–Italian (1585);
(viii) German–French–Dutch–Latin–Spanish–Italian (1595, 1607).

The remarks made above concerning the first, second, and third positions from the left apply also, because (vi) was published in Antwerp, (vii) in Basle, and (viii) in an unknown place (which is, of course, no valid argument). However, the significance of the extreme right-hand position is obviously not corroborated by these editions. The wish to place the Romance languages together here leads to the placement of Italian in the rightmost position, although it is certainly not of particular importance. This means that the extreme right-hand position is by itself ambivalent; it depends on the language which fills it whether it is of more or less importance than the other languages.[50]

All editions, except one, have the Latin title first. The edition of 1576, however, has a French first title.

There are two special cases that deserve mention. In 1602 a Latin–Czech (Bohemian)–German–French–Spanish–Italian edition was printed at Leipzig. And in 1646 an edition with Polish was printed in Warsaw. Having influenced the western part of the European Continent—The Netherlands, Belgium, the Rhine region of Germany, France along the Rhine valley, and Switzerland—the dialogues and word-lists of Noel de Berlaimont also began to find readers in the Slavonic countries. They even became independent of their regional origins, because the 1602 edition no longer lists Dutch texts and words.

There are twelve editions with seven languages. All of them contain Latin, the two German languages and English, and the three Romance languages. This means that all languages of potential interest for learners in Western Europe are now together. With one exception, the Dutch–English–German group comes first, the Latin–Romance group comes last. The edition of 1600, the exception, places Dutch first, then Latin and the Romance languages, then German and English. In

---

[50] Anyway, these deliberations depend on the assumption that the editors and/or printers of the various editions had deliberate ideas about what they were doing. I believe that they did, but this does not of course exclude the possibility that somebody acted irrationally or had ideas in his mind different from my own.

all cases, except the last one mentioned and the 1616 edition, English is placed in the second position from the left, that is, the most prominent position for the language to be learned. Generally speaking, in these editions with as many as seven languages, the grouping was obviously determined more by linguistic criteria than by others, but leaving Dutch as the national source language in its proper place. However, placing English between Dutch and German, and not as the last member of this group, was certainly also an act of national preference. As a partner of commerce, for example, England became more important than all other countries (see below).

Most editions with seven languages were printed in the Dutch area (Antwerp, Liège, Leyden), one (1595) in Frankfurt, two (1608, 1610) in Geneva. All titles place Latin first.

Finally, there are fifteen editions with eight languages. They add Portuguese. Invariably they have the sequence Latin–French–Dutch–German–Spanish–Italian–English–Portuguese. The placement of Latin shows that they were addressing a linguistically unspecified population. The languages then followed according to their didactic importance: French (the original foreign language of the bilingual editions), the two German languages, the remaining two Romance ones, and English. Portuguese was obviously added at a place where, from the printer's point of view, it was most convenient to do so. All of these books published between 1598 and 1631 appeared in the Dutch-speaking area (Delft, Vlissingen, The Hague, Amsterdam, Antwerp, Middelburg), 1639 saw the first edition to be printed in London. The 1646, 1656, and 1692 editions came from Venice and Bologna, that is, from the Italian-speaking area which had already developed into a centre of textbook production for Northern Italy and the south of France, Germany and the Slavonic-speaking area.[51] With two exceptions, the titles of these editions with eight languages were Latin. The 1662 edition had a Dutch title, the 1639 one, already mentioned as the one printed in London, had an English title. It reads:

New Dialogues or Colloqvies, And, A Little Dictionary of eight languages. Latine, French, Low-Dutch, Spanish, Italian, English, Portuguese. A Booke very necessary for all those that Studie these Tongues, either at home or abroad. Now perfected and made fit for Travellers, Young Merchant and Sea-Men, especially those that desire to attain to the uese of these Tongues. London, Printed by E. G. for Michael Sparke junior, and are to be sold neere the Exchange and in Popes-head Palace, 1639.
[Title repeated in Latin, French, and Dutch. Publisher etc. only in Latin.]   (BL 629.a.3.)

The Berlaimont story (Caravolas 1994, 256–60) is one of the several astonishing cases where a textbook spread over almost all of Europe, within the boundaries of those countries which were politically of importance at the time, without changing its substance. It is a case where the unity of European culture, across all language boundaries, comes to the fore.[52] It also shows the way in which English slowly claims its position as an important European language (Stein 1989*a* and 1991*a*).

---

[51]   See Chapter 9.   [52]   See Chapter 9.

If we assume that in each print-run some 300 copies[53] were produced, a total of 30,000 copies must have been extant in predominantly Western Europe between 1530 and 1700. This is certainly an impressive number. Bearing in mind that other textbooks were in print at the same time, we must conclude that the textbook market was enormous in relation to a population of which, by present-day measures, only a small percentage could read and an even smaller one was interested in learning one or several foreign language(s).

The various differences that can be found in the many editions do not change the nature of the textbook. The following two examples are illustrative of this.

EXAMPLE (1), THE 1576 EDITION

Colloqvia Et Dictionariolvm Sex Linguarvm: Teutonicae, Latinae, Germanicae, Gallicae, Hispanicae, & Italicae: eas linguas discere volentibus, vtilissima. Cornelio Valerio Vltraiectino, interprete latino.

Ghemeyne gespreche / oder Colloquia / mit einen Dictionario in sechs sprachen: Niderlendish Latinish Teutsch Frantzosisch Spanish vnd VVelsh: gar nutz vnd dienstlig de selbe sprachen zu lernen. Alles mit grosser fleyß / vnd arbeit zu samen bracht.

Antverpiae, Apud Henricum Henricium, ad Coemiterium B. Mariae, sub Lilio. 1576. Cvm Privilegio Regio.

(WF P 214 Helmst. 12°.)

There is no page numbering; the book has about 488 pages. The book is printed across the sheets. Six columns are printed side by side: (Low) Dutch, Latin, (High) German, French, Spanish, Italian. English is missing, but the preface explains that Latin might be exchanged for it because of its importance: '*quia in quibusdam loco latinae linguae, substitui Anglicam, cuius etiam non paruus est, ob freque[n]s eius nationis apud nos commercium, vsus.*' In fact this did not happen, although English is mentioned later as if it were the seventh language. In the very short lines which each column allows, the preface explains the necessity of knowing foreign languages. Note that the following quotation is arranged in twelve lines exactly as in the book, then for the sake of convenience it is presented as continuous text:

Zu dem Leser.
Lieber leser /
diß buch
ist so nutz
vnd gutt /
vnd der gebrauch
dessen
so hochnotig /
das seine wurde
auch von gelerten leuten
nicht gnug
kan gepreisen werden: [etc.]

---

[53]   For similar calculations see Chapter 9, 315–17, and Chapter 10, 385.

dan es ist niemands in Franckreich / noch in diesen niederle[n]de[n] niemands in Hispanien
noch Italie[n] der kauffma[n]schaft treybet in diese Niderlenden: der nicht dieser sechs
sprachen bedurftig / so hier inne beschrieben und ecklaret sein: dann so iemant kaufmanshaft
treibt / oder zu hoefe lebt / oder dem krieg folgt, oder zu lande reiset / so solte er wol behuefen
einen dolmetshen / zu einer ieden dieser sechs sprach: . . . VVer hett iemals erlangtt mitt einer
sprachen / frembder Nationen freundtschafft? wieviel sein irer reich worden ohne wissenshaft
vieler sprachen: wer kann land vnd stedte wol regieren / da er nur allein seine [Mutter?] sprahe
weis? . . .   (*3^v–*6^v.)[54]

Trading is the first and certainly the most important of the reasons for learning foreign languages but, interestingly enough, an issue like friendship also
comes into play. The town to be governed must have been a multilingual town like
Antwerp or Bruges.

It is suggested in the preface that a learner who does not want to learn the
whole book by heart should select an appropriate part. According to the author,
the possibility of doing this makes the book as useful as it is agreeable for the individual. Today's interest in this sentence is certainly that memorizing the whole
book was obviously supposed to be possible. There then follows the table of
contents:

Tafel dieses buchs.
*Diß buch ist sehr nutz Niederlendish / *English / Lateinish / Hochdeutsh / Frantzosish /*
Spanish / vnd Italianish / zu lernen lesen schreiben / vnd reden: welches geteylet ist in zwey
teill: das erste ist geteylet in vier Capittel deren drey sein mit personen als Colloquia. Das erste
Capittel ist eine gasterey von zehen personen / inhaltend viel gemeiner reden / die man zu tishe
brauchet. Das ander Capittel ist von kauffen vnd verkauffen. Das dritte Capittel ist von
shulden zu mahnen / Das vierde capittel, ist wie man briefe / vorshreybungen / quittantzen
vnd obligatio[nen] machen soll. Das ander teil / begreift viel eintzelner wortt / die man taglich
bedarff in reden / gesetzt nach dem ABC.   (2^v–4^v.)[55]

The dictionary is alphabetical with Dutch as the leading language. Unusually,
verbs are in the majority, then adverbs, and only then nouns. This means the
reader is not given a world of objects but a world of more general actions which
make the use of foreign languages necessary. The dictionary is not limited to the
words used in the dialogues. There then follow lists of the conjugational paradigms, and pronunciation rules. They are given in French for French, Italian, and
Spanish, in Italian for German. With the exception of German there are also lists
of the various declensional paradigms.

Admittedly, the choice of topics for the dialogues allows one to speak of the
onomasiological principle in only a very broad sense. The overriding intention is
to present the language in a natural context. This entails semantically related
vocabulary anyway. But the onomasiological principle is, as it were, always wait-
ing around the corner, as can be shown by a closer look at the texts (see below).

---

[54] For translation see the 1598 edition below.
[55] For translation see the 1598 edition below.

EXAMPLE (2), THE 1598 EDITION

Colloqvia Et Dictionariolvm Octo Linguarvm, Latinae, Gallicae, Belgicae, Teutonicae, Hispanicae, Italicae, Anglicae, Et Portvgallicae.
Liber omnibus linguarum studiosis domi ac foris apprimé neceßarius.
Colloques ou Dialogues, auec vn Dictionaire en huict languages, Latin, Flamen, François, Aleman, Espaignol, Italien, Anglois, & Portuguez: nouuellement reueus, corrigez, & augmentez de quatre Dialogues, tres profitables & vtils, tant au faict de Marcha(n)dise, qu'aux voiages & aultres traffiques.
Colloquien oft tsamensprekingen, me eenen Vocabulaer in acht spraken, Latijn, Fransois, Neerduytsch, Spaens, Italiaens, Engelsch, ende Portugijsch: van nieuwe verbetert ende vermeerdert van vier Colloqien, seer nut ende profitelijk tot der Coopmanschap, reyse ende andere handelinghen.
Delphis. Ex officina Brunonis Schinckelij. Anno 1598. Vendantur Amstrodami in aedibus Cornelij Nicolai.
(WF 107 Gram. 12°.)

There is no page numbering; the book has about 444 pages. The book is printed across the sheets. The left-hand and right-hand pages have four columns each. Left: Latin, French, Dutch, German; right: Spanish, Italian, English, Portuguese. The sequence of languages is rather unusual, in particular because it disrupts the Romance family. Obviously for easy readability, each column is printed in different type: Roman, italics, Gothic, Roman, etc. Dialogues cover pages 1 to 147^v, there then follow alphabetical word-lists. The preface of this book follows the 1576 edition (see above) with the exception of a few words and expressions. This is the English rendering:

To the Reader.
Beloved Reader / this booke is so need full and profitable / and the vsance of the same so necessarie / that his goodnes euen of learned men / is not futilie to be praised for ther is noman in France / nor in thes Nederland / nor in Spayne / or in Italie / handling in these Netherlands / which had not neede of the eight speaches that here in are written and declarede fer whether that anu doo marcha[n]dise / or that hee do handele in the Court / or that hee do solve the warres or that hee be a travelling man / he should need to have an interpretour for som of these eight speaches. ... wo hath euer ben able to fet[ch]h [with] one speach / the frindship of sundry nations? Hou many are ther becom rijche / without the knowledg of diuers languages? who can wel rule Landes and Cities / knowing none other then his language mother toug onlie?   (A5^r–A8^r)

The table of contents shows that four new chapters have been inserted since the earlier edition:.

This booke is very profitable for to learne to reade write / and speake Flemmish / English / Highdutch / Latinish / Frensch / Spannish / Italia[n] a[n]d portugallish the which is diuided in to twoo partes. The first part is diuided in to eight Chapitres: of wher seuen are set by personages / as Colloquies.
The first Chapitre is a dinner of ten persons / and conteineth many common speaches which are vsed at the table.

The second Chapitre is for to buye and sell.
The third Chapitre is for to demaund ones debtes.
The fourth Chapitre is for to aske the way / with other familiar / Co[m]munications.
The fift Chapitre be commen talke being in the Inne.
The vi. chapiter. co[m]municat[ion] at the oprysing.
The vij. Chapitre / proposes of marcha[n]dise.
The eight Chapitre / is for to learne to indite lettres / or missives / obligations / quitances / and contracts.
The second part conteineth many single woordes seruing to daylie communication / set in order of the A.B.C. (B2ʳ–B4ʳ.).

The first three dialogues and the eighth are identical to those in the previous edition, except for some details. The others are new although quite as conventional, as is obvious from the fact that they appear in many dialogues. Indeed, these eight chapters become the pattern for all following books of this kind for almost 200 years.

Again, the dictionary is arranged according to the Flemish alphabet, although this language appears only in the third column of the left-hand page. The entries are precisely the same as those of the 1576 edition. This is also true for the preface to the second book with its interesting remarks on learning. This is the English rendering:

Heere beginneth the second booke.
The Prologe of the second Booke.
After that you haue seene in the first booke / the maner for to learne to speake Dutch / English / Highdutch / Latinish / French / Spanish / and Italian by many commun speaches / as a patron: so haue you now in this second Booke / many commun wordes / set after the order of the A / B / C / etc. as stuff for to make other sayings by your self. Therefore / when as you will translate any sentences out of the Dutch in to Englisch / Highdutch / Latinish / or Italian / so haue you nothing els to doo / but to marke with what letter that the woorde beginneth / which you will findt / and to seeke ther fore woorde after woorde. And when you haue found the wordes / yo my then ioyne them together / like as you haue seene in the first booke. But for to ioyne them well / it weere needful that you knewe the maner to alter sentences in to many times / and diuersitie of perso[n]s: that it is to saye / by Coniugations the which mee for your profit / wil shortlie set fourth more amplie in six languages. (T4ʳ–T6ʳ.)

All the dialogues are notably conventional as regards their topics. Obviously, the authors and/or editors, not only those of the Berlaimont editions but those who published textbooks containing dialogues, knew the relevant literature and thought themselves obliged to stay within its boundaries. This has, of course, certain consequences for the reliability of the so-called facts that are mentioned.

The more natural dialogues are, the more they move away from the onomasiological principle. Or, from the opposite point of view: the accumulation of semantically related lexemes, which is the gist of the onomasiological principle, tends to render any dialogue unnatural and stiff. But the teaching dialogues of the sixteenth and seventeenth centuries can, in any case, not be compared with what we expect from twentieth-century textbooks. The following is an attempt to show the onomasiological principle working, as it were, inside the exchanges of dialogues.

'*A dinner of ten persons*'[56] has a somewhat repetitive structure because the scenes: arrival in a house—invitation for a meal—eating and drinking—departure occur several times. Verbal stereotypes for welcoming and saying good-bye, for toasting and pledging abound. We also read of family quarrels with stereotypes for reproaching and apologizing. The onomasiological arrangement applies to phrases rather than to lexemes. Note these examples:

cover the table—set on the salt—fetch trenchers, goblets and napkins—fetch [= buy] bread— fetch wood—whet the knives—put water into the laver; bring the salad and the salted flesh [= meat]—fill us to drinke—go fetch potage—take your potage—bring here bread—bring here mustard—give me the beer-pot—looke if the pastries and the tarts be brought—fetch the roast-meat—carve up the shoulder—bring hither radishes, carrots and capers; bring clean trenchers—bring us the fruit with the cheese—let us drink after the grace—bring a faggot.

These batches of vocabulary, embedded mostly in verb phrases (VP + NP, etc.) and imperatives, are interrupted by stretches of dialogues on drinking habits and, though rarely, on topics outside eating and drinking.

'*for to learne to buy and sell*' is to be found in dialogue books of any provenance, even such books as can hardly have had any direct influence on each other. They may, of course, go back to one common source, namely Caxton (Verdeyen 1926, vol. I, LXIII–LXXI, see below). The central topic is offering cloth, then haggling over the price, refusing to sell, or giving in. Typical phrases are:

I have here good cloth, good linen cloth, goodsilk, camelot, damask, velvet—I have also good flesh [= meat], good fish, good herrings—here is good butter and good cheese of all sorts.

The debate on prices names the various kinds of coins: shillings, pence, stuvers, guilders, pounds, and uses plenty of adjectives like *low, high, dear*, etc.

'*for to demande debtes*' contains hardly any onomasiological stretches of dialogue. The only words worth mentioning are those pertaining to merchandise: money, to pay, to tarry, patience, pledge, to owe, compassion, to his surety, to swear, etc.

'*for to ask the way with other familiar communications*' is again almost void of onomasiological elements. It is the introduction to the next dialogue '*Common talke being in the Inne*'. Its rather dramatic scenes are: arriving at an inn—looking after the horse—eating and drinking—making company with other guests— going to bed, including a timid erotic offer to the chamber-maid. Again this

---

[56] The linguistic substance of the following analyses is taken from the reprint (Verdeyen 1925–1935) of: *Colloquia Et Dictionariolum Septem Linguarum, Belgicae, Teutonicae, Anglicae, Gallicae, Latinae, Hispanicae Et Italicae. . . .* [Title repeated in French and Dutch] *Antverpiae, Apud Franciscum Ficardum, sub signo Angeli. 1616.* The recent critical re-edition of one of the eight-language versions by Riccardo Rizza *et al.* 1996 contains many careful text emendations.

sequence of scenes is highly stereotypical as it occurs in all comparable textbooks. It gives occasion for the inclusion of batches of vocabulary in the onomasiological way. Note, for example:

have you a good stable, good hay, good oates, good litter—take his saddle—undo his tail—take his halter—water the horse—take the horse to the smith.

The supper-scene is mostly concerned with drinking habits and the home countries of the travellers, France, England, and Germany, and includes the prayer, 'God, preserve us from civil wars'. The scene in the bedroom again gives occasion for relevant phrases. Note:

a good featherbed—the sheets are clean—warm the bed—warm my kerchief—bind my head—cover me well—draw the curtains—the chamber pot—the privy—put out the candle— kiss me once.

'*Communication at the uprysing*' contains very similar topics, namely, looking after the horses, clothes, breakfast. New in comparison to the preceding dialogues are phrases of the following kind:

There is a fair maid, a fair woman, a fair man.—[He] is the noblest, the hardiest, the most honest, the wisest, the richest, the most humble, the most courteous, the most liberal [gentleman] of the country.—She is the fairest, the most honest, the most cast, the best, the happiest, the unhappiest [woman] of the towne.—She is betrothed, she is a widow, she is a good housewife, she has a good dowry, she has a good marriage.

Such sentences disregard the idea of a natural dialogue and offer expressions which stand in a formal paradigmatic relation to each other, irrespective of their meanings.

'*Proposes of marchandise*' repeats the first dialogue in many respects. Various kinds of cloth are offered and the price is negotiated. This leads to expressions for the various kinds of cloth: velvet, satin, damask, fustian, worsted, buckram, sersenet, silk. There is an interesting series of statements on coins:

this Angel is too short—this French Crown is too light—these Shillings are clipped—this Ducat is not of weight—this Crown is not current—this Royal is base gold—this daulder is not of good silver—this Real is not of good Metal.

The practical value of such expressions is obvious.

The *dictionariolum* of some 1,060 words is arranged according to the alphabet and so outside the onomasiological topic. Yet, it deserves a short comment.

The word-list is arranged alphabetically according to the Dutch entries. The translations are arranged according to the sequence of languages, in the 1616 edition, for example, German, English, French, Latin, Spanish, and Italian. The dependence of this word-list on the *Gesprächsbüchlein Romanisch und Flämisch*, edited in 1854 by Hoffmann von Fallersleben, has been convincingly shown (Verdeyen 1926, vol. I, LXIII–LXXI). This means that the alphabetical word-list was at least partly culled from a source the dialogues of which largely followed the onomasiological principle.

This may be why the small dictionary of the Berlaimont textbook is not solely alphabetical. First of all, it is arranged according to word-classes, with verbs in first position, followed by adjectives and indeclinable lexemes. The large number of verbs makes the small dictionary particularly valuable, because all the others suffer from a preponderance of nouns. The formal arrangement is the so-called A-order, that is, it is only the first letter of a word that is considered when words are listed. This permits words also to be arranged additionally according to some other order, such as the topical one. Under C, for example, we find (Dutch and English entries only):

coninck	*a king*	*canoninck*	*a chanon*
conninginne	*a queene*	*capellaen*	*a chaplin*
cardinael	*a cardinal*	*coster*	*a sexton*

and:

cock	*a cooke*	*cleermaker*	*a tayler*
cuyper	*a cooper*	*cousmaker*	*a hosyer*

Under S we find:

schrijnwercker	*a ioyner*	*schrijuer*	*a writer*
slootmaecker	*a lockyer*	*schipper*	*a shipper*
smidt	*a smith*		

and:

schaep	*a sheepe*	*salm*	*a salmon*
simme	*an ape*	*snock*	*a pyke*
slange	*an adder*	*sperwer*	*a sparowe hake*
slack	*a snayle*	*swaen*	*a swanne*
steur	*a sturgeon*	*swalue*	*a swallowe*

Clearly these are topical word-groups. Obviously, the author did not trust the alphabet entirely to serve his didactic purposes well. This can also be seen from word-pairs, that is *ad hoc* opportunities to give the word-list a semantic order as, for example, in *schipman a shipman—schoenmaker a schomaker;* or *tonghe a tongue—therte the heart.* In each case, and in many more, the second member of these pairs was inserted because of its affinity to the foregoing one and not because the alphabet necessitated this.

There are several more such embedded word-groups, all of them, like the ones quoted, belonging to the fields of the professions or crafts, animals, and parts of the body. They are indeed the topical domains which generally show the toughest cohesion in onomasiological dictionaries.

4.4.3 Integrated dialogue books, printed in England

The following dialogue books, all of them of the integrated type, have been chosen for comment in order to demonstrate the great variety of such books, obviously depending on the foreign language to be taught and the predilections of the authors. This brings to light the many variations that occurred within the boundaries of the book-genre (Caravolas 1994, 105–12).

THE DVTCH SCHOOLE MASTER

The Dvtch Schoole Master. Wherein is shewed the true and perfect way to learne the Dutch tongue, to the furtherance of all those which would gladlie learne it.
Collected by Marten le Mayre, professor of the said tongue, dwelling in Abchurch lane. At London Printed by George Elde for Simon Waterson. 1606.
(WF 101.18 Gram, 12°.)

The book has 105 pages (not numbered), including the title. The English part is printed in Roman type, the Dutch part in Gothic. The dialogues are printed in two columns, the English version on the left, the Dutch version on the right-hand side.

The *Dvtch Schoole Master* is an integrated book, but no topical glossary. There are twelve pages of rules for pronunciation, thirty-eight pages of grammar, mostly pertaining to verb morphology, thirty-eight pages of dialogues, and thirteen pages of religious texts. At first, the preface speaks of learning both languages, but then the purpose of the book is narrowed down to learning Dutch. Besides eager learning, the advice is given to win over a Dutchman for daily conversation, to go to church and listen to a sermon, and to read the Bible. The religious bias is confirmed by the collection of prayers, the articles of faith, and psalms at the end.

The dialogues start with '*To buy and sell / te coopen ende vercoopen*'. This is a scene which seems indispensable in this type of book after Caxton: bargaining over the price and the kind of currency to be given for a piece of cloth. Interestingly enough, it is, almost without exception, cloth and no other merchandise that causes the difficulties. In the case of the *Dvtch Schoole Master*, an English customer with an accompanying person wants to buy it somewhere in the Netherlands from a Dutch merchant. The vocabulary always concerns the quality of the ware and the price.

'*Familiar Speeches / Ghememer redenen*' gives a chance to quote greetings for all times of the day. '*Of kindred / Van maechschape*' consists of the question '*How do my father / Hoe vaert myn vader*' and attached to this is a list of words with thirty-one names for family relationships. '*Of Time / Unden Tyt*' does the same with the question '*When saw you them? / Wannaer saech dise?*' and two more questions with the various possibilities of telling the time as answers.

'*Of the day / Van den Dach*' again uses this system in order to introduce the time on the clock, the names for the days of the week, and remarks on the weather.

The same system—few questions with plenty of possible answers either in word-lists or in conversational phrases, and devoted in clusters to one relevant domain of everyday life—is employed in:

  (a) *The Table / De Taeffel* (word-list with names for dishes),
  (b) *The Taylor / Den Cleermaker* (more conversation than word-list),

(c) *The Shoemaker / De Schoenmaker* (more word-list),

(d) *The Barber / De Barbier* (more conversation),

(e) *Of Playes / Van Speulen* (a game of cards),

(f) *Of Musicke / Van de Musicke* (almost only conversation),

(g) *The euening and going to bed / Deu avont ende slapen gaen* (conversation in an inn),

(h) *The rising of men / Het opstaen van mannen* (conversation and word-list on clothes and toilet utensils),

(i) *The rising of women / Het opstaen der vrauwen* (the same on garments and clothes),

(j) *Of the Inne / Van de herberghe* (questions and answers, mainly about horses),

(k) *For to ask the way / Om den wech te vraghen* (only conversation on a journey to London),

(l) *The dayes of the weeke / De daghen van derweke* (only a word-list).

The sequence of topics is unusual because, as a rule, the course of a day from morning to night is preferred, but the topics themselves are quite conventional, in particular arriving, dining, and staying at an inn. They centre around the difficulties of travelling and of living in a foreign country. The practical method of combining topical lists of words with conversation is obvious. The interest in nature, most of the arts and crafts, and the world of artificial objects, for example, in houses, which was constitutive for early colloquies and *nominales* and even in Caxton, has disappeared. The dominant interest in conversing with people is to find the way in a foreign environment. Yet these dialogues are much more onomasiological in the narrower sense than the dialogues in the Continental books instigated by Berlaimont.

THE FRENCH LITTLETON

The French Littleton: A Most Easy, Perfect And Absolvte Way To learne the French tongue. Set Forth By Clavdivs Holyband, Gentil-homme Bourbonnois.
London, Printed by Richard Field, dwelling in the Blacke Friers. 1607.[57]
(WF 103.5 Gram, 12°.)

The author's name is a pen-name for Claude de Sainliens. The book has 203 numbered pages. The text is in Latin throughout, with the English words and texts italicized. Like *The Dvtch Schoole Master*, *The French Littleton* is an integrated book. After 'The Epistle Dedicatorie' there follow dialogues (10–91), a topical word-list (92–110), prayers, the articles of the creed and other religious texts only in French (103–10), an essay on dancing, also only in French (111–39), rules for pronunciation in both languages again, declination and conjugation in both languages (184–201) and, finally, a list of French words difficult to pronounce (202).

In the 'The Epistle Dedicatorie' the author explains that, stimulated by his book

---

[57] The first edition of this book was 1566. The choice of the 1607 edition was purely accidental.

The French Schoole maistre (first printed in 1573), he wants to show '*the depth of the French language*' to the English nation. He chooses a small book size '*that it might be easier to be caried by any man about him*'. (4.) This suggests that the book was meant to be used when travelling.

The English dialogues are printed on the left-hand pages, the French dialogues on the right-hand ones. The first dialogue, '*Of Scholers and Schoole. / Des Escholiers & Eschole*' (10–30), creates a scene to be found in several books of this kind: Parents want their children to learn Latin and French. There are teachers who cheat, but Holyband is a good teacher. There then follow the activities of pupils from morning to night, including exhortations and penalties for idlers. Some questions have structurally built-in alternatives and allow different answers, comparable perhaps to modern pattern practice, for example, '*Can you speake French? / Latin? / English? / Italian? / Spanish? / High Dutch? / Scottish?*' (14). The alternatives are printed in a column with a brace. Whereas the activities from getting up to going to bed and the scenes in school are quite standardized, the following piece of advice is not, but betrays rather a reflection on the methods of learning:

Rehearse after supper the lesson vvhich you vvill learne to morrovv morning: and reade it sixe or seven times: you shall see that to morrovv morning you vvill learne it easily and soone, after you have repeated the same but tvvise. Repétez après souper la leçon ke vous voulez apprendre demain matin: et lisez la six ou sept fois: puis ayant dis voz prières, dormez la dessus: vous verrez ke demain au matin, vous l'aurez apprinze aizément, et tost: après l'avoir seulement repetée deux fois. (30.)

There then follows a dialogue '*For Travellers. / Pour Voyagers*'. (30–4.) It contains conversations on the road and questions concerning the right way to different French towns. The speaker is a peasant who has lost his money in the war. Everybody is afraid of highwaymen. Finally, there is a rest and the arrival at the town.

Subsequently, we have the traditional dialogue '*Of the Inne. / Du Logis*'. (34–50.) Topics are again the horses that have to be looked after and choosing a meal. There are even more questions here with alternative elements, for example, with reference to kinds of wine. This means that there is no natural conversation here but an enumeration of structural elements for it. The scene is no longer France but London. People converse about meals. They speak about measures of capacity and of coins and compare them with each other, for example: '*The denier of France, is vvorth halfe a farthing of England . . .*'. (48.) This is continued in a dialogue '*Of the weight. / Du Poids*' (50–2), which includes a controversy about forged money. Many alternatives are offered.

The following dialogue on '*Rules for Merchants to buy and sell. / Pour Merchands, acheter & vendre*' (52–66) leads to the inevitable market scene. However, whereas the conversations so far have been quite realistic, this one dissolves into a chain of possible utterances which follow each other with only loose semantic coherence. Occasionally, words in paradigmatic relation to each other are given in great numbers within one sentence, for example, in the following market scene:

You have no velvet, cloth, satin of such colour as I do lacke: [with] kersels Flanders dying: blacke, vvhite, yellow, violet, changeable, tavvnie, brovvne, red, skie colour, scartlet, blew, migren, greene, murrey, grey, orange, unvvatered, hamlet, vvatered, damaske, vvosted, buckram, sarsenet, Millan fustian, cloth of gold, of silver, and cypres? / Vous n'avez point de veloux, de drap, de satin de telle couleur que j'en demande: des creseaux [avec] teinture de Fla[n]dres: de noir, de blanc, jaune, violet, changeant, tanné, brun[!] rouge, pers, escarlate, bleu, coleur de migraine, verd, moirée, gris, orange, camelot sans onde, ondoyé: damas, ostade, bougran, taffetas, fustaine de Milla[n], drap d'or, drap d'argent, et crespe?   (56.)

There is again bargaining, this time without success, because of the price. It is afterwards brought to a successful end with a more obliging merchant.

These conversations are followed by '*Proverbs. / Proverbes*'. (66–91.) 'Golden rules' are given, wise sayings, etc. of very different kinds, broken down into groups by headings. In between we find dialogical exchanges between somebody and 'Maister Claudius' who utters these wise *dicta*. There are also ironic remarks, for example under the heading, '*Things against nature / Choses contre nature*': '*A Faire maiden without a lover. / Une belle fille sans amy. An old usurer without money. / Vn vieil usurier sans argent.*'

The topical word-list (92–103) gives the names for parts of the body, relatives, the days of the week and the months, and finally holidays. This means the list gives standardized vocabulary in rather closed sets.

The book is not homogeneous. The conversations and word-lists are quite traditional. The religious texts at the end do not really agree with the general tendency to teach merchants and travellers. The phonetic part is unusually elaborate. The essay on dancing is quite unique. Could it be that, together with the exhaustive wine list, it shows a national stereotype? A practical approach, together with the lack of attention to nature and objects that do not directly concern the foreign traveller, characterize *The French Littleton*. At the same time, the book has its own way of making the onomasiological principle a didactic tool by arranging it in the paradigmatic way.

DIALOGI GALLICO-ANGLICO-LATINI

Dialogi Gallico-Anglico-Latini. Per Gabrielem Dugres, Linguae Gallicae in Illustrissima & Famosissima Oxoniensi Academia haud ita pridem privato munere Praelectorem.
Editio Tertia, priori emendator. Accesserunt huic editioni, ejusdem Authoris, Regulae pronunciandi; ut & Verborum Gallicorum Paradigmata.
Oxoniae, Excudebat A. Lichfield; Anno Dom. M.DC.LX.
(WF Kl 69, 8°.)

The book has 178 numbered pages of conversations and six non-numbered pages of index giving the titles of the twenty dialogues.[58] Thus, it is fairly extensive and

---

[58] Bound together with Dugres' dialogues is a book on French grammar by Henry Leighton (Oxford, 1662).

totally confined to dialogues. The texts are arranged in three columns, French, English, Latin, from left to right. The print changes from Roman (French) to italics (English) to Roman (Latin). Of course, the question immediately arises of what function the Latin version of these dialogues is supposed to have.

The dialogues are embedded in clear scenes which give them meaning. But the text is full of possible variants which, semantically speaking, can be coherent or contradictory in the conversation, because the author merely wants to show many possibilities of questions and answers. This technique disrupts the normal flow of speech. Note, for example:

JE desire fort: Je suis fort desireux: j'ai un fort gra[n]d desir: j'ai gra[n]d enveie d'apprendre á parler françois, Anglois, Hespagnol, Italien, Alleman, Grec, Hebreu.
Ne connoissez vous personne, qui montre cette langue?
Oui Monsieur j'en connois un, qui est fort honneste homme, fort qui habile, & fort expert.
I Doe much desire: I am very desirous; I have a great desire; I have a great minde to learn to speak French, English, Spanish, Italian, High-Dutch, Greek, Hebrew.
Doe you know no body that teaches that tongue?
Yes Sir, I know one, that is a very honest man, and hath very good skill.
Maximè exopto: summo teneor desiderio: Maximum me capit desiderium: summus mihi incedit animus linguae addisce[n]dae Gallicae, Anglicae, Hispanicae, Italicae, Germanicae, Graecae, Hebraicae.
Nullus ne tibi innotuit istius institutor linguae?
Maximè domine: innotuit mihi quidam summopere honestus juxta ac peritissimus. (1.)

The flow and the sequence of dialogues are quite traditional. (a) gives the search for a teacher, as quoted, and an agreement on the hours of the lessons. The importance of grammar is stressed as different from and better than mere learning by heart, which is an astonishing statement to be issued within a textbook with dialogues. (b) gives general remarks on the teaching of French. Note (English version only):

For besides that there are an infinite number of good French bookes which are not translated into English: that tongue is now, and has almost been ever in great account almost through all Europe: and wee scarce account him a compleat Gentleman, but to have something wanting to the perfection of a Gentleman of rank, and fashion, that is ignorant of the French tongue. (18.)

Whereas these two dialogues reflect on the generalities of teaching, the following conversations are topic oriented. They have quite detailed and informative titles.

(c) '*Forms of saluting one another, of asking how one doth: also the names of kindred and allies, and of the most part of diseases*'. Among other items, this contains the names of relatives and of diseases, the latter in considerable detail and according to some rough order, namely, attacks of fever; diseases of the head, the respiratory tract, the heart, the belly, and of digestion, that is, from the head downwards; gout, measles, etc. It seems as if this list of diseases was taken from some other source.

(d) '*Ordinary complements when one intreateth another to be cover'd: To sit down: when one asketh news: when one will take his leave; when one asketh another whither he goeth*'. In addition, this enumerates houses and countries people want to go to.

(e) '*Complements of one that biddeth, inviteth a friend to dinner, &c. The thankes, and corteous excuses of him that is invited: a litle discourse between him that inviteth, and his Land-lady, the ceremonies in going and in washing*'. This stresses generally the importance of conversation and polite speech.

(f) '*Compliments betweene him that inviteth, and him that is invited before they sit at the table. The entertaining of one at table, and the complements they do use in it. The names of meates, and of poultry eaten. How one must carve meat*'. This contains, besides stereotypical phrases, information about polite manners: do not sit down, before the master and the lady of the house do; always have your knife in a sheath; in France men carve the meat, in England women do this; polite behaviour is also important for scholars, who are not married and live in colleges; importance of table talk, only animals eat without speaking.

(g) '*Manners of drinking one to another: the colours, sorts and qualities of wine as well good as bad, and many other like discourses, talks, ordinarily used in drinking, and in Taverns, the name of fruits commonly served on the Board*'.

(h) '*The rising from the table. A trick never to forget to put up his knife. A words of Tobacco. To sit by the fire. Complements to invite one to go to walk. Thanks of one that has been guest to another. Complements and excuses of him that has had him at dinner, or at supper. Forms of intreating one to do his commendations to another*'.

(i) '*Talks used in walking. To ask, and to answer what a clock it is. Of the weather*'.

(j) '*Of time, of the daies, and most noted holy daies in the year. Of the moneths. Of the day of the week. Of daies of the month, and so of the numbers called Ordinall, and of those which are called Cardinal numbers. Complements between one that is to go a journey, and his friend*'.

The preceding dialogues treat ways of polite behaviour with quite unusual detail. Whereas these conversations can be imagined as taking place between the same people and anywhere, however, a change of scene and persons now takes place. After the major topic of behaviour, the topic of a journey to (France), in fact from Dover to Calais and into the country, is the background to the following conversations.

(k) '*A Discourse betweene a passenger and a shipmaster. The names of the chiefest winds, and some other things concerning nauigation*'.

(l) '*To ask for a lodging. Many short discourses needfull for one that is in an Inne. The reckoning. The changing of a piece of gold. The names of the several kinds of coins, monies*': the object of bargaining is poultry this time (a true exception).

(m)'*Of hiring of horses. To put on ones boots*'.

(n) '*To get up on horseback, how one must set on horseback. Some qualities of a horse. To ask the way, and some other talk by the way, or in travelling*'.

(o) '*The going to bed. The rising in the morning. The names of the cloaths or garments*'.

(p) '*To keep a place in the coach, or in the wagon. The view of a town. The journey from Paris to Saumur. Where one may lye at Saumur. To ask of his host where one may have a chamber ready furnished, or where they take boarders. Of strangers which speak alwaies their mother tongue in strange countries*'.

(q) '*To ask of one be at home. To tell one that there was one to ask for him. That one asked for him. To intreat one to come in. And other ceremonies to that effect*'.

(r) '*Of the house, and of all things belonging to it*': a walk through a house with many words, many more than in the previous dialogues, for the things to be seen there.

(s) '*Of man, and of his outward, and inward parts*'. This is no longer a conversation but a list of words without syntagmatic embedding. Occasionally, a sentence is inserted. Towards the end, general terms for the organism appear in defining sentences, but these are not dialogical. Nearly three of the five pages pertain to the human head.

(t) '*Of the Draper, Taylor, Barber, Shoemaker, Dauncingemaster, Fencer, and cobler*'. These are, again, dialogues conducted with craftsmen when doing their work.

(u) '*Forms of Selling and Buying*'. This gives speech patterns but no object is named. It gives also addresses in letters.

This sequence of conversations is quite unusual. The dialogues incorporate a great deal of vocabulary and are, thus, onomasiological almost in the full sense. Occasionally, we are reminded of Caxton and his way of contextualizing lists of words. Note, for example, a question and answer exchange on colours:

Of what colour will you have it? / Of a lively, lasting colour; of a changeable colour, a colour that changeth quickly; of an incarnation; of a mouse colour, silver colour; of yellow, colour of gold. Of a pale colour, of an ash colour. Of a peach leaf colour. Of a gay colour. Of a sad colour, Of a brown colour, of a black colour, white red, tauny, green, yellow, blew, or azure, sky colour, gray colour. (158.)

It looks as if the adjectives were taken from an onomasiological dictionary.[59]

The detailed coverage of ways of polite behaviour in the first ten dialogues provides one of the very few cases where a textbook for language learning reminds us of a book of courtesy. The academic background of the author and some

---

[59] On the other hand, colour adjectives would be differently arranged in such dictionaries. See Chapter 7.

remarks on table manners lead one to assume that he has the colleges (perhaps of Oxford, where the book was printed) and possibly the bad habits of people living there in mind. This background may also account for the unusual third, Latin, column. It is noteworthy that the ceremonial aspects of behaviour in society and, in particular, the verbal complexity of small talk on almost all such occasions is treated here in great detail. This may again point to an academic background behind these conversations.

Finally, many of the dialogues are communicative in a very modern sense. Often, the chain of utterances in a given situation—the structural element which constitutes a conversation and which always includes a dramatic element—is disrupted in order to give, with several variants, what would nowadays be called speech acts, that is, ordinary compliments, invitations, accepting invitations, etc.

NOUVELLE METHODE POUR APPENDRE L'ANGLOIS

Nouvelle Methode Pour Apprendre l'Anglois. Avec Une Nomenclature, Francoise & Angloise; Un Rercueil D'expressions Familieres; Et Des Dialogues, Familiers, & Choisis. Par le Sieur Guy Miege.
A Londres, For Thomas Bassett at the George near S. Dunstan's Church in Fleet-street. 1685.
    [Subtitle for pages 39–85:]
Dialogues Familiers; Pour demander ses Necessitez. Familiar Dialogues, To ask for Necessaries.
    [Subtitle for pages 87–142:]
Dialogues Choisis Sur divers Sujets. Selected Dialogues Upon divers Subjects.
(WF Kn 66, 8° (see also Alston 1974, vol. ii, nos 181–5).)

The grammatical part has 119 numbered pages plus five pages of '*Table Des Principales Matieres*'. The following part of the book has its own numbering, the onomasiological part covering pages 1–38, the '*Collection of Familiar Expressions*' pages 39–43, the dialogues 45–142. With the exception of a few pages in the grammar, the book is printed in two columns on each page, the French words and sentences in Roman and the English words and sentences in italics. The book is carefully printed and reads more easily than others.

The author of this book has quite a professional background. Guy Miège, a Swiss from Lausanne, came to England in 1661. At home he had edited a book on foreign-language teaching. In England, he devoted himself entirely to teaching French native speakers English by publishing dialogues and a nomenclator, a grammar, and a book on the English commonwealth. At this time, many French refugees had flocked to England, because Louis XIV had revoked the Edict of Nantes and textbooks for learning English written by French speakers were in great demand (Howatt 1984, 54–60). He became a great friend of the English language, praising it in almost nationalistic tones (Hüllen 1995b and 2002, 201–18; slightly different Loonen 1991, 93).

Obviously, his dialogues are part of his lifelong didactic deliberations; they were not just produced *ad hoc*. This does not mean that they were not meant for practical purposes. Miège obviously had a comprehensive, well-thought-out concept of foreign-language teaching in which dialogues played an important part. The extracts will show this. Uniquely among books of this kind, dialogues are here broken down into two groups which differ in topics and in their intellectual level. There are '*Dialogues Familiers; Por demander ses Necessitez. Familiar Dialogues, To ask for his Necessities*' (45–85) and '*Dialogues Choisis Sur divers Sujets. Select Dialogues Upon divers Subjects*' (87–142).

The '*Familiar Dialogues*' are devoted to these topics:

(a) '*About asking the way*', that is, the way to London.
(b) '*To lie in an Inn*': looking after the horses; ordering a meal, in particular poultry; bargaining about the appropriate price.
(c) '*About taking a lodging*': here again bargaining about the price.
(d) The same.
(e) '*Between the Traveller and the Coachman*': obviously, the coachman is ordered to take the luggage from the inn, where the first night was spent, to the lodging.
(f) '*Between the Travelour and his Landlady*': a conversation while the room is being prepared.
(g) '*Between the Travellour and the Maid of the House*': conversation on washing, going to bed, getting up. Note, for example: '*Do but tell me whereabouts is your convenient House. / You will find it in a back Yard.*'
(h) '*About giving of Linnen to be washed*': again bargaining about the price, this time with the washerwoman.
(i) '*The washer-woman's Cheat*': the washerwoman has disappeared with all the garments and clothes.
(j) '*About buying of Linnen*': the usual bargaining. This conversation is longer than the previous ones and, different from these, contains lists of words.
(k) '*To get a Sute made*'.
(l) '*To buy a Hat, Periwig, Gloves, Stockings, and Shoos*'. In this and the two previous conversations there are many words pertaining to clothing. There are dialogues with different partners.
(m) '*The Travellour agrees with his Landlady for boarding*': on meals to be taken together.
(n) '*A Table-Dialogue*': on dishes, drinks.
(o) '*To ask for one at his House or Lodging*'.

The dialogues are natural in the sense that they present conversations which a newcomer to London would probably have to conduct. This pertains to their contents and, in particular, to their sequence, which shows a loose coherence. This is standard in such conversations, though here somewhat livelier than in others. The episode with the stolen clothes is an ingenious trick to add another realistic chain of conversations. It is only after (k) that the coherence of topics and happenings becomes rather disrupted. In spite of this realism, the conversations themselves are rather stilted and filled with ready-made phrases. Obviously, the author wants to maintain a certain level of style. Note, for example, out of (l):

Si vous voulez un Soulier fort, & de bon service il vous coutera cinq Chelins. If you will have a good-strong, and lasting pair of Shoos, 'twill cost you five Shillings. Voyons. Prenez la mesure. Well. Take my measure. Si je les trouve à mon gré, nous nous accorderons assez. If I like 'em, we shan't disagree. Où est vôtre Logis, Monsieur? Where is your Dwelling, Sir? Donnez moi du Papier, de l'Encre, & une Plume, & je vous laisserai mon Addresse. Give me some Paper, with a Pen, and Ink, and I shall leave you my Direction. Demain je vous attendrai sur le Soir. Tomorrow I shall expect you in the Evening. Ne me manquez pas de parole. Do not fail me. Monsieur, je serai à vous, sans faute.   (79.)

The '*Select Dialogues*' are devoted to the following topics:

(a) '*Of the Air of England, and its Influences*': the sun and the fog, the mild climate.
(b) '*Of the Buildings, and Fewel of England*': great stability of houses, sea-coal.
(c) '*Of the English Food*': a discussion of the pros and cons of beer and wine, understood as a competition between French and English tastes. Note, for example:

Il faut premierement vous ôter Prejugez que vous avez contre la Biere. En suite il sera plus aisé de vous defaire de ces Entêtements que vous avez pour le Vin. Vous saurez donc, qu'en Angleterre on fait de toutes sortes de Biere, de la petite, & de la forte. / I see I must first shake off from your mind those Prejudices you have against Beer. And so you will so much the more easily be weaned from that conceited opinion you have of Wine. In Order to which, you must know, that in England they make all sorts of Beer, both small and strong.

(d) '*Of the Use of Brandy, Coffee, Tee, Chocolate, and Tobacco*'.
(e) '*Of Coffee-houses, and the Uses a Stranger may make of them*': among other topics, on newspapers ('*every Day it comes out, viz. on Munday and Thursday*'), smoking, drinks.
(f) '*Of Clubbs, and of the English Custom for ever yone to pay at his Club*': in this conversation the Englishman convinces the Frenchman of the advantages of the English habits.
(g) '*Of the English Money*': many coins are mentioned, together with their values.
(h) '*Of London, and of the Way to it from Paris through Calais*': whereas, up to now, the conversations must have taken place in London, this one only makes sense if we assume that it happens in Paris.
(i) '*Of the principal Curiosities of London*': the scene is London again, buildings, the Great Fire of 1666. There is a heading in between: '*A Continuation of the Dialogue*'. There then follow: '*Of the Post-days in London*'; '*Of the Peny-post*'; '*Of the English Calendar, and Style*'; '*Of some particular Days, observed in England*'.

All these conversations are much longer than those in the previous group and are, as is obvious, devoted to more general topics. The style is much more ambitious, but also less dialogical, because there is more description and argument in the speeches. This means that the language is less permeated by cliché and routine. The fact that conversations are broken down into two clearly differentiated groups shows that the author has his own opinion about the learning of a foreign language. For him, it consists of the practicalities of everyday life, and also of a minimum of cultural adaptation, depending on relevant knowledge. It is a rather modern programme that underlies these dialogues.

A DOUBLE GRAMMAR FOR GERMANS TO LEARN ENGLISH, AND FOR
ENGLISHMEN TO LEARN THE GERMAN TONGUE

Zwey-fache Gründliche Sprach-Lehr, Für Hochteutsche, Englische, und für Engelländer Hochteutsch zu lernen; darin alle Lateinische Wörter zur Sprach-lehr gehörig ins Hochteutsch und English übersehzt sein: Es ward darin gehandelt vom Ursprung, Gründen under-wisen zu reden der Englischen Sprach, mit einem Namen-Buch und Täglich vorfallenden nothwendigen Gesprächen. Es ist darbei gefügt alles was ein Ausländer zu Versaillien in Franckreich, und Engelland sehen kann, in einem kurtzen begriff vom standt des Römischen-Reichs.
Alles fleissig zusammen getragen, und in den Truck verfertiget, durch Henricum Offelen, J. V. Doctorem, wie auch Frantzösischer, Englischer, Spanischer, Italienischer, Lateinischer, und Hoch-und Nederteutscher Sprachen Professorem.
Tot Londen, Gedruckt voor den Autheur, en zijn te koop by Nathaniel Thompson, in dem ingangh van Old Spring Garden by Charing-Cross. 1687.
(WF Kn 72, 8° (see also Alston 1974, ii, 348).)

The book has 136 + 269 pages. The first title page with its (presumably) elaborate English title is missing.

As the title page shows, this book is exceptional in that it comprises in one volume an English grammar written in German and a German grammar written in English. The latter is one of the very rare cases in the seventeenth century, probably the second oldest of its kind after Martin Edler's grammar of 1680 (Hüllen 1996*b*). It has its own subtitle: *The German Or Highdutch Grammar. . . ., Composed by Henry Offelen, Doctor in Law, and Professor of seven Languages. London: Printed for the Author. 1686.*[60] This part of the book has its own page numbering. Latin and English words are printed in Roman letters and italics, German words are printed in Gothic.

The book is also exceptional among our sample texts because it has a German author who, by the way he introduces himself, shows his involvement in the German scene as *Sprachmeister*, foreign-language teacher (and sometimes professor), at a university or a *Ritterakademie*.[61] His rather boisterous way of claiming expert knowledge in five foreign languages, besides the two kinds of German,

---

[60] Note that the year of publication is one year previous to that given on the general title page of the book.
[61] *Ritterakademien* were schools founded by the German lower nobility for their youth in order to save themselves the cost of the otherwise desirable educational travel and stays at European courts; they were the first to introduce modern language teaching on a fairly regular basis. However, foreign language teachers there ranked on the same level as teachers for riding and fencing. This is why they were called *Sprachmeister*, like *Reitmeister* and *Fechtmeister*.

attracted stinging criticism even in the eighteenth century, for example by Gottsched (Hüllen 1996*b*).

Whereas the English grammar for Germans consists of this grammar only, the German grammar for Englishmen consists of the grammar itself, a '*Namen-Buch. A Vocabulary*', and a part '*Von Gespraechen. Of Dialogues*'.[62] It is the latter part (189–268) that is interesting in the present context.

The dialogues are printed in two columns, the English version on the left-hand side, the German version on the right-hand side of the page. Except for the last three, the dialogues are quite short, as a rule taking up not more than two pages and sometimes not even a whole page. All of the conversations construct a loose chain of actions from arrival to settling down in London:

(a) *Between a Sea-man and a Gentle-man*, (b) *To ask the Way*, (c) *Being in an Inn*, (d) *With a merchant about a Bill of Exchange*, (e) *About taking a Lodging*, (f) *Of Eating and Drinking*, (g) *Of Buying and Selling*, (h) *With a Taylor*, (i) *With a Shoo-maker*, (j) *With a Coach-man*, (k) *With a Horse-Courser*, (l) *Between a sick Gentle-man, his Servant, and a Physician*, and (m) *With a Landreß*.

The topics of (k)—the visitor wants to ride to Windsor and Oxford—and (l) are rare in such dialogues. One special characteristic of the German visitor in England is that he haggles over every single price that is offered to him whereas bargaining is usually limited to just one scene on the market when cloth is bought.

The brevity of the dialogues does not provide many opportunities for introducing long series of words according to the onomasiological principle, although the situations naturally demand a semantically related vocabulary. But every now and then it comes to the surface, for example when the host of an inn answers the question, '*Have you got any good (Meat) victuals?*' by, '*Yes, sir, as good as any is in England; there is good Beef, good Mutton, good Veal, good Pork, boyled and Roasted*' (197), or when the German customer enters a shop, asking, '*Have you got any good Cloath, Ribbands, good Hats, good Gloves, or Stockings?*' (199).

The last three dialogues are of a different kind:

(n) '*Between two Gentlemen of strange Countries, and first of France*' (209–15),
(o) '*Of England*' (215–34),
(p) '*About the present State of Germany*' (234–69).

Their unusual length shows that they are not conversations meant to be exercises for learners on how to cope with everyday situations. Rather, they provide information about the three respective countries and their culture at that time. Very occasionally this approach provides an opportunity for a compact word-list. Note, for example:

Menagery is a place, where there are all kinds of strange Beasts of forreign Countries, as, Cassi, Wanes, Ostriches, Bustards, Pelicans, Egyptian Hens, Arrabian Ducks, China Pheasants,

---

[62]   The 'æ' in *Gespraechen* also has an umlaut (ǽ).

Indian Geese, Indian Cows, Barbary Goats, Moscovy and Polander Cats, Persian Camels, a Hog of the Empire and Monometapa, and several others. (211–12.)

All three dialogues mention famous towns and buildings in the three countries, and make occasional observations on society and law, and odd habits. The conversation on France deals almost exclusively with Versailles. A certain prejudice against the French is obvious. That the dialogue on England was written specially for this book, to be published in 1686/1687, is shown by the mention of the hard winter of 1684 when the Thames was frozen.[63] Information on English currency is given in detail. The question '*Have they good Victuals in England?*' triggers another cluster of related lexemes. Note:

There's Bread and Meat in Plenty, and very cheap; good Veal, Mutton, Lamb, much Venison, Ducks, Phesants, Partridges, Hares, Rabbets, good Chickens, and small Birds, good Ale and Beer; some Beer is stronger than Wine; there grows no Wine in England; but they have plenty from France, twelve Pence a Bottle; Canary two shillings a Quart; Rhenish-Wine, Mead, Sider, Brumswick Mum, Tea, and Coffee. (222–3.)

There are long explanations of '*Coffee-Houses*' and '*Clubs*'. The third, the longest, of these conversations elaborates on the German Emperor and the Electoral Princes, on the Diet and the *Hansestädte*, on Luther and the Reformation, on the war against the Turks, etc. This means that the dialogue is much more state and history oriented than the two preceding ones. It is not surprising that, as the author is German himself, the portrait of his country contains a certain amount of self-congratulation.

The dialogues in Offelen's double grammar are perhaps more interesting from the political and historical point of view than from their character as veiled onomasiological collections of vocabulary. But the occasional clusters of words that we do find show that the onomasiological principle is always at hand when the semantic nature of the vocabulary allows it to be.

Our comments on selected books containing dialogues in English and one or several other language(s) show the standardization of this part of textbooks, but also the amount of variation that was still possible within the framework. The dialogue is not only a conventional and indispensable part of foreign language teaching and learning, there are also indispensable topics and situations within such dialogues. The books vary tremendously in size. They range from small, pocket-size *ad hoc* productions to elaborate parts of a well-planned textbook system. This means that there is behind them a great variety of didactic considerations. Again, this means that the degree to which the onomasiological tradition is integrated into them varies. Quite frequently, the conversations are simple and only situationally orientated. Whereas the Continental examples are almost entirely lacking in evidence of onomasiological principles, there is not one book among the English examples with dialogues in which the onomasiological origin

[63]   The Great Fire of London in 1666 is also mentioned.

of this textbook-genre does not, at least occasionally, emerge. In such cases, the conversations are used as vehicles for vocabulary. It is arranged into certain domains of experience, semantic clusters which still show old patterns of encyclopaedic world knowledge. The extent to which this happened depends on the predilections of authors. Textbooks always convey some knowledge about the world around them, even if they are meant to be utterly practical.

It is certainly noteworthy and might form the start of an interesting didactic discussion that all the authors of the books analysed were not native speakers of the English language.

4.5 The question of social reality

4.5.1 General

It is obvious that glossaries, in whatever shape they appeared, are a valuable source for our knowledge of cultural history. The living conditions of people, their arts and crafts, their knowledge of nature, legal principles, the division of the secular and the spiritual—all these topics appear in the word-lists and the social reality in the background can be filtered out of them by historiographers with the benefit of hindsight. As the glossaries give the names for things and ideas, we assume that these things and ideas must have been known to people just as the names obviously were.

However, it is too easy to assume that glossaries and word-lists within dialogues realistically mirror the world of their time.[64] They represent a tradition of words rather than of things. Many of these words were originally taken from classical authors and then handed down from word-list to word-list. They certainly also contained names of things which themselves remained unknown. There were many names of plants and animals which nobody had ever seen. There were names of diseases of which people had heard but from which nobody suffered. Households hardly ever had the elaborate equipment which is talked about and, except for the royal households, certainly never all the servants that are mentioned. Glossaries and word-lists presented all the knowledge of the time, as was to be found in books, including the unicorn and the griffin, but they presented its social reality only to a very limited extent. In the Middle Ages and for a long time afterwards, knowledge was largely determined by books and authorities, not by experience. If we try to read glossaries from the relatively modern aspect of social reality, and this is what we are almost automatically prone to do,

---

[64] The same is true for other representations of reality which we find at the time. Chronicles would use the same woodcut to designate quite different cities because they were what could be called *typologically correct*. The same happened with portrait figures or the illustrations of plants. Nevertheless such publications eventually paved the way for an individualistic and realistic illustration technique. See Eisenstein 1983, 58–60.

we must be very careful when filtering the socially real out of the merely verbal information. In order to do this we must find the related lexemes belonging to the semantic field of an entry, including its synonyms and antonyms. Moreover, we must quote syntagmas with collocations on the clause level (e.g. adjective and noun) and on the sentence level (i.e. subject and predicate). Finally, we must describe the referents in some detail. All this is hardly possible without in-depth studies in historical lexicology (Reichmann 1985, 243–8). Definitions of meanings according to present-day structuralist principles certainly do not suffice.

Sometimes, however, onomasiological works contain their own hints which can show historiographers at least part of the way they have to go.

4.5.2 Crafts and professions

Caxton's *Dialogues* are a very interesting case in point, in particular the long passage where as many as 116 proper names are used to present typical dialogues in the context of a journey including a stay in an inn (twenty-eight cases), and to speak of the arts and crafts (the remaining eighty-eight cases). The latter are actually referred to in the old title *Livre des mestiers*. A typical entry reads:

David le lormier Est ung bon ouurier
De faire selles, Frains, & esperous,
Et ce quil y affieret.
David the bridelmaker Is a good werkman
For to make sadles, bridles, and spores,
And that thereto belongeth.   (33, 21–5.)[65]

Actually, such lists of arts and crafts are standard in topical glossaries. *Aelfric's Colloquy* (Wright 1884, cols 89–103) is almost totally concerned with the callings of agricultural labourers. In the vocabulary of the Junius MS (Wright and Wülcker 1884, cols 104–67) we find eighty-three entries under the heading 'Nomina omnium hominum communiter' which, starting with *Imperator* 'casere' and *Basileus* 'kining', contains mostly political offices according to the Roman hierarchy, but ends with ten entries giving the names of artisans like 'Carpentarius "wænwyrhta"' and 'Lapicidina "stanhywet"'. This arrangement indicates that the entries are actually meant to represent not social reality but an ideal order with the emperor at the top and the worker at the bottom. In *Mayer's Nominale* of the fifteenth century, which is contemporary with Caxton, there is a chapter, 'Nomina artificium' with as many as 159 entries, of which twenty-two do not, however, actually belong to this domain. Another chapter, 'Nomina artificium mulierum' has eighteen entries, and a third, 'Nomina operariorum' has another fourteen entries. The total of 169 entries shows the extraordinary diversity of callings at that time. Nevertheless, this is an abstract system rather than social reality. The tradition of

---

[65]   From now on I will give only the English version.

arranging the names of dignitaries and professions according to the medieval three estates, and this means according to a generally accepted natural order, was widespread before Caxton, at his time, and even later.[66] Perhaps the best-known example is *Das Ständebuch* of 1574 with woodcuts by Jost Amman and verses by Hans Sachs. In its preface the idea is maintained that there is a fixed order in society just as in nature. The system of crafts and professions is made and maintained by God. This is why everybody should (be) in his place *'wol zufriden seyn'*. The order of the *Ständebuch* is the following: (i) the ecclesiastical hierarchy, (ii) the secular hierarchy, (iii) the learned professions, that is, intellectuals and artists including people who contribute to their work, (iv) traders, (v) producers of food, (vi) producers of clothes, (vii) people who care for the human body, (viii) workers with metal, (ix) workers with other materials, (x) workers with wood, (xi) various, (xii) musicians, (xiii) fools. This order suggests a world where everybody has his or her proper place with the Pope at the top and the fool at the bottom.

4.5.3 Caxton's list

However, in contrast to the examples mentioned and others, Caxton's list of arts and crafts has some distinctly recognizable signals which point to the social reality underlying the *Dialogues*, that is, towards life in Bruges.

First, there is the selection of crafts and the fact that a convincing order is actually missing. Caxton gives the names for the ecclesiastical and secular hierarchies too, but he gives them outside his deliberations on *mestiers*. Here, their sequence seems accidental, or local, as does the selection. Twenty-three crafts belong to the group of people who provide clothes and garments in one way or other. This means that twenty-three crafts are significant for Bruges as a wool town. The other groups are much smaller. They are less specific and can be seen as dealing in particular with crafts of interest to people, especially foreigners, who live in this town: providers of food (7), mechanics working with metal (7), other mechanics (7), people in the hostel business (6), men important for trading operations, such as the *'proctour'*, the *'keeper of tour'*, the *'tollar'*, the *'usurer'*, the *'broker'*, and the *'changer'*. There are, of course, a number of other callings which cannot be seen as typically Brugian in any respect. But the clearly one-sided selection is certainly indicative of the realistic quality of the dialogues.

Second, according to their contents, the entry articles[67] can be broken down into four clearly distinguishable groups, namely (i) articles which simply speak of the activities of the person (craftsman) whose proper name is its headword, (ii) articles which add some special personal feature to the activities of this man or

---

[66]   The authoritative treatment of this topic is Huizinga 1965 (chap. III). Although he speaks only of France and the Low Countries, the author paints a picture of general validity on 'The hierarchical concept of society'.

[67]   I adopt this lexicographical term which, in application to Caxton's texts, has a meaning different from the usual one but is self-explanatory.

woman and which betray a personal acquaintanceship between the speaker (teacher) and that person, (iii) articles which directly connect the person's activities with the speaker's business, and (iv) articles which speak about persons as private individuals and in no other capacity. The first three groups are fairly evenly distributed with twenty-five, twenty-four, and twenty-eight cases each.[68] With ten cases, the fourth group is much smaller.

Group (i) comes closest to an objective definition, i.e. the function that, generally speaking, entries have with their translations in glossaries. There is here no reference to the social reality of Bruges, though it cannot be excluded. Note these examples:

Euerard the vpholster / Can well stoppe / A mantel hooled, / Full agayn, carde agayn, / Skowre agayn a goune, / And all old cloth.   (34, 13–18.)

Felice the silkewoman / maketh so many purses / And pauteners of silke; / For she is thereof a maistresse.   (36, 20–3.)

Martin the grocer / Selleth many spyces / Of all maners of poudre / For to make browettys, / And hath many boxes paynted / Full of confections, / And many pottes / Full of drynkes. (41, 12–19.)

Group (ii) adds a special, sometimes very personal, touch to the defining explanations, making us see the individual person behind the craftsman or artisan. Note these examples:

Conrade the sherman / He oweth to shere; / He taketh of the elle foure mytes / Syth that the sheremen / Hadde theyr franchise.   (32, 13–17.)

Clarisse the nopster / Can well her craft. / 'Syth whan hath she lerned it / Cloth for to noppe?' / 'What axe ye? / She was ther with rocked. / She hath good to do / That she wynne moche, / For she is moche licherous.'   (33, 12–20.)

Natalye the wyf of the stewes / Kepeth a good styewe, / The moste suffysante of the cite; / They goon thedyr to be stewed / Alle the strangers. / She duelleth / After the walle of the white freris. (42, 27–33.)

The personal touches attached to the descriptions of craftsmen and women are of a very different kind. In the case of Conrad, they refer to the fact that 'sheremen' are now members of a guild and, thus, take a higher price. In the case of Clarisse, they refer to her whole life and a very personal trait of her character. Finally, in the case of Natalye, they refer to her dwelling place. Similar touches can easily be detected. They all depend on a personal acquaintanceship of the speaker, who is a citizen of Bruges, with the craftsman or woman. They very often make an evaluation. A dialogue within an entry, presumably between the speaker and somebody else, underlines their personal style.

Group (iii) has entries which directly connect the activities of the respective person with the business of the speaker. Note these examples:

---

[68] It goes without saying that it is sometimes difficult to allocate an entry to one of these four groups, although in most cases the criteria are fairly clear. In four entries there is a dialogue inside the entry article, which gives it an additional noteworthiness. But I have not treated such entries as a special group.

Colard the goldsmyth / Oweth me to make my gyrdle, / A gyrdle nayled / With siluer, weyeng xl. pens, / And a triacle box.   (31, 33–8.)
Qvyntyne the tollar / Hath taken of me / A pound of grotes / More than he ought to take / Of right tolle. / So shall I drawe me / Vnto the receyuour / For my right to requyre.   (44, 29–35.)
Xristrian the colermaker / Maketh to me a coler; / Then shal I haue two coliers / For my horses of the plowh.   (46, 26–9.)

The business connections between the speaker and the craftsmen and women are obvious. The speaker establishes himself as a person of the town who pursues his various own businesses which involve other people.

Group (iv) does not refer to people as craftsmen, but to persons who have their own personal problems. The majority concern women. Colombe, who is lame, went away when the speaker tried to kiss her. Clemence complains about her step-father. Clare is blind and asks for her bread. Ermentin is sick and his urine must be taken to the doctor. Philipote is a thief and sitting in prison. Gertrude died on this very day and will be buried. Lucie is a bastard. Pieryne is *'the shrewest girl I know'*. Xristine has a daughter and complains that the locksmith does not acknowledge her child. The social character of these problems is obvious (and almost timelessly modern). An exception is the entry on Kylian, who is the saint in Paradise with this name.

These observations seem to prove that, on the one hand, Caxton's *Dialogues* use the onomasiological principle of glossaries in all their abstractness which is the logical consequence of a bare list of words, that is, as names. On the other hand, they make entries more concrete, towards social reality. We can find hints of this in the dialogues themselves. Of course, the next step would be to verify these hints by research into the facts of cultural history, wherever possible.

4.5.4 Geographical names

Another way of directly mentioning the social reality of the world of the *Dialogues*, not just of Bruges, is Caxton's technique of introducing geographical names. During a scene in which a customer and a merchant bargain about the price of a piece of cloth, *'Clothes of many maneris, / Of many tounes . . .'* (18, 24–5) are mentioned. The English towns given are London, York, Bristol, and Bath. Twenty more towns of the region around Bruges, with Paris as the most southern one, follow. Likewise, fairs are mentioned—on the Continent Bruges, Antwerp, and Bergen; in England—Stourbridge, Salisbury, Cambridge, and London. This technique of making something geographically concrete is also used in the part where dignitaries that represent the Church and the state are named. As mentioned, Caxton separates this list from the long list of craftsmen and women in Bruges. In the list of *'The prelates of holy chirche'* (22, 15) he first mentions the Pope, who dwells in Avignon, although he should live in Rome, the emperor and empress who *'Is quene of almayne'* (22, 27), the king of France who *'Is the most riche kyng / Of tresour that lyueth / Beyonde the see'* (22,

28–30),[69] and finally the king of England who '*Is the most myghty and riche*' (22, 33). There then follows a series of more kings without any epithets (of Spain, Aragon, Sicily, Navarre, Bohemia, Poland, Denmark, Portugal, Scotland, Naples, and Jerusalem). Next comes a list of archbishops and bishops with their sees (among them Canterbury, York, Cologne, Reims, Rouen, Mainz, Trier, London, Winchester, Chester, Lincoln, Paris, Liège, Cambray). These lists may not be too instructive. Yet they are illustrative of the author's tendency to locate ecclesiastical and secular dignitaries somewhere in the real world. His predilection for the south of England and the country between the rivers Rhine and Maas is obvious. This is the region that would be of most interest for the wool trade.

The result of such analyses is that Caxton's *Dialogues*, while being traditional and abstract in many respects, contain a number of clear signals which point towards the social reality of Bruges and the country around, namely, that of Flanders and the south of England. This gives the whole text a limited documentary quality. In fact, there are some ways to corroborate this. For example, the topography of the town, as far as it is recognizable, agrees with a map of Bruges of 1562, which is still extant (Gessler 1931, 14). Moreover, there is an interesting passage on money which helps to identify the social reality of Bruges and Flanders in general. Obviously, various kinds of currency were accepted here in business. Note:

'What moneye / Gyue ye to me?' / 'Good moneye; / Thise ben grotes of englond; / Suche ther be of flaundres; / Plackes and half plackes; / The olde grotes of englond / Which be worth v pens; / The newe be worth foure pens; / Ye ought well to knowe, / That so moche moneye receyue.' / 'Ye saye trouthe, sire.' / 'But you had leuer / Rynysh guldrens, / Scutes of the kyng, / Ryallis nobles of englond, / Salews of gold lyons, / Olde sterlingis pens.' / 'This is all good moneye; / Ye, and I may gyue it oute?' / 'Yes, ye shall gyue it oute well / Within the toune / And all aboute the contre / In all peny worthes, / In all marchandyses.'   (17, 18–40; 18, 1–2.)

4.5.5 Realism in dialogue books

Together with *Manière de langage*, Caxton's *Dialogues* are a first example of a new type of foreign-language textbook. They were meant for travellers and, from hindsight, gave Caxton's book its third name.

Manière de langage and Caxton are supposed to have introduced and paved the way for a realistic method of foreign-language teaching and learning, breaking away from the Latin-dominated method which worked with grammar, word-lists, and, mostly literary, texts. Although at this time Latin was not a dead language as we understand the term to-day, it was not taught and learned by performance either. But this was the principle of the new kind of textbook. And the realistic

[69]   The translation 'Beyonde the see' is one of Caxton's many mistakes; the French text says '. . . qui vist / De la la (!) mer'.

quality of Caxton's *Dialogues* was certainly meant to support this principle. It is possible that the new method was suggested because the preferences of people who learned a foreign language became different. They now were traders, merchants, even craftsmen who did business all over Europe. It may be asked to what extent the dialogue books of the following centuries use the same realistic technique and whether they can also be understood as sources of our historical knowledge.

The answer to this question is disappointing. The dialogue books, in fact, use a very limited set of scenes, with little variation. Many of them are present in some parts of Caxton's *Dialogues*. Among the canonical scenes are: asking one's way to London, Paris, etc.; arriving at an inn, asking for the horses to be looked after, for a meal, for accommodation; getting up and having breakfast; selling and buying in the market, bargaining over the price, mostly successfully, but sometimes not; looking for a teacher, behaviour at school; having a meal, etc. As a rule, the haggling over the price concerns cloth, but sometimes food. These scenes provide an opportunity for many semantically related words to be introduced, for example, those for food, for dishes, for wine, for kinds of cloth, for money. They hardly ever contain a really original element. Just as in Caxton, many dialogues in the later books are nothing but embedded word-lists. They relate to the traditional domains of the glossaries such as, for example, names of relatives in the family, diseases, animals, and plants. In spite of their naturalistic composition, the dominant concern of the dialogues is obviously still onomasiological, in that they give the names for things in a fairly abstract way, as in a dictionary. It is not communication *hic et nunc*. This means that, just as we must be on our guard not to mistake the medieval system of concepts and names for the social reality of life, we must also be on our guard not to mistake the standard scenes and dialogues for this reality. In this respect, the later textbooks often fall back even behind Caxton.[70]

This is not to deny that some of the textbooks have individual features which may be understood to be dependent on the special circumstances under which and for which their authors wrote the dialogues. Guy Miège's *Dialogues familiers; Pour demander ses necessitez / Familiar dialogues, To ask for necessaries* (1685), for example, introduce much cultural information about both countries. As the author does this by means of comparison, he cannot avoid what we today would call national stereotypes. Gabriel Dugres' *Dialogi Gallico-Anglico-Latini* (1660) show the academic background of an Oxford don. The author complains about the bad table manners of men in college and is very much concerned with polite verbal behaviour in general.

---

[70]   The logical consequence of this is that the vocabulary of dialogues, like that of the earlier glossaries, need not be the one in general use. As the best sources of dictionaries are older dictionaries, and of dictionary-related texts older texts of this kind, it is easy to imagine that some words may have been transferred from generation to generation without ever being accepted by people. This phenomenon is well known in the hard-word dictionaries of the seventeenth century; we would probably also find that this is true of the older glossaries and dialogues. Large-scale research is needed to verify this.

Dependable facts which would allow similar conclusions are fairly few in number. The scenes in the streets, in hostels, in markets are quite general and very similar, wherever they happen. Occasionally facts do appear such as, for example, another explanation of currency. Note the following overview of English coins which Miège (1658) gives:

- A Jacobus or Broad Piece is twenty-three Shillings (*'this is the best Gold in England. But now a days 'tis kept in private Purses'*).
- A Crown is sixty Pence (*'threescore'*) or five Shillings (*'the most common species'*).
- A Half-crown is thirty Pence or two Shillings and Sixpence (*'most common'*, *'hitherto silver, but now also brass'*).
- One Shilling is twelve Pence (*'most common'*, *'now also brass'*).
- Nine Pence (*'all bent, with the Harp stamped on one side'*).
- Sixpence three Farthings (*'scarce'*).
- Sixpence (*'most common'*).
- Four Pence Halfpenny or the Groats (*'either old or new'*).
- Threepence (*'rare as groats'*).
- Twopence (*'rare as groats'*).
- A Penny is four Farthings (*'the rarest of all'*).
- A Farthing (*'hitherto brass, but now tin'*).
- Twenty Shillings are four Crowns are one Piece, or one Pound Sterling.
- Two Crowns are ten Shillings are an Angel.
- Thirteen Shillings are four Pence are a Mark.
- Half a Mark is a Noble.
- But: Pound Sterling, Angel, Mark, Noble *'be no Species now a days'*.

It is, of course, interesting that Miège enumerates as many as twelve different coins. How careful we must be in evaluating this piece of information, however, is shown by the fact that the reference to *'the old and the new Groats'* appears in 1685 (Miège) and also in Caxton, that is, in a text which originated around 1340. We do not know whether this passage was in the earliest edition of Caxton, but it was there before 1483, two hundred years earlier than Miège. The complicated reality that lies behind such details is shown in the relevant entry of the *OED* (*groat*):

A denomination of coin . . . which was recognized from the 13th c. in various countries of Europe. . . . The adoption of the Du[tch] or Flemish form of the word into English shows that the 'groat' of the Low Countries had circulated here before a coin of that denomination was issued by the English sovereigns.

According to the same source, the English groat was coined in 1351–2, and ceased to be issued for circulation in 1662—twenty-three years before Miège's book appeared. Unless we find some additional clues like those found in Caxton, Miège's dialogues and many others must be regarded as didactic materials standardized rather than as documentary sources.

5

Treatises on terminology

1. General

So far, explanations and quotations have shown an obvious proximity of ono-masiological works to encyclopaedias. But there is also a proximity to treatises which use the onomasiological principle within scientific disciplines with (more or less) strictly systematized terminology such as those that began to appear in the sixteenth century.

These treatises ranged from the art of letter writing to cookery, from husbandry to seafaring. During the sixteenth and seventeenth centuries, a plethora of such works appeared on the market covering all domains of life and having the general aim of making expert knowledge public, because this knowl-edge had hitherto mostly been developed and handed down from generation to generation only in élite circles like monasteries, universities, or learned societies.[1] This tendency is in accordance with the general trend of the secularization of knowledge and of its application to and for the sake of the general good. Francis Bacon (1561–1626) was the most eminent and widely read promoter of this idea.[2]

---

[1] At the same time many alphabetical dictionaries for the learned professions and for the crafts, for trade and commerce appeared which had the same intentions. See Osselton 1999.

[2] Many treatises of the kind discussed here appeared prior to Bacon's works. This shows that the idea of applied scientific knowledge, generally attributed to Bacon, is in fact much older and may have been adopted by him from earlier popular literature. See Whitney 1990.

For the authors of treatises this meant in many cases translating the linguistic form of this knowledge from Latin into English. In other cases it meant writing in English on matters which had never been written on before in the vernacular. Making this knowledge public was done under the general maxim that it alleviated the difficulties which usually appeared with the application of theoretical knowledge to practice and so served the general good, even the entire nation. Giving names to phenomena which were well known as such, either by folklore or by experience, or translating unintelligible terminology, or even inventing new and convincing ones were the most important methods used by this kind of text.

There is a collection of 133 examples of such treatises with terminological glossaries printed between 1480 and 1640 (Schäfer 1989; Osselton 1999). Of these, fifty-two are arranged 'systematically',[3] fifty-five according to the alphabet, fifteen in the order of occurrence in the text, and eleven according to some different principle. It is remarkable that the large number of 'systematic', that is, topical, glossaries of terminology is devoted to scientific areas with their own strict principles of order, namely mathematics and geometry (13), cosmography (8), geographical and historical names (7), medicine and anatomy (6), grammar and rhetoric (5), military actions and armoury (4), coins and measures (3), and some others. Although the individual intentions of each single glossary still have to be assessed, it is obvious that such topical ('systematic') glossaries at that time prefigured what nowadays would be called *scientific nomenclature* (Hüllen 1994a, 36–7).[4]

Speaking of the *onomasiological principle* instead of onomasiology indicates that such treatises deviate in some way from onomasiological works proper, as the dialogues also do. In particular, this pertains to the rule that onomasiological dictionaries start from known meanings in the shape of lexemes which serve as explaining ones (*explanantia*) and then move to new, hitherto unknown lexemes—names (*explananda*). In treatises on terminology this order is retained only in so far as the general context—the book as a whole—presents facts of everyday experience which are given new names and explanations. The act of name giving itself, that is, what appears in the *micostructure* of a dictionary, occurs as a rule in the way in which semasiological dictionaries proceed. Thus, a hitherto unknown name is presented and complemented with either a known name or an explanation, or both. But the most distinct mark of semasiological dictionaries, the alphabet, is of course not observed.

The onomasiological principle is most distinctly to be found in the fact that the treatises are lexeme centred and that the lexemes (names) to be introduced appear in semantically coherent clusters (which would be called *macrostructure* in a

---

[3] This is Schäfer's term.

[4] Of the remaining fifty-five alphabetical glossaries, nine contain hard words in a general sense, two general archaisms, and one words of courtesy, which makes twelve; seven are devoted to names (general and place), six to medical terms, some of them called *popular*, five to theological and Biblical terms, five to plant names, some of them called *popular* again, five to classical antiquity, four to beasts and hunting, four to law, and some others.

dictionary) which, again, presuppose the general and well-known order of reality to which the book as a whole is devoted.

Treatises which introduce terminology also differ from the usual onomasiological dictionary in that they lack its inherent universalism and are highly specific. The proximity to encyclopaedias is replaced by a proximity to specific academic and scientific disciplines. They aimed to be comprehensive within a clearly demarcated field of knowledge. Of course, this again mirrors the difference between the aims of dictionaries and of such works. Dictionaries serve general language education, whereas treatises of the onomasiological kind serve training in some specific skill.

Another difference between onomasiological dictionaries and treatises which employ the onomasiological principle is that the latter do this in varying degrees of density. There are scientific disciplines which consist of nothing but a system of precisely defined terms. Well-known examples are rhetoric, grammar, and mathematics. Highly specialized fields of practical work like navigating sailing boats are also of this kind. On the other hand, there are fields of human activity, like sheep rearing or medical treatment, where terminology is couched in the reality of non-systematic natural conditions. This means that some treatises are onomasiological to a high degree, that they are almost contextualized dictionaries, whereas others contain only pockets of onomasiological denomination.

All the treatises that have been selected for lexicographical analysis here, in order to show their onomasiological elements, have their place in various historical contexts—the history of husbandry, rhetoric, mathematics, and seafaring. These contexts will be largely disregarded. Only the lexicographical structures which are embedded in these texts are of interest. The selection[5] cannot be anything else but arbitrary and could be replaced by a different one. It is meant to be exemplary.[6]

Although the treatises on terminology move away from the theory-driven activities of universities and monasteries, they are not out of contact with this world. It is a traditional idea that crafts are parts of the liberal arts. In their connection with mathematics, for example, they constitute the curriculum of the *quadrivium*. In medicine, agriculture, navigation, architecture, etc. the combination of rational knowledge and manual skills is obvious. The authors of many treatises are eager to show these links (Whitney 1990).

5.2 Husbandry

5.2.1 The boke of husbandrie

[The boke of husbandrie] *Here begynneth a newe tracte or treatyse moost profytable for all husband men: and very frutefull for all other persons to rede.*

---

[5] The selection is stimulated by but not wholly taken from Schäfer 1989.
[6] Outside these historical contexts, such treatises have so far only been investigated as source texts for the beginnings of English monolingual lexicography. See Schäfer 1989.

[Colophon:] *Thus endeth the boke of husbandrie. Imprinted at London in Fletestrete by Rycharde Pynson printer unto the kynges noble grace. With priuilege to hym graunted by oursayd souerayne lorde the kynge.*
[Assumed date: 1523]. *'The boke of husbandrie'* is the running title. The anonymous author is John Fitzherbert.
(BL C.71.b.27. 4°.)[7]

The book is printed in black letter throughout. It has regular paragraph marks. The front page bears a wood cut of two ploughing farmers.

The original of the reprint (Fitzherbert 1882) from a copy in the Bodleian Library is an elaborated version of the 1523 edition which appeared in 1598. This is the source of the passages under analysis here. The definitions and descriptions of horses' diseases have grown considerably in length in this edition, but a smaller number of diseases is treated, namely sixteen vs. thirty-nine. The following remarks relate to the 1523 edition, which comes nearer to a commented word-list than the later one.

The book is divided into 150 chapters, listed in *'The table'.* It describes the work to be done by a husbandman, a farmer, all the year round. Four main divisions may be discerned, the first dealing with tilling the field and growing crops, the second with keeping animals, the third with doing work around the house and in the orchard, and the fourth with the work and conduct of *'husband'* and wife in a gentleman's household. All the descriptions rest on some theological and moral presupposition stated at the beginning, according to which it is the fate of human beings to labour and eventually to have a chance of becoming rich if certain rules of conduct, among them, above all, keeping measure, are observed. The book is obviously meant to be a conduct book as well as a treatise on agriculture. In the first edition the four divisions are not mentioned in *'The table'*, but in the edition of 1598 they are.

All this has nothing to do with an onomasiological arrangement of technical terms. The points of reference are not lexemes with a complementary explanation, which would be an arrangement at least similar to a commented word-list. The whole is an explanatory and descriptive text which, because of its topic, uses much concrete vocabulary. This is even the case in chapters, for example, on the daily work of women, where the theme quite naturally leads to long enumerations of words denoting quite precise activities.

On some occasions, however, the onomasiological principle nevertheless becomes operative. The book starts with a description and explanation of the functions of a plough, the most important tool of husbandry. The fourth chapter, *'To knowe the names of all partes of the plough'*, has the following introductory sentences:

Men that be no husba[n]des may fortune to rede this boke ye knoweth not whiche is ye plough beam / the sharebeam / the plough sheth / the plough tayle / the stylt / the rest / the sheldbrede

---

[7] For editions, reprints, etc. see Schäfer 1989, vol. I, 20. There were ten editions before 1600, one in 1767, and the reprint by Skeat (Fitzherbert 1882).

/ *the fenbrede* / *the roughstaues. The plough eare* / *the plough fote or coke* / *the share* / *the culture or plough mall.*   (aii^v/aiii^r.)

The author then goes on to explain these words in turn, in the 1598 edition even with the help of a drawing. This is an arrangement which will be found in later dictionaries, elaborated in great detail when lexemes belonging to one clearly demarcated domain are gathered under one headword.[8]

Even closer to a commented onomasiological word-list comes a series of short paragraphs dealing with the diseases of horses (fi^r–gi^r, or ff. xxxii^r–xxxvi^r, in the later edition chaps 39–53, pp. 74–81). It is even marked in 'The table', because the relevant paragraphs are not headed with phrases like the others, stating what people should do, but merely with the names of diseases which are in need of explanation. As in a dictionary entry, the paragraphs all start with a name, that is, a lexeme, and give a complementary short definition and explanation. Note, for example, the first two:

The lampas. In the mouth is the la[m]pas: and is a thicke skyn[n]e full of blode hangyng ouer his tethe aboue that he may nat eate.
The barbes: The barbes be lytell pappes in a horse mouth: and lette hym to byte these two ben soone holpen.   (fi^r.)

There are thirty-nine diseases treated in this way, most of them afflicting the head (the mouth and eyes), the fore- and hind-legs, and a few of them the belly of the horse. The general context of husbandry is established by the remark that bad keeping and ill treatment are a cause of many of the diseases. There is an almost stereotypical promise that the sickness can be easily cured. Almost all the diseases mentioned affect the skin or are to be seen in the mouth or the nose of the animal. No organic defects, such as colic or cough, or bruises, broken bones, and the like are mentioned. Most of the entries cover between two and five lines, a few are longer.

The following is a selection of the names of diseases and their explanations which in most cases start with a sentence like 'Something is a sore and . . .':

Pursy *apereth at his nosethyrlles,*
Glaunders *cometh of a heat and a soden colde and apareth at his nosethyrlles and bytwene his chall bones,*
Stranguyllion *it woll ryse and swell in dyuers places of his body as moche as a ma[n]nes fyst and woll breke by it self if he be kept warm,*
Blyndnesse *A horse woll waxe blynde with labour and that may be cured be tyme,*
The cordes *appereth before the forther legges of the body,*
Amalander *appareth on the forther legges in the bendyng of the kne behynde: and is like a scabbe or a scall,*
A **splent** *is the lest sorance that is that alway co[n]tynueth except lampas,*
Morfounde *cometh of riding fast tyll he swete . . . and apereth vnder the houfe in the hert of the fote,*

---

[8]   See, for example, Chapter 7 on James Howell's *Lexicon Tetraglotton* of 1660.

The wormes they ly in the great paunche in the belly of the horse and they ar shinyng of colour lyke a snake,
A curbe maketh a horse to halt sore and apereth vpon the hynder legges,
Mylettes and apereth in the fete lockes behynde and causeth the heer to shede thre or foure inches of length,
Atteynt is a sorance that cometh of an ouer rechyng if it be before: and yf it be behynde it is of the tredyng of an other horse the which may be sone cured,
The scabbe and it is a scorfe in dyuers places of his body.

Fitzherbert's book belongs to a genre which, by virtue of its topics and intentions, deals with very concrete matters and, in so doing, must use concrete language. It belongs to one great domain of reality, a fact which automatically gives the language used a semantic cohesion. This domain is part of human experience. The book as a whole, thus, comes close to the onomasiological principle with its primacy of the object world, but it is itself no part of it yet, except in the places mentioned.

5.2.2 The English Husbandman *and* The English Hus-wife

The English Husbandman. The first Part: Contayning the Knowledge of the true Nature of euery Soyle within this Kingdome: how to Plowit; and the manner of the Plough, and other Instruments belonging thereto. Together With The Art of Planting, Grafting, and Gardening after our latest and rarest fashion. A worke neuer written before by any Author: and now newly compiled for the benefit of this Kingdome.
By Garuis Markham. London: Printed by T.S. for Iohn Browne, and are to be sould at his shop in Saint Dunstanes Church-yard Fleetestreete. 1613.
(BL G.2383. 1–4. 4°.)

The English Hus-wife, Contayning, The inward and outward vertues which ought to be in a compleat woman. As, her skill in Physicke, Cookery, Banqueting stuffe, Distillation, Perfumes, VVooll, Hemp, Flax, Dayries, Brewing, Baking, and all other things belonging to an Houshould. A Worke very profitable and necessarie, gathered for the generall good of this kingdome.
Printed at London by Iohn Beale, for Roger Iackson, and are to be sold at his shop neere the great Cunduit in Fleet-streete. 1615.
There is no mention made of the author, but the book is bound together with *The English Husbandman 1613*.
(BL G.2383. 4°.)

These are the first and third parts of Markham's *A way to get Wealth* of 1631, a compilation of several of his works in six parts, each with its own title page, pagination, and register. There were eight editions before 1700.

Garuis (also: Garvase, Jervis) Markham (?1568–1637) was a prolific writer, who nevertheless dealt almost exclusively with one topic, husbandry and horsemanship. He is said to have imported the first Arab horse into England. His book on the English husbandman is a comprehensive treatment of the subject. Although the various title pages for the parts of the book are slightly misleading, the whole treatise is recognizably divided into a first book containing: '*A Former Part, before the first part: Being an absolute perfect Introduction into all the Rules of true Husbandry . . .',* (seventy pages, not numbered); *'The First Part Of The English Husbandman: Contayning, the manner of plowing . . .'* and *'The Second Part . . . Contayning the Art of Planting, Grafting and Gardening . . .'* (132 pages, numbered). There then follows *'The Second Booke of the English Husbandman. Contayning the Ordering of the Kitchin-Garden, and the Planting of strange Flowers: . . .',* (105 pages, numbered anew). This makes a total of 307 pages in densely printed quarto format.

It is in the nature of a treatise on this topic that it contains mostly descriptions and rules on what to do on a farm all the year round. However, the text also makes use of techniques which were later to become typical of onomasiological word-lists. Furthermore, it is, to a large extent, structured in a way which repeats semantically cohesive word-lists, for example of animals and plants, this time however with the author's special arrangement according to the general intentions of his book. It is these features which deserve our attention.

The *'Former part'* deals mainly with the plough and ploughing according to the different kinds of soil. This repeats Fitzherbert's way of introducing the plough as the most important tool of husbandry: *'. . . for if hee know not how his Plough be made, nor the seuerall members of which it consisteth, with the vertue and vse of euery member, it is impossible that euer hee should make a gwd furrow, or turne ouer his ground in Husbandly manner'* (B2^r). This is why every part of the plough is represented with a drawing and named. With the exception of the first, *'the Plough-beame',* all other parts are named in exactly the same way: *'The second member or part of the Plough, is called the skeath',* *'The third part is called the Ploughs principal hale',* *'The fourth part is the Plough head',* *'The fifth part is the Ploughs spindels',* etc. till the eleventh part (B2^r–B3^r). A similar technique is used for explaining a special tack which allows the farmer to harness four horses or even more in front of a plough and make them pull it to the best of their strength, if the soil is heavy with clay. The complicated tack is given in a drawing (C3ii^r) with all its parts numbered, and these parts are then named and described in the following text. This technique foreshadows systematic ways of naming objects as, for example, employed by Comenius[9] and, even today, in countless textbooks. In Markham's book it is repeated whenever the text demands it, for example when the usefulness of a different kind of plough or some other instrument is explained.

When reading the second book on *'the Ordering of the Kitchin-Garden, and the Planting of strange Flowers: . . .',* it soon becomes obvious that in the background of all its explanations stands a collection of relevant plants as we find them with their names in the older glossaries and also in the dialogues for language teaching. In this case, however, the names are integrated into the overall context of the activities of a husbandman. According to the *'Table of all principall matters contayned in this Booke'* they are:

[9]   See Chapter 10, 395.

Pot-Hearbes: Of Beets, Of Land-Cresses, Of Parceley, Of Sauery, Of Time, Of French Mallowes, and Cheruil, Of Dill, Of Issop, Of Mints, Of Violets, Of Basil, Of sweet Marioram and Marigolds, Of Strawburyes, Of Borrage and of Buglosse, Of Rosemary, Of Pennyroyall, Of Leekes, Of Onions.

Hearbes . . . which are to be eaten, but especially are **medicinall** *. . .:* Of Arage, Of Lumbardy Louage, Of Fennel, Of Anyse, Of Comyn, Of Colyander, Of Rue, Of Organy, Of white Poppye, Of Germander, [etc.].

Sallet-Hearbes: Of Lettuce, Of Spinage, Of Sparagus, Of Colworts, Of Sage, Of Purslaine, Of Artichocks, Of Garlicke, Of Raddish, Of Nauewe, [etc.].

Flowers: Of Roses, Of the Damask Rose, Of the redde Rose, Of the White Rose, Of the Cynamon Rose, Of The Prouence Rose, Of Lauender, Of the white Lilly, Of the wood Lilly, Of the Flower de Lice, [etc.].

The names of the plants are printed in the margins, allowing the eye to travel over them and to read them as a list with the effect of gaining an overview of the whole chapter. The relevant texts are enumerative in character and sometimes give subdivisions of the species marked in the relevant part of the margin. They are, although written in continuous prose, still close to a word-list. Whereas the book as a whole is printed in black letter, the entries in the margins and the corresponding lexemes in the texts are printed in Roman type. This has the effect of a headword of a dictionary entry. Remarks about the plants' treatment in the garden follow the statement of their names. Note, for example (entries in margins printed first and bold):

'*Of all sorts of Pot-herbs*'. *Of Endiue and Succorie. Now for your Pot-hearbs, which are most generally in vse, they be these: Eindiue and Succorie, which delight in moyst ground, and will endure the winter. Bleete of which there be two kindes, Red and White: this Hearbe neuer needeth weeding, and if he be suffered to shed his seed it will hardly euer to be got out of a Garden.*
'*Of Beets*'. *The Beets, which must be much weeded, for they loue to liue by themselves, and if they grow too thicke you may take them vp when they are a finger long in their owne earth, and set them another bed, and they will prosper much better.*
'*Land-Cresses*'. *Then land Cresses, which is both a gwd Pot-hearbe and a gwd Sallet-Hearbe: it loueth shadowie places, where the Sunne shineth least, and standeth in need of little dung.*
'*French Mallovves*'. *Then French-Mallowes, which will ioy in any ground, and are quicke of growth.*   (17 and 18, D $^{r-v}$.)

The passages quoted give a good impression of the length and the style of paragraphs devoted to one plant. Sometimes paragraphs are longer, for example the (not quoted) one *On Parcely*. Generally speaking, texts on medical herbs and *On Sallet-Hearbs* and also those on flowers are slightly longer than the ones quoted. Of course, in all these texts the particular state of knowledge pertaining to the plants and flowers mentioned emerges. Note, for example, the following remark with its traces of the Galenic medical concepts of humours and temperatures:

'*Of Anise*'. *Anise is hot and dry, it dissolueth humores and obstructions, and is very comfortable to weake stomacks, it delighteth in a gwd and lwse mould, and is to be sowne in the height of the Spring onely.*   (22, D3^v.)

The proximity of these texts to mere word-lists is quite obvious.

Garuis Markham's book on *The English Hus-wife*, which does not show the author's name on the title page, is another case in point. The '*Table*', unaccountably speaking of a '*Second Book*', is unusually extensive because it lists not only chapters but all the entries in the margins which mark the chain of thoughts. Of course, the '*English Hus-wife*' must be perfect in all respects:

> To conclude, our english Hus-wife must be of chast thought, stout courage, patient, vntyred, watchful, diligent, witty, pleasant, constant in friendship, full of god neighbour-hood, wise in discourse but not frequent therein, sharpe and quicke of speech, but not bitter or talkatiue, secret in her affairs, comfortable in her counsailes, and generally skilfull in all the worthy knowledges which doe belong to her vocation, of all, or most parts whereof I now itende to speake more largely.   (4, R2ᵛ.)

This is done by elaborating '*Her vertue in House-hold Phy[si]cke*', '*Her skill in Cookery*', '*Of Wooll, Hempe, Flexe and Cloth*' and '*Dairie-work*' in four chapters. At least the first two chapters turn out to be long, enumerating lists of everything that is known in the fields of medical treatment and of cooking.

After some general ideas about the importance of '*House-hold Physicke*' for the family there then follow thirty-five pages covering as many as 124 ailments, with as many remedies to cure them. First we find the several kinds of '*fever*' which we today know to be the several kinds of malaria, and the '*plague*'. Then the list continues with the headache and slowly moves down the whole body to the abdominal tract, as is usually done in similar lists. There then follows another list of equal length, which is less well ordered but contains health problems which are rarely treated, like stitches and dead flesh. As is natural, the remedies often give many names for substances to be used. The paragraphs are rather stereotypical, almost all of them beginning either with '*For the yellow Iaundisse*', '*For the dropsie*', '*For pain in the spleen*' or with '*To increase a womans milke*', '*To make a pouder for the collicke*', '*To stay the flux of the Rhume*'. Note as an example:

> To make a pouder for the collicke and stone, take fenell, parseley seede, anyseeds, and carrawayseeds, of each the waight of sixe pence, of gromel seede, saxifrage seed, the roots of filipendula, and licoras, of each the waight of xvii. shillings, good waight, beat them all to powder and searsse it, which wil waigh in all 25. shillings and 6. pence: This powder is to be giuen in white wine and suger in the morning fasting, and so to continue two howres after; and to take of it at one time the waight of ten pence or twelue pence.   (20, T2ᵛ.)

The significant aspect of this collection of methods of medical treatment, whose prescriptions will probably be of the greatest interest to historians of medicine, is its unrelatedness to the original problem, the skills of housewives, which makes it develop into a quasi-professional treatise. Indeed, at the beginning the author stresses that he does not want to make housewives asssume the name and the knowledge of practitioners, but that he only wants to '*relate vnto her some approued medicines*' (5, R3ʳ). However, he then does the contrary.

The second chapter, on cookery, goes even further along this way towards a collection of relevant names. The author announces that he will write down '*a short Epitome of all that knowledge*', that is, the knowledge which a housewife must command, and gives long lists of the names of plants to be sown in the garden in the months between January and August. Note, for example:

In February in the new of the Moone shee may sow Spyke, Garlicke, Borage, Buglose, Cheruyle, Coriander, Gourds, Cresses, Marioram, Palma Christi, Flower-gentle, white Poppy, Purslan, Radish, Rocket, Rosemary, Sorrell, Double Marigolds and Time. (37, X3ʳ.)

The feature of sheer enumeration, almost '*too tedious to nominate*' also appears in the following:

First then to speake of sallats, there be some simple, and some compounded; some onely to furnish out the table, and some both for vse and adornation: your simple Sallats are Chibols pilled, washt cleane, and halfe of the greene tops cut cleane away, so seru'd on a Fruit-dish, or Chines, Scallious, Radish-roots, boyled Carrets, Skirrets, and Turneps, with such like serued vp simply; also, all young Lettice, Cabage lettice, Purslan, and diuers other hearbes which may bee serued simply without any thing, but a little Vinegar, Salletoyle, and Sugar: Onions boiled and stript from their rinde, and serued vp with Vinegar, Oyle, and Pepper is a good simple Sallat; so is Samphire, Beane-cods, Sparagus, and Cucumbers, serued in likewise with Oyle, Vinegar and Pepper, with a world of others, too tedious to nominate. (39, X3iiʳ.)

The chapter provides some 128 recipes, by no means all of them as full of details and names for ingredients as the one quoted. But the tendency is still, obviously, to give the whole range of possibilities by amassing names.

5.3 Rhetoric: *A treatise of Schemes and Tropes*

A treatise of Schemes & Tropes very profytable for the better vnderstanding of good authors, gathered out of the best Grammarians & Orators by Rychard Sherry Londoner.
Wherevnto is added a declamacion, That chyldren euen strapt fro[m] their infancie should be well and gently broughte vp in learnynge. Written fyrst in Latin by the most excellent and famous Clearke, Erasmus of Roterodame.
No publisher mentioned, no year. Handwritten (old): '1550'.
(BL C.122.a.37. 8°.)
[Colophon at the end of the epistle:] *Geuen at London the xiii. day of Decembre. Anno. M.D.L.*[10]

Richard Sherry, whose dates are unknown, was a headmaster of Magdalen College School in Oxford. His chief work is *A Treatise of the Figures of Grammer and Rhetoricke* (1555). His earlier book is introduced by an '*Epistle. To the ryght worshypful Master Thomas Brooke Esquire, Rychard Shyrrey wysheth health euerlastynge*'. The author starts with the observation that many new and strange words

---

[10] For editions, reprints, etc. see Schäfer 1989, vol. I, 23–4. There is a facsimile edition by Hildebrand (Sherry 1961).

have entered the English tongue and are becoming familiar by use. To them belong '*Paraprasis*', '*homilies*', '*vsurped*', '*abolyshed*', and others, among them '*schemes*' and '*tropes*', that is, the words of the title of his book. He welcomes this development because it enriches the English language, makes it '*copyous and plentyfull that therein it maye compare wyth anye other whiche so euer is the best*' (Aii^v). It (the development) has been brought about by people like John Gower (d. 1408), Geoffrey Chaucer (?1340–1400), John Lydgate (?1370–1450), and Sir Thomas Wyatt (1503–42), but also by the '*ryght worshipful knyght syr Thomas Eliot*,[11] *which first in hys dictionarye as it were generallye searching oute the copye of our language in all kynde of wordes and phrases*' (Aiii^r). This betrays the fact that Richard Sherry saw his own work not only in connection with those creative minds who introduced the new vocabulary into the English language but also with the first lexicographer who intended to make it intelligible to and popular with the common speaker. He certainly favours the influx of new, that is, hard, words because they enrich the sciences and the arts. His own book on schemes and tropes '*came in place, and offered it selfe, demed to be bothe profitable and pleasaunte if they* [= the new words] *were gathered together, and handsomelye set in a playne order, and with theyr descriptions hansomely put into our Englishe tongue*' (Aiiii^r). This characterizes the method of the treatise: (i) a collection of new words belonging to one topical domain, (ii) an order thought to be plain, (iii) the translation of Greek lexemes into Latin, which would become Latinized English words, and (iv) descriptions, that is, definitions, paraphrases, and examples with reference to word meanings.

Sherry's sources, as far as mentioned, were, among others, Quintilian, Cicero, Mosellanus, and Erasmus. The intention of his book was to enable people to use plain language '*sithe the proper vse of speach is to vtter the meaning of our mynd with as playne wordes as maye be*' (Avi^v/Avii^r). In contrast to the usual dichotomy of plain vs. hard, *plain* in this case means the exact knowledge of word meanings, even when we are compelled '*to speake otherwyse then after common facion*' (Avii^r). This pertains to the vocabulary of schemes and tropes. Knowledge of them is necessary to understand good writers, including the Holy Scripture.

Richard Sherry's primary ancient source was the *Rhetorica ad Herennium*, which he does not mention, underpinned with material from the neo-classical intermediaries, which he does mention (Sherry 1961, ix).[12] The author is not concerned with rhetoric at large, but only with its third part, elocution or style, which is the '*prvncipall parte of rhetoriqve*' (Avi^v). Style is the decoration of the expression of thought, and decoration is brought about by the application of

---

[11] Sir Thomas Elyot (?1490–1546) is the first known author of an alphabetical Latin–English dictionary. Moreover, he is the first to have used the word *dictionary* as the name of a word-list, that is, in the present sense. See Stein 1985, 140–56.

[12] Text by an unknown author, for a long time attributed to Cicero. Known since Hieronymus (348–430), also called *Rhetoric Secunda* or *Rhetorica Nova*. Doubts as to its authorship started in the fifteenth century. Nothing is known of the addressee. See Nüßlein 1994, 328–30.

tropes and figures to common language. This idea was widespread in Renaissance linguistic deliberations. Moreover, singling out elocution (and delivery) from the five chapters of rhetoric conformed with the influential ideas of Ramism in which elocution and pronunciation were treated as belonging to rhetoric, whereas invention, disposition, and memory belonged to logic. Charles Butler, in his *Rhetoricae* of 1598, also held this opinion (Salmon 1996), but others like Thomas Wilson in *The Arte of Rhetorique* (1553), Henry Peacham in *The Garden of Eloquence* (1577), and George Puttenham in *The Arte of English Poesie* (1589) adhered to the old five-part concept.[13]

What the macrostructure is for an onomasiological dictionary the general design is for this treatise. It is what brings the whole text close to a topical word-list. Sherry starts with a lengthy explanation of '*Eloquucion*', differentiating between (1) '*wordes considered by them selues . . .*', and (2) '*wordes . . . when they be ioyned together*' (Bi[v]) and explaining the '*three kyndes of style or endyghtynge*', namely '*The greate, the small, the meane*' (Biii[r]). He then divides and subdivides the two groups, and quotes a great number of matching rhetorical terms in clusters which match the subdivisions. For the overall coherence of this system of terminology and definitions see Table A.6, which shows the system but does not mirror the sequence of explanations in Sherry's text.

In all, eleven clusters of terms match the sub- and sub-subdivisions of rhetoric. Typically, each entry consists of a Greek lemma printed in the margin, a translating Latin lemma which opens the explanatory sentence, a word, a definition, and an example or a classical reference. Frequently, but by no means always, the Latin lemma is given also as an English hard word. Unlike the black letter print of the whole book, the Latin lexeme is set in italics. Sometimes the Greek and the Latin term are erroneously reversed. Occasionally, explanations of two or more entries are linked together by stating that the subsequent entries are to be subsumed under the preceding. This arrangement, although not printed in columns, comes very near to the usual dictionary entries with the lexemes in the margin as headwords. Typical entries read:

[Margin:] **Mycterismus.** [Text:] *Subsannatio, a skornyng by some testure of the face, as by wrythinge the nose, putting out the tongue, pottyng, or suche lyke.*   (Ciii[4][v].)

[Margin:] **Tautologia.** [Text:] *Inutilis repeticio eiusdem, is a vayne repeting agayn of one word or moe in all one sentence, whyche faute by takynge lytle heede, Cicero also fell into, as in the oracion for Aulus Cluencius. Therefore that iudgeme[n]t was not lyke a iudgeme[n]t of Judges.* (Ci[r].)

[Margin:] **Epitrope.** [Text:] *Permissio, permission, when we shew y[e] we geue & grau[n]t any thyng altogether to a mans wyll, thus: Because al thynges take[n] a way, only is left vnto me my body & mynde, these thynges, whych only ar lefte vnto me of many, I graunte the[m] to to*[!] *you and to your power.*   (Diiii[r].)

---

[13] For this context in general see Howell 1961, *passim*, and for Sherry's '*Schemes and Tropes*' in particular Howell 1961, 125–36. Howell points out that, on the one hand, Sherry's book appeared too early to be really influenced by Ramus, whose influence began to spread after 1543; on the other hand, Sherry conceived of rhetoric as the Ramists did (Howell 1961, 127).

However, with the '*second order*' (2.22), '*that greate declaracion of eloquence, called of Quintilian and Cicero, the orname[n]ts of sentence*' (Dvii^v), the style of entries changes. In the entries pertaining to the '*first order*' the explanatory parts have already become much more elaborate, and include not only definitions and examples, which are naturally much longer now, but also evaluative remarks. In some cases they extend to over half a page. Finally, explanations develop into a text in its own right with lexemes in the margin only as eye-catchers for the chain of thoughts. There is no longer regular correspondence between Greek terms and their Latin translations. This means that this chapter is not similar to a topical dictionary of rhetorical terms but is a treatise proper. It closes with '*A copious heaping of probacions*' (Evii^v) which have their own order recognizable from the entries in the margin. There then follows the translation of Erasmus's *Education of Children*, mentioned in the title of the book.

Note the following selection of entries in their clusters.[14]

First cluster pertaining to the '*Ffigure of Diccion*':[15]

Prothesis, *Appositio, apposicio[n], the putting to;*
Apheresis, *Ablatio, the takynge away;*
Epenthesis, *Interpositio, added betweene;*
Syncope, *Consicio, is cutte from;*
Proparalepsis, *Preassumpcio, is added to.*

Second cluster pertaining to '*Ffigure of construccion*':

Prolepsis, *Presumpcio, a takynge before;*
Zeugma, *Iunctio, ioynyng;*
Silepsis, *Concepcio;*
Epergesis, *Appositio;*
Hyperbaton, *Transgressio.*

Third cluster pertaining to '*Ffaute*', obscure:

Acyrologia, *Improprietas;*
Pleonamus, *Superabundancia, superfluous words;*
Tautologia, *Inutilis repeticio eiusdem, vayne repeting again;*
Homiologia, *Sermo ubique sui similis, the whole matter is all alyke;*
Amphibologia, *Ambiguitas.*

Fourth cluster pertaining to '*Ffaute*', inordinate:

Tapinosis, *Humiliatio, the dignitye of the thyng is diminished;*
Aschiologia, *Turpis loquutio;*

---

[14] The number of rhetorical terms in the clusters varies between two and forty-two. For practical reasons, I limit myself to five as *pars pro toto*.

[15] In each, the first term (bold) is the Greek, sometimes Latin, one given in the margin of Sherry's book and the second term is the Latin translation. There then follows, where appropriate, the English hard word and/or that part of the defintion which comes near to a translation, either by use of the Latin lexeme or by a translation into some other lexeme. I follow strictly the sequence and spelling of Sherry's entries, even where obvious mistakes occur.

Aschematisto[n], Male figuratum;
Cacosyntheton, Male collocatum;
Soraismus, Gumulatio, mynglyng [of diverse languages], *wordes be naughtelye ionyned.*

Fifth cluster pertaining to 'Ffaute', barbarous:

Barbarismus, [no Greek entry], *a worde is either naughtely wrytten or pronou[n]ced co[n]trary to the ryght law & manner of speakinge;*
Solecismus, Inconueniens structura, vnmete and vnconvenient ionynge.

The sixth and seventh clusters pertain to '*Vertue*', '*or as we saye, a grace or dygni-tye in the speakinge, the thyrde kynde of Scheme*' (Ciii[r]). They differ with reference to the two kinds of '*Vertue*': '*Proprietie, and garnyshyng*'. Under the first come the two entries '*Analogia, Proportio, proporcion*' and '*Talis, Extensio*'; under the second only one entry, '*Sinthesis*', which is not translated but elaborately defined.

There then follow the entries pertaining to tropes. The eighth cluster is sepa-rated from those pertaining to figures:

In figure is no alteracion in the wordes fro[m] their proper significations, but only is the oracion and se[n]tence made by the[m] more plesau[n]t, sharpe and veheme[n]t, after y[e] affecio[n] of him that speketh or writeth: to y[e] which vse although tropes also do serue, yet properlye be they so called, because in them for uenecessitye or garnyshynge, there is a mouynge and chaung-ynge of a worde and sentence, from theyr own significacio[n] into another, which may agre wyth it by similitude.   (Ciiii[r and v].)

The entries of this cluster are:

Metaphora, Translatio, translacion [seven kinds];
Catachresis, Abusio, abuse;
Metonomia, Metonomya, Transnominacion;
Synekdoche, Intellectio, Intellceccion [nine kinds];
Periphrasis, Circuicio.

The ninth cluster pertains to '*an inuersion of wordes, where it is one in wordes, and another in sentence or meanynge*' (Cvii[r]). Its entries are:

Aenigma, Sermo obscurus, a riddle or dark allegorie;
Ironia, Dissimulatio, mockyng;
Sarcasmus, Amara irrisio, a bitter sporting, a mocke;
Astysmus, Festiua urbanitas;
Mycterismus, Subsannatio, a scornyng.

The tenth cluster pertains to '*The fyrst order of the figures Rethoricall*' (Cviii[r].) The entries read:

Epanaphora, Repeticio, repeticion;
Antistrophe, Conuersio, conuuersion;
Symploce, Co[m]plexio, complexion;
Anadiplosis, Reduplicatio, continent rebeatsyng;
Synonimia, Nominis co[m]munio, co[m]munion of the word.

The last cluster of terms pertaining to '*that greate declaracion of eloquence, called of Quintilian and Cicero, the orname[n]ts of sentence*' (Dvii^v) need not be mentioned because it does not follow the onomasiological arrangement.

Apart from its last part, Sherry's *Treatise* has traits in common with topical word-lists which are amplified by definitions, examples, and references. Because of this it represents a move in the direction of a non-alphabetical, defining diction-ary. Besides the recurring elements of entries, this is corroborated by their order of sequence, which is dictated by the rhetorical tradition, but which, lexicograph-ically speaking, gives the book an overall cohesion in which every lexeme has its proper place. Indications of this are sometimes to be found in the explanations when they refer to each other and, in so doing, justify their own place. Note, for example, the explanation to '*Homiologia*', following '*Tautologia*', quoted above, with the introductory sentence: '*Sermo ubique sui similis, a greater faute then the other, is when the whole matter is all alyke, and hath no varietie*' (Ci^r).

Sherry's treatise 'is highly prescriptive. It was born in an age of rules. So much so, that the rhetorician who named his rules and tools was not out of rapport with the period. This accounts for the rigidity, the love of classification, and the schematic presentation of the work. It is nothing more than a highly organized dictionary of ancient, medieval, and Renaissance schemes and tropes.' (Sherry 1961, vi.)[16] This is certainly a correct and just appreciation of Sherry's work as an example of the great rhetorical tradition in sixteenth-century England. What, according to Hildebrand, appears in it as a limitation, however, illustrates its merits in another tradition, that of the onomasiological principle which depends on the principle of classification and the schematic presentation of material, and even on the rigidity of method which were all mentioned in the above quotation.

A treatise on rhetoric is not a practical one in the narrow sense. The topic has nothing to do with the common man. Yet, it is practical in so far as it helps the non-Latin reader to understand and enjoy literature which is written in the spirit and with all the techniques of rhetorical figures. It is part of the movement to adapt the vernacular to tasks which hitherto were reserved for Latin-speaking intellectuals.

5.4 Geometry

5.4.1 The pathway to Knowledg

The pathway to Knowledg, Containing The First Principles of Geometrie, as they may moste aptly be applied vnto practice, bothe for vse of instrumentes Geometricall, and astronomicall

---

[16] In contrast to the *DNB*, Hildebrand in his introduction to Sherry 1961 is of the opinion that our treatise and not that on grammar and rhetoric of 1555 is the author's chief work. Howell 1961 devotes the longer part of his analysis to the earlier of Sherry's books.

and also for proiection of plattes in euerye kinde, and therfore much necessary for all sortes of men. . . .
[No author given, but the dedication to Edward VI signed:] *Robert Recorde.*
[Colophon:] *Imprinted at London in Poules churcheyarde, at the signe of the Brasen serpent, by Reynold Wolfe. Cum priuilegio ad imprimendum solum. Anno Domini M.D.L.I.*
(BL C.82.b.8. 4°.)

Other editions appeared in 1574 and 1602. There is a facsimile edition (Recorde 1974).

Robert Recorde (?1510–58) was a mathematician of distinction. He was the first writer on arithmetic, geometry and astronomy to use the sign '=' ('equals'). *The Castle of Knowledge* (1556), a book on astronomy, was known to Shakespeare. He died in prison, where he was probably kept because of debts.

It goes almost without saying that introductions to such scientific disciplines whose very nature it is to consist of a strictly defined system of interrelated terms must start with definitions and explanations of these terms in an order which, according to the principles of the discipline, are adequate. This means that, within the narrow limits of these disciplines, such introductions make use of the onomasiological principle, bringing the proximity of onomasiology and terminology into the open. The most obvious discipline is mathematics with its several branches.

Before embarking on the definition and explanation of terms, Robert Recorde is eager to deliberate, at first on a rather philosophical and then on a rather practical level, on a problem of major importance. In his '*Epistle*' to Edward VI he philosophizes about the human wish to obtain '*felicity*' which can only be done by becoming knowledgeable. Referring to Aristotle and Solomon, this means for him above all and '*before al other arts*' a '*taste of the mathematical sciences, specially Arithmetike and Geometry*' (ji\u1d5b). For Recorde, they are the basis of the seven liberal arts, and they are also most helpful, for example, in surveying and building.[17] The king is lucky '*in that your Maiesty was borne in the time of such skilful schoolmaisters and learned techers*' (jii\u02b3), among whom the author certainly counts himself. He intends to write more books '*in the Latine tongue and also in the Englsyshe*' and prides himself on the fact that the present book '*is the firste that euer was sette forthe in Englishe*' (jii\u1d5b). This is a programme of general education, in particular for people ignorant of Latin (Watson 1909, 296–304, 337). Note:

And I truste (as I desire) that a great numbre of gentlemen, especially about the courte, which vnderstand not the latin tong, or els for the hard nesse of the mater could not away with other mens writyng, will fall in trade with this easie forme of teachyng in their vulgar tong, and so employe some of their tyme in honest studie, whiche were wont to bestowe most part of their time in triflyng pastime: . . . . (jiii\u02b3.)

'*The Preface*', which is addressed to the reader, strikes a much more practical note. '*Carpenters, Karuers, Joyners, and Masons, doe willingly acknowledge that they*

---

[17] For the history of this idea see above and Whitney 1990.

can worke nothyng without reason of Geometrie' (jiv^v). Furthermore, merchants, goldsmiths, tailors and shoemakers, weavers, clockmakers, etc. are in need of geometrical knowledge, whose importance is then shown with reference to historical examples. Both texts bear testimony to the fact that the author sees his book as offering a treatise for the general education of the public. Apart from the courtiers, who were perhaps mentioned more as a matter of courtesy to the king, this pertains mainly to craftsmen and artisans.

It is the introductory part, headed '*The definitions of the principles of Geometrie*', which systematically provides the terms of the discipline. According to the entries in the margins they are:

A poincte, A lyne, A streghte lyne, A crokyd lyne, an Angle, A righte angle, A sharpe corner, A blunt or brode corner, A platte forme,[18] *A plaine platte, A crooked platte, A bodie, Depenesse, Cubike, A globe, A bounde, Forme, Fygure, A centre, A ground line, A perpendicular, A plume lyne, Parallelys, Gemowe lynes,*[19] *Concentrikes, A twine line,*[20] *spirall line, A worme line, A touch line, A corde, Circum ference, A diameter, Semidiameter, A cord, or a stringlyne, An archline, A bowline, A cantle, A semye circle, A nooke cantle, A noke, An egge fourme, A tunne or barrel forme, An axtre or axe lyne, A yey fourme, A triangle, Isopleuron,*[21] *Isosceles,*[22] *Skalena,*[23] *Quadra[n]gle, A square quadrate, A longe square, A losenge, A diamond, A losenge lyke, Borde formes, A squyre,*[24] *A round spier.*

All the definitions are connected with each other and are accompanied by drawings. The definitions are followed by conclusions, and these are followed in a second book by '*Theoremes*'. The terms are given concise definitions, with short elaborations following. The book is printed wholly in italics, only the terms themselves are set in Roman type, so they stand out by themselves and can easily be found as the eye travels down the page. Note, for example:

A poynte or a Prycke, is named of Geometricians that small and vnsensible shape, whiche hath in it no partes.
A Straight lyne, is the shortest that may be drawenne betweene two prickes.
A sharpe angle is so called, because it is lesser than is a square angle, and the lines that make it, do not open so wide in their departynge as in a square corner, and if thei be drawen crosse, all fower corners will not be equall.
([Margin:] A bounde) I mean therby a generall name, betokening the beginning, end and side, of any forme.
A touche lyne, is a line that runneth a long by the edge of a circle, onely by touching it.   (A–B)

The arrangement of the book does not differ much from that of modern introductions to geometry. Nevertheless, it deserves mention because it stands at the historical beginning of a development which has led to generally accepted routines. In its time, *The pathway to Knowledg* must have been an exemplary novelty with its systematic development of terminology in the English language

---

[18] Two-dimensional.   [19] Parallels.   [20] A line twisting around a body.
[21] Greek letters (type of triangle).   [22] Greek letters (type of triangle).
[23] Greek letters (type of triangle).   [24] '*Two long squares ioyned togethir*'.

employing all the precision which geometry as a discipline demands. Moreover, the book has to be seen as an attempt to make this terminology known to people who, up to then, were barred from mathematical knowledge because they were unable to read Latin.

5.4.2 A Regiment for the Sea

A Regiment for the Sea: Conteynyng most profitable Rules, Mathematical experiences, and perfect knowledge of Nauigation, for all Coastes and Countreys: most needful and necessary for al Seafaryng men and Trauellers, as Pilotes, Mariners, Marchants. &. Exactly deuised and made, by William Bourne.
Imprinted at London, nigh vnto the three Cranes in the Vintree, by Thomas Dawson, and Thomas Gardyner, for Iohn Wight.
[Colophon:] *Imprinted at London nigh vnto the three Cranes in the Vintree, by THomas Dawson, and Thomas Gardiner, for Iohn VVyght, dwelling at the North dore of Paules. Anno Domini. 1577.*
(BL. 55.d.26. 4°.)

There were six editions until 1620 and a reprint in 1963 edited by Taylor (Bourne 1963).

William Bourne (or Bourn) (d. 1583) was probably a ship's carpenter and a self-taught mathematician, who published almanacs and treatises on gunnery and navigation. His *Regiment for the Sea* is an outstanding example of the application of mathematical knowledge to practical purposes. In the '*Epistle*' he stresses that his book '*is not altogether gathered out of other bookes, but that the greatest part is deuised and practised by mee*' and that he addresses not the '*cunnyng and learned sort*' (Aii^v) but the late beginners. This means William Bourne did not plan to contribute anything to the body of mathematical knowledge as it was cultivated at the universities. He planned to write a book for practical sailors whom he must acquaint with the names and uses of the principles of navigation. In '*The Preface to the Reader*', after stressing the importance of navigation for England's well-being, he reiterates this idea:

And albeit the learned sorte of Seafaring men haue no neede of this booke, yet am I assured that it is a necessary book for the simplest sorte of Seafaring men: for that they shall find here the names of the circles in the sphere, with the names of diuerse things meete for Nauigation, togither with their vses, which the most part of Sea men doo mistake or missecal. (Aiii^v.)

This address to the unlearned reader is again complemented by the confession that he, the author, does not belong to the '*learned persons*'. William Bourne obviously wrote as a practitioner for practitioners.

The larger part of the book is made up of calendars for many years and tables on how to determine the time according to the position of the sun and the moon, how to measure the inclination of the sun either from the north or the south of the equator, how to reckon the longitude and latitude of one's position, how to measure distances, how to use the compass, etc. All this is called a '*Regiment for the*

Sea'. In order to go through these techniques, a knowledge of the various factors in the calculations is needed, and this knowledge is to be introduced by some terms—the names and their meanings. Note the following head of the introductory chapter:

The names of certaine things necessary to be knowne of them that are Mariners or Seafaring men, meete to be knowne of them that doo practise Nauigation, as this: the names of the circles of the Sphere, and what they are, and their vses: and also the names of other things belonging thereunto, and what they are, and their vses.   (1, A^r.)

The chapter consists of twenty-eight sections that mention and explain the main terms in the following way. Each section has a heading printed in italics with the term to be defined, then the definition itself in black letter, then another heading, '*The vse of . . .*' again in italics and another explanatory text again in black letter. The second paragraph '*The vse of . . .*' is sometimes but not often missing. Note, for example, the fourth and ninth sections:

4. What the circle or Tropick of Cancer is, being a Parallel circle fixed.
The tropicke of Cancer, is the greatest declination that the Sunne dooth come vnto the Northwardes, and then is our longest Sommer dayes, and shortest nyghts.
9. What the line Ecliptick is.
The line Eclipticke, is a circle in the very middle of the Zodiack, the which, the very middle or center of the Sun doth go vpon.
The vse of the line Ecliptick.
The vse of the line Ecliptick is this, if that the Moone or any other starre, be vnto the North part therof, then it is sayd, that they haue North Latitude, and if vnto the Southe part, then they haue south latitude: and also by this circle called the line Ecliptick, is knowne the Eclipse of the Sunne and the Moone.   (Aii^r, Aiii^r.)

The definitions and explanations of '*vse*' quoted here are among the shortest, but they rarely cover more than a third of a page. This means they are generally concise. An exception to this is the longer sections 26 and 28, which deal with the general problems '*What nauigation is*', '*The vse of Nauigation*', and '*What manner of persons be meetest to take charge of Shippes in Nauigation*', which have no explanations concerning '*vse*'.

Chapter 1 ends with a section, not numbered, which explains the '*Equinoctial Circle, being 360 degrees in compasse*', and specifies all directions with thirty-two names for the various winds. For these thirty-two points the numbers of degrees and minutes are given, as well as their equivalent in hours, minutes, and seconds. A drawing of the compass with all its details accompanies these explanations.

This being done, the basic concepts and their names, necessary for navigation, have all been elucidated and the rest of the book provides rules, methods, and tables for the calculations to be done. The majority are accompanied by drawings.

The close of the book, the twenty-second chapter, deals with the special difficulties when sailing through the Channel and approaching the coast of Cornwall.

5.5 Seafaring: A Sea Grammar

For a long time, the language of sailors has been, and it still is, one of the most original and most complex professional registers which exists in English. Because of the political and commercial importance of the seafaring nation of Britain, it exercised a great influence on the relevant registers of other languages. The world-wide acceptance of sailors' English, as is shown in Johann Hinrich Röding's *Allgemeines Wörterbuch der Marine in allen europäischen Sprachen nebst voll-ständigen Erklärungen* (1793), has for centuries prefigured the world-wide accep-tance of air-traffic pilots' English which we observe today.

At the beginning of this development we encounter a book by an extraordinary character and, consequently, of great interest. It was written by Captain John Smith of Jamestown. It is appropiate, first of all, to follow the history of this book which has caused an almost unparalleled linguistic impact in the world. There are four versions to be noted:

(1) *An Accidence Or Path-way to Experience. Necessarie for all Young Sea-men, or those that are desirous to goe to Sea, briefly shevving the Phrases, Offices, and VVords of Command, Belonging to the Building, Ridging, and Sayling, a Man of Warre; And How to manage a Fight at Sea. Together with the Charge and Duty of every Officer, and their Shares: Also the Names, VVeight, Charge, Shot, and Powder, of all sorts of great Ordnances. With the vse of the Petty Tally.*
Written by Captaine Iohn Smith sometimes Governor of Virginia, and Admirall of New England. London: Printed for Jonas Man, and Benjamin Fisher, and are to be sold at the signe of the Talbot, in Aldersgate streete. 1626.
(BL C.31.d.17. 4°.) Another edition appeared in 1636.

(2) *A Sea Grammar, With The Plaine Exposition of Smiths Accidence for young Sea-men, enlarged. Diuided into fifteene Chapters: what they are you may partly conceiue by the Contents.*
Written by Captaine Iohn Smith, sometimes Gouernor of Virginia, and Admirall of Nevv-England. London, Printed by Iohn Haviland, 1627.

This is a much enlarged edition of (1). There are two reprints of this edition. In Smith (1968) footnotes were added and also comments on the text, which has modernized spelling and which is partly arranged differently from the original, for example, in order to make direct speech and dialogues visible in print. The other reprint, Smith (1970), has an introduction by the editor, K. Goell.

(3) *The Sea-Mans Grammar: Containing Most plain and easie directions, how to Build, Rigge, Yard, and Mast any Ship whatsoever. With the plain exposition of all such terms as are used in a Navie and Fight at Sea. Whereunto is added a Table of the Weight, Charge, Shot, Powder, and the dimensions of all other appurtenances belonging to all sorts of great Ordnance. With divers practicall Experiments in the Art of Gunnery. Also the Charge and Duty of every Officer in a Ship and their Shares: With the use of the Petty Tally.*

Written by Captain John Smith, sometimes Governour of Virginia, and Admiral of New England. Imprinted at London, and are to be sold by Andrew Kemb, at St. Margarets Hill in Southwark, 1653.
The British Library copy has handwritten '1652' as a correction of the printed '1653', and added 'Novemb. 6'.   (Microfilm copy, BL E.679.(9). 4°.)

According to the usual preface '*To the Reader*', this book was edited by somebody whose name is not given, because it '*has long since [been] published by Captain John Smith*'. The table of contents contains the headings of fifteen chapters and adds the remark: '*The exposition of all most difficult words seldome used but amongst Sea-men: where you finde the word in the margine in that break against it; you shall find the exposition so plainly and briefly, that any willing capacity may easily understand them.*'

(4) *The Sea-Mans Grammar and Dictionary, Explaining all the difficult Terms in Navigation: And The Practical Navigator and Gunner: In Two Parts. Containing, I. Most plain and easie Directions, to Build, Rigg, Yard, and Mast any Ship whatsoever. With the manner of Working of a Ship in all Weathers:—And how to manage a Fight at Sea:—Also the Charge and Duty of every Officer in a Ship, and their Shares—And the use of the Petty Tally. (or Shooting in great Ordnance and Morter-Pieces:) Wherein the Principles of that Art are plainly Taught both by Arithmetical Calculation, and by Tables ready Calculated—With the Compositions for the making of several Fire-Works useful in War both at Sea and Land.—And an Appendix how by several Geometrical ways to take Heights, Depths, and Distances, Accessible or Inaccessible. By Captain John Smith, Sometimes Governour of Virginia, and Admiral of New England: Now much Amplified and Enlarged, with variety of Experiments, since his Time, made by several Experienced Navigators and Gunners. London; Printed, and are to be sold by Randal Taylor near Stationers Hall, MDCXCI.*
(BL 51.c.8. 4°.) The preface is signed 'B. N.' Other editions appeared in 1692, 1699, and 1705.

Apart from frequent, but nevertheless minor, changes in spelling, the tables of contents, that is, the headings of chapters, are identical, with the exception of chap. 14, in this, in the 1653, and in the earlier editions. It deals with '*The names of all sorts of great Ordnance*', and may have been omitted in the 1691 edition because this has a whole treatise on gunnery annexed to it (which will be ignored). This edition adds two alphabetical tables instead, 'Of the Names of all the Parts or Members of a Ship' and 'Explaining all the Principle Sea Terms used in Work of a Ship', bringing the number of chapters to sixteen. After the table of contents of the treatise on gunnery there follows a fold-out page printed in four columns, 'A Description of a Ship with all her Tackling', giving a numbered list of the technical terms of the rigging. Facing it is, on another fold-out page, an etching of a ship with the matching numbers attached to all the parts of its rigging.

Except for minor changes, for example of articles, the margin entries and the texts of all the editions mentioned are identical, even in the arrangement on the pages, which often varies only by one word or a few lines. The 1691 edition, however, has changes in the fonts.

'Although Captain Smith passed his adult life in the time of James I and

Charles I, he was truly an Elizabethan.' (Smith 1970, V.) This statement refers to his love of voyages and adventures which, prior to his famous stay in Virginia, took John Smith across western and eastern Europe to North Africa—everywhere engaged in wars and battles. After returning to England in 1604, he set out for Virginia in December 1606, acted as one of the founders of Jamestown, was elected president of the colony, and stayed there until October 1609. The famous Pocahontas story, whatever its truth, occurred about Christmas 1607. A second voyage to New England ended in disaster and he never set foot again in the New World (Gill 1968).

The most astonishing fact is perhaps that this man of the sword and the pistol could afterwards become a man of the pen. His descriptive reports on Virginia, New England, and the Summer Isles became the most important source of European knowledge of the life of the indigenous population and the immigrants in those English colonies. He drew the first map of that country, which was used by the early Pilgrim Fathers.

With all his travelling and fighting experience, John Smith was well equipped to write the first extensive book on sailors' language. The connection between seafaring and war was obviously natural at that time. His *Accidence*, later *Sea-Grammar*, became very popular and saw augmented editions in 1653, 1691, 1692, and 1699. For a fair historiographical judgement it is important to know how much John Smith relied on Henry Manwayring's book on sailors' language (see below). He obviously had access to its unprinted manuscript version (Smith 1970, XIII).

The various titles of the book were possibly taken from Gervase Markham, who published *A Souldiers Accidence, Or An Introduction Into Military Discipline* in 1625, and *The Souldiers Exercise: In Three Books*, containing, besides the *Accidence, The Souldiers Grammar* in 1635 (and 1639). An *accidence* is a primer, just as a *pathway* is, and a *grammar*, in this case understood metaphorically, is a body of more advanced rules of the art under description. The term *dictionary* is likely to be read as indicating the two alphabetical lists in the 1691 edition. Thus, the titles simply show the intentions of the author on two levels of proficiency of readers.

These envisaged readers are '*many young Gentlemen and Valiant spirits of all sorts, who do desire to trye their Fortunes at sea*' (1626, A2^r). It is the inexperienced young captain (1691, 59) or '*A young Gentleman that desires command at Sea*' (1691, 65). All of them could use the *Sea-Grammar* as a handbook or quasi-dictionary in order to achieve the same linguistic knowledge as experienced officers and sailors. Of course, the inexperienced sailor would not read a book like this but would gain his knowledge by practice. The author stresses *passim* that he is experienced with ships of all kinds and has seen many vessels and can judge their good and bad qualities.

Indeed, John Smith's book on navigation comes closer to the onomasiological principle and its various lexicographical techniques in word-lists than many others. It starts from a clearly demarcated domain of reality which has its own complicated order and, in the 1691 edition, is given pre-linguistically as a picture. In the fashion which would become world famous through Comenius' *Orbis pictus*,[25] the pre-linguistic pictures are connected with language by Arabic numbers which link the parts of the illustration with their names in an accompanying list. Moreover, in that same edition all the words explained in their proper nautical places are to be found in a sequence according to the alphabet, but only in A-order, in two appendices which makes it easy to spot each of them and to have it explained in its narrow semantic context. This device was later used, for example, in the alphabetical dictionary of William Lloyd which accompanies the '*Tables*' in Wilkins' *Essay*,[26] again in Comenius and, later, in *Roget's Thesaurus*, where it is to be found even today.

Moreover, the descriptions and deliberations are attached to a number of lexemes, which are given in the margins. The remark after the table of contents in the 1653 edition, even if dropped in the later one, points to the fact that the intention of the book is indeed word explanation and that the facts described and explained in the explanatory text are, in fact, word meanings. The entries in the margins thus serve as 'pathfinders' of headwords, half-way, as it were, between the text itself and the alphabetical word-list. They replace the headwords in the common onomasiological dictionaries. This is why they can be taken as starting-points, for example, for quantitative analyses. The 1691 edition stresses their intention by its print. The book, including the entries in the margins, is set in the usual Roman type, but the words in the text which correspond to the entries in the margins are in black letter and bold so that the eye, by lexeme-hopping, may glance over the text as if it were a dictionary arranged in the usual order of a list.

As a rule, one sentence is devoted to the explanation of one headword. These sentences are, of course, of various lengths and may be rather long and elaborate. Several headwords may also be clustered in one explanatory sentence, frequently by way of enumeration. Towards the end of the book, explanations tend to follow their own momentum more and to lose co-ordination with the entries in the margins. But, on average, the co-ordination of syntax and explanation, that is, of formal and semantic units, is quite obvious. Many sentences, but by no means all, start with the *determinandum* in the subject and add the *determinans* in the predicate. Naturally, this only applies where the word to be explained is a noun. These are the ones where the lexicographical character of the text is most obvious.

Note the following examples of these various observations (entries in the margins given first):

A dry-Dock. A **Dock** *is a great pit or pond, or Creek by a Harbour side, made convenient to work in, with two great flood gates built so strong and close, that the* **Dock** *may be dry till the ship be built or repaired, and then being opened, let in the water to float and lanch her, and this is called a* **dry-Dock**.

---

[25] See Chapter 10.   [26] See Chapter 8.

*A wet-Dock. A **wet-Dock** is any place where you may hale in a ship into the oze out of the tides way, where she may dock herself.* (1.)

*Sockets. Low Counter. Upper Counter. Brackets. **Sockets** are the holes wherein the Pintels of the Murderers of Fowlers go into. The hollow Arching betwixt the lower part of the Gallery and the Transome, is called the **lower Counter**; the **upper Counter** is from the Gallery to the Arch of the round House, and the **Brackets** are little carved Knees to support the Galleries.* (11.)

*A Bulk-head. A **Bulks-head** is like a seeling or a wall of boards thwart the Ship . . . .*

*The Stearage. Great Cabin. The **Stearage** room, is before the **great Cabin**, where he that steareth the Ship doth always stand, ...*

*The Tiller. Rudder. The **Tiller** is a strong piece of wood made fast to the **Rudder**, which is a great Timber somewhat like a Plank . . . .*

*The Bread-room. The **Bread-room** is commonly under the Gun-room, well dried or plated.* (11, 12.)

*A Ship overmasted. Taunt-masted. Under-masted. When a Ship is built, she should be masted, wherein is a great deal of experience to be used so well as art; for if you **Over maste** her, either in length or bigness, she will lie too much down by a wind, and labour too much a hull, and that is called a **Taunt-mast**, but if either too small or too short, she is **Under-masted** or low-masted, and cannot bear so great a sail as should give her true way.* (15.)

There are chapters where one headword after another is introduced in rapid sequence, with short explanatory sentences. Examples are chap. VI '*What doth belong to the Boats and Skiffe, with the definition of all those Thirteen Ropes which are only properly called ropes belonging to a Ship and the Boat, and their use*', and chap. VII '*The Names of all sorts of Anchors, Cables, and Sails; and how they bear their proportions, with their use: Also how the Ordnance should be placed, and the Goods stowed in a Ship*'. The two pages and seven lines of chap. VI contain as many as thirty-one entries in the margins with corresponding words in bold print, and the four and half pages of chap. VII as many as eighty-five. Note these examples:

*The Entering-rope. Bucket-rope. Bolt-ropes. Port-ropes. Jeare rope. The **Entering rope** is tyed by the Ships side, to hold by as you go up to the entering Ladder, cleats, or wailes. The **Bucket-rope** that is tied to the Bucket by which you hale and draw water up by the Ships side. The **Bolt-ropes** are those wherein the Sails are sowed. The **Port-ropes** hale up the Ports of the Ordnance. The **Jeare-rope** is a piece of Hawser made fast to the Main-yard.* (27.)

There are also chapters which deal with relatively few headwords explained in greater detail, which means with rather long descriptions and explanations sometimes extending over half a page or even more. Note, for example, the second part of chap. X, '*Proper terms for the Winds, Ebbs, and Eddies, with their definitions, and an estimate of the Depth of the Sea, by the Height of the Hills and the largeness of the Earth*', where there are only seven margin entries on seven pages. In this part, theories '*touching the reasons of Ebbs and Floods*' (48) are discussed, that is, ideas rather than named objects. Something similar happens in chap. XII, '*Considerations for a Sea Captain in the choice of his Ship, and in placing his Ordnance. In giving Chase, Boarding, and entering a Man of War like himself, or a defending Merchant-man*', which has only seven margin entries on almost five pages.

It is difficult to determine the exact number of words explained, even if a word-for-word count were to be made. The sixty-six pages of the 1691 edition of the book (seventy-six of the 1627 edition, not eighty-six as erroneously numbered) contain some 685 entries in the margins with corresponding explanations. About forty of these entries in the earlier edition, however, are not denotative. They indicate actions to be described and have no corresponding lexemes. Note, for example: '*How they diuide the company at sea, and set, and rule the watch*' (38). The denotational character of margin entries is underlined by the fact that this non-denotational one was changed into a subtitle of chap. IX in the 1691 edition. The same thing happened to the margin entry '*How to handle a ship in a storme*' (40). The deliberate lexicographical intentions of the editor of the later edition is demonstrated by the fact that he recognized the difference in functions of margin entries of his original and set them right. This, however, reduces the number of words explained, compared with the entries of the earlier edition. However, this number is boosted by some chapters, like, for example, chap. IV: '*The names of all the Masts, Tops, and Yards belonging to a Ship*', where we find not one entry in the margins but where the text is largely nothing but a wordlist. In this chapter there are twenty-eight lexemes which have no corresponding entries in the margins. A similar case is chap. XIV, '*The names of all sorts of great Ordnance*', which in the 1691 edition is dropped altogether (see above). Moreover, the explanations often use words which are not indicated in the margins, but which have nevertheless to be counted among the terms of the sea dictionary, even if they are not thoroughly technical. Again, the lexicographical precision of the later edition, in comparison to the earlier ones, is demonstrated by the fact that these words receive a sort of secondary highlighting by being italicized. Note, for example:

*The Gunner with his Mate, and quarter Gunners. The Master **Gunner** hath the charge of the Ordnance, and Shot, Powder, Match, Ladles, Sprunges, Worms, Cartrages, Armes and Fire-works . . . .* (34.)
*The Carpenter and his Mate. The **Carpenter** and his Mate, is to have the Nails, Clinches, Roove and Clinch nailes, Pikes, Splates, Rudder-Irons, Pump nails, and Leather, Sawes, files, Hatchets, and such like . . . .* (34/35.)
[Without entry in the margin.] *Compasses so many Pair and sorts as you will, an Astrolobe Quadrant, a Cross-staffe, a Back staffe, an Astrolobe, a Nocturnal.* (65.)

The mentioning of food to be taken on board provides some thirty lexemes without entries in the margins. Obviously, it is hard to decide whether they count among the explained words or are taken for granted.

In spite of such difficulties, it seems safe to say that the *Sea-Grammar* contains about 630 denotative entries in the margins with corresponding explanations in the text and that several hundred more words appear in these explanations so that the vocabulary presented onomasiologically exceeds 1,000 words. This means that the book counts among the most comprehensive presentations of the register of seafaring at its time.

The order in which the words are presented and explained is, first, determined by the ship itself as a complicated system of instrumental objects. Secondly, the author imposes his own order on the sequence of words and in so doing gives his book a semantic cohesion which connects word explanations with each other and likewise the chapters which contain these word explanations in their own order. As is to be expected, this semantic macrostructure is not perfectly homogeneous. Nevertheless, it is easily recognizable.

The first part of this macrostructure concerns the techniques of building a ship and preparing her for departure. It is strictly adhered to and clearly discernible in the sequence of chapters I to VIII and their titles. The second part, consisting of the remaining seven chapters, is less strictly organized. Its framework is a sea voyage.

After mentioning the place where a ship is built, the docks (chap. I), the text explains in great detail the timber work to be done, moving from the keel, the stern and the stern-post to all the parts of the hull and the planks including the orlop and the decks. This (chap. II) is the longest chapter with the largest number of lexemes explained. Technical details of carpentry, like 'culver-tailing', are mentioned. The reader is able to watch the carcass rise slowly in the dock with carlings, loopholes, and hatches, and with objects on deck like the capstan, pumps, and ladders. He is led through the ship's quarters, etc. After the body of the ship has been completed, the size of the masts and yards is determined in proportion to the size of the whole vessel (chap. III), then they are named (chap. IV), and, finally, the tackling and rigging are named and explained, too (chap. V). Many of the objects are not only given with their details, but are also explained in their various functions and the ways they are handled. The ship being completed, the accompanying boats and the ropes are given (chap. VI) and then the anchors, cables, and sails, including deliberations on where to place the guns and goods (chap. VII). At the end of this section, the tasks of the captain and every officer on board are defined (chap. VIII), which, as it were, makes the vessel ready to sail.

As compared to the matter-of-fact-definitions of the first part, the second adopts an almost narrative tone, at least intermittently. The very first sentence of chap. IX, for example, reads:

Steep-Tubs. It is to be supposed by this [i.e. the state arrived at in the preceding chapters] *the Ship is victualled and manned, the Voyage determined, the steep-Tubs in the Chains to shift their Beef, Pork, or Fish in salt water . . . ; Stearing. Cunning. but before we go any further, for the better understanding the rest, a few words for steering and cunning the Ship would not be amiss.* (37.)

This is done with reference to good and dangerously bad weather (chap. IX). Then a more abstract style is adopted (chap. X), with names for the winds and tides and with ideas on how the depth of the sea can be measured. This develops into a small treatise of its own with the Bible and classical as well as contemporary authorities being quoted. It is indicative of the attitude of the author that he depends on the *'Scriptures, the experience of Navigators, and reason in making estimation of the depth of the Sea'* (49), all three sources making him not only take into account the height of hills above the land but also the height of all the dry land above the sea. After this the good and bad conditions of ships are explored (chap. XI). As if all the deliberations necessary for a successful voyage were only now finished, the *'Considerations for a Sea Captain in the choice of his Ship'* are mentioned at last (chap. XII), together with the habits of pirates and the methods of fights at sea (chap. XIII). In the 1627 edition there then follow the names of all the guns, which are dropped in the 1691 edition, and, finally, in both editions there follow some details on the shares of officers on board, the instruments, the food.

The change in tone of this second part as compared to the first becomes obvious from the dramatic device of inserting direct speech and even dialogues, for example, in chap. IX, which in the reprint of the 1627 edition (Smith 1970) was italicized and even arranged as a conversation. Generally speaking, it is more personal and narrative, although the sequence of chapters lacks the strict development and chain of actions which distinguish the first. However, the general intention of conveying factual knowledge by explaining word meanings and of facilitating this with the help of some natural order is still adhered to, even if interrupted by such deliberations as the ones mentioned on measuring the depth of the sea.

The onomasiological principle of John Smith's book stands out, for example, against Henry Manwayring's alphabetical *Sea-Man's Dictionary* of 1667,[27] of the same period. The fact that Smith's book was reissued more than once indicates that it was popular, and remained in demand (Osselton 1999). In his preface *'Shewing the Scope and the vse of his Book'*, Manwayring addresses the same group of inexperienced people who want to learn the art of navigation and gunnery. Whereas John Smith did not explain his intentions and method in a general announcement, Manwayring does, and it goes without saying that he finds his method superior. He does not, however, make an explicit comparison. Apart from the alphabetical arrangement, his programme is identical to John Smith's. Note:

These Words, Termes, and Proper Names, which I set down in this Book, are belonging either to a Ship, to shew her parts, qualities, or some things necessary to the managing and sailing of her, or to the Art of Gunnerie (for so much as concerns the use of Ordnance at Sea,) and those which are familiar words, I set them down; if they have any use, or meaning about a Ship, other than the common sense: And in expounding them, I do shew what Use, Necessity, Commodity, discommodity, wherefore, and how things are done, which they import: And therewith the Proper Terms, and Phrases, with the different uses, in any kind appertaining to that word; which for better and easier finding out, and to avoid confusion, I have brought into an Alphabet. (Ae[r and v].)

---

[27] *The Sea-Man's Dictionary: Or, An Exposition and Demonstration of all the Parts and Things belonging to Ship. Together with An Explanation of all the Termes and Phrases used in the Pratique of Navigation. Composed by .... Printed by W. Godbid for G. Hurlock, and are to be sold at his Shop at St. Magnus Church corner in Thames street near London-Bridge. 1667.* (BL C 142.dd.33.) There was another edition in 1670 and a reprint in 1972.

With its 132 closely printed pages, Manwayring's book covers much more ground than Smith's and contains more vocabulary. His entries, which are almost always of article length, start with the lemma printed in italics, which is followed by exhaustive explanations. Within these, the lemma, when repeated, is always italicized.

Manwayring moves away from strict alphabetization by constructing *nests*; thus, synonyms, compounds, or other related words are mentioned together with one governing headword. So the entry '*Anchor*' mentions its different parts ('*The Ring, the Eye, the Head, the Nutt, the Beam or Arm, the Shank, the Flooke, to which belongs a stock by which it is made to take hold*'), as well as different kinds of anchors ('*kedge, stream anchor, first, second, or third anchor, sheet anchor*'). We find all of these terms also in the relevant chapter of Smith's book, in this case even in the same sequence. Thus, some of John Smith's chapters and some of Henry Manwayring's entry articles, particularly the long ones, do not actually differ too much from each other.

It is easy to imagine in which different contexts the various terms, which are explained in both books, appear. Manwayring goes out of his way to couch the terms and phrases in useful factual relations and natural situations of speech. For Smith it is much easier to do this simply by the arrangement of entries. We need not speculate which book was the more successful. Manwayring was convinced that he could make anybody '*a better Sea-man*' than those who had gone to sea '*two or three years together*' by reading the book '*over with him, and be content to look sometimes at a Model of a Ship*' (A2ᵛ), and this in six months.

6

John Withals' dictionary for young boys (1553)

6.1 The author

In the article signed by 'S. L.' in the *Dictionary of National Biography*, exactly one sentence is devoted to the author: 'Withals or Whithals, John (*fl.* 1556), probably a schoolmaster, was author of an English–Latin vocabulary for children.' The year given as 'fl.' is that of the second edition of his dictionary. The rest of the article deals with its history as a popular schoolbook. Some dates, obviously depending on Wheatley (1865), deviate from what it was possible (for me) to verify in the British Library. The summarizing sentence, 'Withals's *Short Dictionarie* became a standard school book' is nevertheless true.

Also having no information about the author but appreciating his work is DeWitt T. Starnes (1954, 167–8), who speaks of an 'obscure schoolmaster' whose dictionary was a 'most successful venture'.

6.2 The dictionary

Withals' dictionary was indeed a most successful book for almost eighty years (Watson 1968, 392–4; Green 1997, 92–4). This was the result of its own value for the purpose of teaching, but also of constant re-editing and augmentation. From this results a history of the book which is interesting and significant in itself.

6.2.1 Titles of the various editions

(1) *A shorte Dictionarie for yonge begynners. Gathered of good authours, specially of Columnel, Grapald, and Plini. Anno. M.D.LIII.*
The colophon reads: *Imprinted At London In Fletestrete. In the Hovse Of Thomas Bertheleth. Cum priuilegio ad imprimendum solum.*
(BL.106.d.21. 4°.)
    The title of the 1556 edition is identical; the colophon, however, reads: *Imprinted At London, By Iohn Kingstvn, For John Waley and Abraham Wele. 1556.*
(BL 131.ff.38. 4°.)
    The title of the 1568 edition is again identical, yet there is still another colophon: *Imprinted at London in Fletestreete by Henry Vvykes.*
(BL 142.bb.19. 4°.)
    According to the BL catalogue, there is another 1568 edition which, however, has no entry in the STCs and has no title page. From the text of the dedication to Edward Grindel, Bishop of London, it is to be inferred that this is the first revised edition by Lewis Evans.
(BL 1578/2750.)

(2) *A Shorte Dictionarie most profitable For Yong Beginners, The Seconde tyme corrected, and augmented, with diuerse Phrasys, & other thinges necessarie therevnto added: By Lewys Euans. London 1574.*
The colophon reads: *Thus endeth this Dictionarie, verie necessary for Children: Compiled first by J. Withals, and novv the seconde time corrected and set foorth by Leuis Euans.*
(BL C.131.ff.37. 4°.)
    The title of the 1581 edition is very similar, except for '*the thirde time corrected and augmented*'. The colophon is different, mentioning Thomas Purfoote as the printer.

(3) *A Shorte Dictionarie in Latine and English, verie profitable for yong beginners. Compiled At The First By Iohn Withals: afterwardes reuised and increased with Phrases and necessary additions by Lewis Evans. And nowe lastlie augmented with more than six hundred rhythmi- call verses, wherof many be prouerbial, some heretofore found in olde authours, and other- some neuer before this time seene or read in the Latine tongue, as hauing their originall grace in English, by Abraham Fleming. VVhat is added in this edition which none of the former at any time had, these markes* ¶*[aragraph] may sufficiently shewe. Printed at London by*

Thomas Purfoote, and are to be sold at his shop without Newgate, over against Saint Sepulchers Church. 1586.
(BL 106.d.10.4°.)
　　The title of the 1599 edition is similar.　(BL 131.ff.36.)

(4) *A Dictionarie In English And Latine for Children, and yong beginners: Compiled at first by Iohn Withals, (with the phrases, and Rythmicall, and prouerbiall verses &c. which haue ben added to the same, by Levvis Evans, and Abr. Fleming, successiuely.) And (newlie) now augmented, with great plenty of latine words, sentences, and phrases: with many propre Epigrams: Descriptions: Inscriptions: Histories: Poeticall fictions besides. Framed (all) to their yong vnderstandings which be learners in the Latin tongue, to leade them on to riper knowledge, with delight. By VVilliamn Clerk. Printed at London by Thomas Purfoot. Anno Dom. 1602.*
(BL 1568/3662. 4°.)

　　This edition is smaller in format than previous ones, but with 465 pages plus 'The Table' it is indeed much larger than the previous editions, even those which were 'enlarged' in comparison with the first. The 1608, 1616, and 1634 editions have very similar titles—*A Dictionarie in English and Latine, deuised for the capacity of Children, and yong Beginners*—and are the same in size.[1]

6.2.2 General

A shorte dictionarie for yonge begynners by John Withals, published in 1553 and reissued no less than sixteen times by 1634, is a bilingual dictionary with English–Latin entries.[2] The editions under examination can be grouped into four batches, a first (1553, 1556, 1568), a second (1568, 1574, 1581), a third (1586, 1599), and a fourth (1602 and later). The third batch brings some, the last a considerable increase in size.

　　In the first edition, each right-hand page is numbered, so that '87' actually numbers 174 quarto-pages. The 1586 edition is unnumbered, but has 232 pages. The 1602 edition is somewhat smaller in format and has 464 numbered pages. All editions have two English–Latin columns printed on each page.

　　According to its title and to its introductory text, John Withals' dictionary was planned as an aid to learning Latin. This makes the English–Latin sequence of the entries remarkable. The dictionary is to be used by beginners who as yet know no or only little Latin. Its teaching and learning concept must have been that Latin should be learnt via the familiar English. This is an idea not to be taken for granted at a time when Latin was supposed to be the only means of learning a language at all, including one's mother tongue.[3]

---

[1] For the two editors Lewis Evans and Abraham Fleming see Green 1997, 94.

[2] See Hüllen 1994*b*. The following observations are taken from notes copied from the first edition of 1553, from which all the quotations come. I follow the original exactly in spelling and punctuation, also where obvious misprints occur, but not in line arrangement.

[3] Earlier English–Latin (alphabetical) dictionaries are *Promptorium parvulorum* (1440, printed 1499) and *Catholicon Anglicum* (1483, not printed). See Stein 1985, 77.

In the 1586 edition, where the name of the dictionary is changed to '*in Latin and English*', the arrangement of entries is the same as in the previous and the following editions, whose titles revert to '*in English and Latin*' from 1602 onwards. The reversed sequence of languages in the title of the 1586 edition must be regarded either as an error, or perhaps as an advertising trick for those who preferred the old order.

The method of printing and arranging the entries is basically the same in all editions. From 1602 onwards, however, every entry opens with inverted commas, but does not close with them. Moreover, the entries collected under each headline are now followed by a section headed 'Vers.' (for *versus*?) which contains predominantly phrases, sometimes purely in Latin, sometimes purely in English, and sometimes translated in both directions, although such phrases are by no means absent from the previous entries.[4]

The 1553 edition has a table of headings arranged according to the alphabetical order at the beginning, and a list of adjectives, also according to the alphabetical order, at the end. Moreover, there is a list of numbers in their own order. The 1574 edition, however, has the table of contents in the topical order in which the vocabulary is arranged. Sections are grouped together in such a way that a higher ranking system of topics becomes visible (see below). Adjectives and numbers, this time including a list of figures, are arranged as previously. The 1586 edition has no table of headings at all. It has adjectives and numbers, including figures, as in previous editions, and in addition '*Certaine Phrases for Children to vse in familiar speeche*' in English and Latin. Note, for example:

I am punished for my folly, Pretium ob stultitiam fero.
I haue marred all, Perturbaui omnia.
From the beginning to the end, Ab ouo viq[ue] ad mala.
He is his secretary, Est illi ab aure.

Furthermore, there is a list of '*Illustres quaedam sententiae ex optimis autoribus selectae*', in Latin and without translations. From the 1602 edition onwards, we again find the table of headings in the order of their appearance, either at the beginning or at the end of the dictionary, and in the 1616 and 1634 editions an extensive appendix with adjectives, names of historical importance, epigrams, proverbs, all in alphabetical order, which however is frequently discontinued. There are also numbers. Entirely new in these editions is a '*Breuis et succincta verborum Nomenclatura*' with lists of the most important headwords according to some topical order, which, however, is not the order of the dictionary. As compared to the foregoing dictionary, this '*nomenclatura*' is almost totally stripped of all phrases and additional explanations and reduced to bare English and Latin lexemes in juxtaposition to each other.

Whereas in the early and in the augmented editions before the turn of the

---

[4] A possible explanation for the two types of entries would be mnemonic considerations: lexemes to be learned by heart versus phrases simply to be read. (G. Stein, personal communication.)

century Withals' dictionary was indeed a short one for beginners, it slowly grew into a full-sized and ambitious dictionary after 1600. This growth is, of course, reflected in the growing number of lexemes culled by the author and his later editors, although it is not so easy to say what these numbers exactly are. The article in the *DNB* gives an estimate of 6,000 words. We are not told how this number is arrived at, nor is a distinction made between words and entries. The remark that the total of 6,000 is 'a small number when compared with . . .' Palsgrave (1530: 19,000), Huloet (1552: 26,000), and Levins (1570: 9,000)[5] is beside the point, in that the intentions of the dictionaries compared are not taken into consideration. Obviously the author of the biographical article is inclined to think that a great number of lexemes makes *per se* a great dictionary.

If we assume an average of thirty entries per page, the first edition has some 5,220 entries *in toto*. However, some entries give more than one lexeme, either as *explanandum* or as *explanans*. We find, for example, '*A ryde, henge, or gimew of a dore or other, planula ferrea*',—three English lexemes explained by one Latin. On the other hand, we find '*A walkyng place, ambulacru[m], vel deambulatorium*', that is, two Latin lexemes, even if etymologically related to each other, explaining one English one. This means that the number of English and Latin lexemes is in fact much higher than the number of entries. Until we have an accurate word-for-word count which takes these intricacies into consideration, it seems justifiable to assume that the dictionary has some 8,000 to 9,000 lexemes as *explananda* and as *explanantia*. With the 1602 edition the adjective *short* is rightly dropped in the title, though, hardly rightly, the dictionary retains its restrictive purpose for children and beginners. If we assume an average of forty entries per page, this edition has some 18,400 entries *in toto*. The technique of giving several synonyms in one entry seems not to have been applied excessively here, so the estimated number of lexemes we have to add is, relative to the first edition, not so great.

6.2.3 Overview of the macrostructure

The following overview was copied from the 1574 edition, with the page numbers omitted.

The sky;[6] *Planetes, tymes, partes of the yeares and elementes with thappurtena[n]ces.*
The Ayer [no entry], *windes, partes of the worlde, Byrdes, Bees, and Flyes, with thappurtenances.*
The water, Sea, Fyshes, shippes, **Earth,** *and mettalles, with thappurtenaces.*
Serpentes, wormes, the Feilde, foure foted beastes, a parke, with thappurtenances,
The partes of a horse [no entry], *Hogges, Heardmen, Husbandman, Tylling of the lande, instruments of Husbandrye, the names of the corne, the Fielde, with that belongeth.*

    [5] John Palsgrave: *Lesclarcissement de la langue francoyse* (1530), Richard Huloet: *Abecedarium Anglico Latinum* (1552), Peter Levins: *Manipulus vocabulorum* (1570). See Stein 1985 for Huloet and Levins, and Stein 1997 for Palsgrave.
    [6] The highlighting is introduced by me (W. H.). It corresponds to the following overview.

*The Medow, Trees, Fruites, Vyneardes, wynes, Hearbs, Spices, **Myller**, Baker, and Brewer, with that belongeth.*

The Fisher, Fouler, Hunter, Vytaller, Smithe, and Carpenter, with that belongeth.

The Mason, other craftesmen, the Cloth maker of linnen, sylke, the Clothe maker of wolle, the weauer, Fuller, Dyer, colours of clothe, Shearemen, Draper, Taylor, Sempster, Gouldsmithe, Coyner, Broderer, and Coryer, with that belongeth.

*The shoemaker, Cobler, Botcher, Barber, water bearer, **Housinge** for Husbandmen, the stable with that peteyneth* [no entry], *a towne, Uillage, Deyrye house, Houses of office, a bake house, Brewe house, and Buttrye, with that belongeth.*

The pantrye, wyne celler, Ewry, Lardy house, Kechin, Banquet, Potage, Sauce, Meate, white meate, Officers, a haule, a bed chamber, a Bathe, with the appurtenances.

*A wardrope, apparayll, Clothing for women, a **Citie**, housing in towne, and the place where the lawe is ministred.*

*Places where Maisteryes, and playes be shewed, playce where Marquet is kepte, the stewes, places for Execution, and Correction, a ruler in the prouince, the Mayre of a towne, the Schole. Strife, and wrong, the **lawe**, with the ministers, the **Churche**, with the Ministers, and seruauntes.*

*Diuine seruice, Religion, Playing with Instrumentes, the instrumentes of Musicke, Minstrels, the names of **Kindreddes**, and of affinite.*

*The partes of the **Body**, and vncleanesse of the same, with the vncleannesse of the Soule, and of ages, &c.*

*O[f] sickenesses, **Battayle**, the instrumentes of Battalye, a Physicion, Potecary, and Chirurgian, with thappurtena[n]ces.*

*The fiue **wittes**, a Journey, together wyth adiectives, some belonging to the bodye, and some to the minde.*

It is not difficult to make the semantic order of this overview visible with an arrangement of descriptive terms:

[A world]	C3 city
A1 universe	[D society]
A2 elements	D1 law
[B three elements, nature]	D2 church
B1 air	D3 family
B2 water	[E life and death]
B3 earth	E1 human body
[C man]	E2 war
C1 crafts	E3 senses
C2 housing	

For a comment on this macrostructure see below.

6.2.4 Origin of vocabulary

No author of a dictionary works without taking notice of his predecessors. Almost by definition, every general dictionary must include the lexis of previous works and then add more lexis and/or give it a different profile by making it instrumental for certain purposes, for example teaching.

In the title of his dictionary, John Withals acknowledged his indebtedness to 'good authors', of which he gives Grapaldi,[7] Columella,[8] and Pliny (?23–79) by name. This is somewhat misleading, because Francesco Grapaldi in his *Lexicon de partibus aedium* (1494) exploited Columella and Pliny in his turn. So did Ambrosius Calepinus (1440–?1510), whose Latin dictionary (1502) was the best known source of Latin vocabulary at Withals' time and was almost certainly consulted by anybody who was writing a dictionary which included Latin. This must have been the case with Withals, although he does not mention him. Moreover, there are John Stanbridge's *Vocabula* (1496) and *Vulgaria* (1508) which, though never mentioned either, were certainly well known to the author of an introductory English–Latin dictionary of the middle of the sixteenth century, because they were so similar in their intentions—teaching Latin to English beginners—and in their method—the topical arrangement of entries. Stanbridge, too, made use of Pliny and Columella. In his in-depth study, Starnes (1954, 167–83) names a dozen lexicographers whom Withals probably exploited and proves this by quoting parallel entries (Stein 1985, 197–8). Among them are Sir Thomas Elyot, who is indeed mentioned in the '*Prologue*', and William Turner (d. 1568), author of an *Avium historia . . .* (1544) and a herbal with names in Greek, Latin, English, Dutch, and French (1548). Some of the entries, arranged in parallel by Starnes, are certainly striking, as, for example: Withals: '*The Chapiter of a piller, a little pilour, set upon a greater, Epistylium*'; Elyot/Cooper (see below): '*Epistylium, lii . . . the chapiter of a pyllour, or a littell pillour sette upon a greatter*'. Other parallel entries are less convincing even if almost identical, as for example: Withals: '*A head, caput tis*'; Stanbridge: '*Hic caput tis, the head*'. With or without Stanbridge, Withals could not have omitted the word (head) and he could have hardly given it a different gloss (*caput*).

Without going into more details of the provenance and sources of Withals' dictionary, it seems important to say that the 'obscure schoolmaster' obviously had a good knowledge of the pertinent Latin lexicography and took his entries from such famous authors as Grapaldi, Calepinus, Stanbridge, Elyot/Cooper (Stein 1985, 140–56), and others who provided him with the special vocabulary of zoology and botany, and that he must have been aware of a tradition of topically arranged words which he found in John of Garland's *Dictionarius* (1220) and Stanbridge's two books, but also in Iohannes Paludanus' *Dictionariolum Rerum Maxime Vulgarium, in Communem Puerorum Usum . . .* (1549) for Latin, Flemish,

---

[7] Francesco Mario Grapaldi (1465–1515), famous for his book *De partibus aedium* (1494), in which he describes the rooms of a house, but also many objects in this house, human behaviour and other items in loose connections with the rooms, like, for example, animals. A precise comparison between the vocabulary of this book, to whose later editions an alphabetical dictionary was appended, and the word-entries in Withals would certainly be worth while. See Green 1997, 53.

[8] Lucius Junius Moderatus Columella (first century AD) wrote *De agricultura* (60 AD).

and French (Starnes and Noyes 1946, 203) and possibly in other such vocabularies which have not come down to us. After all, this tradition was old and to be found in many places in Europe and must have been a matter of general information for those who were interested in teaching. Grapaldi also belongs to it, although Withals did not follow his very special method of grouping words according to the objects which can be found in rooms, stimulated by the mnemotechnic devices of the *ars memorativa*. That Withals has sections with names for such objects in rooms may be explained by similar word groups in the topical vocabularies of Garland, Stanbridge, and others.[9]

6.3 'The Prologve' and 'The Preface'

In his 'Chronological notices of the dictionaries of the English language', Henry B. Wheatley (1865, 220) remarks: 'This work is more a vocabulary than a dictionary, as the words are not in alphabet, but are classified and thrown under various heads, by which means we gain a curious insight into the manners of the times'. Besides some remarks on various editions and on the popularity of the book, which seem to have been the basis for the article on Withals in the *DNB*, he gives examples of the various heads and a long quotation from the 'Prologve', obviously however without noticing that both features of the book give it its special property as a schoolbook.

In the 1553, 1556, and 1568 editions 'The Prologve' is addressed '*To the ryght worshipful syr Thomas Chaloner knight, and clerke of the kynges maiesties priuie counsaile*'. Besides the usual expressions of devotion, it mentions that the addressee had helped Sir Thomas Elyot (1490?–1546), the first known author of a Latin–English dictionary (1538, Stein 1985, 140–56) to finish his work. This indicates that John Withals sees himself in the context of the dictionary making of his time, whether semasiological or onomasiological.

For the greater part, the text contains ideas about the value of knowledge, as testified by the ancients, and the duty of individuals to serve their country, which the author is willing to do with his book. There then follows a passage in which he explains the intentions of the topical arrangement of his dictionary:

These thynges considered, I haue resorted to the most famous and ancient authours, out of the whiche as out of cleare fountaines I haue drawen as diligently as I coulde, the propre names of thynges conteyned vnder one kynde, and disposed them in such ordre, that every childe beying able to reade, may with little labour perfitely imprinte them in memory: whiche shall not be only profitable for them nowe in theyr tendre age, but hereafter when they shalbe of more iudgement and yeres, it shalbe vnto them a singular treasure: for the lacke whereof they shalbe compelled, as I hauve herde many profounde clerkes both in disputacion as also in familiar

---

[9] For the sources of extensions and augmentations in the later editions, in particular after 1600, see Starnes 1954, 176–83.

communicacion to vse in the stede of the proper and naturall woorde, a paraphrase or circum-
locucion.   (Aii$^{r \text{ and } v}$.)

This is one of the rare occasions in which an author of a sixteenth-century dictionary does not take the topical arrangement for granted as profitable for learning,
but stresses it and gives reasons for using it. This may be because he wants to mark
his dictionary as something special, for example in comparison to the dictionary
of the previously mentioned Sir Thomas Elyot, or because he follows his own
method of foreign-language teaching and is in need of justification. The central
idea is obviously that the words should be arranged in the dictionary in the very
same order—semantic proximity—in which the things, denoted by these words,
are experienced in reality. In the light of the onomasiological tradition, this preface shows that it is a gross misunderstanding to regard Withals' dictionary as 'a
case for considering such an arrangement as downright destructive of intellectual
gain' and to ask: 'why break up a topic into such tiny morsels, spread nilly-willy
(other than alphabetical) through a fat volume?' (Green 1997, 57). There were
good reasons for doing this.[10]

The 1574 edition has a short '*Epistle*' to the '*Earle of Leycester*', which contains
no remarks on the arrangement of the dictionary. Neither do the following
editions, till the new editor, William Clerk, exchanges the '*Epistle*' for '*The Preface
to this last Edition*' in 1602, which also appears in the subsequent editions of 1608,
1616, and 1634. In this '*Preface*', the topical arrangement is again, and even more
clearly, debated and expressly juxtaposed to the alphabetical:

And though it [= the dictionary] leadeth not, as do the rest, by way of *Alphabet*, yet hath
it *order*, and *method* both, and the fittest *order*, and the fittest method for yong beginners:
for Example, he that would find the *Sunne*, the *Moone*, the *Starres*, or any such other such
excellent creatures aboue, he may looke for the *Skie*: that is more readie here, for his capac-
itie, and that is their place, and there they be readie for him in *English*, and *Latin* both: or
so many of the[m] at the least, and more, than be commonlie talked of. Aghaine, *it is night,*
it is day, it is light, it is darke, it is cleare, it is clowdie, &c. these do pertaine to the *Skie*, and
there is the English and Latin of them, and other such speeches: and not for them alone,
and such as those alone, but some other *sentences, prouerbs*, and *sayengs* of the Skie besides:
as, *if the Skie falleth: the Starres haue their vertue*: and the like. And he that would haue a
forke, or a *rake*, or a *rack*, or a *maunger*, or any thing else within, or without, may looke in
their places of *Husbandrie*, and *Huswiferie*, these haue their titles in this worke with their
appurtanances. The like of Birds, and Beasts, &c. Of these, their sayings more, or lesse,
some graue, some light, some ciuil, some vplandish, some homelie, none vnseemelie, all
familiar, and profitable in their vse.   (Aiv$^{r \text{ and } v}$.)[11]

---

[10]   Besides, the volume was far from being fat and many sections of entries were no 'tiny morsels'.
The author, who thinks that alphabetization is the only measure of progress in lexicography, does not
explain why, in his opinion, 'there would be distinct disappointment following the appearance' of
Withals' dictionary because of its non-alphabetical arrangement and yet it had tremendous success as
'the best-selling dictionary of the century' (Green 1997, 92).

[11]   Italicization in this quotation follows the original closely to make the passage intelligible in its
references to reality, but also to the entries and the sections of entries in the dictionary.

6.4 The microstructure

The syntactic microstructure applies to the single entry. Typically, it consists of an English lemma, which may be taken from any word-class. However, as with all dictionaries of this kind, the vast majority of entries are nouns. There then follow adjectives which, in the case of this dictionary, have their own alphabetical list at the end, but also occur in the preceding chapters. Verbs are relatively rare, although not altogether absent. The increase in the size of the dictionary in the later editions is mainly due to entries of verbs and verb phrases (see below). After a colon, the English lemma is complemented by one or several Latin lemma(ta). The English lemma is printed in black letter and bold, the Latin equivalent in Roman type. In most cases, the lines that follow but belong to the English lemma as the headword of the entry are indented. But there are also entries where each line starts at the left-hand margin. English nouns are always accompanied by a definite or indefinite article. Latin nouns are given in the nominative plus the genitive ending, Latin adjectives in the masculine plus the feminine and neuter endings. Latin verbs appear either in third person singular present, or in the first and second person present plus first person perfect and past participle. This, of course, provides the users of the dictionary with the information that would be essential for the grammatical part of the lessons. Lemmata and their translations can either be simple (one word) or complex (a phrase). Sometimes a lemma is complemented by several Latin lexemes, which are either synonyms or homophones. Sometimes a Latin or English and Latin explanation is added, which can also point to homonyms. Thus, the following entries are typical:[12]

A body, corpus, oris.
The formost part of the head, sinciput, pitis.
The whole busshe of the heare, coma, mae, caesaries, ei.
Blacke beard, niger, gra, gru[m].
A countinaunce, vultus, tus. Phisonomia, dicitur facieci & corporis forma.
Fro[m] the shoulder to the elbow, lacertus, ti. Sed lacertus is also a lisarde.

Sometimes an entry starts with a Latin lemma which, however, continues the translation or explanation of the previous entry. In this case, it is usually not indented, but it is not printed in black letter either. That is, it is half-way between a new headword and the continuation of the previous entry. Note:

A nose, nasus, si.
Nasutus, ta, tum, longe nosed. Aliquando reprehensores & derisores, significat.

The sequence English–Latin was certainly meant to be advantageous for the beginning learner of Latin, but the dictionary is obviously conceived from the

---

[12] Examples are taken from the subchapter, 'The partes of the body', 71–3.

point of view of the Latin language and its lexicalizations. Whereas the English headwords are very often phrases of sometimes considerable length, the Latin translations are usually monolexemic as, for example, in:

the space betwene the browes, intercillium, lij.
The ioygnyng of the necke to the body, iugulum, li.

In these cases, the linguistic starting-point for the entry is certainly the Latin lexeme, not its English equivalent, although this precedes the other one in print.[13] This corroborates Starnes and Noyes' (1946, 203) observation that Withals borrowed numerous entries from Elyot and simply reversed their order.

There are also purely Latin entries. Perhaps John Withals did not know the matching English word, perhaps there were pedagogic reasons for omitting the English version, because, after all, Withals compiled a dictionary for children, that is, for small boys, to be used in schools. Note the two successive entries:

The pricke, virga, virilis i. membra genitale.
Preputium, est pellicula, in summitate penis, que glandem tegit.

Sometimes, no reason can be found for why the sequence of languages is reversed. The chapter on religious virtues, for example, consists of thirteen entries, of which eight (*Fides, Spes, Charitas, Iusticia, Prudentia, Fortitudo* (twice), *Temperantia*) are English translations of Latin headwords, and five (*Obedience, Loue ordinate, Deuocion, Pitee, Peace*) are Latin translations of English headwords. Note also the following examples, of which the first one is, on the basis of the way it is printed, to be taken as one entry:

A bell, campana, nae, vel campanula, lae. [new line, but not indented:] *Tintino, is, iui, vel tintino, nas, to rynge.*
The claper of a bell, malletus campanarius.
Pulso, sas, to ringe or knocke. Vnde pulsator, toris.

Perhaps the systematicity of the sequence of the two languages is less regular than one would expect and like to have it.

The various editions differ considerably in their entries. Note, for example, the very first entry, '*The skie*':

1553: *The skie, hic ether, ris. Sed ether quandoque elementum ignis, quandoque aerem significat.*
1574: *The skye, aether, ethera.*
1586: *The skie, aether, aethera.*
1602: *The Skie, skies, firmament, element, Heauen, heauens, of ye same signification, Aether, tis, rem, vel ra, in accus. sine plural. m. g. Coelum, li, n. g. Coeli, lorum, plural. m. g. Astra, n. g. plural. of Aster vel Astrum, tri, n. g. Polus, li, Olimpus, pi, m. g. Aether, et Astra, Polus, Coelum dicatur Olimpus.*

---

[13] The relation between the English and the Latin lexemes in entries changes in the subsequent editions. This fact deserves a special investigation.

6.5 The macrostructure

6.5.1 General

The macrostructure applies to the dictionary as a whole; more precisely, to the sequence of its sections. It is for an onomasiological dictionary what the alphabet is for the semasiological. It is the search programme by which dictionary users arrive at the entry they want to learn something about. In contrast to the alphabet, which works by virtue of its own formal system and is itself meaningless, the macrostructure (what could be called the *onomasiological alphabet*) has to be conceptually understood, because it has a meaning in itself which alone provides the search programme for the use of the dictionary. This is why the compiler of an onomasiological dictionary must make its semantic macrostructure intelligible. The compiler must assume that a number of ideas common to (most) users of the dictionary guarantee its usability. Being *common* means these ideas are supposed to be *natural*. If there is no such self-explanatory cognitive commonality, dictionary compilers will try to convince their readers that their ideas are indeed the correct and natural ones.

Historiographers who analyse dictionaries read and understand their semantic macrostructures as the master-plan according to which the dictionary author compiled his work. Its most informative signal is the arrangement, that is, the sequencing, of entries and groups (sections) of entries. This sequencing is, as it were, the surface appearance of the ideas which guided the author in his work and about which he assumed either that he shares them with the dictionary users or that he can convincingly show their correctness. The latter applies to authors who justify the order of their dictionary analytically, for example, in introductory remarks to its sections. This is the case with Adrianus Junius.[14] There may also have been ideas at work of which the compiler himself was not conscious. In such cases, historiographers who uncover such ideas through analysis understand more of his work than the author himself did. As a rule, they understand it as a product of its time, coloured by the *Zeitgeist* as every historical artefact is.

In spite of minor changes and a considerable increase in size, the semantic macrostructure of the dictionary, as recognizable in the 148 titled sections of the first edition, continued to be the same during all the editions in the following years under examination. This is why this semantic macrostructure can in fact be considered in its first version only. The overview of the 1576 edition, although not exactly repeating the headings, mirrors this macrostructure almost perfectly. There are only a few cases where the grouping can be amended.

First of all, the sections and corresponding word-groups show a movement *from above to below*, that is, from the sky to the earth and what is below it, and also

---

[14] See Chapter 9, 353–60.

a movement *from outside to inside*, that is, from the world of observable objects and facts to the human organism. This need not be interpreted as having theological significance. On the contrary, there is a conspicuous absence of theological and ecclesiastical terms in Withals' dictionary, in particular there is no mention of God at the beginning—as is the case in so many other dictionaries of this type. Hell, however, is mentioned in connection with '*The Earth*', in the 1556 edition as a separate section entirely in Latin, in later editions as part of '*The Earth, and that belongeth to it*'. The entries pertaining to '*Hell*' are of a decidedly classical character, except perhaps for the entry '*The Diuell, Diabolus, Satan, vel Satanas, daemon*' (1602, 51). Here, as also at the beginning with its names for the universe, the zodiac, and the planets, the dictionary shows that it was meant to serve the learning of classical Latin and that its entries were '*[g]athered of good authours*'.

The beginning of the dictionary, then, pertains to the cosmos at large and to its two essential categories, space (stars), and time (year, month, and day). There then follow the four elements, providing another classical scheme of order, which will be the structuring principle for all the succeeding sections on nature. They centre around 'air' (winds, birds, insects), 'water' (sea, fishes, ships), and 'earth' (metals, creeping animals, four-footed animals, cultivation of landscape, agriculture) and obviously reserve 'fire' for man, but without indicating this by an entry.

The world of man is broken down into arts and crafts, houses and life therein, and cities—domains which show individuals in relation to objects which they manufacture and use for their well-being. There then follow societal aspects with reference to the law, the Church including music, and the family. The last topic is the human body as the seat of life, endangered by death, and of the senses.

Apart from the four great domains of reality, the sequence of topics shows that there are still other categories of order at work. These include the kingdoms of nature (the inanimate, organic, animate, and human kingdom), and the difference between the natural which is given and the artificial which is man-made.

The grouping of sections in the 1574 edition does not always follow these divisions in all strictness. But sometimes its very deviations from them are in themselves telling. Moreover, clever relational links and associations between the domains and subdomains create the impression of continuity. For example, the sections centred around the element 'earth' group together, first, inanimate nature, then animate nature outside agriculture, then the same as it relates to the central activities of agriculture, namely, herding animals, tilling the soil, growing corn, and finally animate nature in relation to the more refined branches of agriculture such as, for example, wine growing and the cultivation of herbs. This provides an excellent point of departure for the world of human activities with their related crafts, namely those providing food, those manufacturing objects out of wood, iron, stone, and those that manufacture clothes plus their paraphernalia. So the reality of 'earth' with everything belonging to it is linked to rather than separated from the world of man with its crafts. (Here, admittedly, the caesura between '*smith*' and '*carpenter*' in one word-group and '*mason*' and others in another does not make sense.) The same happens with crafts and craftsmen and the houses in a city in which they work, and moreover with public functions in a town and the houses in which they are performed. These are set apart from the individual house with its rooms in terms of how they serve the most essential needs of men, namely eating and sleeping. A very similar link is established between divine service and music, even such music as is not performed in churches.

A reading of the semantic macrostructure of any dictionary, as has been practised here with reference to Withals' work, depends on the assumption that onomasiological word-lists, unlike alphabetical ones, present themselves as texts with an all-embracing communicative intention. If readers concatenate the entries, they will discover this intention via the coherence that binds individual entries together in their minds.

In the case of Withals, this intention was certainly to give an overview of the world as he saw it and thought it fit for learning Latin as a foreign language. The world-view that becomes apparent is determined by his experience of the objective world and by the author's own life within society, but it is also determined by his knowledge of those ordering schemata which have a philosophical basis, although they were probably current as folklore. In spite of the many traces of scientific thinking which we find, a dictionary must not be taken as a philosophical treatise. At least, this seems obvious for Withals' work.[15] His dictionary presents knowledge in the way in which a teacher would present knowledge to a class of boys. The didactic particularity is that he judges this arrangement of words to facilitate the learning and presumably also the teaching process. This comes close to a psycholinguistic idea: the words of a language must be ordered in the minds of learners in the same way in which reality is (supposed to be) ordered. This concept of learning a language via the learning of reality, that is, learning words as names for things and not just as words, is generally credited to Comenius and his successors.[16] Withals' dictionary and other earlier topical glossaries and dictionaries suggest that the idea is in fact much older, although it received its philosophical and didactic underpinning only from the Bohemian educator.

6.5.2 The nomenclator in the edition of 1616

The '*Nomenclator*' of the 1616 edition has the following headings:

Celestials—De caelo—Nomina Dearum—Nomina Deorum—De Homine—De membris humanis—De Militia—De Civitatibus—De Ventis—De Navigatione—De Piscibus—De Agricultura—De Arboribus—De Oleribus—De Avibus—De Bestijs—De Aedibus—De Magistraibus[!]—De Medicina—De Carne—De Potionibus—De Habitatione—De Supellectile—De Artificibus—De Aureis—De Argenteis—De Aereis—De Pellibus—De

---

[15] See, however, the analysis of Wilkins' '*Tables*', in Chapter 8.
[16] See Chapter 10.

Diuitijs—De Temporibus—De Diebus festis—De Spectaculis—De Bellarijs—De Moribus—
De Institutione Artis Grammatice—De Serpentibus.

The question arises of why the editor of the 1616 edition and subsequent editions added a '*Nomenclator*' with a different ordering of vocabulary. The term had come into being on the Continent for onomasiological dictionaries which were compiled not as schoolbooks but for general rhetorical education. They mirrored the new Humanistic culture of the sixteenth and seventeenth centuries and often arranged old and new languages side by side. One of the most popular was, for example, the *Nomenclator* of Adrianus Junius.[17]

The '*Breuis et succincta verborum Nomenclatura*' could have been modelled on these nomenclators and, if this is true, could have been an attempt at updating Withals' dictionary, which was now half a century old. Indicative of this is the sequence of the initial chapters, starting with the sky, followed in classical fashion by the names of the Gods, and then by '*De homine*' and '*De membris humanis*'. The human organism was placed in last position by Withals, but it is now placed almost in initial position, preceded only by the universe and the gods. Moreover, outstanding human activities, namely '*De studijs*' and '*De Ludo Literarum*' with entries which breathe the Humanist spirit, follow, together with warfare, life in a city, and navigation. (The section on the winds is a preparation for '*De Navigatione*'.) Only then comes the world of nature with fish, agriculture, trees, herbs, beasts, which preceded the world of man in Withals' arrangement. Here they could be understood as standing under the dominion of man, because the nomenclator goes back to typically man-related domains like medicine, eating, housing, working, clothing. Admittedly, the order of the domains and of the corresponding word-groups in this nomenclator becomes confused towards the end, in particular when the last chapter but one deals with '*De instructione Artis Grammaticae*', which makes sense in a schoolbook, and the last chapter itself with '*De Serpentibus*', which can only mean that these animals were forgotten at their proper place. But it is undeniable that this added nomenclator shows a world different from that of the dictionary itself and that it is almost totally the world of human beings, their achievements, and their activities. Thus the permanent criticism, which was later raised against topical dictionaries, namely that in comparison to alphabetical ones they do not have a reliable, but only a time-dependent order of entries, becomes visible here, because the editor finds it necessary to correct the semantic macrostructure of the work which he has edited himself. The book, as it were, overtakes itself in the course of its succeeding editions.

6.6 The structure of selected sections and topics

The following analyses are meant to be exemplary. They illustrate which insights can be gained by deconstructing the series of entries on the mesolevel. The lead-

[17] See Chapter 9, 353–60. The *OED* lists as a first source for the lemma in the present meaning: '1585. Higins (title), The Nomenclator or Remembrancer of Adrianus Junius, Physician.'

ing questions of the investigations chosen are: (1) How did (and does) the arrangement of entries help the dictionary user to find a certain lexeme? (2) How can we interpret the position of a section relative to other sections and its own structure as an indicator of the author's intentions? (3) How does the expansion and augmentation of the various editions of the dictionary show in one special section? (4) Which insights into cultural history of a kind which is still interesting today can we gain from a question which cuts across (almost) all sections of the dictionary? Of course, many other such questions could be raised and reflected on.

6.6.1 Houses

The sections of the dictionary which are marked by a special heading, in English and Latin, in upper case letters, bold print, and the usual spatial arrangement constitute a level between the microlevel—individual entries—and the macrolevel—the dictionary as a whole—and can be called appropriately the *mesolevel*. Whereas the macrostructure of the dictionary constitutes its semantic unity, the mesolevel constitutes its pragmatic one.

The sections of onomasiological dictionaries have their own pragmatic order, which is almost never indicated in print or by similar means but emerges after an attentive and close reading from the sequence of entries. This order depends on the domain of reality which the lemmata of a section denote. This means that each section has its own order. There may be similarities between these topic-dependent orders, like the movement from the general to the specific or from the outside to the inside, or, whenever a time-related process is implied, from its natural beginning to its natural end. But beyond such very abstract similarities the order of chapters varies according to the nature of the topic.

For using the dictionary, the macrostructure indicates the path which the users have to follow in order to find the section in which the lexeme they are looking for may be found. Then the *structure* of the section between the macro- and the microstructure has the same function on the middle level in that it directs the dictionary user to the place of the lexeme itself. The microstructure, finally, marks the syntactical way in which the information sought is given. This actually means that the mesostructure—the section of the dictionary—is the prototypical unit to work with, after the macrostructure has provided some general guidance.[18]

An illustration of this can be found in the section, '*The partes of housynge with*

---

[18] It seems unreasonable to give this middle structural level a term which is compounded and, thus, marked and which is in its meaning deictically dependent on the names of the two levels between which it is sandwiched. This is why I use an unmarked term, and speak of the *structure* of a section, as distinguished from the *macrostructure* of a dictionary, that is, the totality of its chapters, and of the *microstructure* of the entries. For the analogy of macrostructure, structure, and microstructure to the semantic, pragmatic, and syntactic structure of a text, see Chapter 1, 22–7.

that belongeth. Partes aedium, cum appendicibus'. We assume that somebody is looking for the entry '*A tyle, tegula, lae.*'

The general overview will lead the dictionary user quickly to domain C2 *Housing* (see section 6.2.3), located between '*Crafts*' and '*City*'. Admittedly, there are several chapters here which might contain the entry, and to them also belong some in the domain '*City*'. It is a matter of experience in using the book how quickly the right chapter is found whose title clearly indicates that parts of houses are listed here, and this is what the dictionary user is looking for.

Ninety-six entries await inspection.

A first cluster of six entries gives general words for building (the activity and the results) and builders, for example '*Building, aedificium, vel structura.—Architectura, edificandi scientia'.* There then follow another ten entries giving names for the foundations including the special points where posts have to be erected, namely the corners and entries. Examples are: '*A flore or foundacion whervpon buildyng is set, fundamen, fundamentum, vel solidamentum—A base, a prop, a shore or pile, to vnderset with, sublucum vel spira'.* This cluster stimulates the idea that the entries may be ordered in the way in which a house is built. Indeed, the next group, consisting of fourteen entries, provides names for the walls and materials out of which they are built (six entries) and for doors in them (eight entries). There are some lemmata with wider but related meanings, like, for example, '*The walles about a towne or citee, murus, ri, & moenia, nium, in plu.—He that kepeth the dore, hostiarius, rij'.* But such extensions are not extraordinary. The following entry, '*The inner parte of a house, penetrale'*, suggests that the order of lexemes can also be guided by the opposition outside/inside which may follow the way in which a house is built, but which may also be an order in its own right. This is a cluster of ten entries which gives names for parts of doors and windows as seen from the inside, for example: '*The hookes, that the dore or window hangeth vpon, cardo, dinis.—The barre of a dore, pessulus etiam dicitur'.*

As tacitly assumed, the lexemes read so far pertain to buildings which are lived in in an ordinary way of accommodation. The next cluster of fifteen entries, however, obviously pertains to a church or perhaps a monastery building. In this respect the replacement of this cluster here is odd with respect to the preceding and also to the following entries. They continue to give the names of the inner parts of an ordinary house, thirteen in all, which mainly comprise stairs with ropes, a gallery, and '*A walkyng place, ambulacru[m], vel deambulatorium'.* If we follow this system, this walking place must have been on top of the stairs or right under the roof (where indeed it is found as '*gallery'* in the old houses still extant).[19] The next cluster of twenty entries pertains to this, including the gables as seen from the inside. It is here that the entry '*A tyle, tegula, lae'* appears in its natural slot, but also more entries with similar meanings. Note:

---

[19] This observation makes me think that Withals has an English house in mind and not a Roman one.

A holow tile, imbricium, & in plu. imbrices, quales habe[n]t in italia. Et regulae collicie, per quas aqua in aliquod vs defluere potest.
Imbrices, tiles laide ouerthwart betwene other tiles, Tego, gis, xictum, to couer,
Pauyng tile, asarotum, ti.
A shyngle, scandula, lae. Alij scindulam vocant, Scandulo, las, to shyngle.

This means our dictionary users can not only inform themselves about the Latin equivalent of one English lexeme, they can also do this with reference to a small field of semantically related lexemes, and they can even add encyclopaedic matter-of-fact knowledge to their linguistic information.[20]

The chapter ends with a cluster of five entries on the decay and repairing of houses. As an afterthought they suggest that the sequence of activities in building a house was indeed the most powerful guiding idea for the arrangement of the whole chapter. Three more entries are odd.

'*The partes of housynge with that belongeth*' is a typical example. It shows the effect of a topic-dependent order. This is cleverly chosen in so far as it combines the building of a house with the way anybody would have to go when inspecting it. It also shows the deviations from such natural sequences that always occur. The reader with historiographic hindsight may gain some knowledge about the practice of house building and the interior of a house at the time when the dictionary was written.

6.6.2 The human body

Vocabulary for the anatomy and the organs of the human body appears in almost all onomasiological word-lists and dictionaries. There is hardly one without it. In the observation of reality, which was the basis of vocabulary collecting, the human body was obviously so central that no word-list or dictionary would do without the relevant words, irrespective of the special intentions which these word-lists and dictionaries would follow.

A close analysis of the pertinent entries provides another example of how to understand the overall design of an onomasiological dictionary and its dependency on the knowledge of the time. A series of guiding questions may be raised:

(1) How great is the number of lexemes denoting parts of the human body, absolutely and in relation to the overall number of lexemes in the source? This can help us to understand the nature and the quality of medical knowledge and the importance it was given in the context of a comprehensive word-list.

(2) In which order do the lexemes denoting parts of the human body occur? This can help us to understand the underlying folkloristic and/or scientific concept.

---

[20] We may assume that the eyes of our imagined dictionary users travelled quickly over the entries as soon as they found that their sequence followed the natural order from the ground floor to the roof, that is, as soon as they adopted the visitor's perspective.

(3) In which position is the word-group denoting the parts of the human body located compared to other word-groups of similar importance and semantic coherence? This position should be defined in relation to the whole dictionary and in relation to immediately preceding and succeeding word-groups. This can help us to understand the place that man is allocated in the world which the author of the dictionary has in mind. This can also help us to understand the intention(s) which the author followed in culling and compiling his entries. Comparable word-groups are names of animals and plants, of arts and crafts, and others.

Of course, not every source answers all these questions in a satisfying way.

The section '*The partes of the body*' is placed at the end of the general overview from above to below and, thus, marked negatively. It numbers some 210 lexemes on three pages, equivalent to 1.7 per cent of the whole dictionary. With a total of 148 chapters this is at least a medium degree of elaborateness. The direct vicinity of chapters on 'family' (preceding) and 'sickness, war' (succeeding) shows, however, that the anatomy of the human body is not awarded an importance of its own as it would be in, for example, an anatomical approach. It is one section of several sections on life and death.

Within the section on the parts of the human body two distinct principles of succession are to be found, which, however, are not always strictly adhered to. A higher level (of the section, not of the dictionary) is arranged according to conceptual medical criteria, a lower level according to observable anatomical criteria. The former are scientific (in a modern sense) because they show an understanding of the whole body as a unity, the latter are experiential. This does not, however, mean that only visible or palpable parts of the body were named.

Both principles are shown at work in the following overview. Descriptive terms (underlined) have been added. Digits in brackets give the number of entries under one general term, but also within a clearly delimited group. This shows how little or how much detail the relevant entries contain.

<u>Body</u> (1)
body
<u>Head</u> (68)
upper part including hair (24), forehead, eyes (11), ear (4), face (14), mouth including its interior, speech (15)
<u>Throat, neck</u> (9)
throat, neck (9)
<u>Shoulders to fingers</u> (31)
shoulder (3), armpit to hand (13), fingers (15)
<u>Trunk</u> (64)
breast, back (10), organs, materials (24), navel, lower part of belly (14), leg to feet (16)
<u>Interior parts</u> (15)

bones (5), various (10)
Form (of body) (2)
misshapen, form (2)

From the arrangement of entries we receive clues as to the author's anatomical theory of the human organism. There is only the one lemma 'body' as a holistic term. There then follow the names of the parts of the head. All relevant word-lists start with them and then proceed from head to foot. So does Withals' list. Starting from the shoulders, the arms, hands, and fingers are named, then returning to the shoulders the list continues from there down the trunk. Other lists do this differently, for example proceeding from the head to the base of the trunk and then naming the parts of the arms and legs.[21] There is also a medical concept revealed by the fact that the organs of the breast and the pelvis are named by several series of words and are included in the treatment of the middle and lower part of the trunk, even if the sequence of lemmata within these series is not particularly convincing. On the one hand, this technique stresses the difference between outside and inside, on the other it keeps to the natural sequence from the upper to the lower part of the trunk. At the end we find words on a more abstract level. They give the names for blood, bones, joints, etc. and reveal the beginnings of a more scientific nomenclature. However, the order of lexemes is almost arbitrary here and their number small. We must also remember that, besides the section on the human body, there is another one with words for the five senses.

The way in which entries follow each other within these groups, that is, on a lower level, is determined by visual observation. Very rarely is there deviation from this guideline. In such cases the compiling author was obviously motivated by associations. Note, for example, that the last entry pertaining to the hair of the head is followed by 'A heare of the body'. The principle of visibility is also abandoned when first the general name of an organ or a clearly delimited area of the body, like 'face', and then the names of its parts are given—as is the case with ear, face, and nose. This is a sign, if only a rudimentary one, of the medical concept that the body is a large unit consisting of smaller units. Of course, this elementary piece of medical knowledge is as old as Galen and nothing astonishing. Associations also come into play when the names of organs are followed by names of their functions, when, for example, 'breath' and 'voice' follow the entry 'lungs'.

The words in this section name only parts of the anatomy and of bodily organs. Eighteen entries pertaining to the hair of the head must, in this list as in others, be numbered among them. Very few lemmata are beyond the limit of factual description. They are, as a rule, motivated by some Latin lexicalization. Note, for example: '*The quickenesse of the sight / acies, ei.—A hole (in the foot) / calx, cis*'. An even closer inspection would be able to reveal the precision and quality of medical knowledge which becomes visible in this word-list. This would

[21] These differences may also be influenced by the routines of *post mortem* examinations.

demand a comparison between this and other dictionaries and/or scientific texts of the time.[22] But even a less close inspection shows that this is the work of a compiler of words who does not intend to spread special medical knowledge, but who wants to teach his learners Latin. This is why all explanations are missing. The functional relations between lungs, breath, and voice do not demand any special knowledge but merely everyday experience.[23]

6.6.3 'A banquet with that belongeth'—*in three editions*

A comparison of the variants of one section as presented in various editions can reveal its identical and its variable parts and, in so doing, can confirm the structure of the original dictionary as well as the guidelines for its subsequent revisions. The fairly short section on meals in the 1553, 1586, and 1602 editions lends itself to this kind of analysis, as these editions stand at the beginning of the first, the third, and the fourth batch, the second having so few alterations that a comparison with the first is not really worth while (except for this statement).

In all editions under analysis the section occupies a semantically convincing place in the domain C2 (see section 6.2.3) between a section on the kitchen (the place where victuals are prepared), and a section on potions (the other essential kind of food prepared in the kitchen). In all three editions its title is hardly appropriate, because, according to its entries, the section does not deal with a banquet or anything similar, but with the meals of the day.

In the 1553 edition the title is in Latin, '*Conuiuium cum appendice*'. The section has eighteen entries, twelve of which have an English lemma, each translated by one or several Latin lemma(ta). Note: '*Grace, consecratio mensae. Consecro, cras.—A supper, coena, nae.*' The remaining six entries have a Latin lemma which is translated by an English one. In four of the six cases, this Latin lemma continues a lexeme which had appeared in the translation of a preceding entry. Note: following on '*A supper, coena, nae*' we have '*Coenula, a light supper*' and two more exploiting the same lexeme, even if interrupted by the entry '*A costly supper, saliaris coena*', which again seems prompted by '*A supper, coena, nae*'. The two entries with Latin lemmata mentioned are '*Coeno, nas, aui, & coenatus sum, Coenito, tas, to suppe, or to eate supper*' and '*Coenaturio, ris, coenare cupio*' (the last being all in Latin). Of the two following Latin entries one ('*Commessatio*') is again all in Latin, and one ('*Hospes*') has an English gloss. Some entries are quite short, like some of the ones quoted, some have longer explanations. Note: '*A guest, co[n]uiua, uae, coepulo, lonis, conuictor, vel sodalis, qui vescitur eadem mensa.*' There are two entries which start with an English lemma, wander through a Latin translation, and end up with another English lemma. Note: '*A straunger of another*

---

    [22] A comparison with the lists in McConchie 1997 would be useful.
    [23] See Chapter 9, 353–60, with its analysis of a section on the human body in Hadrianus Junius' nomenclator.

countrei, aduena, nae, peregrinus, extraneus, & alienigina, nae. Discumbo, bis, cubui, bitum, & Acumbo, to sitte downe at the table.' This means that in fact not twelve but fourteen English lemmata are explained. Finally, there are five lines which by virtue of the print are marked not as entries in their own right, but as belonging to the preceding entry whose Latin lexeme they take up. Note, for example: *'Poto, tas, to drynke for pleasure'*, which belongs to *'Drynkyng at any tyme, potura, rae'.* This increases the number of Latin lemmata explained to eleven.

Without exception, the headwords of entries are nouns, occasionally embedded in noun phrases which contain adjectives or adverbs. They can also appear as a gerund, as in: *'Eatyng or drynkyng after diner'*. Six Latin and corresponding English verbs appear at the end of an entry which starts with a noun. Note: *'A diner, prandium, dij. Prandeo, des, sus, sum, to dyne.'* This means they are dependent entries. There are two entries with verbs as Latin headwords (*'Coeno, nas, aui ...—Conuiuor, varis...'*).

All this is quite typical of the varying arrangements of entries in Withals' dictionary. They show that he was somehow torn between an English and a Latin dictionary, although the sequence *English lemma—Latin translation* is clearly dominant. The general observation is confirmed that in by far the greater number of cases Latin lemmata, whether they occur as headwords or as translations, are monolexemic, whereas many English lemmata consist of phrases. This can only mean that, in compiling the dictionary, John Withals took the Latin word as his point of departure and then looked for the adequate English word, even if the entry starts with it. Note: *'Drynkyng at any tyme, potura, rae.—Conuiuor, varis, to make feasts.'* Of course, the author of the dictionary was dependent on the vocabulary he found in the authors for the reading of whom he had to prepare his boys. But this means that, conceptually speaking, it is a Latin–English dictionary turned round in print, with which we are dealing.

The section has a clear position in the onomasiological structure of the dictionary, but it also has a very clear pragmatic structure in itself, which becomes apparent to anybody who peruses it from beginning to end. The first entry (*'Grace'*) stands by itself. There then follows a cluster of six entries pertaining to daily meals with a certain stress on supper. Again, we find another cluster, this time of five entries introducing words for eating and drinking outside the conventional meals. Finally, a cluster of six entries introduces persons who either arrange or are invited to a meal. In this cluster the entry *'A newe yeres gifte or present, strena'* is odd. Some encyclopaedic information is included in the translations, for example that grace is said before a meal, that the main meal is in the evening, that *'Drynkyng at any tyme'* is connected with drinking *'for pleasure'*, that strangers from other countries are guests whom you entertain at a meal, etc.

In the 1586 edition the title is in English, *'A banquet with that belongeth'*. The section has thirty-seven entries. The most important observation is that all the entries of the first edition, in the arrangement that they were given there, have been preserved. The structure of the section has thus been kept intact. Some of the new entries seem to have been added only because they turn lemmata into independent headwords which, in the first edition, were subsumed under a different headword. Note the new entry: '*To dyne, Prandeo, prandes, sus, sum*', which formerly appeared under: '*A diner, prandium, dij. Prandeo, des, sus, sum, to dyne*'. This certainly makes the dictionary easier to use for beginners. On principle, entries now follow the sequence *English lemma—Latin translation*. This also applies to those entries which, in the first edition, had been given the other way round. Moreover, an earlier all-Latin entry is now given together with its English translation (though not always with the same meaning). Note, for example: '*Commessatio, onis, dicitur cibus, potusq[ue] quacunq[ue] hora, qui ex luxu sumitur*' is now: '*A rere supper, Commessario, onis*'. All this facilitates the use of the dictionary by beginners and makes it much more an English–Latin dictionary than the first version had been. An exception are eight newly inserted proverbs which are first given in their Latin and then in their English version. Note:

Absint offensae cum sit celebratio mensae, Let quarelling and offence goe, when grace is saying at the table.
Si non aegrotat, bene mingit, qui bene potat, Hee pisseth well that drinketh well, if he be not sicke and ill at ease.
Dium conuiuaris, caueas ne multa loquatis, Where thou art eating at other mens boordes, take heed and beware to speake many wordes.

The remaining added entries are, with rare exceptions, verbs entered in association with nouns. Note: '*To say grace, Consecro, cras*', associated with: '*Grace, Consecratio mensae*' or: '*To sit tipling al day long, Totum diem potare*'. One of the exceptions is '*A dinner without wine, Prandium canium, abstemium*', associated with '*A diner, Prandium, dij*'.

The principles of arranging entries in print and differentiating between black letter and Roman type are unchanged.

Onomasiologically speaking, the 1586 edition thus leaves the chapter under analysis intact. It does not change its semantic structure and does not add new information. Only those lexemes are added which have a clear relation to other lexemes. The edition moves away from the predominance of nouns, without really abandoning it, and it proceeds in the English–Latin arrangement which was advertised in the title from the first version onwards.

The 1602 edition keeps the English title of the section and has fifty-four entries. Again, all the entries of the two previous editions examined are retained. So is the principle of moving from the English lemma to the Latin translation, with the exception of proverbs. The newly added entries leave the structure of the section intact. The entry '*Grace*', for example, which stood by itself in 1553 and had three entries in 1586, now has six. Added entries are again mostly, but not exclusively, verbs. Participles now also belong to them, which brings word-forms into play which are equivalent to adjectives. In the case of '*Grace*', for example, the three added entries contain one infinitive form ('*To blesse and praise . . .*)', and the two participles *'blesseth or praiseth'*. Occasionally, explanations are given which were absent in the 1587, but not in the first edition. But whereas they were there given in Latin, they are now rendered in English. Note, for example:

To inuite one of his friends to dinner, Vocate ad prandium amicos. And Inuito, tas, is to bid, or inuite to dinner, supper, breakfast, or banquet. Such a bidding, Inuitatio, onis, f.g. and Inuitamentum, ti, n.g. and inuitatus, tus, m.g. signifieth the same.

The example quoted is arranged in the 1602 edition as if it were three separate entries, a technique which is employed several times and makes the increase in entries seem greater than it is. The same happens to the following, which in the first edition would certainly have been printed as one entry:

A dish, or platter seruing for the meat at the boord, Discus, ci. m.g. The word is in vse for a quoit, which they cast, and play with, and sometimes it signifieth a table of state, sometimes a table cloth, as of old. Est Discus ludus, discus quoque regia mensa. Discus seutella: discus quoque sit tibi mappa.

Interpreted in this way, it would be justifiable to say that the section has only fifty entries. Besides the verbal lemmata, more nouns are also introduced, but all fit into the original structure.

The general result of this comparison is that (a) the original semantic structure of the section analysed has been remarkably stable over the decades; (b) the entries have now become exclusively arranged in the English–Latin sequence, with the exception of proverbs; and (c) the store of lemmata is mainly, but not exclusively, enriched with verbs and verbal phrases. The encyclopaedic information in the three variants seems unchanged, although the linguistic information has, of course, increased.

6.6.4 *The world of women*

GENERAL

The situation of women in society is at present being generally (sociologically) researched,[24] linguistically analysed,[25] and politically debated, preferably with reference to our own time (e.g. Tannen 1990). In addition, the historical background of present-day conditions is being explored.[26] Historical documents are

---

[24] See e.g. the volume edited by Connell-Ginet, Borker, and Furman 1989 and the monumental five-volume *History of Women*, edited by Duby and Perrot 1992–4.

[25] The linguistic discussion was started by the seminal books of Robin Lakoff 1975 and Mary R. Key 1975, although a number of papers appeared earlier collected, e.g., in Thorne and Henley 1975. It centres around *gender and sex* (e.g. Baron 1986, Graddol and Swann 1989) and the role behaviour of men and women in speech and conversation (e.g. Coates 1986, Preisler 1986). For a commentated bibliography see Thorne, Kramarae, and Henley 1983, for a recent survey of the state of the art Hellinger 1995, who has also written a German and English comparative study on *'feministische Linguistik'* (1990).

[26] For arguments with material taken from the history of language see e.g. Baron 1986.

being sifted to determine what they can contribute to our modern interest in and knowledge of this problem.[27] When examining a topical dictionary to find out how the world of women is represented in it, we raise a question which the compiler of the dictionary would probably never have raised and would hardly have understood. This is why a present-day enterprise like this one touches on essential questions of historiographical methodology. Is an analysis of a sixteenth-century dictionary in the light of a twentieth-century interest legitimate? It is indeed if we assume that a historical text is marked by more features than the author meant to express in it. The interest of the twentieth century can shed light on the context of a sixteenth-century document which has hitherto been over-looked and which may have been overlooked even by sixteenth-century people, including its author. This makes the question anachronistic in the strict sense. But in this case anachronism is something creative.[28]

The decision in favour of anachronism as a productive method of historio-graphical work has some far-reaching consequences. It requires that our picture of the past depends to a great extent on our interests in the present, that a common opinion about the past is not so much a consensus about so-called historical truth, but a consensus about what to look for when doing historical research.

On the other hand, historiography must not deteriorate into sheer interest-driven arbitrariness.

The following analysis of a sixteenth-century dictionary with reference to the way in which it presents the world of women is meant to illustrate the possibil-ities of a creatively anachronistic question directed towards a historical product of topical lexicography.

THE RELEVANT ENTRIES

The entries under A ('world'),[29] devoted to the reality of nature, give no opportu-nity for differentiations between masculine and feminine, either as a natural or a social fact. The entries under B ('nature') do so in a few cases, limited to the king-dom of animals, where, naturally, sex is a biological condition of life. In '*Birdes aboute the house . . . Aves villatice*' (B1),[30] for example, female functions like hatch-ing eggs are mentioned (6[r]), whereas in '*Four footed bestis. Animalia quadrupedia*'

---

[27]   See e.g. the sourcebook pertaining to the Middle Ages edited by Amt 1993, and Hull 1996.

[28]   *Creative anachronism* should indeed be made a central term in the methodology of historiogra-phy. 'The answer is that a fixed past is not what we really need, or at any rate not all we need. We require a heritage with which we continually interact, one which fuses past with present. This heritage is not only necessary but inescapable; we cannot now avoid feeling that the past *is* to some extent our own creation. If today's insights can be seen as integral to the meaning of the past, rather than subversive of its truth, we may breathe new life into it' (Lowenthal 1985, 410). The term *creative anachronism* is taken from this book. For a more complex treatment of this problem see Hüllen 1998 and 2002, 29–42.

[29]   For the function of A, B1, B2, etc. see section 6.2.3 above.

[30]   Section titles are given in English and Latin, but occasionally shortened. In the original, some are rendered only in English, some only in Latin.

(B3) and '*A parke*' (B3) we find very few differentiations, fewer than nature would allow. Note:

A dere, damma, me
A hert, ceruus, ui . . .
A male goate, caper, pri
A female goate, capra, prae, capella, lae.
A dog, canis, nis . . .
A bitche, canis faemina.   (15ʳ.)

Where human beings are mentioned, the words mostly appear in the masculine form. The question to be discussed is whether this is a generic gender or indeed means *(male) man.* Note in '*A ship with other water vessels. &c*' (B2):

The patrone of a galey, trierarcha
He that keepeth the wharfe, portitor, toris . . .
The gouerner of a ship, nauclerus, ri, vel nauticus, ci.
A mariner. or man of warre on the sea, or shipman, classiarius, rij, nauta, vel nauita.   (10ᵛ.)

Intuitively speaking, the masculine gender in these and in many subsequent cases mirrors a field of activity which was dominated by men and, thus, denotes the male sex. Entries like '*rower, diver, swimmer*' have certainly also to be understood as masculine in gender and sex.

We find the same in '*Heardes men haywardes, sheapherdes, with such other, as kepe cattel. &c*' (B3) with ten entries (out of eighteen) for human beings. Where the English word would formally allow a dual gender, its Latin translation and sometimes English pronouns in explanatory phrases disambiguate this, at least superficially, in favour of a male meaning (e.g. '*A messanger, nuncius, tabellarius*', 17ᵛ). The first feminine entry is to be found in '*The husband man with such other as labour in husbandry. Agricola cum his qui agriculturam exercent*' (B3):

The bailie, or he that ordreth the husbandry, villicus, ci
Villica, cae, the woman in like office, cuius officium dicitur villicatio.   (18ᵛ.)

This first entry to denote a woman by her social responsibilities belongs to those where the headword refers back to the Latin part of the previous entry, and may thus be motivated linguistically. As, on the other hand, the pedagogical interest of all the entries of the dictionary lay in identifying their referents, we are certainly justified in understanding *villica* as indeed denoting a woman in an acknowledged social role.

After the entries on agriculture, the word-groups under C ('man') consist almost totally of words denoting human beings and, thus, offer plenty of opportunities to differentiate between masculine and feminine, male and female, as gender and sex. Generally speaking, this is the more so as word-lists are highly specialized where crafts are concerned (C1), enumerating some 120 different denominations. But by far the greatest number of them are again masculine forms. The following is an exhaustive list of the feminine forms:

A baker, artocopus, pistor, ris: pinsor, soris, panifex: panificus.
Pistrices dicuntur mulieres pauificae, quae panem faciunt . . . .   (30ᵛ.)
A carder. carminator, vel carminatrix, & vel carminarius.   (35ʳ.)
The weauer, textor, toris, & textrix, tricis
A semster or shepster. Sutrix, cis.
A launder, lotrix, tricis. Lauo, uas, to wasshe.   (36ᵛ.)

Pistrices may again have a partly linguistic motivation from the previous entry, but *carder, weaver* and *semster* are, as words, perfect examples of dual (generic) gender having, in these cases, female meanings as is proved by the Latin translation.

The word-groups on crafts are followed by ones on houses including villages and towns (C2) with buildings which fulfil public functions. We find here some plurals, like *oppidani* and *pagani*, which cannot be disambiguated. Otherwise the entries mostly name objects and, if human beings, males. However, '*A deirie house: or chese house, with his vessels, and that perteineth. Domus lactaria. domus casearia*' (43ᵛ) contains the following three entries:

Lactarius, & lactatrix, qui cibos ex lacte conficit
A wase or wreath to bee laide under the vessel, that is borne upon the head, as women use, cesticillus, vel arculus.
The women that beare suche vessels upon their heads, be called, mulieres caniferae.

Note that *lactarius* and *lactatrix* are given only as Latin lexemes. Otherwise, all the roles that people play in the house are, at least linguistically, attributed to men, among them fourteen different kinds of servants (52ʳ⁻ᵛ), for example:[31]

He that beareth meate fro the kechyn to the table, discophorus, dapifer, ti.
Lectistrator, & lecticonsinuator, he that maketh the bed, vel lectisterniator.   (55ʳ.)

Other entries are indifferent with reference to men or women, but can, if compared with the official rules for women's conduct at that time, be intuitively attributed to men, as for example:

Drynkyng at any time, potura, rae.
Poto, tas, to drynke for pleasure.   (49ᵛ.)

A new aspect of the dichotomy *masculine* vs. *feminine, male* vs. *female* is revealed in the two subsections '*Clothinge or apparell for men. Ornatus. tus. vestitus. tus*' (54ᵛ–56ᵛ) and '*Clothynge for women*' (56ᵛ–57ʳ). The first has ninety-five entries, the second only twenty-six. Clothes for men are enumerated roughly in the sequence of dressing, starting with '*nudus, -a, -um, naked*'. Twenty-six lexemes name items of clothing (*A sherte, A typpet, A hose, A gerter, A breache,* etc.), fifteen more name shoes (*A shoe, Sculponex, A slipper,* etc.). Twenty lexemes name accessories (*A gyrdle, A combe, A garland, A hood, A crowne,* etc.). Another twenty

---

[31] The serving and other offices in the house which are mentioned indicate clearly that no everyday household was in the mind of the compiler of the dictionary but either Roman models or a stately household of his own time.

lexemes speak of different kinds of gowns and twelve more of jewellery (*A braclet, A rynge, A perle*).

Clothes for women are also enumerated roughly in the sequence of dressing, with only eleven lexemes for items of clothing and fifteen for kinds of cloth and headwear (*A smoke, A stomacher, An apron, A gowne, A fillet, A kercher, A necke kercher or partlet, A pinne*, etc.). No underwear is mentioned. The two word-groups obviously follow two different principles. Whereas the clothes for men, with many lexemes merely naming different kinds or colours of garments, are meant to display splendour and fashion, the clothes for women stress decorum and their social status. Note:

Castula, a vesture to couer naked women in the hotte house.
Peplu[m], est palla faeminea picta, a mournyng vesture.
A cavil to couer the heare of the head with, as maidens use, reticulum crinale, ve retiolum

The city and its houses (C) and places that serve some public function (the mayor's house, the wrestling place, the prison, the school, even the market) (C3) are a man's world, as is to be expected. Again as is to be expected, '*The stewes, with baudes. harlottes, and theues*' (59ʳ⁻ᵛ) are a world with the two sexes in characteristic roles. Note among thirteen entries:

A baude, leno, nonis.
A flaterer, adulator, toris.
A harlot or common woman, meretrix, cis, lupa, ae.
They that haunt the stewes, dicuntur gauiones. Scort[at]or, toris, to haunte harlottes.

Predominantly masculine and male are also all the offices in the city, including the servants. Note the following few differentiations and undecided plural forms (60ʳ):

A maister of houshuld, dominus, ni. pater familias . . .
A maistresse, hera, re, domina.
Housholde servauntes, atrienses.
A page, assecla.
Circu[m]pedes, lakeies or waityng seruantes.
A maiden seruant, famula, lae.
A woman seruant with other together, conserua, uae.
A bonde man, seruus, ui.
A bonde woman, ancilla, cosmeta.

Entries under D ('society') are devoted to the law, the Church (D2), and the family (D3). Church offices (twenty-six in all) are masculine and male, except:

An abbesse, abatissa, sae.
A nounne, sanctimonialis, & monialis, lis, vel cistercina. virgo.

Whereas there is an entry, '*An abbote, abbas, tis. i. pater*', there is none for *monk*.
'*The names of kynrede. Nomina consanguinitatis*' (69ʳ–70ʳ) show a continuous

symmetrical division into the two sexes. But there are interesting additional entries. First, there is a generic meaning of the Latin word *homo*.

A man, vir, homo, nis.
But homo is indifferent to man, woman or child, whiche is a reasonable creature.

Secondly, the entries for *father* and *mother* have additional explanations which give their biological roles as understood at the time:

Gigno, nis, genui, itum, to begette.
Parere, signifi. foetum emittere, quod foeminarum est.

Thirdly, *son*, but not *daughter*, has two additional entries:

He that is first borne, primogenitus, ti.
He that is borne after that his father is deade, posthumus, mi.

Lastly, *sister*, but not *brother*, has the additional entry: '*A virgin or maiden, virgo, ginis*'.
    Names for ancestors are given in exact pairs of sometimes highly specialized terms. Note:

A grandfathers great grandfather, tritanus
A grandmothers great grandmother, tritaria.
My brothers sonnes sonnes sonne, trinepos.
My sisters daughters daughters daughters trineptis.

Similarly to the previous word-group, '*The names of affinitee, with the appertinences. Nomina affinitatis, cu[m] appendicibus*' (70^r–71^r) show a division into the two sexes in many cases, but also interesting deviations from this principle. All entries, besides the last groups on witches, soothsayers, etc., centre around marriage and wedlock. Except where words name details of the birth of babies, the point of view is masculine. Thus, the entry '*A louer, amator*' has no feminine counterpart. The following entries, however, have:

He that hath the ordre and rule of the weddyng house, pronubus . . .
Pronuba, bae, is the woman hauyng like rule.
He that marieth, sponsus, si.
She that is maried sponsa, sae. Sponso, sas. Desponso, sas, & despo[n]sor, saris, to make promise of mariage.

The first of these entries is again a case where the feminine form is first given in Latin and may be triggered by the previous entry. In the second entry mentioned, this cannot be decided.
    The following three entries show a remarkable difference in the definition of presents given by a husband or wife:

The dowry geuen in mariage for the womans part, dos, dotis.
Dotale dicitur, quod ad dotem pertinet.
Presentes or geftes, as men use to geue at Christmas, or new yeres daie, apophoreta dicuntur.

In the word-group on the birth of children, the point of view is naturally biological and feminine. The sequence follows roughly the natural development: *Childe bearynge, 'The birth of a childe, Abortus, Puerpera, bipera, A childe borne with the feete forwarde, A midwife, A nursery, A nurse'*. An exception is '*A man gelded*' after the entry '*Childe bearings*'. Moreover, the following masculine entry, solely in Latin, seems noteworthy: '*Alumnus, proprie qui ab aliquo alitus est. Aliqua[n]do pro filio sumitur*'. Some entries on breastfeeding conclude this word-group.

Entries under E ('life and death') begin with those in '*The partes of the body. Partes corporis*' (E1). There are 199 entries here, but only sixteen pertain to one sex only, three pertaining to men's beards and six to their genitals, three to women's breasts and four to their genitals.

The following subsections do not yield any new insights. Human vices, called pedagogically '*Uncleaness of the body / Uncleanesse of the soule with fylthy qualitees*', are either unspecific or, when personified, masculine (*A kisser, A lier, A barbiter, A debate maker, An usurer, A sleper*), which again raises the question of the dual gender. An exception, though hardly noteworthy, is '*A lemman, concubina, ae / A common woman, meretrix*'.

The entries of '*Aeges. Aetates*' are likewise unspecific. An exception is '*An old man, senex, nis*' which has no feminine/female counterpart. The following word-groups relating to sicknesses, warfare, surgeons, and travel represent a male world. Note, however: '*The god of battaile, Mars, tis. / The goddesse of battaile, Bellona, nae.*' The entry strikes one as almost odd in the semantic world of the dictionary, but it is obviously geared to the classical texts learners were preparing to read.

The Latin translations of adjectives give the endings of all three genders. This sometimes influences the post-lemmatic explanations as in '*Good, as good man, woma[n], or other thing, bonus, na, num*'. But masculine definitions prevail, as in '*Worthy, as he that deserueth preyse, dignus, na, num*'.

COMMENTARY

With hindsight it becomes obvious that the selection of relevant entries has been guided by some heuristic principles. The first is knowledge of the male/female dichotomy in nature. The second is knowledge of the masculine/feminine dichotomy in language. This knowledge, however, is modified by the observation that biological and grammatical meanings often do not coincide, that grammatical meaning is just as often a matter of nature as it is a matter of convention. Part of this observation is the awareness of a so-called *generic gender*, which, in the languages investigated here, regularly means a general, that is, a male as well as a female, meaning of a masculine word-form. This awareness is actually the effect of the third principle, the knowledge of the masculine/feminine dichotomy in society. This knowledge is again modified by our present-day awareness of the discussion which, broadly speaking, maintains that women in society, most of all in its legal and professional system, are either consciously suppressed or in fact overridden by men and that this state of affairs is the result of a long historical process.

In trying to evaluate the relevant entries identified by applying these three principles in various combinations, some rough divisons can first be made. There are semantic areas whose referent worlds are either clearly masculine or clearly feminine like seafaring or warfare on the one hand and everything around prostitution on the other. There are other areas, like the animal world or the biological facts of the body, where the distinction is factual. Entries in these areas do not pose any problems.

Much more interesting are those areas where the roles of feminine members of society, even if rooted in biological facts, adopt a societal significance. They pertain to: (1) the roles of men and women in husbandry, artisanship, business, and the like, (2) clothes, and (3) the status of sexes in the family.

Admittedly, in this dictionary men were dominant in the world of husbandry, artisanship, and business as in almost all public domains, but women were excluded from them to a lesser extent than one might expect. This fact need not, however, be mirrored linguistically. The statutes of guilds, for example, are almost regularly couched in masculine terms, although all historiographical works agree that women, alongside their husbands, or as widows, or even (!) independently, worked in many crafts and in some of them even predominantly (Amt 1993, 194 ff.). The fact that most of the entries here still adopt the masculine form and masculine pronouns in explanations does not then mean that there were no craftswomen of these kinds but that, in a book like a learning dictionary, they need not be mentioned (in English or in Latin), obviously because they worked in a world that was legally and conventionally laid out for men. If we assume this to be a valid statement, the occasional feminine form in the dictionary would stand out as an exception. It would signify something beyond societal normality. The odd feminine form, thus, does not have little importance, as a quantitative evaluation might suggest; it has, on the contrary, great importance.[32] This might, for example, explain the entries *villica* and *maistresse*.[33] From the late fourteenth century onwards, there was almost everywhere a certain percentage of female heads of households[34]—a fact important enough to be mentioned by the compiler of the dictionary. The female meanings of *baker*, *carder*, *weaver*, *semster*, and women working on dairy farms, recognizable only by the Latin translations, would then point to the fact that the number of women working here was higher than in other crafts. This conforms to general historiographical statements on this matter.[35] According to these, cloth production, food production (excluding butchery, but

[32] Strictly speaking, statements such as these, like some other statements to follow, have significance only for the world of the dictionary under analysis. They contribute to our general knowledge of the problem, although they do not allow direct generalizations.

[33] See: 'In the country, a wife had a right to her husband's real property. In the city, she could, alongside her husband, hold title to substantial wealth in merchandize and capital' (King 1991, 49–50).

[34] King (1991, 29) speaks of one case (Trier, Germany, towards the end of the fourteenth century) of almost one-third.

[35] See Amt 1993, where these and other crafts (fullers, goldsmiths, brewers) are mentioned as being almost exclusively carried out by women. Also Opitz 1992.

including brewing), and washing had almost exclusively been in female hands since the late Middle Ages. A very similar case surfaces in the entries concerning domestic services. Domestic workers were recruited to a large extent from young unskilled girls, eventually developing into the largest occupational group in urbanized society (Hufton 1993).

At first sight, the disproportion of entries in '*Clothinge or apparell for men*' and in '*Clothynge for women*' is astonishing. After all, the opinion that a love of fashionable dresses is something typically female was common in the Middle Ages as well as in the Renaissance. The extravagances of court life in this respect are well known (Hughes 1992). A dictionary for young boys learning Latin would, of course, not be concerned with them, just as it would set itself certain limits for detailed entries about, for example, underwear. The quantitative disproportion may signify a pedagogical reserve *vis-à-vis* the contemporary general moralizing interpretation that the elaborate dresses of women placed their chastity in doubt and created seductive effects for men. Still, the choice of entries may also betray something else.

The great diversity of fashionable clothes for men is obviously meant to signal their social status. The restrictions on wearing velvet or silk, on having one's clothes embroidered with silver or gold, on dyeing one's coat scarlet, or on trimming it with certain kinds of fur, such as ermine, are well known (Hull 1996). Some of them were only abandoned in the French Revolution. Only men of rank and wealth were entitled to wear such materials and colours. When in *The Taming of the Shrew* master and servant change clothes, they exchange a multi-coloured hat and cloak for a plain one (I. i. 207 and IV. i. 81), and when, in the same play, Vincentio meets his son's servant in his son's clothes, he exclaims: '*O fine villain! A silken doublet, a velvet hose,/a scarlet cloak, and a coppatain hat!*' (v. i. 57–9). Men's apparel, ultimately dictated by a love of splendour and vanity as all fashion is, served as a signal of its wearer's place in the social hierarchy. The number and kind of entries within this word-group seem to corroborate this fact.

Vanity as a motive of fashion with respect to women's dresses is hardly alluded to in the dictionary. Instead, at least some of the entries in the relevant word-group show that women's clothes served as signals of another kind, within a second social system, namely that of the phases of a woman's life, which consisted of maidenhood, married status, and widowhood. The two marked phases, before and after married life, are represented by lexemes and, thus, prove to be at the focus of attention. In Withals' dictionary, the entries on clothes prove that men and women were defined according to at least two different sets of principles, namely, men according to the feudal hierarchy of those who fought, prayed, and worked, women according to the state of their restricted sexual life (King 1991, 23).

This is also proved in the word-group giving lexemes for family relations. *Virgin* is defined with reference to 'a maiden', not with reference to a boy. Two entries pertaining to boys (*primogenitus* and *posthumus*) can be accounted for by legal interests. So can the later entry *alumnus*. Girls were, of course, also first born or born after their father's death or were adopted, but this fact did not create legal problems, such as those of inheritance. Marriage as a legally organized transaction with far-reaching consquences is also to be found behind the entries:

He that marieth, sponsus, si,
She that is married sponsa, sae. Sponso, sas.
Desponso, sas, & despo[n]so, soris, to make promise of marriage.

This must not only be understood as betraying the emotional dependence and passive role of women in marriage. The contemporary reading will have understood that the promise of marriage was a legally binding act on the part of the groom which caused an equally binding act on the part of the bride's parents, namely, the promise of a dowry. The relevant entry follows immediately. Its being mentioned in an English–Latin learning dictionary for not yet marriageable boys shows the public importance of this legalized convention which moved hard sums and real property and was the source of potential loss and potential gain respectively for the families involved.[36] When Petruccio thinks of '[t]aming the shrew', his first exchange of opinion with her father concerns the dowry: *'Then tell me, if I get your daughter's love, / What dowry shall I have with her to wife?'* (II. i. 119–20). The following lines of this conversation, moreover, show a potential source of wealth for widowed women. After the death of their husbands, who had, of course, the right to control their wives' dowry, they would get their property back for their own disposal and perhaps their husbands' property, too.

As the main purpose of marriage was to produce a new generation in the family, entries on childbearing and giving birth cannot be absent. Nine entries are, however, not very many. *'Childe bearynge'* and *'The birth of a childe'* are general. *'Puerpera'* and *'bipera'* have an obvious importance at a time when frequent pregnancies were the rule. *'Midwife'*, *'nursery'*, and *'nurse'* show feminine roles in this context. Conspicuously absent is *doctor*.[37] *'Abortus'* and *'a childe borne with the feete forward'* probably appear not only because of their obvious medical meanings. Delivery of a stillborn child or a deformed foetus or any irregularity in giving birth was superstitiously associated with unfavourable meanings.[38] In Shakespeare's *King Henry VI* (Part 3) and *King Richard III*, Richard Gloucester attributes his own ugliness, which is the visible form of his wickedness, to the circumstances of his own birth, a breech delivery and, moreover, a premature one.[39] The following

[36] See King 1991, 26 ff. Since the Reformation, the rival churches insisted more strongly on the idea that the marital act should be consensual and should mirror the love between Christ and his church. Still, negotiations on dowries continued to play an important role, the more so the wealthier the families involved were.

[37] This is obviously a gap in the dictionary, because the role of male and female doctors in obstetrics is generally acknowledged. See e.g. King 1991, 47 ff.

[38] As a case study see the relevant passages in Warnicke 1989.

[39] *'For I have often heard my mother say / I came into the world with my legs forward'* (3 *King Henry VI*, v. vi. 70–1) and: *'I, that am curtail'd of this fair proportion, / Cheated of feature by dissembling Nature, / Deform'd, unfinish'd, sent before my time / Into this breathing world scarce half made up.'* (*King Richard III*, I. i. 18–21). A further anomaly is that Richard was born with teeth; see 3 *King Henry VI*, v. vi. 75. Obviously, Shakespeare heaps the difficulties and anomalies of birth up as he does Richard's deformities and, of course, his vices.

entries in the dictionary on breastfeeding point to a case of major interest at the time. It ensured the babies' health and, where difficulties arose, led to the widespread practice of hiring wet-nurses. At the same time it was a means which regulated new pregnancies.

6.7 Final remarks

Withals' dictionary is an outstanding work of sixteenth-century English lexicography. Gabriele Stein (1985, 194–204) attributes this fact to (i) the concentration of the word-list on a core vocabulary, (ii) its being geared to the native English tongue of the users, (iii) the systematic order of the topical arrangement, (iv) the 'communicative arrangement' of entries, which are often linked to each other by associations, and (v) limited but essential information concerning grammar and problems of word-meaning in the case of homonymy. Moreover, the dictionary carries on the onomasiological tradition in England by following its semantic orientation and improves on it in its lexicographical method. Watson (1909, 164–5) comments on its being used as a textbook for the teaching of natural history in schools. Besides Comenius's *Janua linguarum* and *Orbis pictus*, it is the only dictionary which he mentions in this context. Whereas Garland and Stanbridge were largely, though not entirely, still bound to the technique of interlinear glossing, Withals used an arrangement in columns, which at his time was reserved for alphabetical dictionaries. By using the word *dictionary* he made it clear that his book belonged to this genre like any other, that is, like alphabetical ones. Lastly, the arrangement of the two languages as well as the '*Prologve*' and the '*Preface*' give the dictionary a theoretical underpinning in foreign-language didactics. Withals followed a time-honoured tradition, not because it was there but because it made sense in his practical work. He was a language teacher who knew what he was doing and why.

7

James Howell's dictionary for the genteel
(1660)

7.1 The author

James Howell's (?1594–1666) place of birth in Wales is uncertain. He matriculated at Jesus College, Oxford, in 1610 and took his degree there in 1613. He was appointed steward of a glassware factory in London. In this capacity he travelled to Holland, France, Spain, and Italy in order to obtain materials and skilled work-men for the firm. It seems that this experience laid the foundations of his later linguistic knowledge and interests. He held various posts in the orbit of the court and some noblemen, which brought him political missions, for example to Spain. He was a friend and regular correspondent of Ben Jonson, Lord Herbert of Cherbury, and Sir Kenelm Digby. Politics, languages, and travelling were the topics of his extensive publications.

Howell's political attitudes were somewhat equivocal. He supplied a commendatory poem to *Eikon Basilikė, the Portraiture of His Sacred Majesty in his solitudes and sufferings* (1649), which, purporting to be written by Charles I himself, created an aureole around the House of Stuart after the regicide. By order of the Long Parliament he was incarcerated in the Fleet from 1643 to 1651 because of his political attitudes but probably also because of personal debts. During these years he attempted to gain Cromwell's favour, but approached the court again after the Restoration. He dedicated the *Lexicon Tetraglotton* (1660) to Charles II in the very year of the Stuarts' return to the throne. He died unmarried.

'Howell is one of the earliest Englishmen who made a livelihood out of litera-ture' (*DNB*).[1] His publications mirror his lively interests in current affairs and his rare mastery of modern languages, including his native Welsh. *Instructions for forreine travell* . . . (1642), re-edited as *Instructions and directions for forren travell* . . . (1650) (Alston 1974, vol. iii, 767–8) contain general observations on French, Spanish, Italian, and German. His greatest success were the *Epistolae Ho-Elianae. Familiar Letters Domestic and Forren divided into Sundry Sections, partly Historical, Political, and Philosophical* (1645), of which Alston (1974, vol. iii, 142–54) and the BL catalogue together list thirteen editions between 1645 and 1754 and five later reprints (1880, 1890, 1896, 1903, 1907). Some letters (19, 27, 55–60) deal with European languages, including English. Howell's revision and expansion of *[A] French–English Dictionary. Compil'd by Mr Randle Cotgrave. With Another in English and French . . . . London, Printed by W. H. for Luke Fawne, and are to be sold at his shop at the sign of the Parrot in Paul's Church-Yard* appeared in 1650. It is noteworthy among the alphabetical dictionaries of two languages because the main body of entries is annexed with several lists of topically arranged words under the revealing introductory sentence: '*For the ease of the French Student, and the further advancement of his memory, the heads of some species are collected and annexed hereunto.*'[2]

The German Diet on the Ballance of Europe (1653) is a rare piece of early travel literature in which James Howell advanced the idea of the ethnic individuality of peoples through an imaginary discussion among German noblemen. Although their speeches for and against various European nations abound with clichés on

---

[1] For a bibliography see Vann 1924.

[2] *Arms* (thirty-three entries), *Birds* (seventy-five entries), *Colours* (twenty-eight entries), *Dogges* (fifteen entries), *Fish* (seventy entries), *Hawkes* (twenty entries), *Flowers & Herbs* (twenty-seven entries), *The members of the body* (seventy-one entries), *The Moneths* (twenty-two entries, including days of the week, seasons, etc.), *Numbers* (seventy-seven entries), *Trees* (thirty-six entries), *The vest-ments of the body* (twenty-three entries), *The winds* (eight entries), and onomatopoetic French words. As is obvious, the topical word-groups as such are ordered according to the alphabet. (Cotgrave 1650, WF 16.3 Gram. 2°.)

so-called national character, the speakers subscribe to the idea that every nation has its own merits and foibles.

The *Lexicon Tetraglotton* appeared in 1659/1660.

Finally, there is *A new English grammar, prescribing as certain rules as the language will bear, for forreners to learn English* ... (1662) among the linguistic works of James Howell, which contains an English, but also a Spanish (that is, Castilian), grammar and a Portuguese–Spanish–English vocabulary.

7.2 The dictionary

7.2.1 General

James Howell's dictionary of four languages is divided into three parts, an alphabetical and an onomasiological one,[3] and a part listing proverbs. As frequent in the seventeenth century, the general title lists these parts of the book in the way of a table of contents. The general title reads:

Lexicon Tetraglotton, An English–French–Italian–Spanish Dictionary: Whereunto Is Adjoined A large Nomenclature of proper Terms (in all the four) belonging to several Arts and Sciences, to Recreations, to Professions both Liberal and Mechanick, &c. Divided into Fiftie two Sections; With another Volume of the Choicest Proverbs In all the said Toungs, (consisting of divers compleat Tomes) and the English translated into the other Three, to take off the reproch which useth to be cast upon Her, That She is but barren in this point, and those Proverbs She hath are but flat and empty. Moreover, There are sundry familiar Letters and Verses running all in Proverbs, with a particular Tome of the Brittish or old Cambrian Sayed Sawes and Adages, which the Author thought fit to annex herunto, and make Intelligible, for their great Antiquity and Weight: Lastly, there are five Centuries of New Sayings, which, in tract of Time, may serve for Proverbs to Posterity.
By the Labours, and Lucubrations of James Hovvell, Esq;
London, Printed by J. G. for Cornelius Bee, at the Kings Armes in Little Brittaine. 1660.

Each of the three parts has its own title including place and years of printing. The title of the onomasiological part reads:

A Particular Vocabulary, Or Nomenclature In English, Italian, French, and Spanish. Of the proper Terms belonging to several Arts and Sciences, to Recreations, to common Professions and Callings both Liberal and Mechanick, &c.

---

[3] Publishing an alphabetical and a topical dictionary together as one book was not unusual. It certainly was a means of securing the greatest possible success for a book on the market. A well-known example is John Rider's *Bibliotheca scholastica* of 1589, which actually contains three types of dictionaries: an English–Latin alphabetical dictionary, a topical English–Latin dictionary, and a Latin–English *index alphabeticus*. However, the overriding principle is still the alphabet. Whereas the first and the third part of the dictionary amount together to some 1,000 pages, the second part has only thirty-four pages. See Stein 1985, 333–52, Green 1997, 101–4.

Vocabulario Particolare, ò Nomenclatura Italiana, Francese, Spagnuola, Inglese, Delli Termini proprii, à qualunque Arte & Scienza, alle Recreationi, & Professioni cosi Liberali, come Mechaniche, &c.
Vocabulaire Particulier, Ou Nomenclatvre, Françoise, Italienne, Angloise, Espagnole, Des Termes propres aux Arts, & Sciences, aux Recreations, aux Vocations Liberales et Mechaniques, &c.
Vocabulario Particvlar, o Nomenclatura Española, Inglese, Italiana, Francese, De los Terminos proprios a las Artes y Ciencias, a las Recreationes, y Vocationes Liberales y Mechanicas, &c.
Labore & Lucubrationibus Jacobi Howell Arm; Mariduensis.
. . .
London Printed by Thomas Leach, 1659.
WF Kb 15.4, fol. (see also Alston 1974, vol. ii, 108–10).

Note that the sequence of languages and also the year of publication differ in the general title and in this subtitle.

The book of about 1,000 folios has no numbered pages. The onomasiological part (which is the only one under analysis here) covers about 390 of them, and has two printed columns. It has proved almost impossible to estimate the number of words it contains (unless they are counted one by one). As the size of entries varies from two lines to lengthy articles, there is a range of from five to fifty per page. Assuming an average of twenty-five entries, we would arrive at a total of 19,000 to 20,000 headwords. However, as will be shown later, the microstructure of many entries precludes an estimation such as this, which is only valid for showing that the dictionary is indeed of monumental size.

The four languages follow each other according to the subtitle of the onomasiological part, not according to the general title. The type is Roman and italic (that is, the English entry is printed in Roman, the Italian translation is italicized, the French one is in Roman, and the Spanish one is in italics). In titles as well as in entries, the languages are unsystematically separated by a semicolon or colon. Entries are clearly marked typographically, because the second and all the following lines of each entry are indented so that every first line stands out visibly as the beginning. Each of the fifty-two sections has its own subtitle in the four languages.

According to the BL catalogue there was only one edition.

7.2.2 Overview of the onomasiological part

The dictionary[4] is introduced by a detailed table of all fifty-two sections, each in the four languages. This table is the best and most concise overview of the macrostructure. Note:

A Table Of the several Sections comprized in this Nomenclatvre; Tavola delli Capitoli compresi

---

[4] Henceforth 'the dictionary' means the onomasiological part of the dictionary, unless specified otherwise.

in questa Nomenclatvra; Table de Chapitres compris en ceste Nomenclature; Tabla de los Capitulos comprehendidos en esta Nomenclatura.[5]

SECTION I[6]

An Anatomy of the outward, and inward parts of humane body; Una Notomia delle parti interiori ed esteriori del Corpo umano; Una anatomie des parties interieures, & exterieures du corps humain; Una Anatomia de las partes internas, y externas del cuerpo Humano.

SECTION II

Of horses, and horsemanship, with the peculiar terms, and apurtenances thereof; I cavalli, & la cavallerizza con i suoi termini; Les chevaux, & l'ecurie avec leurs termes; Los cavallos, y la cavalleriza con sus terminos.

SECTION III

Of Hunting, or Venery, with their proper terms, and of the wild beasts and dogs that serve for that sport; Le fiere, & la lor caccia, con i termini proprij di quella; La venetia, ou la chasse avec les propres termes d'icelle; Las fieras y su caça, ó la montaria con sus terminos.
Of other wild Beasts.
Hunting Doggs, and their severall kinds. I Cani da Caccia; Les Chiens de Chasse; Los Perros de Caça.

SECTION IV

Of Fawconry, or Hawking, and all birds of prey; La struzzeria, ó falconeria, & gli ucelli di rapina; Les oyseaux de proye, & la Fauconerie; Las Aves de rapiña, y la Falconeria.

SECTION V

VVar and Souldiery, with the military terms thereof; La guerra, & i suoi termini; La guerre, & ses termes; La guerra, y sus terminos.

SECTION VI

Sea-faring affairs, and navigation, with their multitude of terms; La Navigatione, & termini marineschi; La Navigation, & termes de la marine; La Navegacion, y terminos marineschos. More particular terms of Navigation, as also of the Winds, of the Laws, and Punishments at Sea &c.

---

[5] The titles of sections were copied from this table. In some cases, there are slight, mostly shortened, variants used in the book. In-between titles which do not appear in the table were copied from the book. In the course of my deliberations, when various sections of the dictionary are analysed, I take the headings from the book. This accounts for a few inconsistencies. In all cases, I have refrained from inserting bracketed exclamation marks even where obvious errors occur. For practical purposes I give the first seven sections in full and the following ones only in their English rendering. Unlike the original, I end this rendering with a full stop. Otherwise I follow faithfully the original spelling and punctuation.

[6] Sections I to XX are numbered with Arabic numerals, the following sections with Roman numerals. I use Roman numerals throughout.

SECTION VII

Orders of Knight-hood throughout Christendom, either Regular, or Secular; Ordini de Cavaglieri per tutta la Christianità, Regolari, & Secolari; Ordres de Chevaliers par toute la Christiente Reguliers, y Seculiers; Ordines de Cavalleros por toda la Christianidad, Reglares, y Seglares.

SECTION VIII

Religious Orders, and cloistered reclused Monks, Fryers, and others, according to their Antiquity and Names, &c.

SECTION IX

Ecclesiastical Dignities, and Titles in the Roman Church.

SECTION X

The differing Sects, and Opinions in Christian Religion, with the ages, and times of the Sectaries.

SECTION XI

Buildings, and Terms of Architecture.

SECTION XII

Houshold-stuff, or the movables of a House.

SECTION XIII

A Library, or Bibliotheque.

SECTION XIV

Vtensils, or things belonging to the Kitchin.

SECTION XV

Instruments, and terms belonging to a garden, & Orchard.

SECTION XVI

Garden-herbs, or herbages, and roots.

SECTION XVII

Grain and corn of all sorts.

SECTION XVIII

Wines and drinks, with their appurtenances.

SECTION XIX[7]

Beasts, or flesh for the first course. Domestick, or tame house-beasts.

---

[7]   By mistake, the section is numbered XVII.

SECTION XX

Birds and poultry of all kinds.

SECTION XXI

The degrees, or differences of age and persons.

SECTION XXII

Reprochful, reviling, or opprobious terms.

SECTION XXIII

Infirmities and diseases incident to men and women. The particular Diseases of every member apart, and of womens.

SECTION XXIV

Consanguinity, Kinred and Affinity.

SECTION XXV

Cloath, and other stuffs to make apparrel. Colours of all kinds.

SECTION XXVI

Jewels, precious stones, and others of esteem. Metals and Minerals.

SECTION XXVII

Musick, with the terms and instruments thereof.

SECTION XXVIII

Of common sports and playes, with their terms.

SECTION XXIX

Of a Journey and the appurtenances thereof.

SECTION XXX

Husbandry, and country terms.

SECTION XXXI

Fencing, and the terms thereunto belonging.

SECTION XXXII[8]

Fortification, with its terms. Perfume, odors, and sweet smells.

---

[8] By mistake, the section is numbered XXXIII. Its subsection is numbered XXXII, but the following section continues with XXXIII. This means that '*Perfume, odors, and sweet smells*' has actually no number of its own. See below.

SECTION XXXIII
Habits, or apparrel for men.

SECTION XXXIV
Womens apparrel.

SECTION XXXV
Birds and Fowls for hawking.

SECTION XXXVI
Fish and the terms of fishing.

SECTION XXXVII
Spices for sauce.

SECTION XXXVIII
An Orchard, or hortyard, and fruit trees.

SECTION XXXIX
Singing, or cage-birds.

SECTION XL
VVeights and measures.

SECTION XLI
Forrest trees, and woods.

SECTION XLII
Reptils, worms, and insects.

SECTION XLIII
The table, and the meat thereupon.

SECTION XLIV
Arms defensive, and offensive.

SECTION XLV
Common Names belonging to men, with their Etymologies.

SECTION XLVI
Common names of women, with their Etymologies.

SECTION XLVII
Heraldry, or Armory, and the blazoning of Arms, with their proper terms.

SECTION XLVIII

Terms of Chymistry, and the obscurest explaned.

SECTION XLIX

A City, or Town, &c. with the Tradesmen, and Artificers thereof, and the proper terms of their Craft, and Tools, &c.

SECTION L

The several sorts of Citizens, Trades, and Handicrafts, &c. in a Town.[9]

SECTION LI

Other mechanical Trades and their proper terms, and tools.

SECTION LII

A Gradual Epitome of the Universe, or whatsoever is comprehended in Trismegistus Circle, or is above it.

7.3 Introductory texts and address to dictionary users

As usual, the dictionary is introduced by some general texts, namely, poems and an essay *'To the tru Philologer, Touching the English (or Saxon) with the three Sororian Toungs, French, Italian and Spanish; . . .'.* The onomasiological part is prefaced by its own address to its users: *'To the knowing.[!] Reader, Touching the Matter, and Method, of the ensuing Nomenclature.'*

The poems and essay contain some overlapping arguments concerning the origin and development of languages, the relation of words to reality and of words to ideas, and the special features of the languages concerned. We encounter the well-known assumption that all the Teutonic languages, including English, are 'tough' whereas the others are 'soft'. English is traced back to German and, beyond that, to the beginning of all languages, that is, to Hebrew and even to Adam. The three Romance languages, including their various dialects, are traced back to their mother tongue Latin. It is noteworthy that these historical derivations are given more descriptively than evaluatively, that is, the author does not combine them with judgements on which language is the better or the less good one (Hüllen 1995*b*).

All this is hardly original. Nor is tracing the history of English by quoting the Lord's Prayer in various versions. For Howell, English has reached a state of perfection at his own time *'. . . by adopting to herself the choicest, best sounding, and significanst words of other languages, which in tract of time were enfranchized,*

---

[9] There is an in-between title here: *'Touching sorts. and tasts of wines look in the particular Section of wine.'*

and made free denizons as it were of England by a kind of Naturalization' (ₓₓʳ). The great number of these adopted words, Howell explains, came from French, but also from the other two Romance languages *'Insomuch that she may be sayed to be Dutch*[10] *embrodered with French and other toungs, or she may be sayed to be like one that gathers sweet flowers out of divers banks, and beds to make a nosegay'* (ₓₓʳ). This leads to the idea that in the alphabetical dictionary the etymological affinity of the words, made visible by their simple arrangement in lines, *'will prove a great advantage to Memory in regard of the affinity and consonance they* [= the languages] *have one with another in thousands of words'* (ₓₓ2ʳ). This will facilitate memorizing *'all the fower with more ease'*. Although this seems to place all four languages on the same level, James Howell ranks them in a significant way. In his *poema gnomicum* he compares the dictionary to a cart: *'tis like a frame on divers wheels, / One follows still the other at the heels, / The smooth Italian, and the nimble Frank, / The long-lunged Spanish march all in a rank, / The English head's them, so commands the Van'* (ₓ2ᵛ).

According to the address to the users of the onomasiological part, it is the author's primary aim *'to give every thing its due, genuin and proper peculiar term'*, and to do this for the benefit of *'all Writers, Poets, Orators, Lawyers, specially Divines, who use to illustrat things by familiar similitudes, and fetch them sometimes from mechanical trades'* (++++++ʳ). This strikes a note slightly different from the general introduction, although it is not totally absent there. Now the aim of the dictionary lies within the bounds of rhetoric and eloquence, in particular for such persons as have to speak in public. Obviously the author sympathizes with people who illustrate their ideas with *'familiar similitudes'*, wherever they are taken from. In any case, the genuine proper and peculiar term is also the familiar one for those who know. This places Howell in a line with other representatives of a plain and direct style who favour 'naked' words with clear denotations, avoiding similes as well as metaphors and preferring the language of craftsmen and artisans to that of 'wits'. These persons were to found the Royal Society in the very year of the appearance of James Howell's dictionary.[11]

But the author also mentions 'gentlemen' as a particular group of dictionary users whom he wants to provide with special terms, for example, of hunting, fishing, horse breeding, falconry, heraldry, architecture, husbandry, etc. Together with the first aim of providing people with genuine and precise terms, this proves that the nomenclature does not really cover specialized domains, that is, it is not *special* in the modern sense of *English for special purposes*, but addresses a certain section of society, namely, the gentry with its particular interests and modes of living and with its particular, rather practical style. The general title as well as the subtitle of the nomenclature had already suggested this by mentioning 'arts and sciences' and linking them with 'recreations' and *'common Professions and Callings both Liberal*

---

[10] 'Dutch' here has the older meaning of 'Deutsch', that is, Low German. See Chapters 4 and 9.

[11] See Hüllen 1989, in particular the chapter on Sprat's *History of the Royal Society*, 98–113.

and Mechanick', that is, connected with books and with tools. One paragraph of the introductory essay is even more detailed and more direct in this respect:

The second Volume is a large Nomenclature of the peculiar and proper termes in all the fower languages belonging to severall Arts, to the most generous sort of Recreations, to all professions both liberall, and manuall from the Engineer to the Moustrapmaker, from the Merchant Adventurer to the cryer of matches. (..2^r.)

There then follow all the domains of a gentleman's life which have already been mentioned. In fact, the nomenclature contains the general, rather practical, vocabulary of a special section of society. This is why the majority of its sections cover areas of reality which are present in many nomenclatures of the time. We can also confirm this statement by comparisons between the alphabetical and the onomasiological part of the dictionary. The headwords occur in both, decontextualized in the alphabetical and semantically embedded in the onomasiological one.

Noteworthy among the general deliberations on the aim of this onomasiological dictionary is the fact that it seems to apply more to native English speakers in the use of their mother tongue than in the use of the other three. This is at least suggested by a sentence like '*the prime part of eloquence is to give all things their proper termes*' (..2^r.). Nothing is said about translations, their technique and their problems, and the need for using foreign languages in England or elsewhere, etc. This again points to the fact that the author collected his vocabulary with a special group of people in mind, whose members he addresses as '*the knowing Reader*' and who are the group to which he himself belonged or, at least, worked for.

Among this group must also have been people interested in '*Terms of Chemistry*', defined as '*the Hermetical, or Paracelsian art*', from which words are collected in Section XLVIII. Moreover, people must have been interested in '*whatsoever is comprehended in Trismegistus Circle, or above it*', from which words are collected in Section LII. These two sections are unique in the non-specific onomasiological dictionaries of the time, both in England and on the Continent. The group of people interested in these topics is certainly to be found among scientists. In these sections, more than in others, it is again the mother tongue which attracts at least as much attention as the translations because, in each case, a difficult, that is, a *hard*, English word is given first in one or several easier rendering(s) and only then in the other three tongues. This brings at least the English parts of the entries closer to such alphabetical dictionaries as were designed to translate hard English words into easier ones, that is, such words as are intelligible to people who do not have foreign languages at their command.[12] Both sections will be analysed later.

Finally, James Howell's interest in first, and not so much in foreign, language information and competence is corroborated by entries in which a whole series of

---

[12] Parts of this section are indeed ordered alphabetically. For hard-word dictionaries see Lehnert 1956, Landau 1984, 35–43, and Hüllen 2004, 119–60.

semantically related English headwords (a *Wortfeld*)[13] is juxtaposed not with translations of each of them but just with a summarizing expression in Italian, French, and Spanish. Note, for example, in section LI (with reference to a printing press):

The cap, the cheeks, the head, the nut and spindle, the bar, the bolts, the hose, the garter, the forelock, the shelves, the platin, the plate, the pan, the hooks, the catch, the coffin, the flank, the sockets, the tympane, the gallows of a Press; Le parti della Stampa; Les parties de la Presse, Las partes de la Emprenta.

A consequence of this technique is that the number of English headwords is much higher than the number of their Italian, French, and Spanish translations.

7.4 The microstructure

The microstructure applies to single entries. In Howell's dictionary they are of varying size. Regularly, they contain an English headword[14] and three translations. The headword is frequently but not always followed by a synonym or a post-lemmatic explanatory phrase, which may or may not appear in several or in all of the following translations. On rare occasions, one or several or all of the translations are furnished with synonyms or explanations which are not attached to the headword. This means the four versions can be but need not be exact word-for-word translations. They are often just semantically equivalent expressions. Note the following typical entries, taken from section I:

The Bones: Le offa: Les os: Los huessos:
The Bonage, or all the bones: L'ossame, ossatura, cioe, tutte l'ossa del corpo insieme: La carcasse c'est a dire tous les os du corps ensemble: Todos los huessos del cuerpo junctos.
To be dazzled; Haver le traveggole à gli occhi, cioé, quando pare che davanti à quelli si habbia come moscioni ò cordicelle; Avoir la berlue, c'est quand il semble avoir devant les yeux come des mousches, où cordes; Vizlumbre, cegajez.

The headword is either one word of any class, though predominantly nouns and verbs, or a nominal or verbal phrase (Adj + N, 's + N, Inf + Compl). Almost all the nouns start with a definite or an indefinite article, uncountable nouns and nouns in the plural with no article. Infinitives start with *To*.

The relations between headwords and the post-lemmatic explanations seem to defy any systematization. Of course, some kind of synonymity is intended. The

---

[13] For the term and its history see Chapter 1, 18. I am using it in the meaning of: *a not clearly delimited cluster of lexemes, corresponding to a relatively homogeneous domain of physical or mental reality, which stand in various semantic relations to each other and can all be subsumed under one general archilexeme.*

[14] Very occasionally a Latin headword with an English translation appears, for example '*Deceptio visus, or the Deceit of the eye*' (section I).

two well-known stylistic levels of English, the Germanic and the Latinized, certainly play an important role. But no clear guideline for the relation of head-word and synonym is discernible. Note such differing but fairly typical examples, taken from section I, as:

'To let Blood, open a vein, or phlebotomize', 'Dander, or scruff of the head', 'To nurse or give suck', 'To christen or baptize'.

A special type of entry is constituted by a series of headwords, semantically related to each other, which either is complemented by a word-for-word transla-tion into the three other languages or, as already explained above, is comple-mented by merely a summarizing expression. Depending on one's viewpoint,[15] these series of headwords can be regarded as having related meanings or as a *Wortfeld*. They constitute an independent semantic level between the topical section and the single entry. Note the following typical headwords, all taken from section III, part *'Of other wild Beasts'* (see below):

A Lion, A Crocodile, A Dormouse, The Lions den, The trump or trunk of an Elephant, A caltrop, or Engin of three iron points to hunt the Wulf, To couch or rear a wild Boar, The barr, the Beam, branch, advancers, pawlm and spelters of a Deers head, The fewments or dung of a deer, the lesses of a Fox, or Badger, the spraints of an Otter, the crotells of the Hare, &c.

Note that '*&c*' is part of the multi-member headword. Moreover, note a typical entry with several headwords and summarizing translations from section LI:

The cover, the frame, the movement, the key, the spring, the vice, the plyers, the riveting tounges, turning benches, the balance, the click, the cock, the ratchet, the fusie, &c. of a watch: Parti dell' horologio; Les parties d'un horloge; Las partes de un relox.

There are, however, also entries where the translations express more information than the headwords do. Note an example taken from section XIII:

An Emblem; Vn Emblèma, coorpo con un motto, ó vogliam dire con l'anima, unitamente signifficanti un concetto; Vn emblèm, un corps avec un mot, signifians ensemble quelque conception; Emblèma, &c.

The number of such entries, however, is relatively small.

Generally speaking, Howell's technique of writing entries is very *ad hoc* and pragmatic. He changes their microstructure depending on the nature of the lexemes. His primary interest seems to be lucidity of meaning, the conveying of not just words in four languages but also of matter-based or idea-based knowl-edge. With this interest he fulfils the prime aim of an onomasiological dictionary, which is the presentation of knowledge in and with the help of a certain order, not just of languages in so far as this knowledge is incorporated in lexemes.[16] The last

---

[15]   The difference of viewpoint lies in the ambiguity of the term *synonymy*, which refers either to the fact that a number of words with different meanings are semantically related to each other, or to the fact that a number of semantically overlapping words are separated by shades of meaning.

[16]   For the difference between linguistic meaning and general meaning or world knowledge see Chapter 1, 7-11.

two examples with their '*&c*' show this clearly. As soon as the meaning of the headword is established clearly in English or in a translated version, the further mentioning of lexemes becomes unimportant. Exactness of translation is not always Howell's main concern.

There are, furthermore, entries which do not have any precise lexeme in the function of a headword at all, in English or in the languages of translation, but contain simply a common expression which denotes something worthy of denotation. Note from section I: '*The white of the eye, The corner of the eye towards the nose, The corner of the eye towards the temples*'. In these cases, the translations are literal renderings of the headword/head-expression, that is, none of the four languages offers a lexicalized form for the contents expressed. The motive for inserting these entries is, thus, truely onomasiological, springing from meanings as parts of general knowledge, irrespective of whether there exist or do not exist lexicalized names of them. This does not preclude the fact that the motive for doing this is also eminently practical, for example for doctors, that is for people who describe faces or treat them.

7.5 The macrostructure

The macrostructure applies to the dictionary as a whole; more precisely, to the sequence of its sections. It is for an onomasiological dictionary what the alphabet is for the semasiological. It is the search programme by which the dictionary users arrive at the entry they want to learn something about.

The fifty-two sections of the *Lexicon Tetraglotton* contain the whole '*catalogue raisonné de l'univers*' (Sidarus 1990*a*, 348) which is the backbone of the onomasiological tradition. God, the universe, the three kingdoms of nature, mankind, society with its important institutions, namely, family, state, and church, the arts and sciences, the world of artificial objects—all the great topics of onomasiology are here. This makes the *Lexicon Tetraglotton* one dictionary of many. However, it also has its own arrangement of topics which gives the dictionary its individual profile.

Obviously man is the measure of this work. The first section is devoted to his[17] anatomy, not to God or the universe. The following sections, at least up to section XL, contain lexemes that pertain to man's socially organized world, predominantly in the country. Obviously, the societal stratum of noblemen is focused on, who enjoy hunting, fishing, and warfare and whose domestic life is marked by a certain opulence and by leisure pursuits. This establishes nine clearly demarcated topical domains of vocabulary.

---

[17] As is to be expected, the world of old dictionaries is dominated by (male) men. I cannot but follow this general outlook. Yet, wherever it makes sense, masculine definitions should be understood as being of generic meaning.

(1) Human anatomy (I);

(2) Activities of gentlemen (II. horsemanship, III. hunting and beasts, IV. falconry, V. soldiery, VI. seafaring and navigation);

(3) Christian society (VII. orders of knighthood, VIII. religious orders, IX. ecclesiastical dignitaries, X. controversies in the Church);

(4) Houses and their surroundings (XI. buildings, XII. household goods, XIII. library, XIV. kitchen, XV. garden, XVI. herbs, XVII. grain);

(5) Meals (XVIII. drinks, XIX. meat and domesticated beasts, XX. poultry);

(6) Qualifications of persons (XXI. age, XXII. reprehensible characteristics, XXIII. diseases, XXIV. consanguinity);

(7) Clothes (XXV. cloth and colours, XXVI. jewels, metals, and minerals);

(8) Pastimes (XXVII. music, XXVIII. sport, XXIX. journeys, XXX. husbandry, XXXI. fencing, XXXII. fortification, XXXIII. apparel for men, XXXIV. apparel for women, XXXV. hawking, XXXVI. fishing, XXXVII. spices, XXXVIII. orchard, XXXIX. birds' voices);

(9) Weights and measures (XL). This section XL is an appendix as often added to the main body of entries, giving closed sets of lexemes combined with closed systems of meanings, typically weights and measures, numbers, days of the week, months, etc.

There is a distinct caesura after section XL. The following eight topical domains of vocabulary, most of which consist of only one or two sections, have no convincing order and look like later additions and supplementations:

(10) Nature (XLI. Trees, XLII. Insects): judging by the placement and by the numbers of lexemes in comparison to other onomasiological dictionaries, this domain looks like two appended lists of words for which there was no fitting slot available anywhere else. For Howell, metals and minerals, plants and animals either are obviously part of human life (as in XV, XVI, XVII, XIX, XX, XXVI, XXXV–XXXVIII), or are, almost casually, to be put into some unsuitable place because the author finds it obligatory to mention them.

(11) Table and meat (XLIII) is actually a supplement to (5) Meals; just as

(12) Arms (XLIV) is a supplement to (2) Soldiery (V).

(13) Names (XLV. names of men, XLVI. names of women) would be in their proper place here as a second appendix after (9) Weights and measures, if there were no other sections intervening.

(14) Heraldry could have found a much more fitting place in (3) Christian society (for example, in VII. Orders of knighthood).

(15) Chemistry (XLVIII) is indeed extraordinary because it covers a highly specialized topic for which an adequate place could be found only if terms of other sciences were also collected in the dictionary. But this is not the case. The same holds true for (17) Universe with its vocabulary '*out of Trismegistus circle*' (but see below).

(16) City (XLIX. tradesmen and artificers, L. citizens, trades, LI. mechanical trades, tools) is again a case with its own problems, because, generally speaking, its lexemes represent a world which ranks among the most important and most elaborately treated domains in other onomasiological dictionaries. But this is not the world of Howell which, on the contrary, focuses on the country life of the gentry, not on the town life of citizens, although he shows great interest in the language of the artisans. It seems to have been difficult to combine these two perspectives. So the respective entries did not find their fitting slots, which would have been after or inside (4) Houses and their surroundings.

(17) Universe, already mentioned, provides the vocabulary for God and the world as a whole, which in most dictionaries is found at the beginning. It is at least fortunately placed in this last section, because this position is almost as prominent as the first.

James Howell's onomasiological dictionary mirrors the human activities of a social group which is clearly defined by its lifestyle, its amusements, and its scientific interests. The natural order of this area of reality repeats itself in the order of sections, by which a kind of practical encyclopaedia for the people concerned is created. In this respect it differs sharply from other onomasiological dictionaries which, for example, predominantly mirror the reality of the objective world. This requires that in such dictionaries metals and minerals, plants, in particular herbs and trees, as well as animals, wild or domesticated, appear in their own right as representatives of the three kingdoms of nature, but not as objects of human activities and pleasures. The shortcomings of the *Lexicon Tetraglotton* in its second part (after XL), discernible against the backdrop of its own semantic macrostructure, are, of course, the result of the contradiction existing between the traditional universalism of all onomasiological works and the limits of the personal approach and perhaps of the abilities of the author.

Similar to the way in which the unity of the dictionary is broken down into two parts with a clear caesura between them, we find many sections divided into two sub-sections, where the first presents a topical domain in a fairly strict order whereas the second either supplements the first in details or adds a second related topical domain which could, for some reason, not be integrated into the first. Thus, several sections have a second subtitle without numbering, and one even has a third. This applies to sections III, VI, XIX, XXV, XXVI,[18] where, for example, words for colours are added to words for clothes and words for metals and minerals to words for jewels.

It is difficult to determine on the reasons for this technique. Sometimes it is certainly used simply for patching up faults. Sometimes the compiler of the

---

[18] Section III even has two additions with their own subtitles. A special case is the section 'Fortification' (numbered XXXIII instead of XXXII). Its subsection *'Perfume, odors, and sweet smells'* is very likely erroneously placed and should have its own number.

dictionary will have found himself torn between his own interests or purposes and the onomasiological tradition which made it obligatory for him not to leave out certain topical areas. The following analyses will also show that William Howell sometimes simply follows a model.

7.6 De Noviliers' *Nomenclatvra* and Howell's *Lexicon*

James Howell is not the author of the onomasiological part of the *Lexicon Tetraglotton* in the proper sense. He made use of Guillaume Alexandre de Noviliers'[19] topical dictionary in Italian, French, and Spanish (1629) by prefixing its entries with English headwords and adopting these entries literally in by far the most cases. Thus, they appear as translations of English, although Howell's English headwords are actually translations of them.[20] More important, the topical arrangement of sections is not Howell's achievement but his forerunner's or that of other authors standing behind him.

This fact may be disappointing for the evaluation of James Howell as a linguist, in particular because he acknowledges his debt to the Frenchman rather hesitatingly. After speaking of the '*extraordinary Labor*' of his enterprise, he admits: '*I confesse to have had some single helps in divers things that did facilitat the Things, and Monsieur de Novilliers did contribute more than any*' (++++++^{r}). Leaving aside the question of authenticity, however, the relationship between Howell and de Noviliers is of interest, because, as is to be expected, there are deviations of the later book from the earlier one, and it is these deviations that give Howell's intentions an even clearer profile. The title of de Noviliers' book reads:

Nomenclatvra Italiana, Francese, E Spagnvola. Con i tèrmini proprij ciascun Capìtolo. Nomenclatvre Italienne, Françoise, Et Espagnole. Auec les termes propres de chacun Chapitre. De Gvillavme Alexandre De Noviliers, Clauel. Nomenclatvra Italiana, Francesca, Y Españòla. Con los tèrmonos pròprios de cada Capitulo. Con licenza de' Superiori, e Priuilegio. In Venetia, MDC XXIX. Appresso Barezzo Barezzi. Ad istanza dell' Autore.

The book (WF 45.5 Gram, 4°) has 411 numbered pages printed with two columns. There are 51 *capìtoli*, that is, one fewer section than in Howell's dictionary. Very

---

[19] The BL catalogue registers this author also under *Clavel*, which however seems to be a geographical name. Other libraries (Bibliothèque Nationale, Wolfenbüttel) use 'de Noviliers'. I was unable to obtain further information. According to Howell, when acknowledging his help by de Noviliers, and according to the official *imprimatur* of the dictionary by the Venetian authorities, de Noviliers was, as his name suggests, a Frenchman. The fact that he published in Italy and put the Italian lexemes first in his dictionary might suggest that he lived in Italy. The catalogue of the Bibliothèque Nationale, however, also refers to the name Guglielmo Alessandro de Novilieri. The usual French and Italian biographical reference works and indexes do not contain any entries.

[20] This explains why so many headwords are not lemmata but phrases. The author was bound in his choice by the Italian / French / Spanish lexemes. I cannot say anything about how the Italian / French / Spanish translations of headings and headwords which are not taken from de Noviliers' book were arrived at. No other edition can be traced from which they could have been taken.

conveniently for the reader, entries are numbered within each. Howell obviously took over Roman numbers for counting the sections as well as the typographical arrangement of entries—a regular alternation between Roman, italics, and Roman again. Generally speaking, entries are shorter in the earlier book, because there are fewer synonyms and explanations. But there are, of course, exceptions to this, as will be shown below.

De Noviliers merely speaks of '*Nomenclatvra*' (etc.) whereas Howell mentions arts and sciences, recreations, and professions both '*liberal and mechanic*'. This may be just a matter of advertisement on the Englishman's part, but it shows where his intentions lie. He has the writers, poets, orators, lawyers, and divines in mind, and most of all the *gentlemen* who are interested in these arts and sciences, recreations, and professions. In this, de Noviliers precedes him in his short address speaking of the '*Caualiere, & anche all'altre persone ben nate e gentili*' (a3ʳ) whom he wants to provide with the right words, being asked to do so by the Italian Academy, in particular that of Padua. But otherwise no mention is made of any special group(s) of people envisaged by him as users of his book. In particular, merchants and artisans are missing.[21]

Howell made some interesting changes to the macrostructure, when he incorporated the older dictionary into his more comprehensive work. Looked at from the outside, Howell's sections on religious orders (VIII), sects (X), apparel of women (XXXIV), names of men and women (XLV, XLVI), heraldry (XLVII), chemistry (XLVIII), citizens (L), trades and tools (LI), and the universe (LII) have no counterparts in de Noviliers' book, whose sections on '*Le cose superiori*' (I), '*Il colori*' (VIII), '*Gli odori, & i profumi*' (XI), '*I fiori*' (XIX), '*Gli animali domèstici*' (XXIII), '*I cani da càccia*' (XXXIII), '*Altre fiere*' (XXXVII), and '*Le cariche*' (XLV) have no counterparts in Howell's. Many of these inconsistencies are easily resolved. '*Il colori*' is in fact part of Howell's section XXV, attached to cloths, etc. '*Gli odori, & profumi*' is sandwiched between Howell's sections XXXII and XXXIII and was obviously placed there in error. '*I fiori*' was integrated entry-for-entry into Howell's section XVI which contains names for garden herbs, etc. '*Gli animali domestici*' was made part of Howell's section XIX, which deals with meat for eating. '*I cani da caccia*' is part of Howell's section III, names on hunting. So is '*Altre fiere*'. '*Le cariche*' seems indeed to have been missed out with no reasonable explanation to be found.

However, there are some significant reasons to be found for other alterations. For example, de Noviliers' section XXXIX '*Le dignità spirituali*' contains 218 entries pertaining to the ecclesiastical hierarchy, churches and monasteries, liturgy, etc. It is not astonishing that the vocabulary presented here looks very Roman Catholic. Preparing his book for a country which prided itself on being foremost in reformed theology and which had just passed a period of religiously

---

[21] There is little to say about the microstructure. Both books have the two columns and the change of print. In the earlier one lines are not indented.

motivated civil war, Howell could certainly not simply accept this 'Papist' vocabulary. He divided it into three sections, the first (VIII) giving in sixty-four entries many more details and explanations on religious orders for his readers than the Frenchman and Italianate de Noviliers, who could presuppose them as being well known. The second (IX) gave a very short selection of only twenty-four what could be called Catholic entries, and the third (X) provided sixty-nine entries with names for all kinds of heretics whom de Noviliers did not mention at all. Thus 157 entries in the English dictionary take the place of 218 in the Italian (etc.), sixty-nine of these being newly introduced. The Reformed Howell retained only eighty-eight headwords from the 218 of the Catholic de Noviliers.

Howell took over all the entries from '*I vestiti*', which are in fact only men's clothes, and added another section on apparel of women (XXXIV), thus showing that his gentleman's world was not of one sex only. After all, he lived at the time of Restoration comedy, and the lexemes chosen for men's and women's apparel do not remind us of simple people, either. Names of men and women are often to be found in the appendices of dictionaries. So there was a good reason to include them. Heraldry and chemistry are domains of interest easily explainable from motives which have already been given.

Howell's sections XLIX,[22] L, and LI on '*A City or Town*', '*The several sorts of Citizens*', and '*Other Mechanical Trades*' are again special cases. They match '*La città, gli offiziali, & offizij publici, e gl'artefici*' (XLI) of de Noviliers, but it is only at the beginnings of section XLIX (Howell) and XLI (de Noviliers) that similarities are visible. Altogether, there are 339 original entries to be seen against 407 later ones. Although some entries occur in both books, each is obviously placed in a different context. De Noviliers mentions extensively administrative, judicial, and academic vocations, whereas Howell is more interested in merchants, money business, and crafts. Together with the names for men and women who work in these businesses and crafts, he mentions the materials they work with, their tools, and their products. It is here that we find many entries with clusters of lexemes obviously not standing in a synonymous relation to each other but rather constituting a semantic domain. Note, for example: '*A Wyre drawer; Tiratore de metalli; Trayeur de metaux; Tirador de metales*'. And immediately following is the entry:

A hammer, nippers, a rowl pin, an oyl-stone, bobbins, purling wyers, a spangle tool, a tool to cut oaes, rocket, or small rowles, a serpentine, an anvil, files, the racer, a burnisher, &c; Gli stromenti del tiratore de metalli; Les outils de trayeur de metaux; Los instrumentos del tirador.

There are about forty such *Wortfeld*-entries in section LI, which totals 170 entries. They show clearly that the interest of the author is focused on first-language competence rather than on the translations, which he simply omits. Of course, this is the world of craftsmen and artisans in whose language James Howell was particularly interested, because it was the model of the kind of language he

---

[22]　In the book erroneously given as XLXIX.

wanted to improve and to spread in his work. No wonder that in this case he deviated widely from his source.[23]

Howell's last section, *'A Gradual Epitome of the Univers'*, has changed places with de Noviliers' first section, *'Le cose superiori'*. The later dictionary repeats the earlier almost entry-for-entry. There are five omissions in Howell's section which can all be regarded as simple errors. One further omission shows that the English author had quite precise ideas on what to offer his readers. He left out entry 61 with its country-related information:

vn grado, contiente ottantasette miglia, e mezzo d'Italia. un degre, sont vingtneuf lieués & vnsixiesme de lieue (ou quatre vingts & sept milles & demy d'Italie) a trois milles pour lieue. vn grado, contiene ochenta y sieet millas, y media de Italia, que son poco menos de veyntee y dos leguas de España, a quatro millas por legua.

But he did not leave out entry 159, which is perhaps as country specific: *'il gran caldo del mezzo giorno. La chaleur du midy, ou du my-iour. la sièsta'*.

Two very long entries on the calender (188, 189) were drastically shortened. Obviously de Noviliers' classical knowledge on this topic was thought to be too precise for English readers. Three additions (between 40 and 41, 73 and 74, and between 98 and 99) are inconspicuous. The idea of the *'Epitome of the Univers'* is underlined by moving de Noviliers' entry 33 (*'il cielo Empiréo, la stanza di Dio, e dei Beàti'*) to the beginning and adding three entries (*'Hell, or the remotest place from Heaven, Gehenna', 'Devils, infernal Fiends, or Cacodaemons', 'The Center of the world'*) at the end, thus completing the idea of the enveloping universe as different from *'le cose svperiori'*. But otherwise de Noviliers' dictionary, although not mentioning Trismegistus at all, seems to have satisfied the English adaptor and his philosophical outlook.

There remains the question of placement. De Noviliers obviously followed the onomasiological convention, well founded in theological and philosophical traditions, of starting from *above* and recreating the world in words from there in what would appear to him a natural order. Howell, however, placed men first and then stressed their fields of activities or their fields of knowledge. De Noviliers covers the universe first, then the human world, nature, and societal institutions, to which belong wars, navigation, the arts. Howell starts with men and then covers the activities of the representatives of a certain class, including their favoured sciences which are meant to explain the world. Admittedly, there is no conflict of principles between the two authors, rather one of accent because de Noviliers also sees nature in connection with mankind, not as an independent domain of reality. It is a pity that, in rearranging de Noviliers', by and large, convincing system of sections for his own purposes, Howell made, at least in some parts, such a mess of it.

---

[23] With one exception (see below) I did not try to find the sources for these entries which abound with technical vocabulary. But they are certainly there and traceable.

7.7 The structure of selected sections and topics

7.7.1 Terminology: section, cluster, group

The term *macrostructure* applies to the dictionary as a whole, that is, to the arrangement of sections. The term *microstructure* applies to the entries in all sections. The term *structure* applies to each section; more precisely, to the sequence of its entries in so far as they form related groups. It is the name of the mesolevel[24] between the dictionary as a whole and the single entry. Judging from the clear typographical markers, the three levels *dictionary*, *section*, and *entry* are clearly differentiated. But in fact the organization of Howell's dictionary is more complex. Within the macrostructure we have already differentiated between the two large parts I–XL and XLI–LII, and within them seventeen groups of sections which have their own coherence. Also within the microstructure we have already differentiated between the one-headword entry and the multiple-headword entry. These differentiations depend, of course, on how closely we look at our object and which categories we choose to apply. Within the structure of the section we will find various other differentiations, depending on the semantic cohesion of the lexemes, which depends on the nature of the topic. These differentiations vary between clearly demarcated *groups* of lexemes and loose *clusters*. They are in no case marked typographically.

The structure is for each section what the macrostructure is for the whole dictionary. It is the search programme by which dictionary users arrive at the entry and, thereby, the lexemes they are looking for. In a way, lucidity and intelligibility are required here even more than on the macrolevel. This is particularly difficult because, on this level, it is hardly traditional to use typographical, visible signs. At least James Howell refrains from doing so. Other dictionary compilers fall back on such aids, for example by printing certain headwords in the margin.

Of course, James Howell's way of imposing an inherent, non-marked order on his entries demands great attention from the readers, who cannot just glance through the list of words in order to find the lexeme they are looking for. This is the more so, because the grouping and clustering of entries is different in each case. They depend on the semantic relationship between lexemes. The order of lexemes pertaining to human anatomy is naturally different from the order of lexemes pertaining to warfare or navigation, and horticulture has an order different from that of clothes. Several analyses of sections will be given to show this.

The sections of the *Lexicon Tetraglotton* vary very much in length. The longest is thirteen pages, the shortest just half a page. The longer a section is, the more

---

[24] I do not want to speak of a 'mesostructure', because the natural and primary reading unit for the dictionary user who searches for orientation is indeed the section. Thus it seems justifiable to give it the unmarked label 'structure', reserving the marked labels for the macro- and microlevels respectively.

important its semantic structure is. A page or so is scanned very quickly, even if there is no perceptible order between its entries. Longer sections must provide clarity, which enables the dictionary users to find the entries they are looking for.

The selection of sections and topics to be chosen for analysis cannot be anything but *ad hoc* and accidental. Each treatment is meant to be exemplary in any case. As the length of sections is critical for the use of the dictionary, it must be a powerful guideline for our choice. Although each section deserves a close reading, it is justifiable to treat the twenty-five very short ones cursorily with only two examples (XXV, XXVI), not because they do not have any order but because they reveal it to the attentive reader without difficulties. This is why analyses of different degrees of elaboration will in fact be limited to a choice of the very long (I, VI, LII), the medium-sized (V, XLIII), and the short (XXIII, XLVIII) sections.[25] Apart from this formal guideline, each of the sections chosen for analysis presents itself because of some speciality, either in its contents or in its arrangement. These specialities will be mentioned in the course of each analytical argument.

7.7.2 Section I: man

In Howell's eyes, '*An Anatomy of the Inward and Outward parts of Humane Body*' is obviously a section of great importance. In contrast to de Noviliers, not only is it located first, but with 454 entries it is also the second longest section of the whole work. Only the section on hunting and game is longer.

All onomasiological treatments of the vocabulary of the human body have one principle of arrangement, from head to feet. Within this order, there are many minor, but at the same time significant variations. The order of Howell's first section is one of them.

Its title already deviates from the usual. The dichotomy between *inward* and *outward*, between *invisible* and *visible*, is indeed the guideline of almost all word-lists of the human body. Presumably, it was the first principle of scientific anatomy when it emerged in classical Greece. But it is rarely expressed in the (sub)titles of a dictionary and, in the case of Howell, it certainly betrays the scientific groundwork of his lexicographical work. This is corroborated by three observations. *First*, there is a first and a last word-group of entries arranged around the others like a frame. The first (group (i)), thirty-eight entries, is devoted solely to the inward parts, which are kept together, as it were, by men's skin. The last (group (vi)), forty-six entries, though not so homogeneous as the first, is devoted to those principles and faculties which, according to the knowledge of the time, constitute the human organism. Both word-groups are dominated by what we would now call a scientific view which is functional (group (i)) and conceptual (group (vi)). *Second*, groups (i) and (vi) both differ from the

---

[25] The special relation between Howell's and de Noviliers' dictionaries means that everything that will be said about a section of the one also pertains to the other, unless stated otherwise.

word-groups (ii) to (iv) between them, which give words for the visible or palpable parts of the organism—head, body, and limbs, 302 entries in all. They are dominated more by observable experience than by scientific knowledge. This is still a scientific, but a descriptive rather than a functional-conceptual approach. *Third*, group (v) is a special case. In sixty-nine entries it contains words with distinctly non-scientific, that is, everyday and common, meanings that make the scientific style of the lexemes of groups (i) and (vi) and groups (ii) to (iv) stand out even more clearly. The functional-conceptual and descriptive approaches are, thus, complemented by a pragmatic one. This gives the whole section a tripartite structure between theory and practice whose patterns, however, vary because of their intertwining and overlapping.

The overall structure of the section reads thus:

- group (i): inward organs (thirty-eight entries),
- group (ii): head and face (160 entries),
- group (iii): body, legs to feet (sixty-five entries),
- group (iv): face, shoulders, arms to hands (seventy-two entries plus an unrelated cluster of five entries pertaining to the breast),
- group (v): *curriculum vitae* (sixty-nine entries),
- group (vi): organic principles (forty-six entries, consisting of twenty-seven entries on principles, interrupted by fourteen unrelated entries, followed by five entries on death).

This arrangement is interesting, but at the same time hardly convincing, because in groups (ii)–(iv) it disrupts the usual sequence of giving names of the parts of the human body from top to feet. If we compare the sequence of entries in Howell's dictionary to that in de Noviliers', we immediately see what has happened. For some reason, possibly because of a mistake, Howell interrupted the sequence of entries pertaining to the head after '*The countenance, or face*' and went on with words pertaining to the body ('*The stomack*'), which later forced him to go back to the face. De Noviliers is indeed very systematic in the sequence of his entries. Moreover, Howell inserted the sequence of entries pertaining to the *curriculum vitae*, which is not in de Noviliers at all, at a place which it is difficult to justify. This insertion is, of course, highly significant for Howell's practical interests, but in terms of the order of entries it is certainly ill chosen.

Moreover, note the following details of entries.

Functional explanations in the post-lemmatic units, not in the lemmata themselves, are particularly frequent in word-group (i), for example (English version of entries only):

The Braino, r[!] *seat of the Animal Spirits;* . . .
The Heart, or source of the vital Spirits; . . .
The Liver, or fountain of blood.

The three functions of the organs are conscientiously differentiated as *seat, source,* and *fountain*. The following entry, '*The Lungs, or Lights;*' does not have a functional explanation, but is followed by a new entry, which serves the same purpose:

The Breath, or respiration . . .
To Breath, or fetch breath.

Other functional explanations are:

The Arteries, or ligaments whence is the pulse and movement of the vital spirits; . . .
The Blood or the seat of the Spririts: . . .
The pores through which the sweat and hair come out of the body.

The philosophical (anthropological) orientation of the last word-group (vi) can best be shown by an *ordered quotation:*[26]

Of a sanguine humour; A colerick homour; A flegmatick humour; A melancholy humour.
Hot; Dry; Moist; Cold.[27]
The three faculties of life; The natural faculty; The vital faculty; The animal faculty.
The five outward senses; The sense of seeing; The sense of hearing; The sense of smelling; The sense of tasting; The sense of touching.
The growing or vegetable soul; The sensitive soul; The rational, or humane soul.
The imagination; The faculty of memory; The understanding; The faculty of will.
The spirit, or intellectual part; The soul, or immortal part.

What we find in these entries of word-groups (i) and (vi) are the principles and the terminological skeleton of Galenic medicine as it was popular for many centuries, including the Paracelsianism of the seventeenth century, and a Platonism that appeared, for example, in Robert Fludd's (1574–1637) writings. The Platonic opposition between the natural and the rational, the notion of different souls and their faculties as explained in Aristotle's *De Anima* and the description of the outward and inward senses according to St Augustine's *De Trinitate* lead to an easily discernible grouping of lexemes which proves to be quite traditional.

There follow five entries on death and dying, which betray the fact that the whole section on man also follows the cycle from birth to death, which has not become apparent so far. This also occurs in other onomasiological dictionaries and is not merely to be accounted an afterthought on Howell's part.

In the three word-groups (ii), (iii), and (iv), lexeme meanings are strictly limited to what can be observed by the eye or touched by the hand. This principle is sometimes even pedantically adhered to. Note the following sequence:

forehead—eye-brows—distance betwixt the eye-brows—eyelids—hair of the eyelid—three humours of the eye—apple [= pupil] of the eye—hollow of the eye.

---

[26]   This is a sequence of selected quotations with my own arrangement of lines which is meant to make visible, without further explanation, which entries of the dictionary belong more closely together than others.

[27]   The eight preceding entries are inserted oddly inside the group which is devoted to the *curriculum vitae*.

It is noteworthy here that the general term *eye* (commonly meaning all the details taken together, except 'forehead') is not even introduced, the author favouring rather a strict sequence of its parts. Admittedly, this is not always the case.

The systematic sequence of entries can best be demonstrated by another ordered quotation.[28] This will, moreover, show the way in which everyday and common vocabulary is deliberately integrated into the more scientific and descriptive one. Note:

The Head; The skin of the head; The forepart;
The hair; [colours (five entries), properties of hair (five entries), trimming (five entries)];
The whole head of hair; The tress of a womans hair; Baldness; [hairdressing (seven entries incl. *shave*)];
Young dowl of the Beard; The Mustaches; A Beard; [treatment of beard (four entries)];
neck; A blow or cuff; The crany, or whole head; the seams of the head; the shaven crown of a Priest;
To shake; To nod; A blow on the head.

It is not easy to decide where the dividing line between scientific (descriptive) and common language lies. Colour adjectives for hair like *chestnut, flaxen, black, red, grey*, for example, may still be regarded as descriptive. They can be found in almost all onomasiological dictionaries. However, entries like *Careless uncomb'd hair; Hair scattered up and down; Hair truss'd up* do not denote anatomical or organic meanings, even in the widest sense. Their meanings are determined by statements of people's everyday treatments of their bodies. These examples show that the scientific language of the dictionary lies mostly, though not exclusively, in nouns and adjectives; common language, however, in adjectives and verbs. Note the following group of entries, where descriptive, in a scientific sense, and common vocabulary are mixed:

The forehead; A rugged forehead, or wrinkled; The eye-brows; To frown or look angerly, or proud; The eye-lids;
[colours of eyes (five entries)], *Squint-eyed; The apple of the eye;* [shape of eyes (two entries)]; *The core or foul matter of the Eye; The twinkling of an eye; To eye one; A glance of the eye; To cast amorous glances; To half hoodwink ones self, as the Venetian Dames use to do* [(ten more entries of this kind, including *To weep or shed tears*)].

Strictly descriptive are the nouns *forehead, eye-brows, eye-lids, apple of the eye*. All the other common expressions either contain attributive adjectives or are verbs. There is also an entry where a Latin lexeme precedes the English one (*Deceptio visus, or Deceit of the eye*), which is undoubtedly on the common level but shows that *common* does not mean uneducated. There are similar word-groups pertaining to the other parts of the face, with lexeme entries whose common (not scientific)

[28] Quotations are given in italics; the words in Roman are my own words which summarize several entries.

meanings rest on adjectives, or, even more, on verbs, like *To smile, To yawn, The grinding teeth, To gnash with the teeth, To bite*, etc.

The two other groups ((iii) and (iv)) concerning the body and the limbs are organized in much the same way as the one concerning the head and the face. They follow the visible and palpable parts of the body, inch by inch as it were. But not all word-groups provide the same opportunities for common vocabulary. Among the lexemes pertaining to the body, including legs and feet in group (iv), we find this vocabulary, mostly though not exclusively, with reference to ways of moving. There are three different movements attached to '*The knee*', seven different movements attached to '*The leg*', and even ten different ways of walking attached to '*The feet*'. Note:

To go gropingly and softly—To stumble or trip—To go a tiptoe—To rest on the way—To stand on tiptoe—To stand bolt upright—To go hopping—To crawl on feet and hands—To go backwards—To kick or give a kick.

There is nothing scientific in these verbs.

The following word-group (iv) of the section pertaining (again) to the face, then to shoulders, arms, and legs has as its first entry, '*The air, or countenance of the face*' followed by a cluster of no less than twenty-three entries which give various facial expressions, from colours (*red, bleak yellowish*) to mental states (*troubled, displeased*). Further down in this group are movements of the arms (*To lean upon the elbows*) and of the fingers (*To point with the finger; To spread the fingers; To make mock-signs with the fingers*). They prove that this common vocabulary is, as a rule, attached to one of the foregoing more scientific lexemes and thus always appears towards the end of a cluster of semantically related words.

It is group (v) which gives common words in the densest sequence. A cohesion appears between lexemes in which the *curriculum vitae* of two generations is given as if in a narrative. It starts with *A young man, A young maid*, moves on to *To contract for marriage* and *The marriage, or wedding* and via *To get ones maidenhead, The being with child* leads to *To bring forth*, which marks the beginning of the second generation. There then follow words for well-shaped and misshapen children, for baptism and growth. The entries *A boy pretty well grown, A girl pretty well grown* lead to the end of the second cycle and the point where the third cycle of a generation could begin. This cohesive cluster of lexemes extends over sixty-nine entries.

While the theoretical framework surfaces in the functional-conceptual entries and anatomical observation in the descriptive ones, common experience surfaces in the pragmatic entries. The cycle of generations has, of course, natural links with biological and medical facts. Lexemes denoting meanings in the context of maturity, procreation, and growth can at least be seen to resemble anatomical vocabulary. This would apply to *A marriagable young woman*, but not to *A stale maiden*. There are plenty of lexemes which refer to social events or the folklore associated with them, but which have no anatomical or medical meanings. Note the following:

To contract for marriage—The contract of marriage—To give the goodmorrow to a married couple—To give the good evening.

The last two entries point to customs which may have been more popular in the countries of the translated languages than in England, as the translations show: '*Dar la mattinata; Donner l'aubade; Dar el alvorada*'; '*Dar la serenata. Donner la serenade; Dar musica*'.

Other entries were probably included in this dictionary because they denote facts with legal consequences. Note, for example:

A legitimate son—A natural son, or bastard—A supposed child—A found child—A postume, or born after the fathers death.

These and other entries can only have found their way into a dictionary because they were of general importance at the time. They already appear in earlier Latin dictionaries.[29]

In spite of its shortcomings, section I of the dictionary, called, '*An Anatomy of the Inward and Outward parts of Humane Body; Una Notomia delle parti Interiori ed esteriori del Corpo umano; Une Anatomie des parts interieures et exterieures du Corps Humain; Una Anatomia de las partes internas y externas del Cuerpo Humano*', sets the pace and the tone for the dictionary as a whole, because it combines philosophical concepts with accurate description and embeds both in the everyday world of human actions and suffering.[30]

7.7.3 Section V: war

With 206 entries this is a long section, though it is one of the shortest of the long sections. It is clearly divided into two almost equal parts, with a ragged end. The first part consists of exactly ninety entries which constitute in their sequence a closely forged chain of thought. It starts with the declaration of war. Then the assembling of an army is given, followed by the army's divisions and units, with many lexemes for the old Roman armies. This betrays Latin dictionaries as sources. Subsequently, we find words for battle array, the different parts of an army in battle, and the fight itself, ending in victory. All this is brought to an end with the burial of the dead, the exchange of prisoners, and thanks to God.

Without any kind of external caesura, the word list then goes back to *A great and mighty battail*, with which the first sequence of entries started. In ninety-four more entries it now puts together another chain of thought whose main topic is the siege of a town, including the long presence of an army in the country caused by this siege. The main phases are the charge, artillery fire, surrender, and marching away.

---

[29] Some irregularities of group (v) may go unnoticed.
[30] This analysis of Howell's first section should be compared with Chapters 6 and 9 where sections of other onomasiological dictionaries on the same topic are treated.

The ragged end contains words for the dissolution of the army, but also for duelling, military commands, perhaps in connection with an execution, and military music, altogether twenty-two entries. Such trailing entries are to be found almost invariably at the ends of sections.

Howell's section V follows de Noviliers' section XLVI entry for entry with a few exceptions. There is no discernible reason for the omission of the few entries of the earlier dictionary which are not in the later one. Perhaps the omission is simply erroneous.

7.7.4 Section VI: sea

This section is a very long one, containing 373 entries. There is no need to prove that navigation is an indispensable topical area for a dictionary like the *Lexicon Tetraglotton*. There is a caesura between the first 223 entries and the rest, marked by its own subtitle. As was found in the analysis of the macrostructure, the second part adds to and supplements the first part, as the subtitle itself indicates.

The first part is divided into three word-groups. It moves from (i) *sea, weather, banks and shores, ports* (thirty-six entries), to (ii) *kinds of ships* (149 entries), and (iii) *voyages* (thirty-eight entries). This means that, in the first place, the scene and natural conditions are set with the help of lexemes that can be regarded as prototypically associated with navigation, not only by sailors but also by the layman. Such general introductions to topical areas of onomasiological dictionaries are frequent. Then follow many lexemes denoting parts of ships, people working and the work to be done there, the manoeuvring of ships and their movements in the water, crews including galley slaves of centuries gone by, the tasks of ships in trade (in peacetime), and war and others, arranged according to a superimposed order. In group (ii) this order is: *kinds of ships*, namely, *small boats* (twenty-one entries), *galleons as men-of-war* (forty-three entries), and *merchantmen* (eighty-five entries), and in (iii): *voyages*, namely, *launching, preparation for voyage, voyage itself, crew during voyage* (thirty entries) and *wind, shipwreck* (eight entries). Thus, the superimposed order is a taxonomy in group (ii) and a time-related chain of events, a *story*, in group (iii).

This first part of the section is taken over from de Noviliers almost entry by entry, with seventeen entries missing and three added. There is no tendency discernible in these alterations, except perhaps in the last two added ones which bring the topic to a natural end: '*Wrack'd goods found on the sands or the sea shore*' and '*To escape shipwreck a straddle upon some plank*'. It is astonishing that the adoption of entries from de Noviliers stops here. His entries 237 to 272, which mostly deal with manoevering a ship in the wind, have been dropped entirely.

The second part of the section with its own subtitle is obviously meant to supplement the first, either by adding more lexemes to semantic groups already mentioned, sometimes even repeating entries, or by introducing other groups for which no adequate slot had been provided so far. The first applies, for example, to lexemes pertaining to *anchor, sails, ropes, pumps* (twenty-four entries) and to *manoeuvring, repairing* (twenty entries). It particularly applies to lexemes pertaining to kinds of wind, where the meagre six entries of the first part are supplemented by twenty-five more. The following group of lexemes on *movements of boats under special weather conditions* (twenty-two entries) and *manoeuvring* (five entries) are in fact related to the foregoing entries pertaining to kinds of winds, so that a group with its own cohesion comes into existence. The second applies to *ship in port, ships' guns* (seventeen entries) and *offices on board* (twenty-one entries). There are also two unrelated clusters of lexemes (six and ten entries respectively), the last one being the ragged end which frequently and typically closes a topical section. It is worth while quoting it because of its interest in English, not in the other languages:

Flotsam, Jetsam, Lagam,[31] *and Shares, the first are goods floating on the Sea after a Ship-wrack; the second are goods cast out in a storm; the third goods that lye in the bottom; the last goods due to many; Termes de la loye navale; Termini della legge nautica; Terminos de la ley naval.*[32]

There are quite a number of entries in this section which consist of a series of lexemes constituting a semantically related domain, but complemented only by a summarizing expression in the other three languages. Such collective entries have their own complex microstructure, constituting a level of their own between the structure of the section and the microstructure of the one-headword entry. An enormous amount of factual knowledge goes into these collected entries which probably escaped most general dictionary users but which must have been appealing to the expert. Note the following entry where this can be shown clearly:

The keel, the first and lowest timber, the stem, the stern, the fashion pieces, the rungs or ground timber thwart the keel, the limber holes, the floor, the rungheads, the howle, the ribs, the sleepers, the spurkitts or spaces 'twixt the timbers, the garboard which is the first outside plank next the keel, the run, the trunnions, the choodings, viz. the planks fastned to the ships stem, the transom which is a timber lies thwart the stern, the buttocks, &c. Les parties originelles d'un navire; Le parti piu originali de vna nave; Las partes primetas de vn navio.[33]

The first ten entries of the second part of section VI, from which the one quoted above is taken, show an obvious parallelism to one of the most famous treatments of the language of navigation of Howell's time, John Smith's *Sea-Grammar*, which can be called a contextualized onomasiological word-list.[34] The parallelism between the quoted entry and chap. II of the *Sea-Grammar* is even more striking. Note the following extract from the latter:

The first and lowest timber in a ship is the keele, to which is fastened all the rest; this is a great tree or more, hewen to the proportion of her burden, laid by a right line in the bottome of the

[31] Probably *laysam*; the lexeme is not in the *OED*.

[32] In this section the sequence of languages differs from the others with French first and the others following.

[33] The entry is from the second part of the section, '*More particular names of navigation*'.

[34] Compare these ten entries and the *Sea-Grammar*, 29–30. See Chapter 5, 159–67.

docke, or stocks. At the one end is skarfed into it, the Stem, which is a great timber wrought compassing, and all the butt-ends of the planks forwards are fixed to it. The Sterne post is another great timber, which is let into the keele at the other end somewhat sloping, & from it doth rise the two fashion peeces, like a paire of great hornes, to those are fastened all the plankes that reach to the after end of the ship, but before you vse any plankes, they lay the Rungs, called floor timbers, or ground timbers, thwart the keele. (1627, 2).

In the margin of the *Sea-Grammar* we find the words, '*The Keele*', '*The Stem*', '*The Sterne*', '*The fashion peeces*', '*The Rungs*'. Howell has '*The keel, the first and lowest timber, the stem, the stern, the fashion pieces, the rungs or ground timber thwart the keele*'. This proves that he modelled his entry on Smith's description, taking its main lexemes which are mentioned in the margin, but also taking lexemes from Smith's descriptive text. In all, twenty lexemes of a series of twenty-eight are identical in Howell and Smith, leaving out two groups of lexemes and an isolated one, but adding none.

It looks as if James Howell, after exploiting de Noviliers in the usual way, suddenly abandoned this book and turned to another source, not before round-ing the first part off with two entries of his own pertaining to shipwreck.

The value of this observation is actually not that James Howell used some expert collection of technical terms in order to cull words from it for his diction-ary. There is, after all, no other way of doing this. The value of this observation is that one entry in Howell corresponds to two full pages of Smith's descriptive text, which shows the extraordinary density of the collective entries in the *Lexicon Tetraglotton*. Moreover, it shows that these entries have their own order which, in the case under analysis, could be given with the title of chap. II of John Smith's *Sea-Grammar*: '*How to build a ship . . . also how they are fixed one to another, and the reasons of their vse*'. Generally speaking, the second parts of sections do indeed sometimes give the impression of afterthoughts but, as this example shows, these afterthoughts need not be haphazard.

7.7.5 *Section XXIII: diseases*

This is a short section. In spite of its brevity it is divided into two parts, each with a title. Again, it has a structure all its own.

The second subtitle, '*The particular Diseases of every member apart, and of womens*', will astonish the reader, because the first part of the section already lists diseases according to the organs which are affected, and the second part is actu-ally ordered according not to 'members' but to organs. This time, it is in the microstructure where the difference lies.

The first part (110 entries) starts, like many sections, with the most general phenomenon of the topical domain, here: of being ill, that is, fever. Sixteen entries are devoted to it, in particular to the different kinds of malaria (*A Tertian, A double Tertian, A Quartan, A double Quartan, A quotidian*, etc.). There then follow more, fairly general diseases which attack the head, for example *The Headache, The vertigo*,

Madness. This leads to sicknesses of the eyes, nose, ears, and throat (thirteen entries), and seven more pertaining to the respiratory tract, especially colds. *Melancholy, or black choler* leads to a group of eighteen entries which give diseases of the stomach, heart, liver, and the intestinal tract, plus the following four rather unsystematic entries: 'A *disease in womans dugs*', '*The mother, or a suffocation of the matrix*', '*Swooning*', '*The coqueluchoe, or a fever with a cough*'. The next is a cluster of lexemes denoting diseases which affect the whole body, not just one organ. Eight of its entries give names for gout and for paralysis, eleven, though rather unsystematically, for infectious diseases, for example measles, including '*Faintiness, or feebleness after sickness*'. Seventeen entries are devoted to infections of the skin and venereal diseases, including *plague* and *canker*. Finally, we find seven entries for symptoms inflicted by force or caused by dirtiness. There then follows the typically random ending: '*Dislocation, or a bone out of joint*', '*The Cramp*', '*Kibes*', '*Corns on the Toes*', '*A gauling*'.

All these entries together can be thought of as the inventory of the layman's medical experience or the symptoms a practising doctor might daily be confronted with. The sequence is almost self-explanatory, following the natural order from top to bottom, moving from the general to the particular, from parts of the body to the whole. For a modern reader it is astonishing how few words are devoted to ailments caused by wounds, bruises, broken bones—afflictions from the outside and caused by force. Probably they were regarded as falling not within a doctor's, but rather within a barber's duties. The lexemes are not *hard* words, that is, not doctors' special language, but common ones. An entry like *plague* appeals to general knowledge, not to experience, because the users of Howell's dictionary would only later have a chance to really experience the plague, at least in London. But since the description of the plague in Athens by Thucydides this disease was well, if only vaguely, known and dreaded.

The second part has a rather different microstructure. It consists of multiple entries devoted to:

Diseases of the Head;—of Breast and Lungs;—of the Heart;—of the Stomach;—of the Liver;—of the Bowels;—of the Spleen;—of the reins and Bladder;—of the Joints;—of the eye;—of the Ear;—of the Nose;—of the Tongue;—of the Teeth, and Throat,—Gums;—Diseases belonging to women.

Entries consist of an English lexeme followed by a Latin one, which, according to the typography, belongs to the headword, that is, the English part, of the entry. There then follow the three languages of translation. Sometimes the Latin expressions are themselves translated and explained in English, this time printed in brackets. Note, for example:

Diseases of the Tongue, Inflammatio, gustus laesus, Paralysis (Palsey,) Ranula sub lingua (a swelling;) Inflammatio, gustus laesus, Paralysis, Ranula sub lingua; Maladies de la langue, Inflammatio, gustus laesus, Paralysis, Ranula sub lingua; Inflammatio, gustus laesus, Paralysis, Ranula sub lingua.

The Latin terms lead to many repetitions in the entries, as the example shows.

Whereas the first part of the section seems to be directed towards the layman and his common understanding of diseases, this second part is obviously meant for the doctor, who moves to and fro between Latin and the vernacular, in his own studies as well as in his treatment of patients. Note as a longer example:

Diseases of the Bowels, The Colique, Iliaca passio (the voiding of excrements at the mouth,) Astrictio alvi, Lineteria (the smoothness of the guts,) Caeliaca affectio (when there are pappy stooles,) Diarrhaea (a thin scouring,) Dysenteria (the bloody Flux,) Tenesmus (or soreness of the fundament,) Fluxxus hepaticus, Lombrici (the worms,) the Hemorroids.

The expert approach of such entries is emphasized not only by the Latin and Greek terms, but also by the distinct systematization. Admittedly, the first part also has its own system which becomes quite clear after a close reading. But it is inherent in the order of entries, and not indicated in the headword of each entry. This latter method is certainly more for the expert.

Only a few lexemes of the second part also occur in the first. This first part is an almost exact copy of de Noviliers' section V, with two omissions and a shift of entry 8 to the beginning, all of them without importance. The second part, however, is independent of this source.

7.7.6 Sections XXV and XXVI: colours, metals, and minerals

Both of these sections are very short and need little comment. Both are divided into two parts, each with a title. Section XXV gives lexemes for clothes and apparel first, then lexemes for colours. These two semantic domains are near enough to each other to justify their being included in one section. Moreover, colours constitute a semantic domain which is present in almost all onomasiological dictionaries. In section XXVI the proximity of jewels to minerals and metals is much less convincing. The first parts of these two sections need no explanatory reading. But their second parts do.

The colours are arranged into three clearly discernible clusters, primary colours, mixed colours or colours defined by comparison, and metaphorical colours. The primary colours follow each other prototypically, that is, according to their salience in the mind as can be detected by psychological experiments, or according to their emergence in languages with a limited vocabulary (Berlin and Kay 1969). This sequence is: white, black, red, green, blue, yellow. They are given together with certain shades, like '*white*' and '*whitish*'; '*black*' and '*blackish*', '*red*', '*russet*', '*crimson*', and '*dark red*', etc.

In their comparisons and their characterizations, the mixed colours show folkloristic imagination at its best, for example: '*Isabella colour*', '*Violet colour*', '*Orenge colour*', '*Dove-colour*', '*Couslip colour*', five entries for grey, '*Changeable colour*', '*Tawny*', '*Mace colour*', '*Minim colour*', '*Rose colour*', '*Brimstone colour*', '*Peach colour*', '*Vermilian*'. Metaphorical colours are represented, for example, by '*A gay lively colour*' and '*A faded colour*'.

Something rather similar happens to the enumeration of metals and minerals. Again we have three clearly discernible clusters. First come what could be called elementary metals, again in a prototypical sequence which seems to include a measure of their value: gold, silver, tin, copper, brass, lead, iron. They are given in groups centring around the metal proper, like, for example, '*gold*'; '*massie grains of gold*'; '*carat, or finest gold*'; '*coarse gold*', '*an ingot of gold*', etc. They are followed by chemical substances like '*orpiment*', '*arsenick*', '*sulpher*', and '*bitumen*'. Finally, we find entries for such trivial substances as '*Itching powder*', '*Gun-powder*', or '*A mineral salt*'.

In these two sections, Howell follows de Noviliers almost without any exception.

7.7.7 Section XXXVIII: fruit-trees

Generally speaking, fruit-trees are listed extensively in onomasiological works. Their common experience in everybody's life accounts for this fact. In Howell's dictionary, however, the section on fruit-trees is a short one, with its 161 entries. It is broken down into three clearly discernible word-groups (without subtitles or other typographical indications), namely: (i) orchard, (ii) fruit-trees, (iii) fruit(s).

Group (i) consists of twenty-nine entries pertaining to the growing and grafting of fruit-trees and to their organic parts, from the root to the fruit-bearing tree. The sequence of lexemes is dominated by the idea of growth in the transitive sense, not as something natural but as something intentionally stimulated and cultivated. Here, trees are the object of practical gardening rather than of natural history.

Group (ii) consists of forty-seven entries pertaining to fruit-trees, again broken down into three clearly discernible subgroups. In subgroup (ii–1) are ten entries for indigenous trees and kinds of trees. Their sequence is: apple, pear, cherry, plum, apricot, peach. In subgroup (ii–2) are twenty-eight entries with names of kinds of foreign trees and of uncommon indigenous trees: first '*fig*', then trees difficult to identify (such as melicoton-tree, lote or nettle tree, meddler-tree, arbute or strawberry-tree), followed by '*mulberry*', various kinds of nut-trees, '*olive*', '*pomegranate*', '*orange*', '*caper-tree*', various kinds of palm and pine. In subgroup (ii–3) we find nine entries for vines and vine growing, which to our understanding pertain to fruit but no longer to trees. This sequence is again prototypical in the psychological sense, in that it proceeds from the best known, most common, and most typical example of the abstract concept inherent in the term *fruit-tree* to the least typical, least common and least known. It proceeds from the generally accepted to the rarely accepted, from the familiar to the foreign, from the most to the least representative of its kind (Rosch 1978, Lipka 1987, Taylor 1989).

Group (iii) consists of seventy-nine entries pertaining to fruit, this time broken down into four subgroups. In subgroup (iii–1) eight entries are given with names of fruits as organic items, comparable to part (i) with its entries pertaining to trees. The entries of subgroups (iii–2), (iii–3), and (iii–4) are ordered in exact parallelism to those in the subgroups of (ii), namely indigenous kinds of fruit (kinds of apples, pears, cherries, plums, apricots, etc.) (twenty-four entries), foreign kinds of fruits and such as are difficult to identify (figs, etc.) (thirty-seven entries), and finally ten entries with names of kinds of grapes. Names of trees in (ii) and names of their fruit in (iii) are sequenced in exact genus-to-genus order, notwithstanding the occasional insertion of the names of details, like '*The kernels of fruits*', '*The rind*', '*The stalk*' of pears, or '*The kernel within the stone*' of peaches.

There is the inevitable ragged end, comprising six non-fitting entries like '*strawberry*' or '*melon*'.

This section of the dictionary does not contain any synonyms or explanations, merely names. It reads like the lexical skeleton of a short treatise on orchards. It should be remembered that the growing and grafting of trees was of no small interest in Howell's time. It was a topic of the applied sciences in the mainstream of Baconianism and as such also favoured, for example, by the Royal Society. In 1662 John Evelyn, for example, delivered his paper *Sylva, or A discourse of forest-trees, and the preparation of timber in His Majesties dominions*, which was published under this title in London in 1664 and had many re-editions. In the same year, John Evelyn issued his famous *Kalendarium hortense: or, The gard'ners almanac; directing what he is to do monethly, thoughout the year*. It became a most popular book with nine editions before the end of the century.[35]

Generally speaking, the seventeenth century saw an increasing interest in gardening and landscaping which resulted in the large parks, including orchards with exotic plants and trees, around the great houses of the aristocracy (Webster 1975, 546–8). It was also a topic of Puritan millenarianism with its concrete ideas of building the Garden of Eden in England. Note, for example, Ralph Austen's book on the practical and the spiritual use of an orchard, whose title gives the general interests and tendencies in the treatment of this topic, which may also have guided Howell's work:

A *Treatise of Fruit-Trees Shewing the manner of Grafting, Setting, Pruning, and Ordering of them in all respects: According to divers new and easy experince; gathered in ye space of Twenty yeares. Whereby the value of Lands may be much improved, in a shorttime [!], by small cost, and little labor. Also discoverig some dangereous Errors, both in ye Theory and Practise of ye Art of Planting Fruit:trees With the Alimentall and Physicall use of fruits. Togeather with The Spirituall use of an Orchard: Heldforth[!] in divers Similitudes betweene Naturall & Spirituall Fruit: trees: according to Scripture & Experience. By R[alph] Austen. Practiser in ye Art of Planting. Oxford printed for Tho: Robinson 1653.*

The same Ralph Austen, together with Samuel Hartlib, wrote a petition on the improvement of forestry and fruit-tree husbandry to Oliver Cromwell as Lord Protector.[36]

---

[35] Numbers of editions of the Kalendarium according to the BL Catalogue.
[36] Printed as Appendix VI in Webster 1975, 546–8.

But then it must be pointed out that in this section Howell again follows his Italian model quite closely. Twelve of de Noviliers' entries are missing, but no reasons for the omission are discernible. Obviously, gardening was an Italian area of interest just as much as an English one, but certainly there without Puritan overtones.

7.7.8 Section XLIII: meals

With 220 entries, this section is a short one. This is noteworthy because, in contrast to many others, it is arranged in one meaningful chain of lexemes from beginning to end. The sequence of this chain is determined by the order of dishes as they appear during a banquet. (The term *meat* in the title means 'food, dish'.) The first entry indeed is 'A *Treatment, feast, or banquet*' followed, as usual, by ten very general ones giving names for the meals of a day from breakfast to supper. The seven subsequent entries are of the pattern '*To wash the hands*', '*To say grace*', '*To sit at table*' and demonstrate a cultivated style of eating. There then follows an elaborate menu: ten entries for starters, thirty-four entries for different kinds of bread including the food served with it. Two entries on salads lead to '*The first dish*', meaning the first main course, which is represented by twenty-seven entries for meat dishes, above all pies and puddings. Sixteen more entries are devoted to wine and drinks, including such lexemes as '*To drink by gulps*' or '*To drink greedily*', which again point to the fact that the social reality behind these vocables includes good, and criticism of bad, table manners. The subsequent ten entries pertain to boiled meat. The following '*A confection of grapes*' seems odd because the enumeration first turns to '*Dishes between*', before it approaches desserts. The 'dishes between' consist of meat and poultry (twenty entries), toast, butter, and egg dishes (sixteen entries), then '*Pease pottage*' and '*Beans beaten small*', fish (eight entries). The following seventeen entries for cheese and milk lead to thirty sweet desserts, introduced by '*A tansie*', '*Pap*', '*Fourmenty*', '*Honey*'. Finally, we have some odd entries: '*Meat well-seasoned, well cooked*', '*Burnt meat*', '*A pittance, or allowance*', '*Pitance*'. The very last four entries are again part of the all-embracing order. They pertain to clearing the table and saying grace.

It is astonishing that the translation of Italian, French, and Spanish vocabulary on cooking into English does not cause any real difficulies. Howell follows de Noviliers closely, as usual, with only a few, obviously accidental, omissions. '*Vna minestra, ò zuppa*', '*minestra di maccherato*', and '*di lasàgne*' are elegantly translated into '*Pottage with bread put in*', '*Broth of maqueroons*', and '*Pancakes*'.

As a contribution to the historiography of cooking in England, this chapter of an onomasiological dictionary might well be compared with historical recipes. Note, for example, this menu of a seventeenth-century meal copied in Haseley Manor, Isle of Wight:[37]

---

[37]   Haseley Manor was owned by King Harold in 1066 and seized by William the Conqueror in the same year. Among its later owners were Henry VIII and Sir Thomas Fleming, Lord Chief Justice of England (1608). The menu is taken from a brochure displayed in the house.

first meat course: roast capon, roast swan, roast heron, swan neck pudding, boar's head and tusks, pheasant, cygnets, pork chop.

second meat course: roast coney, curlew, roast woodcock, roast partridge, larks, roast snipe, venison, peacocks.

first fish course: eels in saffron sauce, baked herring, milwell tales, pike, baked lamprey, roast purpoise, salmon belly, fried minnows.

fourth course: hot apples and pears with sugar candy, wafers, ginger columbine, quince in comfit.

A 'subble' (sculptured food decorations representing the four seasons), followed each course.

7.7.9 Section XLVIII: chemistry

This section is unique in an onomasiological dictionary such as the *Lexicon Tetraglotton*. The very title explains that translation from English into three other languages is not its main purpose but the explanation of 'the obscurest' terms of chemistry. This time the entries are ordered according to the alphabet. However, four and a half pages out of five are devoted to the first letter A, followed by other initial letters in sharply decreasing frequency. There is only one entry starting with O. At the end, the alphabet becomes confused. The first entry reads:

The Art of Chymistry, or the Hermetical, or Paracelsian art; Arte Chymica, ò Hermetica; Art Chymique, Hermetique, ou Paracelsienne; El Arte Chymica, Ermetica, ò Paracelsica.

The following entries consist of special terms for substances (elements), sometimes in quite idiosyncratic English, sometimes also in Latin, and followed by an English rendering which is easier to understand. This sequence of words is repeated in three translations. Note for the English part of the entries:

Abric, Kibrit, Chybur, is Sulphur;—Achamech, is dross of silver;—Adorat, four pound weight;—Aethnici, fiery spirits;—Alech, vitriol;—Auiadum, The regenràt man;—Aqua philosophica, sublimated vineger;—Aquila Philosophorum, metals reduced to their first matter;—Athanor, or Athanar, a chymical, oir spagyrical furnace;—Discus solis, Quicksilver out of gold;—Filius unius diei, Faenix, the Philosophers stone;—Alkahest Paracelsi, a liquor that Penetrates, and transmutes all bodies; etc.

From the middle of page three, right-hand column (from: 'Aqua philosophica, sublimated vineger; Aceto sublimato; Vinaigre sublimé; Vinagre sublimado' onwards), the special chemical term is no longer repeated, only the explanations are translated. The whole reads as if an attempt had been made to incorporate a (probably short) chemical glossary into the onomasiological dictionary, which then proved impossible and was aborted, but not eliminated.

The whole section may be an after-effect of the rise of Paracelsianism in England from the beginning of the century and, almost dramatically, after 1640 which, however, occurred more in medicine than in chemistry, with which it is linked in Howell's dictionary. In the 1640s, Paracelsian medicine was welcomed by representatives of the Puritan revolution (Webster 1975, 273–83), for whom it was the new way of treating sickness in contrast to the traditional one according to Galen. There had been popularizing writings on Paracelsus with explanations of his terms at the beginning of the century, and at least four translations of Paracelsus's writings appeared between 1650 and 1660. Howell's strangely aborted section may have been an attempt to serve those people who were interested in Paracelsianism. Among them were not only doctors and chemists but also pansophic philosophers like Robert Fludd or scientists in the Puritan movement like Samuel Hartlib. Howell's section on the human body, however, does not show this modernistic approach.

7.7.10 Section LII: universe

The last section is one of the five very long ones and, thus, qualifies by its sheer quantity as very important. It is indeed unique in its topic and the intentions which are expressed in it. '*A Gradual Epitome of the Univers, or whatsoever is comprehended in Trismegistus Circle, and is above it*' recalls section XLVIII, in its association with a scientific discipline which is, as a rule, ignored in a general dictionary. The last section of the work strikes the same note of appealing to a tradition which would certainly not be alive in everybody's mind, including even the genteel in the country.

The 226 entries are devoted to God, the universe, the weather, space, and time. Looking at the meanings of lexemes, it becomes obvious that they create an ordered image of the world from *above* to *below*, similar to the order of the first chapter of many other onomasiological word-lists and dictionaries. James Howell gives his work a clear architecture in placing the chapter on man first and the chapter on God and the world last in his dictionary. Although the two lexemes do not occur, the schema of the microcosm and the macrocosm comes to mind.

In fact, section LII does not contain any vocabulary which could only be attributed to Trismegistus. The number of entries on God and the world, however, is much greater than usual and their lexemes are more specific. As in all the other sections, it is easy to break the word-list down into semantically related groups, although there are no external signs for the reader.

Group (i) starts with '*The Empyrean Heaven, the theater of God Almighty*', an entry which combines Aristotelian and traditional, that is, rather medieval, Christian terms. There then follow twenty-four entries with lexemes pertaining to God and the hierarchy of angels and terms for the clerical hierarchy of the Church. '*Eternal bliss, or beatitude*' follows. The ten entries of group (ii) deal with the creation of the stars, starting with '*chaos*' and ending with '*zodiac*'. This repeats the Biblical story of the creation of the world and establishes a link between group (i) (God), and group (iii) (cosmology). This has twenty-one entries on the sun, the stars, the meridian, the poles, zenith and nadir, and the four elements, a combination of lexemes which integrates the idea that the *mundus naturalis* is made up of the four elements with rather a precise knowledge of astronomical facts, an area in which the entries come nearer to the body of knowledge connected with the name of Trismegistus[38] than anywhere else. In the astronomical part, special terms abound, such as *equinoctial, tropic, arctic, antarctic, polar star, Pleiades, the cross* (of the south), *the horizon, meridian, spheres of the planets, zenith, nadir, eclipse,* etc. They certainly betray a knowledge of the Hermetic tradition, though most of them have generally accepted meanings in our time. Others are closer to this tradition. Note, for example:

Meteors of flying fishes;—Chariots and beams of fire;—Flying dragons of fire;—There are Meterological impressions seen in the air, as armies fighting, ships, &c.

The following group, (iv), deals with the elements fire, air, and water, but not with earth, presumably because it is not encompassed by the *Trismegistus circle,* that is, it does not belong to the universe outside the human world. Thirty-two entries give lexemes for the sun, the moon, meteors, phenomena in the sky (i.e. fire), and for thunderstorms and tempests (i.e. fire combined with air). Twenty-five entries give lexemes for dew, rain, ocean, fog, ice, and hail (i.e. water). In their connection with each other, certain metereological concepts emerge concerning the cycle by which water comes down to the earth as dew and rain, fills the oceans, and rises again as fog in order to start this cycle anew. Fifteen entries give lexemes for air and wind, including earthquake, which was thought of as a tempest within the earth. Group (v) contains the various aspects of time, space having extensively been dealt with in the astronomical group. Fifteen entries pertain to the four seasons and the weather, which is treated in all onomasiological dictionaries as something cosmological and almost directly connected with God. Forty-four entries pertain to the year and its days, including the names of saints and calender names. They are partly historical like '*The Calends, or first day of every month*' and '*The Ides are eight for every month*', partly highly specific. Note, for example:

A bissectil;[39]. . . ,
A climacteric yeer, which is every seventh; . . . ,
A lustre, or five years; . . . ,
An Olimpiad or fower years; . . . ,
An Indiction, or 15 yeers; . . . .

This topic has a follow-up in thirty-five entries on the holy days of the Church, but also birthdays and secular holidays. The cycle of holy days starts with '*The Annunciation of our Lady*' and then runs through the liturgical year of the Church.

---

[38] The so-called *Corpus Hermeticum,* which originated possibly in Alexandria in the first to third centuries, was called after the 'three times greatest' God Hermes who, in this case, was identified with the Egyptian God Thot. It had been well known since the beginning of the thirteenth century. The 'Book of the twenty-four philosophers' on God and the cosmos influenced European philosophy, in particular of the Neoplatonic kind. Meister Eckhart, Nicolaus Cusanus, Giordano Bruno, and Gottfried Wilhelm Leibniz were influenced by these texts. See below.
[39] A leap year.

This means the cycle of holy days has the birth, life, and death of Christ as its centre. Three entries make up the last part, namely:

Hell, or the remotest place from Heaven, gehenna; . . . ,
Devils, infernal Fiends, or Cacodaemons; . . . ,
The centre of the world; . . . .

This last section of the dictionary blends highly specific language with common language, very much in the same way as the first section did, although there are no such clusters of lexemes as the ones which yielded the two cycles of a *curriculum vitae*. Of note is the large number of entries in which the headword is complemented post-lemmatically by an explanatory synonym or by a whole phrase, and also the large number of entries which do not have a lexeme as headword at all but merely consist of a descriptive expression or even longer sentence.

This last section of the dictionary is comparable to the first, its counterweight, in that both show traditional chains of concepts and terms which were present in Howell's seventeenth century, though certainly not in everybody's mind. Broadly speaking, this applied to anthropological terms in the orbit of Galenic medicine and Platonic, Aristotelian, and Plotinic ideas about the nature of man. Apart from the microcosm–macrocosm dichotomy, which looms in the background, the last section contains pre-Socratic ideas about the zodiac and its influence on the conditions of human temperaments, which we found earlier in lexemes of section I, and the pre-Socratic assumption of four elements as the material of all being. We find the Aristotelian concepts of the spherical structure of the cosmos together with Plotinus' fundamental idea that the nature of things is determined by their distance from God, which places the Devil and Hell in the centre of the earth. Finally, we find the image of hierarchical choirs of angels around God, invented by the Pseudo-Dionysius writings[40] and handed down through the Middle Ages as a stable tradition of theology as well as of popular piety. This means that section I and section LXX together reveal a tradition which is generally called Neoplatonic and which extends from the pre-Socratic philosophers via the peaks of Greek philosophy, Dionysius, and St Augustine through the medieval tradition as far as the Renaissance philosophers in the tradition of Trismegistus (e.g. Pico della Mirandola (1463–94) or Agrippa von Nettesheim (1486–1535)) and the Neoplatonic thinkers of the English seventeenth century such as, already mentioned in this context, Robert Fludd. It is not really important whether James Howell had this philosophical tradition in mind or took it from one or several sources. What is important is that he considered the whole web of anthropological and cosmological thoughts and their terms important for the users of his dictionary.

---

[40] Originated in the fourth to sixth centuries and falsely attributed to Dionysius Areopagitica (first century AD).

7.8 Final remarks

Our analysis of the *Lexicon Tetraglotton* is not meant to be exhaustive. Its main interest is rather to show methods of a possible analytical treatment which would cover all details of the book. One aspect of this, which has been totally neglected here, would be to assess the adequacy of the translations.

Because of its comprehensiveness and its size, the *Lexicon Tetraglotton* comes nearer to the idea of an encyclopaedic dictionary as we know it today than any other English one analysed in this book. It also comes nearer to the idea of a thesaurus, because of the combination of an alphabetical and a topical part. This is why it can serve as a proof of the adequacy of the three-level approach that has been chosen as a method of analysis on the basis of text-linguistic arguments.[41] Each of these levels presents a set of phenomena of its own. The macrostructure shows the dictionary's place somewhere in the intellectual history and in the tradition of the genre. It constitutes the semantic dimension, which is a specific feature of onomasiological dictionaries. The microstructure shows the formal order in which the linguistic material of the dictionary is presented within its smallest unit, the entry. It constitutes the syntactic dimension of the dictionary. The units of a dictionary are what the sentences are in a text. Finally, the structure shows the special arrangements of sections which are determined by the general coherence of vocabulary and by the needs of the dictionary users. It constitutes its pragmatic dimension.

The semantic dimension of the macrostructure shows the *Lexicon Tetraglotton* in its era-dependent contents. The syntactic dimension of the microstructure would, if intensively investigated, show many problems and intricacies of the translations between the four languages. Perhaps the pragmatic dimension on the mesolevel of this comprehensive dictionary is the main surprise of our analysis. Every section proved to have its own order. The dictionary's semantics and syntax are presupposed by the users, yet its pragmatics follows many local rules. For the dictionary user the structure of the sections is perhaps more important than the macro- and microstructure.

Although, depending on the topic, the order on the mesolevel is typically varied, there are general principles discernible which are at work here. Among them are, first, *elementary orientations* which make people say and write 'life and death', 'day and night', 'outward and inward', etc. and not the other way round. The many phenomena that pertain to such dichotomies are ordered accordingly. Obviously, these orientations are the same as those which govern the all-pervading metaphors of our daily language (Lakoff and Jonson 1980) and depend on deeply rooted behavioremes of the human mind. There is no exception to them, apart from humour, irony, sarcasm, or other provocative use of language, but

---

[41] See Chapter 1.

these do not occur in the dictionary under analysis. In their own way, they pervade all sections of the dictionary, whatever topical order these sections have.

Secondly, *natural observations* are among these principles. They appear, for example, in the fact that the human body is described from head to feet and not in some other order, or that the utensils in a kitchen are enumerated in the way in which an observer, entering by the door, sees them (section XIV). The sequences which evolve out of these observations are normally also without exceptions. Yet they are not of the same compelling nature as the elementary orientations are. There are sometimes exceptions to the sequence when the interest of the diction-ary compiler demands them. As observations mostly depend on the visual sense, they naturally apply to all chapters concerned with perceivable domains of reality.

There are, thirdly, *natural schemata* which are regularly observed. They are similar to natural observations in that they combine something objectively given with the normal human perspective of perceiving it. But they pertain to closed sets of phenomena only, like numbers, the names of the months and of the days of the week, or the directions of the winds according to the compass rose. These schemata are man-made, that is, traditional, but of a very compelling nature, although their fields of application are small. They may organize reality in differ-ent ways. The divisions of the year, for example, are different when taken from the liturgical cycle of the church or from the secular calender. Among such schemata we also include hierarchical systems like those of ecclesiastical or worldly offices or of military or nautical ranks.

Fourthly, *traditional concepts and classifications* usually pervade the sections of an encyclopaedic dictionary. Most prominent were the four classic elements till they were replaced by some other tradition, or the three natural kingdoms of ancient natural history. They are traditions with an extraordinarily long range, even exercising a certain, perhaps folkloristic, influence when overtaken by new insights. But we also include among them the typology of scientific disciplines, for example in section XIII on books. Unlike the first three principles mentioned, which never seem to change, traditional concepts and classifications are subject to change in the course of time.

Fifth and last, clearly delimited *units of actions* are in many cases made the organizing principle of sections. Among them are: a fight on the battlefield from beginning to victory; or a meal from laying the table to giving thanks. The life cycle of generations is a unit of action on a high level of abstraction. As is also to be seen in classical literature, ensembles of static objects are sometimes turned into units of actions in order to faciliate enumeration. Thus, all the parts of a ship appear in a natural sequence when the process of building the ship is given. A section on men's clothes (XXXIII) starting with '*A shirt, A wascot, Drawers, Stirrop-hose*' and words for breeches and stockings indicates that the image of dressing for going out, presumably for a ride, is at work here. A section on women's clothes (XXXIV) starting with '*Slippers, A gown, A Busk, A gorget*', and words for doing one's hair shows that this time the image is that of a woman undressing in order to attend to her toilet. Such principles sometimes get lost in the middle of the way through the relevant vocabulary, as they indeed do in the two quoted sections, just as they sometimes only appear at the end, when, for example, the long list of words pertaining to the human body is rounded off with lexemes pertaining to death.

These five principles, and certainly more, are at work in all the sections of the dictionary, although their affinity with some sections is closer than with others. Of course, they overlap and are subject to definition. Their formal and highly abstract nature allows their application to many, almost to all, domains of reality. Calling the structure of the mesolevel of onomasiological dictionaries *pragmatic* is corroborated by these observations, because pragmatic phenomena of language use are, generally, understood to be highly context sensitive but, at the same time, deeply rooted in behavioural properties of human communication.

8

John Wilkins' comprehensive thesaurus of English (1668)

8.1 The universal language context

8.1.1 General

By definition a universal language is intelligible to everybody, irrespective of their mother tongue. Many learned men of the seventeenth century engaged in plans to construct a semiotic system that would achieve this goal, among them Francis Bacon (1561–1626), Johannes Amos Comenius (1592–1670), René Descartes (1596–1650), Athanasius Kircher (1602–80), Gottfried Wilhelm Leibniz (1646–1716), and others. In Britain particularly this idea found many adherents, mainly centred around the Royal Society, founded in 1660. Among them were Francis Lodwick (1619–94), George Dalgarno (?1626–87), Samuel Hartlib (d.?1670), and John Wilkins (1614–72).

---

[1]   The explanation of the use of quotation marks for 'difference' is given in note 31.

A universal language was envisaged in terms of either *universal characters* or a *universal language*. With universal characters there would be a writing system constructed so that everybody could read it in their own language as they could read digits, mathematical signs, or the symbols of the zodiac. Thus, it would not replace native languages but build a bridge between them. A universal language would involve the transformation of a writing system into a new phonological system which, if generally adopted, would replace all other languages. Each part of the written sign would be transformed into a sound.

The idea of a universal language was based on one definite philosophical condition, namely the assumption that there is a universal grammar and a universal lexicon with which a universal phonology can be associated.[2] This linguistic universalism was given a theological garb. Adam and Eve were endowed with a perfect language in Paradise. They could converse with God and all their progeny could do the same and, in addition, they could communicate with each other. This perfect communication was disrupted by Babel, although the structures of universalism in languages were not entirely lost then. Endeavours of erudite men in the seventeenth century aimed at restituting the old Paradisial state among men.

Philosophically speaking, this theological argument was an epistemological and linguistic apriorism. Ways of thinking and of apprehending the world were thought of as being basically the same for all mankind. It needed a commonly accepted way of expressing both in order to ensure universal communication. John Wilkins, whose work will be dealt with more fully than that of all the others, put it thus:

As men do generally agree in the same Principle of Reason, so they do likewise agree in the same Internal Notion or Apprehension of things. That external Expression of Mental notions, whereby men communicate their thoughts to one another, is either to the Ear, or to the Eye. . . . So that if men should generally consent upon the same way or manner of Expression, as they do agree in the same Notion, we should then be freed from that Curse in the Confusion of Tongues, with all the unhappy consequences of it. (1968, 20.)

Besides the ever-present theological argument to reinstate original linguistic perfection (Eco 1995), there were other secular arguments which made the idea particularly interesting for England in the seventeenth century (Salmon 1979). It was the time when English colonization and commerce began to spread all over the world and necessitate communication with people of different tongues. It also was the time when the new sciences were developing in many parts of insular and continental Europe and required an easy method of communication, since Latin had lost so much of its former usability. It was very much the same with Reformation theology. Religious education in the wake of the Comenian works stressed the idea of a universal language as the expression of a universally *pansophical* world.[3]

---

[2] The proximity of this statement to the general scheme of generative transformational grammar is quite intentional.   [3] See Chapter 10.

Moreover, more accidental developments awoke the general interest in the techniques with which universal characters and languages could be constructed. There was a long-established skill in shorthand, which had already been used during the Elizabethan era to write down plays and publish them in pirated editions. During the Puritan era it was also used for copying sermons. There was a long-established interest in cryptography, useful for such divergent purposes as communication between high-ranking members of the Church, alchemists, and the opposing parties in the English civil war (Strasser 1988). Finally, there was a general awareness of the nature of the linguistic sign and the possibilities of long-distance communication.[4]

The English universal language movement has been well researched in monographs devoted to one author (e.g. Lodwick ed. Salmon 1972, Asbach-Schnitker 1984) and to the general nexus of the time (e.g. Funke 1929, Knowlson 1975, Slaughter 1982, Large 1985, Hüllen 1989). They are complemented by many essays devoted to special problems (e.g. Salmon 1979, Cram 1980, 1989, 1990; papers in Subbiondo 1992). Philosophical and grammatical deliberations are in the foreground of these works. Our concern, however, is the proximity of universal language projects to onomasiological dictionaries. The *universal lexicon*[5] inevitably adopted the form of a topically ordered word-list or dictionary which was arranged in such a way that it presented the lexemes as intelligible to everybody through this arrangement. According to the general apriorism which formed the background to all universal language schemes, it was thought to be the common way in which people apprehended the world. This world was identical to the sum of all physical and mental objects, called by Wilkins 'things and notions'. Lexemes were names for these. Thus, the universal lexicon of a universal language was nothing other than a list of words arranged 'philosophically'. It is, although in a quite different context, the basic idea that underlay onomasiological dictionaries.

Most of the adherents of the universal language idea did not contribute much to it besides some general deliberations. This is particularly true for the most eminent men of the century, Bacon, Descartes, Comenius, and Leibniz. Only two works appeared in England which elaborated the general idea in greater detail, George Dalgarno's *Ars signorum* (1661, repr. 1968 and, in Latin plus a translation by Cram and Maat, 2001) and John Wilkins' *Essay Towards a Real Character and a Philosophical Language* (1668, repr. 1968). It is with these two works, but mainly with the latter, that the problems of onomasiology in the context of universal languages will be discussed.

---

[4]   For Wilkins' role in this semiotic interest see below.

[5]   I am using the word *lexicon* in its modern meaning of 'lexis in the mind' because the universal language planners thought of mental facts before they transformed them into written grammars and dictionaries. As most of them never realized their plans (see below), only a few made the transition from the *universal lexicon* to the *universal dictionary* or *universal thesaurus*.

8.1.2 George Dalgarno's Ars signorum

George Dalgarno (?1626–87), born and educated in Aberdeen, moved to Oxford in 1657 where he set up a grammar school. He continued to live there, except for two stays on Guernsey, as Master of Elizabeth College. His ideas on a universal language were widely disseminated in Britain by a group of people who later became the founding members of the Royal Society. Among them were Samuel Hartlib and John Wilkins, with whom he collaborated for some time on the *Essay* of 1668. He propagated his own ideas in broadsheets, which are still extant (see below), and in the book, written in Latin, *Ars signorum, vulgo character universalis et lingua philosophica . . . Londini, excudebat J. Hayes, Sumptibus Authoris; Anno reparatae salutis, 1661.* Besides writing on a universal language, Dalgarno wrote on teaching the language to the deaf and dumb in *Didascalocophus, or, the deaf and dumb man's tutor . . .* (1680).[6] There are various manuscripts on topics related to universal languages in the Bodleian Library and Christ Church, Oxford (Cram 1996; see also Alston 1974, vol. iii, nos. 785–6, vol. vii, nos. 283–5, 287a–9).[7]

George Dalgarno states the aims of his book in the descriptive part of its title. Like all universal language planners, he saw his first task, concerning the word-list of the new language, in classification. '[D]o not consider separately things which are not to be separated, namely the logical and the grammatical[8] parts', the reader is warned (A6^r). Later on, this principle is explained in full:

Since however signs are made by us to stand for things, it is wholly in accord with reason that the art of signs should follow the art of things. Just as I believe that metaphysics and logic constitute one single art, so grammar differs from these only in as much as the sign differs from the thing signified; and since these are thus interrelated, the same body of knowledge should underlie all of them. . . . [T]he grammarian must assign names to things according to the ideas and logical rules derived from the external nature of things themselves. This regular series of things is commonly called the Praedicament.   (177)

According to this statement, the first task of the language planner is classification (Lodwick, ed. Salmon 1972, 105–10). The rules for doing this are given using Aristotles' doctrine of ten categories, which were called *predicament(al)s* in general logic. It is a testimony to the conceptual proximity of onomasiological dictionaries to this philosophical system that, at least in his autobiographical

---

[6] Both texts and unpublished papers (broadsheets) reprinted in Dalgarno 2001, *Ars Signorum*, with a translation by D. Cram and J. Maat, from which I quote. It is only the foldout table 'Lexicon Grammatico-Philosophicum . . .' which I use from the Scolar Press reprint of 1968. In a pocket of the binding this reprint also preserves two of the broadsheets mentioned.

[7] There is no monograph on Dalgarno yet, but he is regularly mentioned in general treatments, in particular his split with John Wilkins, who referred to his services in the preface to the *Essay* of 1668 without mentioning his name. The best concise introduction to his work is Cram 1996; see also Cram 1980. Dalgarno's ideas on a universal language varied in different phases of his life, a fact which will not be discussed here. See the introduction to Dalgarno 2001, 1–79.

[8] *Grammatical* here pertains to linguistic structure in general, not to syntax only.

sketch, which was discovered by David Cram (Dalgarno, 2001, 353–90). Adrianus Junius's *Nomenclator* was (also) counted among the sources of the universal language idea by Dalgarno. But he made the condition 'that the fewest number of words possible be used, so that the vocabulary of this language which comprises them does not grow excessively large' (A7ʳ). This means that what is good in philosophy is not good in the planning of a universal language. In philosophy perfection in constructing 'a series of things . . . as regards number and method' (187) would make sense, although it cannot be achieved even here. Dalgarno has quite a dynamic, even historical understanding of human knowledge, assuming that it increased (and still increases) in the way in which mankind increased after Adam and Eve (185). In matters of a universal language, setting up 'the predicamental line by an orderly series of genera and species, such that they could be denoted by distinct primitive names' (193) would be quite wrong. 'The reason for this is that the number of primitive words would be almost infinite.' (193.) Consequently, a 'middle course (which proves best in many things)' is advocated to assign

a select number of principal notions, drawn from the first and foremost sciences . . . , namely those that refer to the most common respects of things, and to take these as primitive and to impose radical words to signify them, from which the names of other complex things can be derived.   (193)

The 'art of signs does not admit of strict philosophical rules' (195).

Dalgarno's 'middle course' results in his 'Grammatical-Philosophical Lexicon', described as a:

Table of things, or the most simple and universal notions, both artificial and natural, corresponding to the most general reckonings and considerations, arranged in predicamental order; according to the meanings of which names are to be established not at random, but by art and rational consideration, making use of the analogical relationships between things and signs; from which the names of all other things and notions which are more complex and more particular are formed, either by derivation or composition, in one or more words, according to certain general and systematic rules, following grammatico-philosophical analogy; such that the names thus formed contain descriptions of the things themselves which correspond to nature.[9]

Dalgarno uses only five 'predicaments' to start his scheme with: *ens*, split into *substantia* and *accidens*, both fused into *ens completum vel concretum*, which is split into *corpus* and *spiritus*, both again fused into *ens compositum*, which is *homo*. The further classification deals with *ens (completum vel) concretum*, under the two dominating terms *substantia* (= *concretum*) and *accidentia*. With the exception of

---

[9] Translation of the Latin text of the fold-out table of *Ars signorum* (1968). I refrain from a close interpretation of those parts of the text which pertain to the idea of a universal character, here called 'analogical relationship'. Consequently, I also refrain from explaining the idea of the *alphabet*, to be taken literally, which equates special letters with special general notions of things as given in the *Lexicon*. Translation slightly different in Dalgarno 2001, 153.

two, all the classes pertain to the category *concretum physicum* (= *corpus*) and *concretum compositum* (= *homo*), only *anima* and *angelus* pertain to *concretum spirituale*.[10] Note the series of classes pertaining to *ens physicum*:

- *Concretum mathematicum*: e.g. geometrical units, figures.
- *Concretum physicum*: e.g. elements, plants, brutes as species, in their parts, in their anatomy.
- *Concretum artificium*: e.g. food, buildings, ships, tools, musical instruments, arts, arms.

Note the series of classes pertaining to *accidentia*:

- *Accidens commune*: e.g. cause, mode, perfection, comparison.
- *Accidens mathematicum*: e.g. dimensions, positions, sites.
- *Accidens physicum generale*: e.g. general types of movement.
- *Accidens qualitas sensibilis*: e.g. five senses, general and vegetable (organic) states.
- *Accidens sensitivum*: e.g. general states, movements, faculties of the soul, passions.
- *Accidens rationale*: e.g. intellectual acts, habits, expressions, signs, will.
- *Accidens oeconomicum*: e.g. societal relations, contracts, obligations.[11]
  - *Accidens politicum*: e.g official relations, justice, crimes, war, superstition.
                                    (fold-out table in Dalgarno 1968 and 2001)

This classification of things and their concomitant words can be taken as part of a universal language scheme (which it was meant to be) and as the ordering plan of an onomasiological word-list (which it was unintentionally to become). Understanding it as part of a universal language scheme, Dalgarno's opinion becomes obvious that a language like the one envisaged by so many people of his time had to rely mainly on the systematicity of thinking. Only a core of words was given in their 'philosophical' order, then language users had the task of developing their universal lexical competence on their own by using procedures which were generally known. The author mentions derivation and composition, obviously taking them as universally valid. To use a modern term, Dalgarno's concept was structural and generative. It was here that the rift between him and John Wilkins was bound to occur, because Wilkins' concept, as will become obvious (see below), was structural and taxonomic. He was not concerned with the number of words his language would contain. His ambition was to develop the semantic component of a universal language to perfection so that people could use it as a huge store of ready-made expressions (lexemes). Whereas Dalgarno was more on the side of logicians, Wilkins inclined to the side of scientists. Astonishingly enough, the rift between Dalgarno and Wilkins mirrors a rift in

---

[10]   I cannot decide where Dalgarno places '*Deus . . . id est Causa prima*'.

[11]   In the list that assigns letters to each class the *accidens oeconomicum* is called *accidens commune alias servile* and is placed after *accidens politicum*.

present-day linguistics, where language is either reconstructed by generative, that is mental, universal rules or described by as many concrete data as possible.

From the lexicographical point of view, Dalgarno conceived of a type of word-list or dictionary which is very rare in the history of lexicography. Yet it is not totally unknown. Hugutio of Pisa (*fl.* 1200), for example, wrote his well-known *Magnae derivationes*, an alphabetical dictionary of Latin root-words which the user was supposed to enlarge with the help of affixes and of composition. German monolingual lexicography started in the sevententh century with lists of so-called *Stammwörter* (Hüllen 1990*a*) and lists of expanding particles. Obviously, the idea of the generative dictionary was in the air. Admittedly, however, it hardly played a role in onomasiology. For Dalgarno the idea was natural because he relied totally on the universality of linguistic rules.

Apart from his position in the universal language movement, George Dalgarno is a historical example of the onomasiological idea of arranging words according to philosophical principles. These principles were taken from the Aristotelian tradition, probably as taught at his own time by the philosophers of the universities (see below), but adapted in a quite personal way which was guided by what Dalgarno thought feasible for the practice of a universal language. His classes, which correspond to the section level in onomasiological dictionaries proper, are semantically quite similar to them and allow comparisons. Within the framework of universal language planning, onomasiology entered a philosophical stage which it had never had before.

8.2 John Wilkins' '*Tables*'

John Wilkins was an outstanding and most influential figure in seventeenth-century England. He was in turn or in tandem a scientific experimenter, founder member of the Royal Society, linguist, politician, bishop. Most of all he was a promoter of the new sciences which he wanted to reconcile, if necessary, with theology. In *Mercury; or, the Secret and Swift Messenger* (1646, repr. 1984, see also Alston 1974, vol. vii, nos. 277–9)[12] he treated all the semiotic ideas that caused and mirrored the general interest of seventeenth-century English intellectuals in a universal language. He also supported the plain style movement in preaching. His life and his works have been extensively researched (Shapiro 1969, Aarsleff 1982, Hüllen 1989, papers in Subbiondo 1992, Subbiondo 1996).

8.2.1 The semantic component of Wilkins' universal language

By far the most important book of the English universal language movement in the seventeenth century is:

---

[12]   See the elaborate introductory essay by Asbach-Schnitker in the reprint of 1984.

An Essay Towards a Real Character, And a Philosophical Language. By John Wilkins D.D.
Dean of Ripon, And Fellow of the Royal Society. London, Printed for Sa: Gellibrand, and for
John Martin Printer to the Royal Society, 1668.
Folio, pp. 454, bound together with:
An Alphabetical Dictionary, Wherein all English Words According to their Various
Significations, Are either referred to their Places in the Philosophical Tables, Or explained by
such Words as are in those Tables. London, Printed by J. M. for Samuel Gellibrand and John
Martin, 1668.
Not numbered, Aaa[1]–Ttt[3] [pp. 152].
There is a reprint (1968, see also Alston 1974, vol. vii, nos. 277–9).

The *Essay* presents the semiotic construction of a universal language with a degree
of detail and elaborateness which surpasses all other constructions of the kind. Like
the others, this universal language had a semantic, a syntactic,[13] and a graphemic as
well as a phonological component, because it was planned as having a universal
character as well as a universal *language*. The communicative function of the signs
is guaranteed by the fact that they represent reality as it is, a hypothesis which
presupposes the idea already mentioned that all human beings have an identical
comprehension of this reality. Wilkins makes this presupposition without further
explanations.[14] For him, *reality* comprises '*all things and notions*', that is, the physical and the mental worlds in their order. Indeed, it is not reality in some *essence*
but in its intrinsic order which Wilkins makes the basis of his language.

The chief Difficulty and Labour will be so to contrive the Enumeration of things and notions,
as that they may be full and adaequate, without any Redundancy or Deficiency as to the
Number of them, and regular as to their Place and Order.   (1968, 20.)[15]

The semantic component consists of a huge 'philosophically' ordered
thesaurus[16] of all those objects, mental and physical, which can be given names.
The syntactic component consists of a system of natural rules by which the
semantic units are combined into propositions. Both are a priori linguistic structures which are to be found in an imperfect state in all natural languages and,
therefore, can be proved for (and by) any of these, for example for (and by)
English. Thus, the semantic component of this character and philosophical
language is a universally organized thesaurus of words which uses English lexemes
almost only as dummies for universal meanings. The effect is that this universal
language is intelligible to every speaker of a natural language by means of *natural*
translation.[17]

---

[13]   For the absence of the pragmatic component see below.
[14]   '*As men do generally agree in the same Principal of Reason, so do they likewise agree in the same*
Internal Notion or Apprehension of things.' (Wilkins 1968, 20.)
[15]   Note the difference of this statement to Dalgarno's 'middle way'.
[16]   I am using the term *thesaurus* in this case in order to indicate the special position of Wilkins'
'*Tables*' in onomasiological literature and because they became the point of departure for Roget's
Thesaurus, first published in 1852, as has often been stated. See Hüllen 1989, 238–40; 2004, 285–91 and
passim.
[17]   This term does not occur in Wilkins.

In order to construct his universal language, John Wilkins had to lay linguistic foundations pertaining to universal grammar, universal lexicology and semantics, universal phonology, and universal graphemics. As his scheme proved to be erroneous in the long run, it is a sad fact that Wilkins' achievements in these fields never found the appreciation which they deserved.

This is particularly true for the semantic part of his universal language. In fact, the '*Tables*', the ordered list of words, are one of the most important onomasiological works in the English tradition, and certainly the most subtly and elaborately constructed one before 1700. But their lexicographical value has barely been recognized, except by Dolezal (1983,[18] 1985, 1986, and 1987). Dolezal (1987) and Subbiondo (1977) have drawn attention to Wilkins' proximity to structural semantics. It is the '*Tables*' as a most important case of onomasiological lexicography[19] that will be treated here, and not any other aspect of John Wilkins' universal language plan. This is why the analysis is subjected to the same analytical categories (macrostructure, microstructure, pragmatic structures)[20] as all the other onomasiological works are.

8.2.2 The macrostructure

The macrostructure of John Wilkins' thesaurus pertains to the word-lists as a whole. It is of a semantic nature and determines the way in which the word-lists make a statement about the world. In contrast to other onomasiological works, namely, dictionaries in the narrow sense of the word, the macrostructure of Wilkins' thesaurus evolves out of the structural interplay between three levels, the '*chapters*', the '*genera*', and the '*differences*' (see below). Whereas the chapters and genera are missing in the usual onomasiological dictionaries, the 'differences' take the place of their *sections*.

CHAPTERS AND THE GENERAL SCHEME

The best known representation of the macrostructure of John Wilkins' thesaurus is '*The General Scheme*' (chapter I of '*The Second Part, Containing a regular enumeration and description of all those things and notions to which names are to be assigned*'). It contains the forty genera[21] of the '*Tables*'[22] in a special type of printing and arrangement which is highly indicative of the internal structure of these '*Tables*', that is, of an English thesaurus in fact. However, the macrostructure is not only determined on the level of genera. On a higher level, there is its integration

---

[18] Dolezal (1983, 1–177) is the most elaborate of these treatments.

[19] Under the title '*Die Suche nach dem onomasiologischen Alphabet*' I examined this aspect of the historiography of Wilkins for the first time in Hüllen 1989. Naturally, readers will find an overlapping of ideas and arguments between that work and the present treatment. However, the latter was conceived and written as an independent chapter in the course of elaborating my ideas on onomasiology.   [20] See Chapter 1.   [21] Wilkins writes '*genus's*'.

[22] I differentiate between '*Tables*' and tables, that is, between '*The Second Part Containing Universal Philosophy*' of the *Essay* and its formal, or typographical, arrangement. Wilkins himself always speaks of '*Tables*'. Occasionally, the sense of what I write applies to both usages.

into the second part of the book to be observed and, on a lower level, the order of 'differences' and species. Difficulties in recognizing the general order arise from the fact that the '*Tables*' are actually not tables at all but a continuously flowing text which is divided up in various ways, by typographical devices such as paragraphing, breaking of lines, indenting, two kinds of bracing, numbering in various ways, varying fonts, and capitalization. Increasing the intricacies of this system, the ways of numbering and the variety of fonts have several functions. Unfortunately, on a considerable number of occasions these techniques are practised inconsistently or erroneously. Readers have to be aware of this complicated semiotic system if they want to understand the '*Tables*' for what they are, namely, tables and running text at the same time.[23]

Part two of the *Essay* is divided into eleven chapters (I–XI)[24] which set out the most abstract level of systematization:

- **Chapter I** comprises genera I–IV containing the *transcendentals*, the general notions which determine all the subsequent principles of order. They include 'discourse', that is, 'words' as opposed to 'things'.
- **Chapter II** comprises genera V–VI containing God, the creator, and the creation, that is, the world observed collectively.
- **Chapter III**, together with all the following chapters, is devoted to the world observed distributively. It comprises genera VII–IX containing the inanimate elements under the 'predicament', that is, the category, of substance, which is also the heading of the three next chapters.
- **Chaper IV** comprises genera X–XIV containing the vegetative species.
- **Chapter V** comprises genera XV–XVIII containing the sensitive species.
- **Chapter VI** comprises genera XIX–XX containing the significant parts of vegetative and sensitive species.
- **Chapter VII** comprises genera XXI–XXIII containing various phenomena belonging to 'quantity', a category which is subsumed under the category 'accident'. So are the following four chapters.
- **Chapter VIII** comprises genera XXIV–XXVIII containing various phenomena belonging to 'quality'.
- **Chapter IX** comprises genera XXIX–XXXII containing various phenomena belonging to 'action'.
- **Chapter X** comprises genera XXXIII–XXXV containing various phenomena belonging to 'private relation'
- **Chapter XI** comprises genera XXXVI–XL containing various phenomena belonging to 'public relation'.

---

[23] The only thorough analysis of the 'Semiotics of the Tables' is in Dolezal (1983, 38–51). My own analysis, besides using a different method, deviates in a number of details from this.

[24] '*Chapters*' have the same place in the following analysis as *sections* do in the preceding analyses of the various onomasiological glossaries and dictionaries. It seems appropriate to retain Wilkins' own term.

The strongest ordering factors in this division into chapters are (i) the Aristotelian categories, called predicaments (substance, accidence, quantity, quality, action, and relation), (ii) above them in the logical hierarchy highly abstract terms such as 'being', 'notion', 'thing', 'creator', 'world',[25] and (iii) the traditional division into the three kingdoms of the inanimate, the animate/vegetative, and the animate/ sensitive. On this level the human species as the rational animal remains invisible (see below). All this means that the division into chapters shows the very traditional and common store of philosophical terms which are at Wilkins' disposal.[26]

It is only in the '*General Scheme*' that the forty genera are given Roman numbers. This system of numbering does not reappear in the tables themselves. Here it is the differences which have Roman numbers, starting anew with each genus.

The central logical operation by which John Wilkins unfolds his overviews on all levels is binary opposition. It is applied in almost every line of the 265 folio pages. However, the procedure is not used in a very strict sense. Quite often, there are ternary and quarternary oppositions hidden away in the typographical arrangement and, more importantly, very often the oppositions are not oppositions in the logical sense at all (see below). In such cases, the (would-be) oppositions often have no opposing members in the formal sense of *plus/minus* or *yes/ no*, these being replaced by *similar to*, or they have no opposing members in the sense of *either/or*, these being replaced by *more/less* (Dolezal 1983, 157–61). Wilkins saw the problem himself:

[The] Species are commonly joyned together by pairs, for the better helping of the Memory (and so likewise are some of the Genus's and Differences.) Those things which naturally have Opposites, are joyned with them, according to such Opposition, whether Single or Double. Those things that have no Opposites, are paired together with respect to some Affinity which they have one to another. Tho it must be acknowledged that these affinities are sometimes less proper and more remote, there being several things shifted into these places, because I knew not how to provide for them better. (22.)

---

[25] In general logic this is the difference between *praedicabilia* and *predicaments*. Wilkins does not use the former term. See below.

[26] We might argue that Wilkins' interest in natural history, mainly biology, does not pertain to the traditional but rather to the modern type represented by naturalists like Willughby and Ray (see below). This would mean that there is a mixture of traditional and contemporary principles to be found in his classifications. This mixture will appear in other respects, too, for example with reference to lexis. Dolezal (1983, 58) is right to speak of two kinds of classification, although I would not call them *artificial* and *natural*. In the framework of an a priori epistemology there is no difference between artificial and natural. Rather it is the methodological antagonism between a priori rationalism and a posteriori empiricism which becomes visible here. We must not forget that Wilkins was neither a philosopher nor a naturalist *sui generis*, his aim being to construct a universal language. Nevertheless, he was aware of the problem. Note:

Vvhereas men do now begin to doubt, whether those that are called the Four ELEMENTS be really the Primordia rerum, may they here be taken notice of and enumerated, without particular restriction to that Notion of them, as being only the great Masses of natural Bodies, which are of a more simple Fabric then the rest. (56.)

That Wilkins 'knew not better' is as unconvincing as his statement that the binary opposition was mainly a means of memorization. Rather, the binary opposition is the central logical idea of the tables, well known to the author and popular in traditional as well as in contemporary philosophy from the Porphyrian tree of knowledge to Petrus Ramus.

The '*General Scheme*' uses several kinds of semiotic devices which indicate the chain of logical thoughts that run through the text. The most important of them are:

(1) Roman print for the explanatory text.
(2) *Italics* for defined terms, mostly but not always in opposing pairs.
(3) CAPITALS for the names/terms of the genera with their Roman numbers.[27]
(4) Indenting of lines marking logical branches below a binary opposition.
(5) Square braces on the left-hand side binding terms together which are located on the same logical level, although they have several terms on lower levels between them.
(6) Round braces also on the left-hand side either linking opposing pairs which follow each other directly, or linking the various genera that belong to one category, that is, a chapter.

It is important for readers to comprehend this extraordinary system in order to appreciate the complexity of the hierarchically operating thoughts that were at work in the author's mind when he was working on this part of the book. As we understand the '*Tables*' to be the ordering system of a comprehensive thesaurus of the English language, this means that we here face an onomasiological system of unprecedented complexity.[28] The best way of understanding it is to *look* at '*The General Scheme*' and compare the explanations given above. (See Fig. 8.1.)

A clarification of the complex system may be achieved with the help of modern decimal numbers, retaining the differentiation between Roman font and italics, but restricting the syntagmatic structure of the text. This numbering replaces Wilkins' graphical devices for signalling the logical structure of his scheme. Numbers with the same numerical depth are the ones which Wilkins links either with square or with round braces. For example, 1 and 2, i.e. (all things) *general* and (all things) *special* belong together, just as 2.221 and 2.222, i.e. *substance* and *accident*, do. (See Table A.7.)

The choice of varying fonts in Wilkins' original text also now discloses its

---

[27] It is difficult to decide whether the use of capital initial letters has meaning and cohesion beyond what was taken for granted at Wilkins' time. In the '*General Scheme*' this is certainly not the case, as the capitalization of *God* or *Universal* does not deviate from the norm; but in the texts that constitute the following tables it looks as if Wilkins used this kind of capitalization as another means of logical marking. See below.

[28] For the connection between these differentiating devices and the procedure of structural semantics, which can be found in Wilkins *avant la lettre*, see below.

All kinds of things and notions, to which names are to be assigned, may be distributed into such as are either more

General; namely those Universal notions, whether belonging more properly to

                             ⎧ GENERAL.   I

Things; called TRANSCENDENTAL ⎨ RELATION MIXED.   II

                             ⎩ RELATION OF ACTION.   III

Words; DISCOURSE.   IV

Special; denoting either

  ⎧ CREATOR.   V

  ⎩ *Creature*; namely such things as were either *created* or *concreated* by God, not excluding several of those notions, which are framed by the minds of men, considered either

    ⎧ *Collectively*; WORLD.   VI

    ⎨ *Distributively*; according to the several kinds of Beings. whether such as do (belong to

Substance;

  ⎧ *Inanimate*; ELEMENT.   VII

  ⎨ *Animate*; considered according to their several

    ⎧ *Species*, whether

      ⎧ *Vegetative*

        ⎧ *Imperfect*; as *Minerals*, ⎧ STONE.   VIII

                         ⎩ METAL.   IX ⎧ LEAF.   X

                     ⎧ HERB consid. accord. to the ⎨ FLOWER.   XI

        ⎩ *Perfect*; as *Plant*, ⎨ SHRUB.   XIII ⎩ SEED-VESSEL.   XII

                     ⎩ TREE.   XIV

      ⎧ EXANGUIOUS.   XV

      ⎨ *Sensitive*; ⎧ FISH.   XVI

         Sanguineous; ⎨ BIRD.   XVII

                   ⎩ BEAST.   XVIII

     Parts; ⎧ PECULIAR.   XIX

          ⎩ GENERAL.   XX

Accident;

  ⎧ *Quantity*; ⎧ MAGNITUDE.   XXI

             ⎨ SPACE.   XXII

             ⎩ MEASURE.   XXIII

             ⎧ NATURAL POWER.   XXIV

             ⎪ HABIT.   XXV

   Quality; whether ⎨ MANNERS.   XXVI

             ⎪ SENSIBLE QUALITY.   XXVII

             ⎩ SICKNESS.   XXVIII

    ⎧ SPIRITUAL.   XXIX

   Action ⎨ CORPOREAL.   XXX

    ⎪ MOTION.   XXXI

    ⎩ OPERATION.   XXXII

                     ⎧ OECONOMICAL.   XXXIII

             Private. ⎨ POSSESSIONS.   XXXIV

                     ⎩ PROVISIONS.   XXXV

   Relation; whether more

                     ⎧ CIVIL.   XXXVI.

                     ⎪ JUDICIAL.   XXXVII

             Publick. ⎨ MILITARY.   XXXVIII

                     ⎪ NAVAL.   XXXIX

                     ⎩ ECCLESIASTICAL.   XL.

FIG. 8.1   Wilkins: The General Scheme

Source: Wilkins 1668, 23.

sense. If we regard the whole scheme as a series of logical decisions, capitals always mark the last and italics the intermediary ones. Within the linguistic method of structural semantics, we could say that the meaning of the last statement in the logical chain consists of a configuration of the intermediary statements, which function as semantic markers, plus the last one which functions as a distinguisher. Thus, the meaning of FISH is not *fish* in the usual lexico-semantic understanding, but *creature/(considered) distributively/substance/animate/species/sensitive/sanguineous/fish*. The last slots of the scheme provide the distinguisher and are cover terms for the entire chains of the logical deductions.[29]

Wilkins' semiotic system of indicating the structure of his tables is not without faults (as will occasionally be mentioned later). However, exceptions from the rules may have their good reasons. For example, the fact that HERB (2.22121121) is capitalized, although it is not a last slot proper, certainly signals that the following—CONSIDERED ACCORDING TO LEAF; TO FLOWER; and TO SEED VESSEL (2.22121121 1–3)—are looked upon as subgenera of HERB. The typographical shape, here, replaces a theoretical explanation.

GENERA AND 'DIFFERENCES'

Wilkins' '*Tables*' have a three-level structure. Their names are obviously taken from traditional logic.[30] At the same time this structure mirrors Wilkins' interest in the system of natural history, more precisely, biology, where the ordering of plants had become a major task for scientists, following the extraordinary expansion of knowledge in this field. The limitation to forty genera with six 'differences'[31] and nine species each was, of course, dictated by practical reasons and, as Wilkins knew himself, without systematic justification. It was in the tables concerning animals and plants that the system broke down in practice (see below).

In the tables the Roman numbering of genera, as applied in the '*General Scheme*', is abandoned. Instead, the genera appearing in one chapter are numbered with Roman digits, beginning in all eleven cases with Roman I (one). These numbers are given in the margin, together with a paragraph sign (§). There then follows an overview of the various 'differences', also numbered with Roman digits. Again, these appear in the margin together with the name of the 'difference', but without the paragraph sign. The heads of genera always appear in a running heading at the top of each page, and only sometimes in bold capitals heading the relevant table, in this

[29] This seemingly over-subtle analysis will be of importance for the understanding of the microstructure of the thesaurus. See below.

[30] Traditional logic is, of course, a wide and complex field of thought with many differing positions. But it seems justifiable to me to use this imprecise reference because Wilkins seems to have relied more on a general knowledge of logical procedures than on any concrete work treating logic (or rhetoric). See below.

[31] Throughout the subsequent discussion, *differences* will be enclosed in quotation marks ('differences') to indicate that this is the terminological use of the lexeme, which differs from the common use.

case often combined with the preposition '*of*' as, for example, in '*Of Herbs*', '*Of Trees*', etc. Thus, in the '*Tables*', in contrast to the '*General Scheme*', capitalization of whole words (and sometimes of phrases) is used for all three levels of the deduction. The terms that lead from one level to another are, however, printed in italics.

Many genera are explained in an introductory text, either with the help of a synonymous term or with an opposite term (antonym), that is also in the binary way, although this is not marked with the usual arrangement of indented lines and round braces. Whereas the synonymous terms are often given all in capital letters, too, the relevant antonyms are marked with a new typographical convention, namely italicized capitals. This technique is sometimes also used in introducing the 'differences'. Capital initial letters are used for words of greater semantic weight than the surrounding text. This is in accordance with the spelling conventions of the time, however, and should be interpreted here as a consistently used means of expressing the lower-level importance of some word. This leads to a five-stage typographical system for expressing semantic and logical importance: Roman, Roman with capital initial letters, italics, capitals (full word), and italicized capitals (full word). Note, as an example, the introductory sentence of ECCLESIASTICAL RELATION (284):

Under this Head of ECCLESIASTICAL RELATION (*Clergy, Spiritual, Church*) are comprehended the several Notions and respects belonging to a Church-state. By *Church* is meant a Society of men as agreeing in the same kind of inward apprehensions of, and external demeanour towards, the Divine Nature: to which may be opposed the word TEMPORAL, *Civil, Humane, Secular, Lay, Profane.*[32]

The marked words are generally of special importance for the logical and semantic deductions that follow.[33]

The following is an overview of the second level, the 'differences', of each genus of chapters I and V. Again, Wilkins introduced the divisions and integrated them into normal flowing text which can be quite lengthy and in most cases introduces many criteria for the divisions that follow (see below). I will strip this text of almost all of its syntagmas and reduce it to a bare minimum, always using, however, Wilkins' own words in his own (sometimes inconsistent) spelling. The names of genera and their spelling in the '*Tables*' deviate quite frequently from the '*General Scheme*'. I follow the running headings at the top of each page. I adhere to the new typographical rules, as explained above.[34] For a full overview see Table A.8.

---

[32] For the sake of illustration, Wilkins' use of various fonts is shown in this quotation. All other quotations have been changed into italics to conform with the general practice in this book.

[33] Nevertheless, many cases of doubt, and certainly of error, occur.

[34] For the sake of brevity and readability I generally avoid repeating determinations on a lower level which have already been mentioned on the higher one. In this case a dash is inserted. I have tried to render this shortening in such a way that the oppositions remain clear and the chain of statements is intelligible, if the reader realizes the context on the level of 'differences'. In cases of doubt I must refer the reader to the original and/or reprint.

(Chapter I)
TRANSCENDENTALS GENERAL
I KINDS
II CAUSES
III *Differences*, more ABSOLUTE and Common
IV *Differences Relative to Action*: THE END
V—THE MEANS
VI MODES.

TRANSCENDENTALS MIXT
I QUANTITY, considered more GENERALLY
II—more restrained to CONTINUED QUANTITY
III—to DISCONTINUED QUANTITY
IV QUALITY, considered more LARGELY
V—more STRICTLY
VI WHOLE *and* PART.

TRANSCENDENTAL RELATIONS OF ACTION
I more *General* SIMPLE
II more *General* COMPARATE
III more *Special*; denoting *Kinds of Action, Solitary,* BUSINESS
IV—*Social,* COMMERCE
V denoting EVENTS
VI denoting ITION.[35]

DISCOURSE (LANGUAGE)
I *Parts of it, More Simple,* ELEMENTS
II—*less Simple,* WORDS
III Kinds of it, *proper* to GRAMMAR
IV—*proper* to LOGIC
V COMMON TO BOTH
VI MODES of it.

(Chapter V)
OF EXANGUIOUS ANIMALS
I *Lesser usually called insects,* [generation] *analogous to that of other animals,* [with] NO
FEET OR BUT SIX feet, WITHOUT WINGS
II—SIX FEET and WINGS, or MORE feet THEN [sic] SIX
III—[generation] *Anomalous,* DESIGNED TO FURTHER TRANSMUTATION
IV—[with] *severall mutations,* [with] NAKED WINGS
V—[with] SHEATHED WINGS
VI *Greater, Hard,* CRUSTACIOUS
VII—TESTACIOUS TURBINATED[36]
VIII—NOT TURBINATED
IX *Greater,* SOFT

[35] 'The action of going'. This explanation and others in my subsequent notes are taken either from the *OED* or from Wilkins' own explanatory texts or marginal notes.
[36] 'Consisting of a cone-like cavity in a spiral'.

OF FISH

I *Viviparous*[37] and skinned, [with] OBLONG and roundish figure
II—FLAT or thick figure
III *Oviparous*,[38] *Salt water*, [with] *finns on the back* whose *rays* are *Wholly soft* and flexible
IV—*partly soft* and partly *spinous*, having TWO FINNS
V—ONE FINN
VI *Salt water, Figure*, OBLONG
VII—FLAT
VIII—*Salt water*, CRUSTACIOUS COVERING
IX *Oviparous, Fresh water*, scaly.

OF BIRDS

I *Terrestrial, dry land*, CARNIVOROUS
II—PHYTIVOROUS[39] *of short round wings*
III—of *long wings* having their *Bills* LONG AND SLENDER
IV—SHORT AND THICK
V—*insectivorous*, having *slender streight bills*, the GREATER KIND
VI—the LEAST KIND
VII *Aquatic*, living *About and* NEAR WATER PLACES
VIII—*In waters*, FISSIPEDES[40]
IX—PALMIPEDES.[41]

OF BEASTS

I *Viviparous*, WHOLE FOOTED
II—CLOVEN FOOTED
III—*clawed or multifidious*,[42] NOT RAPACIOUS
IV—RAPACIOUS, CAT KIND
V—DOG KIND
VI OVIPAROUS.

At first sight, the overview of the 'difference' level of the '*Tables*' seems to repeat the overview of the '*General Scheme*' with more concrete, but still rather abstract terms. Yet, the terminological and the encylopaedic material now begins to appear which fills the formal categories (predicaments) that lead to the genera. Four comments seem appropriate.

The first is that the first three genera provide the epistemological tools with which the genera that follow will operate. These include abstract terms like 'kind', 'cause', 'end', 'means', and 'mode', which will appear time and again in the tables, as well as 'quantity', 'quality', and 'action' (although not 'relation'), which are the ordering principles of genera XXI to XL. Wilkins seems rather dubious about the success of this epistemological introduction:

The right ordering of these Transcendentals is a business of no small difficulty; because there is so little assistance or help to be had for it in the Common Systems, according to which this part

[37] 'Animals bringing forth young in a live state'.
[38] 'Animals bringing forth young as eggs'.   [39] 'Feeding on vegetables'.
[40] 'Animals having divided toes'.   [41] 'Animals having toes united by a membrane'.
[42] 'With toes'.

of Philosophy (as it seems to me) is rendred the most rude and imperfect in the whole body of Sciences. (24.)

He apologizes that '*because of the streightness of that method which I am bound up to by these Tables it will so fall out, that several things cannot be disposed of so accurately as they ought to be.*' (24–5.) Indeed, the first three genera are not a precise presentation of the terms to be used later, rather they are a more general epistemological introduction to '*Universal Philosophy*'. As such, however, they are highly significant for the tables as a thesaurus. They prove that Wilkins' word-lists are ordered categorially, when he speaks of '*all things and notions*' for which he collects the names. At least in these early chapters of the '*Tables*' he does not present a world of things, real or mental, but one of ideas according to which the world of things and notions can be patterned. In later chapters this will change.

Genus IV on language, though it does not present terms of epistemology, fulfils however the same function. Language is the epistemological prerequisite for a '*Natural Philosophy*'. This pertains to its structural means (the enumeration of which makes this table a perfect specimen of language theory according to the Ramistic method) as well as to the strategies in logic and rhetoric which language performs. Both will be used frequently in the tables that follow. There is no other onomasiological work before 1700 which follows the principle *epistemology before ontology* so extensively as Wilkins' tables do.

Secondly, the two genera that follow, on God and the world as a whole, are still outside the '*things and notions*' to which the categories of thinking with the help of language can/must be applied. In them Wilkins shows the Christian basis of everything he writes. (After all, he was a high-ranking cleric of the Church of England.) It is the Christian world of God and the universe, spirit and body, heaven and hell which we are given, including the contemporary vision of the stellate cosmos and the formations of the terrestrial and aquatic regions of the earth. Although within a less sophisticated theoretical framework, these domains of vocabulary can be found in many introductory sections of other onomasiological dictionaries.

Under the 'difference' I SPIRIT we find as a third entry SOUL, and subsumed under this 4. VEGETATIVE, 5. SENSITIVE, and 6. RATIONAL (51). *Man* is not mentioned, but for anybody who can read, this is the first mention of the special situation of humans in the hierarchy of things. 'Difference' V ANIMATE PARTS OF THE WORLD has the entries 1. MINERAL, 2. PLANT, 3. HERB, 4. ANIMAL, and 5. MAN (54) and through them confirms this special situation which will be tacitly present in all the following tables but which is otherwise curiously absent in them.

Thirdly, with the chapters III to V the tables change drastically. This is now ontology. We are given the objects of the inanimate, animate, and sensate kingdoms of nature. The ordering ideas are the four classical elements, which include phenomena of the weather, and the kingdoms of nature. Inside these general schemata the tables are devoted to tangible and observable things. All this is very much in the tradition of onomasiological dictionaries. The subsumption under the category of substance is almost a formality.

Obviously John Wilkins was very much concerned with the tables which enumerate plants. It was, of course, the general progress in biology during his life-time, which he came to know through his collaborator John Ray,[43] that caused this interest, but also his scruples about the ways of drawing up the respective tables. Hence he prefaced chapter IV with a text '*Of Plants, the difficulty of enumerating and describing these*'.

I design in these following tables to take notice only of the chief families of Plants, to which the others are to be reduced. In the descriptions of which, there will be no small difficulty, by reason of their great number, and the want of proper words to express the more minute differences betwixt them, in respect of shape, colour, tast, smell &c. to which instituted languages have not assigned particular names. I mention this by way of Apology for the several defects, which I am sensible of in the following tables.   (67.)

Wilkins also apologized for the reduction of species to nine, which he found necessary, among other reasons, '*because the just number of them is not yet stated, every year producing new ones*' (67), and went on to enumerate twenty-three possible criteria by which plants could also be classified and which might be expressed periphrastically. Moreover, he rejected his earlier system of distinguishing '*plants for pleasure*', '*plants for nourishment*', and '*plants for medical purposes*' as '*not so truly philosophical*' (69). His final solution was conventional as well as new. The distinction of herbs, shrubs, and trees is part of traditional knowledge of natural history, as introduced by Pliny, but in particular the tables listing the distinctions of herbs according to leaves, flowers, and seed vessels come closer than any others to the scientific endeavours of his own time, mainly represented by John Ray's work (see below). His authority was strong enough for Wilkins to give up his strict scheme of six 'differences' and nine species in each genus. The table on herbs according to their leaves lists nine 'differences', with fifteen, six, sixteen, thirteen, ten, thirteen, eight, seven, and ten species; the table on herbs according to their flowers also lists nine 'differences', with seventeen, sixteen, fourteen, fifteen, fourteen, seven, seventeen, six, and eight species; the table on herbs according to their seed vessels again lists nine 'differences', with five, seven, fifteen, fifteen, thirteen, eleven, eleven, ten, and nine species each.[44]

The tables on animals show very much the same mode as those on plants.

---

[43] After part of the plates of the *Essay* had been burnt in the Great Fire of London in 1666, John Ray helped Wilkins in drawing up new tables of plants and animals, not however without doubts about whether the artificial restriction to six 'differences' and nine species would allow him to mention all the species known at that time in their proper places.

[44] Of course, we also find irregularities in the tables of other genera, in particular fewer than nine species under one 'difference'. But Wilkins never takes such pains as with plants to stress the difficulties of classification, not even with animals where his scientific ambition can be assumed to have been as highly developed as with plants.

Wilkins' ambition to classify them adequately depends on traditional as well as on (for him) modern principles.[45] There is no table on human beings as a species of beasts. Only genus XX OF GENERAL PARTS, that is, anatomical and organ parts which are common to all beasts, contains lists of names for the liquids and materials, for the exterior parts (head, trunk, and limbs) and the interior parts of the body, which in almost all other onomasiological works are reserved for lists concerning human anatomy.

Fourthly, even more than the subsumption of genera VII–XX under the category of substance, the subsumption of genera XXIV–XL under the categories of quality, action, and relation, but to a certain degree also the subsumption of genera XXI–XXIII under the category of quantity, are an almost purely formal matter. It is true that the 'differences' of the last mentioned genera have a common affinity to quantifiable relations: one-, two-, and three-dimensional figures, that is, the contents of geometry; temporal and spatial relations, and the various measures, including numbers, the English monetary system, and the calendar, including the '*AGE of LIVING Creatures (as particularly applied to Men . . .)*'. But the following genera seem to have no direct semantic affinity at all to the formal categories after which they are called.

Chapter VIII deals with the mental faculties of humans, their senses, their dispositions of character and of the body. It deals with virtues in various domains of life, namely, social, intellectual, and religious; and also with manners and politeness, experience via the senses, and with diseases. This means that *quality* here pertains to anthropological states.

Chapter IX deals with the religious, rational, voluntary, and emotional life of humans. It deals with movements carried out by parts of the human body and by the body as a whole,with agentive motions like walking, with organic, often non-agentive, motions like sneezing, including 'recreation', that is, games and sports, and with crafts, arts, and trades. This means that *action* here pertains to human behaviour and activities in the world, often observed under societal conditions.

Chapter X deals with consanguinity, marriage, and personal relations in society, and their consequences for behaviour. It deals with the object world of houses, vessels, furniture, with food and clothes and the materials that are involved in them. This means that *relation private* here pertains to the order of human life in society.

Finally, chapter XI deals with hierarchies in the state and in society and with obligations springing from these. It deals with the legal, the military, the naval, and the ecclesiastical system, the persons acting in them and the actions performed by them. This means that *relation public* pertains to certain clearly demarcated domains of life.

If we disregard the categorially orientated classification of '*things and notions*'

---

[45] I refrain from commenting on the chapter on Noah's Ark, because, interesting as it is in itself, it is of no importance for the tables as a thesaurus.

in Wilkins' tables, we find a sequence of topics which is indeed typical of and conventional for comprehensive onomasiological works in general. We can call them:

(1)   God and the universe.
(2)   The four elements.
(3)   The kingdoms of nature, with an almost covert treatment of human beings.
(4   Anthropological states.
(5)   Arts, crafts, and trades.
(6)   Family and societal organization.
(7)   Houses, vessels, furniture.
(8)   The legal domain of society.
(9)   The military domain of society.
(10) The naval domain of society.
(11) The ecclesiastical domain of society.

This rather traditional list of topics[46] disregards the epistemological introduction of the first four genera. Speaking of the traditionality of the '*Tables*' does not diminish the amount of erudition and systematic thinking that went into them. It simply proves their closeness to the onomasiological principle and technique in general.

8.2.3 The microstructure

The microstructure of John Wilkins' thesaurus pertains to the entries on the level of species.[47] It is of a syntactic nature, that is, it pertains to the formal regularities of these entries, which are the building-blocks of the whole thesaurus in the same way as sentences are the building-blocks of a text.[48] It will be found that the microstructure of the thesaurus is quite different from the microstructure of onomasiological dictionaries.

SEMANTIC SLOTS AND SYNONYMS

Wilkins' word-lists denote '*All kinds of things and notions, to which names are to be assigned*' (23) in his universal language. This means that they are meant to be universally valid. The English (and sometimes Latin) lexemes used in them merely take the place of the potential lexemes of any other language. This presupposes that all languages run semantically parallel to each other, because they give names

[46]   A comparison of this list of topics with the several overviews of onomasiological dictionaries presented in this book proves its traditional substance. See (mainly) Chapters 6, 173, and 7, 216–17, and *passim*.

[47]   In the following discussion, quite subtle and intricate matters will be described and analysed. Therefore it is advisable to read my deliberations with the original/a reprint alongside in order to check or verify (or confute) the intended meanings of my statements.

[48]   See Chapter 1, 23.

to the things and notions of the world which are recognized by people in the same way. '*As men do generally agree in the same Principle of Reason, so do they likewise agree in the same Internal Notion of Apprehension of things.*' (20.)[49] To show this is the task of philosophy:

> It being the proper end and design of the several branches of Philosophy to reduce all things and notions unto such a frame, as may express their natural order, dependence, and relations.' (1.)

This philosophical underpinning of the word-lists gives each entry its significant slot.[50] It is determined in its meaning by the place in which it appears in the tables.[51]

> The principle design aimed at in these Tables, is to give a sufficient enumeration of all such things and notions, as are to have names assigned to them, and withall so to contrive these as to their order, that the place of everything may contribute to a description of the nature of it. (289.)

However, in spite of this universal aim, Wilkins mainly uses the English language and, by appending an alphabetical dictionary of the English lexemes which appear in the tables, he shows his serious interest in his mother tongue (Dolezal 1983, 62). Already in '*To the Reader*' he thanked William Lloyd for drawing up this diction-ary, '*which upon tryal, I doubt not, will be found to be the most perfect, that was ever yet made for the English Tongue*' (c[r]). Obviously, Wilkins saw his (and William Lloyd's) work in the tradition of English lexicography.

This has repercussions for the syntactic nature of each entry. It consists struc-turally of: (i) the indication of individual semantic slots in a comprehensive system, which are normally split into a positive and a negative position; (ii) two English lexemes, semantically opposing each other, which fill the split slot and which Wilkins calls '*Radicals*'; and (iii) an optional series of English synonyms according to a special system (see below). I call (i) and (ii) together the *slot entry* which is indicated by lexemes, the positive position printed in capitals, the negative position printed in italicized capitals. I call (iii) *synonyms* in the position of *comple-mentation*. They are printed in italics. The slots have Arabic numbers, which start anew with each 'difference', their two positions being linked with each other by round braces. There are exceptions to these rules. The slots are sometimes not split

---

[49] Wilkins also gives a list of words which are not universal but era and culture dependent, for example names of dishes, clothes, dances, etc. (295–6).

[50] The term *slot* is taken from tagmemic grammar, where it signals a place in a (sentence) struc-ture into which a certain class of items, structures of a lower scale, can/must be inserted. This is called the *slot-and-filler technique*. My use of the term is unspecific with reference to tagmemics, signalling the place in a comprehensive semantic system where a semantic meaning, independent of its lexical-ization, is to be inserted.

[51] The proximity of this statement to Saussure's *valeur* is obvious. The term *slot* could be replaced by *semantic value* or by *valeur* itself. As the intention of the present explanation is, however, to make Wilkins' overall system in its typographical representation understandable, I prefer the more neutral lexeme *slot* to the others, which carry associations to modern structural semantics.

into a positive and a negative position, but merely state the positive one. The entries are combined with each other by a running text in which their logico-semantic relations to each other are explained in the same binary way in which the slots themselves are split (see below). Moreover, the technique of using square braces to the left and of indenting lines, both indicating logical inclusion and subsumption, clarify the logico-semantic hierarchy. The techniques of round bracing, numbering and capitalizing the slot entries, and italicizing the synonyms highlight the entries in such a way that the eye can travel over each page of the book and, while ignoring the explanatory text, simply read, as in a dictionary proper. The thesaurus has some 2,000 slots of this kind.[52]

For an illustration of the somewhat bewildering complexity of the typographical means employed in the Essay see Fig. 8.2.

The first feature that meets the eye when one reads the series of synonyms complementing the slot entries is the great variation in their number. In the epistemological genera I–III they are extremely numerous. Note, for example, genus I:[53] TRANSCENDENTAL GENERAL, CAUSE, slot 5:

ADJUVANT *Help, Aid, Assistance, Succour, Relief, Support, Advantage, auxiliary, subsidiary, avail, conduce, promote, farther, stand in stead, supply, accomodate, serve, Co-adjutor, abet, take ones part, stand by, a stay to one, forward, minister, relief, back one.*
IMPEDIENT, *hinder, Obstacle, Remora,*[54] *Clog, Bar, debar, obstruct, cumber, Rub, Check, Dam, Luggage, Lumber, Baggage, Prejudice, Disadvantage, foreshow, lett, stop, Disservice, stay, stand in the way, trigg, keep back, restrain, with-hold, interfere.*

In genus IV DISCOURSE, however, there are no synonyms at all or only very few of them in the 'differences' on the parts of language, but more, though still a smaller number than in the quotation, in the 'differences' on grammar and logic. Note, for example: WORDS, slot 5 and COMPLEX GRAMMATICAL NOTIONS, slot 9:

SUBJECT.
PREDICATE,[55] Attribute, ascribe, impute.

And

PLAIN, *Evident, Perspicuous, clear, express, obvious, easie, facil, explain, explicate, unfold, illustrate, open, make out.*
OBSCURE, *Dark, abstruse, riddle, aenigmatical, deep, profound, hard, difficult, mysterious, intrigue.*

The following genera, V–VII, are of a very similar microstructure: either there are no synonyms at all, or a minimal number, just one or two, or else a very small

---

[52] General count of lexemes according to the alphabetical dictionary that accompanied the *Essay.*
[53] For easy identification I use the genera numbers of the '*General Scheme*'.
[54] 'Obstacle, hindrance, impediment, obstruction'.
[55] Note that PREDICATE is (rightly) not italicized in spite of the binary arrangement. A predicate is not the opposite of a subject.

V. EVENT.　　V. The General name for that which follows upon Actions, especially as it relates to the end for which Actions are done, is EVENT, *Upſhot, iſſue, reſult, emergence, accrue, occurr, come to paſſ, fall out, befall, betide, enſue, prove, redound, happen, light, ſuccede, Luck, Fortune, End, Sequel, Succeſſ, incident, coincident, intervene, ſupervene, take effect, how fares, goes, ſpeeds it, come of it, come to good or to naught.*

Tranſcendental relations of Action belonging to *Event*, may be diſtributed into ſuch as do concern the

{ *Exiſting* or *not exiſting of the End* deſigned.

1. { OBTEINING, *Acquire, get, procure, attain, reach, gain, compaſſ, recover, take, win, catch, come by, pick up.*
{ FRUSTRATING, *Fail, diſappoint miſſ, defeat, deceive, elude, croſſ, come ſhort of, ſhift off, put by, of no effect, to no purpoſe, vain, void, nullity.*

Good or *Evil* accrewing to us by it, with reſpect to the

{ *Increaſing* or *Diminiſhing of our Poſſeſſions.*

2. { GAINING, *Lucre, Advantage, Profit, Emolument, Stock, the proceed, acquire, get, win, recover, extort.*
{ LOOSING, *Dammage, decrement, detriment, diſadvantage, diſprofit, wrack, ſpoil, hurt, hinderance, out of ones way.*

Diminiſhing or *Increaſing of our Want.*

3. { SAVING, *Sparing, take up.*　　(*ſumptuary, run out.*
{ SPENDING, *Lay out, beſtow, expend, diſpend, expence, charges, coſt,*

Continuing, or *not Continuing of a thing in our Poſſeſſion.*

{ *Imperfect* ; denoting the *Endeavour* and care *we uſe* about it, whether *any* or *none.*　　(*poſitory*

4. { LAYING UP, *Treaſuring, Preſerving, Stow, Hoord, Store, Repoſitory*
{ SQANDRING, *Laviſh, profuſe, careleſſ, miſpend, embezel, waſt unthrifty, ill husbandry, ſpendthriſt, flying out.*

{ *Perfect* ; Conſiſting in the *Good* or *Ill ſucceſſ* of ſuch Endeavour.

5. { KEEPING, *Preſerve, retain, Cuſtody, holding, promptuary, Cellar.*
{ LOOSING, *Perdition, loſſ, wrack, ſhed, ſpil.*

Applying of a thing ; whether more

{ *Simply* ; denoting the *applying* of a thing *to its proper end,* or *the not applying of it ſo.*

6. { USING, *Imploy, improve, exerciſe, occupy, manage, treat, handle, entertain, uſeful, ſerviceable, ſtand in good ſtead.*　　(*hand.*
{ ABSTEINING, *Forbear, refrain, ſpare, withdraw, wean, hold ones*

{ *Relatively* ; as to that *ſatisfaction* or *diſſatisfaction* of mind which we have in the *uſe of a thing.*

7. { INJOYING, *Fruition.*
{ BEING SICK OF, *Nauſeate, loath, tedious, ſurfet, weary of.*

{ *Reſult of ſuch application,* in the *diminiſhing* or *increaſing* of our

{ *Pain.*

{ REFRESHING, *Recreate, relieve, recruit, relaxation, refection, Bait.*
{ WEARYING, *Laſſitude, tyring, tedious, faint, fatigue.*

{ *Hinderances.*

9. { QUIETING, *Tranquillity, reſt, compoſe, ſedate, ſerene, ſtill, calm, ſet or be at reſt.*
{ TROUBLING, *Moleſt, diſturb, annoy, diſquiet, incumber, infeſt, terrupt, peſter, cumber, turbulent, ſtirs, coil, broil, turmoil, garbou, perturbation.*　　VI. The

FIG. 8.2　Wilkins: Event
Source: Wilkins 1668, 42.

number. In genera VIII–XVII, on inanimate materials, plants, and animals, the slot entries cease to be complemented by synonyms. Very rarely is the lexeme (in capitals) followed by one or two words: for example, MERCURY is followed by *Quick-silver*, NAVELWORT by *Wall-pennywort*, DAMES VIOLET by *Double Rocket*, RAIA OXYZYNCHOS by *Maid*, etc. (66, 79, 100, 133). The reason is obvious. In contrast to the earlier and later genera, these genera have deductions that end with the terminology of various scientific disciplines. Terms in a closed set hardly need to be complemented by synonyms. If such scientific terms are complemented at all, it is by folkloristic names. (The reverse is also true.) Consequently, genera XXI–XL, which do not deal with the taxonomies of nature, are similar to the earlier ones in that in most cases the number of synonyms following the slot entries is either very small or else very large. It is exceptional to have no synonym at all or an extraordinarily large number of synonyms, as in the entry quoted. Generally speaking, the number of synonyms stands in directly inverse relation to the concreteness of the slot entry. A non-ambiguous, precise lexeme in the slot entry does not need to be complemented by synonyms. Greater ambiguity and semantic fuzziness lead to a greater number of synonyms.

WORD-CLASSES AND ʻ*TRANSCENDENTAL PARTICLES*ʼ

The second feature of the synonyms that meets the eye is their seemingly irrational order. In his comment on the tables (289–96) John Wilkins offers an explanation in terms of his ideas on '*Natural Grammar*'. This is a philosophical grammar, applicable to all languages. Its first part is the '*Doctrine of Words*', that is, a system of word-classes. According to this 'Doctrine', all words are either '*Integrals*', that is (in modern terminology) content words or '*Particles*', that is, structure words. Either integrals are '*Nouns*', which are either '*Substantives*' or '*Adjectives*', or they are '*Adverbs derived*'. The set does not have any verbs. They are defined as adjectives combined with the copula,[56] which is the only essential and perpetually occurring '*essential Particle*'. (The other particles are of no interest here.) Substantives, adjectives and derived adverbs each appear in three possible modes, called '*Neuter*', '*Active*', and '*Passive*'. Applied to (a) things, (b) action or passion, and (c) persons, this 'Doctrine' actuates a generative process which determines the structural potential of word-classes any language can have, irrespective of which word-classes are actually to be found, for example, in Latin or English.[57] For the explanation of this structural potential, which has redundant parts, Wilkins starts with substantives neuter as (in modern terminology) the unmarked form, which he calls '*Radical*' (298–304). The following is an overview of the potential of word-classes:

---

[56] The same explanation appeared in the Port Royal grammar of 1660 and in Dalgarno's *Ars signorum* (1661). In the following century it was taken up by quite a number of grammarians, for example John Brightland and Charles Gildon in *A Grammar of the English Tongue*, 1711; Jenkin T. Philips in *An Essay Towards an Universal and Rational Grammar*, 1726; Joseph Priestley in *A Course of Lectures on the Theory of Language and Universal Grammar*, 1762, and others, among them James Harris in *Hermes*, 1751.   [57] Wilkins consistently uses Latin and English lexemes as examples.

(1) The substantive of a thing has (a) a radical form, such as *heat, light,* (b) a derived form for 'action', for example, *the heating, the enlightening,* and for 'passion', for example, *the being heated, the being enlightened,* (c) another derived form for 'person', for example, *the heating person* (e.g. *fireman*), *the enlightening person* (metaph. *teacher*) for the agent, and *the heated* (e.g. *burnt*) *person, the enlightened person* (metaph. *disciple*) for the patient.

(2) The substantive of an action has (a) a radical form, for example, *feeding, spitting,* (b) a derived form for 'person', for example, *the feeding person, the spitting person* (e.g. *nurse, spitter*) for the agent, and *the person fed* (e.g. *baby*), *the person spat at* for the patient, (c) another derived form for 'thing', for example *the feeding thing* (e.g. *food*), *the spittle.*

(3) The substantive of a person has (a) a radical form, for example, *judge, king* for the agent, and *judged* (e.g. *defendant*), *governed* (e.g. *subject*) for the patient, (b) a derived form for 'action', for example, *judging, governing,* (c) another derived form for 'thing', for example *a judging thing* (e.g. *law*), *a reigning thing* (e.g. *government, police*).[58]

Wilkins goes on differentiating the system on the basis of the categories *substance, quality,* etc. that govern the tables, although this is not done consistently and his distinctions are often far from convincing. The whole project, in present-day linguistics to be situated at the intersection of structural semantics and word formation, is interesting not so much in itself but in the overriding idea that language can be subjected *in all its aspects* to one structural principle. As the slots of the tables are understood in an abstract categorial way, all word-classes can actually be placed there, because they are governed by the same categories.[59] But, probably for the sake of easier intelligibility, Wilkins rules that all slot entries are to be understood *'as being simple Substantives'* (299). He knew, of course, that there are semantic transformations between words, for example those generated by rhetorical figures, which cannot be accounted for by either of the two systems. This is why he drew up a third which changes the word meanings by so-called *Transcendental Particles.*

> *Those particles are here stiled Transcendental, which do circumstantiate words in respect of some Metaphysical notion; either by enlarging the acceptation of them to some more significa-tion, then doth belong to the restrained sense of their places: or denoting a relation to some other Predicament or Genus, under which they are not originally placed.* (318.)

The table of *Transcendental Particles* is developed in the same way as the seman-tic tables, using a significant selection of their categories and general terms in binary deductions and ending in binary slot entries. This system is also supposed to be universal. It systematizes the semantic relations between lexemes denoting

---

58 All examples are Wilkins'.
59 This is one more reason why slot entries have to be read in a double way, that is, as abstract slots at the end of logico-semantic deductions and as lexemes.

something in the literal or the metaphorical way (e.g. *light* and *evident*), or a thing and the place where it is found (e.g. *metal* and *mine*), or an operation and an instrument (e.g. *painting* and *pencil*). For a shortened version of the whole system, arranged with decimal numbers, and for examples, see Tables A.9 and A.10.

This system of *Transcendental Particles*, which Dolezal rightly calls 'a highly sophisticated linguistic device' (1983, 72), accounts for the semantic relationships which are well known to present-day lexical semantics. They fall into the domains of metaphors and metonymies, collocations, means of expressing cases (in the sense of Fillmore) like object, agentive, instrument, cause, by way of word derivations, etc. The *furor logico-semanticus* with which Wilkins systematizes these phenomena and applies the same categories and distinctive terms as in his '*Tables*' may amuse us. But it shows the high-flying ambition that is behind the semantic dimension of his universal language, and consequently behind the thesaurus. It is his endeavour to construct a universal system for the lexis of all human languages, represented by English, a comprehensive, all-embracing network of determinations which, if realized, would be a universal matrix of everything people are able to express linguistically. This network has three determining matrices: the first is the deductive system of abstract terms, genera and 'differences' which generates the logico-semantic slot entries; the second is the system of word-classes, mainly integrals, and the third is the system of *Transcendental Particles* which generates meaning transformations between lexemes. These three embrace the semantic potential which any language can have. In fact, Wilkins moves here in the direction of thoughts which Descartes expressed critically and, later, Leibniz envisaged ambitiously on the possibilities of a universal language for all mankind.[60] Wilkins' thesaurus is the first historical example of the onomasiological idea being made the basis of language in general and, thus, being taken to a rationalistic extreme.

The series of synonyms which complement the slot entries of Wilkins' tables have to be seen in the context of his ambitious aim and the steps he took to realize it. By definition, synonymous words are those lexemes which are to be derived from the same slot entry in the tables and which can, furthermore, be determined according to the two systems of word-classes and *Transcendental Particles*.

It is not at all certain whether Wilkins himself realized the structural dimensions of his '*natural philosophy*' and '*natural grammar*'. He did apply the two additional systems to the series of synonyms with which he complemented the slot entries, but, admittedly, he only did this in a very sketchy way, just as the series of synonymous lexemes, presumably, are often hastily put together and difficult to follow. In his '*Explication of the Fore-going Table*' (289–96) he illustrates how the entries (species) of his '*Tables*' had to be read. It seems useful to present two examples:

---

[60]   For Descartes see Hüllen 1989, 188–90 (letter of Descartes to Mersenne of 20 November 1629); for Leibniz see Pombo 1987, 83–91, and *passim*.

(1) The radical PAST (*time past*) (186, 292) is complemented by:
  —the adjectives (without closer characterization): *expired, former, foregone, over, out*;
  —the adverbs (without closer characterization): *already, heretofore, out*;
  —the adverbs plus T(*ranscendental*) P(*article*) diminutive: *even now, a-late, erewhile, a little while ago*;
  —the adverbs plus TP augmentative: *long since, a great while ago*.

(2) The radical MEMORY (196, 292) is complemented by
  —the verbs (without closer characterization) *commemorate, record, recount*;
  —the verbs plus TP endeavour: with reference to present: *recollect, recal, call/come to mind*, with reference to future: *con over, getting by heart, [getting] by rote*;
  —the verbs plus TP cause: *put in mind, suggest, [cause to] remember*;
  —the substantives plus TP sign: *memorial, memorandum*;
  —the adjective passive (without closer characterization): *memorable*;
  —the adjective neuter (without closer characterization): *mindful*.

I have subsequently attempted to map the series of synonyms of a radical on to the system of word-classes and TPs:

(3) The radical FORTITUDE (207) is complemented by:
  —the substantive (without closer characterization): *courage*;
  —the substantives plus TP augmentative: *valour, prowess*;
  —the substantive plus TP like: *manhood*;
  —the substantive plus TP aggregate: *puissance* [= armed force];
  —the adjectives plus TP cause: *stout, undaunted, resolute*;
  —the adjective plus TP officer: *redoubted*;
  —the adjective plus TP power: *bold, daring*;
  —the adjective plus TP augmentative: *valiant*;
  —the adverb(ial)s plus TP metaphor: *in heart, of spirit*;
  —the adverb(ial)s plus TP like: *manly, manful, sturdy*.

It is obvious that Wilkins did not exploit all the determinations which he could have derived from his own ideas on 'Natural Grammar'.

It would certainly be impossible to try to analyse even a fragment of the lexemes occurring as synonyms in the tables according to these systems. It is worth bearing in mind Wilkins' ambition to systematize the vocabulary comprehensively, not only on the level of fairly precise word meanings but also in the undergrowth of semantic shades and cross-references. The fact that Wilkins did this with a great corpus of English lexemes and appended an English alphabetical dictionary to his *Essay* shows that he was thinking not only of his universal language plan but also of English as a vernacular language. In fact, he introduced the idea of a comprehensive and monoglot onomasiological dictionary of that language into lexicography (possibly without being aware of it) and also deliberated on the necessary order of synonyms to be used as the explanatory synonyms (*explanantia*) in a work like this.[61]

Among other things, this means that John Wilkins followed two principles which pointed in opposite directions. We might call this the 'Wilkins paradox' (Dolezal 1983, 8). The one principle was structural (in modern terminology), exploring the semantic potential of any language, the other was empirical (again in modern terminology), exploring the lexis of the English language.[62] Very possibly, Wilkins was aware of this opposition inside his own work, but he may have underestimated its profound importance. His disagreement with Dalgarno, for example, had its roots in this problem.[63]

In a way better geared to present-day typology, although painted with a very broad brush, we can distinguish fourteen types of synonymity in the tables (Hüllen 1989, 217). Of course, this typology, whose origin in modern descriptive grammar and case theory is obvious, would be susceptible of much refinement, and totally different typologies are certainly possible.

(1) Synonymy of nouns or noun and adjective: *being—entity, multitude— many.*

(2) Antonymy of nouns or noun and adjective: *person—nobody, accent— elevate.*

(3) Synonymy of nouns belonging to different frames: *thing—affair, matter, business.*

(4) Synonymy of an individual and a collective noun: *person—party.*

(5) Synonymy of nouns denoting a class and members of a class: *fiction— romance, tale.*

(6) Synonymy of nouns denoting persons/things and their properties: *person—age.*

(7) Synonymy of nouns denoting persons/things and their places: *judge— bench, court.*

(8) Synonymy of nouns denoting persons/things and instruments: *notary— roll.*

(9) Complementarity between nouns denoting persons: *advocate—client.*

(10) Synonymy of noun and verb: *appearance—show.*

---

[61] Peter Mark Roget knew very well what he was doing when he chose the *Essay* as his model for his *Thesaurus*. However, it is still unlikely that he understood all the intricacies of Wilkins' project, as the introduction to the first (and subsequent) edition(s) to his *Thesaurus* shows. See Hüllen 2004.

[62] In his *Essay*, 295–6, Wilkins speaks of words which cannot be provided for by his universal language system. Among them are titles of honour, degrees of professions, etc., that is (in modern terminology) culture-specific terms and names for things '*continually altering*', like games, drinks, tunes (see above). This shows the author's sense of linguistic reality. On the other hand, it also shows his underestimation of such facts, because he did not realize the historical relativity of these lexemes and, thus, the total blindness of his own ideas to the historicity of language (which, admittedly, became a notorious topic of linguistic thinking only in the nineteenth century).

[63] See the discussion of *Ars signorum* above.

(11) Synonymy of nouns denoting persons and verbs denoting actions: *accuser—impeach, tax, prosecute.*

(12) Synonymy of nouns denoting the outcome of actions/processes and verbs denoting actions/processes: *fiction—forge.*

(13) Synonymy of nouns denoting instruments and verbs denoting actions/processes: *name—nominate.*

(14) Antonymy of nouns denoting the outcome of actions/processes and verbs denoting actions/processes: *appearance—vanish.*

8.2.4 Using the thesaurus

GENERAL

John Wilkins' thesaurus is different from other onomasiological works in that every single entry is accounted for by a multi-branched logico-semantic deduction. The systematic method used on the levels of the macrostructure (thesaurus as a whole, genera, 'differences') is carried through to the level of the microstructure (species). Essentially, this systematic method consists of a large set of well-defined terms brought into a system by way of a deduction performed in (mostly) binary distinctions. This is a great achievement indeed.

[T]here is a fundamental congruency of structure from Table to Table. In short, the structure marks the boundaries of the levels of hierarchy; this technique produces an abbreviated and concise method of definition. It has the further benefit of graphically portraying semantic relations of words within and between the hierarchies of meaning.   (Dolezal 1983, 55.)

The 'fundamental congruency of structure' even appears in the discursive introductions and explanations of the tables. They are recognizably patterned. There are two standard propositional forms for introducing these tables. Either a synonym of the 'difference' to which the table is devoted is given, or the 'difference' is defined by exactly those divisions into which it branches. Each of these two patterns has its subpatterns (Dolezal 1983, 97–100). Moreover, discursive explanations of the classificatory tables show three patterns: reasons are given why a member is subsumed in a certain slot, or reasons are given why a natural member is nevertheless excluded, or a general explanation of the table is offered (Dolezal 1983, 87–97). In spite of considerable variation in phrasing, this leads to a 'fundamental congruence' of the chains of thoughts.

All this makes it doubtful whether we can speak of 'pragmatic' structures, placed between the semantic macrostructure and the syntactic microstructures, in the thesaurus at all. Every single entry (microstructure) is justified in terms of the semantic cohesion of the whole work (macrostructure). Whereas the users of an onomasiological dictionary are asked to construct the coherence[64] of a batch of

---

[64] For the difference between *cohesion* and *coherence* see Chapter 1, 22–3.

entries with the help of their encyclopaedic knowledge and thus to reconstruct a
tacitly assumed pragmatic structure, the users of this thesaurus simply have to
follow the long logical path from the beginning of 'all things and notions' to any
entry. Comments on different ways of using the thesaurus will clarify in which
way we can, nevertheless, speak of its pragmatic structures.

INTERMEDIATE LEXICAL STRUCTURES

In '*An Advertisement To The Reader*' of the alphabetical dictionary, which is
appended to the *Essay*, the author explains the appearance of the lexeme *corruption*
at various places in the tables. His explanation is corroborated by its entries in the
dictionary itself. According to both sources, this is the meaning of ***corruption***:

1.   [primary meaning, denoting the being or making of a thing evil or
         worse]
1.1   [by admixtion of some bad thing] > ***defiling***
1.2   [by privation . . .]
1.21   [. . .of being] > ***destruction***
1.22   [. . .of usefulness] > ***spoiling***
2.   [secondary meaning, applied to . . .]
2.1   [. . .thing, natural in varying degrees] > ***infection, decay, putrefaction***
2.2   [. . .thing, moral, general] > ***unholiness, viciousness***
2.3   [. . .thing, moral, special] > ***unchastity, bribery.***

According to the relevant '*Tables*' the word-group ***corruption: defiling; destruction; spoiling; infection, decay, putrefaction; unholiness, viciousness; unchastity,
bribery*** is defined with the following abstract terms:
   *general/special, degree (more/less); being/making, admixtion, privation, thing,
natural, moral (evil/good), usefulness.* Note the definition of these terms in the
following genera:

general/special: T[RANSCENDENTAL], I, 4;
degree: T, VI, 8;[65]
being: T, I, 1;
making: T, II (synonym for *cause*);
admixtion: T, III, 8 (synonym for *commixtion*);
privation: T, III, 3;
thing: T, I, 2;
natural: T, III, 7;
moral: T, III, 2 (antonym for *corrupt*);
useful(ness): T A(CTION), V, 6.

This proves that the abstract terms in the tables can indeed serve to deduce the
meanings of a lexeme. However, in no case is there a direct connection between

---

[65]   The dictionary says erroneously 'VI, 6'.

these terms and the lexemes that appear as a group. It seems advisable to look for the slots where they are located in the relevant tables. Note:

defiling: T M(IXED) V (Quality considered more strictly), 7 (synonym for *defilement*)[66] with the synonyms: *Filthiness*,[67] *Impurity, unclean, fowl, squalid, bedawb, besmear, bewray, contaminate, slabber, slubber, smear, soil, sully, pollute, daggle, slurry, smutch, smutt, stain, alloy, embase, dash.*

destruction: A(CTION) S(PIRITUAL) I (of God), 4 with the synonyms: *Perdition, Confusion, Bane, Devastation, Loss, pernicious, subvert, undoe, ruine, confound, extirpate, abolish, bring to naught, stroy, destroy, cast away, perish, cut off, wast, consume, dissolve, exterminate, extinguish, fall, gone.*

spoiling: TA II (Comparate), 9 with the synonyms: *Marring, corrupting, deprave, impaire, raze, scrape, cross out, sleight works.*

infection: S(ICKNESS) I (General Causes), 1 with the synonyms: *Contagion, taint, catching, run, spread, diffuse.*

decay: N(ATURAL) P(OWER) V (corporeal, relating to the individual), 4 (synonym for *decaying*) with the synonyms: *consume, wear, wast, drooping, fading, out of heart, flagging, languish, break, fail, goin down, fall away, bring down/low, decline, impair, quail, abate, molder, pine, wither, perish, spend, corrupt.*

putrefaction: NP V, 2 (synonym for *putredness*) with the synonyms: *Rottenness, Corruption, purulent, tainted, unsound, moulder, festered, addle, Matter, rankle, suppurate, putrefie, Carrion.*

unholiness: H(ABIT); V (infused, moral), 2 with the synonyms: *Wickedness, Iniquity, Impiety, Ungodliness, Prophaneness, Corruption, Sin, Miscreant, graceless, Caitiffe.*

viciousness: M(ANNER) I (virtue). The lexeme *vice* appears as the opposite of *virtue* in the general introduction to this 'difference', with the synonyms: *Sin, Crime, Dishonesty, Trespass, Transgression, Fault, Failing, Infirmity, Oversight, wicked, Improbity, Turpitude, unrighteous, unjust, bad, naught, vile, base, loose, evil, ill, corrupt, venial, heinous, debauched, lewd, lawless, licencious, foul, flagitous, enormous, profligate, Miscreant, Ruffian, Caitiff, Villain, Rakehell, Libertine, defile, pollute.*

unchastity: M II (relating to body), 7: with the synonyms *Incontinence, Wantonness, lascivious, unclean, obscene, ribaldry, bawdy, lewd, light, dishonest, corrupt, defile, deflowr, incest, rape, ravish, viciate.*

bribery: R(ELATION) J(UDICIAL) IV (faults, not capital), 6 with the synonyms: *Corruption, dawbing.*

The terms that define the relevant 'differences' (given in round brackets) can easily serve as a terminological bridge between the fairly abstract terms that determine the genera and the lexemes. All of them could be found in the relevant genera. More valuable, however, is the observation that the synonyms of the slot entries which appear in the semantic variants of *corruption* constitute a word-group consisting of smaller word-groups, which is dispersed through the tables and

---

[66] The dictionary says erroneously 'V, 6'. The letters give the genera, the Roman numbers the 'differences', the Arabic ones the species, either in the positive or the negative position. Words after the Roman numbers (in round brackets) indicate the terms that define the species.

[67] Wilkins writes '*Filthineß*', and similarly in other words.

makes intermediate lexical structures visible which extend across genera and 'differences'. Indeed, users of the tables can arrange these intermediate structures themselves, depending on the lexeme from which they start. Their number is obviously almost unlimited, and our example is just one possible case given to show the principle. These intermediate pragmatic structures are *pragmatic* in a special way because they depend on the correlation of meaning segments, that is (in modern terminology), lexical markers, which is not provided for in the numerous deductions which semanticize the slot entries. If Wilkins had been an extreme rationalist who allowed only one lexeme in a slot, these intermediate structures would not appear. But as, in spite of all his rationalist ambitions, Wilkins was also an empiricist who observed linguistic reality and enriched his slot entries with synonyms, he allowed for lexical structures which extend across his own systematization.

8.2.5 Reading selected 'differences'

GENERAL

What the section is in an onomasiological dictionary proper, the 'difference' is in Wilkins' thesaurus. It is the textual unit which the users have to consult in order to be able to find an entry. Its embedding in higher-ranking units like the genera and the thesaurus as a whole can easily be found, not least by the *'General Scheme'* at the beginning and the overviews introducing each genus, which function like the *'General Scheme'* on a lower level. Moreover, there are the indications in the margin.

For the experienced and interested reader the perusal of any 'difference' is almost always a rewarding enterprise. It shows the whole machinery of the thesaurus at work. It also shows its limitations, and the one experience is just as valuable as the other. Both together form a picture of an author who is grappling with two interfering principles of linguistic semantics, namely the top-down order of lexis which would, ideally, lead to an all-covering logico-semantic deduction whose paths each end in one and only one pair of lexemes with clear meaning demarcations—the aim of Wilkins' universal language—and the bottom-up order of lexis which in fact is a vast collection of denotations ruled by encyclopaedic meanings and the pragmatic needs of human communication. If we measure Wilkins' ambitious aim against his performance in the *Essay*, we realize how, in certain domains more than in others, the structure of language with its mixture of consistency and inconsistency finally gained the upper hand over the plan of an artificially perfect language.

The pragmatic structures of an onomasiological dictionary are defined as regularities which serve the communicative needs of language users and which cannot be accounted for by semantic and syntactic regularities. In the case of Wilkins' thesaurus they are less dictated by everyday language use. The author's philosophical aims and methods preclude this. Rather, they are dictated by the author's knowledge of facts and ideas and by predilections which may not even have been conscious to him, and which could not be incorporated into his tables.

The following *reading protocols* were written with the aim of showing such overshooting regularities. They may be language (i.e. English) dependent or universal. Certainly, no pedestrian criticism is meant in any of the cases. Wilkins' spelling and the semiotics of the *Essay*, including the meanings of capitals, italics, numbering, braces, indentation, are strictly observed.[68] The selection of the 'differences' for close readings is motivated by the wish to show some of the different ways in which pragmatic structures are worked into the tables. This pertains to general societal experiences (*event*), to biological means of description (*herbs*), and to philosophical presuppositions (*virtues*). Many other domains of basic assumptions could be found. The meaning of the lexeme *pragmatic* presupposes that the number of such assumptions is virtually limitless, just as the number of conditions that determine human actions and thoughts is limitless.

EVENT

EVENT (see Fig. 8.2) belongs to the logical domain of the tables. It is part of the third genus, TRANSCENDENTAL RELATIONS OF ACTION, more precisely the fifth 'difference'. According to the introductory text and the synonyms, '*it relates to the end for which Actions are done*'.[69] In present-day terminology we would integrate the topic into a theory of action (or a theory of planning, of strategies, etc.). With nine slot entries, all of them binary opposites, the table follows the rules which Wilkins set himself. As always (see above) in this logical domain, the slot entries are complemented by an extraordinarily large number of synonyms.

The most abstract distinction, indicated by a long square brace, is between '*Existing or not existing of the End* designed' and '*Result of such Application*'. However, following the print and the chain of thoughts we find that there are in fact four distinctions here, besides the two mentioned, '*Good or Evil* accruing to us by it' and '*Applying of a Thing*'. The nine slot entries fit perfectly into these distinctions. Looking at their meanings we detect that Wilkins is thinking of a very special kind of 'end for which actions are done', namely everything that can be subsumed under 'possessions' which must be 'saved' or 'layed up' and which can be 'applied' and consequently 'enjoyed'. Note the entries:

(1) OBTEINING / *FRUSTRATING*[70] under '*Existing or not Existing . . .*', (2) GAINING / *LOOSING*, (3) SAVING / *SPENDING*, (4) LAYING UP / *SQUANDERING*, and (5) KEEPING / *LOOSING* under '*Good or Evil . . .*'; (6) USING / *ABSTAINING* and (7)

---

[68]   There is one more typographical device to be observed, namely a double bar printed vertically in the sentences which introduce entry slots and/or link two of them. These bars indicate that a binary branching of the semantic deduction follows. So it typically occurs before the word *either*.

[69]   This and all following quotations are taken from *Essay*, 42.

[70]   In giving the numbered slot entries I occasionally skip logical subbraces.

INJOYING / *BEING SICK OF* under 'Applying . . .', [8] REFRESHING / *WEARYING*[71] and (9) QUIETING / *TROUBLING* under '*Result* . . .'.

Some of the most characteristic synonyms are:[72]

(1) *acquire, win/fail, come short of;* (2) *Profit, Stock/disprofit, spoil;* (3) *Sparing, take up/expence, cost;* (4) *Treasuring, Store/misspend, ill husbandry;* (5) *preserve, retain/loss, spill;* (6) *occupy, manage/refrain, spare;* (7) *Frutition*[73]*/tedious, fatigue;* (8) *recreate, relieve/tyring, faint;* (9) *Tranquility, rest/disturb, annoy.*

Logically, the table is certainly convincing. The terms that are used for distinctions could be looked up in their definitions in other tables. The slot entries serve as distinguishers measured against the more abstract characterizations that introduce them. The binary oppositions are clear. And yet the slot entries and the (selection of) synonyms betray a context which, in terms of present-day sociology, might be called *bourgeois culture* and which is not prepared by the logical deduction of the table at all. This means we encounter tacit pragmatic conditions of thinking in this table.

HERBS BEARING MANY SEEDS IN A BUTTON

HERBS BEARING MANY SEEDS IN A BUTTON (see Fig. 8.3) belong to the scientific, more precisely the biological, domain of the tables. It is part of the eleventh genus, HERBS ACCORDING TO THEIR FLOWERS,[74] in fact it is the ninth 'difference'. The numbers of 'differences' subsumed under this genus and also the eight slot entries are anomalous, as is the case in most of the biological tables (see above). With one exception, slot entries have no synonyms at all because they are terms of a biological taxonomy. The Latin versions of this taxonomy are given in the margin. Thus, instead of synonyms we have one taxonomy replaced by another. In accordance with the binary method, slot entries, with two exceptions, are given in pairs. But they are not in opposition. This is why the second position of each slot entry is, rightly, not italicized.

The most abstract distinction, indicated by a long square brace, is between *Leaf* and *Seed*. A closer look, however, reveals that this is in fact a division into three, with the criterion *Flowers* in between. This distinction follows the accepted biological principles of taxonomy. Note the entries:

(1) WILD TANSY AVENS, (2) CINQUEFOIL / TORMENTIL, (3) ANEMONY / PASCH FLOWER under '*Leaf*'; (4) CROW-FOOT PILEWORT, (5) ADONIS FLOWER under '*Flowers*', and (6) MALLOW / HOLYHOK, (7) MARSH MALLOWS / TREE MALLOW, and (8) VERVAIN MALLOW under '*Seed*'.

ANEMONE is the only slot entry with a synonym, namely *Wind-flower*.

---

[71]   The number (8) is erroneously missing.

[72]   I admit that my selection of synonyms introduces an element of subjectivity. However, a large-scale comparison of all synonyms proved impossible for practical reasons. Note that for Wilkins any word-class may serve as a synonym of the slot entry.

[73]   If, as in this case and in later cases, only one synonym is mentioned, the entry contains only this one.   [74]   All quotations are from *Essay*, 95.

Chap. IV. *Herbs according to their Flowers.* 95

IX. HERBS bearing MANY SEEDS together IN A cluſter or BUTTON, may be diſtinguiſhed according to the | IX. HERBS BEARING MANY SEEDS IN A BUTTON.

Leaf; into ſuch as have

Winged leaves; || either that whoſe leaf is *underneath hoary* and of a ſilver colour.: or that whoſe *leaves* are *broad at the end*, having little *pinnulæ towards the bottom* of them, *bearing a burr*.

1. WILD TANSY. / AVENS.

Fingered leaves; *growing from the ſame point of the foot-ſtalk*; || either *five*, having a *flower* conſiſting of *five leaves*: or *ſeven*, the *flower* conſiſting *of four leaves*.

2. CINQUEFOIL. / TORMENTIL.

But one leaf upon the foot-ſtalk of the flower, and but *one flower*; || either that whoſe *leaves* and *ſtalks* are generally *more Smooth*: or more *Hairy*, the head after the flower is faded, being covered with long woolly locks.

3. ANEMONY, *Wind-flower*. / PASCH FLOWER.

Flowers; whether moſt commonly

Yellow; ſhining as if varniſhed, bearing their ſeed in a rough head; || either that whoſe *flower* doth generally conſiſt *of five round pointed leaves*: or that whoſe *flower hath eight or nine leaves blowing early*.

4. CROW-FOOT. / PILEWORT.

Red; having *leaves like thoſe of Camomil*.

5. ADONIS FLOWER.

Seed; in a *head of a* round flat *cheeſe-like figure*; || either that which is

Of *rounder leaves*; the *Leſs* or the *Greater*.

6. MALLOW. / HOLYHOK.

Of *hoary ſoft leaves*; || either the *leſs* growing *in Marſhes*: or the *greater by the Sea*.

7. MARSH MALLOWS. / TREE MALLOW.

Of *jagged leaves*;

8. VERVAIN MALLOW.

FIG. 8.3 Wilkins: Herbs according to their flowers
Source: Wilkins 1668, 95.

This is certainly almost the easiest case of a deduction imaginable. However, the author finds himself compelled to add fairly elaborate descriptions to the criteria *leaf, flowers,* and *seed,* in order to arrive at his slot entries. Note, as examples:

Added to *Leaf*: [herbs as have] *Winged leaves; // either that whose leaf is underneath hoary and of a silver colour: or that whose leaves are broad at the end, having little pinnulae towards the bottom of them, bearing a burr.*
Added to *Flowers*: *Yellow; shining as if varnished, bearing their seed in a rough head; // either that whose flower doth generally consist of five round pointed leaves: or that whose flower hath eight or nine leaves blowing early.*
Added to *Seed*: *in a head of a round flat cheese-like figure; // either that which is * Of rounder leaves; the Less or the Greater. * Of hoary soft leaves; // either the less growing in Marshes; or the greater by the Sea. * Of jagged leaves.*[75]

The careful marking of words by italics shows that this table contains many more distinguishing criteria than the author could insert in it. Probably they could not be systematized. The description added to *leaf* and quoted above contains five such criteria. There are two other descriptions containing four criteria each, namely:

Fingered leaves; growing from the same point of the foot-stalk; flower consisting of five leaves; flower consisting of seven leaves.
But one leaf upon the foot-stalk of the flower; but one flower; leaves and stalks more Smooth; leaves and stalks more Hairy.

Of these only 'winged leaves' and 'fingered leaves' can be seen in a systematic relation; all the other criteria are biological particulars that resist a logico-semantic deduction using the binary method. Things are very similar with the descriptions added to *flowers* and *seed.*

As in the previous reading protocol, we are given information which does not come from the tables. However, unlike the first example, it is not tacit (as pragmatic structures in onomasiological works normally are), because Wilkins expresses it with great care. It pertains to the great number of visible phenomena which are used in biological taxonomy.

HOMILETICAL COMMON VIRTUES

HOMILETICAL COMMON VIRTUES (see Fig. 8.4) belongs to the social domain of the tables. It is part of the twenty-sixth genus MANNERS, more precisely its fourth 'difference'. With nine slot entries it has a regular size, just as the whole genus does, with six 'differences'. All entries are given in opposing pairs, which is according to Wilkins' own norm, but each time the negative position of the pair is divided into two positions again, which is not the normal case. The slot entries have a large, many even an extraordinarily large, number of synonyms.

---

[75]   * = new line with a slot entry in between.

The name of the 'difference' refers to manners, more precisely: virtues, in conversation. '*HOMILETICAL Vertues more COMMON, are such vertuous habits as are required in men of all degrees and conditions for the regulating of their mutual Conversations*.'[76] The table deals thus with the rare topic of the ethics of language use in society.

The most abstract distinction, indicated by a long square brace, is between a '*Profitable*' and a '*Pleasant*' conversation. Each of the two is broken down again following criteria on lower levels. The homiletical virtues of the profitable conversation concern either *matter* or *manner*. Concerning matter they tend to '*the preservation of Truth*' or '*of Peace*'. Concerning manner these conversations regulate human behaviour '*in due respect of Things or of Persons*'. The homiletical virtues of the pleasant conversation regulate either '*Our Outward carriage towards others, both Actions and Speeches*' or '*Our Words and Speeches*' either in 'More serious' or in '*Less serious*' debates and matters.

This is a perfectly clear order, each higher position branching into two lower ones. The distinctive criteria are all well grounded in the first epistemological genera of the tables. The slot entries appear under (i) *Truth*, (ii) *Peace*, (iii) *Things*, (iv) *Persons*, (v) *Outward carriage*, and (vi) *Words and Speeches*. Note the entries:[77]

(1) VERACITY / *LYING: OVER-SAYING* // *UNDER-SAYING*, (2) FIDELITY / *UNFAITH-FULNESS*: OFFICIOUSNESS // *TREACHERY* under (i),
(3) PEACABLENESS / *UNPEACABLENESS: TAMENESS* // *CONTENTIOUSNESS* under (ii),
(4) FRANKNESS / – :*TOO MUCH OPENNESS* // *RESERVEDNESS*, (5) TACITURNITY / LOQUACITY under (iii),
(6) GRAVITY / *VANITY: FORMALNESS* // *LIGHTNESS* under (iv),
(7) COURTESY / – :*FAWNING* // MOROSENESS under (v),
(8) COMPLACENCY /–: *ASSENTATION* // *MAGISTERIALNESS*, (9) URBANITY / –: SCURRILITY // *RUSTICITY* under (vi).

Some of the most characteristic synonyms are:

(1) *Truth/Hyperbole, brag* // *Dimunition, disparage*, (2) *trusty, loyal/Fawning* // *perfidious, undermine*,[78] (3) *Quietness, Concord/TAMENESS*[79] // *Strife, Controversie*, (4) *Freeness, plain* / *Tell-tale, blab* // *coy, demure*, (5) *staunch, close* / *Babbling, talkative*, (6) *Seriousness, sober* / *fond, foppish* // *flashy, Petulance*, (7) *mannerliness, civility* / *obsequious, smooth* // *cynical, rude*, (8) *soft, popular* /*Flattery, fawning* // *Arrogance, pedantical*, (9) *Facetiousness, jocular* / *Abusiveness, Vice* //*Clownishness, blunt*.

---

[76] This and all following quotations are from *Essay*, 210–11.

[77] Regularly slot entries have a positive and a negative position (capitals and italicized capitals). I indicate this difference by a slash. Different from this arrangement, in the entries displayed here each negative position again branches off into two positions which oppose each other but together stand in opposition to the higher positive position (thus both italicized capitals). I indicate this second difference by a double slash. The transition from the higher to the lower pairs of positive and negative positions is indicated by a colon. See Fig. 8.4.

[78] Slot-entry (1) is headed '*Declarations* or Assertions', slot entry (2) '*Obligations* or Promises'. Note how near such characterizations are to present-day notions in speech-act theory.

[79] There is no synonym.

IV. HOMI-LETICAL COMMON Vertues.

IV. HOMILETICAL Vertues more COMMON, are such vertuous habits as are required in men of all degrees and conditions for the regulating of their mutual Conversations. Not that the other Vertues before specified, are not likewise necessary to this end: but that they do not so directly and immediately tend to it as these others do which are styled HOMILETICAL. To which may be opposed INSOCIABLENESS, *Barbarism.*

These are distinguishable into such as render our Conversation; either *Profitable* to each other: which may be considered according to the *Matter*; such as tend to the preservation of

Truth; either in our

Declarations or Assertions.

1. { VERACITY, *Truth.*
   { LYING, *Leasing,* { OVER-SAYING, *Hyperbole, Boasting, Ostentation, forge, fib, flam,* { *tion, vapor, crack, brag, vaunt, swagger, Rofalse, perjury.* { *domontade.*
                     { UNDER-SAYING, *Detraction, Diminution, disparage, traduce, depreciate.*

Obligations or Promises.

2. { FIDELITY, *trusty, true, loyal.*
   { UNFAITH- { OFFICIOUSNESS, *Fawning.*
   { FULNESS. { TREACHERY, *perfidious, false, faithless, unfaithful, untrusty, disloyal, Recreant, Traitor, Ambodexter, betray, falter, undermine, prevaricate.*

Peace.

3. { PEACEABLENESS, *Quietness, Concord, Accord, Agreement, Union, appease, atone, pacifie, reconcile, compose, take up, compromize, still, calm, set at peace, part a fray.*
   { UNPEACEA- { TAMENESS.
   { BLENESS. { CONTENTIOUSNESS, *Strife, Dissension, Discord, Variance, Controversie, Difference, Broils, Contest, Combustion, Debate, Division, Bickering, litigious, quarrel, wrangle, clash, jarr, brabble, jangle, Garboil, Odds, Brangling, Conflict, Squabble, Brawling, Cavilling, captious, Incendiary, Barreter, Boutefew, Shrew, Scold.*

Manner; such as regulate our Carriage with a due respect of

Things; in

Saying what is fit to be said.

4. { FRANKNESS, *Freeness, plain, open-hearted.*
   { TOO MUCH OPENNESS, *Tell-tale, Blab,*
   { RESERVEDNESS, *shy, nice, coy, demure, staunch, wary, close.* ✱

Concealing what is fit to be concealed.

5. { TACITURNITY, *staunch, close, still, counsel-keeping, secrecy, silence.*
   { LOQUACITY, *Babbling, Garrulity, talkative, babble, blab, chatter, gabbling, tattle, prate-tile.*

Persons; in observing a just Decorum.

6. { GRAVITY, *seriousness, sober, demure, sage, stayed, earnest, settled, solid.*
   { VANITY, { FORMALNESS, *Coxcomb, fond, foppish.*
   { { LIGHTNESS, *flashy, Freak, Levity, Petulance.*

Pleasant

{*Pleasant* to each other ; serving to regulate

  {Our *Outward carriage* towards others, both Actions and Speeches, is
    to a Facility for Converse, together with our desires and endea-
    vours by all honest wayes to please others, and care, not to offend
    them.

7. {
    { COURTESY, *Comity, mannerliness, civility affability, kindness, hu-*
      manity, gentle, fair, humane, benign, tractable, smooth.
    { FAWNING, *Assentation, Adulation, obsequious, smooth, glavering,*
      gloze, cogg, cajole, curry favour, collogue, wheedle, crouch, creep-
      ing, scraping, flatter, sooth, clawing, Blandishment, Parasite, Sy-
      cophant, Claw-back.
    { MOROSENESS, *curst, crabbed, cynical, froward, churlish, uncivil,*
      boisterous, rude, sullen, surly, unmannerly, hard to please, humor-
      some, rough, harsh, sour, testy, snappish, dogged, currish, waspish,
      tetchy, wayward, peevish, pettish.

{Our *Words and Speeches* ; either in

  {*More serious* debates ; making due allowances to others, affording
    them just liberty.

8. {
    { COMPLACENCY, *Civility, smooth, soft, popular,*
    { ASSENTATION, *Flattery, glozing, soothing, fawning, mealy-*
      mouth'd, trencher-friend.
    { MAGISTERIALNESS, *Arrogance, Imperiousness, Lordliness,*
      masterly, pedantical, rough, over-bear, Roister.

{*Less serious* matters ; by such honest mirth whereby Conversation
  is to be sweetned.

9. {
    { URBANITY, *Facetiousness, Raillery, Drollery, jocular, jocund,*
      merry, Conceit, Jest, Squib, Clinch, Quibble, Wagg.
    { SCURRILITY, *Buffoonry, Abusiveness, Pasquil, Zany, Vice.*
    { RUSTICITY, *Clownishness, boisterous, blunt, barbarous, rough,*
      rude, Kerne, home-bred, Slouch, uncivil, unmannerly, dirty.

FIG. 8.4   Wilkins: Virtues
Source: Wilkins 1668, 210–11.

The arrangement of slot entries calls for two observations.

The first is that, in this table Wilkins follows the classical and medieval doctrine of *temperantia*, of the virtue situated in the middle between two extremes. He introduces the notion 'temperance' in the second 'difference' of the genus 'MANNERS', which deals with 'VERTUES RELATING TO OUR BODIES' and is opposed to 'sensuality'. The meaning of the word seems to refer to wisdom rather than to ethics. The table on the ethics of language use does not introduce the notion of temperance at all, but uses it as an additional criterion, even flouting the binary system, because the first and the second positions of each slot entry are not oppositions, as indicated by the print type, but the second positions are. The 'differences' I–III of the genus 'MANNERS' also employ this arrangement, which signals a general concept of ethics. Obviously, the doctrine of *temperantia* was more important for Wilkins with reference to language use than to other domains of human 'manners'.

The second observation is that it is well known that Wilkins and many others of the monarchist and Latitudinarian party saw the roots of the Civil War mainly in *enthusiasm*, that is, in an uncontrolled manner of theological argumentation. Note from 'The *Epistle Dedicatory*' of the *Essay*:

> To which it will be proper for me to add, That this design [the universal language] will likewise contribute much to the clearing of some of our Modern differences in Religion, by unmasking many wild errors, that shelter themselves under the disguise of affected phrases; which being Philosophically unfolded, and rendered according to the genuine and natural importance of Words, will appear to be inconsistencies and contradictions.   (b^r.)[80]

It is not without historical significance that one aim of the 'homiletical vertues' was to keep the peace. It is not even without historical significance that the topic was included at all in a 'difference' of its own under 'MANNERS' and not under 'DISCOURSE' where it also might have found its proper place. Significantly, the subentry '*TAMENESS*' (under '*UNPEACABLENESS*') has no complementing synonym. But the subentry '*CONTENTIOUSNESS*' has as many as thirty-two, all of which probably had much more concrete meanings in Wilkins' life experience than we can imagine today. Both observations show that the table is determined by criteria outside itself just as much as by its own logico-semantic deductions.

8.3 The background

8.3.1 Logic and rhetoric

GENERAL

In 'The *First Part* [of the Essay] Containing the Prolegomina' John Wilkins mentions in the text and in the marginal notes many authorities who supported

---

[80]   See also Sprat 1966, 112, 152, and *passim*.

his ideas on the origin of languages, their corruption in Babel, their history, the historical course of Anglo-Saxon as well as the historical relation between sounds and letters. These references reveal him as a well-read man, in agreement with many authors of the tradition. However, in 'The Second Part Containing *Universal Philosophy*' there is nothing of this kind. The great task of '*a just Enumeration and description of such things and notions as are to have Marks and Names asssigned to them*' (20) is introduced in one single paragraph of the first part (20–1) and in chapter 1 of the second part (22–5) which, besides '*The General Scheme*' and the overview of '*Transcendentals general*', consists of not quite two pages of text. He describes his division of genera into 'differences' and species and explains the special role of the first six genera which comprehend '*such matters, as by reason of their Generalness, or in some other respect, are above all those common heads of things called Predicaments*' (24). Instead of references to traditional authors we find general complaints about the state of *Metaphysic*, which is of no help either for the discussion of 'transcendentals' or for the ordering of 'predicaments'. This is why the introduction of general terms is '*very short and deficient*' (24) and why the tables cannot be '*disposed of so accurately as they ought to be*' (25).

Wilkins' polemical attack against metaphysics is in agreement with many writers after Bacon. It shows, on the other hand, that he does see his '*Tables*' in the tradition of ancient logic and ontology as it had come down to him through the centuries from the Porphyrian tree to Ramistic schemata of knowledge and whose present state he deplores. Within the universal language programme, onomasiological word-lists thus appear as the direct successors of philosophical tables.

Nevertheless, it seems hard to believe that John Wilkins should have drawn his 242 folio pages of tables from everything in the physical and mental world that could be given a name without any model in mind. Since he raised his criticism against contemporary metaphysics only on a very general level and since his categorial order of tables does not deviate too much from what was traditional, we might assume that he depended more on the usual endeavours of this kind than he makes us believe. It will be a task of future research to study the relevant books and find out the ones which Wilkins may have thought of when planning the '*Tables*' or which he may actually have consulted.[81]

Among them, it is the books on logic and rhetoric, written in Latin and in English and often of an intoductory character, which will most probably prove to be helpful, although they were written by the so-called schoolmen, who were widely despised after Bacon's verdict.[82] They are likely to contain those ideas and patterns of thinking which were in the air, even if they cannot be pinned down to one source. They live on in the Aristotelian and/or the Ciceronian tradition and play a part in the debates launched by Philip Melanchthon (Philip Schwarzert,

---

[81] See Lodwick, ed. Salmon 1972, 107–8 which partly guided my search.

[82] See Bacon, *Works* 1859, III (*The Advancement of Learning*), 286–7. In fact, Bacon does not condemn the 'schoolmen' altogether. They could have proved, he says, 'excellent lights' if they had 'joined variety and universality of reading and contemplation' to their works (287).

1497–1560) and Ramus (Fr. Pière La Ramée, 1515–72; see Howell 1961, Risse 1964). Besides carrying on traditional terminology and method, for example the Porphyrian tree of logical terms, their main concern was how to transcend the language-centred methods of *definition* and *division* in favour of matter-centred methods of making inventories of reality.

Ramism was one of the most influential, if controversial, philosophical movements of the sixteenth and seventeenth centuries. What historiographers judge to be a deplorable deterioration into a scholastic dogmatism and mechanical way of thinking and teaching (Risse 1964, I, 200), may account for its general influence. Although often seen as a philosophical position hostile to the Aristotelian tradition, it could also be combined and made accordant with it.[83] The question has never been raised but is worth while asking how great the influence of Ramism actually was on the conception of Wilkins' tables, in particular because Ramistic works, favouring binarism, have a strictly didactic intention (see Kusuka-Wa 1999, 133).

A number of features are common to the works of English authors of this highly sophisticated and pedagogically minded branch of philosophy (Risse 1964, I, 59–64, 166–72).[84] Among them are the reduction of the five great rhetorical arts to only two, namely *inventio* and *iudicium*, of which the first embraces the logical determination of terms, the second the use of these terms in propositions and sequences of propositions, that is, syllogisms and figures. Among them also are the logical differentiation between *praedicabilia* and *praedicamenta*, of which the former contains those abstract terms (like *being*, *matter*, *form*, etc.) which are preconditions for the latter—the Aristotelian categories—to become real. Special chapters on *definitio* and *divisio* ensure that the logical procedures applied to *inventio* and *iudicium* are precise. A first step from language to reality is then made in defining *loci/places*, where the terms of *inventio* are used to draft a hierarchical inventory of the universe, prefiguring later encyclopaedic projects. A gradient could be defined between the two extremes of *logic* and *encyclopaedia*, with all of the titles in the relevant context being situated somewhere between the two. Note, for example:

Aditus Ad Logicam In vsvm eorum qui primo Academiam Salutant. Autore Samuele Smith . . . *(1627)*.

But:

The Artes Of Logike And Rhetorike, plainly set forth in the English tongue . . . . Written by M. Dudley Fenner (1584).

And:

---

[83] For example, *The Art of Logik, Gathered out of Aristotle, and set in due forme, according to his instructions, by Peter Ramus, . . . Published for the Instruction of the vnlearned, by Anthony Wottoon. . . .* (1626).

[84] This is, of course, also true for other than English authors, but they remain outside the scope of this discussion. See Risse 1964, *passim*.

Logicae Et Physicae Compendivm. Authore Rob[ert] Sanderson . . . (1618).
Petri Molinaei Opera Philosophica—Logica, Physica, Ethica . . . (1645).

Generally, such treatises on logic and rhetoric were written in a tightly knit language which moved pedantically from the definition of one term to that of the next and used binary oppositions to keep the logical deduction in motion. Even where patterned in a sequence of questions and answers for pedagogical reasons,[85] such oppositions, located in the answers, were regularly used to stimulate the next question. Braces were quite often inserted and sentences typographically arranged inside them in order to indicate the binary relations between, for example, sentences and their common dependence on a foregoing statement or definition. There are no tables of the size of those in Wilkins' book, but quite frequently paragraphs or chapters of books are epitomized in a way which prefigures them. This shows that they were obviously in common use as a means to show the typographical indication of the logical or any other order of a text.[86]

We can easily detect these general features of books on logic and rhetoric in Wilkins' work, although his aim was quite different from theirs. The first three genera and genus VI are in the proximity of *inventio*, at the same time repeating the difference between *praedicabilia* and *praedicamenta* in '*such matters, as by reason of their Generalness, or in some other respect, are above all those common heads of things called Predicaments*' (Wilkins 1968, 24). Genus IV, devoted to language as a means of expressing thoughts, is in the proximity of *definitio* and *divisio*. All the genera from VII to XL are *places*,[87] that is, the application of 'predicaments' to reality. Wilkins' '*Philosophical Character*', finally, is in the proximity of '*iudicium*' although its function is, of course, quite different. But it considers the rules of concatenation of terms in order to formulate correct and true sentences, and this is what *iudicium* does.

Besides the general schema of books on logic and rhetoric, Wilkins' *Essay* also employs their typical style in its '*Tables*' by generalizing the use of formal and typographical arrangement, and also in the concise, step-by-step definitions which introduce these tables. In their use of the binary method of definition they are very similar to each other, sometimes only made different by the way of printing. Quite frequently, the introductory texts could easily have been laid out as tables of terms, and the tables could easily have been printed as paragraphs in continuously flowing text. The most general similarity between the treatises on logic and Wilkins' *Essay* is their position between language-centred logic and the reality-centred systematic inventarization of the universe.

---

[85] For example Fage 1632, BL 8467. a. 25. 8°.
[86] This is also true for publications outside the logical and rhetorical domain. See, for example, the elaborate overview with tables of Robert Burton's *The Anatomy of Melancholy* (1621).
[87] Genus V 'Creator' does not fit into this comparison.

BINARISM AND TABULAR ARRANGEMENT

In the following discussion, some individual traits of Wilkins' *Essay* and of the earlier books on logic and rhetoric will be displayed parallel to each other in order to show their similarities, not however in order to show any direct dependence of the later book on the earlier ones. Binarism and tabular arrangement are certainly the features of the literature in the background which reappear most obviously in Wilkins' work. This can be observed in various degrees.

Dudley Fenner

The Artes Of Logike And Rethorike, plainly set forth in the English tongue, easie to be learned and practised: Together with examples for the practise of the same for the methode in the gouerment of the familie, prescribed in the woords of God. . . . Written by M. Dudley Fenner, late Preacher of the worde of God in Middleburgh.
[s.l., s.n., s.d.—1584][88] BL C. 142. b. 22. 8° (see also Alston 1974, vol. vii, nos. 17–18).

Dudley Fenner's (?1558–87) book is noteworthy as a publication of Ramism in England (Howell 1961, 219–21). It consists of two parts, logic and rhetoric, each of which has its own half-title. It presents exclusively determinations of terms by binary bifurcations. Note, for example:

- *reason* is defined as consisting of 'first reason' and 'reason arising from the first';
- *argument* is defined as consisting of 'single or uncompared argument' and 'compared';
- *compared argument* is defined as consisting of 'agreeable argument' and 'disagreeable argument';
- *agreeable argument* is defined as consisting of 'more agreeable' and 'less agreeable'; etc.

The series quoted shows in which way the definitions follow each other and how the principle of binarism with its inherent oppositions is the driving force behind this. There are no tables, but many braces are used in the text to mark the bifurcations. Note:

A Cause is that which giueth some necessarie force for the verie being of the thing caused. {
The one which is without the thing caused, as the making or efficient cause.
The other within the thing caused.

The making cause is a cause [etc. . . . 24 lines]. *The causes that are within a thinge, are those causes which are always inseparablie remaining together for the being of the thing.*

They are two. { *The Matter.*
The Form.

[88] Year according to BL Catalogue.

The matter is a cause of which the thing caused is made; . . . The form is a cause of which a thing is that which it is . . . . (A (6^{r+v}).)

Note the comparable table from Wilkins' Essay ('*Transcendentals General, II: Cause*'):

That which any way contributes to the producing of an effect, is styled CAUSE. . . . That which proceeds from, or depends on the Cause, is styled EFFECT, . . . External, such as are without the Effect. // Internal, such as are within the Effect as its chief constituent parts . . . . MATTER / FORM. (27.)[89]

The parallelism between the two books in the paragraphs quoted is obvious. It does not prove that Wilkins copied Fenner, but it raises the question as to how far Wilkins' binarism represents the method of Ramism as propagated in England.

Thomas Blundeville

The Art of Logike. Plainly taught in the English tongue, by M. Blundeuil[l]e of Newton Flotman in Norfolke, as well according to the doctrine of Aristotle, as of all other modern and best accounted Authors thereof.
A very necessary Booke for all young students in any profession to find out thereby the truth in any doubtfull speech, but specially for such zealous Ministers as haue not beene brought vp in any Vniuersity, and yet are desirous to know how to defend by sound argumentes the true Christian doctrine, against all subtill Sophisters, and cauelling Schismatikers, & how to confute their false Sillogismes, & captious arguments.
London Imprinted by Iohn Windet, and are to be sold at Paules Whare, at the signe of the Crosse Keyes. 1599.
BL 8465 b. 9 (see also Alston 1974, vol. vii, nos. 22–4).

Thomas Blundeville (*fl.* 1561), whom the *DNB* calls 'a writer on horsemanship', dedicated his publications to what we would nowadays call higher education. Obviously he thought of young men living on estates, like himself, as readers. He translated from the Italian and wrote on the education of princes, on maps, on cosmography and navigation, and indeed on riding and horsemanship. His book on logic, in spite of its re-editions in 1617 and 1619, was the least successful of his writings. It is regarded as 'the true work of the English counterreformers who wrote in England to restore scholasticism while preserving some of Ramus's innovations' (Howell 1961, 285).

The most interesting parallel in *The Art of Logike* in which Blundeville seems to prefigure Wilkins' comprehensive enterprise is his explanation '*Of Predicaments. Chap. 6*':

What are Predicaments?
Predicaments are certaine titles or tables conteining all thinges that be in the world: for euery thing whatsoeuer it be, is eyther a substance or accident, and if it be a substance it is found in

---

[89] The double slash shows the caesura of the two parts of the sentence in the arrangement of the table; the subsequent entries under 'external' differ from Fenner.

the table of substance hereafter following: if it be an accident it belongeth eyther to quantity, quality, relation, action, passion, time, place, to be scited or to haue. For these be the tables of accidents, in one of the which euery accident is easie to be found; so that in all there be x predicaments or tables, one of substance and nine of accidents, and these bee called the highest and most generall kindes, albeit there bee others in deede higher then they, called of the Schoolemen Transcendentia, (that is to say) surpassing, as these, Res, ens, vnum, aliqvid, verum, bonum: which may be Englished thus, a thing, a being, one, somewhat, true, good: but forsomuch as these bee not spoken of the other higher kindes according to one selfe significa- tion, but may be diuersely applied, they are excluded from the order of predicaments. (12–13.)

According to this paragraph, 'predicaments' are categories as well as the elabora- tion of these categories in logical tables. This goes together with the author's method of explaining each predicament by an elaborate text and of introducing each of these texts with an overview in the form of a table. Although these two meanings of *predicament* are not to be found in Wilkins, they are not in opposi- tion to his use of the term either. On the contrary, they allocate the tables a def- inite place in the logical framework which is certainly in accordance with Wilkins' intentions.

Blundeville's and Wilkins' basic lists of predicaments are very similar to each other. Note: '*There be fyue, that is to say, Genus, Species, differentia, Proprium & Accidens: which may be englished thus, generall kinde, speciall kinde, difference, propertie and accident.*'(5.) If in Wilkins 'proprium' is exchanged for 'substance', which according to the preceding quotation is allowed, the two lists are actually identical.

There is, however, also a deviation which should not go unnoticed. Blundeville differentiates between what he calls '*words of the first and the second intention*':

Words of the first Intention are those, whereby any thing is signified or named by the purpose and meaning of the first author or inue[n]tor thereof, in any speech or language whatsoeuer it be, as ye the beast we comm[o]nlie ryde is called in English a horse, in latin, Equus, in Italian, Cauallo, in Frenche Cheual. Words of the second Intention are terms of Arte, as a Nowne, Pronowne, Uerbe, or Participle are termes of Grammer: likewise Genus, Species, Proprium, and such like are termes of Logike. (3.)

This difference does not appear in Wilkins' *Essay*, and this may be as significant as the overlaps. The general idea of his comprehensive thesaurus actually was to make the difference between the two '*intentions*' disappear, that is, to give each word the status of a technical term.[90] The most convincing proof of this is in the botanical tables (see below).

Naturally, coincidences between Blundeville and Wilkins appear not only in definitions and the use of terms but also in the tables themselves. One could even

---

[90] Strictly speaking this is only true for slot entries. But when we consider the system of '*Natural Grammar*' which rules the series of synonyms which correspond to slot entries, it also is true for every single word. See above.

call this the test of the conceptual parallels mentioned. There are tables on substance, on quantity and quality (including habit and natural power, passion and figure/form), and on relation distributed through Blundeville's book. They epitomize various of its chapters. They can be compared with the relevant parts of Wilkins' *'General Scheme'*. For a comparison of Blundeville's *'Table of Substance'* (19) with the genera VI to XX (*Creature*, WORLD to *parts of animate species*, GENERAL) see Table A.11 and Fig. 8.1.

However, conformity on an abstract level does not have much significance for the more concrete level of tables referring to accidence as can, for example, be shown by Blundeville's table on *'Naturall power and impotencie'* (28). It deals with the second kind of quality among the tables of accidence. Wilkins' table *'Of Natural Power'* (195–9) is the first kind of quality, his table *'Of Sickness'* (219–25), which belongs thematically to Blundeville's table, the fifth kind. For Blundeville see Table A.12.

A comparison between Blundeville and Wilkins shows that only the former's entries under 2.2 *'power sensitive'* (2.21–2.2125) appear in both works, in Wilkins' as *'Internal Senses'* and *'External Senses'*. Other entries deviate either in meaning or in location, because Wilkins does not consider any innate quality of the body as a *'power natural'*. This is why entries under 1. *'body'* (1.1–1.4), which appear in Wilkins, have a different, that is a psychological, meaning here, and why entries under 2.1 *'power vegetative'* (2.11–2.113)[91] as well as those under 2.22 *'motive'* (2.221–2.223) appear in Wilkins' genera *'Action Corporeal'* (XXX) and *'Motion'* (XXXI). Entries under 2.3 *'power intellective'* (2.31–2.324) mostly appear in Wilkins' *'Action Spiritual'*. An interesting case of semantic ambiguity is 2.323 *'command'*. For Blundeville this is a *'power intellective'*, for Wilkins an *'Oeconomical Relation'* (XXXIII). That is, Blundeville sees commanding as a mental, Wilkins sees it as a societal process.

Such comparisons, which could (and should) be made in greater detail and quantity, prove that, notwithstanding the general dependence of onomasiological word-lists on the categories and the binary techniques of general logic, the shape of tables ultimately depends on the semantic understanding of terms and of lexemes. The integrated ambiguity of natural language always gains the upper hand over the wish for strict systematization.

Samuel Smith

Aditus Ad Logicam In vsvm eorum qui primo Academiam Salutant. Autore Samuele Smith, Artium Magistro. Quarta editio, de nouo correcta, & emendata. Londini Per Guilielmum Stansby. 1627.   BL 527. a. 50. 4°.

Samuel Smith's (1587–1620) conception of logic is scholastic rather than Ramistic (Howell 1961, 193; general 292–8). The interesting point in this case is that this has

---

[91] As far as I can see, entries under 2.12 *'adjuvant power* [to the mind]' do not appear anywhere in Wilkins.

no effect on the principal logical and encyclopaedic framework of the book. Some of its chapters, for example '*De Substantia*', even close with a table in which all the previously defined terms are arranged according to *species, differentia, proprium,* and *accidens* of a genus. The four logical levels are marked by spatial arrangement and the latter two additionally by braces. The table on substance (B2^r) is quite complex and strictly arranged though typographically somewhat difficult to read. For a comparison of the overall order and contents of this table, given with a number code, and a shortened version of Wilkins' genus VI WORLD (51–5), see Table A.13. It is easy to map the two tables on to each other and recognize their far-reaching identity in formal arrangement and in content.[92]

8.3.2 Botanical taxonomy

General logic and rhetoric in the background of Wilkins' *Essay* make the book look rather traditional. The botanical taxonomy to be considered now, however, makes it look rather innovative. It was provided by John Ray.

John Ray (1627–1705) was the supreme European naturalist before Linnaeus. He was educated at Cambridge, where he later became a lecturer in Greek, mathematics, and the humanities. His first botanical publication, the *Catalogus Plantarum circa Cantabrigiam nascentium* (1660) was devoted to the region around this university town. He collected physiological observations during his extensive travels in the British Isles and later, together with his friend Francis Willughby (1635–72), on the Continent. Besides other botanical works (see the Introduction by Stearn in Ray 1981), he published his monumental *Historia Plantarum* (1686–1704) as one result of his travels.

But John Ray was not only a naturalist, he was also a lexicographer. This is attested by *A Collection of English Proverbs* (1670), *A Collection of English Words not generally used* ... (1674), and finally by his *Dictionariolum Trilingue* (1675) (Ray 1981).[93] It is the *Historia Plantarum* and this dictionary which are of interest in the present context. An overview of the former will demonstrate how close John Wilkins is to John Ray, that is, how much his comprehensive thesaurus is planned like a taxonomy of plants. An overview of the latter will demonstrate how close John Ray is to the tradition of nomenclators, which form the general lexicographical background to Wilkins' work.

John Ray's *Historia Plantarum*

Joannis Raii Societatis Regiae Socii Historia Plantarum Generalis, Species hactenus editas aliasque insuper multas noviter inventas & descriptas complectens. In qua agitur primo De Plantis

---

[92]   For such overlappings between Wilkins and earlier (or almost contemporary) writers, see also, for example: *Logicae Et Physicae Compendivm. Authore Rob[ert] Sanderson,* ... *1618.* The eighth edition, of 1672, is contemporary with Wilkins. (BL 1578/2292. 8°.)

[93]   There were also influential theological works from Ray's pen.

in genere, Earumque Partibus, Accidentibus & Differentiis; Deinde Genera omnia tum summa tum subalterna ad Species usque infimas, Notis suis certis & Characteristicis Definita, Methodo Naturae vestigiis insistente disponuntur; Species singulae accurate describuntur, obscura Illustrantur, omissa supplentur, superflua resecantur, Synonyma necessaria adjiciuntur; Vires denique & Usus recepti compendio traduntur. Accesserunt Lexicon Botanicum Et Nomenclator Botanicus Totum opus in duobus Tomis cum Indicibus Necessariis Nominum, Morborum, & Remediorum. Tomus Primus. Londini: Impensis Samuelis Smith & Benjamini Walford Regiae Societatis Typographorum, ad Insignia Principis in Caemeterio D. Pauli. M DCXCIII.
(BL 1505/117. Folio, 983 numbered pages.)

There is a general table, which epitomizes the whole book, between pages 59 and 60, volume one. The main points of interest of this overview of the *Historia Plantarum* in the present context are, first of all, the strict parallelism between it and the relevant sections of Wilkins' *'General Scheme'* and, moreover, the fact that the typographical means of indicating a tabular arrangement with various levels of systematization (as well as by different fonts, above all by square and round braces and Roman numbers) are here *exactly* the same as in Wilkins. Although twenty-five years lie between the publication of the *Essay* and the *Historia*, these conventions remained the same. The universal language schema and the history of plants become almost indistinguishable in their basic principles of ordering.[94] This pertains also to the fact that the tables are actually a long, continuously flowing text whose hierarchical levels of deduction are signalled by typographical means instead of explanations. (See Table A.14.)

John Ray's *Dictionariolum Trilingue*

Dictionariolum Trilingue: Secundum Locos Communes, Nominibus usitatoribus Anglicis, Latinis, Graecis, Ordine Parallelos[95] dispositis. Opera Joannis Raii, M.A. Et Societatis Regiae Sodalis. Londini: Typis Andreae Clark, impensis Thomae Burrel, ad Insigne Pilae auratae sub Aede S. Dunstani in vico vulgo Fleetstreet. 1675.
Reprint. (Ray 1981).

The dictionary is printed in three columns, English, Latin, and Greek. The English lexemes are printed in italics, the countable nouns accompanied by an indefinite or, more rarely, a definite article. The Latin lexemes are printed in Roman type, with genitive and gender morphemes for nouns and the two gender morphemes for adjectives added. The Greek morphemes are printed in Greek letters with the same grammatical addenda as in Latin and a fronted number between one and five to indicate declension classes. The dictionary has some 2,660 entries printed on ninety-one pages.

---

[94] I am not interested in the question of whether the typographical means of the tables were *invented* by the one (whoever) and *copied* (or *retained*) by the other, or *planned* by a third person, for example the printer. Although Ray's book appeared so much later than Wilkins', it is obvious that a monumental work of this kind must have needed a long time for preparation and was already in the mind of Ray when he helped Wilkins with his *'Tables'*. It is the common way of thinking, surfacing in typographical means of expression, which is of interest here.

[95] Written in Greek letters.

There were four editions before 1700 and thirteen more after. All of them are described in Stearns's Introduction (Ray 1981). The original edition of 1675 was followed by a second one in 1685, the third one (1688) appeared with the new title *Nomenclator Novus Trilinguis*, obviously to protect the book against a pirate edition by one 'P. K'. In order to strengthen this protection (Cram 1991*a*), all subsequent editions between 1696 and 1736 bore the title *Nomenclator classicus*.[96]

Ray's trilingual dictionary was a textbook for schools. In fact it was written for the education of Francis Willughby's two boys after their father's death. The later editions are supplied with grammatical paradigms, proverbs, etc. which enhance the schoolbook character of the dictionary for the potential purchaser.

But Ray's trilingual dictionary was also a work for biological purposes. Its origin goes back to a prompt-list which the author and his friend had compiled for gathering linguistic samples on their travels through Britain and the Continent in the 1660s (Cram 1990, 1991*a*). This can in turn be linked with the fact that both helped John Wilkins in writing the biological tables of his *Essay*.

'*The Preface*' shows that John Ray was interested in children who were learning Latin, and presumably Greek.[97] This is proof of his broad interests, given the fact that his genuine field was botany. But already here the naturalist reveals himself. His main concern is with terminological errors, '*especially in the names of Animals and Plants*' (A2). He points out that in many cases English words and their assumed Latin origins or translations do not refer to the same object. In other cases the classification is erroneous, for example when the bat is classified as a bird. It is the correctness of nomenclatures in the two languages which Ray is really thinking of. He admits: '*In the names of Apparel, several sorts of Viands, parts of Buildings, Utensils and Implements of Houshold stuff, Instruments and Tools of Husbandry and Gardening, I have not, nor indeed can I fully satisfie my self.*' (A2[a].) But even in these domains he predominantly thinks of items which either the ancients or the English had or did not have so that nothing can be done other than to make the translations or derivations '*come as near and answer as well one the other as may be*' (A2[b]). This nomenclator '*secundum locos communes*' is in fact a generalized attempt to free English nomenclatures by comparison with Latin (and Greek) from folk errors, which are mostly folk etymologies. Ray's fear is that children absorb the classification system along with their mother's milk, as it were, and that learning to speak and learning to classify scientifically are part of the same enterprise.

---

[96] Dates according to Stearn (Ray 1981), who refers to earlier bibliographies. Cram 1991*a* mentions two more editions in 1692 and 1694 with the title *Nomenclator classicus*. Green (1997, 175) discusses Ray's dictionary together with Bathe, Comenius (the *Orbis pictus*), and Greenwood. Whereas there is a connection between Bathe's *Janua*, Comenius (via his own *Janua* and the *Orbis pictus*), and Greenwood, who used Comenius's pictures in his *Vocabulary*, I cannot see any reason for placing Ray in this group. See Chapter 10.

[97] There is no mention of Greek in the preface, but the author must also have applied all his thoughts to this language and its learners.

One singular feature of the dictionary confirms this aim, its footnotes. There are sixty-seven of them, mostly in the sections on herbs (eight), trees (seven), beasts (seven), birds (eighteen), fishes (fourteen), and insects (four). Most of them deal with questions of etymology, with the adequacy of English and Latin terms, with synonyms in either language, with the problem of missing terms, and with the classification of species. Some are more general cultural annotations. Note the following examples:

Pinks—Caryophyllus:[98] *The Pink and July-flower were not known or at least described by the Antients, they are by the Moderns called 'Caryophilli', as well from the shape of the Flower, together with his Cup resembling a Clove, as from its sent.* (12.)

Barberry-bush—Oxyacanthus: *The Barberry-bush is commonly in Latin called 'Berberis', and is taken by many Herbarists to be the 'Oxyacantha' of Galen, but not of Dioscorides, that being the White-Thorn.* (15.)

Bunting—Emberiza: *'Emberiza' is no antient Latin word, but made by Gesner of the Dutch 'Emmeritz'. This bird is by some named 'Rubetra', and by others 'Calandra'.* (26.)

Wren—Passer, Troglodytes: *This hath been commonly mistaken for the 'Regulus' and 'Trochylus' of the Antients; but now the 'Regulus' is well known to be another Bird less than this, which is also found with us in England, but hath no English name that I know.* (29.)

A Long-Oister—Locusta: *Our Lobster hath been generally but falsely taken for 'Locusta marina'; which mistake ought to be rectified.* (31.)

Grass-hopper—Locusta: *'Cicada' by a general mistake in our Schools hath been Englished a Grass-hopper; whereas 'Cicada' is an Insect of far different make from the Grass-hopper, proper to hot Countreys, not known in England, and having no English name; that usually sits on trees, and sings so loud that it may be heard afar off.* (33.)

These footnotes show Ray, the naturalist, in the garb of the language teacher. In fact, the dictionary has a place not only in the onomasiological tradition, but also in the history of the technical language of biology. It is of interest to note both how few have been the changes in the commonly used English vernacular names for plants and animals adopted by Ray in 1675 and, despite the drastic revisions of their nomenclature and classification by Carl Linnaeus in the eighteenth century, how many of the Latin names have been passed into modern scientific nomenclature, most of them being adopted as specific epithets by Linnaeus himself (Ray 1981, 8). The macrostructure of Ray's dictionary deserves to be given in full:[99]

I. Of Heaven
II. Of the Elements and Meteors
III. Of Stones and Metals
IV. Of the Parts & Adjuncts of Plants
V. Of Herbs
VI. Of Trees and Shrubs
VII. Of the proper Parts and Adjuncts of Animals

[98] I give the lemmata in shortened form, omitting the Greek. The footnotes are quoted literally, italicization sometimes being replaced by inverted commas.

[99] English section titles only.

VIII. Of Four-footed Beasts
IX. Of Birds
X. Of Fishes
XI. Of Insects
XII. Of the Parts of Mans Body
XIII. Of some Accidents of the Body
XIV. Of Diseases
XV. Of Meat
XVI. Of Drink
XVII. Of Apparel
XVIII. Of Buildings
XIX. Of God
XX. Of created Spirits
XXI. Of the Faculties of the Soul
XXII. Of Moral Virtues and Vices
XXIII. Of Kindred and Affinity
XXIV. Of Housholdstuff [!]
XXV. Of a School
XXVI. Of the Church and Ecclesiastical matters
XXVII. Of Husbandry and Country-affairs
XXVIII. Of Warfare
XXIX. Of Shipping and Navigation
XXX. Of Arts Liberal and Mechanic
XXXI. Of Time and its measures
XXXII. Of Number

Most astonishing in this macrostructure is the division into two groups of sections which allocates to 'God' the very unusual position in the middle. Sections I–XVIII deal with the areas of reality, or nature, which can be subjected to a strict order, although it starts to deteriorate with section XV. This is the domain of the naturalist. The sequence of topics is: stars—elements—inanimate nature—organic nature—animate nature—man: body and needs arising from the body—food, clothes, houses. Section II has a subdivision indicated typographically by FIRE, AIR, WATER, and EARTH. Section VII has a subdivision by subtitles (fishes, birds, beasts).[100]

Sections XIX–XXX deal with the spiritual and societal areas of reality which defy a strict taxonomy. The four domains which are clearly demarcated, however, conform to the onomasiological tradition. They are: XIX–XXII: the spiritual world: God and spirits, the soul, morals; XXIII–XXVI: societal groupings: family and house, school, church; XXVII–XXX: fields of activities: agriculture, warfare, navigation, arts and crafts; finally XXXI–XXXII: appendix: time.

The microstructure of the dictionary is as simple as possible: lexemes in parallel columns which are meant to be translations of each other. More information,

---

[100] This subdivision is part of the macrostructure; for the subdivision in section XII see below.

which in other dictionaries is packed into the entries, appears in the singular feature of academic footnotes.

The pragmatic structure of the dictionary has one particularity which, however, may be found in some other nomenclators, too: various sections (V, VI, VIII, IX, X, and XI) are ordered according to the alphabet.[101] The scientific taxonomy being too difficult for teaching, Ray probably thought the alphabet the next best means for this. Moreover, the entries are numbered.

There are some specialities to be mentioned which show in which way the naturalist and the language pedagogue interfered with each other. After eighty-eight entries according to the alphabet in section VI, forty entries follow in the manner of onomasiological dictionaries, giving names for the kinds of fruit that come from the aforementioned trees: general terms (three), common fruits (four), exotic fruits and nuts (fifteen), berries (five). There then follow names of spices (eleven) and the two odd entries 'acorn' and 'gall'. Arrangements like these may also be found elsewhere.[102] The alphabetical order of a total of 114 entries in section VIII is interrupted by word-clusters which each pertain to one species of beasts, namely 'deer' (six lexemes), 'dog' (eight), 'goat' (four), 'hog' (six), 'horse' (thirteen), 'mouse' (four), 'ox' (eight), 'sheep' (ten), 'otter' (six), and 'serpent' (five).[103] Section XI has forty-five numbered entries in alphabetical order, except for two word-clusters pertaining to 'bee' (ten) and 'worm' (six). In all of these cases John Ray obviously did not trust the formal arrangement of the alphabet and preferred a more topically motivated sequence of entries.

All the sections of the dictionary have their own internal order which depends on the topic under discussion and on more general aspects of word collection. As is the rule with these pragmatic structures, they are not signalled by external marks, for example of the typographical kind. There are three exceptions to this. Section XIX, 'God', has, first, a batch of sixteen words on God and philosophical characteristics of divinity followed by batches on FATHER, SON, and HOLY GHOST, marked by capitals. The batch on 'son' presents names of theological terms first, then names of incidents of Jesus' life, then words pertaining to the Last Judgement. Section XXI, 'Of the Faculties of the Soul', is divided by Roman numbers into '*I. Of the Senses and their Objects*' and '*II. Of the Understanding, Will and Affections*'. Each of these two again has typographically marked subdivisions: into SIGHT, SMELL, HEARING, TOUCH and MIND, WILL; and AFFECTIONS. In addition, the first subdivision has an appendix in which twelve nouns are derived from twelve adjectives pertaining to *touch* (e.g. 'hot—heat', 'cold [adj.]—cold' [n.], 'moist—moisture', etc.).

---

[101] Adrianus Junius's *Nomenclator, Omnivm Rervm Propria Nomina* (see Chapter 9) has several subsections in alphabetical order, for example '*arborum nomina*' (115–19) and *infamia* (364–71). The former is understandable, because it is part of natural history; the latter, however, is rather astonishing.

[102] Compare, for example, Howell's *Lexicon Tetraglotton*, see Chapter 7.

[103] I give the first lexeme of each word-cluster. There is one more cluster, 'panther' (five lexemes), which is rather inconsistent.

The last special case is section XII, '*Of the Parts of Mans Body*'. It has an introductory remark:

In setting down the Parts of Mans Body, I shall follow the Division of the late L[ord] B[isho]p
of Chester in his Book of the Universal Character; which is into Homogeneous or similar, and
Heterogeneous or dissimilar Parts; the Homogeneous being subdivided into conteining and
conteined, the Heterogeneous into external and internal.   (34.)

These determinations indeed appear with Roman numbers in the section.
Obviously, Wilkins did not alone take advantage of Ray but Ray also of him.
However, Wilkins' genus XX, '*Of General Parts*', in fact consists of six 'differences',
namely '*homogeneous contained*', '*homogeneous containing*', '*heterogeneous external*
head', '*heterogeneous external trunk*', '*heterogeneous external limm*', and '*internal*'.
Ray conflates them into four, thus tacitly criticizing Wilkins for his redundancy
(everything internal is, of course, contained) and for the application of the binary
method to a field where it is difficult to carry it through. Indeed, Ray's subsections
I ('*homogeneous containing*'), II ('*homogeneous contained*'), and IV ('*heterogeneous*
internal') may well be compared with Wilkins, although the binary co-ordinations
are often changed. But III ('*heterogeneous external*') is independent of Wilkins and
a perfect example of the many cases where names pertaining to the parts of the
human body are arranged from head to foot. Its sequence is so strict that, for
example, '*The Eye-brow—Supercilium, ii, n.*' and '*The Eye-lid—Palpebra, ae, f.*'
come before '*The Eye—Oculus, i, m.*', and this before the following '*The Sight of the*
Eye—Pupilla, ae, f.', '*The White of the Eye—Albugo, inis, f.*' and '*The Corner of the*
Eye—Hirquus, i, m.'. Only after that do we find '*The Hairs of the Eye-lids—Cilia,*
orum, n.'. This is strict ordering indeed. The special feature of this list of the parts
of the human body is an occasional arrangement in front / back pairs, like 'neck—
throat', 'back—breast', and 'backbone—rib'. The method of proceeding from the
head to the trunk to the legs and feet and then adding the parts of the arms and
hands is rather unusual.[104]

All the other sections have a pragmatic structure which subjects the topics to an
ad hoc order and which can only be found by close and attentive reading. The first
and last entries tend to be special, the one as a rule rather general, often a headword
for the whole section, the other often slightly odd. Section XIV, 'Diseases', for example, first lists general terms (five lexemes), then slight diseases of the skin like
'bruise' or 'pimple' (twenty-two), followed by severe diseases which affect the
whole body, like the various kinds of malaria ('ague') or 'consumption' (twenty-
five) and diseases located in special parts of the body, ordered from the head
('cough' or 'hoarseness') downwards to the body ('jaundice' or 'stone') to the feet
('gout') (thirty-two). There then follow names for anomalies of the skin like 'wart'
or 'corn' (eight), and finally words pertaining to doctors and medicine (eighteen).
Section XXV, 'School', first lists general names of persons (five lexemes) and

---

[104]   Compare the relevant analyses of Withal and Howell in Chapters 6 and 7.

pieces of furniture (six) in a classroom, and these are followed by a rather long series (twenty-eight) of words, all pertaining to the diverse parts of books and utensils for writing. There then follows a sequence of terms (thirty-four) referring to the units of written language, spoken language, linguistic exercises in schools, and types of text. These terms give a lively impresson of the curriculum that learners of Latin, who used Ray's dictionary, had to go through. As so often, some odd entries conclude the section: '*truant*', '*dunce*', '*rod*', and '*feruler or palmer*'. The impression of the curriculum is, thus, completed with an impression of everyday problems of school-life.

Section XVII, 'Husbandry', finally, again has a most interesting order of its own. After introductory general terms (five), we find a rather long sequence (fifty-one lexemes) devoted to everything connected with 'field' and another one devoted to everything connected with 'pastures' (twenty-two). The first one arranges its members, that is, words for persons, objects, tools, according to the course of work in the year: 'plough', 'harrow', 'seed', 'harvest', 'stubble', 'cart', 'thresher', 'sieve', 'straw', 'bread-corn'. The second does the same, though not with as strict a sequence: 'meadow', 'hay', 'rake', 'cart', 'garden', 'orchard', 'arbour'. There then follow a batch of entries with the names of utensils that are used for gardening, and another five general terms.

Without any exception, all the sections of John Ray's nomenclator have individual principles of arrangment like the ones mentioned, and they all deserve analysis. Such pragmatic ordering is common to all nomenclators. It increases their usability. At the same time it makes visible the realistic situations in which the authors saw their language patterned, although they had to arrange it in a rather abstract and naked shape, namely a list.

8.3.3 The universal language context, revisited

John Wilkins' scheme of a universal language is representative of an intersection of historically important intellectual traditions, onomasiology among them, with each other and with new developments of the seventeenth century. The former are (i) the idea of a perfect language as it was supposed to have been extant in Paradise, (ii) the Aristotelian–Porphyrian system of logical and ontological classification, (iii) encyclopaedism in natural history, and (iv) the collection of topical word-lists from glossaries to fully grown dictionaries. Traditions (i) and (ii) are of a more theoretical and speculative character, (iii) and (iv) of a more concrete and practical one. Each of these traditions has its own context. That of (i) is the problem of the sign and the referent (semiotics), of (ii) general (classical and scholastic) logic and ontology, of (iii) sciences and universal history, and of (iv) language teaching in the widest sense. They intersect with the new developments, namely (i) general communication by education, (ii) scientific taxonomy, for example in biology, and (iii) new developments in mathematics (algebra). Of these intersecting traditions and new intellectual tendencies only algebra has not been mentioned so far.

In *Vindiciae academiarum* (Ward[105] 1654, repr. 1970) tribute is paid to the '*Symbolicall way, invented by Vieta, advanced by Harriot, perfected by Mr Oughtred and Des Cartes*' (Ward 1970, 20).[106] This pertains to the newly invented method in algebra of expressing not only unknown variables (like x, y, z) but also known ones by letters (like a, b, c) (Hüllen 1989, 163–4), a technique which was thought to overcome the difficulty that a universal language had to operate with such a huge number of signs that nobody could learn and memorize them. Note the statement of Robert Hooke in his *Cutlerian Lectures* (posthumously 1705, 64)):

whereby the whole [Natural] History may be contracted in as little Space as is possible; for this . . . is of huge use in the Prosecution of Ratiocination and Inquiry, and is a vast Help to the Understanding and Memory, as in Geometrical Algebra, the expressing of many and complex Quantities by a few obvious and plain Symbols: And therefore 'twere to be wisht, that we could express the whole [Natural] History in as few Letters or Characters at it has Circumstances, somewhat of the manner of doing which in my second Part.[107]

Mathematicians in the seventeenth century called this kind of algebra *logistica speciosa* (specious arithmetic) and the new kind of symbols *species*. Thus, this term acquired a double sense, meaning non-numerical mathematical symbols as well as logical classifications (Cram 1994*a*, 223–4). In the context of universal languages both senses were conflated into one. John Wilkins used special strokes (written) and letters (spoken) for them.

Yet, John Wilkins used a second set of these *species*, besides those stemming from the Porphyrian tradition and largely preserved in the books on logic by the schoolmen. It is the set of transcendental particles. They pay tribute to the fact that grammar, first of all, distinguishes between the various classes of integrals and particles. They are both, semantically speaking, universal, although formally speaking language specific. But they serve different purposes in the universal language scheme: the integrals cover the area of '*things and notions*', that is, they are the material of collection, the others are means of classification (Cram 1994*b*). The former design the linguistic units of onomasiology, the latter its categorial order.

Thus, it is correct to point out that John Wilkins' universal language is very much dependent on the old principle of onomasiology; but this includes the fact that his order of words, besides following traditional principles, also obeys new and very modern rules of scientific classification (Slaughter 1982). Compared with

---

[105] The book was published by (Set)H (War)D with an introduction by (Joh)N (Wilkin)S as an answer to John Webster's attack on contemporary universities in *Academiarum examen* (Hüllen 1989, 163–6). Therefore it, supposedly, presents the opinions of both authors. It is important to stress this because, later, Seth Ward and John Wilkins did not share the same ideas about the feasibility and necessity of a universal language (Cram 1994*a*).

[106] Francois Viète (Vieta) (1540–1603), Thomas Harriot (1560–1621), William Oughtred (1574–1660).

[107] This second part was never written.

other representatives of the universal language idea, the former—the ency-clopaedic—strain is much more obvious, because it impresses itself in the masses of tables directly on to the eye of the reader. But the algebraic strain is neverthe-less there, as Seth Ward's book had already announced so much earlier. Speaking from the viewpoint of the onomasiological tradition, this means that onomasiol-ogy here merges with new structures in a new context.

C. The European Scene (1400–1700)

9

Multilingual dictionaries and nomenclators

9.1 Early textbook culture

9.1.1 General

In 1477 the first onomasiological dictionary which was not devoted to teaching Latin (or Greek or Hebrew) appeared in Venice as a printed book. It used the new technique for propagating a book-genre which had already been extant in hand-written manuscripts, for example in 1424, and in early prints, for example in 1533. Roughly speaking, the tradition of late-medieval vocabularies terminated at the beginning of the sixteenth century (e.g. with Murmellius's *Pappa*, see below) and gave way to a new tradition of topical word-lists (nomenclators) in the light of Humanist studies (de Smet 1985).

The years between then and 1600 are a phase of that era which is covered by the terms *Renaissance* and *Humanism* and which succeeded the so-called Latin Middle Ages. Among the intellectual activities of the Renaissance and Humanism, language teaching and learning were particularly important and influential.

As their name indicates, the Latin Middle Ages were dominated by the one language of intellectuals, Latin, which may have been less influential in oral everyday communication than we sometimes think but which made a linguistically homogeneous written European culture possible.[1] Theorizing on language was only conducted in relation to Latin, descriptive categories were taken from Latin, and other languages were hardly considered at all. Admittedly, there was a discussion on the roles of Greek and Hebrew as the two oldest 'sacred' languages of Christianity (Eco 1995), but as languages they were next to unknown. The monopoly of Latin was possible on the one hand because of the classical tradition which supplied Europe's post-classical culture with its relevant texts, and on the other, because of the Church which guaranteed this culture's linguistic unity.

This means that, for the people involved, European culture was determined by a *foreign* language from its post-classical beginnings up to the fifteenth century. In spite of its general use as a medium of communication, Latin never achieved the status of a vernacular. In so far as there was education at all in schools, generation after generation had to submit to the necessities of foreign-language teaching and learning. This left its traces in the written culture. For example, among the oldest written fragments of vernaculars in our possession are translation aids for Latin texts, which were obviously used in classes. Bilingual lexicography, as it developed from these beginnings in many European national languages, had the main aim of helping in the learning of Latin, just as grammars were mainly written with this aim in mind. As far as linguistic analysis and description are concerned, medieval book culture was to a large extent a textbook culture.

In spite of the dominance of Latin, there were even in the Middle Ages good reasons for learning foreign vernaculars. There were, for example, many areas in Europe where people used several languages side by side. In the Low Countries there were the dialects of Low Dutch (i.e. present-day Dutch and Flemish), French, and English. In Bohemia there were Czech, Slovak, German, and Hungarian. Moreover, in the twelfth century some vernaculars grew to become a regionally functioning *koiné*, like French for the dominant courtly culture or like German for commerce in Northern Italy and the countries around the Adriatic (Bischoff 1966). There also existed a general awareness of multilingualism on the Continent. The famous collection of legal texts called the *Sachsenspiegel*, written between 1220 and 1235, for example, stated that defendants in court need only answer when spoken to in their own language, and the *Goldene Bulle*, which contained the statutes for the election of the Emperor, demanded as early as 1356 that officials of the *Reich* should have a command of German, Italian, and Czech. There were good reasons, then, to learn foreign languages, even if this hardly happened in the monasteries, the pre-eminent institutions of education at the time.

The British Isles found themselves in a peculiar position because they did not

---

[1] Naturally, this does not apply to those parts of eastern Europe which were dominated by Greek, and temporalily to Spain.

have any language barriers around the country, though there was the internal struggle between English and the Celtic languages, and because the linguistic situation of the country after 1066 demanded foreign-language teaching almost exclusively in French (Lambley 1920, Orme 1973, Kibbee 1991).

When, beginning with Dante's *De vulgari eloquentia* (probably written in Latin between 1303 and 1305), and because of the complex changes in the wake of the Renaissance and Humanism, people became even more aware of the existence and the intrinsic value of many national languages, there was, at least at first, no other way of talking about them than by using the categories and the evaluative measures of Latin. This led to Latinizing grammars (Michael 1970, Padley 1976–88, Robins 1994) and to dictionaries which, in their arrangement, were not only meant to provide meanings for Latin lexemes. Dictionaries came into being which positioned vernacular lexemes before the Latin ones[2] or which gave many vernaculars in parallel columns. Moreover, this development led to a competition between national languages according to their alleged relatedness to Latin and/or to the first language of mankind of which the Bible made mention and which was generally supposed to be Hebrew. The hitherto predominantly philosophical approach to languages, which was interested in their epistemic functions, gave way to evaluative comparisons in which we can find the first traces of national clichés (Hüllen 1996c and 2002, 219–46). National languages were not only evaluated with the notion of perfection as explained in the commentaries on the Bible, but also regarded as the expression of common virtues or vices of the people who spoke them. The Latin unity, which must have always been somewhat abstract when compared to the vernaculars, retreated before the highly complex web of these comparisons without, however, losing its impact on linguistic analysis. This did not happen until many centuries later. The ensuing Humanism, in particular, cultivated the classical as well as the national, the intellectual as well as the vernacular languages of Europe.

Just as the permanent teaching of Latin and its use in ecclesiastical and academic contexts formed the foundations of the Latin Middle Ages, the permanent experience of foreign languages in oral use formed the foundations of comparisons during the four centuries to come and led to the learning of these foreign languages in or, more often, outside schools. This made the production of an extensive dictionary- and textbook-literature necessary (Caravolas 1994, Kaltz 1995). Its practical driving force was the habit of extensive travelling which extended across the whole Continent and which made the learning of foreign languages meaningful and also financially advantageous.

Among the dictionaries of the time, quite a number were arranged onomasiologically. In his bibliography of those dictionaries between the beginning of printing and 1600 which include German as one of their languages, Claes (1977) finds 475 with a non-alphabetical arrangement among a total of 858. Two conditions

---

[2]   See Chapters 3, 4, and 6.

had to be met for the large-scale production of dictionaries in Europe: first, the craft of printing had to be established in many places[3] and, second, there had to be sufficient interest among enough alphabetically educated people to make the production and distribution of such dictionaries rewarding. Turning this argument the other way round, we can deduce from the existence of a sufficient and even astonishingly large number of dictionaries the reality and even the vitality of this interest.

Vis-à-vis the complex relations between Latin and the national languages we should distinguish between three types of dictionaries: (i) Latin or other so-called sacred languages vs. a national language, (ii) Latin or other sacred languages vs. several or even many national languages, and (iii) one national language vs. another, or several languages parallel to each other. Type (i) was obviously meant to serve the teaching of Latin, Greek, or Hebrew. This is even the case, if the national language is the first, the leftmost, to be printed in the dictionary. Type (ii) in all probability was still meant to serve the teaching of Latin (etc.). However, the range of application of this type of dictionary was extended over several linguistic areas, which shows a growing awareness of their vernaculars. This awareness may have been financially stimulated. Moreover, several, even many national languages appeared in parallel and this made visible their presupposed translatability. All this shows that, on the one hand, Latin as the most thoroughly lexicalized (and grammaticalized) language was still the point of departure for learning one or many other languages. On the other hand learning national languages attracted more and more interest. Type (iii) could only be meant for learning one or several foreign vernaculars[4] with the help of a mother tongue.

This typological differentiation presupposes that dictionaries were read from left to right, as seems natural and as we still do today. There are, however, a number of indications which suggest that authors also meant dictionaries to be used from right to left or, provided there were sufficient columns, by column hopping.[5] In 1514, for example, the *Vocabularium Latinis, Gallicis et Theutonicis verbis scriptum* (Claes 1977, No. 233) was published for the first time. In 1543 it appeared under the title *Dictionarius Latinisch, Frantzösisch und Teütsch, fast nützlich und gut, für die Teütschen, die da Frantzösisch, oder Frantzosen, die da Teütsch lernen wollend* (Claes 1977, No. 398). The majority of dictionaries, which constitute a wide and complex filiation (see below), have similar introductory

---

[3] Alda Rossebastiano Bart 1984 lists literature on the history of printing with reference to onomasiological dictionaries. For general information see Steinberg 1961.

[4] Multilingual dictionaries and textbooks are typical of the sixteenth and seventeenth centuries. Caravolas (1994, 64, footnote 28) suggests that 'La Bible polyglotte éditée par les érudits espagnols de l'université d'Alcala peut ainsi être considerée comme le premier dictionnaire polyglotte'. It will probably never be possible to verify this hypothesis. But it is a very interesting thought nevertheless.

[5] The *Hermeneumata* (see Chapter 3) are generally thought to have served the teaching of Latin to Greeks as well as the teaching of Greek to Romans, that is, they are thought to have been used in both ways.

texts. This signals both the traditional position of Latin as the point of departure and the learning of German or French in either direction from the dictionary.

The following is an overview of the most important onomasiological dictionaries from the beginning of printed dictionaries to 1600.[6] It is meant to show how onomasiological dictionaries conquered all European areas with their respective national languages and made the onomasiological principle a widely used practice of foreign-language teaching and learning, of Latin as well as of vernaculars.

9.1.2 Select list of topical dictionaries

'SACRED LANGUAGE'-NATIONAL LANGUAGE

Dictionaries Nos. 1 to 8.2 are onomasiological dictionaries for teaching Latin to Germans. There are far more of these dictionaries on the Continent than of dictionaries of other national languages.

1.   *Wenceslaus Brack. Vocabularius rerum.* Basle: Peter Kollicker, 1483, 4°, fol. ll.[7] 98. Latin–German.[8] Seventeen editions:[9] 1483, 1485, 1486, 1487(3), 1489(2), 1491(2), 1495(2), 1496, 1498, 1501, 1509, 1512.

---

[6] This is not an exhaustive list in the bibliographical sense. It is merely meant to give a general impression of the rich and complex development of printed onomasiological dictionaries on the Continent. The sources are Alston 1974, Claes 1977 (both, in spite of their age and obvious shortcomings, bibliographies of unquestionable value), Bart 1984, Stein 1989a, Stein 1991a, Cram 1991b (unpublished), Lindemann 1995, Niederehe 1995, and various specialized monographs or papers. Titles are simplified and modernized. Only general, not special dictionaries, like, for example, that by Gesner, are listed (with one exception, No. 10.2). In each case, the title, including the name of the printer and the location of the printing shop, and the number of pages (leaves, columns) are those of the earliest copy which could be traced bibliographically. Later editions may be different in all these respects, except in the essential contents of the dictionary. *Edition*, then, means that a copy catalogued in one of the world's libraries varies at least in title and/or colophon from another copy. Variations in places of printing and names of printers are particularly frequent. Dates which are uncertain have been given with the first assumed year, but without any further note. A number in brackets after the date gives the various editions of that year, a date repeated means that one of them is uncertain. As a rule, dictionaries with fewer than three editions have not been included, unless there was some compelling reason, such as an unusual choice of languages. The bibliographies consulted give technical descriptions.

The cut-off date of 1600 has been primarily enforced by the four most elaborate bibliographies, those of Claes, Bart, Lindemann, and Niederehe. A similarly dense bibliographical overview of dictionaries in the seventeenth century is not yet available. However, it is not by accident that the bibliographies impose this cut-off date. The new developments instigated by printing and the new achievements of Humanism had then completed their first period. It should be remembered that almost all bibliographical sources differ on some points.

[7] ll.= leaves, pp.= pages, s.l.= sine loco, s.n.= sine nomine.

[8] The name to be used for 'German' (as it is understood today) poses difficulties. As a rule, dictionaries make a clear distinction between *Oberdeutsch* and *Hochdeutsch* in the old linguistic sense by calling it 'Alemannisch', and 'Niederdeutsch' by calling it 'Teut(h)onick', 'Low German', 'Low Dutch', 'Flemish', or 'Belgick'. *Oberdeutsch* and *Niederdeutsch*, the latter including today's Dutch and Flemish, were regarded as two separate languages (which, linguistically speaking, they indeed are), even where they apply to the present-day area of *German*. Italian dictionary titles and, unfortunately, also Bart (1984) in her comments do not indicate this distinction and always speak of '*tedesco*'. I have seen many, but not all, of the dictionaries mentioned. This is why in some cases I cannot decide which dialect of

2. *Vocabula pro juvenibus.* Leipzig: Konrad Kachelofen, 1492, 4°, ll. 14. Latin–German. Twenty-six editions: 1492, 1492, 1495(4), 1496, 1499, 1500(2), 1501, 1502, 1503, 1505, 1505(3), 1508, 1509, 1511, 1512, 1512, 1514, 1515, 1517, 1522.

3. *Ioa[n]nis Murmellij Ruremu[n]densis. cui titulus Pappa. in quo hec sunt* . . . . Cologne: Quentell 1513, 4°, ll. 32. Latin–German (Low Rhenish dialect). Thirty-two editions, including eight separate editions of the first part, that is, the nomenclator, six of them with a Polish translation: 1513(3), 1515(2), 1515, 1517(3), 1518, 1519, 1520(2), 1521, 1522(3), 1522, 1525, 1536, 1537(2), 1539, 1540, 1543, 1545, 1548, 1550, 1551, 1553, 1560, 1565. (See also Nos. 10.1, 16.1, and 16.2.)

4.1, 4.2. *Joannes Pinnicianus. Promptuarium vocabulorum.* Augsburg: Sylvanus Otmar 1516, 4°, ll. 120. Four editions. In addition, a selection from this dictionary entitled: *Ex Promptuario vocabulorum Joannes Pinniciani variarum rerum vocabula, ad puerorum usum collectum.* Augsburg: Silvanus Ottmar, 1521, 4°, ll. 22. Latin–German. Thirteen editions: 1516, 1520, 1521, 1521, 1522, 1524, 1528, 1530, 1532, 1534, 1535, 1541, 1545.

5. *Sebald Heyden. Nomenclatura rerum domesticarum.* Augsburg: Heinrich Steiner, 1530, 8°, ll. 24. Latin–German. Twenty-seven editions: 1530, 1532, 1533, 1534(2), 1535(3), 1536, 1538(2), 1539, 1540, 1542, 1550, 1550(2), 1554, 1555, 1564, 1566, 1570, 1573, 1580, 1581, 1593, 1595.

6. *Martin Luther. Catechismus, Düdesch unde Latinisch.* Edited by Georg Meier. Magdeburg: Michael Lotter, 1531, 8°, ll. 48. Low German–Latin. Note the sequence of languages. The dictionary is added to the catechism. Eighteen editions, five of them High German: 1531(2), 1535, 1538(2), 1539, 1545, 1548, 1550, 1551, 1555, 1559, 1561, 1562, 1570, 1575, 1579, 1581.

7. *Petrus Dasypodius. Dictionarium voces propemodum universas in autoribus Latinae linguae probatis, ac vulgo receptis occurentes Germanice explicans.* Strasbourg: Wendelinus Rihelius, 1535, 4°, ll. 232. Latin–German. The onomasiological part of the dictionary is added to a semasiological one. Thirty editions, partly with a different sequence of languages: 1535, 1536(2), 1537(2), 1538, 1540, 1540, 1541(2), 1543, 1544, 1547, 1548, 1554, 1557, 1559, 1562, 1563, 1564, 1565, 1569, 1570, 1570, 1577, 1580(2), 1592, 1596(2).

8.1, 8.2. *Johann Byber. Nomenclatura in usum scholae Gorlicensis. Recognita et innumeris rerum vocabulis aucta.* Görlitz: Johann Rhamba, 1572, 8°, ll. 96. Latin–German. Eight editions, from the second edition onwards entitled:

German is meant. In most cases the place of printing gives a valuable clue. Note that 'Teut(h)onic' always means 'Low German' if 'Alemanic' also appears in the dictionary. If it does not, however, 'Teut(h)onic' obviously has a more general meaning. See Loonen 1991, 13–18. The rare *High German* refers to the dialects which are neither *Niederdeutsch* nor *Oberdeutsch*, that is, mostly Thuringian and Saxonian, which became so important for the establishing of standard German after Luther. Languages are only mentioned in my list if they are not clearly discernible from the title of the dictionary.

[9] The number of editions refers only to the sixteenth century. Many dictionaries had more editions after 1600.

Martinus Mylius. Nomenclatura rerum communium in usum tyronum scholae Gorlicensis, studio Johannis Byberi edita, nuncque recognita & locis vocabulisque aliot aucta. Görlitz: Ambrosius Fritsch, 8°, ll. 80. Latin–German. Note that the dictionary was meant to be used in one special school: 1572, 1577, 1578, 1579, 1582, 1590, 1590, 1598.

Dictionaries Nos. 9.1 and 9.2 are the only Latin–French and French–Latin onomasiological dictionaries known before the end of the century.

9.1, 9.2. *Jean Fontaine. Hortvlvs Pverorvm, Pergratvs ac Pervtilis Latine discentibus. Summa capita pagellae sexta & seq. indicant. Petit Jardin Povr Les Enfants, Fort Agreable & profitable pour aprendere Latin,* s.l.: Iean Lertout, 1581. Latin–French. No further edition. In the same year there is a Latin–French edition, whose topical chapters have an alphabetical sequence of entries: *Jean Fontaine. Petit Jardin Pourt les enfans, fort agreable & profitable pour aprendre Latin,* s.l.: Iean Lertout, 1581.

Dictionaries Nos. 10.1 to 10.3 are dictionaries with Greek and Hebrew entries, as well as Latin and German. They also serve the teaching and learning of a (or several) sacred language(s).

10.1. *Petrus Curius. Rerum maxime vulgarium congesta per locos in puerorum gratiam vocabula, Graece et Teutonice interpretata.* Antwerp: Michael Hillen, 1538. A further edition '*repurgata à mendis, et locupletata*' 1543 (filiation of No. 3).

10.2 *Paulus Eberus, Caspar Peucerus. Vocabula rei nummariae, ponderum & mensurarum Graeca, Latina, Ebraica. Additae sunt* . . . . Wittenberg: Joseph Klug, 1549, 8°, ff. 40. This is the only special dictionary listed. It is included because it has a division according to natural history in its second part. Ten editions: 1549, 1551, 1552, 1556, 1558, 1559, 1563, 1564, 1570, 1574.

10.3. *Nicodemus Frischlinus. Nomenclator Trilinguis, Graecolatinogermanicus.* Frankfurt: Johann Spies, 1586, 8°, ll. 283. Six editions: 1586, 1588, 1590, 1591, 1594, 1600 (see No. 24).

'SACRED LANGUAGE'–SEVERAL NATIONAL LANGUAGES; AND VERNACULAR–VERNACULAR

A great number of onomasiological dictionaries which juxtapose Latin (and in rare cases also Greek) and several, in fact up to eight, languages are a filiation of Nos. 11.1 to 11.3, which juxtapose two vernaculars. They eventually extend over the whole Continent. Also No. 12, with its two vernaculars, is dependent on No. 11.1.

11.1, 11.2, 11.3. [Adam of Rotweil]. *introito e porta de quele che voleno imparare e comprender todescho a latino cioe taliano el quale e vtilissimo per quele che vadeno a pratichando per el mundo el sia todescho o taliano.* Venice: Adam von Rodueil, 1477, 4°, ff. 56. Later editions bear the title *Solenissimo Vochabulista e utilissimo a imparare legere per gli che de siderase senza a[n]dare a schola Como eartesa ni e done* . . . . Bologna: Domenego de Lapi, 1479, 4°, ll. 64. Yet another title of the same book is *Libro vtilissimo a chi se dileta de intendere todesco, dechiarando in lingua taliana.* Venice: Manfrino de Monteferrato, 1499, 4°, ff. 24. Eighteen editions: 1477, 1479, 1480, 1482, 1493, 1498(2), 1499, 1500, 1501, 1511, 1513, 1514, 1520, 1522, 1542, 1550, 1555.

12.   [Rosembach, Hans]. *Vocabulari molt profitos per aprendre Lo Catalan Alamany y Lo Alamany Catalan.* Perpignan: Hans Rosenbach, 1502, 8°, ll. 72. Only this edition.

13.1, 13.2. *Introductio quaedam utilissima, siue Vocabularius quattuor linguaru[m], Latinae, Italicae, Gallicae, & Alamanicae, per mundum uersari cupientibus summe utilis.* Rome: Jacobus Mazochius, 1510, 4°, ll. 60. Also: *Vocabularius quattuor linguarum, scilicet Latine, Italice, Gallice, et Alimanice.* Augsburg: Philipp Ulhart, 1518, 8°, ll. 76. Eight editions: 1510, 1516(3), 1518, 1521(2), 1522.

14.1. *Dictionarius trium linguarum, Latine, Teutonice, Boemice, potiora vocabula continens: peregrinantibus apprime utilis.* Vienna: Hieronymus Vietor and Johannes Singriener, 1513, 4°, ll. 10. Probably only this edition.

14.2. *Quinque linguarum utilissimus Vochabulista, Latine, Tusche, Gallice, Hyspan[ic]e, & Alemanice. Valde necessarius per mundum versari cupientibus.* Venice: Melchior Sessa, 1513, 4°, ll. 36. Also with a different choice of languages: *Quinque linguarum utilissimus Vocabulista. Latinae, Italicae, Gallicae, Bohemicae, et Alemmanicae valde necessarius per mundum versari cupientibus.* Nuremberg: Friedrich Peypus, 1531, 4°, ll. 36. Thirteen editions: 1513, 1526, 1529, 1531(2), 1533(4), 1537, 1538, 1540, 1542.

14.3. *Franciscus Mymerus. Dictionarium trium linguarum, Latinae, Teutonicae et Polonicae, potiora vocabula continens.* Cracow: Hieronymus Vietor, 1528, 8°, ll. 46. Five editions: 1528, 1541, 1555, 1570, 1592.

14.4. *Sex linguarum, Latinae, Gallicae, Hispanicae, Italicae, Anglicae, & Teutonicae, dilucidissimus dictionarius.* Augsburg: Philipp Ulhard, 1530, 8°, ll. 98. Also: . . . *Latine, Theutonice, Gallice, Hispanice, Italice, Anglice* . . . . Southwarke: James Nicolson for John Renys, 1537, 8°, ll. 34. Thirty-four editions: 1530, 1531, 1533(4), 1535, 1537, 1541(4), 1548(3), 1549(2), 1553, 1557(2), 1558, 1563, 1564, 1567, 1568(3), 1570, 1570(2), 1579, 1582, 1590, 1595.

Dictionary No. 14.5 is a grouping of six languages different enough to deserve its own number.

14.5. Gabriel Pannonius Pesthinus: *Nomenclatvra sex lingvarvm, Latinae, Italicae, Gallicae, Bohemicae, Hungaricae & Germanicae.* Vienna: Joannes Singrenius, 8°, ll. 28. Five editions: 1538, 1554, 1561, 1568(2).

14.6. *Septem linguarum Latinae, Teutonicae, Gallicae, Hispanicae, Italicae, Anglicae, Almanicae, dilucidissimus dictionarius. Vocabulaer in sevenderley talen Latijn, Duytsch, Walsch, Spaensch, Italiaens, Engels ende Hoochdytsch. Vocabulair de sept langages.* Middelborch: Henrick Peetersen, 1535, 8°, ll. 24.

Note the mentioning of two German languages. Five editions: 1535, 1540(2), 1551, 1569.

14.7. *Octo linguarum, Grecae, Latinae, Teutonicae, Gallicae, Hispanicae, Italicae, Anglicae, Alemanicae dilucidissimum, mirum quam vtilis, nec dicam necessarium omnibus linguarum studiosis.* Paris: Pasquier le Tellier, 1546, 16°, ll. 20. Eleven editions: 1546, 1548(2), 1550, 1552(3), 1558, 1569, 1573, 1580.

The next is the fairly rare case of a dictionary which combines Latin, French and German in its entries.

15.1, 15.2. *Vocabularium Latinis, Gallicis et Theutonicis verbis scriptum.* Lyons: Jehan Thomas, 1514, 4°, ll. 34. The dictionary is part of a book of dialogues. There are four editions, after 1522 sixteen more with the title: *Dictionarius Latinis, Gallicis et Germanicis vocabulis conscriptus et denuo castigatus et locupelatus.* Strasbourg: s.n., 1522, 4°, ll. 44: 1514, 1515(2), 1521; 1522, 1527, 1530, 1535, 1543, 1550, 1550, 1568, 1571(2), 1573, 1575, 1580, 1587, 1589, 1590.

There is also a filiation of Murmellius's *Pappa*, though not as extensive as that of *Introito e porta*.

16.1. *Joannes Murmellius. Dictionarius variarum rerum, cum Germanica atque Polonica interpretatione.* Cracow: Hieronymus Vietor, 1526, 8°, pp. 107. Thirteen editions: 1526, 1528, 1531, 1533, 1540, 1541, 1546, 1550, 1551, 1555, 1564, 1566, 1584.

16.2. *Joannes Murmellius. Lexicon in quo latina rerum vocabula, in suas singula digesta classes, cum Germanica et Hungarica interpretatione.* Cracow: Hieronymus Vietor, 1533, 8°, pp. 207. Probably only this edition.

Two other dictionaries juxtapose Slavonic languages with Latin and German.

17. *Dictionarius seu nomenclatura quatuor linguarum. Latine, Italice, Polonice, et Theutonice, aprime cuiuis utilissimus, cu[m] peregrinantibus, tum domi residentibus, Adiecto vocabulorum indice.* Cracow: Florian Ungler, 1532, 8°, ll. 53. Three editions, a fourth has French instead of Italian: 1532, 1566(2), 1574.

18.1, 18.2, 18.3. *Vokabularz Latine e Cesty a Niemetzky kaz dému mlademu y Staremu welmi potrzebny a vzyteeny. Vocabularius rerum* [Latin, Czech, and German dictionary quite needful and useful for everyone young as well as old]. Nuremberg: Jodocus Gutknecht, 1535, 8°, ll. 32. Four editions. Another edition is *Petrus Codicillus. Wokabulář latinský, Cžeský a německý.* Prague: Daniel Michalek, 1546. Still another of 1560 is entitled: *Paulus Aquilinas. Wokabulář Nomenclatura rerum domesticarum. Ex Petro Dasypodio, Sebaldo Heyden, & Ioanne Piniciano. In usum studiosae iuventutis, Latina, Boemica, Germanicaque lingua.* Olmütz: Joannes Gunter, 1560, 8°, ll. 40. Note the mention of the derivation of the dictionary. After 1566 eleven more editions, entitled: *Petrus Codicillus. Vocabularium trilingue, pro usu Scholarum diligenter & accuratè editum.* Prague: Daniel

Michalek: 1535, 1546, 1550, 1560, 1560, 1560, 1566, 1570, 1575, 1576, 1581, 1582, 1586, 1587, 1589, 1590, 1599.[10]

The following presents the rare combination of Latin, Flemish, and French.[11]

19. *Johannes Paludanus. Dictionariolum Rerum Maxime W[u]lgarium, In Commvnem Pverorvm Vsvm, ex Optimis quibusque autoribus congestum, cum Flandrica & Gallica interpretatione.* . . . Gent: Iodocus Lambertus, 1544. Three editions: 1544, 1549, 1561.

The following (20) is perhaps the most learned and influential onomasiological dictionary, far beyond the usual needs of language learning, which developed a large filiation, each with its own editors. Among them (21.1–21.5) are also concise versions for schools.

20. *Hadrianus Junius. Nomenclator omnium rerum propria nomina variis linguis explicata indicans.* Antwerp: Christopherus Plantius, 1567, 8°, pp. 570. Fifteen editions with various languages—Latin plus Greek, German, Dutch, French, Italian, Spanish, and rarely English: 1567(3), 1569, 1571, 1575, 1576, 1577(2), 1583, 1585(2), 1588, 1590, 1591, 1593, 1594, 1596.

21.1. *Adam Siber. Nomenclatoris Hadriani Junii Medici Epitome.* Leipzig: Johann Rhamba, 1570, 8°, pp. 112, Latin–German. Eight editions, also entitled *Gemma gemmarum*. Also two editions Latin–Flemish and two more Latin–French–German: 1570, 1571, 1573, 1574, 1575, 1578, 1579(2), 1585(2), 1588, 1593.

21.2. *Matthias Schenckius. Nomenclator Hadriani Junii, Medici clarissimi: ad scholarum vsum, pretermissis linguis peregrinis, & mutatis on loco Germanicis, additis deniq; paucis quibusdam rerum vocabulis, accomodatus.* Augsburg: Michael Manger, 1571, 8°, pp. 288. Latin–German. Seven editions: 1574, 1578, 1581, 1585, 1588, 1595, 1599.

21.3. *Theophilus Golius. Onomasticon Latinogermanicum, in usum scholae Argentoratensis collectum.* Strasbourg: Josias Rihelius, 1579, 8°, col. 502. Eight editions: 1579, 1582, 1585(2), 1588, 1589, 1590, 1594.

21.4. *Nathan Chytraeus. Nomenclator Latino–Saxonicus.* Rostock: Stephan Möllemann, 1582, 8°, col. 626. *Saxonicus* means 'Low German'. Ten editions: 1582, 1585(2), 1589, 1590, 1592, 1594, 1596(2), 1597.

21.5. *Daniel Adam von Weleslavin. Nomenclator omnium rerum propria nomina tribus linguis, Latina, Boiemica & Germanica explicata continens, ex Hadriano Junio Medico excerptus.* Prague: Daniel Adam von Weleslavin, 1586, pp. 557. Probably only this edition.[12]

The following is a Latin–German dictionary which might have also been mentioned in the preceding subsection, except that the mention of a Dutch edition suggests that there were two national languages involved.

---

[10]   For the Czech tradition see Chapter 10.   [11]   See, however Chapter 4.
[12]   See Chapter 10.

22. *Petrus Apherdianus. Tyrocinium Latinae linguae.* Cologne: Johann Gymnick, 1575, 8°, pp. 221. Latin–German. Five editions (a Latin–Dutch edition is mentioned for 1552). (1552), 1575, 1579, 1581, 1584, 1591.

The following dictionary (23) has a division according to word-classes and within this a topical division.

23. *Helfricus Emmelius. Nomenclator Qvadrilinguis, Latino Germanico-Graeco Gallicus in Classes IIII Distinctus* . . . . Strasbourg: Theodosius Rihelius, 1592, 8°, col. 420. Later editions have the sequence German–Latin–Greek–French. Three editions: 1592, 1592, 1596.

The following dictionary (24) is a filiation of Frischlin (No. 10.3).

24. *Henricus Decimator. Tertia Pars Sylva Vocabvlorvm Et Phrasium, Sive Nomenclator.* . . . . Leipzig: Michael Lantzenbergerus, 1595. Latin–Hebrew–French–Italian–(High) German–(Low) German–Spanish. It is the third part of: *Sylva vocabulorum et phrasium* (1595) and *Secunda pars sylvae vocabulorum et phrasium* (1595), 8°, pp. 1049, both of which are alphabetical. Note the monumental size of the book. Probably only this edition.

9.1.3 Textbooks and the book trade

The select list of topical dictionaries described in the preceding section provides evidence of the size of the book market.

The first category (Latin (etc.)–vernacular) contains a total of 90; and the second and third categories (Latin (etc.)–several vernaculars; and vernacular–vernacular) together comprise a total of 216 editions.

This is indeed an astonishing number. We do not have any dependable information on the number of copies in each print run. For the years around 1480, the numbers 100 (minimum) and 1,000 (maximum), the average 300–500 (Brandis 1984) or 400–500 (Bennett 1970, 224) are mentioned, '*darnach eine deutlich steigende Tendenz*' (Brandis 1984, 187).[13] The editor[14] of *Vocabulari Català-Alemany* (1502) speaks of '*einigen hunderten[!] von Exemplaren*' (Stegmann 1991, 9). If we take this to mean 300, which agrees with Brandis's numbers and is still a moderate assumption, we arrive at as many as 91,800 copies which, given the circumstances of the time and the number of people who could read,[15] looks almost unbelievable.

---

[13] These numbers do not pertain to dictionaries, but there is no reason for not transferring them to this genre. Brandis claims that 1480 is a turning-point in the history of printing, because the printed book, from that date, took over from manuscripts and incunabula and printing became a craft and an art of commercial importance. This statement can certainly by applied to dictionaries. See also Hupka 1989, 14, who speaks of between 200 and 1,000 copies of lexicographical works. Furthermore see Steinberg 1961, in particular, 'On early bestsellers', 139–45, and Eisenstein 1983, 9.

[14] The Catalan–German successor of *Introito e porta* attracted more critical and philological analysis than other books of the kind. See Michatsh 1917, Colón 1983, and Stegmann 1991.

[15] Eisenstein 1983, 30 states that 50 per cent of people were literate, more in urban areas than in rural areas.

Some books, like Luther's catechism or the erudite dictionaries that followed in the wake of Humanist studies, were certainly not distributed purely regionally and must have been produced in print runs of many more than 300 copies in each case. After all, Luther's translation of the *New Testament* sold 5,000 copies between September and December 1522 (Steinberg 1961, 144), and 50 new editions up to 1526. Though the demand for this particular book was certainly a special case in the given situation, we must bear in mind that a copy of the Bible was much more expensive than a copy of the catechism. This fact certainly had its impact on the number of copies sold.

Contracts between the printer Richard Pynson and John Palsgrave from 1523 and 1524 speak of 750 copies of *Lesclarcissement de la langue francoyse*, not an onomasiological work but a grammar including a bilingual alphabetical diction-ary (Stein 1997, 7 and 20). It is a book of outstanding quality devoted to foreign-language teaching and learning which found its way into English and French libraries. Other dictionaries, admittedly, may have been of a much more limited use. But even an assumption of a smaller average number of copies per print run leads to such high sums that the importance of this book-genre at and for its time is proved. From the incunabula period onwards, schoolbooks have indeed proved 'the most profitable branch of the publishing trade' (Steinberg 1961, 139). For the succeeding one hundred years it was a regulation of the Stationer's Company that the numbers of grammars, primers, and catechisms should not exceed 2,500 or, under certain conditions, 3,000 copies a year (after Stein 1997, 40). In order to gain a comprehensive picture we must also remember that onomasiological dictionar-ies were only one genre of books for learning foreign languages.[16] There were alphabetical dictionaries and the widely distributed books of dialogues (collo-quies), which sometimes also contained short topical word-lists, more often however such lists being arranged alphabetically. For the Latin–German so-called *Vocabularius ex quo*, for example, of which, in addition to manuscripts, not less than forty-eight printed editions appearing between 1467 and 1505 are to be found, we have a balance sheet of the publisher and bookseller Peter Drach from Speyer (Schnell 1986) who sold 991 copies between 1480 and 1503. But only one-third of the balance sheets of this businessman is extant, and towards the end of the sixteenth century the sale of the *Vocabularius ex quo* is said to have 'exploded'. There is no reason to assume that selling figures for such alphabetical dictionar-ies should have been much different from those of topical ones.

Another example is the many books that go under the name of Noel de Berlaimont from Antwerp.[17] His first book appeared in 1530 and produced, over the following 200 years, a filiation which was perhaps even more productive than

---

[16] For the different book-genres in the context of foreign-language teaching material see Kaltz 1995. For the *Janua linguarum* by William Bathe and Johannes Amos Comenius and their respective adaptors, another widely used textbook in the form of an onomasiological dictionary (of sentences), see Chapter 10.

[17] See Chapter 4.

that of *Introito e porta* (Loonen 1991). Moreover, there were of course alphabetical dictionaries in all the languages mentioned, including the most successful dictionary of Ambrosio Calepino. This appeared for the first time in 1502 as a Latin dictionary with occasional Greek entries. It grew into a dictionary family with, eventually, eleven languages. Niederehe (1995) lists as many as eighty-five various editions (see also Labarre 1975). If, as previously, we assume each edition to have had a print run of 300 copies, these two titles would add another 55,500 copies to the corpus of works which served the needs of foreign-language learning in Europe between 1470 and 1600. These books must have been a powerful factor in European culture (and commerce).

Unlike Latin books for which folio volumes were preferred, and which could be read only with the help of special book-stands, a small format, mostly octavo, became popular for onomasiological dictionaries. Their binding was simple and, as a rule, without decoration. They could be carried, when travelling, in the sleeve of a coat so that they could easily be consulted at any time. They were obviously meant for learning outside study-rooms.

Of course, we do not know precisely how the various derivatives of *Introito e porta* found their way across Europe. We know the authors' names only from the original version and its Catalan adaptation. There are no patrons recognizable,[18] neither persons nor institutions, as is the case with the *Liber in volgaro*. The only statement we can safely make is that the wide distribution of books for foreign-language learning must have mirrored people's needs and wishes in this respect. Wide travelling was not unknown at the time and had even been popular earlier. There had been the Crusades and there still were mercenary armies. There was the Continent-wide ecclesiastical invigilating and visiting system organized by the Church. Monastic orders settled all over Europe. There were regional and trans-regional trading routes which crossed many linguistic borders. There existed an extensive system of pilgrimages, and of course the travels of German Emperors and their entourage from north to south. The activities of Humanists were, almost by definition, transnational. All this caused a great number of people to move through Europe and cross linguistic boundaries. The number of books available on the market, including all those titles which have been lost for ever and which certainly outnumbered those that have come down to us, proves how quickly the printing market reacted, within its time-given limits, to these activities. Seen from the point of view of today's book market, the habit of re-editing simply filled the gap in an effective system of transporting books. Some geographical centres evolved: centres of printing like Cologne and Nuremberg, centres of general trade like Frankfurt; Paris, and Cracow were centres of national learning. Multilingual regions had their own centres, for example, in Antwerp, Strasbourg, and Prague.

---

[18] In England the production of books for the teaching of French, other than onomasiological ones, was recognizably sponsored by members of royalty and the nobility, such as Henry VII and Henry VIII, the Duke of Norfolk, and the Duke of Suffolk (Stein 1997, 56).

Augsburg, Vienna, and Lyons were trading centres whose routes led into countries with several foreign languages. Dictionaries of Latin (or Greek or Hebrew) vs. German were printed in places evenly distributed throughout Germany; other dictionaries were predominantly printed in Italy, the south of Germany, and adjacent countries, with the exception of Rostock. Towards the end of the sixteenth and in the seventeenth century Antwerp became a leading centre of the printing industry.[19] As the internationalization of intellectual life across linguistic borders is generally attributed to the spread of printing, this means that above all the members of the trade themselves profited from it. The many editions of one book in all relevant linguistic areas of Europe point towards the internationalization of the printing trade but also to the continuance of the regionalization of readers.

The choice of languages shows, first of all, the still strong position of Latin. Many people learned it because of its own importance or used it as the mediating language for learning other national languages. Besides this, the choice of languages covers almost all the regions of Europe quite evenly. Initially we have Italian and Catalan, the leading *linguae francae* of the eastern and western Mediterranean. There then follows French as the most important vernacular after German on the western part of the Continent. The Hungarian, Czech (Bohemian), and Polish territories received their importance from the central political positions of Vienna and Prague, and from Germany's interest in colonization. Finally, Low Dutch, today's Dutch and Flemish, appears. It became even more popular with the growing importance of these regions in the turmoils of the Reformation and the Thirty Years War. England is added last, its language having only marginal European importance in these centuries.

The arrangement of languages in the onomasiological dictionaries obviously followed systematic as well as accidental principles. Among the systematic principles are the leftmost position of Latin, the side-by-side grouping of the Romance languages, and the frequent rightmost position of (Low or High) German, in particular if English or a Slavonic language is included. As the rightmost position is almost as marked as the leftmost position, it shows in these cases that English or the Slavonic languages were learned via German, not via Latin (Stein 1989*a*). The reasons for this convention were possibly the fairly easy translatability of English and Low German and the general knowledge of German in the Slavonic-speaking areas.

The existence of onomasiological dictionaries, as explained here, proves by the number of books and by the choice of languages as well as by their wide geographical distribution that, after the end of the Latin Middle Ages, Europe was not separated into mutually exclusive domains, but became polyglot for an important, though not particularly numerous, part of the population. This will

---

[19] Compare the list of places of publication with the two maps in Eisenstein 1983, 14 and 15, which show the spread of printing from the beginnings to 1500. Obviously the printing of textbooks for the learning of vernaculars—a genre of books grossly neglected by historiographers—was a normal activity of the trade. There is no mention of them, for example, in Eisenstein 1983, although the author sometimes speaks of 'schoolbooks'.

also have raised the level of alphabetization. The awareness of foreign national languages and the endeavours to learn them on such a large scale became a part of Europe's culture, proving that it continued to be a unified Continent even though the Latin linguistic unity had been lost and would from now on be of ever-decreasing importance. The new awareness of vernaculars was certainly not nationalism in any representative meaning of the word; it was rather a deliberate internationalism. It will require more studies to decide in what way, if at all, it paved the way for later national thinking and the claiming of vernaculars as a national property (Eisenstein 1983, 81–2).

It is in this context that English made its appearance on the Continent as one language among many. The tongue of this country which lay on the north-west-ern edge of the Continent and hardly interfered with its politics, except in parts of France, then came into contact with the tongues of other countries. There must have been a general need for this, otherwise it would not have happened.

9.2 Latin dictionaries for the *trivium*

The use of nomenclators for ordinary language teaching was certainly part of the general context of providing linguistic knowledge concerning learned but also trivial topics. The Humanists wanted Latin to become a means of general commu-nication. Nomenclators became quite popular in the German-speaking regions (Germany, the Netherlands and Switzerland). Here the late-medieval glossaries were followed by glossaries and dictionaries in the Humanist tradition.[20] Among them are the works by Johannes Murmellius and Sebaldus Heyden, by Petrus Dasypodius and Josua Maaler, and not least the authors that adapted Adrianus Junius's *Nomenclator* of 1565 in various ways (see above and below).[21] They testify to the slow growth of a common vocabulary across the many German dialects. In Germany, and also in the Romance countries (Lindemann 1994), topical works were more popular than in England, where interested people probably imported them from the Continent. This is a historical fact to be derived from the bibli-ographies (see above, also Müller 1882, 7). Of course, nomenclators are a priceless source of information about school-life.

---

[20] The analyses of all the following word-lists and dictionaries are restricted to comments on their macro- and microstructures. This is mainly done for practical purposes. Comments on the relevant pragmatic structures would have been much too extensive. Moreover, because of the elementary char-acter of some word-lists, an analysis of their pragmatic structures would not yield any results beyond what has already been stated in the preceding chapters. Examples are all taken from the German context, which is assumed to be representative of continental Europe in general (de Smet 1979 and 1985, Wiegand 1998). See Müller 2001. For an overview on the teaching of foreign languages here see Caravolas 1994, 121–65.

[21] Oldest manuscript of the *Vocabularius ex quo*: 1410, first print: 1467. First print of *Pappa*: 1513, last print: 1565. First print of Heyden 1530, last print: 1590. First print of Dasypodius: 1535. First print of Maaler: 1571. First appearance of Junius: 1565, subsequently many adaptations. According to de Smet 1985.

The macrostructure of an onomasiological dictionary establishes a particular kind of textual cohesion upon which the dictionary users, be they teachers or learners, can construct their ideas of coherence.[22] Besides the formal arrangement and the choice of languages it is this cohesion which marks the difference between dictionaries for learning Latin or one of the other sacred, in effect academic, languages and for learning one of the European vernaculars. A look at the contents of dictionaries will help us to recognize the differences and, at the same time, the overlaps. Thus, a content-oriented analysis can support the idea of the unity in diversity of European culture in the centuries that succeeded the Latin era.

In the *trivium*, grammar was one of the *artes* and *grammar* meant Latin grammar (Stammler 1960, vol. 2, 1127–35). So Latin was at the same time the topic and the medium of teaching. Grammars according to Donatus described the language and used it. Alphabetical glossaries were used as translation aids, topical glossaries as aids for constructing texts. The examples to be quoted show a certain homogeneity which proves that they were taken from a common store of linguistic (Latin) knowledge. Yet the choice of topics to which lexemes belong and their arrangement vary to a certain extent as can be shown. The three dictionaries selected for this purpose are among the most influential of their time.

9.2.1 Vocabularius (rerum) Registrum vocabularii sequentis

Vocabularius (rerum) Registrum vocabularii sequentis. Augsburg: Günther Zainer, [not later than 1474].   (WF Gram. 30.5 fol.)

This is the oldest example of a Latin–German dictionary as a nomenclator.[23] It is an incunabulum. The Wolfenbüttel copy has no printed title. There is a librarian's handwritten note: *Vocabularius ex quo Cop. 6326*, which does not agree with the title mentioned above given to the book by Claes (1977, No. 4). The book has 274 pages. With an average of ten entries per page, it contains some 2,740 lexemes. The printing is in Gothic type for Latin as well as for German.

The microstructure of this dictionary is quite variable. Latin lemmata are translated into German, then often, though not always, an explanatory Latin sentence is added. It either describes the meaning or, more frequently, derives it according to the etymological principles of the time. Such explanations can be quite elaborate and may cover as much as half a page. Very often two related Latin

---

[22] See Chapter 1.

[23] For a complex treatment of early Latin–German dictionaries, alphabetical as well as onomasiological, as sources for the *Deutsche[r] Wortatlas*, see de Smet 1968 and 1985. Filiations and interrelations and also word-geographical aspects of dictionaries are treated here in considerable detail, in particular in relation to Junius's *Nomenclator* (see below).

lemmata are complemented by one explanation. As is usual in an incunabulum, there are many abbreviations.

Typical entries are:

Faber / schmid / dicitur om[n]is artifex in materia dura subiecta duris instrumentis opatis et laborans ut in lignis lapidibus et metallis. Et diuersificantur secundum diuersam speciem materie subiecte.
Ferrifaber / eysen schmid / qui laborat et opatur.
Faber ferrarius / in ferro.
Cuprifaber / kupffer schmid / qui laborat et opat[ur] in cupro.
Aurifaber /golt schmid.   (49.)
Arthocrea / krapff / Est panis habens carnes concisas simul in pasta decoctas et dicitur ab artos id est panis et creos id est caro.   (80.)

The macrostructure of the dictionary is given at the beginnings with the headings of sixty-two sections. However, the arrangement is not very systematic although it betrays certain predilections. To start with, three sections are devoted to man. There then follow sections devoted to clothes, buildings of various sorts, and, above all, to instruments or equipment. However, the latter are arranged according to a sequence which is hard to understand. Note, for example, the heads of sections 16 to 35:

De nominibuis significantibus vtensilia in quibus res seruabiles continentur.
De nominibus significantibus vtensilia quib[us] vtimur circa equos.
De nominibus significantib[us] mensuras necessarias pro co[m]mutatione rerum qnibus[!] vtimur co[m]muniter.
De nominibus significantibus vtensilia domus
De nominibus significantibus seruatoria et instrumenta pertinentia ad frumenta et pascua
De nominibus significantibus instrumenta pertine[n]tia ad curros et quadrigas.
De nominibus rusticorum et instrumentorum et rerum et vasorum rusticalium plurimorum
De nominibus significantibus ea que pertinent ad scriptores.
De fabris et instrumentis eorum.
De murarijs et instrumentis eor[um].
De nominib[us] ornamentorum et instrumentorum p[er]tinentium ad cultum diuinum.
De nominibus libroru[m] ecclesie pertinentium ad cultum dei.
De nominibus locorum vbi solent sepelire corpora humana.
De nominibus locorum et instrumentorum penaliu[m] que malefactoribus pro pena infliguntur.
De nominibus intrumentorum quibus lusores vsuntur.
De nominibus intrumentorum artificialium quib[us] vtimur ad consonandum consonantias musicales.
De nominibus cultorum agrorum et eorum que pertitent ad culturas agroru[m].
De nominibus significantibus potus humanos et que pertine[n]t ad tales et instrume[n]tis vinitor[um] vel viniariorum.
De nominibus mollitorum et instrumentis eorum.

There then follow ten more sections on craftsmen and their particular equipment.

The vocabulary closes with a quite rare, though not unique, feature, six sections on well-known species of animals and plants, arranged '*secundum ordinem alphabeti*'.[24]

Obviously, the unifying principle of the *Vocabularius* is *man* and the *human world*, in particular that of objects and equipment. Entries on natural history, predominating in almost all other vocabularies, are added almost as an afterthought with no trouble being taken to give them a sensible, that is, an onomasiological, order.

9.2.2 *Brack,* Vocabularius rerum

[Wenzeslaus Brack,] *Vocabularius rerum.* [Strassburg: Schott 1489.]   (WF KB 467.)

The author (*fl.* 1489) came from Liebenwerda in Saxony and was headmaster of the municipal school in Constance. Stammler (1933, col. 272) assumes that his dictionary goes back to a manuscript in Donaueschingen (cod. 56, v.J. 1486, Bl. 37a–128a). In the Wolfenbüttel copy only the title is printed. Author, place, and year of printing are handwritten by a librarian. The book is an incunabulum of 116 pages. The printing is in Gothic type throughout. There are on average twenty-eight entries per page, amounting *in toto* to about 3,200.

In the microstructure the Latin lemmata are complemented either by Latin explanatory paraphrases or by German translations/paraphrases plus Latin ones. Translations are only of one word, but explanations can be rather elaborate. There are also references to classical authors, for example Isidore of Seville and Virgil. Word-classes are indicated. Frequently, but not always, genitive endings are given in the noun entries. There are etymologies in the manner of the sixteenth century.

Typical entries are:

Co[m]plexio. art oder eygene natur auß d[en] vier eleme[n]t eyge[n]schafft.
Melancholica terra sicca et frigida complexio. Inde melancolicus. grauis. tardus. iners. lutei coloris. tristis. Flegma. aquaea. frigida et humida complexio. Et fere omnes mulieres flegmatice sunt.
Sanguinea optima est complexio. aerea. humida et calida.
Aqua sanguineus ad optima aptus. pulcer. amabilis. liberalis. affabilis. prudens. (biii [3]ᵛ.)[25]
Speculum ein spiegel. quia in ipsum species rei recipit[ur].
Crinile krentzlin. a crinibus.
Sertum idem a sertis herbis.
Corono kron. quia circuitu vna.

---

[24] The flouting of the onomasiological order is frequently found, in particular with reference to plants and animals (natural history). See, for example, Hadrianus Junius (below). One of the twenty books of Isidore's *Etymologiae* (X, not devoted to natural history) is ordered alphabetically. In the case of our *Vocabularius (rerum)*, therefore, we need not assume that the alphabetical parts were taken from their own source, although we cannot exclude this altogether.

[25] There is here an obvious reflection of contemporary physiological and medical knowledge, particularly that of the Galen school, which is also to be found in other dictionaries. See Chapter 7.

Diadema kunigklich kron.
Sceptrum kunigklich zepter.
Tridens idem quia tres quasi dentes.
Laurea corona ex auro. in signum triumphi. (dii[1]ᵛ.)
Simeus aff. Simea effin. Nam homini similat.
Elephasantis[!]. *Elephio grece est mons latine quia mole corporis elephantes dicunt[ur].*
Grifes greyff. animal pennatum & quadrupes. Unde Vergil. Iugent[ur] tam grifes equis. tale animal odit naturaliter equum.
Linx luchs. Ex cuius urina Plinio teste. apis ligurius nascit[ur]. Ideo inuidia suam tegit vrinamin arena [et]*c.* (biii[4]ʳ.)

Brack's *Vocabularius rerum* has about 450 more entries than the previous *Vocabularius* and is more detailed in its macrostructure. There are exactly 100 topical sections. There is a considerable overlap between the two dictionaries. Brack's shows its more universal aspect by commencing with twelve sections on the world as a whole (God, time), before proceeding to '*De homine et eius origine atqu[e] eius sexu*'. Moreover, he concludes with fourteen sections on animals, plants, and stones in the usual order of natural history and arranged onomasiologically.

Between these introductory and concluding parts, the seventy-four sections are largely the same as in the earlier *Vocabularius*, at least as far as topics are concerned. Headings are almost always different and so is, frequently, the number of sections devoted to one topic. The earlier vocabulary has three sections on man and consanguinity, the later one has twelve. The earlier one has one section on containers (for liquids, etc.), the later six. This allows for a better and more complex systematization, which, for example, shows in the sections on man in *Vocabularius*:

De homine et de diuersis membris in eo existentibus.
De homine et de diuersis co[n]ditionibus.
De consanguinibus et affinibus.

Against Brack:

De homine ei eius origine atqu[e] eius sexu.
De p[ro]prietatibus hominis interioris et de affectibus.
De integralib[us] et corporalibus p[ar]tibus hominis.
De sanguine.
De complexionibus.
De affinitatibus et gradibus.
De patruis.
De amicis.
De auunculis.
De materteris.
De nuptijs et ex his contractis amicicijs et appendentijs.
Civium et populi vocabula seniorum.

More complex systematization is also to be found in the sections on husbandry.

The number of sections in Brack which do not appear in the earlier *Vocabularius* at all (e.g. *De terre vocabulis, De locis terre, Loca terra inferiora, De itineribus* and *De monachis, Nomina fidelium, De philosophis, De poetis, De magis*) is quite small. So there is a clear dependence of the later vocabulary on the earlier one. This is shown even in occasional inconsistencies, for example the placing of the one or two sections on navigation where they do not have any intelligible locus in the overall arrangement.

Although the two dictionaries cannot be said to be affiliated, the later author, Wenceslaus Brack, must have had knowledge of the unknown former's work or of a common source. This means that, by and large, he agreed with the choice of words which he enlarged in number and systematized more strictly. This also means that the authors largely conformed in their opinion on which factual knowledge, expressed in lexemes, was necessary and useful for learning Latin. Both works were called *Vocabularius rerum*, that is, both were meant to present in words a world of things.

9.2.3 *Murmellius*, Pappa

Ioa[n]nis Murmellij Ruremu[n]densis. cui titulus Pappa. . . . . . [Köln: Quentell 1513.]   (WF Kg 369.)

Johannes Murmellius (1480–1517) belongs to what can be called the second rank of Humanists, behind, for example, Erasmus and Reuchlin. His activities as a member of *Gymnasien* in Münster and Alkmaar testify to the cultural unity that prevailed at that time in the Netherlands, the Lower Rhineland, and Westphalia. He took part in the reform of Latin teaching and the introduction of the teaching of Greek. In relation to the former he wrote and published some twenty-five schoolbooks, among them *Pappa*, besides many other classical works like introductions to Boethius and Aristotle. The bibliography of his publications has forty-seven items (Reichling 1880, 131–65). Unfortunately, a new edition of his works omits the dictionary, although it is praised as an attempt at realistic language teaching (Murmellius 1894, VII). The Wolfenbüttel copy of *Pappa* has 'Köln: Quentell 1513' added by a librarian's hand.

Johannes Murmellius takes a large step forward in the direction of practical teaching. His is an integrated textbook whose parts are indicated on the title-page (Latin text only):

Uariar[um] rerum dictiones cu[m] germanica interpretatione—Oratiuncule varie puerorum vsui exposite—Precepta moralia adiecta interpretatione germanica—Protrita item quedam prouerbia & latino & vernaculo sermone conscripta.—Huios libro addita est ex opere gram[m]atico Jacobi Montani viri litteratissimi forma declinandi per primam [con]iugatio cu[m] vernacula interpretatione.

All the parts—word-list, colloquy, rules of behaviour, proverbs, and grammar—were conceived in the Humanist spirit and conflated into one book. Only the word-list will be treated here.

The quarto incunabulum is of course printed in Gothic letters throughout, in two columns with the usual abbreviations, which however are rare in the lexicographical part. Sections are indicated by majuscules, but not numbered. There are sixty-four pages. The microstructure is very simple. There are no explanations, just Latin lexemes and their (Low) German translations. Macrostructurally this is the first complete, perfectly systematic specimen of its genre. For a full overview of sections see Table A.15.

The macrostructure of this onomasiological dictionary is easy to establish. A first part [1–20], divided into four subparts, can be called *philosophical*. The first subpart [1–3] deals with God, heavenly things, nature, and time. There then follows a second subpart [4] which enumerates the classical four elements in the sequence air,[26] earth, water, but not fire. We can assume that, following the pre-Socratic philosophers, fire was seen as equal to the human 'life-fire' and was thus not mentioned here, nor indeed later when man is being treated. An overview of the countries and nations, which show the world known to the author, concludes this subpart [5]. The sections of the third subpart are devoted to nature in descending order from animals, and plants to inanimate material. Man belongs to the highest species of animals [6]. In the following enumeration of birds, fish, and vermin, three of the four elements reappear [7–11]. The division of plants into trees, herbs, and grass [12–18] also follows classical models. Emphasis is placed on the usefulness of plants for humankind (fruits of trees [13], herbs as spices [17], grain as kinds of grass [18]).

This first philosophical part is followed by a second, *sociological* one dealing with the societal world of humans [21–44], this time in three subparts. The first subpart [21–7] lists names of artificially made objects and, in so doing introduces another categorial division, that of *naturalia* and *artificialia*. Among the latter are churches [21–2], which, significantly, occupy the first place. There then follow houses to live in with their furniture, including food and clothes [23–7]. The following subpart is devoted to ordering systems in society, beginning with consanguinity, continuing with the church-related and state-related hierarchies and leading to the professors of the *artes*, artists, and craftsmen. This sequence shows a societal order which can also be found in other sources, for example in the *Ständebuch* by Hans Sachs (1574). Mention of professions and crafts includes mention of things and equipment with which these people work, for example books. A last subpart lists measures, money, and numbers [35–44]. Because of the extensive listing of numerals it is somewhat formalistic, but must be understood as pointing towards the world of trade. After all, *Pappa* is a textbook for learning Latin with its complicated system of numerals.

The philosophical and sociological part is followed by a third, a *pedagogical* one [45–8]. In it the names of the virtues, the deadly sins, and the so-called four last

---

[26] We also find 'things generated in the air', which are basically phenomena of the weather, among them lightning, that is, fire.

things—death, the Last Judgement, Paradise, and Hell—are listed. This part establishes a symmetry between the beginning and the end of the dictionary. The world appears framed in Christian ideas. The young learners of Latin obviously undergo an education according to Christian principles.

The exact store of knowledge and of convictions, of the availability of objects and of institutional systems, laid down in this dictionary of 1513 could only be correctly judged if we were to look at every single entry. But even without doing this, we can see that Johannes Murmellius attempted to mirror the whole of the world objectively, to the extent that he was able to understand the (modern) term. He used a philosophically based concept of natural order which has classical predecessors as well as the knowledge and experience of his own time. The coincidences and overlaps with the two earlier onomasiological dictionaries no longer signal a factual dependency but originate from the common stock of ideas and objects, of items of knowledge and of experience, of philosophical, that is, classical, categories and religious, that is, Christian, convictions that existed at Murmellius's time. The lexical skeleton of this vocabulary will be found in many later works of the kind, even if in their size and their ambition they go far beyond the aims of a textbook for teaching Latin or other foreign languages. The fact that *Pappa* started a whole family of similar textbooks was certainly a consequence of its lexicographical quality.[27]

Murmellius's textbook was extremely successful (de Smet 1985). Up to 1560 no fewer than thirty-two editions appeared on the market in the Low German and High German regions, with print runs of 1,000 copies (Reichling 1880). Even if this figure is an overestimation, the number of copies printed *in toto* must have been considerable. Among the various parts of the book, the first, the nomenclator, seems to have been even more successful than the others. Proof of this is its eight separate editions, six of them with a Polish translation.

9.3 Textbooks for vernaculars

9.3.1 Liber in volgaro *(1424)*

On the European Continent the cradle of foreign-language teaching textbooks outside the Latin tradition is to be found in Upper Italy, more precisely, in Venice. Its first highlight is a handwritten glossary of 100 leaves which today is to be found in the Österreichische Nationalbibliothek in Vienna (Cod. 12 514) and the Bayerische Staatsbibliothek in Munich (Cod. ital. 261). There are less important copies in the Universitätsbibliothek Heidelberg (Cod. pal. germ. 657) and the Vaticana in Rome (Cod. lat. 1789). They show similarities to other Latin–Italian and Italian–German glossaries (Pausch 1972, 41–8), in particular in the systematic arrangement of vocabulary.

---

[27] Note the metaphorical title *pappa*, 'food for children (beginners)'. For a comparison between *Pappa* and *Introito e porta* see below.

The title *Liber in volgaro* stems from the cover of the Viennese codex. It has been excellently researched and critically edited by Oskar Pausch (1972).[28] Its colophon is dated '16 February 1423', which according to the calendar then valid was in fact that day in 1424.

A painstaking comparison of the handwriting, in particular its irregularities, and of the mistakes that occur shows that the codices in Vienna and Munich are copies by the same scribe of an earlier original which must have been extant in Venice. There are two columns on each page with an average of thirty to thirty-five lines, the Italian lexeme in the left-hand, the German translation in the right-hand position. At the end of the text a '*maister Jorg . . . von nurmberck . . .*', that is, Magister George of Nuremberg, is mentioned as its author. The general assumption is that he was a German *Sprachlehrer* who taught German to Italians at the *Fondaco dei Tedeschi*, a guildhall of German traders and merchants in Venice, founded in 1228, which organized and controlled the lively commercial connections between Southern Germany and Upper Italy with their respective centres of Nuremberg and Venice. The 'German House', of which there are pictures still extant, the linguistic needs which the vocabulary answered, and also the vocabulary of the glossary itself reflect these particularly lively trading connections between the two regions in the quattrocento. The function of the glossary in this respect is corroborated by the Bavarian and Venetian colouring of its language.

The *Liber in volgaro* is, in fact, not a glossary but an integrated textbook. In this respect it has some unique features.

There are no subtitles or other visible caesurae for marking sections. Entry follows entry. This means that the macrostructure of the glossary is not indicated typographically. Nevertheless, we can easily distinguish between four different kinds of entries: (i) they centre around nouns and adjectives, that is, they are noun phrases; (ii) they centre around adjectives and their morphology, that is, they deal with comparison; (iii) they centre around verbs and their morphology, that is, conjugations; or, (iv) they consist of conversations. The first three kinds of entries are intermingled, but by the preponderance of their appearance they also mark different parts of the glossary. First, there is the systematically, though rather loosely, arranged vocabulary, as had become traditional from early glossaries and as would be traditional for the centuries to follow. Microstructurally the greatest number of entries consists of lexemes translated into lexemes, or phrases, that is, nouns with adjectives or genitive postmodifications, translated into compounds or similar phrases. As a rule, nouns have a definite article. Often they are given in the singular as well as in the plural and together with morphologically related verbs. In between the clusters of such entries and, frequently, added to their ends we find sentences, sometimes of a proverbial character, translated into sentences. In many cases they are not triggered by the topic of a word-cluster but by the

---

[28] This monograph (and this means the Viennese version) is the source of most of my own observations and of all quotations. It mentions all analytic literature published up to 1972.

meaning or even the form of just one of its lexemes. But the entries which have just one lexeme in each of the two columns are by far in the majority. This makes the following entries from a cluster on fire and warmth quite typical (1^r and 1^v):

El fuogo	*das fewer*
El fuogo de ciello	*daz himeliß fewr*
El fuogo infernalle	*daz helliß fewr*
Impia vn fuogo	*zunt ein fewer*
Eme uoio scaldare	*Ich wil mich wirmen*
Ele fredo	*Ez ist chalt*
Eho fredo ay pie	*Mich freust an die fueß*
ealle man	*vnd an die hend*
layer	*der lufft*
El vento	*der wint*
El tempo e piu resent	*daz weter is heut chuller*
ancho cha eri	*ben gestern*
Chaldo	*worm haiß*
fredo	*chalt*
Eho piu fredo all naso	*Mich frewst fester an die nassen*
cha alle alltre menbre	*den an die andern glider*

Secondly, adjectives are treated differently in that they are given together with the patterns of their comparisons or other means of expressing a degree. In the cluster just mentioned we find, for example:

Chaldo	*worm haiß*
piu chaldo	*wormer*
Molto chaldo	*gar borm*
Massa chaldo	*ze worm*
Epiu chaldo	*aller birmist*
la chaldana	*die hicz*
Ele Anchuo piu	*Ez ist heut birmer*
chaldo cha eri	*den gestern*

There then follows a similar sequence of entries with *fredo–chalt*.

There is a batch of 216 entries and another of 150 entries (26^v–29^v, 44^r–46^r) in the *Liber* which consist entirely of such adjectives in their various forms of comparison, including related adverbial forms and nouns. Note for example (44^v):

Richo	*Reich*	*Epiu richo*	*Aler reichist*
piu richo	*Reicher*	*Richamente*	*Reichleich*
Molto richo	*gar reich*	*la richeza*	*die reicheit*
Massa richo	*ze reich*		
Pouero	*Arm*	*Masssa pouero*	*ze arm*
Piu pouero	*Ermer*	*Epiu pouero*	*Aller armist*
Molto pouero	*gar arm*	*la pouertade*	*die armuet*
Pouramente	*Armleich*		

Thirdly, there is also a special treatment of verbs. They occur between the entries mentioned so far, usually in the infinitive or as predicates in sentences. But a long series of entries (in fact 819, 51^r–63^r) contains nothing but verbs in their imperative, infinitive, and participle forms, and an even longer one (in fact, 1,569, 64^r–85^v) gives them conjugated in all persons and tenses. Note, for example (51^r):

Commenca Heb an	*Commenzare an heben*	*Chomenzado an gehebt*
Ama hab lieb	*Amare liebt haben*	*Amado liebt hebabt*
Reprende straff	*Reprendere Straffen*	*Reprendudo gestrafft*

Note, furthermore (70^r and 70^v):

e Sento Ich Sicz	*Tu senti dw Siczst*	*Quell senta der Siczt*
Nui sentemo wir Siczen	*Vui senti Ir Siczt*	*Quelli senta die Sitzen*
E sentaua Ich Saz	*Tu sentauy du Sast*	*Quell sentaua der Saz*
Nui sentauano wir Sassen	*vui sentaui Ir Sast*	*Quelli sentaua die Sassen*

E son sentado Ich pin gesessen
Tu e sentado [etc.]
E seraue sentado Ich wer gesessen [etc.]
E era sentado Ich baz gesessen [etc.]
E sentero Ich burt siczen [etc.].

On the one hand, these entries follow the classical morphological paradigm of grammar. On the other, they show that the didactic aim of this language textbook is direct speech with its structural need to use all persons. It certainly is not reading competence with its predominance of the third persons singular and plural.

Fourth and last, there are dialogues (86^r–100^v).

This means that the overall arrangement of the book follows word-classes rather than a convincing onomasiological plan. Nevertheless, the vocabulary focusing on nouns and adjectives has the traditional semantic cohesion. This is supported by the fact that root-words often appear together with compounds and derivations.

Obviously there are several interests combined here, which indeed give the *Liber in volgaro* the character of an integrated textbook for foreign-language teaching and learning. They are: (i) the semanticization of the vocabulary, which is presented in an onomasiological order; (ii) the grammatical morphology of the adjective and the verb, and (iii) the morphology of word formation; finally (iv) language use, which shows in the many phrases, half-sentences, sentences, utterances, and proverbs sandwiched between the word-lists, and in the dialogues.

Given this complex macrostructure, it is difficult to give an approximate estimate of the number of words available for the learner. There are about 2,700 entries with lexemes, which however contain many of the adjectives in three or four variants each. Sixty-five adjectives are given separately with their comparisons. Yet they repeat quite a number of those contained in the topical word-lists. The two batches with verbs contain 220 and forty-six conjugated ones, which are partly identical. It seems justifiable to say that there are some 3,000 semantically independent lexemes here.

In the vocabulary, we find all the criteria of the onomasiological order which are typical of word-lists of this kind, but arranged in a sequence which is frequently hard to understand. The great domains (God, universe, mankind, food, society, artificial objects and tools, church and state, nature, mentality, etc.) are discernible, but arranged rather associatively and in many cases accidentally. The word-list starts with entries on God, the universe, the weather (according to the four elements) (1^r–5^r), there then follow entries on man, the body, clothes, living conditions in houses, comestibles and beverages (5^r–17^r). A third batch of entries pertains to materials (stones and metals) and objects made from them (17^r–18^v). This is fairly traditional, though many deviations occur, for example a section on numbers (14^r–16^r). Between 16^r and 26^v we have a rather disorderly arrangement of entries on various topics, namely food (19^r and 19^v), school and teachers, crafts, medicine, spices (19^v–21^v), town and castle, ship, crafts (again), thieves and murderers (22^r–24^r), music (24^v), arms and what can be done with them (25^r), and finally hostel and butchery, including 'whore', pertaining to the personnel of a hostel (25^v–26^v). There then follow the adjectives together with the patterns of their comparisons, which have already been mentioned. The following sections are relatively systematic: on animals (quadrupeds, vermin and insects, including mice; birds, fish: 29^v–33^r), on trees and their fruits (33^r–34^v), on grain, wine, and other plants (35^r–35^v). The three following batches are devoted to three systems of society: the family (36^r–36^v), the church (36^v–37^v), and the state (37^v–38^r). They are followed by an enumeration of countries and their inhabitants (38^r–40^r). The following entries on a castle, a bridge, a village, a well, a lake, etc. (40^r–41^r) are difficult to bring together. Then clerical offices and divine service are taken up again (41^v–42^v), and also arms and soldierly life (42^v–43^r). There then follows a list of deadly sins and features of negative character (43^v), followed by the second batch of adjectives (44^r–45^v), which include colours. The next is the paradigm of personal pronouns (46^r–46^v). Between them and the list of verbs (in imperative, infinitive, and participle forms, beginning after another list of pronouns on 50^v) we find words pertaining to positive and negative mental states and actions following from them, and diverse other items (46^v–50^r), including parts of the body. Finally, there is the long list with verbs, and the dialogues.

All this shows that there is a clearly universalist tendency in the long word-list, but that the author had no philosophical ambitions whatsoever. He geared the vocabulary to the needs of his learners. As we do not know the exact conditions under which the book was used, whether it was an aid for the teacher and/or working material for his learners, whether there was one or there were many copies available in a class, how the teaching was done, etc. we may overlook important and compelling communicative constraints. Following the names of countries and towns, we find, for example, a chain of entries pertaining to: (i) Christians, heathens, and Jews; (ii) the sea and a town; and (iii) streets, markets, bridges, villages, fords. Why not see in them the vocabulary of a didactic teaching unit, perhaps a journey to France, England, and Flanders, all three names also occurring in this list? As it is very difficult to imagine the day-to-day practice of the teaching that went on, it is also difficult to recognize the semantic and pragmatic links that may be behind such a batch of entries.

Pausch (1972, 53–7) characterizes the linguistic register of the *Liber in volgaro* as fairly vulgar and appealing to a lower-class urban population. Although the selection of words clearly serves communicative ends which are dominated by commercial intentions, it seems justifiable to point out that the general (philosophical) ideas of ordering reality, which were current at the time and which are traditional in older glossaries, are not altogether absent here. They seem to hover in the background. Perhaps they were known to the author, but not deemed essential.

There is no meaningful order beyond two or three entries recognizable in the lists of adjectives and verbs. Opposites like 'healthy / sick', 'rotten / fresh', 'young / old', or like 'to eat / to drink', 'to be asleep / to be awake', 'to read / to write' regularly occur together. But there are no discernible links beyond them and between such groups.

9.3.2 Introito e porta

The book (BSB Inc. c. a. 106 4° Rotweil) does not have a title page in the usual sense. It starts immediately with this text:

qUESTO [!] LIBRO EL DUALE SILBI ama introito e porta de quele che voleno imparare e co[m]prender todescho a latino cioe taliano el quale che vadeno a pratichando per el mundo el sia todescho o taliano: . . . .

The corresponding German text reads:

dIs[es] puch haltet ine[n] den aler kosteleichisten vnd nŭ c zleichisten vund wer lernen wŏlt wăl hisch oder teutsch der findez an dise[n] puch ale di năm vnd wŏrter der ma[n] pedarf zu reden oder zu ne[n]nen ale creaturen di da sind in den vier elementen: . . . .

There is a reprint (1971), prefaced by A. Bart Rossebastiano and another one (1987), edited by V. R. Giustiniani. The book has 112 unnumbered pages (a–g[8]), each printed in two columns, the left-hand one containing the Italian lexemes, the right-hand one the German ones. The type is of course black letter. The colophon reads: *Compiuto Per meistro Adamo de Roduila. Volpracht Durch maister Adam von Rodueil. 1477 Adi .12. augusto.*

This Adam of Rotweil was identified as a German printer, Adam Rot, living in the Abbruzzi at a time when Italian–German trade connections led to the publication of various Italian–German travel books (Bart Rossebastiano, in Adam of Rotweil 1971). We do not know whether he was the author or only the printer and editor of *Introito e porta*, although he is usually regarded as being both.[29] He printed a few more books; in 1481, for example, a *Breviarium Romanum* by Antonio de Stanchis and Giacomo Britannico.

After the introductory text we find some remarks on the pronunciation of letters differing in their acoustical qualities in the two languages, which later found a place in all the derivatives of the book (see below), and then two separate overviews (the macrostructure) of the sections (chapters), first in Italian and then in German. (See Table A.16.)

There is a 'first book', although not indicated as such, with fifty-five sections,[30] called 'chapters', and 'another book' with nine. The section (chapter) titles in the two overviews and those heading the word-lists, where they are only in Italian, are in many cases not identical. Titles heading the word-lists are frequently shorter than those in the overview, German titles in the overview frequently follow the Italian titles heading the lists but just as often are independent of them. However, there are no deviations which would signify any semantic or otherwise important differences. Section eighteen is erroneously numbered '19' in the text without causing a numbering problem.

In the second book, the contents and their arrangement are somewhat confusing. Section (chapter) five, according to the overview, is missing, section six has no title of its own. There is an interposed title '*Dela speranza*' which appears nowhere else. Sections seven, eight, and nine are also headed by short titles, but are not numbered. Not in the overviews but in the book we finally find:

In questo quaderno truovamo de onge chose cio che ma[n]chachi non fosse schripto qui auanti. In disem quintern vint ma[n] noch allerlei was sunst mangelt im puch.

It is not easy to qualify these irregularities. Section nine, for example, is headed 'On the family' in Italian, 'On boys and girls' in German. The five entries in the section corroborate half of the German version, because they deal only with girls. It seems possible that the German overview was worked out after the book had been finished and that its author need not have been the same as the author of the word-lists and the Italian overview. Generally speaking, however, there is no doubt that the book had one author whose Italian way of thinking certainly dominated his German one. There are no surprising irregularities between the Italian lexemes and their translations. The Italian is Venetian, the German is Bavarian dialect.

In the first book, entries are fairly easy to count. Their microstructure is very simple. It consists of one lexeme each, in Italian and in German, mostly nouns, but also adjectives. In the majority of cases nouns are accompanied by definite articles. These word-lists cover seventy-six pages with some thirty entries (Italian and

---

[29] '*Se Rotwil fu, oltre che stampatore ed editore, anche autore dell'* Introito e porta, *non si sa.*' Bart Rossebastiano in Adam of Rotweil 1971, VII–VIII.

[30] 'Chapters' in *Introito e porta* are what have so far been called 'sections' as the unit of the macrostructure of onomasiological dictionaries. See Chapters 1 and, for example, 7.

German) each, which amounts to some 2,340 entries and lexemes in both languages.

The second book has predominantly adjectives in its first two sections, with occasional phrases like *Non me piaxe / Es gefelt mir nit; Me piaxe multoben / Es gefelt mir fast wol.* Section three changes into a series of adjectives with their comparative forms and expressions for varying degrees. Note:

Grando Groß;	*Ultra via über hin;*
Piu gra[n]do Noch grösser;	*Piczolo Clain;*
Multo grando Gar gross	*Wenor winczig;*
Massa grando ze gros;	*Suptil Dun; . . . .*
Ultra la mexura über di mas;	

Besides these adjectives, verbs often appear in the infinitive and participle, like 'make', 'made'; 'do', 'done', but sometimes also in other forms, like the first person singular affirmative or interrogative. Then there is a list of pronouns and prepositions, followed again by verbs in various forms. This list spills over into section four. The series of words pertaining to horses and riding is difficult to understand in this place and looks like an afterthought. The verbs appear occasionally in phrases, which sometimes even indicate a dialogue. Note, for example:

Che vole chomprar was welt ir kaufen;
E voraue chomprar qual che chosa per caxa Ich wolt gern kaufen etzwas für das
                                                                    haus.

As is obvious, entries are very irregular in this second book, but they are predominantly verbal and obviously geared to special situations. The following entries, for example, may be understood as set phrases in a conversation:

La veritade Di warhayt;	*Me par de si Ich man ia;*
El vero Es ist war;	*Ecredo de non Ich glaub nit;*
Accontradir widerreden;	*Ecredo de si Ich glaub ia;*
None vero Es ist nit war;	*Perche non warum nit; . . . .*
Me par de non Ich main nit;	

It is also difficult to understand why the lists of verbs and phrases are once more interrupted by a series of lexemes pertaining to cooking and dishes, and later by lexemes pertaining to sleep. Again the most likely explanation seems that they are an afterthought of the author, after he had almost finished his work.

The second book extends over thirty pages, again printed in two columns with some thirty entries, which makes a total of some 900 entries, but which, as indicated, do not correspond to as many lexemes. A rough count leads to the result that about 150 verbal lexemes are introduced and about fifty adjectival ones.[31] The other entries contain inflectional forms made out of these and phrases.

The governing principle of the second book is certainly not semantic, as is that of the first, but communicative and grammatical.

---

[31] Participles have been counted as verbs.

Naturally, the question as to the relation between the *Liber in volgaro* and *Introito e porta* arises. The two books are fifty-two years apart. It is difficult to judge whether the former's authority was so great that we can assume its being known to the author of the latter, although both originated in the same town. After all, the *Liber* was only a manuscript of which existed a very few copies, if there were indeed any more than we have today.

Judging from its contents, we can assume with some certainty that book two of *Introito e porta* depends on the relevant parts of the *Liber*. The grammatical treatment of adjectives and of verbs, the lists of pronouns, and the insertion of lexemes in phrases, which often appear as set phrases in dialogues, as, for example, before a court, are the same in the two books even if the lexemes and the phrases used differ. Whether this is to be accounted for by Adam of Rotweil's knowing the book of George of Nuremberg itself or whether there was a certain tradition which had established itself after his work in the intervening fifty years we cannot say.

In the preceding first book, that is, the strictly onomasiological part, however, any kind of direct dependence seems unlikely. The lexemes in *Introito e porta* that coincide with those in the *Liber* are such as would be listed in any topically arranged word-list at that time anyway and which do indeed appear in many later publications. They are the common stock of lexemes which, as names for proto-typical objects, form the natural store of words covering the classes of which the macrostructure of any onomasiological dictionary consisted. It may, therefore, be safe to say that *Introito e porta*, the great importance of which for the further development of onomasiological textbooks in the service of foreign-language teaching is an established fact, rests on a tradition which, according to our knowledge, was founded by the *Liber in volgaro* without being its direct successor.

George of Nuremberg, Adam of Rotweil, and Hans Rosenbach (1991) (also: Rosembach) who in 1502 adapted *Introito e porta* to Catalan, were authors of books in which two vernaculars were juxtaposed. This was extremely rare in the fifteenth century and indeed in the next two centuries, because, in spite of all the interest in living foreign languages, Latin would in most cases be the point of reference for learning them. Thus, the many derivatives of *Introito e porta* included Latin. It seems, therefore, appropriate to compare the early Italian–German version, the mother of all onomasiologically arranged textbooks and precursor of a long tradition of teaching and learning vernaculars, with the other tradition which was more interested in the teaching and learning of Latin. It was older than any other type of language teaching and was to run parallel to the new tradition which had established itself during the sixteenth and seventeenth centuries, and indeed to well beyond 1700. The comparison can be made with Johannes Murmellius's Latin–German dictionary of 1513, because it is a singularly perfect case of the Latin tradition.

In *Introito e porta* we discover almost all the sections of *Pappa*, but in a significantly different way. The topics of its macrostructure are not as clearly demarcated. Rather, they follow each other in an associative way. Most importantly, the sections on natural history, so important for and typical of *Pappa*, are missing.

The Italian–German vocabulary, just like the Latin–German one, starts with theological sections, which can be understood as a short philosophical part [1–5]. We even find lexemes for 'hell' and 'devil' here which the later vocabulary lacks. More importantly, a long list giving saints' names [2] and the text of the *Pater noster* [3] have been inserted. They give words and a text of an everyday and practical importance for travellers in a foreign Christian country.

There then follows a long sociological part [6–11] which has a somewhat blurred dividing line at its end. It is introduced by a subpart on the human body [6] which, in contrast to its treatment in *Pappa*, belongs neither to nature nor to the species of animals. This means *man* is introduced at a marked position but without any systematic context. The section includes some lexemes for human activities and clothes. This leads on to the second subpart with the names of patterns of societal order, namely the hierarchy of offices in the state and the family [7, 8; 10], associatively followed by a section on marriage and the family relationships that derive from it [11]. The short section 'On wenches' [9], consisting of '*di diern, das diernlen, das medlein*', and sandwiched between the others, may also have served some tacit practical purpose. The third subpart deals with what could be called practical life [12–18], significantly starting with a section on life in a town and, in particular, with reference to its law courts. There are many entries pertaining to audits and negotiations before the bar. They include a list of the paradigm of *to be*, which is indeed very important for such negotiations ('I am innocent', etc.). Here again we can assume a direct practical interest. The following sections deal with numbers and money [13–14], everyday commodities [15–16, 18], and craftsmen [17]. The last class is not embedded in a comprehensive concept of the strata of society as it is in *Pappa*. The fourth subpart of this second part of the dictionary [19–24] enumerates man-made objects, in particular household goods, dishes, tools, precious stones, and arms. Problems of demarcation start with section 25, which pertains to the world of villages and farmers. On the one hand, this is a new domain of societal reality. On the other, it is the beginning of a series of sections on plants and animals in the usual sequence [26–31], which here appear as the theatrical stage of rural life, not however as an inventory according to the principles of natural history.

The following sections are arranged rather arbitrarily, but probably with the clear purpose of enabling people to communicate in everyday situations. Sheer practical associations link the sections on fish, ships, and wind to each other [32–3]. All three are appropriate for a communication area along the coast. It is again sheer practical associations which motivate sections on countries, towns, and castles [35–6], mostly from Italy. Some odd topics follow, including 'sickness', [40] again of great practical interest when travelling in a foreign country. It is not until sections 41 to 46, also 50, that there is cohesion again in the vocabulary on churches, theological ideas (which formed the pedagogical part in *Pappa*), and schools. As though they had to be given a last chance, sections on the four elements are added, followed by ones on water and, now even, on fire [48–9]. At the very end we encounter vocabulary pertaining to buildings, from the palace to the barn [51–6].

It would not be too difficult to map the parts and subparts of the earlier *Introito e porta* and the later *Pappa* on to each other. Obvious overlaps would become visible which mark the common store of knowledge to be taken for granted at the time and which, viewed with the hindsight of the end of the twentieth century, show the contents of a continent-wide culture of the sixteenth century. The striking differences are of a typological significance. *Pappa* is more theoretical and objective in registering the items of reality in a certain schematic order. *Pappa* is a kind of museum in words. *Introito e porta*, however, answers practical needs. Obviously, the semantic cohesion of a dictionary as a textbook for learning a foreign language was thought less important *vis-à-vis* the practical problems of understanding in a foreign country. A particularly good proof of this is the added section [57] which deals with speech, followed by five more sections [58–60, 62–3] with routine speech-acts, before various other topics, like cooking and sleeping, are taken up. These sections are dominated by verbs and differ sharply from the preponderance of nouns in the preceding parts and subparts. This is consistent with the observation that, generally speaking, the German–Italian vocabulary lists many more verbs than the Latin–German vocabulary does. Concentration on nouns (including adjectives) is a striking feature of onomasiological dictionaries anyway. It seems even more significant of those vocabularies which present a philosophically guided world-view as was usual in Latin schools. Turning towards verbs shows more consideration for the concrete communicative needs of travellers in a foreign country. Within these two different approaches the contents of vocabularies, as constituted by the semantic dimension of word-lists, are largely identical.

9.4 The *Introito e porta* derivatives

Introito e porta is one of the few textbook families which governed the learning of vernaculars in Europe for many decades.[32] Although certainly designed for self-study, the various editions are most likely also to have been used in schools that were not connected to the Church or the universities with their aims of Humanist education. Other textbook families of similar extension and importance are the one called *Colloquia et Dictionariolum*, following the pattern originated by Noel de Berlaimont, and the various *Januae linguarum* propagated by Johannes Amos Comenius, his forerunners, and followers.[33] The historiographically most interesting feature of all these

---

[32] For the sequence of languages and the interdependencies of the various editions see Stein 1989a. For editions including English see also Alston 1974, vol. ii, nos. 1–23.

[33] See Chapters 4 and 10 respectively.

textbook families is what could be called their internationality, that is, the fact that they applied certain ideas about foreign-language learning in the same way to all the relevant languages of Europe. These common ideas centred more around lexis and communicative phrases than around grammar, which was a prerogative of teaching Latin in the classical way. Of course, there are also examples of vernaculars being taught with the help of elaborate grammatical descriptions, as the famous *Lesclarcissement* of 1530 (Palsgrave 1969) shows (Stein 1997). On the other hand, the communicatively orientated textbooks even included Latin without giving it the special status of a sacred or classical language. The onomasiological principles of organizing the lexis of various languages shows a far-reaching cultural unity of the Continent, in spite of its many linguistic boundaries.[34]

The *Introito e porta* derivatives are all very similar. The books are of a small size, so they can be carried around and consulted when necessary. They contain about 3,000 words, printed in parallel columns. This gives the simplest microstructure imaginable: the lexemes of four, five, six, seven, or eight languages are supposed to be translations of each other. The macrostructures of the various editions are identical. There are only some variations in the so-called 'second book'. As in *Introito e porta* there is no onomasiological order here in the strict sense, because this part is not lexeme centred but lists phrases in an order which often seems rather unconvincing.

The titles of the various editions are quite elaborate and show in their polyglot manner the wide areas where the books were supposed to be used (and sold). Their connection with the original author Adam of Rotweil was soon lost, in particular if the name of a later editor was mentioned. Note, for example, the title of this five-language edition:

Quinq[ue] linguaru[m] vtilissimus Vocabulista. Latine. Tusche. Gallice. Hyspanice. et Alemanice. Valde necessarius per mundum versari cupientibus. Noviter per Franciscum Baronum maxima diligentia in lucem elaboratus.—Vocabulista de le cinq[ue] le[n]gue. Cioe Lati[n]a Toscana. Fra[n]zosa. Spagnola. & Todesca.—Vocabulaire de cincq lengues. Latin. Italien. françoys. Spagnol. et Aleman.—Vocabulario de cinco lenguas. Latina. Italiana. Fra[n]cesa. Espagnola. & Alemana—Vocabular funfferley sprachenn. Latin. Wuellch. Franczosysch. Hyspanisch. vndt Deutzsch. Cu[m] privilegio.
[Colophon] *Impressum Veneijy Anno domini. 1533.*

These derivatives of the original *Introito e porta* were certainly better known as a type of book than by the name of their editor or even original author.

The 'Introduction', which appears in all editions, states the aims of this text-book. Note the German and French versions of the five-language edition mentioned above (WF 34. Gram 4°):

Dysen aller nutzlichste[n] vocabular zue lerne[n] lesen de[n] dye es bege[e]r sunder chule zugan als wyhant wercksleuth od weiber auh mag darinne lernen ein deutzscher latinn welsch

---

[34] See the elaborate stemmas in Bart 1984.

vnd fra[n]zois vnd eyn itlicher von yhn deutzsch de[n] in dise[m] buch sint behalten alle
name[n] vocabel u[n]d wort di ma[n] mag spreche[n] in ma[n]cherley hande.

Dies buech heisset einn pforth odder ein an weisu[n]g zu lernan deutzsch odder welch d[?] do
vast noth ist den die in viel lande handeln welle[n] sie sei deutzsch oder welsch aber es ist
etzlich [?] te scheidt yin A.b.c. vnd wer die nit weiß der kan nit wol wellisch lesend ye vindet
ma[n] hernach geschriben. als. wo du vindest ein a so ließ es nit vor ein a. sunder vor dise sill-
ben ae.

Ite[m] vo du vindest ein. u. vor einen laute[n] buchstaben so liß eß vor ein w. Item wo du
vindst ein. x. so liß es vor ein. s. vnn wo du vintst. ch. dz liß vor ein. lc. vnn vnn[!] wo dit
kumniet sch das ließ vor die sylben se.

Vres vtil vocabulaire / pour ceulx qui desirent apre[n]dre: sans aler a le scole / come artisans &
fem[m]es. En core le Fra[n]çoys / peult apre[n]dre Latin / Italien / Spagnol / & Aleman: Et
chascun deulx peult apre[n]dre fra[n]çoys: pour quoy en ce liure si se co[n]tienne[n]t tous les
noms vocables & paroules que on peult dire en plusieurs manieres.

Se liure se apele entree & porte de ceulx q[ue] veule[n]t apre[n]dre & apre[n]dre[!] Fra[n]çois
ou Italia[n]: le quel est de gra[n]t vtilite pour ceulx q[ue] vo[n]t praticant pour le mo[n]do /
ou soit fra[n]çoys Italia[n] Spagnol ou Alama[n]: q[ue] veult tres bien ente[n]dre &
co[m]pre[n]dre ces q[a]tre le[n]gages: il faut scauoir les differe[n]ces des l[et]res a.b.c. En ce
poit q[ue] trouvera [?]ssa dariere script en ce p[re]sent liure, La p[re]miere l[it]re de
differe[n]cce si est. c. le q[e]l lyras pour s. qua[n]tt si sera ala fin du mot: comme fosse
come[n]ce. Et [?]eillement ou tu troueras en françoys. ch. il fault pronu[n]cer per z. come
dimc[?]chen. d[?]mca. Et ou au milieu du mot sera s. no[n] la fault pronuncer: mes dire com
est elle ni [?]ut point. Come seroit a dire il est & qeilleme[n]t vosrtez; pour quoy fault
pnu[nc]er / il et r votre: r aussi aultre q[ue] no[n] fault pronu[n]cer. l. r ou sera. s. ala fin il
fault fere com[m]e est dit de c. non pronu[n]cer. verbi gr[?]a in casa delli todeschi ala maison
des alema[n]s cio aleman.[35]

This 'Introduction' stresses the usefulness of the book for people like craftsmen and women who would usually not attend a school but had to trade in foreign countries. Thus the *Vocabulista* were clearly set apart from the Latin vs. vernacular vocabularies which were geared to the needs of schools. Consequently, the envisaged users were not bookish people who lived in monasteries or at universities, but they were, of course, people able to read and to write. This simply shows how little alphabetization coincided with the acknowledged institutions of education and certainly with modern ideas about the so-called upper and lower strata of society.

We also find the idea that the word-lists can be read and used from left to right, or from right to left, or by column hopping. In the first paragraph, Spanish is

---

[35] 'This [is a] most useful vocabulary to learn how to read for those who want it without going to school as, for example, workmen or women. Also from it a German can learn Latin, Italian, and French, and each of them German. In this book there are all names, vocables, and words which one can speak in various ways. This book is called a gate or an instruction on how to learn German or what is necessary for those who want to trade in many countries, be it German or Italian. But there is a difference in the A.b.c. and whoever does not know this cannot read Italian correctly [in the way in which] you find it written later on. For example, where you find an a, do not read it as an a but as the syllable ae. Moreover, where you find a u in front of a letter [indicating] a vowel read it as w. Moreover, where you find an x, read it as s and where you find ch read it as lc, and where comes sch read this as the syllable se.' (My translation of the German version, W. H.)

forgotten in this respect, in the second only German and Italian are discussed, probably a trace left over from the original *Introito e porta* version in these two languages. Although the French version does not forget Spanish, it also concentrates on French and Italian. The remarks on differences of the phonetic qualities between German and Italian as well as between French and Italian letters show, as is to be expected, that the teaching of pronunciation (of which we know hardly anything) is strictly tied to spelling. Finding in this dictionary an early treatment of phonetic differences is a fact worth mentioning in itself.[36]

The following is a fairly detailed overview of the macrostructure of a six-language edition, confined to English headings and English entries. It shows the world incorporated into these textbooks with all its concepts and ideas, its objects and images, and proves in what way the onomasiological principle employed here appealed to the mental faculties of learners, in particular to their awareness of the natural conditions of communication. The edition is:

Sex Lingvarvm Latinae, Gallicae, Hispanicae, Italicae, Anglicae & Teutonicae, dilucidissimu[s] Dictionarium, mirum qvam vtile, ne dicam necessarium omnibus linguarum studiosis.
Omnia (optime Lector) bona fide recognita casti[!] *gataq[ue] deprehendes.*
Tigvri apvd Froschou. M. D. LXX.
(Wb 105.6 Gram. 8°.)

The small size of the book makes it very convenient for carrying around. There are no numbers for the 178 pages, which again contain between 2,700 and 3,000 entries. Three columns (Latin, French, Spanish) are printed on each left-hand page, three more columns (Italian, English, (Low) German) on each right-hand one. English and German are printed in Gothic, the other languages in italics. Sometimes there are run-on lines. Entries are one-to-one, without any explanations or synonyms. Typical entries look like the following:

DOmus	*Maison*	*CAsa*	*LA casa*	*A House*	*DAs hauß*
habitatio	*habitation*	*habitacion*	*le habitationi*	*a dwellynge*	*die wonung*
Cella	*chambre*	*camara*	*la camera*	*a chambre*	*die kammer*
Habitare	*demeurer*	*habitar*	*habitare*	*to dwell*	*wonen*
Vaporarium	*estune*	*estufa*	*la stufa*	*a whote house*	*die stub.*
(Chapter xx, 1–5.)					
Somnus	*somne*	*sueno*	*somno*	*slepe*	*der schlaaff*
Surgere	*se leuer*	*leuentar*	*leuare*	*to arise*	*aufston*
Ire dormitum	*aller coucher*	*yr a dormir*	*andar a dormire*	*to go to bed*	*schlaaffen gon*
Ientaculum	*desieuner*	*colation*	*la colatione*	*brekfast*	*ein morgen essen*
Prandium	*dtsner*(!)	*comer*	*il disinare*	*a dynner*	*ymbiß*
(Chapter xxi, 29–34.)					

---

[36] The first follow-up of *Introito e porta* to include French appeared in 1510 (see above). Systematic attempts to describe French pronunciation start in 1530 with Palsgrave's *Lesclarcissement* (Stein 1997, 67).

Apart from the first entries of each chapter, lexemes do not start with capitals. Sections often begin with a general term taken from the heading, followed by another similar lexeme, which is sometimes an adjective, sometimes a verb. Note, for example: '*warre—Krieg*', '*to fyght warre—kriegen*' (xxxviii), '*sycknesse— Kranckheit*', '*sycke—kranck*' (xl).

The following is a fairly detailed overview of the dictionary with some selected comments:

1. '*The first Chapter is of God / of the trinite / of power / and of richesses*'.
   Twenty entries, starting with '*God—Gott*', ending with '*idoles—goetzen*'. The holy Trinity, divine attributes, but also '*pouerte—armut*', '*a poore man—armer mensch*'. Few noun phrases and adjectives.

2. '*The ii. chapter is of the sai[n]ctes / and of their names*'.
   Sixty entries. First, '*holy—heilig*', etc., then '*Apostles—zwoelffboten*' and their names. Forty-two men's names; thereafter: '*Maydenheade—mag- thumb*', '*a mayden—maget*', and nine women's names; finally, '*a mayden— meytlin*'.

3. '*The iii. chapter of the Pater noster and Aue Maria*'.
   The two prayers appear on forty-four lines. The syntagmatic texts are broken down into as many speech units.

4. '*The iiii. chap. of the deuel / of hell and of purgatory*'.
   Eighteen entries with theological concepts, e.g. '*in the darknesse—im finstern*', '*chastened—gestrafft*', also '*death—todt*'. There are seven adjectives or participles in this section.

5. '*The v. chapter of tyme / yeare / moneth / weke / and daye*'.
   Eighty-eight entries, a very long section. The first one is, as so often, the keyword of the heading, followed by its adjectival form. In other cases the keyword is given in the singular and then in the plural. Here: '*Tyme—Die Zeyt*', '*temporall—zeytlich*'. First, eight entries of a general nature, among them '*in the beginninge of the worlde—im Anfang der Welt*'; then twenty- two entries for year, month, day, among them also '*Almanack—kalender*'; '*[y]mbringe dayes—die fronfasten*' is translated into the other languages as '*quatuor tempora*'. Following the four seasons, fifteen holy days in the order of the ecclesiastical year starting at Pentecost and ending at Easter. Among them '*shroftday—fastnacht*'. Then '*marriage-day*' and eighteen entries on workdays, including the days of the week, with special empha- sis on labour. Finally thirteen variations, such as,'*one dayes tour—tagreyst*', '*it must be done—es muß geschaehen*'. Generally speaking, the section is loaded with theological meanings. There are more adjectives, verbs, and temporal adverbs here than usual.

6. '*The vi. chapter of man / and of all the partes of him*'.
   With 129 entries this is quite a long, and this means an important, section. Eight lexemes with general meanings, then anatomy in the usual

sequence from head to foot. Eighty entries in all. Head, shoulder to arms and hands, then back to body, down from the shoulders, first front, then back. Stomach and kidneys as the only invisible organs between visible parts of the body. Finally seventeen entries pertaining to blood, organs, functions of the body. After the eighty entries on the human body another twenty-five pertaining to breathing, coughing, singing, etc., among them nine verbs. Finally fifteen entries pertaining to clothes, without any order.

7. 'The vii. chap. of the Emperor / and his pouwer'.
   Twenty-one entries giving titles and words used in courtly life.
8. 'The viii. chap. of the empresse and gentel women'.
   Five entries.
9. 'The ix. chap. of seruantes'.
   Eleven entries with general meanings like servant and maid, but also: 'a chylde—ein kind', 'chyldren—die kinder', 'a man chylde—ein maennlin', 'a woman chylde—ein wyblin'. This may signify an unusual societal position of children.
10. 'The x. chap. of grand father and of all the kynred'.
    Thirty-eight entries. Family relationships symmetrically from 'olde grand fater—Aene' through the generations. One entry 'a husbande—ein eemann', but nine entries pertaining to married women, including 'a vyrgine—junfrauw', 'a hande mayden—eerjungfrauw', 'a harlotte—ein hur'.
11. 'The xi. chap. of mariage'.
    Twenty-four entries: 'mariages—Hochzeyt', 'a brydegroome—der breutigam', 'a bryde—die braut', 'to mary—vermaechlen', 'a dowry—heim-steur', 'a widower—witling', 'a widowe—witwe'; four entries on in-laws; then 'good father—der geuatter', 'good mother—die geuatter', 'a mydwife—die hebamm', 'a nursse—die saugamm', 'to mary—heyraten / mannen', 'a babe—unredenkind', 'babes—kindlin', 'frendshippe—freündtschafft', 'mariage—die ee', 'patrimony—vaeterlich gut', 'natyue cuntrye—vatterland', 'a generacion—geschlecht', 'heretage—erbschafft'. This selection may give an impression of circumstances, developments, and concepts which were important in connection with marriage.
12. 'The xii. chap. of cities / iudges / and officers'.
    131 entries, among them twenty-two on citizens, streets, and gates in town; twenty-seven on prison, the death penalty, sentences in court, among them parts of a discussion before the court like 'i haue reason—ich hab recht', 'thou hast no reason—du hast unrecht', 'wherefore—warumb', 'there-fore—darumb'. Twenty-two entries are difficult to group together like 'commmountie—gemeinschafft', 'bynd these together—bind diß zusamen' (what?), 'merite—verdienst'. Thirty-six entries pertaining to merchandiz-ing, goods, utility, politeness, among them as many as nineteen verbs. They can be taken together with the previous group to form fifty-eight

mixed entries on everyday life in town. Finally twenty entries with conjugated forms of *to be* and some imperatives.

13. *'The xiii. chap. of symple and double noumbre'.*
    Eighty-nine entries with numerals, fourteen entries with measures and coins.

14. *'The xiiii. chap. of golde / sylver and of all other metalles'.*
    Fourteen entries: gold, silver, copper, tin, brass, iron, and objects made from these.

15. *'The xv. chap. of spyces'.*
    Twenty-six entries: spices, but also sugar, soap, cotton, figs, apple, silk.

16. *'The xvi. chap. of occupynge and marchandise'.*
    Thirty-six entries: useful objects; eight entries: cloths, mirror, containers.

17. *'The xvii. chap. of marchauntes and crafftes me[n]'.*
    Thirty-six entries on professions and crafts. A few objects in connection with them. Moreover: *'expositoure—tolmetsch'.*

18. *'The xviii. chap. of colours'.*
    Twelve entries.

19. *'The xix. chap. of housholde stuff and clothes'.*
    Twenty-five entries: besides *'houshold stuff—Haußrath'* only garments. First nineteen for men's clothes, then six for women's clothes.

20. *'The xx. chap. of house'.*
    A total of forty-seven entries for parts of a house, beds, containers to keep valuables in, rooms, tools, mostly for the kitchen. There is an odd sequence of six entries meaning 'break'.

21. *'The xxi. chap. of bread and wyne and other thynges to be eaten'.*
    Fifteen entries for basic food, twenty-two for eating, drinking, but also fasting. Eleven entries pertain to the chain of actions constituted by 'supper—sleeping—breakfast'.

22. *'Das xxii. chap. of craftes and their instruments'.*
    Sixty-two entries, among them five pertaining to 'smith', eleven to 'taylor', nine to 'cobbler', three to 'glue', eighteen to 'crossbowman', seven to 'carpenter', nine to 'mason'. There are also the beginnings of a dialogue: *'I haue hit the marke—ich hab das zyl getroffen', 'not i—ich nit'.*

23. *'The xxiii. chap. of precious stones'.*
    Twenty-one entries, among them thirteen on precious stones, then: *'leade—bley', 'an ymage—bild', 'the ymage of the virgyn Mary—das bild der jungfrouwen Maria', 'meel—mael', 'coddes—kleyen', 'grunsch, darve or past—teyg, pest', 'dregges—hepffen / truesen', 'to grende—malen'.* The last five entries on meals are obviously misplaced.

24. *'The xxiiii. chap. of wapens'.*
    Thirty entries on arms, but also warriors and hunters, plus fencers and jugglers.

25. *'The xxv. chap. of villages and of hussbande men'.*

Fourteen entries on tools in agriculture.

26. '*The. xxvi.* [!] *of the gardyn and all his frutes*'.

Seventy-three entries show the importance of this section. Among them are eighteen on vegetables, twenty-two on orchards, including fruit-trees, two various, eight on vineyards, twenty on fields and meadows. The cluster of 'orchard' has a meaningful arrangement, starting with '*hege—zaun*', '*a arccharde—baumgart*', followed by the names of trees which are inside the fence.

27. '*The xxvii. chap. of wood and of his appertenance*'.

Twenty-three entries, among them: four general, nineteen names for trees.

28. '*The xxviii. chap. of beàstes*'.

Twenty entries.

29. '*The xxix. chap. of wormes*'.

Fifty-one entries, among them domestic animals and poultry.

30. '*The xxx. chap. of byrdes and of thier kyndes*'.

Forty-one entries, among them six general (wing, quill, etc.), nineteen kinds of birds, including 'bat', eight kinds of poultry, including 'pigeon', four other kinds of birds, including birds of prey, and four general (feather, tail, etc.).

31. '*The xxxi. chap. of fishes*'.

Fifteen entries, among them five general, including angling, then ten kinds of fish, including whale and dolphin.

32. '*The xxxii. chap. of shippes and nauies*'.

Eight entries on parts of a ship. Then: '*in the grounde—am boden*', '*in the lod gynge*[!]—*in der herberg*', '*in the house—im hauß*'. These may be read as three entries pertaining to the end of a sea journey.

33. '*The xxxiii. chap. of the ayer and wyndes*'.

Twenty entries on the weather.

34. '*The xxxiiii. chap. of hylles and valleys*'.

Thirteen entries on geographical phenomena. Last entry: '*earth quake—erdbidem*'.

35. '*The xxxv. chap. of countreys*'.

Twenty-two names of countries in Europe, also regional names from Germany. No Spanish version. Moreover: '*ethiopia—moren land*' and Greece.

36. '*The xxxvi. chap. of cities*'.

Fourteen entries with names of towns: Rome, Sienna, Florence, Bologna, Ferrara, Venice, Mantua, Milan, Naples, Constantinople, Basle, Cologne, Bruges, Paris. The first ten still show the horizon of Venice as the first place of publication of this type of textbook, the others name four towns on the western Continent famous for their printing trade.

37. '*The xxxvii. chap. of christendome and the infideles*'.

Eight entries: Christians and heathens, including Jews and Turks; three entries: heretics, apostates, sodomites. The attitude of the author or his predecessors here appears (in modern terms) rather liberal.

38. *'The xxxviii. chap. of warres / batayles and players'.*
Twenty-nine entries, among them twelve on war and peace, seven on thieves, etc., three on witches and whores, four on stealing and gambling, and four utterances from conversations: '*i haue lost x. gyldens in playenge—ich hab verloren x. floren mit spilen*', '*thou sayest troute but so is it not done—du sagst die warheit. es ist aber nit geschehen*'.

39. *'The xxxix. chap. of mynstreles and musyciens'.*
Twelve entries on instruments, dice, cards, etc.

40. *'The xl. chap. of weaknesses and syckenesses'.*
Thirty-seven entries, among them twelve on diseases and their symptoms, nine on phenomena like blindness or baldness, seven on extreme behaviour like trembling and dying, eight on healing and helping.

41. *'The xli. chap. of the seuen deadly synnes'.*
Eight entries.

42. *'The xlii. chap. of the fiue wyttes'.*
Six entries, all verbs.

43. *'The xliii. chap. of the seuen workes of mercy'.*
Eight entries given as infinitive plus noun phrase, for example, '*To lodge the straungers—die froembden beherbergen*'.

44. *'The xliiii. of the x co[m]mandementes'.*
Twelve entries in the biblical form.

45. *'The xlv. chap. of study and of schole'.*
Twenty-one entries, among them three on studying and schools, three on doctor and pupils, six on writing. Then: '*priyuilege—freyheit*', '*the seuen scyences—die siben künst*', '*temporall lawe—das weltlich recht*', '*spirituall lawe—das geistlich recht*', '*the holy scripture—die heilig gschrifft*', '*physicke—die natuerlich kunst*', '*to teache—underweysen*', '*to learne—lernen*', '*he can the bookes well—er kan die buecher wol*'.

46. *'The xlvi. chap. of the offyce of churche'.*
Fifty-one entries, among them thirteen nouns denoting ecclesiastical offices and four adjectives denoting piety, etc.; moreover expressions like '*he kepeth the catolycke faythe—er hat ein rechten glauben*', '*he is a good christen man—er ist ein guter christ*'. Twenty-five entries give names for objects in churches and monasteries as needed for a Catholic service (e.g. '*sensors—rauchfaß*', '*hoste—die hosty*'), four verbs on praying, weeping, etc., and two odd entries. Occasionally we find articles in front of these lexemes, German as well as English, but there is obviously no system behind this.

47. *'The xlvii. chap. is of water and licoure'.*
Thirty entries on all occurrences of water, including snow; also river names (Rhine, Danube).

48. *'The xlviii. chap. of fyre and heate'*.
    Twenty-four entries on fire, sky, weather, also angels, among them eight verbs on burning, etc.
49. *'The xlix. chap. of obedyence'*.
    Nineteen entries on good and evil. Almost equal numbers of nouns, adjectives and phrases. It is difficult to establish coherence between them. Some phrases read as if spoken in a confession: *'thou sayst trouth—du sagst waar'*, *'my faut—mein schuld'*, *'my de ter*[!]*—mein schuldner'*, *'conscynce—das gewissen'*, *'he hath a good conscynce—diser hat ein gut gewissen'*.
50. *'The l. chap. of madde folcke'*.
    Six entries on foolishness, etc., among them four adjectives.
51. *'The li. chap. of palaces'*.
    Five entries on palaces and houses. The section looks odd.
52. *'The lii. chap. of the cellar wyth that perteineth tothem* [!]*'*.
    Thirteen entries on basements, drinks, hostels.
53. *'The liii. chap. of the kytchen'*.
    Fifteen entries on kitchen, utensils for cooking.
54. *'The liiii, chap. of the chambre'*.
    Nine entries, all on spinning.
55. *'The lv. chap. of the barne and corne'*.
    Ten entries on grain.

The preceding sections were not mentioned as belonging to a *'liber primus'*, but there now follows: *'Liber Secvndvs, de nominibus & verbis, secundum eorum significationes'*.

1. *'The i. chap. of wordes'*.
   126 verbs in the infinitive and forty participles without recognizable cohesion. Only immediately succeeding entries belong together, such as, *'to see—sehen'*, *'to heare—hoeren'*, *'to hope—hoffen'*, *'to despayre—verzweyf-flen'*, *'to laugh—lachen'*, *'to wepe—weinen'*, *'to slepe—schlaaffen'*, *'to dreame—traumen'*, *'to watche—wachen'*.
2. *'The ii. chap. of names'*.
   Forty-eight entries, a little more coherent than in the previous chapter. There are larger patches of loose cohesion. After two general entries there follow twenty-five pertaining to speech-acts, astonishingly followed by twenty-five pertaining to horses and stables. The ones after them have no recognizable order.
3. *'The iii. chap. is of adiectyues pronomes and aduerbies'*.
   118 entries without semantic order, as above. After forty-six adjectives there follow more grammatical entries: inflected pronouns, interrogative pronouns, adverbs of place, prepositions. In between, adjectives again, without recognizable order.
4. *'The iiii. chap. of speches'*.

Syntagmatic phrases with recurring elements taken from conversations. Sometimes in a dialogue, but without a chain of arguments. Extending over twenty-two pages. With an average of eighteen entries per page this amounts to a total of about 390 entries. Examples:

do after my minde—thu nach meinem sinne, i will not, ich wil nit, wherefore wilt thou not?—warumb wilt du nit? it pleaseth me not—es gefalt mir nit, it pleaseth me wel—es gefalt mir wol.

9.5 Nomenclators in the spirit of Humanism

9.5.1 Aristotelians

Nomenclator is predominantly the name of topical glossaries which were collected in the spirit of Humanism. The name started to be used in the late sixteenth century and became popular in the seventeenth. Nomenclators had a strong bias towards the classical languages, although they also listed one or even two and occasionally many more vernaculars. In this case the classical languages, however, were the leading ones. Nomenclators were based on a strict and precise systematization and did not arrange vocabulary according to the presumed necessities of everyday communication. It is the strict method of arrangement, the scholarly character of the macrostructure, which gives the nomenclator its Humanist tinge.

They are of at least two kinds. The first served foreign-language teaching in very much the same way as the other topical dictionaries do, primarily the teaching of Latin or Greek, but also of vernaculars. They take very seriously the importance for language teaching of semantic cohesion, and realize it in their own way. In function, they are didactic nomenclators, and it is sometimes difficult to draw a clear line between them and onomasiological dictionaries.

The second kind has a broader spectrum of functions. It arranges lexemes in such a way that a system of knowledge comes into being which can be used to find the words one knows but cannot remember, which can help to distinguish between synonyms and, thus, improve the stylistic quality of language use and which, moreover, teach people to think logically in thematic frames. These nomenclators also have their place in foreign-language teaching and learning, as a rule on a higher academic level than the others. But they are also useful for general education, including one's own language. Although they mostly appear in a classical and at least one vernacular language, they serve their purpose, too, when monolingual. In a broad understanding of the term, this purpose can be said to be rhetorical.

What follows is an analysis of two influential nomenclators whose macrostructure is clearly marked as scientific in the Humanist sense by their proximity to Aristotelian categories. The subtlety of their semantic order surpasses that of other dictionaries. This is why they were selected for analysis.

FRISCHLIN'S *NOMENCLATOR TRILINGUIS*

Nicodemi Frischlini Nomenclator Trilinguis, Graecolatinogermanicus, Continens omnium rerum, quae in probatis omnium doctrinarum auctoribus inueniuntur, appellationes: quarum aliquot millia nusquam sunt obuia.
Opvs Nova Qvadam Methodo, Secvndvm Cathegorias Aristotelis, non sine labore maximo concinnatum. Et Qvarto Iam, Nova Vocabvlorvm Germanicorvm Hisce In Regionibus vsi tatotum accessione, te cognitum, atqua a mendis omnibus diligentissime repurgatum.
Cum Gratia & Pruilegio Caesareae Maiestatis.
Francofvrti Ad Moenvm, Excudebat Wolffgangus Richter, Impensis Ioannis Spiessij. ANNO M. DC.
(WF 53.4 Gram. 8°.)

The book consists of an *Epistola Dedicatoria* (nineteen pages), an *Epistola*, etc. (four pages), the index (seven pages), all of them without page numbers. There then follow 466 pages of the dictionary with twenty-five entries per page on average, amounting to a total of about 11,650 entries. They are not printed in columns but in run-on lines: first the Greek lemma, then the Latin, and then the German translation. Occasionally there are two or even more synonyms given. The printing is in Greek, Roman, and Gothic type. The absence of columns prevents the dictionary from being read other than from left to right. This gives the Greek lemma its marked position. Each entry consists of an article which complements this lemma. The index with its 178 headings is very elaborate. It even contains cross-references, for example in Caput LXXXV: 'De numeris . . .: *Nomina substantiua temporum, quae hinc formantur, habes suo loco.*' (195.) Sometimes we find references to sources, for example in Caput XX: '*De arboribus sylvestribus*': *Ex lib. 1. Dioscorid.*' (57.) Furthermore, we find cross-references from one section to other sections, combined with advice on how to use the book, as for example in Caput XXIII: '*Reliqua repete ex cap. 122. de Vinitoribus.*' (66) or in Caput CXXII: '*Repete huc cap. 23 de Vite*' (267).

The index and the headings in the dictionary are not always identical, although they have the same meaning. Note, for example, Caput XXXVII: Index: '*De Volucribus aeris minoribus*', but in the dictionary: '*De avibus minoribus*' (99). Sometimes the German translations are missing. There are also errors in the page numbers.

Frischlin's dictionary is of almost monumental size. Its first edition appeared in 1586. Its Humanist spirit shows in the reference to Aristotelian categories, in the philologically accurate cross-referencing, and in the minute and strict systematization, which is faultless and supersedes that of most other similar works (Müller 2001, 379–84, 423–27). For a full overview of its macrostructure see Table A.17.

The list of 178 headings is imposing proof of the author's all-embracing concept of world order. Aristotelian categories, which are mentioned in the title, do not emerge overtly in the dictionary as they do in other dictionaries (see below). Rather, they surface in the order, that is, the macrostructure of the dictionary, itself. The following overview reveals the structure of this otherwise irritating order:

A	God (1)
B	nature (2–65)
B 1	universe, nature, space, time, elements (2–12)
B 2	kingdoms of nature (13–65)
B 21	inanimate: metals, stones (13–14)
B 22	organic: plants (15–32)
B 23	animate: animals (33–65)
C	man (66–178)
C 1	rationality (66–76)
C 11	philosophical (66)
C 12	sex, age, affections (67–8)
C 13	virtues, mainly justice, and vices (69–76)
C 2	world of men: knowledge and labour (77–147)
C 21	learning (77–91)
C 22	ailments (92–106)
C 23	pictures, colours (107)
C 24	crafts (108–47)
C 3	world of men: society (148–78)
C 31	houses (148–50)
C 32	family (151–4)
C 33	towns, countries (155–6)
C 34	church (157–9)
C 35	justice, state (160–9)
C 36	war, peace (170–6)
C 37	play (177)
C 38	death (178)

It is the usual hierarchy of the universe, of nature and of society, as is to be found in many older glossaries and dictionaries, expressive of the general philosophical thought of the time and which originated from the classical cosmogony, including Aristotle. The leading concepts of the relevant philosophical tradition are in some cases introduced in sections of their own which, thus, provide an ordering function for other sections.

Section 16, for example, with its sixty-eight entries, consists of a long list of lexemes pertaining to dishes, drinks, feeding, digestion, liquids of the body, diseases. Among them are entries like '*cholericus*' and '*phlegmaticus*' which belong to the context of the dominant Galenic medical theory. Otherwise the entries are only loosely clustered. In a very similar way, sections 16 to 59 present the whole concrete world of nature with all its genera and species. But the preceding section (15) had already presented the framework of the philosophical concepts in which the entries of section 16 and the following ones find their proper, systematic, places. Section 15 has twenty-seven entries, of which ten pertain to life, the soul, age. There then follow (Latin versions only): '*anima nutriens, anima sentiens, facultas mouens, intellectus, ratio*', and other, very similar ones. The next section (16), but also section 34, use the general terms mentioned and translated in section 15 ('*facultate nutritiua et generatiua, facultate motiua*') as headings under which many relevant concrete items are collected. Moreover, sections 15 and 33 list the general terms which mark the hierarchy of objects and animals in the world: 15, '*planta, arbor, frutex, herba, animal, homo*'; 33: '*animal, fera, auis, volucris, piscis, serpens, vermis, insectum, animal quadrupes, homo*'. Later on, all these entries are used as headings of sections in the dictionary without any further explanation.

Of similar interest is section 66, '*De Anima RATIONALI, & de Homine*'. Its spelling with capitals, unique to the dictionary, obviously indicates its importance. This justifies a full quotation (Latin and German versions only):

	Intelligentia—Verstand
Mens, Intellectus—Gemuet	*Animus—Sinn*
Animulus—Sinnlin	*Virtus—Tugend*
Animosus—Sinreich	*Scientia—Wissenheit*
Ratio—Vernunfft	*Sciens—Wissenhafft / wissend*
Rationalis—Vernuenfftig	*Sapientia—Weißheit*
Orati, Sermo—Red	*Sapiens—Weiß*
Verbulum—Woertlein	*Prudentia—Fuersichtigkeit*
Cogitatio—Gedancken	*Prudens—Fuersichtig*
Consideratio—Bedencken	*Consilium—Raht*
Ratiocinatio—Außrechnung	*Sententia—Meynung*
Recordatio—Das	*Cognitio—Erkaenntnuß*
Hindergedencken	*Iudicium—Urtheil*
Conceptus animi—Das	*Experientia—Erfahrung*
besinnen / Nachdencken	*Ars—Kunst*
Voluntas—Will	*Homo—Mensch*
Institutum, Propositum—Das	*Homunculus, Homuncio—*
Fuernemmen	*Menschlin*
Alacritas, Studium—	*Humanus—Menschlich*
Frewdigkeit	*Corpus—Leib*
Affectio—Mut / Anmutung	*Anima—Seel*

By giving the names of the faculties of the human soul and the traditional doctrine of cardinal virtues, these terms pave the terminological way for the next ten sections.

Finally, we find that the sections on crafts, which are full of concretely denoting lexemes, are time and again interrupted by sections with entries on a more general level. Note, for example, section 116 for metal, 118 for food, 136 for garments, and 144 for wood and other materials. Something similar is to be found in section 150 for houses.

Nicodemus Frischlin's *Nomenclator* is certainly indicative of the erudition of its author and of the encyclopaedic and systematic thought of the Humanists in general. At the same time, the dictionary was certainly constructed with didactic purposes in mind. The author (1547–90) was a popular, if unfortunate philologist and Latin teacher of the time. He was best known for his Latin verse and plays, which brought him praise and much trouble. Later historiography saw his real merits in his Latin textbooks, which he had to write in order to make a living after he had been dismissed from the faculty at Tübingen. Among them, his *Grammatica latina* (1585) and his *Nomenclator trilinguis* (1586) are the most outstanding. It was obviously the opinion of this erudite man that all the achievements of Humanist philology had to go into the making of textbooks and, thus, into the teaching of classical languages.

DICTIONARIUM LATINO-GERMANICUM

Dictionarium Latino-Germanicum Omnivm Qvotquot Vbivis In Qvacvnqve facultate, tam liberali quam mechanica, vsurpantur nominum atque formularum. Non Pverorvm Dvntaxar, Sed & studiosorum utilitati seruire iussum. Ex Nomenclatore Iuniano methodice compendioseque digestum.
Ordentliche Verzeichnuß und Außlegung aller und jeder Woerter / wie dieselbige so wol bey den Gelehrten / un[d] in den Schulen / als auch bey jedem Gewerb und Handthierung in ublichem Brauch geredt und außgesprochen werden / Teutsch und Lateinisch.
Francofvrti, Apud Egenolphum Emmelium. M. DC. X.
(WF 87 Gram. 4°.)

No author is mentioned, but in fact it is a re-edition of Matthaeus Bader's adaptation of Junius's *Nomenclator* (see below) for teaching purposes (1598) (Müller 2001, 363–70). The book has 632 numbered pages with twenty-two entries each on average, amounting to a total of almost 14,000 entries. This means the nomenclator is of monumental size. The printing is in Roman type and in very bold Gothic. The microstructure is complex. As a rule, entries consist of one Latin lemma and its German translation. The overviews which introduce books (i) and (ii) do not always coincide with the headings in the dictionary.

The most striking feature of this nomenclator is its macrostructure according to Aristotelian categories. Frischlin made these categories a covert ordering system for the contents of his onomasiological dictionary. They now appear on the surface and are used as the schematic headings that divide the whole book into its sections. This makes the classical Aristotelian categories the main heads of this dictionary: *substance* (*liber primum*), *accidence*, namely *quantity, quality, relation, action* and *passion, where, when, situation, habit* (*liber secundum*). The mass of experience which is reported in this, as in any, onomasiological dictionary, is not only guided by some philosophical principle in the background, but openly subjected to a system of philosophical categories. Although we must always remember that dictionaries are collections of words and not philosophical tracts, a macrostructure like this moves any dictionary in the direction of a philosophically organized *summa* filled with the numerous items of an encyclopaedia.

This impression is even heightened by the fact that, in this nomenclator, categories are introduced by a Latin definition and that sections, that is, semantically related clusters of lexemes, begin with a general definition. There is one exception to this. There is no definition of 'substance' in general, but one of 'God': '*qvi omnium bonorum autor est, & nulli subest praedicamento*', followed by definitions of the most general lexemes of sections devoted to *substantia*. Note the following examples:

In the first book '*On substance*':
Sydera seu asterismi [as a subsection of '*Substantia corporea simplex*']: '*Asterismus est firmamento constellatio quedam, representans formam alcuius animalis, vel figuram alterius rei.*' (8.)
De arboribus & fructibus [as a subsection of '*Substantiae corporeae mixtae*']: '*Arbor est planta stipite nascens, in iustam altitudinem, constans ramis, folijs, trunco seu stipite, & quadoq[ue]. fructu.*' (91.)
In the second book '*On accidence*':
Quantitas: '*Quantitas adiacens est creaturae, quo distinguitur ab alijs, magnitudine & numero. Magnitudinis autem species 3. sunt, Linea, Superficies, Corpus.*' (266.)
Qualitas: '*Qualitas comprehendit ea, quae rebus insunt vel adiacent. Insunt autem vel naturaliter, vel fortuito, vel arte introducuntur.*' (310.)
Relatio: '*Relationum tres sunt classes, Ordinationes, Collationes, Applicationes. Ordinatio complectitur omnes functiones & munera publica, itemq[ue] personas.*' (360.)
Actio: '*Actio est applicatio agentis ad patiens: qua fit mutatio aliqua in patiente. Omnes autem actiones, vel sunt DEI. Eaeq[ue] vel internae vel externae. Vel sunt Creaturarum. Creaturarum, vel sunt spirituales, vel corporales. Corporae actiones, vel sunt naturales, vel voluntariae, vel violentae. Naturales porro vel sunt inanimatarum, ve animatarum. Voluntariae vel mentis sunt, vel voluntatis. Vtraeq[ue] vel sunt Politicae, vel Ecclesiasticae, vel Oeconomicae.*' (434.)
ubi: '*Praedicamentum ubi, Indicatio loci in quo res aliqua sit vel contineatur. Id autem triplici modo contingit. Vel Repletiue, ut DEUS. Vel definitiue, ut Essentia Spiritualis creata. Circumscriptiue, ut omnia corpora naturalia. Loca autem vel sunt Naturalia: vel fortuita: vel mixta.*' (535–6.)
Quando: '*Tempus est nummeratio alicuius motus: secundum prius & posterius. Et sumitur vel Absolute, qua[n]do significat duratione[m]: ac tum proprie ad prima[m] Quantitatis speciem est referendum: Vel Relatue, cum significat rem, quae est vel fit in tempore. Itaq[ue] vel est Infinitum, ut aeternitas, Ewigkeit / carens initio & fine, vel Finitum. Finitum vel est Naturale, vel Voluntarium.*' (596.)
Situs: '*Omnis Situs vel est Naturalis, vel voluntarius, vel fortuitus. Naturalis, quem DEUS unicuiq[ue] corpori attribuit, ut: Terrena ad terram tendunt: Aera aeri, Ignea, igni, Aetherea, aetheri, se consociant. Voluntarius, cum pro arbitrio animantis mutatur Situs, ut Statio, seßio. Mixtus, partim naturalis, partim voluntrius. Hic rursus duplex est: Fortuitus, ut: Situs urbium, aedificiorum, columnarum, &. Casualis, qui praeter naturam fit: ut ruina aedificij, Terra motus.*' (606.)
Habitus: '*Decimum & postremum praedicamentum ab Aristotele to echein* [Greek letters] *inscribitur. Et est . . . : Substantiae circa substantiam posito. Pertinent igitur ad hanc classem: Omnia vestitus genera, quaeq[ue] instructum, ornatum & tegumentum significant.*' (614.)[37]

---

[37] '*Stars or* [the world of] *stars*: [The world of] stars is a certain constellation in the sky representing the form of some animal or the figure of [some] higher thing.
  On *trees and fruits*: A tree is a plant growing with a trunk, in proper height, with firm branches and leaves, stem or trunk, and sometimes with fruit.

These defining texts provide a skeletal conceptual system for the macrostructure[38] of the dictionary. (See Table A.18.) Its first book is not very much different from the others, except that it is more exhaustive and more subtly differentiated. The categories which in other glossaries and dictionaries are covert are turned outside and made overt. This is quite different in its second book. In particular verbs and adverbs, which had so far almost regularly been neglected, now find a proper place. The mental faculties of men, their actions and passions, are allocated new places in the macrostructure, or appear here for the first time. Place and time lead to some repetitions of lexemes. In particular, '*praedicamentum situ*' is rather problematic. This part looks unfinished; many entries are only in Latin.

An onomasiological dictionary can certainly not go much further without losing its character as a dictionary and taking on that of an encyclopaedia or *summa*. Later encyclopaedias and natural histories like those by Konrad Gesner and John Jonston did take this step.

Quantity: Quantity belongs to a creature [and] it is distinguished by it from others by size and number. There are, however, three kinds of size: line, surface, and body.

Quality: Quality embraces what is in things or [goes] with them. Inside, however, it is either natural or by chance, or [it] is artificially put inside.

Relation: There are three classes of relations: appointments, engagements, and inclinations. "Appointment" embraces all functions and public offices, and also persons.

Action: Action is an active engagement to [something] passive: which effects a change in [something] passive. But all actions are either of God. And they are either internal or external. Or they are of creatures. Creatures are either spiritual or corporeal. Corporeal actions are either natural, or by the will, or by violence. Moreover, the natural [actions] are either of inanimate or of animate [creatures]. The [actions] by the will are either mental or by the will. And both are political or ecclesiastical or economic.

Where: The category where should be the indication of the place in which something is [located] or contained. This, however, exists in three modes. Either complete like God. Or defined [= delimited] like created spiritual essences [= angels]. [Or] bounded like all natural bodies. Places, however, are either natural, or accidental, or mixed.

When: Time is the counting of some motion: according to prior and posterior. And it is assumed [to be] either absolute when it signifies duration, and then it is rightly referred to the first species of quantity [= God]: or [it is assumed to be] relative when it signifies the thing which is or is to be made in time. Therefore it is either infinite, like eternity . . . , without beginning or ending, or finite. Finite [time] is either natural or from the will.

Position: All position is either natural or from the will or accidental. [It is] natural [to anything] which God attributes to one and the same body, like: terrestial [things] tend towards the earth: aerial [things] consociate with air, fiery [ones] with fire, ethereal with ether. [It is position] from the will when it [= position] is changed for the judgement of [somebody] animate, like standing, [or] sitting. [Position] mixed is partly natural, partly from the will. This is again twofold: accidental like the site of towns, buildings, [and] columns, and casual which may happen outside nature like the ruins of a building [and an] earthquake.

Manner: The tenth and last category from Aristotle is inscribed to echein [Greek letters]. And it is [performed with the help of] arranging substances around a substance. Therefore they pertain to the following classes: all kinds of clothes and which serve as equipment, decoration, and protection.' (My translation, W. H.)

[38] The overview does not follow the headings and subheadings of the dictionary literally, because the way in which they are printed is rather irritating. The lines written flush with the left-hand margin are in fact my own, whereas the indented lines coincide with sections of the dictionary. However, I use only such lexemes as occur in the dictionary.

9.5.2 *Hadrianus Junius's* Nomenclator *(1567) and its English adaptation*

THE *NOMENCLATOR*

Nomenclator, Omnium Rerum Propria Nomina Variis Linguis Explicata Indicans: Multo quàm antea emendatione ac locupletior: Hadriano Iunio Medico Auctore. Antwerpiae, Ex officina Christophori Plantini, Architypographi Regij. M.D.LXXVII.
Colophon: *Antverpiae Excudebat Christ. PLantinvs Architypographvs Regivs, Decimo Kalend. Septembris, Anno M.D.LXXVII*
(PC. 8°.)

The book appeared in 1567 and went into many editions, such as the one in 1577 (see Alston, vol. ii, II, nos. 70–80); in fact, it was perhaps the most successful and widely acknowledged nomenclator published in the sixteenth century. At the same time, it was probably the most erudite book of its kind, enriching the headwords and their translations with quite elaborate explanations. This is why simplified editions for use in schools appeared later. Junius's *Nomenclator* was translated into even more than its original nine languages, for example into Czech by Daniel Adam of Weleslavin (1598),[39] and its derivatives served as sources for more derivatives. Matthias Schenckius in his adaptation *Nomenclator Hadriani Junii Medici clarissimi accomodatus ad usum scholarum* (Augsburg 1571), for example, made use of Adam Siber's *Nomenclatoris Hadriani Junii Medici Epitome* of (Leipzig) 1570,[40] and may have used Siber's adaptation again for his editions of 1573 and later. Moreover, Adam Siber was used by Theophilus Golius in the *Onomasticon Latinogermanicum, in usum scholae Argentoratensis collectum* (Strasbourg, 1579, see Claes 1982, Müller 2001, 349–70).

The author, (H)Adrianus Junius (Adriaen de Jonghe, 1511–75), was called the most learned Dutchman after Erasmus. This pertained not only to his activities as a doctor of medicine, a degree which he obtained in Bologna—the most famous faculty of medicine at that time—but to classical learning in general. He travelled widely in Europe, spent about ten years in England as the personal physician of the Duke of Norfolk, and later lived in Haarlem and Middelberg. In 1548 he had already published a *Lexicon Graeco-Latinum*, before his multilingual nomenclator came out in 1567 (Loonen 1991, 91).

The entries of this nomenclator have a highly complex microstructure. They consist of a Latin lemma and Greek, 'Allemannisch' (i.e. High German), 'Belgian' (i.e. Flemish), French, Gaelic, Italian, Spanish, and English translations. Not all of these languages are present in each entry. In particular English is frequently missing in the early editions. Entries vary enormously in length, depending on whether and in which languages they give translations and additional explanations. Moreover, references to the classical sources of the Latin words, varying

---

[39] See Chapter 10, 368–71.
[40] For the selection of and the changes to Junius's vocabulary by Siber see Ludin 1898.

considerably in length, take up space. Two columns are printed on each page. The Latin lemma is printed in Roman type, Latin explanations and references in italicized type. German and 'Belgick' are printed in Gothic, all other languages again in Roman type. The lemma, the first line of each entry, is printed flush with the left-hand margin, all the following lines are indented, but run on within their entry. Languages, except for Latin and Greek, are indicated by capital letters, thus 'AL.' for 'Alemanice', 'G.' for 'Gallice', 'B.' for 'Belgice', 'IT.' for "Italice" etc. Typical entries, of the shorter size, read thus:

ECCLESIA est coetus Christi fidelium, ecclesia [Greek letters]. *AL. Ein versamlung der Christen. B. Een vergaderinge von Christenen / een Christelijke ghemeynte. G. Vne assemblee, esglise. IT. La chiesa. H. Yglesia.* (220.)

Calendae. Horat. Primus cuiusque mensis dies, a calendo, id est vocando, quod tunc Senatus conuocaretur; vel quod tunc debitares calarentur per praecones ad dissoluenda nomina. kalendai [Greek letters] *Plutarc. AL. Der erst tag eins ietlichen monats. B. Den eersten dach des maents. G. Le premier iour d'vn chascun mois. IT. Il primo giorno del mese. H. El primero dia de qualquiet mes.* (259.)

After the title page and the royal warrant, there are listed the authors from whom the explanations of the lemmata in the dictionary were taken. The majority are classical authors, with relatively few patristic theologians.

The main body of the dictionary comprises 432 pages containing classified entries broken down into a '*tomus prior*', a '*tomus posterior*', and an appendix. The first '*tomus*' consists of fifty-nine sections (according to an overview at the end; the dictionary itself has six additional subtitles, but two that are listed are missing), and the second '*tomus*' has twenty-six sections. The appendix has twelve sections with proper names in alphabetical order. The number of entries per column varies between four and twelve. An alphabetical index of sixty-five pages, not numbered, registers all the Latin lemmata explained, about 150 per page. They amount to some 13,000, which would be an adequate estimate for the total number of entries.

Nineteen introductory and linking texts in Latin are inserted between the sections in the two main parts of the book. Unfortunately, this technique is discontinued after section ten in the second part. Instead, two texts by a censor are to be found, criticizing the dictionary because heathen and heretical words have been used for notions of theology and the Church. There is one more final text by the author explaining why he has given a list of national and geographical names. The whole book has an air of philological erudition and accuracy. It is a multilingual dictionary, because its entries have the main purpose of translating Latin lexemes into those of other languages, but because of its elaborate explanations it is moving in the direction of an encyclopaedic dictionary. However, it is the nineteen introductory and linking texts which really capture our attention. It is not claimed that the ideas which they contain are, historically speaking, new. It is, however, claimed that they allow us an unprecedentedly direct insight into the ideas of a sixteenth-century lexicographer when planning the macrostructure of his dictionary. Whereas we usually have to infer these ideas from the arrangement of topics and the sequence of lexemes, supported by the hindsight of the historiographer, we can, in this case, read them from the author's own words.[41]

The author strikes a very individual note right at the beginning. The first section is not devoted to God, the sky, the stars, etc., as would be traditional, but '*De re libraria & libroru[m] materia*'. The introduction (1) gives the argument: Words are names for things. They are produced by the voice and received by the ear. They are prevented from being forgotten by writing and made common property by printing. If forgotten, they can be recovered from books. This is why the first section turns to books, '*mutis quasi magistris*'.

This small passage contains noteworthy ideas. It bases the dictionary on an inchoative theory of language. With its words, language attaches names to things (Waswo 1987). The dictionary contains these names, that is, the world-in-language. It contains human knowledge made transferable by language and retrievable by the great achievement of the time, printing. Thus, the dictionary does not follow any natural order accessible to observation and experience, as earlier glossaries did. It follows the knowledge of a 'mute master'. It is not a simple mirror of the world but a thesaurus of knowledge. The high appreciation of books becomes apparent. They make knowledge accessible to everybody.

This leads directly to the idea that man should be the topic of the next section (11), because he alone '*animi cultum è libraria supellectile haurire datum est*'. Thus, the differentiation of humans is not the usual one between the angels and the animals, but their being knowledgeable with the help of books. This places them at the focus of the dictionary.

Consequently, the following sections are devoted to domains of the world in so far as they do service to humans: animals because they work for them, feed them (quadrupeds, birds, fish), give them delight (birds), or are simply useful (insects) (29); the fruits of the earth and of trees (59), because '*haec verò pabulis reparando, hominibus adiumento esse, operisque adminiculari queant*'; finally cereals, herbs, and trees for the same reason (82). This sequence of sections deviates from other nomenclators which follow the well-known order of natural history or the four elements.

As, besides food, there is nothing more important for humans than clothes, they are the candidates for the next section (119). An undertone of moral criticism intrudes here because of people's vanity: '*seculorum vitio, luxus cònturbatione*'. However, this provides a chance to add a section on colours (134).

After food and clothes, accommodation is the next necessity (138), somewhat artificially combined with a section on ships (163), which the Greeks called movable houses. The whole is completed by '*instrumentorum omnis generis classibus*' (169) because, metaphorically speaking and interestingly enough, the coping-stone ('*colophon*') of a house is what can be made out of it. Somewhat artificially, a section on warfare is introduced (205) via the idea of danger (property, life, etc.)

---

[41]   Occasionally, we find small Latin texts within subchapters, but they will be disregarded.

and, after that, a chapter on sacred buildings: '*tamquam coronide*' (220). The very last section of this first part of the nomenclator is devoted to money, weights, and measures because they are needed for providing, improving, and decorating all the objects used in a house (225).

Thus, in the first '*tomus*' of the dictionary we have a fairly tightly linked chain of thought allowing the author to assemble many groups of words which, traditionally, belong to topical lexicography, such as parts of the human body, the names of plants and animals, of dishes and clothes, as well as of colours, the parts of houses, tools and other equipment. But they are in a sequence different from the traditional one and the reason for their being in the dictionary is different from what one would infer from older word-lists and glossaries.

After this, the author declares that he wishes '*pausam facere*'. For his new start he begins '*à primis mundi elementis*' (252), fire, air, earth, and water, but only in general and mostly with reference to the celestial universe. He then goes on to the units of time (257) because time started with the creation of the world. Another section deals with the elements as they are revealed in the world, mainly with earth and water (263). '*Telluris intimae officina*' is the topic of the next, that is, metals, because they belong to the earth. Interestingly enough, the author explains that he is not going to discuss whether they do humans good or not, he only plans to give the names (283). The following section is devoted to diseases (294) because they arise from '*modo aut immoderatione*' of the elements. Finally and consequently, the names of medicines are collected.

Here, the technique of inserting arguments for each succeeding section unfortunately terminates. But the ones we have suffice to show that in this second '*tomus*' of the dictionary a different principle of selection is at work. It is the more traditional idea of scanning the universe from *above* to *below* with the four elements as guidelines. Even diseases and, indirectly, their remedies are determined by them.

The sections, no longer introduced by comments, are devoted to God and spirits, clerical and profane offices, arts, crafts, and professions, crimes, and family relationships. The placement of '*De Deo & spiritibus*' after instead of before the elaborate treatment of the elements is unusual, and the words of the censor may have to do with this. But the sections that follow all pertain to human society and are traditionally placed after the sections pertaining to the universe and nature.

The most important result of the analysis is that Adrianus Junius compiled his *Nomenclator* following two quite different principles. At the time of the origin of the dictionary, the first principle would have been the modern one, taking into account a new approach to human knowledge. The second principle would have been fairly traditional. Whatever the reasons for this, the special case of Junius's dictionary is that the author conveys not only words and their meanings, but also the system itself according to which these words are arranged. This is indeed a scientific way of approaching a lexicographical task.

THE ENGLISH ADAPTATION OF JUNIUS'S *NOMENCLATOR*

An English adaptation of the nomenclator was published in 1585. Its title reads:

The Nomenclator, or Remembrancer of Adrianus Iunius Physician, diuided into two Tomes, conteining proper names and apt termes for all thinges vnder their conuenient Titles, which within a few leaues do follow: VVritten by the said Ad. Iu. in Latine, Greeke, French and other forrein tongues: and now in English, by Iohn Hig[!]ins: VVith a full supplie of all such vvords as the last inlarged edition affoorded; and a dictional Index, conteining aboue fourteene hundred principall words with their numbers directly leading to their interpretations: Of special vse for all scholars and learners of the same languages. . . . .
Imprinted at London for Ralph Newberie, and Henrie Denham. 1585.[42]

The book has the same macro- and microstructure as the original. The nomenclator proper numbers 539 pages with an additional alphabetical index listing some 13,000 Latin lexemes in three columns per page on 118 pages. The index was prepared by Abraham Fleming (?1552–1607). The printed design is the same as described above. The bridging texts between the sections are retained in Latin.

The entries have a Latin headword, followed in many, though not in all, cases by quotations from classical authors. Then a Greek translation, a French translation, and, finally, the English translation appear. This means that, besides the two classical languages, this adaptation of Junius's nomenclator contains only French and English lexemes, the English always being the last one. The languages are not tagged. A typical entry reads: '*Articulus, iunctura & nodus me[m]bri, artridion* [Greek letters], *Iointure, A ioint or knuckle*'. (21.)

As in the original, the size of entries varies enormously. As regards the French and English translations, we find three versions: (i) the French and the English lexemes are (roughly speaking) equivalent in number and meaning; (ii) a short French translation, and a lengthy English one which adds an explanation; and (iii) the French translation is missing altogether. There is no entry without an English rendering. Note the following consecutive entries:

Literae laureatae . . . Lettres ioyeuses enuoyees du camp, ou qui annonçent la victoire. Letters of victorie obtained against the enimie. (type i)
Apostoli [. . .] Letters of appeale: letters missiue: dimissories. (type iii)
Epistola aduentoria . . . Lettre gratulatoire. Letters gratulatorie, or letters sent to ones freend for his welcome in his waie homeward. (type ii) (9.)

The frequent Latin explanations, which occasionally go into considerable detail, are part of the microstructure of the original. But the English explanations, in particular where they outgrow the French translations, seem to point to a special endeavour of the English translator in order to explain the Latin (and Greek and French) lexeme(s) and, perhaps even more importantly, the matter in its meaning. Note:

---

[42] Copied from a film by University Microfilms, library reference number 20822. For editions including English see also Alston 1974, vol. ii, nos. 70–80.

Musculus, Plin. mide. Muscle. A muskle or fleshie parte of the bodye, consisting of fleshe, veines, sinews and arteries, seruing specially to the motion of some parte of the bodie by meanes of the sinews in it.   (21.)

In an entry like this the English translator was obviously eager not simply to give an English word for a Latin one, but to give more detailed information to his readers than the mere translation of the Latin lemma would provide. It is difficult to say whether this is a general tendency or just accidental. However, the general impression is that the translator is not just interested in rendering the Latin lemma as closely as possible, but that he has his own interests in the language and in the matter signified by the lexemes. Quite often he realizes his translation into English not only via the Latin lexeme but also via the French one. Note the following consecutive entries (Latin, French, and English only):

Homo, ab humo dictus / Vn homme / Man and woman.
Homuncio, homunculus, homulus / Petit homme / A little man.
Mas, masculus / Masle / Malekind or mankind.
Femina, femella, mulier / Femme, femelle / Womankind, or a woman.
Mulier sterilis, infoecunda / Femme sterile / A barren, unfruitfull or childless woman.
Mulier foeta, grauida, praegnans / Femme grosse d'enfant / A woman with child.
Foetus . . . / Le fruit & porteé de femme / The fruite of a woman, that she beareth in hir great belly.
Puer, a pueritate / Enfant, garçon / A childe: a boy.   (16.)

Note furthermore the following selected entries which contain examples of translations of the French lexeme:

Penvs / Prouision de viures de la maison / All kind of food either to be eaten or dronke: prouision for housekeeping: store of victuals.
Commeatus / Viures / Commons, table diet, either at an ordinarie, or at home in a mans owne house.   (76.)

The following entry is a good example of the fact that the quotations from classical authors, which follow the Latin lemma, do not merely show classical erudition but serve to provide synonyms which match the headword. The English translation, with the help of the French, makes every effort to include these synonyms in its lexeme or phrase. Note, for example:

Annonam flagellare, Plin. vexare & onerare, Vlpian. incendere, & excandefacere, Varro. vastare, Lamprid Faire ou cauler la cherté. To enhaunce the price of victuals: to make them deere, or to spoyle and make waste of them.   (77.)

Sometimes the French part of the entry is missing. Note the consecutive examples:

Pirum Pomponianum . . . / A brest peare, resembling the fashion of a woma[n]s breast.
Pirum regium . . . / A king peare with a very little stalk.
Pirum signinum . . . / A red peare or sand peare.
Pirum superbum . . . / A water pear.
Pirum Venerum . . . / A Venus or faire louely peare.   (99.)

In such cases the translator cannot fall back on the French rendering and explains a word-meaning with obvious elaboration. Note:

Voluta . . . in capitulo quod propendet circuli tortilis ad modum, aut cincinni crispati / That in the head or chapter of a piller, which sticketh out or hangeth ouer, in maner of a writhen circle, or a curled tuft being a kind of worke of leaues or some such denise turning diverse wayes: some saye it is the square table of stone set vpon the chapters of pillers. (204.)

In cases like these the Latin paraphrase and the English translation both serve a certain cultural understanding. Note again, for example:

Confarreatio, Vlpian. Matrimonij ritus, quando farre conuenitur in manum, certis verbis, & decem testibus praesentibus. A kind of solemnising of matrimonie, when with a cake of wheate, the parties were handfasted, with certayne words spoken. and ten witnesses present. (537.)

The Latin as well as the English text obviously served to make something intelligible which could not be inferred directly from the Latin lexeme. There are, however, also cases where extensive explanations in the Latin part have not been taken over in the translations. '*Ebenus*', for example, is explained with a text longer than a whole column of a page, but is not translated into French at all, and into English simply by '*The ebene tree*' (150).

Without a minute analysis it is, of course, impossible to say whether these observations occur consistently. But it seems obvious that the English translation regularly observes the headword as well as the synonyms, that is, those added to the headword and those given as quotations from classical authors, and in many cases also the French translation, using it as a guide for the choice of the appropriate English lexeme. On average the French rendering of the word meaning is very much shorter than the English rendering.[43]

It is also obvious that the translations do not present the kind of English which is infiltrated with Latinate vocabulary. After all, this English version of Junius's nomenclator is one of the most elaborate and erudite onomasiological dictionaries to be written in the Humanist spirit and to include English, even if it did originate outside the country. This was the time when the influx of classical Latinate words into the English language was still very great. But the translator was obviously not ambitious in this respect. In a plainly understandable way, he characterized and circumscribed many words for which he could have found a *hard* lexematic equivalent. This accounts for the fact that many more phrases occur as translations than lexemes. Note, for example:

Maender, Virgil. In veste acu picta operi labyrinthorum adsimilis & inextricabilis filorum aut etiam clauorumqui illigantur ductus. [no Greek entry] Bordure d'habillement entortilée. A welt, hem, or border winding in and out this way and that way like a chuerne, &c.

The lexeme *meander* does not occur, although, according to the *OED*, it made its first appearance in English in this meaning in 1576. Likewise '*Siphon*' is translated

---

[43] I did not make a comparison with the Greek rendering; but its general brevity, compared with the other languages, is perfectly obvious.

as '*The tap, faucet, or pipe whereout liquor runneth*', not as (Engl.) *siphon* (237); '*Lardarium*' as '*A larding stick, wherewith Cookes vse to drawe lard through flesh*', not as a derivation of or compound with (Engl.) *lard* (241); '*Conchae*' as '*Shells wherein painters put their colours*', not as (Engl.) *conchs* (255); '*Colossus*' as '*A goodly great image, large & tall, and bigger than a man*', not as (Engl.) *coloss(us)* (307); '*Sulphur*' as '*Naturall brimstone, or brimstone digged out of the earth, and that never felt fire*', not as (Engl.) *sulphur* (408).[44] These examples were, of course, randomly selected, and many counter-examples can be found. It also depends on the lexical domain, which coincides with a domain of reality, whether the English translations are nearer to or farther away from the Latin sources. Sometimes we find the Latinate and the English lexeme side by side, as in '*Magistratus*' translated as '*A magistrate or superior*' or '*Senatores*' translated as '*The Senators, Aldermen, and Burroughmaisters of a citie*' (486).

The English version of Junius's nomenclator certainly deserves a detailed study of the translation techniques employed in it and the position it occupies in the history of the English language of its time.

The macrostructure of the English adaptation is slightly different from the original in the first book, listing sixty-three titles instead of fifty-nine, because some subtitles, which did not denote a section originally, are here used in this capacity. There is, however, no semantic change involved in this. In the second book the macrostructures of the two versions are identical. For the macrostructure of the English version see Table A.19.[45]

---

[44] According to the *OED*: *siphon* has been known since 1659, this is after the translation of Junius, but the word was in the air; *lard* has been known since 1330; *conch* since 1398; *coloss* since 1561, around the time of the translation; *sulphur* since 1390.

[45] For other relevant dictionaries in the German-speaking area of the sixteenth century, see Müller 2001, in particular chap. IV, 285–427, with a detailed chronology (286–90).

The case of Johannes Amos Comenius

10.1. The onomasiological tradition in early Czech lexicography

Perhaps *the* outstanding mark of foreign language teaching between the last third of the fifteenth century and 1700 is its European internationalism. Grammar was thought of in the framework of a unified set of traditional terms in every linguistic region (country).The methods of arrangement and, thus, the semantic structure of onomasiological glossaries and dictionaries remained the same, although more and more European languages were involved. The unity of the larger part of the Continent, which had linguistically been guaranteed for seven centuries by the one language of intellectuals, Latin, did not break apart when more and more vernaculars rose to prominence. Rather, Europe became a multilingual unity as it had been a Latin unity before.

This is why the historical development of foreign-language teaching and learning can hardly be adequately treated in historiography according to nations (Caravolas 1994) but only as a Continent-wide homogeneous intellectual movement. The best proof of this fact is Jan Amos Komenský (Johannes Amos Comenius, 1592–1670) who cannot possibly be approached otherwise than as a European figure. This does not preclude his having deep roots in the Czech tradition of theological and philosophical thinking and also in the tradition of Czech lexicography. As *the* great figure of education and of lexicography at the end of the seventeenth century, he can only be understood as a mind which was formed in the setting of his early life, Moravia, and then expanded all over the countries of the European Continent. But even in his youth there is nothing special in the fact that he studied in Germany (Herborn and Heidelberg). During his years as an adult his growing European attitudes were not least brought about by the fate which forced him to leave his own country and live as a refugee in Poland, Hungary, Sweden, England, and the Netherlands.

Before the advent of printing, lexicography which involved the Czech (at that time called *Bohemian*) language started in the usual way. Latin texts were glossed, then the glosses were collected in alphabetical and topical glossaries (Flajšhans 1926, X–XXXII, Brauner 1939, 3). From the fourteenth century on, this led to book-sized collections the aim of which was the explanation of Latin vocabulary to Czech learners. The lexicographical development was accompanied by the general cultural efflorescence, in particular in the Caroline period[1] whose clearest sign was the foundation of the *Universitas Carolina* in 1348.

It is certain that Johannes Amos Comenius, who himself worked for forty years on an alphabetical dictionary of the Czech language, was aware of this tradition, certainly of its historical highlights. In order to understand the lexicographical work of this genius of his century, it is appropriate to look briefly at the lexicographical tradition which, at least partly, made him and prefigured his own achievements (Přívratská 1994).

10.1.1 Claretus of Prague

The pre-eminent lexicographer of the early fourteenth century was Bartoloměj z Chlumce, called Claret(us) (Magister Bohemarius Bartholomeus de Solencia, *fl.* 1379) of Prague (Přívratská 1994). His *Bohemarius* (*Bohemář*), probably written before 1350, consists of about 1,000 hexameters, each of which explains two or three Latin nouns, thus glossing some 2,500 foreign lexemes. The rhythmic language with a regular caesura in the middle of each line was certainly meant to help memorization and gave the glosses a pedagogical aspect. The overall arrangement of topics reads thus:[2]

Proemium
I. De Deo et mundo
1. *De Deo et celo* 2. *De aere*

---

[1]   Charles IV reigned 1346–78.
[2]   The following overview and the quotations are taken from Flajšhans 1926 (NL Praha 54C 1281), 'Bohemarius', 31–72, 'Glossarius', 73–202. Titles and brackets have been added by the editor.

II. De aqua et piscibus
3. De aqua 4. De piscibus
III. De volucribus
5. De volatilibus
IV. De terra et animalibus
6. De terra 7. De animalibus 8. De bestiis 9. De vermibus
V. De arboribus, plantis et seminibus
10. De arbore 11. De plantis 12. De arbutis 13. De semine
14. De frumentis 15. De herbis 16. De radicibus
VI. De homine et stirpe
17. De hominibus 18. De membris 19. De languoribus 20. De progenie 21. De ferculis 22. De vestibus
VII. De civitate et ecclesia
23. De domo 24. De rebus domesticis 25. De utensilibus 26. De ecclesia 27. De civitate 28. De armis
VIII. De artificibus
29. De opificibus 30. De textoribus 31. De sutoribus 32. De fabris 33. De militibus 34. De nautis
35. De scriptoribus
Conclusio

Note as an example of the microstructure of entries this extract from section 3:

3. De aqua
Hinc aqua sit woda, *flumen* rzyeka, *mare* morze;
Lacus sit yezero, *sed palus dico* moczydlo;
Stagnum sit przyerow, *sentina* luzye *memento;*
Torrens prud, *fluvius* potok, *fons* studnycze *[dicta].*
Est puteus stbel, *limpha* wrchowysscze *vocatur;*
Est limphus clococz, *piscina sit tibi* rybnyk,
Obstagium yez, *vir vorax,* produch *cataracta,*
Brzyeh *ripa, margo sit* ohlubnye, struha *rivus,*
Situla dic okow, *libra* waha, *tibi [sit] pons* most.
Ladula lawyczka, *glacies* led, *lama* prohlub[ina];
Procelle wlny, *caribdis* strzyess, *kraque massa;*[3]

---

[3]   '*3. On water*
The water be woda, *river* rzyeka, *sea* morze;
Lake is yezero, *but swamp I call* moczydlo;
Pond is przyerow, *puddle remember [as]* luzye;
Torrent prud, *stream* potok, *spring* studnycze *[is called].*
Well stbel, *limpha* wrchowysscze *is named;*
Rapids are clococz, *fishpond is for you* rybnyk,
Weir [is] yez, *vir whirl,* produch *cataract,*
Brzyeh *river-side, bank is* ohlubnye, struha *brook,*
[For] Bucket say okow, *[for] pound* wahe, *bridge is for you* most.
Foot-bridge lawyczka, *ice* led, *bog* prohlu[ina];
Gales wlny, *abyss* strzyess, *and* kra *mass.'*
I acknowledge with thanks the generous help given to me by Jana Přívratská and Vladimir Přívratský in translating this and the Czech texts that follow. For any errors, I am solely responsible.

The arrangement of topics is the usual one, moving from God and the universe to nature, man, and society. It has been argued that the subtlety of these divisions and their semantic content were taken from Vinzenc of Beauvais' (?1190–1264) *Speculum majus*, written between 1244 and 1254,[4] the most important medieval encyclopaedia (Štěpanek 1976, 297–318). The division of chapters follows the four elements of classical philosophy—water, air, earth, and fire, the last however being reserved for man. Man is seen as a part of nature, but also as creator of his own world in the institutions of society, state and church, and in crafts.

Claretus's *Glossarius* (*Glossař*) is longer than his *Bohemarius*. It contains about 2,700 hexameters with three translated lexemes on average, which amounts to almost 8,000 Latin words. This time they are not only nouns, but also adjectives, pronouns, adverbs, and verbs which, as a rule, however, are used only to fill up a hexameter. The sequence of topics is similar to, though not identical with, that of the *Bohemarius*, the greater length demanding more detailed sections and subsections.

Most noteworthy of the two texts is their pedagogical format which almost turns them into textbooks to be learned by heart. One specific feature supporting this idea is the author's extraordinary habit of starting and ending topical sections with cataphoric and anaphoric lines. Thus each section turns into a clearly delimited (learning-) unit.

It is possible that Claretus followed the example of John of Garland (Brauner 1938: 4).[5] He mentions him in the last line of the section devoted to birds ('*Has dat aves omnes de Garlandia Johannes*'). But in these anaphoric lines many names appear as sources for the vocabulary (e.g. on birds: '*Ambrosius, Plinius volucres dedit hasque Solinus*'), among them the famous historical ones which everybody would expect (Pliny, Galen, St Augustine, Isidore of Seville, Albertus Magnus (1200–80), etc.), and also others of more regional importance. It needs detailed investigations to decide in which way these references have to be understood as serious sources. They certainly increase the book's didactic aspect, because learning from authorities was the method of the time.

There is also a *Vokabulař grammatický* (written after 1360), which has onomasiological divisions, this time not taken from philosophical categories but mainly from the seven *artes liberales* and the crafts. This means that it is not reality, as seen by philosophers, but the principles of education which provide the guidelines. An onomasticon and sections on numbers, again both highly pedagogical, follow. The divisions are:

I. *De grammatica*	I. *Nomina Christi*
II. *De rethorica*	II. *Nomina deorum*
III. *De loyca*	III. *Nomina fluviorum*
IV. *De musica*	IV. *Nomina montium*
V. *De arismethica*	V. *Nomina lapidum*

---

[4] See Chapter 11, 436.   [5] See Chapter 4, 85–7.

VI. De geometria	*VI. Nomina terrarum*
VII. De astronomia	*I. De num. cardinalibus*
VIII. De phisica	*II. De num. ordinalibus*
IX. De theologia	*III. De numer. substant*
X. De medicina	*IV. De numer. multiplic*
XI. De ethica	*V. De numer. adverb*
XII. De mechanica	*VI. De numeracione*
XIII. De artibus	*VII. De cifris.*

Most historiographers of lexicography, like Flajšhans (1926) and Brauner (1939, 5), attribute to Claretus a far-reaching influence on later lexicography and on the development of the Czech language. In the *Glossarius* alone he translated some 8,000 Latin technical terms into Czech. Some of the words he coined are still used today like, for example, *jakost* 'quality', *byt* 'flat, living quarters', *podstata* 'essence, substance', and *tvářnost* 'form, look' (Štěpanek 1976, 299).

10.1.2 The first printed dictionaries

The early sixteenth century saw the first printed dictionaries. One of them is a curious mixture between a grammar and a dictionary, which itself mixes onomasiological and alphabetical arrangements. The book does not have a title page in the usual sense. The library catalogue entry (Prague) reads: *Jan Bosák: Ullis ferme vocabulis . . . . Tento wokabulař Lactifer. Plzeň 1511* (NL Praha 45 A 7 [Tres Rd 2]. 4°). It has 594 pages, which however are not numbered. It is printed in Gothic type. The author is the Franciscan monk Jan Bosák z Vodňan, called Johannes Aquensis (*c*.1460–after 1534). Note the following macrostructure of the dictionary:

Primus liber: 3–175^r; alphabetical, nouns
175^v: *Nomina signoru[m] Zodiaci*
Secundus liber: 176^r–239^r; alphabetical, verbs
in between: 204^r: *De diuersis vocibus animalium*
Tertius liber: 239^v–251^r; alphabetical, indeclinabilia
Liber quartus: 251^v–255^v: *De monstruosis hominibus*; alphabetical
Liber quintus: 256^r–260^r: *De infirmitatibus humani corporis*; alphabetical
Liber sextus: 260^v–265^r: *De arboribus*; alphabetical
Liber septimus: 265^v–274^r: *De herbis*; alphabetical
Liber octavus: 274^v–279^r: *De lapidibus*; alphabetical
Liber nonus: 279^v–286^r: *De auibus*; alphabetical
Liber decimus: 286^v–289^r: *De animalibus*; alphabetical
Liber undecimus: 289^v–292^r: *De piscibus*; alphabetical
Liber duodecimus: 292^v–296^v: *De serpentibus et vermibus*; alphabetical.

This macrostructure is quite unusual. The first three books contain entries according to word-classes. The following ones are onomasiological, but not in the strict sense, because the lexemes collected under a certain topic are themselves ordered alphabetically. This comes close to the much later technique of dictionaries of synonyms or semantically related word-clusters. There is also an unusual selection of topics, at least those concerning man. Although monstrosities and diseases are to be found in many topical dictionaries, it is astonishing to find them here as the only section concerning man. The subsequent sections on nature are the ones we would expect in a fairly small onomasiological dictionary.

The microstructure is quite unusual, too. There are linking remarks between sections which are printed flush with the right margin. Frequently rather long Latin entries occur which are then repeated in Czech. The usual microstructure is: a Latin lemma with grammatical explanations referring to gender, class of declension or conjugation, sometimes a genitive or second person ending, followed by the Latin paraphrase of the lemma and the Czech translation (Brauner 1939, 11–14).

Macrostructure and microstructure suggest that this glossary served lexical as well as grammatical needs in teaching Latin. This means that, didactically speaking, it moves towards an integrated textbook with grammatical as well as lexical information. In this respect it is not unique; there are other dictionaries which have the same microstructure. This fact and the selection of topics may also suggest that the *Lactifer* is actually the Czech version of some other dictionary which has yet to be identified.

Both these facts, pertaining to a well-known source, apply to the two dictionaries of Tomáš Rešl:[6]

Dictionarivm Latinobohemicvm In Vsvm & gratiam studiosae iuuentutis Bohemicae, ex Petri Dasypodij Dictionario, eiusdemq[ue]; recognitione postrema, concinnnatum. Accesservnt Ex Eodem Et nomina locorum, & Amnium in Germania, & alia quaedam, ut sequens pagina indicabit. Praeterea ex eodem adiecta sunt & Forensia, ac seorsim sub unum locum redacta. Authore Reschelino Parocho Ieroschouiense.
Cavtvm est Caesareo Priuilegio, ne quis hoc Dictionarium intra quadriennium imprimat. Impressum Olomucij, apud Ioannem Guntherum. M.D.LX.

The book (Prague NL 45 G 51 [Tres Re 2]. 4°) has an estimated 850 unnumbered pages.
And:

Dictionarivm Bohemicolatinum In Vsvm Et Gratiam Bohemicae Pvbis Iuxta Dictionarium Petri Dasypodij, summa diligentia interpretatum. Authore Thomas Reschelio Parocho Ieroschouiensi.
CAVTVM est Caesareo Priuilegio, ne quis hoc Dictionarium intra quadriennium imprimat. Impressum Olomucij, apud Ioannem Guntherum M. D. LXII.

The book (NL Praha 45 G 222 [Tres Re 3]. 4°) is about half the size of the first one.

Both dictionaries are translations of Petrus Dasypodius's *Dictionarium latinogermanicum* of 1552, which has an alphabetical and an onomasiological

---

[6] I was unable to find any life-dates.

part. In Rešl's 1560 edition, the latter is about one-tenth the size of the former (Müller 2001, 62–73, 203–9 and *passim*). It has the following sections whose entries have themselves an alphabetical ordering:

Titvli Nomenclatvrae Rerum
Vrbium, Regionum, Montium, ac Populorum in Germania, nec non alijs quibusdam locis, nomina.
Flvviorum nomina in Germania, quorum à Latinis scriptoribus fit mentio.
Plantarum, maximé quae Germanis cognitae sunt nomenclatura.
Arborum ac Fructicum [nomina]
Herbarum [nomina]
Frumentorum, & Leguminum nomina
Animalium quadrupedum nomina
Reptilium, seu Vermium & Insectorum nomina
Aquatilium, seu Piscium [nomina]
Volatilium, vel Auium nomina
Partium domus nomenclatura
Vtensilium, siue intrumentorum domesticorum, & uarie suppellectilis nomenclatura
Instrumentorum ad officinas pertinentium, & machinarum nomina
Armorum bellicorum nomina
Rusticorum instrumentorum appellationes
Mensurarum Romanarum, & Ponderum nomina, Bohemicé quantum fieri potuit explacata
Liquidorum [nomina]
Aridorum [nomina]
Geodaeticarum mensuram nomina
Ponderum [nomina]
Numismatum & Summarum rei Numariae nomina
Partium hominis nomenclatura
Habitudinum corporis nomenclatura
Vestium nomina
Ciborum, siue Eduliorum nomina
Potus nomina
Morborum nomina
Partium temporis explicatio Germanicé
Forensium uerborum & loquendi generum interpretatio

In the 1562 edition, which merely reverses the sequence of languages, the sections are the same as in the earlier one, except for some minimal deviations. Only the section on Roman measures is missing. With reference to languages, entries are ordered according to the titles of the dictionaries. The Czech lexemes are printed in Gothic, the Latin lexemes in Roman type. In the later edition the entries are, on average, shorter than in the earlier one. The author probably expected the two versions of the dictionary to be used together, or at least by the same persons. Like their model, Rešl's dictionaries show the spirit of Humanist learning, the Latin–Czech version to be used for translating and analysing Latin texts, the Czech–Latin version to be used for composing them.

10.1.3 Daniel Adam of Weleslavin

The outstanding Czech lexicographer of the second half of the sixteenth century was Daniel Adam z Weleslavína (1546–99), who lived in Prague. He was a student and a professor of history at Charles University, but after his marriage in 1576 became the proprietor of his wife's printing shop, where he produced and published his own dictionaries.

Besides writing some minor lexicographical works, for example a herbal, Weleslavin was the author of four comprehensive dictionaries, two alphabetical and two onomasiological ones, which are all adaptations of existing dictionaries. In 1579 he published the alphabetical *Dictionarium Linguae Latinae Ex Magno Basilii Fabri Thesauro collectum atque concinnatum.* . . . . He must have used the 1572 edition of Basilius Faber's *Thesaurus Eruditionis Scholasticae* with its Latin lemmata and explanations which he complemented with Czech translations (Brauner 1939, 69). In 1586 he edited Adrianus Junius's very popular *Nomenclator Omnium Rerum* of 1567[7] by pruning it down to Latin and German entries and appending his own Czech translations. The title of this edition is *Nomenclator omnium rerum propria nomina tribus linguis, Latina, Boiemica et Germanica explicata continens, ex Hadriano Junio Medico excerptus. Pragae, Daniel Adam von Weleslavin, 1586.*

In 1598, one year before his death, there followed two dictionaries (1598*a* and *b*):

Sylva Qvadrilingvis Vocabvlorvm Et Phrasium Bohemicae, Latinae, Graecae Et Germanicae Lingvae: In Vsvm Stvdiosae Ivventvtis Scholasticae, Natvraliae Methodo Alphabeti Bohemici In ordinem disposita, & Poeticarum phrasium copiosa supellectili locupletata.
Ad Calcem Stylae Adiectvs Est Locvpletissimvs Index Omnivm Vocvm Et Locvtionvm Germanicarum, quibus Bohemica, Latina & Graeca Synonymice explicantur: in gratiam eorum, qui ex Germanicis, Latina & Bohemica discere cupiunt, contextus. Haec omnia nunc primum eduntur studio, opera & impensis M. Danielis Adami à VVeleslavina: Anno M. D. XCIIX.

and:

Nomenclator Quadrilinguis Bohemicolatino Graecogermanicus. Continens Omnium Fermé rerum, quae in probatis omnium doctrinarum autoribus inveniuntur, apellationes. In Qvatuor Classes Distinctus, Quarum Prima Est De Deo, secunda de Natura, tertia de Homine, quarta de Artibus. in usum studiosae Iuuentutis editus, studio, operá & sumptibus M. Danielis Adami à VVeleslavina.
In fine additi duo Indices copiosißimi, Bohemicus & Latinus.
Anno Domine M. D. XCIIX.

The first dictionary is alphabetical, the second onomasiological. Both are adaptations of Helfricus Emmelius's dictionary in that they append a Czech translation of the entries and give them a new order with the Czech lemma in first position. The title of Emmelius's alphabetical dictionary reads:

---

[7] See Chapter 9, 353–60.

Sylva Qvinqvelingvis Vocabulorum et Phrasivm Germanicae, Latinae, Graecae, Hebraicae, Gallicae linguae, in vsum studiosae iuuentutis, facili methodo disposita per M. Helfricum Emmelium VVombacensem, scholae Alzenanae Rectorem. . . . Argentorati Excudebat Theodosius Rihelius [1592]. (BSB Polygl. 60, Fiche Beibd. 1.)

The title of the onomasiological dictionary reads:

Nomenclator Qvatrilingvis, Germanicolatinograecogallicus, In Classes IIII distinctus. Auctore M. Helfrico Emmelio VVombacensi, scholae Alzenanae Rectore [. . .] Argentorati. Excudebat Theodosius Rihelius [1592]. (BSB Polygl. 60. Fiche Beibd. 1)

There is also a Latin–German–Greek–French part in this dictionary with the same title, except 'Latinogermanicograecogallicus'.

Emmelius's nomenclator has a third part, an alphabetical onomasticon of countries, islands, seas, rivers, forests, lakes, mountains, peoples, towns, villages, etc. The alphabetical and the onomasiological dictionaries, the second consisting of three parts, are bound together and are one of the outstanding lexicographical works of the late sixteenth century.

Weleslavin's dependence on Junius and Emmelius is an excellent example of the general interdependence of nomenclators written in the Humanist spirit of Europe in the sixteenth century. Adapting dictionaries in the way in which Weleslavin did was, of course, perfectly legitimate. Other authors did the same, by which method a close proximity of the macrostructures of nomenclators came into being.[8] Besides being a schoolbook, Weleslavin's work was certainly stimulated by the general wish to improve the Czech language of his time. This was, of course, best done by linguistic education. The lemmata are Czech with Latin, Greek, and German translations. At the same time the nomenclator is dominated by Latin. For example, all titles and subtitles are in Latin only. Note the following entries from *Classis II, Caput IIII*, which are typical of the whole dictionary:[9]

DE MVNDO, COELO ET Astris
SWět / Mundus / Welt
Nebe y země, a wsse cožw nich g[es]t, wssecken swět /
    Vniversitas rerum / Himmel vnd Erd, vnd alles was darinnen
Spausta swěta / Machina mundi / Das gebew d(er) welt
Nebe / Coelum / Himmel
Kaule / Globus / Kugel
Žiwlowé / Eleme[n]ta / Element
krsslek zemský / Orbis terrae / Der erden kreyß.
Okolek, okrsslek / Orbis / Der vmbkreyß
Znamenj nebeská, Hwězdnatosti / Astra, sydera / das gestirn

---

[8] An example of this proximity of macrostructures is the astonishing similarity of Weleslavin and Frischlin, for which I have no explanation so far. Henricus Decimator's monumental *Sylva vocabulorum et phrasium cum solutae, tum ligatae orationis, ex optimis & probatis Latinae & Graecae linguae auctoribus. . . . Leipzig . . . Georg Defner 1580*, of whose four parts the third is a nomenclator, may have had a bridging function. It appears as an adaptation of Frischlin's nomenclator of 1586. I know that the dates are inconclusive. See Chapter 9.   [9] Greek translations omitted.

Hwězda / Stella / Stern
Planeta / Planeta, stella erratica / Planet
[three entries: names of stars]
Slunce / Sol / Sonn
Slunečný Blesk / Iubar seu splendor solis / Sonnenglantz
Slunečný drobný prássek, kterýž se w paprslcých slunečných
     spatřuge / Atomi / Sonnen steublin, kleinsts dinglin, welche
     man in der Sonnen stral siehet
[four entries: names of stars])
Měsýc / Luna / Mond
[five entries: phases of the moon]
Swětlo / Lumen, Lux / Liecht
Paprslek slunečný, aneb giných hwězd / Radius / Stral der sonnen,
     oder anderer stern
Tma, mrákota, possmaurno / Tenebrae, Caligo / Finsternueß, tunckel
Stjn / Vmbra / Schatte
Zatměnj Slunce / Defectus, deliquiu[m] aut obscuratio Solis /
     Finsternueß der Sonnen
Zatměnj Měsýce / Defectus vel obscuratio Lunae / Finsternueß des
     mondes
[four entries: points of the compass]
Uhel nebe / Cardo, vertex, polus / Angel des Himmels
Wýchod slunce / Ortus solis / Auffgang der Sonnen
Západ slunce / Occasus solis / Nidergang der Sonnen
[thirteen entries: zodiac]
[three entries: constellations of stars]

   The nomenclator (WF Kb 164. 4°) has 658 columns on 329 pages plus forty-two pages of an index of Czech words, printed in three columns, each column consisting of sixty words. Czech words are printed in Gothic, Latin words in Roman, Greek words in Greek, and German words again in Gothic type. At first sight, the index makes the counting of entries fairly easy. It yields a total of 7,560 Czech words, glossed in the other three languages, which amounts to 30,240 words. Since, however, the synonyms and derivations mentioned in the entries are not listed in the index (at least not exhaustively), the number of words in the dictionary is in fact much greater. There are certainly two or three times as many Czech lexemes as the index suggests. Many entries are given with descriptive phrases, which have their own vocabulary. This makes the counting even more difficult. There are not as many synonyms and derivations in Latin, Greek, and German as in Czech; as a rule not more than two. On average there are between fifteen and twenty entries in one column. This amounts to as many as 13,160 lemmata, a much greater number than that of the Czech words in the index. Of course, whether nouns and derivations following each other are to be regarded as two independent entries is a moot point.
   Whatever result an exact count of Weleslavin's nomenclator will lead to, it seems obvious that the work is quite an extensive dictionary of the Czech

language of its time. In order to evaluate its comprehensiveness as highly as is justified it must be remembered that the alphabetical and the onomasiological dictionaries are companion volumes, that is, that the author approached his task from two viewpoints, achieving noteworthy results in both of them.

Daniel Adam of Weleslavin could only (and did) achieve the high standard of his works by using the method of Latin-based lexicography of his time as it had spread all over Europe in alphabetical and onomasiological dictionaries.[10]

10.2 Comenius on dictionaries

It was the inventiveness of this early tradition, enriched by many other achievements in the field of lexicography in the Europe of that time, which helped Jan Amos Komenský, more often called by his Latin name Comenius, to find his place. (Přívratská 1994, 155.)

Comenius is the probably unique figure for whom a dictionary, alphabetical or onomasiological, was the direct expression of a philosophical and pedagogical idea.[11] Therefore, the making of dictionaries was directly linked to the elaboration of his system of thought. This system is composed of theological, philosophical, linguistic, and pedagogic elements. The theological motivation was certainly the strongest of all, but there were also national overtones, because Comenius wanted the children of his country to enjoy a linguistic education in their own vernacular as he deemed it right and necessary (Čapkova 1968, 55).

For Comenius, the importance of dictionaries resulted from three lines of thought which he had already acquired in his youth from his teachers and from such contemporaries as, for example, Wolfgang Ratke (Ratichius, 1571–1635), Johann Heinrich Alsted (1588–1638), Joachim Jungius (1587–1657), and the Rosicrucians,[12] and which, in one way or another, he adhered to throughout his whole life. They can be labelled *universalist*, *encyclopaedic*, and *panharmonious*. The domain to which these men's ideas pertained was the world at large, conceived of as an ordered entity of details. The domain of their practical work was the individual who achieved harmony of thinking, speaking, and acting by becoming aware of this order.

Even as a young man, between 1611 and 1614, when he studied at the universities of Herborn and Heidelberg, Comenius planned to render the whole world and its intrinsic order accessible to his further ideas and activities by preparing

---

[10] See Chapter 9.

[11] The bibliographical representation of Comenius's works is notoriously difficult. A critical edition, the *Opera Omnia Jan Amos Komenský* is being prepared by the Academy of Philosophy in Prague. An overview of this as yet unfinished huge editorial enterprise is given in Králík 1981. It includes bibliographical references to the works to be included. Urbanková 1959 and Brtová and Vidmánová 1978 give an exhaustive list of all Comenian works to be found in the territory of the Czech and Slovak republics (1959, at that time Czechoslovakia) and elsewhere (1978). For an exhaustive bibliography, up to 1980, of Comenius's works and of secondary literature see Totok 1981, 384–419.

[12] Johann Valentin Andreae (1586–1654): *Chymische Hochzeit Christiani Rosencreutz*, 1616.

three books, (i) a *Theatrum Sanctae Scripturae*, (ii) a *Theatrum universitatis rerum*, and (iii) a *Thesaurus linguae Bohemicae*. This means he planned an inventory of the spiritual world, of the world of objective reality, and of (his mother) language. The *Thesaurus*, an alphabetical dictionary, was to consist of (i) a complete list of names of objects, (ii) a grammar, and (iii) a collection of proverbs. With it Comenius aimed at showing (i) the analysis of reality, (ii) the synthesis of thinking, and (iii) the *'syncrisis'* (his term) of the spiritual and the secular, three methods of reflection in which Comenius engaged to the end of his life (Blekastad 1969, 21–90).

Later, in the years 1618–21, he worked on this book as his *opus principale* under the title *Amphitheatrum*. The part devoted to the world was broken down into the *theatrum naturae* (heaven, earth, and hell, i.e. the universe as a whole according to Comenius's religious convictions), the *theatrum humanum* (i.e. mankind between sin and salvation), the *theatrum orbis terrarum* (i.e. a global geography), and the *theatrum saeculorum* (i.e. a global history). Clearly, these divisions are moving towards the well-known divisions of universalist nomenclators and Comenius's own dictionaries.

Most of the *Amphitheatrum* and the entire *Thesaurus*, on which Comenius had worked for forty years, were burnt in Leszno in 1656 in the turmoils of the war. Of the former only chapters one to nineteen are preserved.

In the course of his life, Comenius deliberated on the role of language for humans again and again, treating the subject in various of his works (Geißler 1959, Kraemer 1977). As an epistemological framework, he developed a triadic arrangement of 'reality, thought, and speech', also called 'object, mind, and language' (or: '*res, mens*, and *lingua*'). In this arrangement one item is not simply the image of the other. The first, *res*, has only itself as a norm, because they exist independently of the others, but *mens* follows the nature of *res* and the nature of itself, and *lingua* follows the nature of *res*, of *mens*, and again of itself (Kraemer 1977, 3–16, Přívratská 1987). Thus, complexity increases between the members of this chain of terms, and language is the most complex of the three, providing insights into the mind and into reality according to its own, linguistic rules. Consequently, it is only by learning these rules that such insights can be obtained. Ideally, learning a language means causing one's mind to operate according to the structure of reality.

But language is not an end in itself. It is the starting-point of action and has to be used as such. In this capacity, as a social activity, language is the central member of another triadic arrangement, namely 'thought, speech, and action' or '*ratio, oratio*, and *operatio*'. The performing instrument of *operatio* is *manus*. The two triadic arrangements in line (*res—mens—lingua—manus*) mark the position of language between reality and the mind on the one hand and its function in society on the other. Moreover, *operatio*, also called *manus*, as an activity in society, leads back to reality, because the result of human activity creates another *res*, thus starting a new cycle. This leads to the arrangement of the terms: *res—mens—lingua—manus—res*, in which the first *res* is the object of thinking, speaking, and acting, and the second *res* is its product. Comenius illustrated this arrangement in the famous schema at the start of his book *Triertium catholicum* which, more than other texts, stresses the tripartite division of his way of thinking. In fact, the *Triertium* is even printed in three columns in which the explanations are given in a parallel position (Comenius 1974, 240–346).

For Comenius, the pedagogue, these philosophical statements have certain didactic consequences. Generally speaking, the language taught must be in harmony with the mind of the learner who is in harmony with reality, and it must lead to such public use of language as influences society in a way which is harmonious with reality again. The method of teaching has to ensure these interconnections (Caravolas 1993 and 1994, ch. 10). This makes certain demands on the teaching material. The harmony between all the members of this chain is grounded in the essential analogy of all the domains of this world, which for Comenius was a fact guaranteed by God.

Comenius treated the problem of language teaching in connection with his philosophical system as well as in practical didactics and textbooks. One consequence in the practice of teaching was that he classified textbooks according to the capabilities of learners. As early as 1657, in the *Didactica magna* (Comenius 1986a) he distinguished between *Vestibulum*, *Janua*, *Atrium*, and *Thesaurus* (the last one being devoted to classical authors, but this stage was later dropped), a typical scheme which he adhered to henceforth.

A most important work explaining these matters is *Novissima linguarum methodus* (Comenius 1957).[13] In it Comenius developed the principles of teaching Latin (or any other language), starting from the nature of language (chaps. I to VII) and then, after pointing out the special role of Latin among all the other languages, sketching out the principles of language teaching in general (chaps. X ff.). In the *Methodus*, Comenius confirmed many teaching principles of his *Didactica magna*. But in contrast to the approach adopted in this earlier book he now addressed learned and erudite readers and adjusted the level of his deliberations accordingly (Blekastad 1969, 422–4).

The *Novissima linguarum methodus* is an extraordinarily rich book which deserves a more detailed comment than can be given here. The greater part discusses the philosophical foundations of adequate language teaching and includes the thoughts of about forty scholars of his time (Sadler 1966, 151). In our lexicographical context only some of those statements will be selected which pertain directly to the two onomasiological works for which Comenius is famous, the *Janua linguarum reserata* (Comenius 1986b) and the *Orbis sensualium pictus* (Comenius 1970b). They will be shown to be lexicographical works which directly express a theological and philosophical idea. But, except for a few remarks, they will not be discussed as textbooks in Comenius's very particular and complex

[13] Written in Lezsno in 1648 and included in *Opera didactica omnia* 1657, vol. I, part II, cols. 1–292; see Kraemer 1977, Helmer 1980, Přívratská 1991.

system of teaching (Caravolas 1994, 339–69). They will be discussed as dictionaries.

At the beginning of the *Methodus* we find the well-known triad:

Tria sunt inprimis, qvibus humanam naturam, supra brutam exaltatam, decoravit Creator: RATIO, ORATIO, & varia liberaqve rerum OPERATIO. / RATIO, est lumen divinum in Homine . . . . ORATIO verò est luminis illius qvidam effluxus, quo Homo ea qvae intelligit, aliorum qvoqve intelligentiae clarè ac distinctè explicat. OPERATIO deniqve, est ea qvae intelligit et loqvitur producendi etiam, si vult, facultas, solertia mirabili.   (1957, cols. 17/18, 6–8.)[14]

After this the divine origin and the confusion of languages in Babel which makes *culturam linguarum* necessary are treated. This is to be done with three instruments:

(1) Nomenclatura Rerum, sive Tabulatura Universi, Verbis aptis contexta. (2) Index Verborum & Phrasium plenus: h.e. Lexicon, seu Dictionarium. (3) Sermonis faciendi artificium certum, h.e. Praecepta de sermonis structura, Grammatica.   (1957, col. 50, 4.)[15]

In toto, this *nomenclatura* shows the work of the supreme architect of the world and of language alike, God. Lexicographically speaking, it is the onomasiological part of the undertaking, the *Index* being planned as alphabetical (and not to be mentioned any more). Before commenting on the *nomenclatura*, Comenius quotes Pliny's history of the world and Julius Pollux's onomasticon (180 AD), thus indicating to his readers the tradition in which he sees his own work. He then explains the *nomenclatura rerum* in a paragraph which he obviously thought to be very important because it is printed entirely in italics:

Condendam suademus, Rerum & Verborum Tabulaturam quandam, Universalem: in qva Mundi fabrica tota, & Sermonis humani apparatus totus, parallelè disponantur; Verbis nempe simplicissimis, & sententiis brevissimis, & serie sic una & perpetua, ut finis nisi in fine non reperiatur: intermediis omnibus (Rebus & Verbis) tàm non nisi suo loco positis, ut nihil idem repeti opus sit: & omnia tamen sint clara, facilia, fluida, ut ad instar historiae cuivis hominum, & legere ista volupe sit, & intellegere promptum. Et quicunqve haec vidisset, legisset, intellexisset, ut certus sit se vidisse Rerum seriem omnem, & intelligere Lingvam totam. (1957, col. 53, 13.)[16]

---

[14] 'There are in particular three [properties] with which the Creator has decorated human nature, exalting it over [the nature of] animals: intelligence, language and various and free action. Thinking is the divine life in man; . . . language is truly a certain outcome of this light, by which man clearly and distinctly explains that which he understands also to the intelligence of others. Action, finally, is the ability of producing, if he wants to, with wonderful skilfulness that which he understands and speaks [of].' (My translation, W. H.)

[15] '(1) A Nomenclature of things or table of the universe by the apt words in context; (2) [An alphabetical] index of words and full phrases, i.e. lexicon or dictionary; (3) The certain art of making speech, i.e. rules of the structure of speech, grammar.' (My translation, W. H.)

[16] 'We suggest putting together [= writing] a certain universal table of things and words, in which the total edifice of the world and the total apparatus of language are arranged in parallel; however, with very simple words and short sentences and in a unitary and homogeneous sequence so that a limit cannot be found except at the end, with nothing put between all the things and words except at its [proper] place, so that it is not necessary to repeat [anything]. And all [things] should be

This passage contains almost all the ideas that pertain to onomasiological dictionaries in the way which became typical of Comenius: their entries represent the world, the human mind, and language, as if there were three lines running parallel. They are arranged in an unbroken chain in which every item finds its proper place. This arrangement gives them clarity and makes them easily intelligible so that people who see and understand them actually understand the world and language *in toto*. Consequently, their expression, which makes use of this understanding, will lead to harmonious communication. As divisions for this *tabulatura*, Comenius suggests: (i) '*naturalia*', the world as created by God (ii) '*artificialia*', the world as created by man; (iii) '*moralia*', the way man treats the world which he is entrusted with; and (iv) '*spiritualia*', everything concerned with religion (see *Methodus*, Comenius 1957, col. 54, 16; Helmer 1980). This is in accordance with Comenius's ideas on *pansophia* which he expressed later in his *Consultatio catholica*.[17] The *mundus naturalis, mundus artificialis, mundus moralis*, and *mundus spiritualis* constitute the state of a harmonious whole.[18] Each of them depends on the nomenclature of phenomena which make up the respective worlds. Thus, *nomenclature*, which is identical with the arrangement of Comenius's onomasiological works, is in fact one of the principles of the pansophical philosophy. It is not merely a lexicographical technique but a philosophical idea.

The division into four classes is certainly not new and can be found in the context of philosophy and natural history in many other authors; but Comenius highlights it by giving it explicit theological reasons. There is also an elaborate explanation of the way in which items should be entered in the *tabulatura*. Not merely the name, but details must be given referring to:

> ... *Qvid sit?, & ad qvid, & qvale, & qvid agat aut patiatur, & cum qvibus vicinis cohaereat, &c unumqvodqve: Nominanda itaqve fuerit Res ipsa tota, cum suo FINE. Tùm ejus partes, tanqvam intrumenta, seu media, per qvae suo fini apta est. Tùm qvid singula ista agant, vel patiantur. Vt nihil in Rebus sit essentiale, qvod non observare, verbisque propriis exprimere, doceantur omnes.* (1957, col. 54, 17.)[19]

---

nevertheless clear, easy [to understand], fluent so that it would be a joy for whomever is to read this and understand [it] promptly as if it were some entertaining narrative. And whoever should read . . . and understand this is sure to see the whole sequence of things and understand the whole language.' (My translation, W. H.)

[17] After being lost and, though occasionally mentioned, unknown in the eighteenth and nineteenth centuries, found in the library of the Franckesche Stiftungen in Halle, Germany, as late as 1935 and printed for the first time in Comenius 1966a.

[18] In the more elaborated explanations of the *Consultatio*, the *mundus archetypus, mundus angelicus, mundus materialis*, and *mundus aeternis* are mentioned in addition to those given above.

[19] 'What is it [to be]? And for what purpose, and for what quality, and what acts or suffers, and with what neighbours is it connected, etc. [and] similar. Therefore the whole thing itself should be named with its purpose. Then its parts as well as its instruments or media which are appropriate to the purpose. Then what these details do and suffer. So that there is nothing in the things but what is essential which everybody would be taught to observe and express with proper words.' (My translation, W. H.)

All this means that the *tabulatura* is not a mere list of items in isolation designated by lexemes; it contains entities which only become what they are in a web of delimitations, meanings, functions, and interdependencies. This is exactly the programme which Comenius realized in the way in which he constructed the sentences of the *Janua* and the *Orbis pictus*. Taken together, they represent the *universitas rerum*.

For Comenius, *res* exist before the mental images which man has of them and these before words (Kraemer 1977, 18–19). Conversely, this means that language, mind, and world have the same extent and cover the same area, provided language use is adapted to the mind, and the mind to reality. Note:

Linguae apparatum (si in sua perfectione spectetur) praegrande qvid esse, ut Mundus ipse, qvem repraesentatum it; & amplum capaxqve, ut Mens ipsa, cujus Conceptibus exhauriendis, & in alterius mentem transfundendis, sufficere debet: & deniqve concinnum qvid, omnia sua tam harmonice contexens & connectens, ut harmoniam Rerum, cujus mensuras in se Animus humanus continet, recte exprimat.   (1957, col. 23, 15.)[20]

This is not only a pedagogical programme for language teaching and language use, it is also a linguistic programme for the construction of a perfect, even a universally intelligible language which has just as many words as there are mental concepts and ontological units in reality.[21] Both transcend the domain of lexicographical thoughts in Comenius's works. He followed the goal of a perfect language in his (unfinished) *Panglottia*, part of the comprehensive *Consultatio catholica*, and the aim of the pan-harmony of man and world in his concept of 'syncrisis', the unification of all human knowledge (Přívratská 1987 and 1989) Note:

Est praeterea usus Analyticae proprius ad Rerum inventiones; Syntheticae ad exseqvutiones; Syncriticae ad utrumqve.   (Comenius 1966a, col. 118, 64.)[22]

'Syncrisis' is Comenius's own term and concept. It depends very much on analogy which can be found by comparison. '*Syncrisis . . . est actio mentis rem cum re conferentis*' (*Lexicon pansophicum*, Comenius 1966b, col. 1232).

In the background of this programme we find the concept of encyclopaedic

---

[20] 'The apparatus of language, if looked at in its perfection, is something very great like the world itself which it will represent; and [it is so] vast and spacious as the mind itself, whose concepts it should interpret and transmit to other [people's] minds, [so that] it is sufficient [for them]: [and that] finally, being skilfully combined, it [= language], so harmoniously contextualizing and connecting all its properties, then expresses rightly the harmony of things whose measures the human spirit contains.' (My translation, W. H.)

[21] For Comenius's ideas on a perfect and universal language see Hüllen 1989, 165–73. He also planned an alphabetical dictionary as a document of a perfect and universal language, giving it the name *Lexicon reale pansophicum*. Its entries consisted of definitions of word-meanings which allocated every word of the human language and every corresponding meaning its 'orderly' locus in the world. The plan, an appendix to *Consultatio catholica*, remained unfinished. See Dvořák 1985.

[22] 'Moreover, the method of analysis is especially useful in finding [= recognition] of things, [the method of] synthesis in making [them], [and the method of] of syncrisis in both.'(My translation, W. H.)

knowledge as it prevailed in the seventeenth century and also the concept of name semantics, in so far as word-meanings were understood to be names for pre-existing things.[23] The authorities for the concept of encyclopaedic knowledge were Genesis, Aristotelian physics, natural history according to Pliny, Galenic anatomy and anthropology, and general knowledge according to Isidore (Sadler 1966, 60–9). Fundamental to all of them were the ideas of *order* and of man as microcosm, that is, as the epitomic repetition of the macrocosm. This is an essentially traditional world-view, as the relevant chapters in the two onomasiological dictionaries also prove, although Comenius was well aware of the new scientific developments (Sadler 1966, 60–4).[24]

Comenius was a theologian and a philosopher, but he was also a practical schoolman. During his first stay at Lezsno (1628–32) he had to teach Latin to children who were hardly able to read and write. What he needed was a simple textbook.

In his *Novissima linguarum methodus* (Comenius 1957, cols. 81/82, 20) he narrates how he came to know the work of the Irish Jesuit, William Bathe (1564–1614), living in Salamanca, who had collected 1,200 Latin sentences, translated into Spanish, in such a way that no word was repeated. This collection had been known since 1605, well before its publication in 1613. It was a textbook of Latin for Spanish learners. It met with great success and was translated into various other European languages. Comenius mentions editions by Isaac Habrecht and Caspar Schoppe(ius) and the translations of Bathe's Latin sentences into English, German, Italian, Greek, and Hebrew (see below). By doing so, he indirectly acknowledged Bathe's priority to the title which he adopted for his own work and which has been associated with Comenius rather than with Bathe ever since. *Vis-à-vis* the many editions and adaptations which appeared of Bathe's original work we must assume that Comenius simply thought he was adding another one, using, as all the adaptors did, the original title with the added adjective *reserata* and a distinctive subtitle.

10.3 *Janua linguarum*

10.3.1 *William Bathe and his adaptors*

Ianva Lingvarvm, Sive Modvs Maxime Accomodatus, Qvo Patefit Aditvs Ad Omnes Lingvas Intelligendas. Indvstria Patrvm Hibernorvm Societatis Iesu, qui in Collegio eiusdem nationis Salamanticae degunt, in lucem edita: & nunc ad linguam Latinam perdiscendam accomodata. In Qva Totius Lingvae, Qvae frequentiora, & fundamentalia sunt continentur: cum indice vocabulorum, & translatione Hispanica eiusdem tractatus.
Salmanticae. Apud Franciscum De Cea Tesa. Anno M. DC. XI.[25]

---

[23] See Chapter 11.

[24] 'In the *Orbis pictus* the illustrations show that he retained the old misconceptions though, in places, he gives evidence of detailed knowledge as, for instance, when he names the thirty-four bones in the hand and thirty in the foot.' (Sadler 1966, 67.)

[25] According to a facsimile copy in O Mathúna 1986: between 78 and 79. Identical with BL C.33.f.7.

The title of *Janua linguarum*, stemming from the imagery of the *ars memorativa*,[26] was invented by the Irishman William Bathe (1564–1614) who lived as a member of the Societas Jesu in the Irish convent of St Patrick in Salamanca. His personal career has been carefully researched (O Mathúna 1986, 33–75). The descendant of an influential Irish family, he worked as a courtier and a lawyer, but mainly as a Jesuit priest carrying out his spiritual and pastoral duties. Among his many interests and activities, questions which we would today call *learning theory* seem to have enjoyed high priority. As a student in Oxford, he studied *ars memorativa* after Giordano Bruno; in 1584 and 1596 two books on music from his pen were printed which also focused on the problem of learning (O Mathúna 1986, 33–75, Caravolas 1984, 1991).[27]

William Bathe published two versions of his *Janua linguarum* in Salamanca in 1611. The shorter version of the book consisted of 1,200 sentences in Latin and Spanish. The full version had an additional word-list of 5,300 lexemes which were taken from these sentences. He had worked for twenty years on both, supported by his brother John. There is evidence that the sentences and word-list were used before their publication, for example in 1605 by Englishmen for attaining a quick knowledge of Spanish (O Mathúna 1986, 81).

The sentences were broken down into sections of one hundred, termed 'centuries', each with its own topic, which however remained rather vague. The first seven topics are of a moral character: 1–100: virtue and vice; 101–200: wisdom and folly; 201–300: temperance and intemperance; 301–400: justice and injustice; 401–500: fortitude and cowardice; 501–600: human actions; 601–700: things turbulent and quiet. The next two topics refer to objects of reality: 701–800: objects with and without life; 801–900: artificial objects. After that the strict order of the book breaks down: 901–1041 are called 'miscellaneous'; 1042–1100 are left blank; they were probably meant for ambiguous lexemes which however could not be explained in short sentences and, not printable on the pages, went into the appendix; 1101–1200 were taken up by a continuous text. The sentences were numbered, arranged in two columns, the Latin sentence printed in Roman type, the matching Spanish sentence in italics. Note these five examples from the first 'century':

Sententiarium moralium. De virtute, & vitio in communi.

. . .

---

[26]   The title of the first printed textbook for the learning of a foreign vernacular, Adam of Rotweil's *Introito e porta* (1477), stems from the same context of images. (Actually *Introito e porta* is not the title of the book but the key words of its first sentence. This, however, does not alter the facts.) See Chapter 9, 331–6.

[27]   O Mathúna 1986 and, on a much smaller scale, Caravolas 1991 are the authoritative recent treatments of Bathe who has not attracted too much scholarly attention. There is also Corcoran 1911, who treats Bathe mainly as a Jesuit. The well-known monographs on language learning (e.g. Kelly 1969, Mackey 1971, Howatt 1984, Caravolas 1994) all mention Bathe, and so do, in comparison with Comenius, the great monographs on the latter (e.g. Geissler 1959, Červenka (in Comenius 1959), Schaller 1967, Čapkova 1968, Caravolas 1984) and, more broadly, historiographical treatments of the seventeenth century (e.g. Webster 1975, Padley 1976–88, Salmon 1979, Hüllen 1989). Our concern here is mainly lexicographical.

10. Sub sordida veste saepe scientia. 10. Debaxo de vil vestido muchas vezes ay sciencia.

11. Nouitas acquirit gratiam. 11. La nouedad adquiere agrado.

12. Reminiscere te omninò puluerem esse. 12. Acuerdate, que eres totalmente poluo.

13. Socius facundus pro vehiculo. 13. Compañero gracioso vale por coche, (esto es aliuia el camino.)

14. Quod scis ignoras, digito compesce labellum. 14. Lo que sabes ignoras, con el dedo aprieta el labio.

15. Declina à malo, & in bono te exercere. 15. Apartate de lo malo, y exercitate en lo bueno.[28]

The examples quoted[29] are typical of the pithy and often proverbial character of the sentential entries and also of their semantic unrelatedness. Very exceptionally, for example in the fifth 'century', some sentences are bound together in a text, here a rhyming hymn on Christ. The vocabulary is taken from Calepino's famous Latin dictionary which appeared for the first time in 1502. There are no derived or compounded lexemes in this collection, only radicals.[30]

During the seventeenth century, Bathe's *Janua linguarum* acquired, with some forty more versions, the status of a textbook used throughout Europe, quite similar to *Introito e porta*, and also to Comenius's two later ones, of which the first bore the same name. As with all of these, it testifies to the lively interest in vernaculars, if always in connection with Latin, and also to the intellectual unity of Europe in this Humanist century that a textbook for learning modern languages via Latin (or the other way round) was applied to most of the influential European languages and printed and used in most of the European countries. Unfairly, William Bathe's name disappeared from almost all of the later versions in favour of that of the new translator and editor. Very likely the reason is that it was not politically correct to advertise a Jesuit author in many, that is the reformed, European countries.

The book was obviously particularly popular in England. Five editions by William Welde, of 1615, 1616, 1619, 1621, and 1623,[31] are known, in which the original Latin sentences are used with English translations. Note the title:

Ianua Linguarum, siue modus maxime accomodatus in qua, totius linguae vocabula, quae frequentiora, & fundamentalia sunt, continentur [by William Bathe]: *cum indice vocabulorum, & translatione Anglicana eiusdem tractatus* [by William Welde].[32] *Excudebat H. L. impensis Matthaei Lownes: Londini 1615.*
(BL C.33.d.14.)

---

[28] '10. Underneath a plain dress there is often wisdom. 11. News brings thanks. 12. Remember that everything of you will be dust. 13. An eloquent companion [is good] for the journey. 14. [Let] what you know to be unknown close your lips with a finger. 15. Turn away from evil and be devoted to good.' (Translations from the Habrecht edition 1629.)

[29] From a facsimile page of the first edition in O Mathúna 1986, 78.

[30] The structure of Bathe's book can probably be best understood in the context of the strict rules which the Jesuits set up for the conducting of classes and for learning languages in all stages of a curriculum. See Caravolas 1994, 313–38.

[31] According to the BL Catalogue and the STC of Pollard and Redgrave 1991. Without giving a basis of calculation, O Mathúna (1986, 107, n. 58) estimates that the editions of 1615, 1616, 1621, and 1623 amounted to at least 5,000 copies, which would be indeed a very large number.

[32] Names of authors inserted according to the BL Catalogue.

Also in London, and in 1617, Johann Barbier published his four-language version with the title: *Janua linguarum, quadrilinguis. Or a messe of tongues Latine, English, French, and Spanish.* In this the Latin sentences and their English translations were printed on the left-hand page and the Spanish and French translations on the right-hand one. The word-list was provided only in Latin and learners were referred to the sentences where they could find the vernacular equivalents. There was a second edition of the book in the same year. Also in the same year Johann Rhenius included Bathe's Latin sentences, without any translations, in his volume *Methodus institutionis nova quadruplex.* There was a reissue of the book in 1626.

Next to be mentioned is the Latin–Spanish–Portuguese version by Amaro de Robero (1623). He used Bathe's word-list, but added many derived and compounded forms. His is the only reissue of Bathe on the Iberian Peninsula.

Isaac Habrecht's *Ianua Linguarum Quadrilinguis*, published in Strasbourg in 1624, gave German, French, and Spanish translations in addition to the Latin sentences. His *Ianua Linguarum Silinguis* of 1629 is important in our context because the editor added Italian and English translations. Note the title:

Ianua Linguarum Silinguis, Latina, Germanica, Gallica, Italica, Hispanica, Anglica. Sive Modus Ad Integritatem Linguarum Compendio Cognoscendam Maxime Accommodatus: ubi sententiarum selectiorum Centuriis duodenis omnia fundamentalia, necessaria & frequentiora vocabula semel, sineque repetitione comprehenduntur. Cvm Introductione, Et Dvplici indice, Latino-Germanico, vices vocabularii supplente. Auctore Isaaco Habrechto, Phil. & Med.D.—Sechsfache spraachen-Thuer Lateinisch / Teutsch / Frantzoesisch / Italianisch / Spannisch / und Engellaendisch: Oder eine Newe vortheilige Weiß / allerhand spraachen auff das aler leichtest zu erlernen: da in zwoelff Hundert außerlesenen spruechen alle urspruengliche / nothwendige / und gebraeuchliche Wort gedachter spraachen ohn unnoethige Widerholung begriffen seynd. Sampt beygefuegtem fernerem Bericht / und zweyfachem Register / Lateinisch / und Teutsch / welches an stat eines Vocabularbuchs zugebrauchen. Argentinae. Sumptibus Eberhardi Zetzneri: Bibliop. ANNO D. DC. XXIX. (BL 627.b.2.)

There were more editions published in England. John Harmar, an Oxford professor of Greek, was responsible for the one of 1626, re-edited in 1627 and 1631, which, besides minor changes in the Latin sentences, added notes with explanations of idiomatic meaning. He planned this *Janua* to be a primer for beginners, but also useful for refresher courses.

The next chapter in this story of a book are the editions by Caspar Schoppius entitled *Mercurius Bilinguis* and *Mercurius Quadrilinguis*. He was the first to identify William Bathe as the author on the title-page ('*Guielelmus Bateus Hibernas opusculum hoc . . . composuit.*') *Mercurius Bilinguis* is a Latin–Italian version, published in Milan in 1628. In 1643 it was re-edited together with a comprehensive Latin–Italian and Italian–Latin dictionary and phrase book, called *Il perfetto dittionario*. There were re-editions in 1649, 1657, 1659, 1672, 1682, and 1684. *Mercurius Quadrilinguis* is a Latin–Italian–Greek–Hebrew and Latin-German-Greek-Hebrew version, which both appeared in Padua in 1637.

Finally Thomas Horne, who later also edited English editions of Comenius's *Janua linguarum reserata*, and his friend Timothy Poole edited in 1634 *Janua linguarum or an easie and compendious Method and course for the attaining of all Tongues, especially the Latin . . .*, with substantial additions to Bathe's text, a Latin–English plus an English–Latin index, and inflectional information. Note that this edition appeared after Comenius's *Janua*. The fact that there was a new edition of Horne's version in 1645 shows that Bathe's book remained in demand, although Comenius's *Janua* was by now well established on the market. There is mention of more editions with up to eight languages, including Czech, 'Slavonic', (probably Polish), and Hungarian, whose existence, however, cannot be verified.

In his introduction, which was reprinted in part in many of the later editions, William Bathe gave a didactic explanation of his book. Judged from today's linguistic knowledge, it is full of surprising insights into the meanings, distribution, and use as well as usage of words. Bathe thought of learners so different from each other as missionaries, ambassadors, scholars, and senior servants in noble households, all of whom needed a command of foreign languages. Obviously he was not thinking of scholarly or scientific language use, but of regular communication situations and oral competence. According to Bathe, there is a 'regular' method of learning this competence by grammar and translation, and an 'irregular' one of learning it by reading and speaking. We would today call the former the grammar-translation method and the latter the direct method. But Bathe claims to have found a 'middle' method for learning languages. A list of basic words was culled according to the frequency of their use by students of *litterae humaniores* (in fact empirically observed in Belgium, where Bathe studied for some time). They were framed in short sentences. A word-list contained numbers which referred to these sentences, so every word could be found in its minimal context. Grammatical rules, in particular explaining concord, were deemed superfluous because they were in fact incorporated in the syntagmas. Bathe maintained that his textbook would do for ordinary language use, although he knew that a language command with scientific ambitions could not be attained in this way. Translation was supposed to serve either the learning of Latin from a vernacular or the learning of a foreign vernacular from Latin. The later editions added the possibility of learning one vernacular from another.

In spite of his almost modern ideas on language and language learning, the author neither gave a reason for the division into 'centuries' nor suggested how the teaching and learning should be done. Concerning the former, he simply mentioned that people on a journey like to have their way divided up by equal milestones. So the whole architecture of the book looks rather artificial. Concerning the latter, it is almost certain that William Bathe was simply thinking of learning the sentences by heart, probably a fixed number per day. This may also account for the rather odd idea that words, except structure words, were not to be repeated. They occur in one sentence only, which created severe problems of style. The neglect of any sort of repetition and exercise which this method entailed only makes sense if the author believed in the absolute reliability of the learners' memory.

The topics of the 'centuries' were, therefore, of little importance for the learning process itself, except that they had to be in accordance with a church-guided education. Bathe says in the introduction: 'There was a difference of opinion for a time between the author and those who collaborated with him in this work concerning the best method for forming the words into sentences. Finally, it was decided that as far as possible morality should be the central theme. This directive was strictly observed as far as the sixth century.' (Translation by O Mathúna 1986, 117.)

Indeed, there are no meaningful connections between Bathe's sentences at all. The first 500 contain only moralizing statements and proverbs, which may be very interesting as a source of knowledge about then current convictions and beliefs. The fifth 'century' gives Christ's passion in sentences. Among the moralizing sentences of the sixth 'century' we find some statements of facts, for example:[33]

514: In der nechsten Handelstatt (Gewerbstatt) laßt uns von Diamanten un[d] Chrystallen berahtschlagen.—Let us aske advise concerning Adamants and Chrystall, in the next Market-tovvne.

522: Das Testament / (oder letzte willen) ist bey mir / in dem Trog / (oder Kisten).—The Testament is in my keeping in a chest.

559: Mein Dochtermann wird mit seinen geschwisterkindern in dem Herbst- unnd[!] Weinmonat bey uns seyn.—My sonne-in-lawe, and his cosens vvill be vvith vs in September and October.

Some sentences are (possibly) not without humour. Note, for example:

638: Ein Rahtsherr gehet daher in einem langen rock.—A Senator goeth in a long govvne.
639: Ob die in der Hoellen seynd / auch discuriren?—Do those that are in hell, discourse?

There are hardly any connections between the titles of 'centuries' and their sentences. Admittedly, in the eighth hundred, more animals are mentioned than in the others, but this does not come near to a natural history approach. The sentences of the tenth 'century' deal with tools, crafts, and edifices, but are still mixed with many other topics. The titles of the tenth, eleventh, and twelfth 'centuries' preclude a semantic coherence anyway.

Probably, William Bathe would not understand this characterization of his book at all, because such understanding is guided by Comenius's later work. For Comenius the semantic coherence of sample sentences was a strict didactic postulate. From historiographical hindsight we might evaluate Bathe's collection of sentences as a typical collection of expressions which would be used in many Latin classes of the seventeenth century.

---

[33] Taken from the Habrecht edition, German and English versions only. (Bathe 1629.)

10.3.2 *Johannes Amos Comenius and his adaptors*

J. A. Comenii Janua Lingvarum Reserata sive Seminarium Lingvarum Et Scientiarvm Omnium. Hoc est Compendiosa Latinam (et quamlibet aliam) lingvam unà cum scientiarum artiumque omnium fundamentis perdiscendi Methodus, sub titulis centum, periodis autem mille comprehensa.[34]

The *Janua linguarum reserata, sive seminarium linguarum et scientiarum omnium* ... (Comenius 1986*b*) appeared in 1631 in Latin and in 1633 in Czech, both in rather poor editions. In their wording and meanings both texts were planned to be as identical as possible, an ambition which often did harm to the structure of the Latin sentences. The contents were taken from the *Amphitheatrum universitatis rerum.*

Comenius's *Janua linguarum* was a success which took its author completely by surprise, because he had meant the first Latin and Czech editions to be tentative ones which he wanted to finalize and combine into one edition if they found a favourable reception. Instead, many translations started appearing in unauthorized versions. It was only in 1657, in his *Opera Didactica Omnia* of that year, that the final authorized version appeared (1957, vol. I, p./col. 250–302). Between the first and this edition, Comenius worked over the *Janua* no less than six times. He produced the editions of Leszno 1631 and 1633 and of Danzig 1633, that is, the editions of the so-called *forma prior*, and those of Leszno 1649, Paták 1652 and Amsterdam 1666, that is, the editions of the so-called *forma posterior*. Červenka (in Comenius 1959, XL) shows that there were seven more editions from Comenius's own hand of the *forma prior*, repeating in one case the edition of Leszno 1631 and in six cases the edition of Danzig 1633. Twenty-two more editions of this first group were published by other editors. Of the *forma posterior* we have six more editions by Comenius himself and three by other editors.

Twenty-five editions of *Janua linguarum* contained English and were published in England (London).[35] As early as 1631, Johannes Anchoran was the editor of a Latin–English–French version:

Porta Lingvarvm Trilingvis Reserata Et Aperta. Sive Seminarium Linguarum & Scientiarum omnium, Hoc est, Compendiaria Latinam, Anglicam, Gallicam (& quamvis aliam) Linguam vnà cum artium & scientiarum fundamentis sesquianni spatio ad summum docendi & perdiscendi methodus, sub titulis centum, periodis mille comprehensa, Latinè primum. Nunc verò gratitudinis ergo in Illustrissimi Principis Caroli Britannicaeque Gallicae & Hybernicae pubis, gratiam, Latinè, Anglicè & Gallicè in lucem eruta, Opera studio, & elucubratione Ioh. Anchorani Theol. Licentiati. . . .

---

[34] Comenius 1986*b*, *Opera omnia*, vol. 15.1, 261–301, notes 490–509. All subsequent quotations are from this edition.

[35] These editions have various titles, besides the original one, for example, *Porta linguarum* ... (1631, 1633, 1639) or *Latinae linguae janua* ... (1656).

Londini, Excudebat Georgivs Millervs Sumptibus Michaelis Sparkes & Thomas Slater. MDCXXXI.

The Gate of Tongves Vnlocked And Opened, Or else A seminarie or seed-plot of all Tongves and Sciences. That is, A short way of teaching and thorowly learning within a yeare and a halfe at the farthest, The Latin, English, French, (and any other) tongue, together with the ground and foundation of Arts and Sciences, comprised vnder an hundred Titles, and a thousand periods. In Latine first, And now as a token of thankfulnesse brought to Light in Latine, English, and French, In the behalfe of the most Illustrious Prince Charles, and of British, French and Irish youth. By the labour and industry of Iohn Slater, Licentiate in Diuinitie.

London, Printed by George Miller for Thomas Slater, and are to be sold at his shop in Black Friers neere the Church. 1631.

This edition was reissued in 1633, 1637, 1639, and 1640.

Thomas Horne translated the Latin text into English (1636), and after a considerable augmentation of this translation by John Robotham the two brought out a Latin–English version probably in 1640 (this issue is no longer extant),[36] then in 1643 and 1647. The re-editions of this version in 1650, 1652, 1656, 1659, 1667, 1670, and 1673 were organized by William Dugard. The 1656 edition was enriched for the first time with an alphabetical index. There is also a Latin–Greek–English edition which appeared without the name of an editor in London in 1662, 1670, and 1685. Besides the editions mentioned, the relevant STCs (Pollard and Redgrave 1991 and Wing 1994) have entries on another seven editions published in Britain (1641, 1647, 1664, 1664, 1665, 1673, and 1674).[37]

The interest in Comenius's work was not even limited by the otherwise rigorous conditions in religion. In 1667 a Latin–Czech–German edition was published by Jesuits in the printing shop of the archbishop in the College St Norbert, Prague, and '*cum Licentia Superiorum*' (Comenius 1667). The title contained the sentence in three languages: '*In qua postrema Editione omissa sunt ea paucula, quae Catholicae doctrinae non satis consona, & Juventuti non explicandaese videbantur*'.[38] The Thirty Years War had destroyed the peace between the confessions of the country, but it had failed to eradicate the influence of Comenius's books.

Other language combinations of *Janua* editions were Latin–French–Italian–Spanish and German (Amsterdam, 1661), Latin–French (Geneva, 1663), Latin–Greek–French (Amsterdam, 1665), Latin–Dutch ('Belgick')

---

[36] It is, however, mentioned in a letter of Philippe Georg Hübner to Comenius of 27 November 1640; see Červenka in Comenius 1959, XXXV.

[37] There is a list of editions of *Janua linguarum* in Britain between 1631 and 1700 besides other interesting aspects of the printing history of Comenius's book, mostly with reference to Dalgarno, in Cram and Maat 1996.

[38] 'In this following edition very few [sentences] have been omitted which seem not to conform thoroughly to the Catholic doctrine and not explainable to young people.' The sentence appears in the Latin, the Czech, and the German versions of the title. A painstaking comparison between this Catholic and the earlier Protestant editions would show how dictionaries are made the tools of ideologies.

(Amsterdam 1666), Latin–Czech–German (Prague, 1669), and Latin–German–French–Italian (Frankfurt, 1673).[39] All this happened in Comenius's life time.[40]

But the popularity of the book did not end with its author's death. *In toto*, no less than 101 varying editions reached the market, published in almost all European towns which housed a printing shop, including, besides the languages mentioned, translations into Polish, Swedish, and Hungarian (Beneš and Steiner 1985*b*, 482–9).[41] If ever there was a European textbook, this is one.[42]

And not only this. Soon after the foundation of Jamestown, Virginia, in 1607, plans were developed there for the higher education of the settlers and also of the natives in New England. John Hartlib's (?–?1670) *A Description of the famous Kingdom of Macaria* ... (1641) and Johann Valentin Andreae's *Rei publicae Christianipolitanae Descriptio* (1619)—and this means also Comenian ideas (Young 1929)—exercised great influence on them, as the correspondence of the first Governor of Massachussetts, John Winthrop the Elder (1589–1648), reveals (Young 1932, 89–95). From the correspondence between John Winthrop the Younger (1606–76) and Robert Boyle we know that *Janua linguarum* was used at the newly founded Harvard University by English and by native students. Comenius, obviously briefed by John Hartlib, took great interest in this development (Young 1932, 93; more details in Acheson 1997), as a letter of his to Andrew Klobusicky of 24 May 1655 betrays.

In 1669, Comenius mentioned (Young 1932, 48) that according to a letter of a Master Golius, which he had received in Leyden, his *Janua linguarum* was being translated into Arabic by a brother of the letter writer living in Aleppo, and moreover into Turkish, Persian, and Mongolian by persons who expressed great interest in further works of his. However, nothing is known about these editions

[39] The various issues have been compiled from Červenka in Comenius 1959, Comenius 1986*b*, 482–9, i.e. the isagoge of *Janua* by Kyralová-Steiner, and the BL catalogue. There is a synoptic edition of six versions edited by Červenka (Comenius 1956). The book, which also contains valuable comments on *Janua*, is written entirely in Latin.

[40] Comenius's encyclopaedic arrangement must have had an intriguing effect on people because the 1643 edition of Bathe's *Janua*, entitled *Mercurius Bilinguis*, published together with *Il perfetto dittionario* by Caspar Schopp (see above), had the sentences regrouped in forty-two units and arranged under encyclopaedic titles like 'De variis partibus seu membris corporis', 'De diversis brutis animalibus', etc. Obviously, the editor believed that this would aid memorization better than Bathe's collection of sentences with its rather formal architecture (O Mathúna 1986, 102).

[41] It is impossible to say how many copies of the book were produced in each print run, so that we can only estimate the total number of copies. As Comenius wrote and printed the *Janua* in connection with specific, local teaching tasks, the number of copies will have been very small, probably below 100. There is simply no way of estimating the numbers of copies that appeared in unauthorized versions. If we assume an average of 300, as with *Introito e porta* and its derivatives (see Chapter 9), we come to the almost gigantic number of some 30,000 copies in almost all European countries. It is only with the *Opera Didactica Omnia*, in 1657, that we can reckon that a larger number of copies in an authorized version were produced. I thank Martin Steiner for information on this matter.

[42] As far as I have been able to ascertain, there is no study on the reception and use of Comenius's works in English schools. Watson (1909, 185 and 189), mentions the *Janua linguarum* and the *Orbis pictus* in the context of teaching natural history and geography in England.

today.[43] Both cases, the American and the Oriental, were certainly taken by Comenius as demonstrations of the missionary value of his book.

In the preface to his *Janua linguarum reserata* (Comenius 1986*b*) Comenius gives the reasons for his book and its structure in thirty-three numbered paragraphs. He complains about the methods of teaching Latin which were current at his time and which were criticized by many authors, such as Juan Luis Vives (1492–1540), Erasmus of Rotterdam, Johannes Sturm(ius), Nicodemus Frischlin(us), Julius Caesar Scaliger (1484–1558), and others. The complaint is that vocabulary and grammar were not integrated, and vocabulary was taught without an understanding of meanings. In paragraphs twelve to twenty Comenius describes his disappointment with Bathe after his initial enthusiasm for the book, mentioning Habrecht's French and German translations, an eight-language edition of 1629, which however cannot be verified today, as well as the general popularity of Bathe in England and Germany. He mainly criticizes the selection of the 1,200 words and their semantic unrelatedness and also the sometimes nonsensical meanings of the sentences in which they are embedded. He expressly agrees with the method of constructing an epitome of the whole language in words and in phrases, which facilitates learning, and he promises to do the same. However, as words are '*signa rerum*' (263, par. 5), this means for Comenius not merely collecting useful words in short sentences for memorization but creating an epitome of reality and one of language in parallel. Paragraph twenty-one contains the most important statement:

Principiò quia mihi inter immotas didacticae leges haec est, ut intellectus et lingva parallelè decurrant semper, et quantum quis rerum apprehendit, tantum eloqui consvescat [. . .] necessariò faciendum putavi, ut rerum ipsa universitas per classes certas ad pueritiae captum digereretur, eoque modo id, quod sermone exprimendum est (res ipsae), imaginativae parti primùm imprimeretur. Factum itaque est, et enati sunt mihi centum communissimi rerum tituli. (1986*b*, 265, par. 21.)[44]

As authorities who confirm this idea Comenius names Cicero and St Augustine.

The following paragraphs deal with details. Some 8,000 words were embedded in exactly 1,000 sentences, as a rule without being repeated, unless the words have several meanings. Synonyms and antonyms were arranged so that they explain each other. There is no word-list, because Comenius planned a comprehensive dictionary as well as a grammar, more textbooks, and a short didactic treatise, so that teachers and pupils would have whatever they needed in one volume. It would be good, Comenius writes, if somebody else could do the same with the

---

[43]   Červenka (in Comenius 1959, V) even mentions Armenian and Abyssinian editions.

[44]   'Because I am convinced under unchanging didactic rules that mind and language always work in parallel and that people understand things in as much as they are used to them, I thought it necessary to establish an orderly universe of things by certain classes to make [it] comprehensible for the boys in such a way that at first is imaginatively impressed [= remembered] what is to be expressed in words, the things themselves. Therefore [this] happened, and 100 common titles of things were created.' (My own translation, W. H.)

texts of classical authors. The separate printing of a German version of this *Janua* was justified by the idea that not everybody would be interested in the former one.

The main point of difference between Bathe and Comenius is obvious. The Irishman had a practical idea which depended on what would today be called *rote learning*. It was responsible for the architecture of his book, its contents being almost selectable *ad libitum*. The Czech used this architecture, but underpinned it with his epistemological ideas. Bathe's book, therefore, is a selection of sentences in a loose order. Comenius's book is an onomasiological sentence dictionary. This is shown by the title (see above). For the *tituli* of the two books and their characteristic differences see Table A.20.

Comenius changes the Bathian architecture[45] of twelve sections ('centuries') with 100 sentences each into 100 sections with a variable number of sentences each. The shortest is section XXXVIII with only one, the longest section LXVII with thirty-three sentences.

The macrostructure of Comenius's *Janua* is almost a model of a clear arrangement. Sections I and C are pedagogical sections addressing the learner and explaining the aims of the language course. They show a symmetrical arrangement, stressing the beginning and the end. There are no divisions between sections II and XCIX, but it is easy to break the ninety-eight sections down into smaller and still smaller units which betray the categorial framework that is behind them. The most obvious division is the one between nature (II–XXIX) and the man-made (human) world (XXX–XCIX). The first seven sections (II–VIII) refer to the universe as a whole. Its categorial guidelines are the Biblical story of creation, the classical concept of the four elements, and general observations concerning the weather and the earth. *Aer* as an element is somewhat neglected. Unlike *fire*, *water*, and *earth* it does not have a section of its own, but is included in '*De Meteoris*'. These seven sections follow the general tendency of the *Janua* to go from the comprehensive to the detailed, from the general to the specific. Besides, they ensure that nature is understood to be God's nature.

The following eleven sections (IX–XIX) refer to nature in the sense of natural history, broken down into the inorganic (IX–X), the organic (XI–XIII), and the animal kingdoms (XIV–XIX). They present the general knowledge of the author's time, mostly derived from Pliny, but also from contemporary authors like Johann Heinrich Alsted or Konrad Gesner (1516–65).[46] Moreover, the sequence of the three kingdoms follows the Aristotelian order. Subsequently, sections XX–XXIX refer to men in so far as they are, as a species, members of the natural chain. Section XX speaks of the various ages, sections XXI–XXV speak of the body and what may happen to it, and XXVI–XXIX, finally, speak of the senses and the mental faculties, that is, *ratio*, will, and emotions. All of them are part of generally known anthropological concepts.

---

[45] For a comparison between the *Janua* by Bathe and that of Comenius see Caravolas 1991.
[46] See the detailed commentary in 1986*b*, 490–509.

The human world is seen as the domain of activities which make life possible (XXX–LIII), of the family (LIV–LVII), of public life (LVIII–LXVII), of academic disciplines (LXVIII–LXXXII), and finally of virtues (LXXXIII–XCVI). It is a characteristic feature of these domains that they do not always have clear delimitations.

Human activities pertain to providing food (vegetarian, XXXI–XXXIV; animal, XXXV–XXXIX; dishes, XL–XLI), to travelling, which includes trade (XLII–XLV), and to providing clothes (XLVI–XLVII). A section on various crafts according to the different materials that craftsmen work with stands by itself (XLVIII), although the preceding sections have already mentioned crafts according to their part in providing the means for living. The house (XLIX–LIII) is presented with its main rooms. It can be regarded as the product of craftsmen, thus belonging to human activities. It can, however, also stand as a topic by itself, or as a part of the succeeding sections on the family for whom it provides accommodation. However this is resolved, the sections devoted to crafts, houses, and family are associatively linked with each other. The family (LIV–LVII) is seen to spring from marriage and to be the basis of the economy.

The domain of public life (LVIII–LXVII) centres around buildings with public functions and the order of the state, which is obviously seen as responsible for peace and war, because a section devoted to them follows immediately. Academic disciplines (LXVIII–LXXXI) start again with (the parts of a) building, namely a school and a museum, that is, a study, establishing a link with the preceding sections on public life in houses, and then proceeding to the trivium and quadrivium, although not in strict order. More so-called modern disciplines like history and scientific disciplines like optics and medicine follow. Finally, all the classical and medieval virtues are enumerated (LXXXII–XCIV). The two sections on 'erudite conversation' and 'games' can be included with them.

There remain three sections (XCVII–XCIX) before the '*Clausula*' (C) which deal with death, God's providence, and the angels. They are the exact symmetrical counterparts to the first three which showed the universe to stem from God and thus to be God's nature. This time, the human world is shown to be God's creation as well, dominated by his providence, with the angels between him, and mankind doomed to death.

Comenius's *Janua* has always been recognized as a lively textbook the direct and precise language of which creates natural images of all the domains of the world (Blekastad 1969, 174–5). It is part of a whole textbook system consisting of the alphabetical *Lexicon januale*, the onomasiological *Janua linguarum*, and the *Grammatica janualis*. The pupil is supposed to work with all three during the process of teaching and learning at this stage.

The *Janua* textbook system is itself included in a wider system the parts of which are geared to the needs of learners depending on their level of proficiency, not their age. It consists of the *Vestibulum*, *Janua*, and *Atrium* (see above), each of which is divided into an alphabetical dictionary, an onomasiological dictionary, and a grammar. It is important for the way in which Comenius planned language teaching that he did not abandon the idea of the systematic arrangement of vocabulary with its philosophical underpinning in any of the three stages (Caravolas 1994, 361–4).

Another consequence of this idea of matching the order of the world with the order of the language to be taught was the principle of not listing words but sentences. Logically speaking, most of the sentences in the *Janua linguarum* are definitions. Typical features of objects are mentioned in order to identify them, frequently in opposition to the typical features of other objects. Linguistically speaking, these definitions make use of common collocations between nouns and adjectives.[47] We also find enumerations of lexemes, for example when members of a species are enumerated. This means that the onomasiological principle is practised not only on the level of sentences but also on the level of lexemes, even if within syntagmas. In other sections actions are described step by step, giving a certain narrative quality to the text. Finally, some sentences are of an exhortatory or moralizing character. Though it would require a sentence-by-sentence and section-by-section commentary on the *Janua* to say something definite about the structure and style of its sections, the following examples can illustrate the principles mentioned.[48] Note the defining style and the collocations:

82. *Lapis comminutus Arena est, que si crassior sabulum et clarea vocatur.*—*A stone bruised or broken in pieces is sand, which if it be thick or grosse, it is called grosse sand or grauell, and round pibble stone, driest sand.*
83. *Saxa humi iacent: siue existant siue lateant, scopuli et cautes eminent.*—*Great stones lye in the ground (whether they be seene or hidden), high rockes and hils ful of great stones appeare on high.*
86. *Tophus arenosus & scaber est.*—*A grauell stone is sandy and rough or rugged.*
87. *Alabastrites candidissimum marmor.*—*The alabaster stone is marble very white.*

Note the enumeration of lexemes:

126. *Herba cauli vel scapo innititur.*—*An hearbe leaneth or stayeth vpon a stalke.*
127. *Es his rapum, napus, caereta, siser, Raphanus maior, Raphanus minor, pastinaca, Brassica, Crambe, Lactuca, Scolymus, Apium (petroselinum) Nasturcium, olera vocantur.*—*Of them a rape, a nanew, a carrot, a skirwike root, a radish, a rayfort, a parsenip, cabbage or colewort, a lettice, an artichoake, or sowthistle. parsly or smallage, water cresses, or nosemart, are called pothearbs.*

---

[47] This linguistic feature stands out even more prominently in the 427 sentences of the *Januae Linguarum Reseratae Vestibulum* (Comenius 1986c), the more elementary form of the *Janua*. Note, for example: '*Montes sunt altis, valles profundae, colles elevati.*' (13); '*Locus est commodus vel incommodus.*' (39); '*Sermo jocosus, vel serius.*' (53). There is also collocation between noun and verb: '*Sol lucet, luna splendet, stellae micant.*' (65); '*Canis latrat, aries arietat, bestia laniat.*' (85).—'Mountains are high, valleys are deep, hills are elevated.—Places are convenient or inconvenient.—Speech is humorous or serious.—The sun shines, the moon is bright, the stars twinkle.' (My translation, W. H.)

[48] All quotations in Latin and English are taken from Anchoran 1631. The French translations are omitted. There is no French title. I am using the facsimile reprint of 1970c.

129. Legumina verò siliquis et valuulis, vt in Faba, Piso, Cicere, Eruo, Vicia, Lente videre est.—And the legums with huskes or cods, and shales or peeles, as may be seene in a bean, a pease, a small pulse, a oare, a vetch, lintels.

Note the step-by-step actions:

553. Mensae mappis stratae disci, orbesque atque quadrae imponuntur, ut & salinum.—Dishes or platters are set and laid vpon the table couered with tablecloths, as likewise rundels or trenchers, and a saltsellar.

554. Apponuntur verò panis collyrae, aut bucceae scissae, & fercula.—But loafes of bread, bunnes, cracknells or simnells, or morsells cut, and messes or dishes of meat are set vpon.

555. Inuitati conuiue a conuiuatore in cenaculum (triclinium) introducuntur.—The guests bidden or inuited, are brought into the parlour by the feast mamaker[!].

Note the exhortatory and moralizing tone:

918. Cvm quo tibi necessitudo est, erga illum apertus sis, sine fraude doloque amicum enim fraudare & fallere quae gloria?—Whom thou art familiar with, be open towards him, without fraud and guile: for what glory is there to beguile and to deceiue, or to deal fraudulently and deceitfully with a friend?

919. Fidelio socio fidus esto: perfidè qui agit, sibi perditi onem machinatur.—Be trustie to a faithful & loyall companion: hee that dealeth perfidiously, deuiseth his owne perdition and ouerthrow.

921. Ab amicitia nihil alienus assentatione.—There is nothing so much against friendship as flattering, or flattery and asssentation,[!].

The question of whether the book lives up to Comenius's own standards as defined in *Methodus* (see above) must remain open. Certainly lexemes do not merely stand as names for items, they are defined in the context of semantically related lexemes. The section on 'water', for example (VII), states that out of humidity come 'springs' which become 'brooks'; they assemble in 'rivers' and 'streams'; without current they become 'still waters'; 'torrents' lead to 'inundations'; there is 'flowing water', 'whirling water', 'precipitating water', 'brine'; where the land ends we have a 'bay', 'promontory', 'isthmus', etc. This is a quite typical sequence of statements which brings together a group of semantically related lexemes. Many sections consist of descriptive miniatures. All of them are quite realistic. Even if it is difficult for the historiographer to find Comenius's philosophical ambitions realized in these texts, they certainly encircle small meaningful domains of reality and represent their interior structure, as far as the language provides lexemes for doing so.

In spite of bluntly teaching a great number of facts, the climate of classroom conversation is occasionally kept alive by interposing questions between statements. This shows a friendly atmosphere between teacher and learner, which is, more so even than in other places, created in the opening and the closing sections. Note, for example the first five sentences:

1. Salve, lector amice. 2. Si rogas, quid sit eruditum esse? responsum habe: Nosse rerum differentias et posse unumquodque suo designare nomine. 3. Nihilne praetereà? Nil certe quidquam.

4. Totius eruditionis posuit fundamenta, qui nomenclaturam naturae et artis perdidicit. 5. Sed id difficile forsan? 6. Est, si invitus feceris aut praeconcepta opinatione teipsum terrueris.
1. Welcome, friendly reader. 2. If you ask what is going to be taught, be answered: to know the difference between things and to be able to designate each with its name. 3. Nothing more? Certainly not. 4. He laid the basis of all erudition who learnt the nomenclature of nature and of art. 5. But this is perhaps difficult? 6. It is, if you do it reluctantly or if you frighten yourself by preconceived opinions.

The opening and the closing sections have quite a marked position in the whole, but we find dialogical elements also at inconspicuous places. In section VI 'On Meteors' we unexpectedly find the rhetorical question (English version only): '*When it lightneth and thundereth, who should not be frightened and astonished?*' (62); in section XXVI 'Of outward senses' the almost teasing: '*Wouldst thou know how anything sauoureth? taste it.*' (325.) Note a similar address to the learner in section XXIX 'Of the will and affections': '*But behold and looke how subject it [the will] is to the affections! how greatly it is now and then troubled therewith! Are good things absent?*' (362–3.) Something very similar can be found in the opening lines of some sections. Note, for example: '*Go to, let us now look into the entrailes.*' (XXII, 'Of inward members', 266) and '*We ought then now to visite and to see also the shops of craftsmen*' (XXX, 'Of things mechanicall in general', 378).

The speaker who is behind these sentences obviously feels as if he were standing in front of a class. He even seasons his teaching principles—this time the change of description into a chain of actions—with a good portion of humour. Note section XLIX, 540:

'*Being to enter & to go into a house, for feare thou shouldst misse the doore, stand still & stop at the entrance, & behold and looke on the forefront: then knock at the gate or at the doore.*'

The dialogical element which emerges in this introduction and, if in a somewhat hidden way, in several entries seems to have been particularly close to Comenius's pedagogical heart because he, later, turned the whole of the *Janua linguarum* into a stage-play, the famous *Schola ludus, seu Encyclopedia viva*, thus producing the unique example of a dramatized dictionary (*Omnia Didactica Opera*, vol. 2: cols. 831–1039).[49] In fact, Comenius also expressed at least the intention of laying out his main work, the *Consultatio catholica*, as a comprehensive dialogue and so turning the system of philosophical concepts into a sequence of conceptual derivation. This means taking the word *consultatio* literally.

Whether the Latin is formally and semantically appropriate for beginners can be queried, certainly, but not only, from today's point of view. Obviously, an enormous amount of traditional and contemporary erudition went into those sentences. Another sentence-by-sentence commentary would probably be able to

---

[49] Eight dramatic plays where a king and his councillors ask experts for the names of various things (plays 1–5 and 8) or where ordinary people talk to each other. They used to be popular in schools. They contain invaluable information on seventeenth-century life.

read Comenius's whole world from the text, his dependence on general traditional thinking, his everyday knowledge, his personal opinions and beliefs.[50]

Certainly Comenius had the one central idea that his work should mirror the order of the world. It is the nucleus of onomasiology. It also was the nucleus of his thinking which he labelled *pansophy* and to which he dedicated much of his work and to which he even subjected his dictionary making. It is symbolized in the well-known emblem which shows the sun, the moon and stars, wind, water, and rain above a flourishing landscape. The motto: *Omnia sponte fluant absit violentia rebus* signals the natural harmony which was not conceived of as something static but as the flow of life in nature. His *Janua* was to reflect this in words embedded in their sentences. Learning a language was to be achieved by becoming aware of this natural order (Blekastad 1969, 459).

10.4 *Orbis sensualium pictus*

10.4.1 *The dictionary*

During the years 1650 to 1654 Comenius lived in Sáros Patak in Hungary in the service of the princely family Rákóczi in order to implement his pedagogical ideas in their schools. There were three successive classes for teaching Latin. However, Comenius faced great difficulties in realizing his ideas. He tried solving them by writing a book called *Lucidarium* (Comenius 1970a) for children to learn about the world and its order by pictures, before they could read properly. He himself sketched the pictures. The book was later to become the *Orbis sensualium pictus* (Comenius 1970b). In a simplifying transposition its contents were taken from the *Janua*. Very young children were merely asked to look at the pictures; the older ones were additionally supposed to read the titles with the help of an illustrated alphabet that preceded the book; and the still older ones were supposed to read the simple sentences which explained the pictures (Blekastad 1969, 535). In 1654, when Comenius was back in Lezsno, the manuscript was sent to the publisher Michael Endter in Nuremberg. There is no proof that Comenius included sketches of the illustrations from his own hand (Pilz 1967, 33–4). Two years later the war forced Comenius to leave Leszno, after all his manuscripts had been burned. From Amsterdam, he tried to retract his permission for Endter to print the *Orbis sensualium pictus*, but the publisher had already had the pictures drawn by one Paulus Creutzberger and the Latin text rendered into German by Siegmund von Birken. It appeared in 1658 without its author's *imprimatur*. It was to become Comenius's most famous textbook for language learning.[51]

---

[50] The commentary in *Opera Omnia* attempts to do this by pointing out where in his other works Comenius makes statements which coincide (or conform) with statements in the *Janua*.

[51] The history of the book is minutely narrated in the notes (by Marta Bečková) to the edition in the *Opera Omnia*, vol. 17, 270–92. They include the hypothesis (by Stánislav Králik) that the German part was written by Comenius himself, who had a perfect command of the German language, and that it was then worked over by Siegmund von Birken.

Comenius's *Orbis sensualium pictus* is the prototype of an onomasiological dictionary, because it presents the *explananţia* prelinguistically and juxtaposes pictorial semantic messages with lexeme forms.[52] This means that the pictures are not illustrations in an ornamental or pedagogical sense but an integral lexicographical part of the dictionary. Although the layout is different,[53] the pictures (theoretically) constitute the left-hand column, the texts the right-hand column of an onomasiological dictionary in its common form. The fact that entries are embedded in sentences represents a certain deviation from this. However, the technique of tagging lexemes with numbers which reappear in the pictures and the italicization of these lexemes makes it abundantly clear that the book is lexeme orientated and, thus, fulfils one of the most important criteria of dictionaries.

For Comenius, using pictures as an instrument of language teaching was probably a simple didactic idea. He had tried his hand at illustrating earlier versions of the *Janua* and *Vestibulum* and approved of illustrated editions, for example by Johann Jakob Redinger (?–1688) in his Latin–German dictionary. According to his own account, he took over the idea of illustrating schoolbooks from Eilhardus Lubinus (Eilhard Lübben, 1565–1621) (Pilz 1967, 17–19, Ĉapkova 1968, 130). In his introduction to a Latin–Greek–German edition of the New Testament Lubinus had floated the idea that children should be educated with the help of pictures (Caravolas 1994, 142–6). However, it seems unnecessary to point to individual authors who influenced Comenius, because illustrating had been in general use for a long time as a prelinguistic way of conveying information (Hupka 1989, Stein 1991*b*). During the first half of the thirteenth century, for example, the so-called *Biblia pauperum* came into existence, besides other book illuminations on theological matters. Between then and the time of the publication of the *Orbis pictus* most of the types of pictures we find there had become popular, like plants (in herbals), animals (in natural histories), astronomical spheres (in encyclopaedias), towns and landscapes (e.g. in Schedel's famous chronicle, Nuremberg, 1493), technical matters (in books on mining, metallurgy, pyrotechnics), anatomy (e.g. in Vesalius, 1543).[54] This means that almost all the woodcuts of the *Orbis* had their forerunners. Moreover, pictures had been in use for a long time in the tradition of *ars memorativa*.

Since Andrea Alciatus's *Emblematum liber* (Augsburg, 1531) many emblembooks with their special arrangement of pictures and texts had appeared on the market. They constitute a Europe-wide tradition, inside and outside book culture.[55] They are particularly well represented in Germany and the Netherlands (Steinberg 1961, 185–6; Höltgen 1986, 23–9).

---

[52] See Chapter 1.

[53] All remarks and all quotations pertain to and are taken from the edition Comenius 1970*b* in the *Opera Omnia*, vol. 17.

[54] There was also a songbook of the Unity of Brethren, whose bishop Comenius was and which contained everyday scenes in richly decorated initials. I thank Dr Bohatcová, Prague, for this information.   [55] For example, in tapestries, grave monuments, and paintings.

Superficially, the arrangement of *emblems* is very similar to the arrangement of the *Orbis pictus*. It consists of *motto, pictura,* and *epigram,* which are comparable to *name* (of section), *picture,* and *entry-text.* In both genres the three elements explain each other mutually. In his 'Praefatio' to the *Orbis pictus* Comenius explains the arrangement of the book by pointing out the three parts:

Libellus est, ut videtis, haut magnae molis, mundi tamen totius et totius linguae bereviarum, plenus picturis, nomenclaturis rerumque descriptionibus.   (59.)[56]

In describing the pedagogical functions of pictures, nomenclatures, and texts, however, Comenius did not make the slightest allusion to emblems in the usual sense. In other works, he shows that he is aware of the existence of emblems proper, as is to be expected.[57] But he seems to regard them as one of at least two means by which the contents of teaching can be illustrated. In his *Didactica magna,* chap. XVII, par. 42, he develops a plan, reminiscent of similar ideas put forth by Tommaso Campanella (1568–1639) in his *La città del sole* (1602) and Francis Bacon (1551–1626) in his *New Atlantis* (1627), that everything to be learned in a classroom should be depicted there '*sive sint theoremata et canones, sive imagines et emblemata*' (Comenius 1986a, *Opera Omnia* 15.1, 116).[58] That *imagines et emblemata,* here and elsewhere, are mentioned side by side betrays the fact that Comenius did not regard one as superior to the other. Historiographically, the two belong to quite different worlds. Emblems construct a religious, philosophical, or mythological world; Comenius's dictionary, however, is a language textbook, although with a distinct philosophical and religious underpinning. So it is difficult to decide whether the structure of *Orbis pictus* is a deliberate, though only formal, adaptation of the emblem technique.

Various methods of illustration were vigorously debated and put into practice in Comenius's own time (Volkmann 1929, Hüllen 1993 and 2002, 159–71). More important than discovering the precise links between Comenius and other illustrators and their methods of illustration is perhaps the recognition of the pedagogue's *general* inclination towards visibility and memorization via the human

---

[56] 'As you see, it is a small book, not a great volume [but] nevertheless the whole world and the whole language, a concise book full of pictures, nomenclatures, and descriptions of things.' (My translation, W. H.)

[57] See, for example, Comenius 1966a, vol. II, *Pampaedia,* chap. XII: 12–13 (cols. 186–7, 116–17) where he mentions emblematic literature. He suggests that a book of emblems be composed which would comprise the most important messages of *pansophia.* It was to be of a small format so it could be carried around. Obviously, Comenius thought of a collection of moralizing proverbs. His *Labyrint světa* is fully dependent on the emblematic method, in particular in Comenius's own drawings.

[58] See also Comenius 1986a, *Didactica Magna,* chap. XIX, para. 37 (*Opera omnia* 15/1, 135) where a similar idea is mentioned. In chap. XXVIII we find the plan of a picture book with Latin inscriptions. The topic has not attracted much scholarly attention; see however Forster 1960.

senses. This leads to the problem of what kind of structural element in lexicography, more precisely: in the *Orbis pictus*, pictures actually are.[59]

Each section of the *Orbis pictus* has a picture and a text in Latin and German (and, in later editions, in different and more languages). The text is divided into paragraphs which were given numbers, obviously by the editor. These numbers are very useful because they draw attention to the fact that the arrangement in print of sentences or parts of sentences is not random.[60] The numbers are printed between the two language columns and, thus, refer to both. The texts are of unequal length, varying between two and twelve paragraphs. Each paragraph is between two and five lines long, a few paragraphs, those which follow the Biblical story (see below), exceed this length by up to twelve lines. The number of explanatory lexemes in each line varies according to the type of section (see below). Disregarding introductory paragraphs, which are cataphoric with reference to those that follow, the natural lower limit is of course one, the upper limit is about ten to twelve. These lexemes are tagged with a number which reappears in the picture, thus identifying their meaning. However, there are also italicized lexemes without a number, which consequently do not reappear in the picture. Note this example from section CXXXVIII on 'royal majesty':[61]

Inter hos [aulici] primarii sunt cancellarius[6] cum consiliariis et secretariis, praefectus praetorii[7], aulae magister[8], pocillator (pincerna)[9], dapifer[10], thesaurarius[11], archicubicularius[12] et stabuli magister[13].

Unter diesen [Hofleute] sind die vornehmsten der Kanzler (Erzsiegelhalter)[6] mit den Räten und Sekretarien (Geheimschreibern), der Marschalk[7], der Hofmeister[8], der Mundschenk[9], der Truchseß[10], der Schatzmeister[11], der Oberkämmerer[12] und der Stallmeister[13].

The chief amongst these [Courtiers], are the Chancellor[6] with the Councellors and Secretaries, the Lord Marshal[7], the Comptroller[8], the Cup-bearer[9], the Taster[10], the Treasurer[11] the high Chamberlain[12], & the Mast. of the horse[13].[62]

Naturally, the number of lexemes in a paragraph tends to be greater where the text presents an inventory of things (see below). In other cases there is an average of two to four lexemes. For Comenius, learning certainly meant learning by heart (though not blindly), at least to a great extent. Paragraphs were certainly planned as learning units and the number of tagged lexemes in them as the learning

[59] Something similar can be said of Comenius's technique of numerical reference between picture and sentence. Zigmund Evenius used it in his *Gottselige[r] Bilderschule* of 1636 (Čapkova 1968, 130). For Evenius and also for Johannes Saubertus see Pilz 1967, 20–7. This is the authoritative treatment of the production and reception of the *Orbis pictus*. For the tagging of words with numbers there are other examples which were in all likelihood outside Comenius's experience. See Chapter 5, 146.

[60] Nevertheless it is difficult to understand that an addendum like this in an otherwise faithful critical edition should go unannounced and uncommented by the editor.

[61] This is the second paragraph of this section, which explains why the numbers start with '6'. In subsequent quotations paragraph numbers will only be indicated by an asterisk. Italicization will be ignored.

[62] The Latin and the German texts are taken from Comenius 1970b (see note 53). The English text, here and in all subsequent quotations, is taken from the 1672 edition by Charles Hoole (see below).

burden that could be assigned to a learner in one step. However, there is no theoretical discussion of this matter with reference to the *Orbis pictus* in Comenius's works.

Paragraphs in print do not coincide with sentences. It is the syntactic structure together with the editorial paragraph numbering which constitutes a subtle system of indicating the intrinsic (see below) order of sections. In section XXX, on serpents and reptiles, for example, the first sentence is divided into three paragraphs: the first is introductory ('Angves *repunt sinuando se*', '*Die* Schlangen *kriechen und krümmen sich*', 'Snakes *creep by winding themselves*'), the second and third give names of serpents according to the places where they can be found. There then follow special cases. Paragraphs four and five name the blindworm on account of its blindness, not of its habitat, and lizards because they have feet. The last sentence is divided into paragraphs six and seven which separate the 'winged serpent' (dragon) from the poisonous (basilisk and scorpion). This means that each paragraph is devoted to a special category of the species of animals presented.

Generally speaking, the flexible mapping of sentences and paragraphs on to each other serves the entry structure on the pragmatic level (see below). This means that the two division systems have a different ordering function in almost every section. Note, for example, the first two and the last two paragraphs of section LXV, on devices, tools for moving and lifting, the other paragraphs being devoted to one tool each:

1. Quantum duo ferre possunt palanga[*] vel feretro[*], 2. tantum potest unus trodendo ante se pabonem[*], suspensa a collo aerumna[*]. 6. Fistuca[*] adhibetur ad pangendum sublicas[*]; adtollitur fune, tracto per trochleas[*], vel manibus, si ansas habet[*].

1. Soviel zweene tragen können an einer Stange[*] oder auf der Tragbahr[*], 2. soviel kann einer vor sich herschiebend den Schubkarren[*] mit vom Hals hangenden Tragriemen[*]. 6. Der Hei (Schlegel)[*] wird gebraucht, einzuschlagen die Wasserpfähle[*]; 7. wird gehoben mit dem Seil, gezogen durch die Werbel[*] oder mit Händen, wann er Handheben hat[*].

One can carry as much by thrusting a Wheel-Barrow[*] afore him, having an Harness[*] hanged on his neck, as two can carry on a Cole-staff[*] or Hand-barrow[*]. A Rammer[*] is used to fasten Piles[*] it is lifted up with a rope drawn by Pullies[*] or with hands, if it have handles[*].

In addition to the syntactic structure, paragraph numbers here point out the difference between what two men and what one man can do, and the downward and upward movement of a pile driver. Both differences are of immense practical importance.

The *Orbis pictus* was designed to be read *in toto*. It is a cohesive text[63] realizing Comenius's general ideas on language textbooks, as concisely defined in the title and explained in the 'Praefatio'. Moreover, it achieves the tasks that were given to onomasiological dictionaries in the sixteenth and seventeenth centuries. The author makes these conditions for using his book quite clear. There is a pre-section

---

[63]   See Chapter 1, 22–7.

'*Invitatio / Einleitung / Invitation*' and a post-section '*Clausula / Beschluss / The Close*' which are set apart from the main body of the dictionary because they are not numbered, proceed in dialogue fashion between teacher and learner, and have the same picture. The teacher announces:

Ducam te per omnia, ostendam tibi omnia, nominabo tibi omnia. Ich will dich führen durch alle Dinge; ich will dir zeigen alles; ich will dir benennen alles. I will guide thee thorow all, I will shew thee all. I will name thee all.

And he resumes at the end:

Ita vidisti summatim res omnes, quae possunt ostendi, et didicisti primarias voces Latinae (Germanicae) lingvae. Also hast du gesehen in einem kurzen Begriff alle Dinge, die gezeigt werden können, und hast gelernt, die vornehmsten Wörter der lateinischen (deutschen) Sprache. Thus thou hast seen in short all things that can be shewed, and hast learned the chief words of the English & Latine Tongue.

'*Invitatio*' and '*Clausula*' draw a clear communicative frame around the presentation of the world, identifying the voice of the speaker, namely, the teacher, and the ear of the listener, namely, the learners. There are two more occasions on which the teacher steps forward and stresses the textual cohesion of the sections. Section XLIV, on gardening, starts with the sentence:

Hominem vidimus; jam pergamus ad victum hominis et ad mechanicas artes, quae huc faciunt. Den Menschen haben wir besehen; itzt laßt uns fortschreiten zur Kost des Menschen und zu den Handwerkskünsten, welche hierzu dienen. We have seen Man: Now let us go on to Mans living, and to Handy-craft-trades, which tend to it.[64]

And section LXIII, on carpenters, starts:

Hominis victum et amictum vidimus; nunc sequitur domicilium ejus. Des Menschen Fülle und Hülle haben wir besehen; nun folget die Wohnung desselben. We have seen Mens Food and cloathing: now his dwelling followeth.

As a cohesive text, the *Orbis pictus* has a semantic macrostructure, which is constituted by the order of sections. Comenius did not provide an overview but, obviously for practical purposes (and possibly against his own intentions in the *Orbis pictus*) he provided an alphabetical index of sections. However, it is not entirely certain whether this index indeed came from his pen. It could have been added during the process of drawing and printing. The *Orbis pictus* also has a syntactic microstructure on the level of its entries, and it has a pragmatic structure, which is constituted by the order of these entries within one section. Strictly speaking, an entry consists of that detail in a picture which corresponds to a lexeme with the same number in the text. But it would certainly be against all the intentions of the book to isolate items from the pictorial and the syntagmatic contexts. Rather, it makes sense that the paragraph in the text, which is numbered

---

[64] This anaphoric remark is also to be found in *Janua linguarum*, chap. 30.

and marked in print by indentation, be considered as the entry unit, together with the corresponding details in the picture. Moreover, the whole pattern of the book makes readers run their eyes over the pictures *in toto* and, consequently, read the texts *in toto*. It is only after this synthesizing perception that an analytical awareness of details can commence. Thus, the process of understanding moves from section level to paragraph level to lexeme level.

The macrostructure of the *Orbis pictus* does not pose special difficulties. It is not extraordinary—in comparison with other onomasiological dictionaries of the time or Comenius's other works, in particular his *Janua linguarum*, whose macrostructure the *Orbis pictus* follows closely. Neither would the artificially constructed entry, the equation of lexeme and pictorial detail, be of any interest. It is the entry paragraphs in their special order within each section and the correspondence between section type and picture type that call for a comment. This means that the need for explanation arises at the pragmatic level of the dictionary.

10.4.2 Text types and picture types

Abstract typologies of pictures have been suggested which classify the information expressed in them. They centre around Peirce's differentiation between *icon, index,* and *symbol* or other criteria like *enumerative, sequential, structural, functional, nomenclatural, scenic,* etc. (Hupka 1989, 184–206).[65] Such systems can be mapped on to each other quite easily. Moreover, their level of abstraction allows the application to many, albeit mostly more modern, relevant works. Yet in the case of a singular book like the *Orbis pictus* it seems preferable to explain the picture types in close proximity to the text types of the dictionary, even if this means that the ensuing system has no general validity but explains Comenius's work and nothing else.[66]

A close look at Comenius's texts at the section level and the corresponding pictures shows that they both belong to one of three types, namely: (i) a *statement* on something, which has its pictorial counterparts in *schemata*; (ii) a *narrative* of something, which has its pictorial counterpart in a *story*; and (iii) an *inventory* of something, which has its pictorial counterpart in a *pedagogical scene*.

Statement, narrative, and *inventory* are three different text types which have their own communicative aims and are marked by adequate linguistic features. Among them are, in particular, the kinds of verbs used as predicates.

STATEMENTS

The propositions of statements are facts, as a rule of general validity, whose truth is maintained. Such facts are, for example, states (*'Multae urbes et pagi faciunt*

---

[65] There is hardly any analytical literature on the topic, besides Hupka 1989 and the much more modest Schulze-Stubenrecht 1990. Moreover, see Stein's 1991*b* review article on Hupka 1989 with her systematization of illustrations in dictionaries, historical and contemporary, according to semantic criteria.

[66] However, the following analyses allow an application also to pictures in Diderot's *Encyclopédie*. See Hupka 1989, 102–7.

regionem et regnum', 'Viel Städte und Dörfer machen ein Land und ein Reich', 'Many Cities and Villages make a Region and a kingdom' [CXXXVII]) or mental notions *('[Deus] summum bonum et solus inexhaustus fons omnis boni', '[Gott] das höchste Gut und alleine der unerschöpfliche Brunn alles Guten', '[God] The chiefest Good, and the only unexhausted fountain of all good things'* [I]).[67] They are also actions *('Pisces natant in aqua', 'Die Fische schwimmen im Wasser', 'Fishes swim in the water'* [II]) and processes *('Procella sternit arbores', 'Der Sturmwind reißet die Bäume nieder', 'A Storm throweth down Trees'* [V]), provided they are not meant as actually happening at the moment but as essential and timeless features of items like species (e.g. fish) or natural phenomena (e.g. wind). Typically, the relevant sections of the *Orbis pictus* contain not one but a chain of statements which, taken together, must be read as a definition of the item which is named as its head. Thus, a series of statements on divine attributes defines 'God' (I), a series of statements on the four elements and the states, processes, and actions of their inhabitants defines 'world' (II), and a series of statements on the processes that make the moon appear in different shapes defines 'phases of the moon' (CV). The messages of the sentences taken together constitute a logical relation between them and the general term, which is the head of the section and the common point of reference. This requires that the order of statements is determined by other factors than temporal sequence. It depends on the topic treated which factors these are. As actions and processes must be taken not in themselves but as the general potentials of items, they often become metonymical or metaphorical. This applies to artistic (e.g. 'arts belonging to speech', XCIX), intellectual (e.g. 'philosophy', CI), or moral (e.g. 'prudence', CX) concepts. In most cases, processes stand for the laws of nature.

Without exception, the statements in the *Orbis pictus* are of a general and theoretical kind. The corresponding pictures are *schemata*, that is, they depict nothing happening *in actu*. They consist either of formal elements like circles, rays, or triangles (e.g. for 'God', I), or of mythological elements like an armoured woman (e.g. for 'bravery', CXIII), or of natural elements like men and women (e.g. for 'the seven ages of man', XXXVI). Some of these pictures mix these elements, for example mythological and natural ones, in the form of a strongly blowing face together with the natural signs of a storm like bending trees and high waves (for 'air', V). Others introduce natural elements, like fighting people expressing anger or cattiness (e.g. in CXV). Readers who understand these pictures in the process of semanticizing the texts must know the meanings of the formal elements and of the mythological figures and they must be able to recognize the metonymic and metaphorical character of realistic representations.

The following group of sections belongs to the type *statement*:

---

[67] The Roman numbers refer to the sections of the 1659 edition in *Opera Omnia* (1970*b*). The numbering of sections in the 1672 edition (Hoole) is one in advance of this because the '*Invitation*', which has no number in the earlier, is counted as 'I' in the later one. There are, furthermore, some other irregularities in the numbering of sections here.

FIG. 10.1   Comenius, section CIII, Global spheres
Source: Comenius 1970*b*.

- **on concepts (A1)**:[68] I (God),[69] II (world), XXXVI (ages), XLII (soul), CVII (terrestrial sphere; also A3), CXIII (fortitude; also A2), CXV (humanity), CXVI (justice), CXIX (consanguinity), CXLIV (religion; also C1), CXLIX (God's providence).
- **on actions (A2)**: XCIX (arts of speech), CI (philosophy), CIX (moral philosophy), CX (prudence), CXI (diligence), CXII (temperance), CXIII (fortitude; also A1), CXVII (liberality).
- **on processes (A3)**: III (heaven), V (air), CIII (global spheres), CV (appearance of the moon), CVI (eclipses), CVII (globe; also A1).

The semantic domains are obvious: God and the human soul, the universe, including the world, as a whole, the liberal arts, and virtues, that is, the world of religion and ethics. The corresponding pictures are all schemata.[70]

The different kinds of schemata are distributed in the following way:

[68]   For the letter and number system (A1, A2 etc., 1.1, 1.2, etc.) see below.
[69]   The English names for topics are taken from the 1672 edition. This accounts for the spelling, including some irregularities.
[70]   An insoluble problem is presented by section CXXXVII (country and government). Its picture is meant as a schema, but is indistinguishable from a pedagogical scene (see below).

- **formal (1.1)**: I (God), III (sky), XXXVI (ages), CIII (global spheres; Fig. 10.1), CV (phases of the moon), CVI (eclipses), CVII (globe), CXIX (consanguinity).
- **Mythological (1.2)**: II (world; also 1.3), V (air), XLII (soul), XCIX (arts of speech; Fig. 10.2), CI (philosophy), CX (prudence), CXI (sedulity; also 1.3), CXII (temperance), CXIII (bravery), CXV (humanity), CXVI (justice), CXVII (liberal mindedness), CXLIV (religion), CXLIX (divine providence).
- **Natural (1.3)**: CIX (moral philosophy; Fig. 10.3), CXI (sedulity; also 1.2).

All the schemata are traditional. A possible exception to this is the one in section XLII (soul), which is special in any case, in so far as the mythological schema is given as a picture, that is, a picture in the picture.

NARRATIVES

Narratives present actions or processes by strictly observing their temporal order. Their most frequent pattern is succession, indicated by the grammatical conjunction, '*and then . . . and then*'. There are also more complicated patterns which interrupt the succession without diminishing its central function as the time axis, indicated by the grammatical conjunctions, '*before . . . after . . . at the same time. . .*'. Narratives constitute a story with a beginning, a chain of changes, and an end.

FIG. 10.2   Comenius, section XCIX, Arts of speech
Source: Comenius 1970*b*.

FIG. 10.3   Comenius, section CIX, Moral philosophy
Source: Comenius 1970*b*.

Actions and processes as contents of narratives differ from each other in that the former has a human agent as the instigator, whereas the latter happens by force of nature. This entails a certain selection of verbs in predicates. There are the verbs, mostly transitive, which have a human agent as subject, and those, frequently intransitive, that have an experiencer or an objective. Action verbs appear more frequently in the active voice; but even in the passive voice agentivity can be signalled, for example, by the context.

Actions either create or change the present state of something. This means they are either effective or affective. Human actions of the kind presented in the *Orbis pictus* are of the kind which consists of a series of subactions. They have to be performed in a certain order, because otherwise the effect or affect of something will not be successful. The narrative of an action presents the subactions from the beginning to the end. The agent may be one or several persons who communicate with each other. As a text, the narrative of an action is marked by adverbials which signal the simple or complex temporal sequence of subactions. Even where they are missing, the sentences that constitute the narrative are tacitly combined by '*and then and then and then, before, after, at the same time*', etc. A typical section whose text presents the narrative of actions is XLIX, 'Bakery':[71]

1. Der Bäcker* beutelt das Mehl mit dem Mehlsieb (Reiter)* und schüttet es in den Backtrog*; 2. alsdann gießet er zu Wasser, macht einen Teig* und knetet ihn mit dem Knetscheid*; 3. darnach formet er Brotlaibe*, Kuchen*, Semmeln*, Brezen (Krengel)* u. dg.; 4. Nach diesem legt er sie auf die Backschaufel* und schießt sie in den Backofen* durch das Ofenloch*; 5. doch zuvor scharret er heraus mit der Ofenkrücke* das Feuer und die Kohlen, die er unten zusammenwirft*. 6. Und also wird Brot gebacken, welches außen hat eine Rinde* und innen die Brosam*.
The Baker* sifteth the Meal in a Rindge* and putteth it into the Kneading-trough*. Then he powreth water to it, and maketh Dough* and kneadeth it with a wooden slice*. Then he maketh Loaves*, Cakes*, Cimnels*, Rolls*, etc. Afterwards he setteth them on a Peel* & putteth then thorow the Oven-mouth* into the Oven*. But first he pulleth out the fire, and the coals with a Coal-Rake* which he layeth on a heap underneath*. And thus is Bread baked, having the Crust without* & the Crumb within*.

The text conforms to the general characteristics of narratives. Moreover, two other features are noteworthy. One is the special position of many last sentences which often have a closing function, but can also have a punch-line effect. Section LXXV on the barber's shop, for example, ends with the sentence '*Chirurgus curat vulnera*', '*Der Wundarzt heilet die Wunden*', '*The Chirurgion cureth Wounds*'—after the barber has inflicted these wounds on the patient by letting blood. There are also first lines which have a special introductory function. Note, for example, the historical remark in section XCV on the bookbinder:

Olim agglutinabant Chartam chartae, convolvebantque eas in unum Volumen. Hodie compingit Libros Compactor . . . , Vorzeiten leimeten sie ein Papier an das andre und wickelten solche zusammen in eine Rolle. Heutzutage bindet die Bücher der Buchbinder . . . , In times past they glued Paper to Paper, and rolled them up together into one Rowl. At this day, the Bookbinder bindeth Books.

The second noteworthy feature is that narratives often expand into inventories, like '*panes, placentas, similas, spiras*', '*Brotlaibe, Kuchen, Semmeln, Brezen*', '*loaves, cakes, cimnels, rolls*', which, strictly speaking, are not subject to any temporal sequence. There are even sections which change their textual type totally (see below). A typical section whose text presents the narrative of processes is VII. 'Clouds':

1. Auf dem Wasser steiget auf der Dampf*. 2. Daraus wird eine Wolke*; und nahe an der Erden ein Nebel*. 3. Aus der Wolke tröpflet (fleußt herunter tropfenweis) der Regen* und Platzregen. 4. Welcher gefroren ein Hagel*, halbgefroren ein Schnee*, erhitzet ein Mehltau ist. 5. In einer Regenwolke, welche der Sonnen gegenübergesetzt, erscheinet ein Regenbogen*. 6. Ein Tropf ins Wasser fallend machet eine Wasserblase*; zu viel Blasen machen einen Schaum*. 8. Gefroren Wasser wird Eis*; gefroren Tau wird genennet ein Reif. 9. Aus schwefelichtem Dampf entstehet

---

[71] Words marked with an asterisk are those that are indexed with a number which also appears in the picture. From now on I do not quote the Latin versions in longer quotations.

der Donner; 10. welcher, aus der Wolke brechend mit einem Blitz˚, donnert und wetterstrahlet. A vapour* ascendeth from the water. From it a Cloud* is made, and a white Mist*.ueer[!] the Earth. Rain* and a small shower distilleth out of a Cloud, drop by drop: Which being frozen, is Hail*; half-frozen, is snow*; being warm is Mil-dew. In a Rainy Cloud, set over against the Suu[!], the Rain-bow* appeareth. A drop falling into the water, maketh a Bubble*. many[!] Bubbles make froth*. Frozen water, is called Ice*. Dew congealed, a white Frost. Thunder is made of a brimstone-like vapour, which breaking out of a cloud with lightning*, thundereth and striketh with lightening.

The pictures that correspond to narratives are *stories*. They consist of several scenic arrangements giving the subactions narrated. They have to be understood as happening one after the other and not at the same time. There are no special signals for this temporal sequence; the viewer has to find the temporal path with the help of the text, just as he has to semanticize the text with the help of the picture. Occasionally, the temporal sequence is indicated by a separation in space of various scenic arrangements. The activities of the quoted section, XLIX, for example, take place in the bakery, but the various kinds of bread are exhibited in an adjacent room.

One of the characteristics of these pictorial stories is that the same person appears several times, because he or she is engaged in several consecutive subactions. But there are two kinds of pictorial stories, a decentralized and a centralized one. In the former the agent indeed appears several times working on several subactions, whereas in the latter the agent appears only once working on one subaction while the preceding and succeeding subactions are indicated by other means, mostly by the objects used for them. But the decentralized narrative is the typical one in the drawings.

In his pictorial stories, Comenius makes use, of course, of a very old technique which is to be found in old altar paintings (of the life of Christ, of the Passion, etc.), tapestries, book illustrations, etc., and which is even today alive in comics. Nevertheless, the readers of the *Orbis pictus* had to learn that what appeared to them as synchronic in space had to be understood as being consecutive in time.

Structurally, a *narrative of processes* is very much the same as a *narrative of actions*, except that man does not have the role of an instigator in it. Man either has disappeared completely, as in section VII which presents the cycle of water rising from the earth, gathering in the clouds, and falling down again as rain; or man is replaced by a machine as in section XLVIII with its representation of a mill; or man is the object of processes which cannot be controlled as in a shipwreck (section XC). As with actions, the narrative of processes consists of subprocesses in a strict order which leads from their beginning to their end.

Pictures as *stories of processes*, just as pictures as *stories of actions*, have to be read as consecutive and not as synchronic. In most of these pictures man does not occur.

Narratives, of actions as well as of processes, have a certain typical quality. They aim at showing something which can happen and which will happen at any time.

However, the liveliness of the narrative, in the text as well as in the picture (story), makes the reader (certainly the child reader) forget this and imagine the actions and processes as happening when they are imagined in the course of the reading act. The following group of sections belongs to the narrative type:

- **of actions (B1)**: XLIV (dressing of gardens [gardening]), XLV (husbandry), XLIX (bread baking; Fig. 10.4), LV (vintage), LVII (feast), LIX (dressing of line [making linen]), LXIII (carpenter), LXVII (mine), LXIV (mason), LXXV (barber), LXXVI (stable), XCI (writing), XCIII (printing), XCV (book-binder), CII (geometry), CXVIII (society betwixt man and wife), CXX (society between parents and children), CXXIV (judgement), CXXVI (merchandizing), CXXIX (burial), CXXX (stage-play), CXL (camps);
- **of processes (B2)**: IV (fire), VI (water; Fig. 10.5), VII (clouds), XII (tree), XLVII (honey), XLVIII (grinding), XC (shipwreck), CIV (planets).

The semantic domains are obvious. They cover arts and crafts and natural or mechanical processes. In cases where an affinity between the topic and human action is not obvious, the author dissolved a static topic into an action as, for

FIG. 10.4   Comenius, section XLIX, Bread baking
Source: Comenius 1970*b*.

FIG. 10.5   Comenius, section VI, Water
Source: Comenius 1970*b*.

example, in section LXVI where the actions of grooming a horse are given or in section CXL where the steps of building a camp are traced.

The corresponding pictures are all stories, twenty-two **decentralized** (**2.1**) and four of them **centralized** ones (**2.2**, sections LIX, LXVII, LXXIV, and CXVIII). There are four exceptions. These pictures do not give stories of actions or processes but their results. They are pedagogical scenes (see below). This applies to section XII, where we see a tree and not the process of growing, which is actually presented in the text. It also applies to section XLIV, where we see the laid-out garden instead of the work done on it in the course of the seasons as the text describes it. It applies again to section CXXX with its presentation of a theatrical scene instead of acting, and finally to section CXL, where not the building of a camp but the finished camp is depicted.

INVENTORY

An *inventory* is a type of text which is hardly ever found in common language use. Rather, it has its place in many kinds of special languages, for example in technology. An inventory lists items in a chain of nominations, which can be, but need not be, embedded in a syntagma. Inventories in the *Orbis pictus* are always rendered syntagmatically. They appear in a fairly simple, but also in a more complex way. The simple cases merely list things of any domain of reality, the complex cases list actions and processes. As a rule, *inventories of things* are series of nouns, frequently with an adjective, within one or several sentences. These series of words can be ordered at random, but in many cases they follow what can be called an intrinsic order, depending on the nature of the domain from which the lexemes are taken. Whatever this order, it is not the temporal sequence of a narrative. A typical section whose text presents an inventory of things is section XCVI, 'A Book':

1. *Das Buch nach der äußerlichen Gestalt ist entweder ein Foliant* oder ein Quartbuch*, in Oktav*, in Duodez* oder in Registerform* oder in Langformat*; mit Klausuren* oder Bändern und Buckeln. 2. Inwendig sind die Blätter* mit zweien Seiten, zuweilen gespalten mit Kolumnen* und mit Randschriften*.*
1. *A Book, as to its outward shape is either in Folio*, or in Quarto*, in Octavo*, in Duodecimo*, either made to open Sidewise*, or Long wise*, with Brazen Clasps*, or Strings*, and Square-bosses*. Within are Leaves* with the Pages, sometimes divided with Columns* and Marginal Notes*.*

Inventories of actions and processes consist of several narratives *in serie*. Within the narratives the order is strictly temporal, but between the narratives it is either random or dominated by an intrinsic order such as can be found in the inventories of things. Typical of an inventory is the conjunction *and*, which may either refer to the act of making the inventory or link the various actions in a very unspecific, but not consecutive, way. Both functions are also realized by the conjunction *or*. The complex structure of these inventories also shows inventories being interspersed inside narratives (see above) or narratives changing into inventories at some point, frequently towards the end. Yet we cannot speak of a narration of inventories, because this would be self-contradictory. Besides, it is difficult to decide how many items must be listed for a narrative to become an inventory, in particular if this is, syntactically speaking, a phrase within a syntagma. In such cases it seems better to say that a section belongs to two different types, i.e. is partly a narrative and partly an inventory. The various sections are quite complex in the various ways in which they combine narration and the making of inventories and demand detailed analyses. The following are examples. Section VIII, '*The Earth*' is typical of a straightforward inventory of things without any overt or covert order:

Auf der Erden sind hohe Berge, tiefe Täler*, erhabne Hügel*, hohle Klüfte (Höhlen)*, ebne Felder*, schattichte Wälder*.*
In the Earth are high Mountains, Deep Valleys*, Hills* Rising, Hollow Caves*, Plain Fields*, Shady Woods*.*

Section LVI, '*Beer-brewing*' is typical of an inventory of actions, consisting of two narratives with the first and the last two lines having an extra function:

1. *Wo man nicht Wein hat, trinkt man das Bier; 2. welches aus Malz* und Hopfen* im Kessel**

gesotten, hernach in Kufen* gegossen, 3. und wann es verkühlet, mit Gelten* in die Keller*
getragen und gefasset wird, 4. Der Branntwein, aus den Weinhefen in einem Kessel*, über
welchen gestellt ist ein Brennkolbe*, durch Kraft der Hitze herausgezogen tropfet durch die
Röhre* in das Glas. 5. Wein und Bier, wenn es versauret, wird zu Essig. 6. Aus Wein und Honig
wird der Met gesotten.

Where Wine is not to be had they drink Beer, which is brewed of Malt* and Hops* in a Caldron*
afterwards it is powred into Vats*, and when it is cold it is carried in Soes*, into the Cellar* and
is put into Vessels. Brandi-wine, extracted by the power of heat from dregs of wine in a Pan*,
over which a Limbeck* as placed, droppeth thorow a Pipe* into a Glass. Wine and Beer, when
they turn sowr, become Vinegar. They make Mede of Wine and Honey.

Note that the two narratives are separated by a full stop with each of them embedded in one sentence. The order of the two narratives is random.

Section LIII, '*Butchery*' is an inventory of three narratives of which the first two have a random order, but not the third. The second narrative changes into an inventory of things.

1. Der Fleischer (Metzger)* schlachtet (metzelt) das Mastvieh* (das magere* taugt nicht zum
Essen), 2. schlägt es mit der Barte* oder sticht es ab mit dem Schlachtmesser*, zeucht die Haut
ab* und zerstückt es 3. und das Fleisch hat er feil auf der Fleischbank*. 4. Die Sau* senget wer
mit dem Feuer oder brühet sie mit heißem Wasser* und macht Hammen (Schultern)*,
Schinken* und Speckseiten*; 5. uberdas allerlei Würste*, Schweiß- (Blut) würste*, Leber-
würste*, Bratwürste*. 6. Das Schmer* und Unschlitt* wird ausgeschmelzt oder ausgelassen.

The Butcher* killeth fat Cattle*, (The lean* are not fit to eat) he knocketh them down with an
Ax*, or cutteth their throat with a slaughter-knife* he fleaeth them*, and cutteth them in pieces,
and hangeth out the flesh to sell in the Shambles*. He dresseth a swine* with fire, or scalding
water*, & maketh gammons*, Pestills* and Flitches*: Besides, several Puddings*, Chitterlings*,
Bloodings*, Liverings*, Sausages*. The Fat* and Tallow* are melted.

Note that again the three narratives are separated from each other by a full stop. The inserted inventory is part of the syntagma that constitutes the second narrative, but is set off from it by a new paragraph number.

Section LXII, '*The Shoo-maker*' is typical of a narrative of action which changes into an inventory of things.

1. Der Schuster* machet vermittelst der Ahle* und des Pechdrahts* über dem Leist* 2. aus Leder*
(welches mit der Kneipe* zugeschnitten wird) 3. Pantoffeln*, Schuhe* (an welchen zu sehen ist
oben das Oberleder, unten die Sohle und zu beiden Seiten die Läpplein), Stiefeln* und
Halbstiefeln*.

The Shoo-maker* maketh Slippers* Shooes* (in which is seen above the upper-Leather, beneath
the Sole, and on both sides the Latchets) Boots* and High-Shooes* of Leather*, (which is cut
with a Cutting-knife*) by means of an Awl* and Lingel* upon a Last*.

Note that the whole section is just one sentence, with the inventory separated from the narrative by a new paragraph number.

The following group of sections belong to **narratives of action** which change at some point into **inventories of things:**[72]

---

[72] There are no narratives of processes which change in this way.

- LIII (butchery), LVIII (flax-dressing), LXI (taylor), LXII (shoo-maker), LXVIII (black-smith), LXIX (box-maker and turner), LXX (potter), LXXIII (wells), LXXX (cooper), LXXXI (roper and cordwainer), LXXXIII (horseman), XCII (paper), CXXVIII (physick), CXXXVIII (regal majesty), CXLI (army and fight).

The semantic domains are predominantly crafts which produce various things. The last two sections give scenes with many details.[73]

The following group of sections belong to **inventories of things (C1)**. It is more numerous than all other groups:

- VIII (earth), IX (fruits of the earth), X (metals), XI (stones), XIII (fruits of trees), XIV (flowers), XV (pot-herbs), XVI (corn), XVII (shrubs), XVIII (birds), XIX (tame fowl), XX (singing-birds), XXI (birds that haunt fields and woods), XXII (ravenous birds), XXIII (water fowl), XXIV (flying-vermin), XXV (four-footed-beasts), XXVI (herd cattle), XXVII (labouring beasts), XXVIII (wild cattle), XXIX (wild beasts), XXX (serpents), XXXI (crawling vermin), XXXII ([amphibia]), XXXIII (river fish and pond fish), XXXIV (sea-fish and shell-fish), XXXVII (outward parts of man), XXXVIII (head and hand), XXXIX (flesh and bowels), XL (chanels and bones), XLI (senses), XLIII (monstrous people), LXVI (house), LXXI (parts of house), LXXII (stove and bedroom), LXXXII (traveller), LXXXIV (carriages), C (musical instruments), CVIII (Europe), CXVI (book), CXXII (city), CXXIII (inward parts of city), CXXXIX (soldier), CXLV (gentilism).

The semantic domains of these sections are, first of all, natural history with its great number of genera and species of plants and animals. Next come artificial objects like houses, vehicles, books, etc. Section CXXXIX enumerates the details of armour, section CXLV pagan gods and goddesses.

The type of picture which corresponds to inventories of things is the *pedagogical scene*. It shows the enumerated items in appropriate surroundings, which are either the interior of a room or an area in the open or, quite frequently, these two adjacent to each other (Figs. 10.6 and 10.7; see below). The pedagogical quality of these scenes consists in the fact that things which belong together semantically appear together only for pedagogical reasons, not because they actually occur together. On the contrary, pedagogical scenes are quite unrealistic. People who look at them have to learn that it is the individual item that counts in these pictures and not the picture as a whole.

Sections XXXVIII, on head and hands, and XLI, on external and internal senses, are special cases because they represent pedagogical scenes as pictures in the picture.

The intrinsic order of inventories, that is, the order on the pragmatic level,

---

[73] I ignore three more sections (LI, bird catching; LVI, beer brewing; CXLIII, siege) with other typological changes.

FIG. 10.6   Comenius, section XCVI, Book
Source: Comenius 1970*b*.

depends on the nature of the items that are listed and can, thus, only be shown by examples. A general feature of this order is that either the sequence of lexemes follows a natural arrangement (*natural* meaning something different in each case) or batches of lexemes do the same. But there are also cases where no order can be found at all. Note the following examples.

Section IX, on fruits of the earth (quoted above), is obviously randomly arranged. Section XI, on stones, first lists common stones (1–4),[74] then precious stones (5–9), then glass (10). The batches have four sentences, three sentences, and one sentence. Of common stones we first learn the names of the materials (1–2), then kinds of stones in random order, then there is a general remark on their 'darkness' (3). The 'magnet'[75] is set off as something special, because it attracts iron (4). On precious stones we first read a general characterization (5), then the names of precious stones (6–7), then about pearls and corals because 'they grow in Shell-Fish' (8), then about amber 'which is gathered from the Sea' (9), and

---

[74] The index numbers give the numbers of paragraphs in the *Orbis pictus*, not the numbers as tags of lexemes.

[75] The fact that 'magnet' is mentioned at all is, of course, of historiographical interest. There are many other such cases in other sections.

FIG. 10.7   Comenius, section CXXXIX, Soldier
Source: Comenius 1970*b*.

finally about glass. The sequence in 6–7 is not as random as it might appear at first sight. Unlike common stones which are 'dark',[76] precious stones are 'clear'. This is first proved by various kinds of colourful stones, namely white, red, blue, green, and yellow ones, in an arrangement that orders colours prototypically (6). There then follows the remark that the light, that is, the colour, of precious stones 'glister' when they are cut 'in fashion'. Thus it turns out that the order of this inventory is, after all, strictly determined in each single sentence. It follows the two dichotomies *natural/artificial* and *dark/clear* and differentiates unmarked from marked conditions, for example places of origin.

The picture follows this order only with respect to the dichotomy *natural/artificial*. The common stones are placed in the open air as part of a landscape, the precious stones are displayed on a table in a kind of showroom, set apart from nature. The arrangement of items in each of these two sections of the picture is, however, quite random.

Section XXI, on wild birds, has an order which is much less tightly knit and also less natural. It subjects the named birds to the human criteria of evaluation and

---

[76]   The English translation for '*obscurus*' is 'ordinary'.

usefulness. The first five kinds of birds are characterized by superlatives of evaluation: the biggest and the smallest, the most despicable and the most sordid, the rarest—ostrich and wren, owl and hoopoe, the bird of paradise (1–2). The next seven birds, (pheasant, bustard, wood grouse and black grouse, quail, snipe and fieldfare), make popular and delightful dishes (3–4). Of the last seven birds, the first two (crane and turtle-dove), are mentioned with their outstanding features, watchfulness and lovesickness expressed by cooing; the others—cuckoo, pigeon, woodpecker, jay, and crow—are only mentioned by name. The evaluative features as well as the characteristics of the crane and dove are folkloristic. [77] Thus the order of this section is rather artificial, though formally quite clear. The picture does not follow this order. It shows all the birds, the small ones sitting on a tree, the bigger ones, arranged according to size, standing on grass. In the case of the crane watchfulness is indicated by a stone in one of its claws (because the bird would warn men of danger by dropping this stone), in the case of the dove lovesickness is indicated by its sitting on the highest branch of the tree (from where it coos to its absent lover). Taken as a whole, the picture is a pedagogical scene with a random display of its details.

Section LXVI, on houses, lists its entries according to the way in which they appear to somebody who walks through a house. First, the details of the front door, seen from the outside, are named (1–3). There then follow the great hall with its columns (4–5), and after that the stairs (6). It comes as a surprise that after this the order of the walk is obviously abandoned, because now the details of windows, bay windows, terraces, and roofs are listed (7–12). This may be a break in the text, but the picture makes good for this in an astonishing way. On the first floor an outward balcony is shown from where you can see in a perfectly natural way what the text says about windows, roof, etc. This suggests that the observer walks in through the door, through the hall, up the stairs, and out on to the balcony, from where he looks at the outward appearance of the building. This seems a perfectly sensible thing to do, because the later sections LXXI and LXXII are devoted to the rooms of a house and to the sitting-room and bedroom respectively. Section LXVI is a perfect example of the close correspondence between picture and text, because the former realistically illustrates what the latter tacitly assumes. In this case it might even be justifiable to classify the picture not as a pedagogical scene but as the narrative of an action, namely a tour through part of the house, except that no human being is mentioned and depicted.

Almost all those sections which are classifiable as inventories of things have their own order which can be subjected to a minute description.[78] They vary and are different from the greater systems that determine the order of the macrostructure. They may appear simply as the sensible and natural way of enumerating

---

[77] I do not make a distinction between *traditional, mythological, emblematic, folkloristic,* etc., though it would certainly make sense to do so. I am sure that Comenius used only those non-literal meanings which he thought to be generally intelligible. See Harms 1970.

[78] In my opinion only sections VIII, IX, X, XV, and XLIII are accidental.

items. Even if this is so, they make these enumerations lucid and intelligible and easy to follow. Moreover, they are full of tacitly made assumptions which are today called *folkloristic* or *everyday knowledge*. They are the background categories of a world-view which is otherwise determined by mythology and philosophy. In most cases they are unreflected—although in a case like Comenius one never knows.

An *inventory of actions*, as explained above, consists of several succeeding narratives which follow each other randomly[79] or according to an intrinsic matter-bound order. Section XLVI, on cattle breeding, for example, narrates what is being done with cattle, sheep, pigs, what is done in the dairy, and what in the shed for sheep. There is a historical introduction (1), the narrative of herding (2–4), of work in the pigsty (5), and of work in the cowshed and the shed for sheep (6–8). Thus the sequence of narratives is subject to an intrinsic order which works with the animals (cattle, sheep, pigs) and the dichotomy *inside/outside*, that is, *pasture/shed*. Note section L, on fishing, which is a perfect text with its clear self-explanatory divisions:

1. Der Fischer* fähet Fische: 2. entweder am Ufer mit dem Angel* welcher von der Angelrute am Faden herabhänget und an welchem klebet die Speise oder das Köder; 3. oder mit dem Hamen (Feimer)* welcher hangend an der Stangen* ins Wasser gelassen wird; 4. oder auf dem Kahn* mit dem Netze (Zuggarn)*; 5. oder mit der Reusen*, welche über Nacht eingesenkt wird. The Fisher-man* catcheth fish, either on the shoar, with an Hook*, which hangeth by a line from the angling-rod, and on which the bait sticketh; or with a Cleek-Net*, which hanging on a Pole*, is put into the water; or in a Boat*, with a Trammel-Net* or with a Weel*, which is laid in the water by Night.

Note section LXXXVII, on swimming, which divides the kinds of movements when crossing water. The last entry has a punch-line effect.[80]

1. Man pfleget auch über das Wasser zu schwimmen auf einem Binsenbüschel*, 2. ferner auf aufgeblasenen Ochsenblasen*, 3. darnach frei durch Bewegung der Hände und Füße*. 4. Endlich haben etliche gelernet Wassertreten*, bis an den Gürtel unter dem Wasser gehend und die Kleider über dem Haupt tragend. 5. Der Täucher* kann auch schwimmen unter dem Wasser wie ein Fisch.
Men are wont also to swim over waters upon a bundle of flags*, & besides upon blown Beast bladders*; and after, by throwing their Hands and Feet* abroad. At last they learned to tread the water*, being plunged up to the girdle-stead, and carrying their Cloathes upon their Head. A Diver*, can swim also under the water, like a fish.

The following group of sections belong to **inventory of actions** (C2):

- XLVI (grazing), L (fishing; Fig. 10.8), LII (hunting), LIV (cookery), LX (linnen-clothes), LXV (engines), LXXIV (bath), LXXVIII (picture), LXXIX (looking-glasses), LXXXV (carrying to and fro), LXXXVI (passing over warters), LXXXVII (swimming), LXXXVIII (galley), LXXXIX (merchants-ship), XCIV

---

[79] In my opinion only sections XXIV, LXXVIII, CXXV, CXXXI, and CXXXVI are accidental.
[80] The word *auch / also* in the first entry is anaphoric to the previous section.

FIG. 10.8   Comenius, section L, Fishing
Source: Comenius 1970*b*.

(book-sellars shop), XCVII (school), XCVIII (study), CXIV (patience), CXXI (society between masters and servants), CXXV (tormenting), CXXVII (measures and weights), CXXXI (sleights), CXXXII (fencing school), CXXXIII (tennis-play), CXXXIV (dice-play), CXXXV (races), CXXXVI (boyes-sport). Two sections, LXXXIX (merchants-ship) and CXXVII (measures and weights), change into inventories of things.

The semantic domains of these sections are human crafts, movements, and work which demand a great number of detailed actions and offer a certain choice of how to perform them.

The corresponding pictures present a **pedagogical scene** consisting of actions (**3.2**). This means that several actions are depicted in one picture which have no temporal relation to each other. People angling on a lake in different ways or engaged in various kinds of hunting do so without any context. Viewers must learn to see the difference between a *story of actions* and a *scene of actions*. In the first kind of picture, actions are performed in temporal succession. In the second kind of picture, they are performed independently of each other. There are no pictorial clues to the intrinsic order of actions, except that the dichotomies *outside/inside* and, in combination with this, *natural/artificial* are regularly observed.

There are only two sections that present an **inventory of processes (C3)**, namely LXXVII (dialls) and CXLII (sea fight). They are structurally similar to inventories of actions, except that either no human beings are involved, as in LXXVII, or humans are treated as objects, as in CXLII. The same can be said of the corresponding two pictures.

There are two sets of actions which are outside this general structural pattern. The first is *'Introduction'* and *'End'* with identical pictures (Fig. 10.9), which have gained world-wide fame. They give the whole book a communicative frame by identifying the voice of the teacher as speaker and the learner as addressee (see above). Second, there are four sections whose texts follow the Biblical story. Among them are XXXV, on man, giving the story of Adam and Eve in Paradise with a picture as a story of actions, and CXLVI, on Judaism, giving the stories of Abraham and Moses. The corresponding picture is divided into six parts with their own frames. Each of them presents a realistic, not a pedagogical, scene either of an action or of a *thing*: Abraham conducting circumcision, Moses receiving the tablets inscribed with the Ten Commandments, people celebrating

FIG. 10.9   Comenius, Invitation and Close
Source: Comenius 1970*b*.

a Passover meal, a priest sacrificing at the altar, the Ark of the Covenant, and the brazen serpent. Section CXLVII, on Christendom, gives a shortened version of Christ's life, again with a corresponding picture divided into six parts. Section CXLVIII, on Islam, tells a story of Muhammed founding the new religion together with a Jew and an '*Arian monk named Sergius*'. The picture shows a conversation between the three, with a mosque and muezzin visible through the window. Finally, the *Orbis pictus* ends with section CL, with a story and a picture of the Last Judgement in the linguistic style of the Revelation and the pictorial style of an altar painting.

10.4.3 Abstract typology and concrete realization

The general pattern of text types and picture types on the level of sections is shown in Table 10.1.

TABLE 10.1 Pattern of text types and picture types in the *Orbis pictus*

	Texts	
Statement on	Narrative of	Inventory of
A1 concepts	B1 actions	C1 things
A2 actions	B2 processes	C2 actions
A3 processes		C3 processes

	Pictures	
Schema	Story	Scene
1.1 formal	2.1 decentralized	3.1 pedagogic
1.2 mythological	2.2 centralized	3.2 several actions
1.3 natural		3.3 several processes

The pattern in Table 10.1 shows that 150 variable texts can be described, on a higher level with the help of three terms (*statement, narrative, inventory*), and on a lower level by means of two sets of terms (*concepts* and *things, actions* and *processes*), the second set used twice. *Concepts* and *things* are the same, the difference between them being +/– *mental*; *action* and *process* are also the same, the difference between them being +/– *agentivity*. The pattern also shows that three picture types correspond to these text types. They depend on the two dichotomies *formal* vs. *natural* and *diachronic* vs. *achronic*. These patterns give the whole book its extraordinary clarity and lucidity.

Comenius planned his pictures to attract the attention of the young learners and to keep them awake ('*Praefatio*', 60). He seems to have overlooked the fact that the picture types which were introduced created new tasks of visual learning. They had to be read like text types. However, as we do not know anything about the co-operation between Comenius, the author, Michael Endter, the publisher, and Paulus Creutzberger, the engraver of the pictures, it may very well be that the preface was written without a knowledge of what the layout of the book and in particular the drawings would look like.

The special appeal of the *Orbis pictus*, in so far as it can be accounted for theoretically at all, however, lies in the fact that the abstract clarity of the pattern of the text and pictures goes together with the enormous richness of concrete nouns and adjectives, which are taken from all domains of reality and life. All the special names for plants, animals, materials, tools, objects, parts of the body, etc. go together with the precise indication of what they look like, how they move, operate, function, feed, breed, grow, etc. Again and again special features are mentioned such as, for example, how useful or harmful something is, where or when it can be found, what people do with it. In comparison to the *Janua linguarum*, the language of the *Orbis pictus* is poorer in verbs, and adverbs are conspicuously absent. This mirrors the more elementary stage of language learning that the *Orbis pictus* is geared to. As so many sentences are definitions, the verb *be* and similar copular verbs ('appear', 'make', 'follow', etc.) are particularly frequent.

The pictures which help to identify the meanings of words so successfully achieve this because of their realism, which has often been praised. People recognize in them what they know from nature. On the other hand, even pictures with such recognizable details are not realistic at all because of the fact that their structural elements are strictly observed. As abstract clarity and concrete richness go together, so do the artificiality of composition and the realism of illustration.[81]

By the nature of their subject-matter, some sections are nearer to theory than others. This pertains, for example, to I, on God, and, XLII, on man's soul. There is also philosophy behind the introduction to section XVIII, on animals, which first gives an idea of 'animal in genere':

1. *Das Tier lebet, empfindet, bewegt sich; wird und stirbt;* 2. *nährt sich und wächst; stehet oder sitzt oder lieget oder gehet.*
A living Creature, liveth, perceiveth, moveth it self; is born, dieth; is nourished, and groweth; standeth, or sitteth, or lyeth, or goeth.

Note that this sentence contains no number indexes referring to the accompanying picture.

One feature that lends the *Orbis pictus* its vividness is the turning of states into actions and, consequently, static descriptions into dynamic narratives. This is, of course, a time-honoured and well-known device of dramatization in literature. Note the different ways in which the four elements are treated: Fire (IV) is presented by a narrative of actions starting with kindling a fire, setting fire to things, causing a blaze, quenching fire, and having ashes left over. Air (V) is

---

[81] There is a parallel to this in the fact that the illustrations of herbals combine realistic details of illustration with a generalizing classification of the various genera. See Hupka 1989, 17; also Ivins 1953, 44.

presented by a few statements which treat the movement of the air as its characteristic. Water (VI) is presented by a narrative of processes between a well and the ocean. The same is done referring to clouds (VII) between steam rising and rain pouring down. Finally, earth (VIII) is presented in a short inventory of the typical forms of the earth's surface.

The intelligibility of the pictures depends to a large extent on the clarity of the three types. This corroborates the well-known fact that visual representations, from the days of Egyptian hieroglyphs on, depend on a structural order which, mostly, goes unexplained. It is presupposed. But, as with the texts, their appeal depends on additional features. Comenius's pictures depend also on their illustrative realism, which was not to be taken for granted at his time. This realism pertains to the many details which the pictures present in interrelationship with the text paragraphs. But the details are almost always situated with a wide horizon. Most scenes are set in a seascape or in a landscape with a hilly background. Almost all the pictures have a sky with dynamically shaped clouds. The scenes which are located indoors are still linked with the reality of nature, in that the house may be set in a landscape, or that a room has windows which allow a view outside. Even if neither of these is the case, the mere fact that windows are drawn make the outside world part of the picture. The dichotomy between inside and outside, between nature and house, is quite obvious. It often goes together with categories of the pragmatic structure, like *natural* vs. *artificial*, but this need not be case.

For texts and pictures alike, the combination of an abstract typology with a wealth of concrete realizations, linguistic and pictorial, seems to mark the special quality of this book.

10.5 English adaptations

The *Orbis sensualium pictus* is one of the most successful books ever published. According to the authoritative bibliography by Pilz (1967) 245 editions appeared between 1653, the year of its publication in Sáros Patak as an experimental sheet in Latin, and 1964. (There may have been more since, though not in Europe, with the exception of reissues, for example, in the USA and Japan.) During the years between 1653 and 1700, a total of fifty-five editions reached the market. Twenty of them were in Latin and German, the languages selected by Comenius himself. After 1700 special editions with the German dialect spoken in Transylvania were produced. The English edition of 1659 was the first translation into a language different from the original arrangement. Seven more English editions appeared between 1659 and 1700.

Other languages than German that appeared before 1700 in varying order as translations of the Latin text were French, Italian, Polish, Hungarian, Danish, Dutch, Swedish, Zipser (i.e. the language of Roma), and Slovak. Most of these editions also contain German, only the seven Latin–English and seven

Latin–Swedish editions do not.[82] For a century and a half, no edition omitted Latin; this happened for the first time only as late as (around) 1817 with a French–German one.

The later editorial history of the *Orbis pictus* reveals it as a truly European book. After 1700, other languages appeared, namely Russian, Slovene, Hebrew, Czech (Bohemian), Greek, Serbo-Croatian. There is one Czech edition in Braille. Doubtless, the *Orbis* has also appeared in non-European languages, such as Japanese. Of course, the book stresses the immense importance of Latin for language learning in Europe. Of the 245 editions, 215 contain Latin. The original Latin–German version enjoyed unbroken popularity for three centuries. Before 1700, the English and the Swedish changed this original to create their national editions and made the *Orbis pictus* a national manual for learning Latin. There are two English versions before 1700 worth mentioning.

10.5.1 Charles Hoole's Joh[annes] Amos Comenius's Visible World

Joh[annes] Amos Comenii Orbis Sensualium Pictus: Hoc est, Omnium fundamentalium in Mundo Rerum, & in vita Actionum, Pictura & Nomenclatura.
Joh. Amos Comenius's Visible World: Or, A Picture and Nomenclature of all the chief Things that are in the World; and of Mens Employments therein.
A Work newly written by the Author in Latine and High-Dutch (being one of his last Essays, and the most suitable to Childrens capacities of any that he hath hitherto made) and trans-lated into English, By Charles Hoole, M.A. For the Use of Young Latine Scholars. Nihil est in intellectu, quod non prius est in sensu. Arist.
London, Printed by T. R. for S. Mearne, Book-binder to the Kings most Excellent Majesty, 1672. (GöL Ling, I 3051 8°.)[83]

Charles Hoole (1610–67) was 'an educational writer' (*DNB*) who held teaching posts all his life. In 1642 he was sequestrated by Parliament, after the Restoration he became chaplain to the bishop of Lincoln. His many popular educational works deal with the introduction to Latin and the publication of school colloquies in English and Latin. He edited Lily's grammar 'fitted for the use of Schools' (1653), a *Vocabularium parvum Anglo-Latinum* (1657), and Comenius's *Orbis pictus* (Caravolas 1994, 78–80).

The book[84] of 308 pages plus ten pages of indexes follows Comenius's original faithfully by using the same woodcuts and the Latin text which is rendered into an English, instead of a German, translation. The pictures are on the left-hand pages.[85] Depending on their length, the related texts follow them and spread to the

---

[82]   These statements follow Pilz 1967, 54–5. Latin is regularly the first language except in two cases, where German is. For the English translation in the left-hand column, that is, in the first position, and Latin in the right-hand column see below.

[83]   Reprints 1967 and 1970.

[84]   For a discussion of this English adaptation in the light of Wilkins' *Essay* see Dolezal 1983, 177–97.   [85]   There is one exception, section LXXXV, 174.

right-hand pages or are printed only there facing the pictures. The texts appear below the pictures in two columns, the English version to the left, the Latin version to the right. The numbers, which refer to the pictures, are not given as superscripts but as normal-size numbers and on the same line with a full stop following (which is irritating for the present-day reader). Note as an example: '*The Camel 5. carrieth the Merchant with his Wares*.', '*Camelus 5. [gestant] mercatores cum mercibus suis.*' [XXVIII.][86] There is no numbering of subsections. However, the division into paragraphs, which follows the numbering of subsections in the original edition, is conscientiously carried through in both languages. The English text is printed in Gothic type, the words marked by numbers in Roman. The Latin text is printed in Roman type, the words marked by numbers in italics.

Comenius's version with a Latin column to the left and a German column to the right was obviously meant to be a textbook for Czech-speaking children to learn Latin or German (potentially via Latin) or both languages. In his '*Praefatio*', Comenius mentioned the multiple functions of his work by saying that it was *one* book in *two* languages like a human being with two types of clothes. We should add that both languages were foreign to the young readers for whom the book was written. Hooles's version with an English column to the left and a Latin column to the right was, however, meant to be a textbook for English-speaking children to learn Latin. Thus, Comenius's famous book with various functions is brought into line with other English textbooks, for example, John Withals' dictionary for young beginners.[87] Read in the normal way, from left to right, it looks as if an English text had been translated into Latin; in fact, however, it was the other way round—the Latin text was translated into English.

It was the obvious intention of the English author to translate the Latin version as closely as possible.[88] He did not want to write a new textbook in the manner of Comenius, he adapted the *Orbis pictus* for his purposes without altering it. There are, of course, minor deviations from the Latin text. A difference of word-order in English, for example, occasionally causes the sequence of numbers, which refer to the pictures, to be interrupted, whereas it continues in its original way in Latin (for example, in LXIII we find numbers attached to the Latin words from 1 to 10, but attached to the English words in the sequence 1, 7, 8, 9, 10, 5, 6, 2, 3, 4; see above; see also CXXXVIII). Other minor changes concern such phenomena as the translation of *obscurus* as 'ordinary' (XII), the insertion of the lexeme '*gloweth*' (V), and the omission of a lexeme (XXVIII). It goes without saying that the translation of a Latin ablative frequently demands the insertion of a preposition in English.

Note XCVII, '*A Book*', which shows such and other minor deviations between the two texts caused by word formation:

A Book, as to its outward shape is either in Folio*, or in Quarto*, in Octavo*, in Duodecimo*, either made to open Side-wise*, or Long wise*, with Brazen Clasps*, or

[86] Note that Hoole's numbering is one ahead of Comenius's numbering.
[87] See Chapter 6.
[88] For the quality of the translations see the examples given above.

Strings*, and Square-bosses*. Within are Leaves* with two Pages, sometimes divided with Columns* and Marginal Notes*.
Liber, quoad formam exteriorem, est vel in Folio*, vel in Quarto*, in Octavo*, in Duodecimo*, vel Columnatus*, vel Linguatus*, cum Clausuris aeneis*, vel Ligulis*, & Bullis angularibus*. Intus sunt Folia* duabus Paginis aliquando Columnis divisa, cumque notis marginalibus*.

English words tagged with numbers are in most cases, but not always, capitalized; with Latin words this happens less frequently. Closer examination may bring to light some more inconsistencies between the original Latin and the English translation, but there can be no doubt that Charles Hoole wanted to render the Latin text as faithfully into English as possible—and nothing else.[89]

The book also contains a translation of Comenius's introduction and a special address, entitled '*The Translator to all judicious, and industrious School-Masters*'. The translation of the introduction is just as faithful and correct as the translation of the book itself, given that the two languages involved sometimes cause minor differences. In the special address, the English author writes of the usual difficulties of memorizing words, when a foreign language is learned ('*to pack up many words in memory, of things not conceived in the mind*'), and praises '*Mr. John Commenius*'[!] for tackling the problem in his own way.

He hath therefore in some of his later works seemed to move retrograde, and striven to come nearer to the reach of tender wits; and in his present Book, he hath (according to my judgment,) descended to the very Bottom of what is to be taught, and proceeded (as Nature it self doth) in an orderly way; first to exercise the Senses well, by representing their objects to them, and then to fasten upon the Intellect by impressing the first notions of things upon it, and linking them one to another by a rational discourse.

Like Comenius himself, Charles Hoole is very much concerned by the decline in the success in language teaching and the harm that is done to young minds by the grammar-driven method in classrooms. The paragraph quoted suggests these remedies: (i) the priority of things to words, (ii) the priority of senses to the intellect, (iii) the natural order of the presentation of things, and (iv) rational discourse with words. Subsequently, Charles Hoole suggests a method of teaching which makes use of these ideas of Comenius. First, the learner is to look over the pictures and their general inscriptions. This represents the priority of senses, via pictures, to the intellect and of things to words. '*By this means he shall have the Method of the Book.*' Second, the learner is to read the text carefully and identify the indexed words in the pictures. Apart from the word-meanings, this will give him a knowledge of orthography. Third, the learner is to learn the titles and descriptions by heart, '*which he will more easily do by reason of those impressions which the viewing of the Pictures hath already made in his memory*'. With the help of his *Accidence*, that is, his elementary grammar, the learner is then to learn the

---

[89] In his address to schoolmasters (see below) he even suggests first translating word by word in order to overcome these divergences.

construing and parsing of sentences. This is certainly helpful for the '*rational discourse*' mentioned above. But the author warns the schoolmasters against over-stressing grammar and rules.

The three suggestions allow an interesting insight into classroom work from the viewpoint of an author who is eager to reform it, just as Comenius was all his life. The *Orbis pictus* is regarded as the object of memorization as a text, in its totality. This text presents knowledge in its natural order. Generally speaking, the success of learning is supposed to rest on the accommodation of teachers and learners to the natural ways of experience. This is the nucleus of a learning theory which is discussed by educationalists even today.

Like the original, Hoole's translation of Comenius proved very successful. There were new editions in 1659, 1664, 1672, 1689,[90] and after 1700 four more. The edition of 1777 bears the number 'twelve'. American editions appeared in 1810 and 1887. A Czech textbook for learning languages became an English one without major adaptations.

10.5.2 *James Greenwood's* London Vocabulary

James Greenwood: The London Vocabulary, English and Latin: Put into a new Method proper to acquaint the Learner with Things, as well as Pure Latin words. Adorn'd with Twenty Six Pictures. For the Use of Schools. The Third Edition. By . . ., Author of the English Grammar, and now keeps a Boarding-School at Woodford in Essex.
London, Printed for A. Bettesworth, at the Red Lyon on London-Bridge. 1713. Price 1 s.
(BL 1568/4124. 12°.) There are no modern reprints.

The book is a small-sized volume of 123 pages. The estimated numer of lexeme entries is about 2,000. The first edition, of which no copy seems to have survived, is commonly said to have appeared 'around 1700'.[91] The third edition appeared in 1713, further editions in 1723, 1752, 1763, 1766, 1767, 1771, 1785, 1791, 1797, 1802, 1807, 1812, 1817, and 1828. The last edition bears the number '24th'.

THE AUTHOR AND '*THE PREFACE*'

After leaving Woodford, James Greenwood (?–1737) was a surmaster of St Paul's School in London till the end of his life. His most famous book is *An Essay towards a practical English Grammar. Describing the Genius and the Nature of the English Tongue*, 1711 with many re-editions. His last work was a collection of poems 'from our most celebrated English poets'. Of his *London Vocabulary* it was said, 'It is, however, nothing more than an abridgment of Jan Amos Komensky's "Orbis pictura" [!]' (*DNB*)—a deprecatory remark which cannot account for the extreme success of the book and which, as will be shown, does not do justice to it either in a positive or in a negative way.

---

[90]   According to the BL Catalogue.
[91]   This is why, for once, I ignore the date line of 1700.

In the title the author stresses his own position as a teacher and as the writer of the *Vocabulary*. This is also what he does in the '*Preface*'. According to this, the selection of words is solely meant to introduce learners to the Latin authors they are preparing to read, of which Corderius, the Latin Testament, Aesop, Cato, Ovid, Erasmus, and others are mentioned by name. Because of its elementary nature, the *Vocabulary* contains only 'primitive Words', that is, no compounds or derivations. Greenwood does not mention Comenius, his obviously admired model, at all. Neither does he discuss Comenian ideas. In the title he speaks of a 'new method'. In the '*Preface*' there is one paragraph which shows his conceptual proximity to Comenian ideas, but in a way which obviously only adheres to the (assumed) practicality of his method, not to its philosophical underpinning:

As to the Method, I have made Choice of the most Natural and Entertaining that the subject is capable of; and distributed matters into such an Order that the Learner may at the same Time and with the same Pains, with the Knowledge of the Words, understand the Things themselves which they express, with their order and Dependance upon one another. And the better to fix both upon the Memory of the Readers, and to give them as clear an idea as possible of what they learn, I have caused little Draughts and pictures to be made of such Things as are known and distinguished by their outward Shapes with References to the Words that mention them. (vi–vii.)

It is, of course, mainly these pictures that gave Greenwood the reputation of having done nothing else but 'abridge' Comenius's *Orbis pictus*.

THE DICTIONARY

The *Vocabulary* consists of thirty-three sections of which I–XXVI are arranged topically and XXVII–XXXIII according to word-classes. In its macrostructure, it conforms with the many other macrostructures of comparable books and thus also with the *Orbis pictus*. (See Table A.21.)

Judged as an abridgement of Comenius's book, Greenwood's *Vocabulary* appears well and conscientiously planned. If he modelled his *Vocabulary* on the *Orbis pictus*, he did it by cutting out many entries and whole sections, by inserting new entries, and by rearranging others. In particular, his rearrangements show a clear sense of strict systematization which even outdoes that of Comenius who, for example, mentions plants (i.e. grass, herbs, corn) first in 'the Fruits of the Earth', then treats metals and stones, then trees and their fruits, flowers, herbs, corn. Greenwood, however, has a clearer sequence from minerals to metals to plants (i.e. herbs), trees, and shrubs.[92] Furthermore, Comenius deals with animals in the sequence: birds, insects, beasts, serpents, vermin (i.e. insects again), fish. Greenwood, however, has the clearer sequence: insects, birds, fish, beasts. Greenwood's more systematic (and perhaps less pedagogical) concept is confirmed by his decision to insert a section on diseases directly after those on the

---

[92]   Defined as plants that do not grow as high as trees do.

parts of the body and the bones, because diseases belong to the organism, whereas Comenius lacks this topic and lists words on deformities and monstrosities as the last section of the group on man.

From the point of view of the *Orbis pictus*, the most drastic cuts occur in the domains of husbandry, crafts, sciences, virtues, various societal domains, etc., as is to be expected. But here, too, we find an extraordinarily clear chain of topics in the *London Vocabulary*: food, clothes, houses, country, that is, the paraphernalia of the individual's life; and school, church, judicial matters, war, naval affairs, that is, institutions and occurrences affecting the whole of society. The two books differ in size, because of the different selection of vocabulary, and, macrostructurally speaking, they differ in the strictness of systematicity, which is more explicitly marked in Greenwood than in Comenius.

There are differences, too, between the microstructures of the original and its epigonal 'abridgement'. They emerge most clearly in the typographical arrangement. Comenius had presented his words in sentences which were *in toto* printed in columns and in which the lexemes were marked by typographical means and linked by numbers to the pictures which semanticized them. Greenwood took up the device of linking lexemes by numbers to pictures, although more rarely. There are many more lexemes without a reference to the related pictures here than in Comenius. The first section '*Things*', for example, which means *general terms* and *universe*, has forty-three words of which only eight reappear in the picture. This ratio is quite typical. Greenwood gives introductory sentences which end in series of words. Whereas the sentences are printed horizontally as usual, the words are arranged vertically in two columns, English on the left-hand side, Latin on the right, with a printed slash between them. Thus, the introductory sentence hardly serves as a semanticizing context, as Comenius's sentences did, but only gives a name to the domain to which the following lexemes belong. These names are often printed in capitals or in bold type. Otherwise the sentences are in italics. The English lexemes are also italicized, the Latin lexemes in Roman type. As a rule, countable nouns are accompanied by an article. As in a good textbook, Latin nouns have marks indicating the length of syllables and nominative and genitive endings including names of gender. Note the following examples of typical entries, which were chosen randomly:

A THING *is*
The World / Mundus, i, m.
A Body / Corpus, ori, n.
The Sky / Aether, eris, n.
A Spirit / Spiritus, us, m. (2.)
A METAL *is all that which is digged and fetched out of the* EARTH; *as*
Gold / Aurum, i, n.
Silver / Argentum, i, n.
Lead / Plumbum, i, n. [etc.] (9.)

Sometimes the sentences run on or are parallel to each other:

TREES *have*
Wood   / Lignum, i, n.
Which hath
A Knot   / Nodus, i, m. (19.)
On the HEAD *is worn*
An Hat or Cap   / . Pileum, i, n. *Or*, Pileus, i, m. *Or*, Galerus, i, m.
A peruke or Perriwig / Caliendrum, i, n.
About the BODY *is worn*
A Close Coat   / Tunica, ae, f.
A Great Coat   / Lacerna, ae, f.
A Riding Coat   / Penua, ae, f. [etc.] (56.)

Sentences of this kind, which are so much poorer and more uniform than those of Comenius, together with the typographical arrangement, stress the dictionary character of the *Vocabulary* more than was the case in the *Orbis pictus*. In reading, first of all the eye is arrested by the two columns in which the words are arranged in the two languages, and only then do the sentences at the top and in between catch the attention of the reader. It would be very easy to ignore them altogether and to use the book only as a dictionary proper. But it would certainly not be advisable to do this.

Admittedly, the first sentence of each section is semantically quite empty. It simply gives the name, which however is also printed as a heading above the picture. But the sentences between the columns also indicate the pragmatic structure imposed on the sequence of entries, which normally goes without any indication and has to be found by the attentive reader. Note, for example, section XVII, '*of Buildings*'.[93]

A BUILDING [1] *Is either for ordinary dwelling in, as* [2]. *Or, for Grandeur or Strength, as* [3]. *Or, for Religious Worship* [2]. *For Warmth, Cleanliness, or Health* [2]. *For selling of Goods in there is* [1]. *For Passage they make* [2]. *For Walking in there is* [2]. *For Passage over the Water there is* [1]. *For Passage for foul Water there is* [1]. *In a Building there is* [4]. *Parts of the House are* [4]. *You go over* [11]. *A Room hath* [2]. *On the Outside of the House appears* [4]. *An House is supported by* [2]. *Doors have* [4]. *Which is opened by* [1]. *Under the House is* [1]. *Out-Houses are* [5]. *A Company of Houses are* [3]. *To a City or Town belong* [5]. *A Building is made by* [13] (58–62.)

Section XVII employs a quite typical technique of using headings, with reference to their length as well as to the numbers of lexemes in between. They seldom exceed ten, and there are quite often not more than two or three. Their order depends on the nature of the domain whose lexemes are listed in the section. They were obviously also taken from Comenius. The technique of abridging can indeed be observed when the heads of sections in the *Orbis pictus* appear as intermediate headings in Greenwood's *Vocabulary*. Note in Comenius:[94]

---

[93]   I give only the sentences; the digits in brackets show the number of lexemes that are subsumed under one heading. This section is slightly anomalous in that there is no introductory sentence.

[94]   Numbering according to the edition in *Opera Omnia*, in spite of the English titles which are taken from the later Hoole edtion.

XXV: '*Four-Footed Beasts, and first those about the House*',
XXVI: '*Heard-Cattle*',
XXVII: '*Labouring Beasts*',
XXVIII: '*Wilde Cattle*', and
XXIX: '*Wilde Beasts*'.

Note in Greenwood:

IX: '*Of Four-Footed Beasts*' with the in-between-titles: '*Cattle is*', '*Labouring Beasts are*', '*Wild Beasts are*', '*Beasts that dwell about the House are*'.

Greenwood obviously follows Comenius, except that the animals about the house have been shifted from the first to the last place of the group (for which one can find good reasons). But Greenwood goes on: '*For-footed Beasts that live as well by Water as Land, are*' (which appear in Comenius's section XXXII) and '*A Number of Small Cattle, as Sheep, etc. is called*' and '*A Number of Big Cattle, as Oxen, etc. is called*'. The two last-mentioned groups in this section are not to be found in Comenius, but in many other onomasiological word-lists of the time. Greenwood continues: '*Beasts have [hoof, horn, tail, etc.]*' and '*Beasts are covered with*' where words were obviously culled from Comenius's much more elaborate and descriptive sentences. Note: Under '*Beasts are covered with*' Greenwood lists (English lexemes only): '*A Bristle*', '*Hair*', '*Shag*', '*Wool*', '*Fleece of Wool*'. In Comenius's section XXVI we find the sentences: '*The Bull, the Cow, and the Calf are covered with hair. The Ram, the Weather, the Ewe, and the Lamb bear wool. The Hee-goat, the gelt-goat, with the Shee-goat and Kid have shag-hair and beards. The Hog, the Sow and the Pigs, have bristles, but not horns, but cloven feet too, as those other have.*' The names of animal species (bull, cow, calf, ram, etc.) had all already been mentioned at the beginning of Greenwood's section IX. The other pertinent lexemes of Comenius's sentences now appear towards the end. This means that all of Comenius's words appear in Greenwood, if somewhat differently grouped. It shows the later author's eagerness for clear systematization that he obviously collected words into subgroups which Comenius had used for general description.

A further example of this eagerness is to be seen in section V, '*Of Trees and Shrubs*'. It coincides with Comenius's section XIII, '*Fruits of Trees*'. Note Greenwood's headlines:

A Shrub is a Plant which riseth not up to the just Bigness of a Tree; such is [11]. *Pome-bearing Trees are* [5]. *Plum-bearing Trees are* [4]. *Berry-bearing Trees are* [4]. *Nut-bearing Trees are* [4]. *Forest-Trees are* [19],[*etc.*].

These divisions indeed follow exactly Comenius's entries. Greenwood gives names to an order which Comenius tacitly assumed. Moreover, these divisions were accepted at that time by botanists as valid for the taxonomy of plants (trees). John Wilkins in his '*Tables*',[95] for example, distinguished between '*pomiferous trees*',

---

95   See Chapter 8.

'pruniferous trees', 'bacciferous trees', 'nuciferous trees', and *'glandiferous or coniferous trees'* (Wilkins 1968, *Essay*, 112).This part of the *'Tables'* was written by the expert John Ray.[96]

The *London Vocabulary* is less of an abridgement and more of an adaptation of the *Orbis pictus*. Where Comenius relied on the pedagogical persuasion of his descriptions, Greenwood obviously relied on strict systematization which sometimes even outdid his much more famous model. This, however, raises the question of whether Greenwood had really understood the gist of the pedagogical matter which Comenius had proposed.

The twenty-five topical sections of the *London Vocabulary* are followed by one section *'On Time'* and by seven more sections according to word-classes (see above). The former lists the names of the phases of the day from morning to night and the names of the days of the week. It has the character of an appendix. The latter deserve mention because, in spite of following grammatical categories, they pick up the lexemes of the topical sections in their own sequence and combine them with the word-classes that have hitherto been neglected. Typical entries read thus:

A THING is
Comely, or handsome / Pulcer, ra, rum
Acceptable / Gratus, a, um
Wonderful / Mirus, a, um
Vain / Vanus, a, um (etc., 89.)
A Body is
Hard / Durus, a, um
Or, Soft / Mollis, is, e
Strong, or firm / Firmus, a, um
Or, Weak / Debilis, is, e
Hollow / Cavus, a, um (etc., 93.)
A Bird uses
To fly / Volare
To sing / Canere
A Fish
To swim / Nare
A Bullock
To low / Mugire
An Hog
To grunt / Grunnire (etc., 101–2.)
(A Man) With his Hand *(uses)*
To take / Capere

[96] Greenwood's *Vocabulary* reminds one of Wilkins' *'Tables'* in yet other respects. The introductory sentences, the intermediate headings, which can be read like a linking text, and the criteria for systematization appear like an elementary form of Wilkins' much more elaborate and ambitious undertaking. A precise comparison between Greenwood and Comenius, but also other writers of the time, would probably allow an insight into the way in which the London teacher of Latin worked with other books to hand.

To snatch	/ Rapere
To give	/ Dare
To hold	/ Tenere
To lay hold of, to catch	/ Prendere (etc., 105.)

It is as if James Greenwood wanted to make good for the fact that he had stripped the lexemes in his sentences down to their root-forms and now aimed to combine and enrich them with collocating words, a goal which Comenius had achieved more naturally in his sentences. This aim returns to sections XXVII to XXXIII their onomasiological character. Note, for example, the following sentences which introduce series of adjectives in section XXVII and which go directly back to sentences or to lexemes in previous sections:

Section I: *A THING is . . .; The Mode, or Manner of a Thing is . . .; A Part is . . .; Nature is . . .; A Thing, as to the Time of its Continuance, is . . .; Things are also, in respect of their NUMBER . . .; A PLACE is . . .; A BODY is . . .; As to its MEASURE it is . . .; AS to its FIGURE it is . . .; A Spirit is . . .; GOD is . . .; A SOUL is . . .; The LIGHT is . . .; The SHADE is . . .; A STAR is . . . .*[97] **Section II:** *The AIR is . . .; The EARTH is . . . ; RAIN is . . . .* **Section III:** *A METAL is . . . .* **Section IV:** *A TREE is . . . .* **Section VI:** *An ANIMAL is. . . . .* Etc.

In this way, the section of adjectives is directly bound to the previous sections which only listed nouns. The same is true of the section on verbs which follows things, God, the elements, the various kinds of plants, the senses of man, the parts of his body, his activities and affections, his professions, his affairs, etc., all of them contained *verbatim* in previous sections. These two grammatical sections are just as much topical, and onomasiological, as the topical sections. The next two sections, on pronouns and adverbs respectively, are arranged according to the pronoun sets in answers and questions. Prepositions, conjunctions, and interjections are merely listed.

TEXT TYPES AND PICTURE TYPES

One of the great achievements of Comenius's *Orbis pictus* was its richness in text types and concomitant picture types, both of which combined the lucidity of three abstract type orders (*statement, narrative,* and *inventory* with *schema, story,* and *pedagogical scene*) and the many realistic details of concrete descriptions (see above). James Greenwood's *London Vocabulary* is much poorer in this respect. As the sentences do nothing but allocate a name to a phenomenon of some sort, the word-lists, that is, the lexicographical part of the sections, take on the main message and the text type regularly amount to a mere inventory. There is only the odd sentence which includes a statement, an action, or a process.

Sometimes we can reconstruct contextual links between the lexemes which, if spelled out, would result in a statement or a narrative. Section I is again a good example. Its entries exceed by far the philosophical substance of the *Orbis pictus*.

---

[97]   There are seven more sentences that do not have a literal reference to previous sections.

Seen in context, they constitute a complex of abstract statements. Note:[98]

A THING hath
A Name, A Sign, A Mark or Note, A Mode or Manner, A Kind, A Part Or Member.
A PART is
An Half, A Fragment or broken Piece, A Crumb or little Piece.
THINGS have also their
Cause, Nature, Fortune, Beginning, End, Order, Time, Number, Place, Space.
A THING is
The World, A Body, The Sky, A Spirit.
GOD created the World out of
Nothing.
In a BODY there is
Matter, Form, Figure.
(1–2.)[99]

A natural sequence of processes is constituted by the entry: *From the FIRE cometh A Spark, Smoke, A Flame, Soot* (4) which follows the phases of kindling, (being) burning, and quenching a flame. Yet, in this case as in the former, the bare way in which the lexemes follow each other gives them the appearance of a naked enumeration or an inventory. This is even more true of all the sections (the vast majority) which list things of the various natural orders. Consequently, from the point of view of text types and picture types, the pictures in Greenwood's book are rather poor and uniform.

There are only three schemata among them: I (cosmos, mixing formal, mythological, and natural elements), X (the ages of man, formal), and XXVI (prepositions, i.e. a special case anyway, formal). All the other pictures are pedagogical scenes, because they accompany inventories.

Scenes of things are II (elements: earth),[100] III (minerals and metals), IV (plants), V (trees and shrubs), VI (insects), VII (birds), VIII (fishes), IX (four-footed beasts), XI (parts of body), XII (bones), XVII (buildings), XVIII (household), and XXV (sea).

Scenes of actions are XIII (diseases),[101] XV (meats and drinks), XVI (apparel), XIX (country), XX (societies), XXI (school), XXII (church), XXIII (judicial matters), and XXIV (war). **Scenes of processes** are three parts of II (elements: fire, air, water).

The semantic domains of these three subtypes of scenes are obvious: (i) objects of natural history and of the environment of human life, (ii) societal actions, and (iii) natural processes. The predominance of inventorizing is stressed by the fact that in IV (plants), VII (birds), and VIII (fish) people acting (a gardener, a bird-catcher, an angler) are part of the picture as if they were just

---

[98]   I refrain from indicating the typographical arrangement in detail and from quoting the Latin lexemes.   [99]   Compare this with the remarks on the grammatical sections above.
[100]   This picture consists of four parts devoted to each of the elements. For the other three parts see below.   [101]   There is no picture referring to section XIV.

things. Their actions are in no way connected with the plants, birds, or fish. Again this predominance is corroborated by the fact that the texts which are accompanied by scenes of actions are predominantly inventories and only rudimentarily indicate actions. Here the parallelism of text type and picture type was obviously disregarded. It adds to the poverty and barrenness of the pictures that they hardly ever include the enveloping world. The greater number are illustrations in an otherwise empty frame. Only IV (plants), XII (bones), XIII (disease), XIX (country), XX (societies), XXI (school), XXII (church), and XXIII (judicial matters) show a natural setting. In the case of XII (bones) this is, however, hardly identifiable.

James Greenwood's *London Vocabulary* does not integrate the pictures in the same way as Comenius does in his *Orbis pictus*. The author's general commitment to 'the new method' by which the word as well as the thing is learned, attributes to the pictures all the importance they have in an onomasiological arrangement. They semanticize lexemes. However, as the *London Vocabulary* is a primer from which English-speaking boys are supposed to learn Latin, the English lexemes are actually not in need of any semanticization. This is why in the end and in contrast to Comenius, they have a more ornamental character. The service they perform for memorizing the Latin lexemes, which are the only ones in need of memorization, may be part of this ornamental function. The author seems not to have understood Comenius's ideas in this respect too well.

Summing up we can say, James Greenwood wrote a succesful vocabulary which was modelled on some general and, most of all, on the pictorial features of Comenius's book, which had become so famous in England. But he seems not to have understood its basic ideas. Rather, he relied on principles, most of all a strict macrostructural order, which had been traditional in this book-genre for a long time. He was nearer to the classical nomenclators than he knew.

D. Reflections on the Topic

11

Towards mental lexicography

11.1 Résumé

Onomasiology is a term belonging to lexical semantics as well as to lexicography. It denotes a mental operation, namely the co-ordination of meaning and language, that is, of semantic matter and linguistic form. It also denotes the technique of listing lexemes according to some order which is not that of the alphabet. *Semasiology* is the corresponding term which denotes the co-ordination of language and meaning, that is, of linguistic form and matter, employing the technique of listing lexemes in the arrangement of the alphabet. As is obvious, the two terms presuppose that meaning and language, matter and form, are separate entities in natural languages which, although bound to each other, can nevertheless be distinguished in abstraction. This presupposition can be proved valid by everyday linguistic behaviour. In using language we can employ either approach. When learning a language, native or foreign, in the manner which St Augustine[1] described in the classical way, we give a name to something of which we have previously become aware, mostly by its being pointed out to us and by the ensuing perception. Indeed, the question 'What do we call this [pointing]?' is with us throughout our life. When we encounter difficulties in understanding, however, again with our native language or foreign ones, we always ask, 'What does this word mean?' Obviously, the mental operations that underlie the onomasiological and the semasiological principles are tied to the natural ways in which we handle linguistic communication, either at the productive or at the receptive end. It is

---

[1]   *Confessiones*, book I.

these observations which raise the dichotomy *onomasiological* vs. *semasiological* above the level of mere academic subtleties.[2] But so do historical facts.

Between the beginnings of post-classical European written culture and 1700 we find the onomasiological principle employed in various genres of text. They are, first, non-alphabetical glosses, glossaries, and their expanded variants which were later to become the norm, that is, dictionaries. In the sixteenth and seventeenth centuries, a special type of these dictionaries was called *nomenclator*. Among nomenclators are, second, John Wilkins' thesaurus, which is the semantic part of his universal language scheme. It is, structurally speaking, closer to onomasiological dictionaries than the other text-genres. We may call these two *onomasiological works in the narrow sense*. There are also genres which employ the onomasiological principle *in a wider sense*. They are, third, treatises on terminology and, fourth, dialogues, either as such or as parts of language-teaching textbooks.

Each of these genres of texts has its special class of authors and addressees and, consequently, its special functions of communication. The strongest one is certainly language teaching and learning,[3] as applied either to native or to foreign tongues, and, among the latter, to the classical ones and to the vernaculars. Within this didactic field, the onomasiological works served the linguistic identification of referents, translation (mostly of nouns and adjectives), and vocabulary acquisition. All three of these imply an accumulation of a general knowledge of the world. This, however, also appeared as an autonomous function of onomasiological works. The knowledge of the world is either general (encyclopaedic—see below), or special (connected with some academic discipline or practical craft, frequently of an innovative kind). What all these functions have in common is that language and knowledge are intimately bound to each other, that, on the one hand, knowledge can only be acquired and expressed by lexemes in their identifying function, that is names (see below), and that, on the other hand, languages can only be learned by making propositions, that is meanings. The universal language subjugates this intimate relation to its own particular intentions.

That knowledge cannot be accumulated without its linguistic expressions and vice versa is certainly a statement of a profound philosophical dimension and, thus, of general validity. But it is also a culture-bound condition of the activities of the European intellect because post-classical European culture was acquired and developed via the acquisition and development of a foreign language, namely Latin (and to a much smaller extent Greek and Hebrew). So the linguistic aspects of knowledge accumulation were much more in the foreground than they would have been in a truly monolingual culture (if there is such a thing).

---

[2]   These statements stimulate a plethora of questions and objections when measured by the yardsticks of modern mainstream semantics. They cannot be dealt with here. Note that my present concern is mainly with the linguistic understanding and description of historical sources.

[3]   More teaching than learning, because up to 1700 the possession of books as learning and study aids was a rarity, in spite of the rapid advances in the printing trade by that date.

More text-genres could have been found which at least imply the onomasiological principle in the way in which dialogues and treatises do. Encyclopaedias, so-called housebooks, vocabularies in travelogues, tracts on education, and others are examples.

The onomasiological tradition, as given prominence in this book by the analysis of outstanding historical examples, is part of other traditions which exist outside the onomasiological principle and technique. They include, above all, the *encyclopaedic* tradition, including philosophy, and the *linguistic* tradition, including grammar and rhetoric. They are furthermore integrated into a *pedagogical* tradition which, however, also exists outside the domains of encyclopaedias and linguistics. On a somewhat lower level of abstraction, the traditions of various disciplines and crafts—of mathematics and navigation, of agriculture and architecture, for instance—come into play. All the various text-genres have their special dependencies in this network which have to be mentioned if they are to be fully understood in their own historical conditions. For the pedagogical tradition this has already been done to a certain, though still rather limited, extent in the course of various analyses. However, the encyclopaedic and the linguistic traditions also pertain to all the historical cases mentioned. This is why they will be sketched here within the limits of a historiographical treatment of onomasiological lexicography. Other traditions in the background of certain text-genres will have to be ignored.

11.2 The encyclopaedic tradition

The *OED* explains the lemma *encyclopaedia* with seven adapted forms as a false reading from Greek, occurring in texts of Quintilian, Pliny, and Galen with the assumed original meaning 'encyclical education', 'the circle of arts and sciences considered by the Greeks as essential to a liberal eduction'. Its present-day two readings are '1. The circle of learning, 2. A literary work containing extensive information on all branches of knowledge, usually arranged in alphabetical order'.[4] As the first source of the first reading Sir Thomas Elyot's (1490–1546) *The Boke Named The Governor* (1531) is given. Its author, 'the great popularizer of Humanism in England' (Padley 1976, 14–15), here advises parents not to content themselves with their children's command of Latin but to have them acquire general knowledge of different kinds: '*whiche of some is called the worlde of science: of other the circle of doctrine / whiche is in one worde of greeke* Encyclopedia' (after Henningsen 1966, 286). As the first source of the second reading John Bulwer's *Chirologia* of 1644 is given: '*Me thought thy Enchiridion, at first view, / seemed like*

---

[4] There is also an entry *cyclopaedia* which, except for quoting different sources, does not add anything to the entry *encyclopaedia*, except that this form of the lemma stresses the element *circle/cycle*, e.g. in 'circle of learning', more than the other one. I shall ignore this entry and the use of the word in English, mainly triggered by Chambers *Cyclopaedia*.

that manual cloud, that swiftly grew, / Till the moist curtain had the heavens o'er spread, / For straightways it became the Encycloped.' (Dedicatory poem by Thomas Diconson to Bulwer 1974, 9.)[5]

The entry in the *OED* is largely corroborated by Henningsen (1966) in his detailed etymological study. He stresses as the central meanings of the lexeme (i) 'general knowledge as taught by the *septem artes liberales*', and (ii) 'the interconnectedness of the items of this knowledge in the shape of a circle or otherwise' (1966, 284, 286–7, and *passim*). Idiosyncratic meanings such as, for example, those given to the term by Johann Heinrich Alsted (1588–1638) and Johannes Amos Comenius, are pointed out. Common to all meanings is the idea that the contents of an encyclopaedia are taken from as many sources as possible and that as much knowledge as possible, ideally a sum total, should be collected. This is why an encyclopaedia replaces many books, even a whole library. The use of the English lexeme from the sixteenth century on attests to the popularity of a tradition which then was already many centuries old but which had not found a generally accepted name.

The classical author who more than others shaped the later European idea of encyclopaedism was the most prominent victim of the Mt. Vesuvius disaster, C. Plinius Secundus (the Elder, 23–79) with his *Naturalis historia*, in which he collected, according to his own words, 20,000 items from 2,000 literary sources. The most prominent post-classical author was Isidore of Seville (*c.*560–636) with his *Etymologiarum sive originum libri XX* (Diesner 1976). Early medieval authors were the Venerable Bede (676–735) with *De natura rerum* (written about 700–20), in the British Isles, and Hrabanus Maurus (*fl.* 842) with *De rerum naturis*, on the Continent. There is a gap in sources between the eighth and the eleventh centuries, which does not mean that no encyclopaedias were written at that time. The twenty or so works which are today regarded as constituting the genre and of which quite a number of manuscripts are extant (Meyer 1984, 468) were written in the eleventh to fifteenth centuries (Zöllner 1976). The outstanding examples are Hugh of St Victor's (*fl.* 1020) *Didascalion*, which besides the liberal arts also introduced the *artes mechanicae*, then the *Imago mundi* of Honorius Inclusus (twelfth century), an English Benedictine monk living in Regensburg who fell back on the classical authors and on medieval chronicles, and Bartholomäus Anglicus' (*fl.* 1230) *De proprietatibus rerum*. He was an English Franciscan monk living in Magdeburg. His work, shaped mainly after Pliny and Isidore, is well known for its strict logic and moreover for its personal ordering of facts (Zöllner 1976, 74–7). It was translated into several vernacular languages. The most eminent book, however, with a pan-European influence was Vincenz of Beauvais' (1190–1264) *Speculum majus*, written between 1244 and 1254. Alexander Nequam not only wrote *De nominibus utensilium* for learning Latin,[6] but also *De naturis rerum*, in

---

[5] *Encyclopaedia* has also become the name of 'a literary work containing extensive information on a special branch of knowledge' such as, for example, in *International Encyclopedia of Linguistics*.

[6] See Chapter 4, 83–4.

which he followed Vincenz in so far as nature is here presented as God's six days' work. In 1481, finally, William Caxton published *The Mirrour of the World*, an English translation of the French *Image du Monde*. It had originally been written as a rhymed poem and then been transformed into a French prose version, which became the source of the most successful English translation.[7]

It goes without saying that a literary genre like this cannot be homogeneous in the variety of works compiled. In spite of this there is a general accordance of contents which goes together with a relative flexibility of arrangement. Typical topics are the universe in its parts, nature in its traditional species, and kingdoms, including man, history in the sequence of the six ages, ethics with the traditional Christian systems of virtues and vices, and the arts according to the *trivium* and *quadrivium*. The sequence of these topics varies. The arrangement: *Creation—nature rendered as God's six days' work—man's history—Last Judgement* shows a strong theological bias, the arrangement: *nature as cosmos—man and society—the Church*, however, a more philosophical one. Naturally, the theology of these encyclopaedias is always that of the Church,[8] the philosophy that of the Greek-Arabic *philosophia perennis*. A special problem are the *artes mechanicae* (Meyer 1995) which have an ambivalent place in these strictly structured domains and were supposed to be inferior because they had no obvious part in the salvation of mankind. On the other hand, they were already part of the classical encyclopaedic tradition, for example, with deliberations by Aristotle, Cicero, and St Augustine, and with such seminal works as Junius Moderatus Columella's (first century AD) treatment of agriculture in twelve books (*De re rustica*, AD c.60) and Pollio Vitruvius' (?84–after 27 BC) treatment of architecture (*De architectura libri decem*, c.25 BC). Moreover, they were legitmate means of salvation, for example, in the monastic world. Lastly, the practical importance of navigation, warfare, dancing, and playing instruments, etc. were objects of everyday experience which could not be ignored by medieval writers. Consequently, the mechanical arts were sandwiched between and connected with the other topics wherever the authors thought fit to do this. This brought specifically culture-bound sections together with the more traditional ones which were largely unaffected by the time and place of the origin of encyclopaedias. This could be done because the integrative structure of these comprehensive overviews was never so strict as to preclude additional sections.

Pliny's arrangement in his *Naturalis historia* largely follows the philosophical principles of the classical world, but also treats nature as the great reservoir of the resources for mankind, for example, by implying pharmacology (McArthur 1986*b*,

---

[7] The authoritative bibliography is Collison 1964; for more analytical literature see Meyer 1984 and 1995, as well as the contributions in *Cahiers d'histoire mondiale* 1966 (Commission internationale . . . 1966) and in Eybl *et al.* 1995.

[8] I cannot detect any significant differences in this respect between works appearing before and after the Reformation. This even includes Luther's catechism. For the adaptations made by the authors of the Jesuit edition of Comenius's *Janua linguarum*, see Hüllen 2000.

43; Meyer 1995, 25–6). After prefatory information (book one), cosmology is treated (book two), and the geography of the world as then known (books three to six). Book seven is devoted to anthropology (the organic properties of mankind), and books eight to thirty-seven to nature: land animals, sea animals, birds, insects, plants and agriculture, medicine taken from plants and animals, metals, painting, and minerals including gems and jewellery. The topic of nature as treated by Pliny was to have a century long effect. Isidore's arrangement of topics in his *Etymologies* shows all the signs of amalgamating pagan and Christian sources of knowledge in his mixture of the liberal and mechanical arts (Whitney 1990, Meyer 1995, 27–8). Books one to five A are devoted to the seven liberal arts plus medicine and the law. Books eleven to sixteen treat nature in the sense of Pliny. Between these two batches of classical knowledge, topics from non-pagan sources are wedged: on chronology (book five B), on books and authorship (book six), on Christian theology, the Church, and pagan concepts (books seven and eight). There then follow the mechanical arts (books seventeen to twenty) in an open series, only loosely ordered according to the material handled (see Table A.22). This procedure of adding on sections was adopted by Hugh of St Victor, Vincenz of Beauvais, Alexander Nequam, and the later authors and, finally, led to the most detailed list of arts and crafts available up to 1700 in the encyclopaedia of Alsted. Common to all these principles of ordering was the intention of presenting a comprehensive image of the whole world. The widespread concept that the world was a book written by God and which was decipherable for those who were able to read it in the right spirit was, so to speak, reversed like an image in a mirror in these encyclopaedias which were intended to be books which contained the whole world and which were written by authors who had previously read and understood the world as God's scripture. This is why various titles were given to those *Weltbücher* such as, for example, *imago, speculum, historia, thesaurus, encyclopaedia*, either stressing the character of these books as reflections of the world and its order, or stressing the richness of their contents in analogy to the richness of God's creation (Henningsen 1966, 322). This is also why we must be careful to interpret the information in these encyclopaedias as being realistic for the time of their origin. This does not diminish their general value as sources of cultural history. But up-to-date information was not their main concern.

The extent and the manner to and in which the encyclopaedic tradition appears in the various onomasiological works evidently vary, according to their intellectual level, the predilections of their authors, their size and comprehensiveness, etc. The classical and Christian heritage in these works is always a *res mixta*. A certain preponderance of Aristotelian categories developed, for example, during the era of Humanism, without touching the Christian element. It also shows in Wilkins' monumental work—actually not always in a convincing way because too many different things are included, for example, under categories like quality, action, or relation. Moreover, the increased attention that is paid to a, then modern, discipline like botany tends to undo the unity of the whole. Works in which vernaculars are more in the foreground than the classical languages are geared to more practical problems, but they still move within the general guidelines of encyclopaedism. Treatises devoted to terminology do so in their attempts at linking various domains of reality with each other—botany with pharmacology, medicine with husbandry, mathematics and geometry with crafts like carpentry or watchmaking, etc. Comenius is a special case in that he uses a theory of encyclopaedism to give his pedagogical ideas a solid base. As a rule, he is regarded as the great innovator of pedagogical ideas; in respect of encyclopaedism he looks rather like somebody who is drawing a *summa* of the past.

Lexicographers are practical people, they are no philosophers. Their minds are mainly set on culling words from various sources and putting them together in a manner which makes sense and which enables their readers to do something with them. At least during the period from the beginnings of post-classical culture to the seventeenth century the encyclopaedic context was the generally accepted way of achieving this. Every single glossary or dictionary analysed in this book can be read in its arrangement as part of the encyclopaedic tradition. This is also true for those genres of text where the onomasiological principle is applied only in a wider sense and where not general knowledge as such but knowledge in a special domain is sought. But even this variant is prefigured in classical literature.

All this testifies to the strength and the general validity of encyclopaedic thinking. It proves that onomasiology is grounded in one of the most stable and most comprehensive traditions that Europe has ever seen. It also testifies to the fact that the boundaries between philosopher and teacher, between linguist and educator, between generalist and specialist, in short between representatives of theory and representatives of practice, were not as rigid as they would later become. This applies to all authors of that time, not only to those who wrote (or published) an encyclopaedia as well as an onomasiologically organized textbook, as Alexander Nequam or William Caxton did.

11.3 The semantic tradition

Lexicographers are no philosophers or encyclopaedists proper, and yet their works are significantly marked by principles of philosophy and encyclopaedic thinking. They are no theoretical linguists, either, and yet their works are also marked by some linguistic principles. This, however, is so only to a limited extent, as compared to the encyclopaedic background.

As is natural for word-lists and dictionaries, tracts on terminology, and dialogues, the linguistic element pertains only to semantics and ignores grammar, although grammar was so much more at the centre of classical and medieval thinking about language. It is the theory of names that comes into play here. Words are names for things, attached to them by men. As early as Parmenides (*fl.* 475 BC) the doctrine was launched that a statement is false if it contains a false name (Kretzmann 1972, 359, and *passim*) and that it is the philosopher's task to find the right one. However, the subsequent discussions on the conventionalism vs. naturalism of names in Plato's *Cratylos* and the relations between thing, mental image, and words in Aristotle's *De interpretatione* did not reach the lexicographers at all. Perhaps it was the Christian variant of the doctrine of names that claimed its place here in opposition to the classical one. It rests on the well-known scene in Genesis 2: 19–20, in which God takes Adam by the hand and asks him to name the plants and animals. Like everything else in Paradise, these names must have been perfect. Again the subsequent discussions of the impact of Babel on this act of Adamitic name giving is not of any concern to the onomasiological lexicographers. They take it for granted that words have referential meanings (Waswo 1987, 3–47), that is, for them reality and language are separated from and co-ordinated with each other, very much like an item of reality and its image in a mirror. This gives reality the precedence of occurrence—reality is first and language is second—and language is right if it identifies the thing meant. Acquiring knowledge is incorporated into this act of identification. The knowledge of the thing without its name is nothing, it is the name which stabilizes it. This is why the word can indeed be taken for the thing itself and can function as a surrogate (Harris 1980, 33–78). '*Nomen dictum quasi notamen, quod nobis vocabulo suo res notas efficiat. Nisi enim nomen scieris, cognitio rerum perit*' (Isidore 1911, 33).[9] A direct consequence of this surrogationalism is that it is enough to have the word if the matching reality is hard to come by, for example when it lies outside human experience. This is why names of things appear which nobody had ever seen, for example the wild animals of India, or the fictitious unicorn.

According to present-day semiotics, the referential relationship oscillates between the magical and the symbolic (Waswo 1987, 29), but there is no reflection among historical lexicographers on its nature. The ordering effect of the encyclopaedic principles, for example of the four elements and the kingdoms of nature, were used to preclude a confused atomism that could ensue from this thing–word approach. The ordering effect of Aristotelian categories was used by those who wanted their dictionaries to have a sound philosophical basis. In all other respects, lexicographers obviously relied on the power of practice in language use. If there was no doubt about the thing meant, the name must be right. Problems like those of synonymy and homophony were well known and pointed out (to a limited extent) in the dictionaries, but they were not regarded as flouting the system. In any case, there are no arguments to be found about such problems.

In bilingual or multilingual dictionaries, the ease with which nomination was taken for granted had its corollary in the ease with which perfect translatability was assumed (Harris 1980, 4). There is no discussion of this topic, either. Except for odd remarks in the case of dishes, dances, folkloristic habits, etc., lexemes are

---

[9] 'A name spoken is like a note because by its word it creates for us the named thing. Unless you know the name, the knowledge of things perishes.'

juxtaposed by what is supposed to be their perfect translatory equivalent. However, it is often the case that monolexemic expressions are translated by multilexemic ones, or nouns and nominal phrases by whole definitions, that is, by sentences. A careful comparison of the translations may reveal many instances which lack structural parallelism on the expressing side. However there is no discussion anywhere of this problem on a metalevel.

The two great theorists of our sample, Wilkins and Comenius, transposed the naively assumed correspondence of thing to word into a theorized one. Wilkins assumed an epistemological apriorism. All men were supposed to have the same notions of things, and a universal language had nothing else to do but to express them. In so far as he treated English words in his thesaurus as representing this universal language, the match between them and reality was guaranteed. Comenius saw all knowledge secured by his religious conviction of a harmonious world as it became obvious in his concept of pansophy.

This straightforward semantic theory explains some of the properties of onomasiological works, most of all their focus on the visible and tangible world. In particular the dictionaries and nomenclators swarm with concrete animate or inanimate lexemes. If at all, the semantic domains are named by generic terms which can still make their readers imagine something concrete like fire, water, birds, quadrupeds, or the like. Note that even the descriptive terms of the Aristotelian categories carry something directly imaginable with them and must not be understood in the abstract way which we prefer today. They were labels of visible and tangible items of meaning which corresponded to people's sensual experience. This is most obvious with words whose referents can be directly localized 'in the world', but it also holds true for other word-meanings.[10] The ontological status of referential meanings is of no interest. Comenius's section titles in the *Orbis pictus* are a perfect example of this visualizability. Reliance on what can be seen and touched as an aid to memory, said to be a special property of classical culture (Ong 1967, 1–9 and *passim*), seems to have been kept alive in these dictionaries. Comenius's decision to explain word-meanings by pictures testifies, of course, to the visuality of this dictionary world in general.

A direct consequence of this is that nouns and adjectives, subsumed under the one word-class of *nomina*, make up by far the majority of entries. *Verbales* are so much in the minority compared to *nominales* that they have been almost over-

---

[10] Another approach to the explanation of the preponderance of nouns in onomasiological dictionaries is the special status of the category *substance* in Aristotelian philosophy as compared to all other categories. This also shows in the so-called *speculative* grammar (see below) at the end of the thirteenth and during the fourteenth centuries when word-classes were grounded in the categories of reality by the *modi significandi*, with the noun regularly mentioned first as signifying substance. But then, these philosophical particularities may themselves be indicative of the general truth that objects, including persons of course, are so much nearer to naive life experience and observation of the world than anything else. Dictionaries certainly express this naive approach much more directly than any philosophical doctrine. Note in this context that Lyons differentiates between 'first-order entities', physical objects, and 'second-order entities', events, processes, and states of affairs (1977, 442–3).

looked so far in research. Things and objectifiable abstract entities are presented, but states, processes, and actions were rather neglected. The number of verbs and adverbs is small in onomasiological works. It is only the practical dialogues which introduce them to a certain extent. The dictionaries by Bathe and Comenius, whose entries are in sentence, not in lexeme form, depend on predicates, of course. However, these sentences are often definitions which use semantically vacuous copulas or linking verbs. The defined items in them, the themata as distinct from the rhemata, are mostly nouns. Clever deviations are found, for example, when certain actions are expressed not by verbs but by the instruments, given as nouns, which are used for them.

Everything said so far shows that historical onomasiological dictionaries were embedded in a semantic tradition which ignored the functional and pragmatic side of language. This is also true for many (not for all) of the dialogues, which are rather unnatural and stiff and abound in defining statements. In modern linguistic terms, these dictionaries confine themselves to what is called *nomination* (Wiegand 1996), and it is not nomination in the sense of mentioning names in discourse but of giving them (almost in the way in which Adam did it) as a means of identification. Though nomination as the leading linguistic principle means a certain narrowness which we would not accept today as a matter of linguistic principle, it is not a linguistic approach entirely foreign to us either. The language of technology and science, in particular of these scientific disciplines which are constituted by rigid terminological systems, is still dominated today by acts of nomination. Think, for example, of the elaborate indexes which list all the names for every single part of a plane. The onomasiological dictionaries up to 1700 had the tendency to treat every-day language as if it consisted of nomenclatures. This makes them important fore-runners of the terminological systems, for example in botany, which came into being in the course of the seventeenth century (Hüllen 1989, *passim*). Wilkins' thesaurus is certainly the most elaborate attempt in this respect. Our analysis has shown, however, among other things, that the author failed.

Our present-day linguistic approach is that language is not secondary to real-ity and does not merely identify what is given 'out there'. It is a regulating factor for the ways in which we become aware of the outside world in its own right. This (ethnomethodological) idea is all but lost to historical onomasiological lexicogra-phers. But in the world of technical devices and artefacts even nowadays reality often has precedence of occurrence and is given a name *post festum*. Among other features, this is one of the most powerful differences between *everyday language* and *language for special purposes*. Up to 1700, onomasiological dictionaries tended to treat everyday language as if it were special.

11.4 The end of speculative lexicography

I propose to characterize onomasiological lexicography up to 1700 by the attribute *speculative*. I understand this label as an analogon to the same word as used in encyclopaedic literature and in the grammatical school of the *modistae* (Bursill-Hall 1963 and 1971, Robins 1990, 84–90 and *passim*, Vineis 1994) during the thirteenth and fourteenth centuries.[11] The gist of this school of syntactic theory is the definition of word-classes in semantic terms which are themselves taken from speculative philosophy, in particular from the Aristotelian tradition of the doctrine of categories. Note, for example:

nomen: a part of speech signifying by means of the mode of an existent or of something with distinctive characteristics . . . .
verbum: a part of speech signifying through the mode of temporal process, detached from the substance . . . .
participium: a part of speech signifying through the mode of temporal process, not separated from the substance. . . .   (Robins 1990, 89.)

Grammar is here not justified by itself, as the art of correct language use, but by a system of logical and metaphysical theories which pertain to the reality outside. It derives its own right by reflecting these systems as in a mirror. The elaborate argumentations of the *modistae* did not actually lead to a grammar which was much different from the traditional one of Donatus and Priscian, but gave it a new theoretical underpinning (Bursill-Hall 1971, 27 and 38). It is in this general relation that the grammar of the *modistae* and onomasiological lexicography have some affinity.

The seventeenth century brought forth such highly elaborated works of speculative lexicography as Howell's *Lexicon Tetraglotton* and Wilkins' *Essay* with its '*Tables*'. But it was also the period in European intellectual history when the encyclopaedic tradition and with it speculative lexicography were eroded. They retreated into the background, much to the advantage of the many academic and scientific disciplines which now claimed rights of their own. These disciplines had already been previously named and delimited, as the works of Petrus Ramus, Johann Heinrich Alsted, and Johann Amos Comenius show. But there they had been integrative parts of a theological context. As the domain of human knowledge they were located between God's creation followed by men's sin on the one hand and the history of the salvation of mankind on the other, and they had the function of preparing and supporting the latter with the help of the acknowledgement of the former. But after the disastrous Thirty Years War and the English Restoration this theological function of scientific and academic work lost its

---

[11]   I know that some scholars have their doubts about this reading of the lexeme *speculative* in *grammatica speculativa*. See, for example, Covington 1984, 139, n. 15. Even if the main meaning here is 'theoretical', as opposed to *grammatica practica*, the question is still open as to why *speculativa* comes to mean 'theoretical'. I take it to be a case of the shift of meaning from the concrete and sensual to the abstract and notional which occurs so frequently. At least, this is not a far-fetched assumption. Note also: '[*Speculative*] must not be taken in its modern sense, but in the more particular sense deriving from the view that language is like a "mirror", Latin *speculum*, which gives a "reflection" of the "reality" underlying the "phenomena" of the physical world. The Stoics had employed the same metaphor' (Lyons 1968, 15).

justification, and the various disciplines came into their own (Schmidt-Biggemann 1995). This is, of course, not the historical development of one year or decade, it permeated the whole century under the label of *scientific progress* and was well on its way at the end. It happened, although the Royal Society, as perhaps the most powerful agent of this scientific progress, maintained that 'the advancement of learning' did not do any harm to religion, on the contrary that it supported man's knowledge of God and promoted salvation.[12]

In the area of lexicography the new independence of academic disciplines made itself felt, first of all, in alphabetical dictionaries. In *The New World of English Words* (1658), for example, Edward Phillips (repr. 1969) mentioned all of them as sources from which he culled his entries:

Theologie, Philosophy, Logick, Rhetorick, Grammer, Ethicks, Law, Natural History, Magick, Physick, Chirurgery, Anatomy, Chimistry, Botanicks, Mathematicks, Arithmetick, Geometry, Astronomy, Astrology, Chiromancy, Physiognomy, Navigation, Fortification, Dralling[!], Surveying, Musick, Perspective, Architecture, Heraldry, Curiosities, Mechanicks, Staticks, Merchandize, Jewelling, Painting, Graving, Husbandry, Horsemanship, Hawking, Hunting, Fishing, &c. (title page.)

Although there is some order detectable in this list from theology to the mechanical art of fishing, it has nothing to do with an encyclopaedic overview of the world. There is no 'speculative' attribute in it. There are many alphabetical dictionaries in the late seventeenth and the eighteenth centuries which show such lists of academic disciplines on their title pages; there are also many which refer to 'arts and sciences' in their titles. Both properties betray the encyclopaedic background from which their vocabulary is taken, although this is no encyclopaedism in the speculative sense.

Onomasiological dictionaries did not, of course, disappear altogether with the end of encyclopaedism. The technique went on, although the backgrounding tradition quickly vanished. In particular in the context of (foreign) language teaching, thematic word-lists remained in use. Books which had been published before 1700 were re-edited and new ones appeared. Ordered word-lists remained a fixed habit in textbooks and have done so till today. Yet within this old technique we now find the new principles of arrangement. In *An Introduction to the English Language and Learning* (1754) Benjamin Martin, for example, no longer ordered his word-lists according to the domains of reality but according to academic disciplines: theology, philology, mythology, philosophy, cosmography, arithmetic, geometry, mechanics, architecture, anatomy, physics, pharmacy, botany (Martin 1979).[13] Generally speaking, the century-old incentive to compile a comprehensive onomasiological dictionary had obviously exhausted itself.[14] It reappeared only 150 years later (in 1852) with *Roget's Thesaurus*.

---

[12] There are relevant passages, for example, in Thomas Sprat's (1966) history of the Royal Society and in Robert Boyle's book on the 'Christian virtuoso'; see Hüllen 1989, 103 and 135.

[13] I thank Astrid Göbels for information on this matter.

[14] Neither McArthur 1986b nor Green 1997 mention one single onomasiological dictionary between 1700 and 1852.

11.5 The beginnings of mental lexicography

Things also changed in the semantic tradition. Indicative of this development is, above all, the *Essay on Human Understanding* which John Locke (1632–1704) published in 1689. Again the statement that lexicographers are no philosophers and vice versa must be taken into account, although in this case the philosopher was even interested in the structure of dictionaries (Hupka 1989, 92–4). But Locke changed the general attitude to knowledge and language so drastically (Aarsleff 1994) that authors could not help thinking and working along the new lines, when onomasiological lexicography made its new appearance. The most basic terms and ideas expressed by Locke will suffice to show this.[15]

For Locke, all human knowledge starts from experience either by the senses (which he calls *perception*) or by observation of one's own mental processes (which he calls *introspection*). Experience causes *ideas* to form in the mind, and these ideas are signified by words. This means that words are always the signs of ideas and never the signs of objects in reality, although it is these objects of reality which trigger them into their existence.

The triad *experience (reality)—mental notion (idea)—word (sign)* is not far away from the traditional epistemological pattern which, since Aristotle, saw the mind in its mediating function between reality and language. But this mediating link now gains a totally new weight.

Ideas are either *simple* or *complex*. The simple ones are caused by sensation through one sense or several senses, or by reflection, or by sensation plus reflection. The human mind is *passive vis-à-vis* their coming into existence. But it takes an *active* role in combining simple ideas to form complex ones, of which there are *modes*, *relations*, and *substances*. Substances are what we usually call word-meanings. They are the main point of the whole framework. The lexeme *gold*, for example, stands in the place of a complex idea into which simple ideas, like 'yellow colour' (by one sense), 'malleability' (by another sense), 'metal' (by reflection), and many others, have been integrated. The human mind has the faculty of extricating certain ideas, simple or complex ones, from the *node* of various ideas and of making them the ordering principle of a *class*, such as 'all yellow objects', 'all malleable objects', 'all objects yellow and malleable', 'all metals', etc. The human mind also has the faculty of establishing relations between at least two objects and of making them complex ideas of their own, such as, for example, 'father' or 'enemy'. Modes are again simple or mixed. Simple modes pertain to one substance, signifying one of its accidentals, such as, for example, 'quantity'. Mixed modes do the same with many substances and lead to concepts such as 'thankfulness', 'responsibility', etc.

---

[15] With a few exceptions, I refrain from giving quotations and references. The definitions are contained in book III of Locke's *Essay* (Locke 1961, vol. 2). It is merely the consequences for lexicography which are of interest. For more subtle information on the matter see Woolhouse 1971, Arndt 1979, Chappell 1994, and Losonsky 1994.

This is an epistemological framework which, being entirely free from metaphysical concepts, places the acquisition of knowledge solely on words. It is their function to bind together the various simple ideas which are integrated into one whole, to act as a *node*. Words are not orientated towards a preordered reality, they *mean* a creatively collected bundle of simple ideas which they stabilize for recording and for communication. Locke stresses again and again that the compounding of ideas is due to the 'workmanship of the understanding' and does not depend on natural coherence (1961, vol. 2, 40). The difference between Locke and Wilkins concerning word-meanings is that Locke's 'ideas' are the creation of the human mind after empirical stimuli, whereas Wilkins' 'notions' are given a priori in the world.

By words, ideas are transported from one mind to another one, and there is no guarantee that the ideas of the latter conform to those of the former. It is a matter of experience and communication (the modern term is 'negotiation') to ascertain this. Communication always underlies correctability. The fact that many people who do not reflect on these problems tend to equate words with things is a misuse of language. Defining a word-meaning is done by retracting the path of construction from the complex idea(s) to the simple ones which function as their building-blocks. Simple ideas cannot be explained, they must be intuitively intelligible. This is why Locke proposed semanticizing them in dictionaries by pictures (Hupka 1989, 92–4). Complex ideas must be clear (intuitively convincing) and distinct (accurately delimited from other ideas). Thus, meaning is referential only for simple ideas and for complex ones in an indirect way. In all other respects it is actually created by the active human mind and has a relational character. Both clearness and distinction are ultimately achieved by the quality of the name given to a complex idea. As the linguistic sign, it must be non-ambiguous and useful in daily communication. As communication is the binding factor of society, many names, that is, many nodes of complex ideas formed of simple ones, are geared to the needs and the interests of this society.

The sum total of all these deliberations by John Locke is that language is not a mirror of reality, and vocabulary is not arrangeable according to any preconceived order. Language can only be presented according to the ideas to which it gives its names. This order is no longer speculative but mental. Locke expresses this idea with an observation which we can find in many linguistic deliberations of later years and centuries:

A moderate skill in different languages will easily satisfy one of the truth of this, it being so obvious to observe [a] great store of words in one language which have not any that answer them in another. Which plainly shows that those of one country, by their customs and manner of life, have found occasion to make several complex ideas and give names to them, which others never collected into specific ideas. This could not have happened if these species were the steady workmanship of nature, and not collections made and abstracted by the mind, in order to naming, and for the convenience of communication   (Locke 1961, vol. 2, 37).

In the ideas of the mind, encyclopaedic thinking now has a new ordering principle. These ideas may even be given alphabetically as can be seen in the great encyclopaedias proper of the time: Ephraim Chambers' *Cyclopaedia, or an Universal Dictionary of Arts and Sciences* (London, 1728), Johann Heinrich Zedler's *Großes vollständiges Universal-Lexikon aller Wissenschaften und Künste welche bishero durch menschlichen Verstand und Witz erfunden und verbessert wurden* (Halle and Leipzig, 1731–50), Denis Diderot and Jean d'Alembert's *Encyclopédie, ou dictionnaire raisonné des sciences, des arts et des métiers* (Paris, 1751–65), and finally the *Encyclopaedia Britannica* (Edinburgh, 1768–71). For a long time, lexicographers evidently did not think of writing new comprehensive dictionaries according to the onomasiological principles under these new conditions. As mentioned above, it took almost 150 years till Peter Mark Roget issued his *Thesaurus*. Its 'Plan of classification' shows the new era:[16]

I **Abstract relations**	III **Matter**
1 Existence	1 Generally
2 Relation	2 Inorganic
3 Quantity	3 Organic
4 Order	IV **Intellect**
5 Number	1 Formation of ideas
6 Time	2 Communication of ideas
7 Change	V **Volition**
8 Causation	1 Individual
II **Space**	2 Intersocial
1 Generally	VI **Affections**
2 Dimensions	1 Generally
3 Form	2 Personal
4 Motion	3 Sympathetic
	4 Moral
	5 Religious

[16] Quoted from Roget 1863, the fifteenth edition, the plan of which, however, is identical with that of the first edition. Of course, it is not implied that Roget's ideas are identical with Locke's. It is the general epistemological framework that counts.

Appendix

The Appendix presents twenty-two supplementary tables intended for readers who wish to obtain a more detailed understanding of the texts analysed in the book.

The tables comprise word-lists and overviews of onomasiological dictionaries. Some are in a foreign language, without translation. The book may be understood without reference to them.

TABLE A.1   Onomasticon of Amenopĕ

<63> god
<64> goddess
<65> male spirit (male blessed dead)
<66> female spirit
<67> king
<68> queen
<69> King's wife
<70> King's mother
<71> King's child
<72> crown-prince
<73> vizier
<74> sole friend (the commonest title of courtiers)
<75> eldest King's son
<76> great overseer of the army
<77> (same)
<78> despatch writer of Horus, mighty Bull (i.e. the king)
<79> chief of department of the Good god (i.e. the king)
<80> first King's herald of His Majesty
<81> fan bearer on the right of the king
<82> (sb) performing excellent works for the Lord of the Two Lands (i.e. the king)
<83> superintendent of the chamberlains of the victorious King
<84> chief of the bureau of his lord
<85> royal scribe within the palace
<86> the vizier and overseer of the cities of Egypt
<87> general (overseer of a general expedition)
<88> scribe of the infantry
<89> lieutenant (substitute) commander of the army
<90> overseer of the treasury of silver and gold
<91> King's envoy to every foreign land
<92> overseer of cattle
<93> overseer of the king's house
<94> overseer of horses
<95> lieutenant commander of chariotry
<96> charioteer
<97> chariot-warrior
<98> standard bearer
<99> chief(s) of the scribe(s) who place offerings before all the gods
<100> overseer of the prophets of Upper and Lower Egypt
<101> the mayors of the towns and villages
<102> the great controllers of His Majesty
<103> (sb) in command of the secrets of the Palace
<104> (sb) at the head of the entire land
<105> deputy of the fortress-commander of the Sea
<106> intendant(s) of the foreign lands of Syria and Cush
<107> scribe of distribution (an army official)
<108> scribe of assemblage
<109> overseer of the river-mouths of the hinterland
<110> chief taxing-master of the entire land
<111> majordomo of the Ruler of Egypt
<112> chief of scribes of the mat (?) of the Great Court
<113> chief of the record-keepers of the House of the Sea
<114> the royal scribe and lector priest as (?) Horus
<115> scribe of the House of Life, skilled in his profession
<116> lector-priest of the royal couch (i.e. throne)
<117> First Prophet of Amun in Thebes
<118> Greatest of Seers of Rec-Atum (title of the high-priest of Heliopolis)
<119> Greatest of Artificers of Him who is South of His Wall (title of the high-priest of Memphis)
<120> Setem-priest of Kindly of face (a second title of the high-priest of Memphis)
<121> overseer of the Granaries of Upper and Lower Egypt
<122> King's butler in the palace
<123> chamberlain of the Palace

<124> great steward of the Lord of the Two Lands
<125> scribe who places offerings before all the gods (see above)
<126> prophets
<127> god's fathers
<128> ordinary (pure, clean) priests
<129> lector-priest
<130> temple scribe
<131> scribe of the god's book

Source: Gardiner 1947, vol. 1.

TABLE A.2 *Aelfric's Glossary*, overview

The overview quotes entries according to Zupitza and Gneuss 1966. This is why they are not arranged in columns. Square brackets [. . .] before and after entries mean that a selection of entries is given. The counting of entries refers to Latin lemmata. An entry is marked by a full stop in the Zupitza and Gneuss edition. This means that numbers of entries and numbers of lexemes do not coincide, because some entries consist of two or three synonyms. The number of Latin lemmata explained is slightly higher. So is the number of Old English lemmata. Lazzari and Mucciante (1984, 22) count 1,290. Inevitably, our choice of lemmata is subjective. It is meant to convey a general impression of the glossary as well as an indication of its topics and subtopics. Subsections within *Nomina membrorvm* and *Nomina domorvm* follow the paragraphs in the same edition.

INCIPIVNT NOMINA MVLTARVM RERVM ANGLICE.
NOMINA
Deus omnipotens, þæt is god ælmihtig, sê wæs ǽfre unbegunnen and ǽfre bið ungeendod. *caelum* heofen. *angelus* engel. *archangelus* hêahengel. *stella* steorra. *sol* sunne. *luna* môna. *firmamentum* roder. *cursus* ryne. *mundus* ꝉ *cosmus* middaneard. *tellus* ꝉ *terra* eorde. *humus* molde. *mare* ꝉ *aequor* sǽ. *pelagus* wîdsǽ. *occanum* gârseeg. *homo* mann. *mas* ꝉ *masculus* werhâdes mann. *femina* wîfhâdes mann. *sexus* werhâd odde wîfhâd. [23 entries]

NOMINA MEMBRORVM
[. . .] *Membrum* ân lim, *membra* mâ lima. *caput* hêafod, *capita* mâ. *oculus* êage. *cor* heorte. *uena* ǽddre, *uenae* mâ. *pes* fôt [. . .] [79 entries]
[. . .] *Patriarcha* hêahfæder. *anachorita* ancra. *coniugium* ꝉ *matrimonium* sinscipe [. . .] [83 entries]
[. . .] *Pater* fæder. *mater* môdor. *filiaster* stêopdohtor. *affinis* ꝉ *consanguineus* siblinge [. . .] [35 entries]
[. . .] *Rex* kyning. *regina* cwên. *dominus* ꝉ *herus* hlâford. *mulier* wîf. *consiliarius* rǽdbora. *rusticus* æcerceorl. *piscator* fiscere. *fidicen* fidelere. *fistula* hwistle. *medicus* lǽce [. . .] [31 entries]
[. . .] *Diues* welig. *felix* gesǽlig. *bonus homo* gôd mann. *capitium* hæt [. . .] [45 entries]
[. . .] *Indigena* ꝉ *incola* inlendisc. *doctor* lârêow. *diploma* boga. *penna* feðer. *gluten* lîm. *scolasticus* scôlman [. . .] [44 entries]
[. . .] *Miser* earming. *paraliticus* bedreda odde sê ade PARALISIN hæfd. *morbus* âdl. *sapiens* wîs. *humilis* êadmôd [. . .] [67 entries]
[. . .] *Vita* lîf. *mors* dêad. *uentus* wind. *dies* dæg. *hora* tîd. *hiems* winter. *hodie* tô dæg. *humor* wǽta. *color* bleoh. *creator* scyppend [. . .] [68 entries]

NOMINA AVIVM

[. . .] *Auis* ł *uolatilis* fugel. *aquila* earn. *merula* þrostle. *alcedo* mǽw. *passer* spearewa oðđe lytel fugel. *auca* gôs. *musca* flêoge [. . .] [46 entries]

NOMINA PISCIVM.

[. . .] *Piscis.* fisc. *cetus* hwæl. *tructa* truht. *muscula* muxle. *concha* scyll [. . .] [19 entries]

NOMINA FERARVM

[. . .] *Fera* wildêor. *lupus* wulf. *equus* hors. *ursus* bera. *feruncus* meard. *mus* ł *sorex* mûs. *ceruus* heort. *bos* oxa. *agnus* lamb. *canis* hund. *peduculus* lûs. *tinea* moðđe [. . .] [74 entries]

NOMINA HERBARVM

[. . .] *Herba* gærs oðđe wyrt. *simphoniaca* hennebelle. *petrocilinum* petersylige. *absynthium* wermôd. *artemisia* mugewyrt. *lilium* lilje. *filex* fearn [. . .] [68 entries]

NOMINA ARBORVM

[. . .] *Arbor* trêow. *cortex* rind. *fructus* wæstm. *populus* byre. *cypressus* næfð nǽnne engliscne naman. *spina* þorn. *silua* wudu. *collis* hyll oðđe beorh. *campus* feld. *latex* burna oðđe brôc [. . .] [83 entries]

NOMINA DOMORVM

[. . .] *Domus* hûs. *ecclesia* cyrice oðđe gelêafful gegǽderung. *cera* wex. *casula* mæssehacele. *dormitorium* slǽpern. *linum* flex. *lana* wull. *lardum* spic. *caseum* cŷse. *artauus* cnîf. *coquina* cicene. *triclinium* bûr. *fortis* strang [. . .] [228 entries]
[. . .] *Sella* sadol oðđe setl. *bellum* ł *pugna* gefeoht. *mucro* swurdes ord oðđe ôðres wǽpnes. *oppidum* fæsten. *urbs* burh. *uilla* tûn. *ferramentum* tôl. *aurum* gold. *marmor* marmstân. *homicida* manslaga. *cadauer* lîc oðđe hold [. . .] [137 entries]
[. . .] *Limen* oferslege oðđe þrexwold [. . .] [67 entries]
[. . .] *Edax* ł *glutto* oferetol. *pudicus* sideful. *scelus* scyld. *pelex* cyfes [. . .] [25 entries].
(Total: 1172 entries.)

TABLE A.3   *Treatise* (c.1280), *Nominale sive verbale* (1340), and *Femina* (1415)

Treatise

Prologue	riddles
parts of body	flowers
clothes	trees
assemblies and voices of animals	birds
the red knight	other animals
country occupation	beasts
weather	carts and ploughs
building a house	breaking things
utensils	feast

Source: Wright 1857 (my own descriptive terms, W. H.).

Nominale sive verbale

parts of the body	some red things
natural noises and actions of men and women	trees
	beasts
assemblies	noises of beasts
building a house	herds of beasts
utensils	birds
winds and storms	flocks of birds
breaking things	noises of birds
puns	parts of plough and cart

Source: Adapted from Skeat 1906.

Femina

De assimilitudine bestiarum	*Semina seminanda*
Quomodo appelluntur secundum eorum voces	*Ars braciatricis*
	Ad prendendum pisces
De proprietatibus infantis	*De tempore yemis*
De partibus capitis	*De nominibus herbarum*
De anteriori parte capitis	*De nominibus avium*
Adhuc de corpore	*De nominibus animalium*
De vestury infantis	*De proprietatibus bige*
De diuersitate nominum	*[De proprietatibus aratri]*
De eodem	*De edificandum domos*
De proprietatibus campi	*De proprietatibus nominum*
De arte pistoris	*De moribus infantis*

Source: Wright 1909.

TABLE A.4   Caxton's *Dialogues*, boundaries within the text

The letters and numbers to the left (A, B, C1, C2, etc.) have been added to the text of the edition to show the arrangement of pre-unit, frame, subunit, sub-subunit, etc. The numbers give the page and line according to the Bradley (1900) edition. Descriptive passages in capitals are my own (W. H.), the other lines are quotations.

A	1.1–3.16	PRE-UNIT: TABLE OF CONTENTS
	1.1	*Hier begynneth the table*
		Of this prouffytable lernynge,
		For to fynde all by ordre
	1.4	*That whiche men wylle lerne.*
	1.5–3.13	TABLE OF CONTENTS*
	3.14	*Ryght good lernyng*
		For to lerne
	3.16	*Shortly frenssh and englyssh*

TABLE A.4   CONTINUED

B	3.17–4.7	FRAME: INVOCATION AND SELF-APPRAISAL
C1	<u>4.8–6.15</u>	SUBUNIT 1: FORMULAE FOR GREETINGS
	4.8	*Now knowe what behouet*
	4.9	*That he haue of alle a partie.*
	4.10–6.13	RULES FOR BEHAVIOUR, FICTITIOUS DIALOGUE
	6.14	*Thus enden the salutations*
	6.15	*And the ansueris.*
C2	<u>6.16–9.10</u>	SUBUNIT 2: OBJECTS: HOUSE, FURNITURE
	6.16	*Now standeth me for to speke*
		Of othir thynges necessarie:
		That is to saye of thinges
		That ben vsed after the hous,
		Of whiche me may not be withoute.
		Of the hous first I shall saye,
	6.22	*On auenture, if it be to doo.*
	6.23–9.9	DESCRIPTIVE VOCABULARY
	9.10	*Here endeth the thirde chapitre.*
C3	<u>9.11–14.24</u>	SUBUNIT 3: OBJECTS: FOOD
	9.11	*Now understande, litell and grete,*
		I shall saye you right forth
		Of an othir matere
	9.14	*The whiche I wyll begynne.*
	9.15–11.15	RULES FOR BEHAVIOUR, FICTITIOUS DIALOGUE
	11.16	*Yet ben ther othir bestes*
	11.17	*Whereof men recche not to ete:*
	11.18–11.32	DESCRIPTIVE VOCABULARY
	11.33	*Now hereafter shall ye here of fissh.*
		Of the fisshes may ye here
		The names of somme,
		Not of alle,
		For I ne wote not
		How alle to knowe;
		Also ne doo not the maroners.
	11.40	*First of fisshes of the see:*
	11.41–12.9	DESCRIPTIVE VOCABULARY
	12.10	*Of othir fishes*
	12.11	*Of the river, [etc]:*
	12.12–12.20	DESCRIPTIVE VOCABULARY
	12.21	*Who knoweth more, name he more;*
	12.22	*For I ne knowe no more to speke.*
	12.23	*Now name we the white mete*
	12.24	*And that wherof is made.*
	12.25–13.2	DESCRIPTIVE VOCABULARY
	13.3	*Of fruit shall ye here named*

	13.4–13.9	DESCRIPTIVE VOCABULARY
	13.10	*The names of trees:*
	13.11–13.37	DESCRIPTIVE VOCABULARY
	13.38	*These ben the potages:*
	13.39–14.2	DESCRIPTIVE VOCABULARY
	14.3	*Thise ben the drynkes:*
	14.4–14.24	DESCRIPTIVE VOCABULARY
C4	14.25–22.13	SUBUNIT 4: COMMERCE
	14.25	*Of othir thinge withoute taryeng,*
		Whiles that I remembre,
	14.27	*I wyll to you deuise and teche.*
	14.28–15.1	RULES FOR BEHAVIOUR
	15.2	*So may ye beginne*
		By suche gretyng
	15.4	*As it is in the first chapitre.*
	15.5–19.16	FICTITIOUS DIALOGUE, DESCRIPTIVE VOCABULARY
	19.17	*Ye shall ansuere*
	19.18	*Also as it is wreton els where.*
	19.19	*Yet shall I not leue it*
		That I ne buye
		Hydes of kyen,
	19.22	*Whereof men make lether.*
	19.23–19.31	DESCRIPTIVE VOCABULARY
	19.32	*Alle in one chapitre.*
	19.33	*For that I am not*
		Spycier ne apotecarie
		I can not name
		All maneres of spyces;
	19.37	*But I shall name a partie:*
	19.38–20.8	DESCRIPTIVE VOCABULARY
	20.9	*Now shall we saye of the oyles.*
	20.10–20.14	DESCRIPTIVE VOCABULARY
	20.15	*I shal bye thinges*
	20.16	*Wherof ben made paintures*
	20.17–21.18	DESCRIPTIVE VOCABULARY (NOT HOMOGENEOUS)
	21.19	*Yet I have not*
		Named the metals
	21.21	*Which follow:*
	21.22–21.29	DESCRIPTIVE VOCABULARY
	21.30	*These ben marchandises:*
	21.31–22.5	DESCRIPTIVE VOCABULARY
	22.6	*Here I shall make an ende,*
	22.7	*And shall saye of graynes:*
	22.8–22.11	DESCRIPTIVE VOCABULARY
	22.12	*Of these things I am wery,*
	22.13	*So that I shall reste me.*

TABLE A.4   CONTINUED

C5	<u>22.14–25.9</u>	SUBUNIT 5: OFFICES, SOCIAL RANKS
	22.14	*But the grete lordes I shall name;*
		The prelats of holy chirche;
		The princes, the grete lords.
	22.17	*Fyrst of the hyest:*
	22.18–24.11	DESCRIPTIVE VOCABULARY
	24.12	*Now comen the names*
	24.13	*Of dukes, of erles*
	24.14–25.9	DESCRIPTIVE VOCABULARY
C6	<u>25.10–47.30</u>	SUBUNIT 6: NAMES, PROFESSIONS, ARTS, CRAFTS
	25.10	*For this that many wordes*
		Shalle fall or may falle
		Which ben not playnly
		Here tofore wreton,
		So shall I write you
		Fro hens forth
		Diuerse maters
		Of all thynges
		Syth of one sith of anothir
		In which chapitre
		I wyll conclude
		The names of men and of wymmen
		After the ordre of a.b.c.,
		The names of craftes,
	25.24	*So as you may here.*
	25.25–31.32	NAMES, PORTRAITS, DIALOGUES
	31.33–47.25	NAMES, (PORTRAITS), PROFESSIONS, ARTS, CRAFTS
	47.26	*I am all wery*
		Of so many names to name
		Of so many craftes,
		So many offices, so many seruises;
	47.30	*I wyll reste me.*
C7	<u>47.31–50.31</u>	SUBUNIT 7: PILGRIMAGE
	47.31	*Neuertheless, for to lengthe*
		That whiche I haue begonne,
	47.33	*I shall saye the beste:*
	47.34–48.40	RELIGIOUS ADMONITIONS
	49.1–50.24	FICTITIOUS DIALOGUE
	50.25	*Lordes, who wolde,*
		This boke shold neuer be ended,
		For men may not so moche write
		Me shold fynde alway more:
		The parchemen is so meke;
		Hit suffreth on hit to write
	50.31	*What someuer men wylle.*

D	<u>50.32–51.31</u>	POST-UNIT 8: NUMBERS
	50.32	*Here after I shall deuise you*
		A litell book that men calle
		The nombre, the which is
	50.35	*Moche prouffytable,*
	50.36–51.31	DESCRIPTIVE VOCABULARY, NUMBERS
E	51.32–52.5	FRAME: INVOCATION AND SELF-APPRAISAL

* Lines 3.11–3.13 do not strictly belong to the table of contents, but it seems justifiable to ignore this, because they are a direct continuation of lines 3.9–3.10. They read: '*Doo diligence for to lerne. / Flee ydleness, smal and grete, / For all vices springen therof.*'

TABLE A.5 Caxton's *Dialogues*, a textual overview

As in Table A.4, the letters and numbers to the left (A, B, C1, etc.) have been added to show the arrangement of pre-unit, frame, subunit, sub-subunit, etc. The numbers give the page and line according to the Bradley (1900) edition. The descriptive passages in capitals are my own (W. H.).

A	PRE-UNIT	
	1.1–1.4	BOUNDARY: OPENING
	1.5–3.13	NUCLEUS: TABLE OF CONTENTS
	3.14–3.16	BOUNDARY: CLOSING
B	FRAME	
	3.17–4.7	INVOCATION AND SELF-APPRAISAL
C	TEACHING UNIT	
C1	SUBUNIT 1	
	4.8–4.9	BOUNDARY: OPENING
	4.10–6.13	NUCLEUS: RULES, FICTITIOUS DIALOGUE
	6.14–6.15	BOUNDARY: CLOSING
C2	SUBUNIT 2	
	6.16–6.22	BOUNDARY: OPENING
	6.23–9.9	NUCLEUS: DESCRIPTIVE VOCABULARY
	9.10	BOUNDARY: CLOSING
C3	SUBUNIT 3	
C31	9.11–9.14	BOUNDARY: OPENING
	9.15–11.15	NUCLEUS: RULES, FICTITIOUS DIALOGUE
C32	11.16–11.17	BOUNDARY: OPENING
	11.18–11.32	NUCLEUS: DESCRIPTIVE VOCABULARY
C331	11.33–11.40	BOUNDARY: OPENING
	11.41–12.9	NUCLEUS: DESCRIPTIVE VOCABULARY
C332	12.10–12.11	BOUNDARY: OPENING
	12.12–12.20	NUCLEUS: DESCRIPTIVE VOCABULARY
	12.21–12.22	BOUNDARY: CLOSING
C34	12.23–12.24	BOUNDARY: OPENING
	12.25–13.2	NUCLEUS: DESCRIPTIVE VOCABULARY

TABLE A.5 CONTINUED

C35	13.3	BOUNDARY: OPENING
	13.4–13.9	NUCLEUS: DESCRIPTIVE VOCABULARY
C36	13.10	BOUNDARY: OPENING
	13.11–13.37	NUCLEUS: DESCRIPTIVE VOCABULARY
C371	13.38	BOUNDARY: OPENING
	13.39–14.2	NUCLEUS: DESCRIPTIVE VOCABULARY
C372	14.3	BOUNDARY: OPENING
	14.4–14.24	NUCLEUS: DESCRIPTIVE VOCABULARY
C4	SUBUNIT 4	
C411	14.25–14.27	BOUNDARY: OPENING
	14.28–15.1	NUCLEUS: RULES
C412	15.2–15.4	BOUNDARY: OPENING
	15.5–19.16	NUCLEUS: FICTITIOUS DIALOGUE, DESCRIPTIVE VOCABULARY
	19.17–19.18	BOUNDARY: CLOSING
C42	19.19–19.22	BOUNDARY: OPENING
	19.23–19.31	NUCLEUS: DESCRIPTIVE VOCABULARY
	19.32	BOUNDARY: CLOSING
C43	19.33–19.37	BOUNDARY: OPENING
	19.38–20.8	NUCLEUS: DESCRIPTIVE VOCABULARY
C44	20.9	BOUNDARY: OPENING
	20.10–20.14	NUCLEUS: DESCRIPTIVE VOCABULARY
C45	20.15–20.16	BOUNDARY: OPENING
	20.17–21.18	NUCLEUS: DESCRIPTIVE VOCABULARY (NOT HOMOGENEOUS)
C46	21.19–21.21	BOUNDARY: OPENING
	21.22–21.29	NUCLEUS: DESCRIPTIVE VOCABULARY
C47	21.30	BOUNDARY: OPENING
	21.31–22.5	NUCLEUS: DESCRIPTIVE VOCABULARY
	22.6	BOUNDARY: CLOSING
C48	22.7	BOUNDARY: OPENING
	22.8–22.11	NUCLEUS: DESCRIPTIVE VOCABULARY
	22.12–22.13	BOUNDARY: CLOSING
C5	SUBUNIT 5	
C51	22.14–22.17	BOUNDARY: OPENING
	22.18–24.11	NUCLEUS: DESCRIPTIVE VOCABULARY
C52	24.12–24.13	BOUNDARY: OPENING
	24.14–25.9	DESCRIPTIVE VOCABULARY
C6	SUBUNIT 6	
	25.10–25.24	BOUNDARY: OPENING
	25.25–31.32	NUCLEUS: NAMES, PORTRAITS, DIALOGUES
	31.33–47.25	NUCLEUS: NAMES, (PORTRAITS), PROFESSIONS ETC.
	47.26–47.30	BOUNDARY: CLOSING
C7	SUBUNIT 7	
	47.31–47.33	BOUNDARY: OPENING
	47.34–50.24	NUCLEUS: RULES, FICTITIOUS DIALOGUE
	50.25–50.31	BOUNDARY: CLOSING

D	POST-UNIT	
	50.32–50.35	BOUNDARY: OPENING
	50.36–51.31	NUCLEUS: DESCRIPTIVE VOCABULARY (NUMBERS)
E	FRAME	
	51.32–52.5	INVOCATION AND SELF-APPRAISAL

TABLE A.6   Rychard Sherry, *A treatise of Schemes and Tropes*

1.   *wordes considered by them selues,* i.e. schemes:
1.1   *Ffigure [of words], i.e. of Scheme ye first part* (Bvr):
1.11   *Ffigure of Diccion,*
1.12   *Ffigure of construcction;*
1.2   *Ffaute,* i.e. *Of Scheme, the second part* (Bviiiv):
1.21   obscure,
1.22   inordinate,
1.23   barbarous;
1.3   *Virtue,* i.e. *the thyrde kinde of Scheme* (Ciiir):
1.31   propriety,
1.32   garnishing.
2.   ropes,
2.1   parts:
2.11   *a mouynge and chaungynge of a word and sentence* (Ciiiiv),
2.12   *an inuersion of wordes* (Cviir);
2.2   *Ffigure of Dianoias, or sentence:*
2.21   *The fyrst order of the figures Rethoricall* (Cviiir),
2.22   the second order, i.e. *the orname[n]nts of sentence* (Dviiv).

Source: Sherry 1550. BL C. 122.a.37.8°.

TABLE A.7   John Wilkins, '*The General Scheme*'

All kinds of things and notions are
1.   more *general*
1.1   belonging to *things* called:
1.11   TRANSCENDENTAL GENERAL I
1.12   RELATION MIXED II
1.13   RELATION OF ACTION III
1.2   belonging to *words*: DISCOURSE IV
2.   more *special*
2.1   denoting CREATOR V
2.2   denoting *creature*
2.21   *collectively*: WORLD VI
2.22   *distributively*
2.221   according to several kinds of beings, belonging to *substance*
2.2211   *inanimate*: ELEMENT VII

TABLE A.7   CONTINUED

2.2212   *animate*
2.22121   according to their *species*
2.221211   *vegetative*
2.2212111   *imperfect*, as *minerals*:
2.22121111   STONE VIII
2.22121112   METAL IX
2.2212112   *perfect*, as plants:
2.22121121   HERB:
2.221211211   considered according to LEAF X
2.221211212   considered according to FLOWER XI
2.221211213   considered according to SEED-VESSEL XII
2.22121122   SHRUB XIII
2.22121123   TREE XIV
2.221212   *sensitive*:
2.2212121   EXANGUI[N]OUS XV
2.2212122   *sanguineous*:
2.22121221   FISH XVI
2.22121222   BIRD XVII
2.22121223   BEAST XVIII
2.22122   according to their *parts*:
2.221221   PECULIAR XIX
2.221222   GENERAL XX
2.222   according to several kinds of beings, belonging to *accident*
2.2221   *quantity*:
2.22211   MAGNITUDE XXI
2.22212   SPACE XXII
2.22213   MEASURE XXIII
2.2222   *quality*:
2.22221   NATURAL POWER XXIV
2.22222   HABIT XXV
2.22223   MANNERS XXVI
2.22224   SENSIBLE QUALITY XXVII
2.22225   SICKNESS XXVIII
2.2223   *action*:
2.22231   SPIRITUAL XXIX
2.22232   CORPOREAL XXX
2.22233   MOTION XXXI
2.22234   OPERATION XXXII
2.2224   *relation*
2.22241   more *private*:
2.222411   OECONOMICAL XXXIII
2.222412   POSSESSIONS XXXIV
2.222413   PROVISIONS XXXV
2.22242   more *public*:
2.222421   CIVIL XXXVI

2.222422	JUDICIAL **XXXVII**
2.222423	MILITARY **XXXVIII**
2.222424	NAVAL **XXXIX**
2.222425	ECCLESIASTICAL **XL**

Source: Wilkins 1968, 23.

TABLE A.8   John Wilkins, Genera

(Chapter I)
TRANSCENDENTALS GENERAL
I KINDS   II CAUSES   III *Differences*, more ABSOLUTE and Common   IV *Differences Relative to Action*: THE END   V—THE MEANS   VI MODES.

TRANSCENDENTALS MIXT
I QUANTITY, considered more GENERALLY   II—more restrained to CONTINUED QUANTITY   III—to DISCONTINUED QUANTITY   IV QUALITY, considered more LARGELY   V—more STRICTLY   VI WHOLE *and* PART.

TRANSCENDENTAL RELATIONS OF ACTION
I more *General* SIMPLE   II more *General* COMPARATE   III more *Special*; denoting *Kinds of Action*, *Solitary*, BUSINESS   IV—*Social*, COMMERCE   V denoting EVENTS   VI denoting ITION.[1]

DISCOURSE (LANGUAGE)
I *Parts of it, More Simple*, ELEMENTS   II—*less Simple*, WORDS   III Kinds of it, *proper* to GRAMMAR   IV—*proper* to LOGIC   V COMMON TO BOTH   VI MODES of it.

(Chapter II)
OF GOD, AND WORLD (*IDOL, ANTICHRIST*)
GOD
[without numbers] FATHER, SON; HOLY GHOST

WORLD
I SPIRITUAL and immaterial   II *corporeal*, CELESTIAL   III *corporeal, Terrestrial, inanimate*, LAND   IV—WATER   V ANIMATE   VI CIRCLES by which [the world] is divided.

(Chapter III)
ELEMENT (METEOR)
I More *simple, Real, Lighter*, FIRE   II—AIR   III—*heavier*, WATER   IV—EARTH   V—*Real*, APPARENT[2]   VI More *mixed*, WEATHER.

STONE (EARTHY CONCRETION)
I *Stones*, VULGAR and of no price   II—MIDDLE-prized   III—PRECIOUS, LESS TRANSPARENT   IV—MORE TRANSPARENT   V *Earthy Concretions*, DISSOLVIBLE   VI—INDISSOLVIBLE

METAL
I *Perfect*, NATURAL   II *Perfect*, FACTITIOUS   III *Imperfect* with reference to METALLINE KINDS   IV—RECREMENTITIOUS PARTS.

TABLE A.8   CONTINUED

(**Chapter IV**)
HERBS ACCORDING TO THEIR LEAVES
I *Imperfect*, wanting essential parts   II *Perfect*, distinguished by the *Fashion of the Leaf, Long, Not flowring,* FRUMENTACIOUS[3]   III—NOT FRUMENTACIOUS   IV—*Flowering,* of BULBOUS ROOTS   V—[with] AFFINITY TO BULBOUS ROOTS   VI distinguished by the *Fashion of the Leaf,* ROUND   VII distinguished by the *Texture of the Leaf,* NERVOUS   VIII—SUCCULENT   IX distinguished by SUPERFICIES[4] of the Leaf, or MANNER of Growing.

HERBS ACCCORDING TO THEIR FLOWERS
I STAMINOUS   II *foliacious, compound flowers,* NOT PAPPOUS   III—PAPPOUS[5] IV—*Simple flowers, umbelliferous,*[6] of BROADER LEAVES   V—of FINER LEAVES   VI *Simple flowers, verticillate,*[7] FRUTICOSE[8]   VII—NOT FRUTICOSE   VIII *Simple flowers,* SPICATE[9]   IX SEED; GROWING MANY TOGETHER IN A Cluster or BUTTON.

HERBS ACCORDING TO THEIR SEED-VESSEL
I divided Seed-vessel, CORNICULATE   II *entire Seed-vessel, siliquous,*[10] *Papillionaceous,*[11] CLIMBERS   III—NOT CLIMBERS   IV—*not papillionaceous,* FLOWERS [with] GENERALLY . . . FOUR LEAVES   V *entire Seed-vessel, Capsulate,* FLOWERS OF FIVE LEAVES   VI—FLOWERS OF THREE OR FOUR LEAVES   VII [flower of one leaf], *campanulate*[12] VIII—*Not campanulate*   IX *entire Seed-vessel,* BACCIFEROUS.[13]

Of SHRUBS
I *Bacciferous, Deciduous,*[14] SPINOUS   II—NOT SPINOUS   III *Bacciferous,* EVERGREEN   IV *Bacciferous,* SILIQUOUS [with] seeds in PODS   V *Graniferous,*[15] DECIDUOUS   VI—EVERGREEN

Of TREES
I *Fruit or Seed in fleshy pulp,* POMIFEROUS   II—PRUNIFEROUS   III—BACCIFEROUS   IV *Fruit or Seed in Hard shell,* NUCIFEROUS   V—GLANDIFEROUS or CONIFEROUS   VI *Fruit or Seed in* SINGLE TEGUMENTS or Coverings   VII WOODS OR BARKS   VIII GUMMS OR ROSINS.

(**Chapter V**)
OF EXANGUI[N]OUS ANIMALS
I *Lesser, usually called insects,* [generation] *analogous to that of other animals,* [with] NO FEET OR BUT SIX feet, WITHOUT WINGS   II—SIX FEET and WINGS, or MORE feet THEN SIX   III—[generation] *Anomalous,* DESIGNED TO FURTHER TRANSMUTATION   IV—[with] *severall mutations,* [with] NAKED WINGS   V—[with] SHEATHED WINGS   VI *Greater, Hard,* CRUSTACIOUS   VII—TESTACIOUS TURBINATED[16] VIII—NOT TURBINATED   IX *Greater,* SOFT

OF FISH
I *Viviparous*[17] and skinned, [with] OBLONG and roundish figure   II—FLAT or thick figure   III *Oviparous,*[18] *Salt water,* [with] *finns on the back* whose *rays* are *Wholly soft* and flexile   IV—*partly soft* and partly *spinous,* having TWO FINNS   V—ONE FINN   VI *Salt water, Figure,* OBLONG   VII—FLAT   VIII—*Salt water,* CRUSTACIOUS COVERING   IX *Oviparous, Fresh water,* scaly.

OF BIRDS
I *Terrestrial, dry land,* CARNIVOROUS II—PHYTIVOROUS[19] *of short round wings*
III—of *long wings* having their *Bills* LONG AND SLENDER IV—SHORT AND THICK
V—*insectivorous,* having *slender streight bills,* the GREATER KIND VI—the LEAST
KIND VII *Aquatic,* living *About and* NEAR WATER PLACES VIII—*In waters,* FISSI-
PEDES[20] IX—PALMIPEDES.[21]

OF BEASTS
I *Viviparous,* WHOLE FOOTED II—CLOVEN FOOTED III—*clawed* or *multifidi-
ous,*[22] NOT RAPACIOUS IV—RAPACIOUS, CAT KIND V—DOG KIND VI
OVIPAROUS.

(**Chapter VI**)
PARTS PECULIAR
I *Plants,* LASTING PARTS II—ANNUAL PARTS III—KINDS OF FRUIT IV
Animals, SWIMMING V—FLYING VI—GOING.

PARTS GENERAL
I *Homogeneous,* CONTANED II—CONTAINING III *Heterogeneous, External,* HEAD
IV—TRUNK V—LIMM VI INTERNAL.

(**Chapter VII**)
MAGNITUDE (EXTENSION)
I DIMENSIONS II MUTUAL RELATIONS III AFFECTIONS in respect of *Figure,*
SIMPLE IV *Compound,* LINEARY V—PLANARY VI—SOLIDARY.

SPACE
I TIME II PLACE III SITUATION

MEASURE (PROPORTION)
I MULTITUDE II MAGNITUDE III GRAVITY IV VALOUR V *Duration* More
GENERALLY CONSIDERED VI—RESTRAINED TO LIVING CREATURES

(**Chapter VIII**)
NATURAL POWER (*IMPOTENCIES*)
I *More particular,* RATIONAL II *Sensitive,* INWARD III—OUTWARD IV *More
general,* SPIRITUAL V—*Corporeal, relating to the good of the* INDIVIDUUM VI—
SPECIES.

HABIT (*DISPOSITION*)
I *States* which reward or enable men for vertuous actions, comprehending the END OR
REWARD OF VERTUE II—INSTRUMENTS OF VERTUE III *Qualifications* which
dispose unto Vertue, AFFECTIONS OF VERTUE, INTELLECTUAL IV—MORAL V
Kinds of vertuous habits, INFUSED, intellectual and moral VI—ACQUIRED INTEL-
LECTUAL.

MANNERS (and CONVERSATION)
I *Wills and Affections, considered more separately* according to Soul and Body, Reason and
sense, [considered] More GENERAL II—More *Particular,* relating to Our BODIES
III—to Our ESTATES or DIGNITIES IV *Conversations, considered as Members of Society,*

TABLE A.8   CONTINUED

More GENERAL and Common   V—More *Particular* towards SUPERIORS   VI—towards INFERIORS.

SENSIBLE QUALITY (OCCULT QUALITY)
I [relating] to the *Eye, Primary* [to] LIGHT   II—*Secondary* [to] COLOUR   III—*Ear*, [to] SOUND   IV [to] TAST and SMELL   V [to] *Touch*, more ACTIVE   VI—more PASSIVE.

SICKNESS (HEALTH)[23]
I CAUSES OF DISEASE   II *Diseases themselves, Common* to the whole Body, DISTEMPERS   III—TUMORS   IV—*Peculiar* to some parts, HEAD, or ARISING THENCE   V—MIDDLE REGION   VI—LOWER BELLY.

(Chapter IX)
SPIRITUAL ACTION
I belonging to GOD   II belonging to the *Soul*, with Reference to the *Understanding*, SPECULATIVE   III—PRACTICAL   IV—with Reference to the WILL   V with Reference to *Fancy* or *Appetite*, SIMPLE   VI—MIXED.

CORPOREAL ACTION
I *more peculiar* to Living Creatures, *Absolute* belonging to VEGETATIVES   II—SENSITIVES   III—RATIONALS   IV—*Relative* to the Outward SIGNS OF PASSION   V—GENERAL Notions belonging to DEMEANOUR   VI *More Common* with other Things, GESTURE.

MOTION (REST)[24]
I *Natural*, of the *whole*, more *General*, Kinds of Animal PROGRESSIVE MOTION   II—more *Particular*, VARIOUS NOTIONS OF GOING   III—of the *Parts*, considered More *Largely*, belonging to ANIMAL ACTION IN COMMON   IV—*restrained* to the Acts of PURGATION   V—EXERCISE VI kinds of VIOLENT MOTION.

OPERATION (*PLAY*)
I More *Common*, relating to MECHANICAL FACULTIES   II—to MIXED MECHANICAL OPERATIONS   III More *Particular*, belonging to AGRICULTURE   IV—to Houses or Utensils, FABRILE Arts   V—to Clothing, SARTORIAN Trades   VI PHYSIC; CHYMICAL, Pharmaceutical Operations.

(Chapter X)
OECONOMICAL RELATION
I Personal Relations of CONSANGUINITY   II—AFFINITY   III—SUPERIORITY or Inferiority   IV—EQUALITY   V Oeconomical Duties referring to *Education*, in WORDS VI—in DEEDS.

OECONOMICAL POSSESSIONS (and REVENUE)
I things *Natural*, LAND   II *Artificial, Buildings*, considered according to their KINDS III—to their *Parts*, GREATER   IV—LESSER   V—things *serviceable for* CARRIAGE   VI FURNITURE; *Utensils*.

PROVISIONS
I *particular references to Food, The kinds of it*, ORDINARY   II—EXTRAORDINARY

III—*The Manner of* PREPARING   IV CLOTHING   V VESSELS   VI COMMON MIXED Nature.

(Chapter XI)
CIVILL RELATION (ANARCHY)[25]
I *Persons* in a political capacity according to their DEGREES   II—PROFESSIONS or Vocations   III CONVENTIONS   IV Things or businesses relating to RIGHTS   V CONTRACTS for the Alienation of our Rights   VI OBLIGATIONS for the Confirmation of our Contracts.

JUDICIAL RELATION
I PERSONS   II CAUSES and Actions   III *Faults* CAPITAL   IV—NOT CAPITAL   V *Punishments* CAPITAL   VI—NOT CAPITAL

MILITARY RELATION (WAR)
I ACTIONS   II EVENTS   III *Persons*   SEGREGATE   IV—AGGREGATE   V *Instruments*, AMMUNITION   VI PLACES.

NAVAL RELATION
I KINDS OF VESSELS   II *Parts of Vessels,* as serve for *Containing,* HULL   III PROGRESSIVE MOTION OR STAYING   IV—RIGGING   V PERSONS   VI ACTIONS.

ECCLESIASTICAL RELATION (TEMPORAL)[26]
I KINDS OF RELIGION   II *Persons* in regard of their ECCLESIASTICAL CALLINGS III—STATES OF RELIGION IV *Actions* belonging to WORSHIP   V—DISCIPLINE   VI INSTITUTIONS.

---

[1] 'The action of going'. This explanation and others in subsequent notes are taken either from the *OED* or from Wilkins' own explanatory texts or margin notes.
[2] 'Appearing meteors'.
[3] 'Resembling wheat or other cereals'.
[4] 'The outer surface of a body'.
[5] 'Seeds lying in down or having downy parts'.
[6] 'Flowers growing in the fashion of an umbel'.
[7] 'Flowers growing in rundles or whirls about a stalk'.
[8] 'Having stalks of a hard cosistency'.
[9] 'Having an efflorescence in the form of a spike'.
[10] 'Containing their seeds in pods'.
[11] 'Flowers resembling a butterfly'.
[12] 'Resembling the figure of a bell'.
[13] 'Seeds included in a juicy pulp'.
[14] 'Parts (leaves, petals etc.) falling off at a particular time of season or growth'.
[15] 'Bearing smaller seeds'.
[16] 'Consisting of a cone-like cavity in a spiral'.
[17] 'Animals bringing forth young in a live state'.
[18] 'Animals bringing forth young as eggs'.
[19] 'Feeding on vegetables'.
[20] 'Animals having divided toes'.
[21] 'Animals having toes united by a membrane'.
[22] 'With toes'.
[23] Should be *HEALTH* (i.e. in italics).
[24] Should be *REST* (i.e. in italics).
[25] Should be *ANARCHY* (i.e. in italics).
[26] Should be *TEMPORAL* (i.e. in italics).

Source: Wilkins 1968, *passim.*

TABLE A.9   John Wilkins, *Transcendental Particles*

I follow Wilkins' spelling closely, in particular his conventions in italicizing and capitalizing. In this table he drops the difference between slot entries printed in capitals and these printed in italicized capitals in order to indicate their oppositeness. Indeed, there are no oppositions here in the binary slot entries, their positions rather complement each other. They are generally printed in italicized fonts. See Dolezal 1983, 72–87, Hüllen 2002, 102–22.

Semantic transformations occur according to

1.	*General essential* respects
1.1	*Comparative, similitude* in *words* or *things: METAPHORE / LIKE*
1.2	*Positive*
1.21	*general* beings, *common essence* or *common circumstances: KIND / MANNER*
1.22	*individual* beings, *irrational* or *rational: THING / PERSON*
2.	General *Circumstantial* respects
2.1	*Absolute; Position* or *Duration : PLACE / TIME*
2.2	*Relative*
2.21	*Effecting* or *representing: CAUSE / SIGN*
2.22	*Being* in *conjunction* or *separate: AGGREGATE / SEGREGATE*
3.	*Special* respects, *substance,* as result from their Application to other Substances for *Enclosure* and service
3.1	*Places,* or *Things: SEPIMENT¹ / ARMAMENT*
3.2	*MEN*
3.21	*Contiguous,* against *Weather* or *Enemies: VEST / ARMOUR*
3.22	More *remote,* more *General* or *Special: HOUSE / ROOM*
4.	*Special* respects, *Figure*
4.1	*Shape alone, Broad* and *Flat,* or *Slender* and *Long*
4.2	*Shape* and *Use*
4.21	*More simple,* for *Operation* and *Containing: INSTRUMENT / VESSEL*
4.22	*Less simple, not necessarily designed for motion,* or *designed for motion: JUGAMENT² / MACHINE*
5.	*Quality*
5.1	*Abstractly,* natural Powers, or *Practical* matters: *HABIT / ART*
5.2	*Concretely*
5.21	personal Qualifications, *Degrees* and *Business,* or *Faculty and Skill: OFFICER / ARTIST*
5.22	*Professions of Manufacture* or *Exchange: MECHANIC / MERCHANT*
6.	*Action* or *Passion*
6.1	*Ability,* or *Disposition* of Thing : *POWER / APTITUDE*
6.2	*Beginning* or *Repeating of* an Action: *INCEPTIVE / FREQUENTATIVE*
6.3	Application of Power, *ordinary* or *sudden: ENDEAVOUR / IMPETUS*
7.	*Relative* notions *common* to *Quality* and *Action*
7.1	*Measures*
7.11	*Great* or *little: AUGMENTATIVE / DIMINUTIVE*
7.12	*Too much,* or *too little: EXCESSIVE / DEFECTIVE*
7.2	*Manner* of a Thing or Action: *PERFECTIVE / CORRUPTIVE*
8.	Affections of Animals

8.1   *Sounds, articulate,* or *inarticulate: VOICE / LANGUAGE*

8.2   *Sexes: MALE / FEMALE*

8.3   *imperfect age, whole* [and part, applicable to animate and inanimate beings]: YOUNG / PART.

---

¹ 'Hedge, fence, limitation of field, etc.'

² Wilkins does not explain the word, and it is not in the *OED*. Obviously he is thinking of something like a plough or a harrow, an instrument which is more complicated than a tool but less complicated than a machine.

Source: Wilkins 1968, 320–2.

TABLE A.10   John Wilkins, *Transcendental Particles*, examples

1.1	*light* and *evident / dark* and *mystical*
1.21	*child* and *offspring / domestic bird* and *poultry*
1.22	*eaten* and *food / idle* and *truant*
2.1	*metal* and *mine / festival* and *holy time*
2.21	*shine* and *polish / wound* and *scar*
2.22	*assessors* and *bench / gathering* and *picking up*
3.1	*water* and *mote / foot* and *horse-shoe*
3.21	*head* and *cap / head* and *helmet*
3.22	*dog* and *kennel / walking* and *gallery*
4.1	*wood* and *board / iron* and *nail*
4.21	*painting* and *pencil / drink* and *cup*
4.22	*printing* and *press / grinding* and *mill*
5.1	*worshipping* and *devotion / arguing* and *logic*
5.21	*city* and *mayor / star* and *astronomer*
5.22	*stone* and *mason / flesh* [= meat] and *butcher*
6.1	[*to be seen*] and *visible*; [*lover*] and *amorous*
6.2	*fire* and *kindle / talk* and *babble*
6.3	*hear* and *listen / rain* and *storm*
7.11	*sea* and *ocean / chamber* and *cell*
7.12	*patience* and *obstinacy / heedfulness* and *carelessness*
7.2	*humour* and *debonair / event* and *misfortune*
8.1	*lion* and *roaring / [language* and *English, Spanish, etc.]*
8.2	*man* and *woman / nun* and *friar*
8.3	*hen* and *chicken / ship* and *prow.*

Note: All examples are Wilkins'. In a few cases, enclosed in square brackets, they are my own (W. H.), because Wilkins gave an explanation but no example.

Source: Wilkins 1968, 320–2.

TABLE A.11   M. Blundevil[l]e, *'Table of Substance'*

This is a shortened version of the table with the typographical devices for signifying hierarchical order replaced by a numerical system. See Table A.7.

Substance is eyther
1.   *without bodie as*
1.1   *an Angell . . .*
1.2   *A Spirit . . .*
2.   *or with body, if it be with bodie it is eyther*
2.1   *Simple, if it be simple it is either*
2.11   *Celestiall as the eleuan heauens and all the starres and planets,*
2.12   *or elementall as*
2.121   *fire,*
2.122   *aire,*
2.123   *water,*
2.124   *earth.*
2.2   *or co[m]pound, if it be compound it is either*
2.21   *living, if it be living it is either*
2.211   *sensible, if . . . called in latin animal, it is eyther*
2.2111   *reasonable as ma[n] . . .*
2.2112   *or unreasonable [as]*
2.21121   *a bird . . . ,*
2.21122   *a four-footed beast . . . ,*
2.21123   *a fish . . . ,*
2.21124   *a creeping beast . . . .*
2.212   *or vnsensible as a plant which is eyther*
2.2121   *a tree . . .*
2.2122   *a shrub . . .*
2.2123   *or hearb . . . .*
2.22   *or vnliving, if it be vnliving it is either*
2.221   *perfect, if it be perfect it is either*
2.2211   *metall . . . ,*
2.2212   *stone . . . .*
2.2213   *or vnperfect as*
2.22131   *liquor . . . ,*
2.22132   *fiery impressions . . . ,*
2.22132   *as or[!] watery [impressions].*

Source: Blundevil[l]e, 1599, 19. BL 8465 b. 9.

TABLE A.12   Blundevil[l]e: *'Natural power and impotencie'*

Naturall power is eyther
1.   *Of the body, as*
1.1   *Health,*

1.2   *hardiness,*

1.3   *nimbleness,*

1.4   *strength.*

2.   *or, of the minde, if it be of yᵉ minde, it is either*

2.1   *Power vegetatiue which is eyther*

2.11   *principal as*

2.111   *Nutritiue,*

2.112   *Augmentatiue,*

2.113   *Generatiue.*

2.12   *or adiuant, as*

2.121   *Attractiue,*

2.122   *Immutatiue,*

2.123   *Retentiue,*

2.124   *Expulsiue.*

2.2   *Power sensitiue is eyther*

2.21   *Comprehensiue which is eyther*

2.211   *Interior, as*

2.2111   *Common sense,*

2.2112   *Phantasie,*

2.2113   *Memorie.*

2.212   *exterior, as*

2.2121   *Sight,*

2.2122   *Hearing,*

2.2123   *Smelling,*

2.2124   *Tasting,*

2.2125   *Feeling.*

2.22   *or motiue which is eyther*

2.221   *Appetitiue which is eyther*

2.2211   *Concupiscible or*

2.2212   *Irascible, whereof spring all the perturbations & passions of the mind, as loue, hate, wrath,*

2.222   *progressiue, as*

2.2221   *to goe,*

2.2222   *to flie,*

2.2223   *to swym.*

2.3   *or power intellectiue, which is eyther*

2.31   *Speculatiue, as*

2.311   *to contemplate,*

2.312   *to vnderstand*

2.32   *or practiue, as*

2.321   *to will,*

2.322   *to nill,*

2.323   *to command,*

2.324   *to chuse.*

Naturall impotencie is eyther

1.   *Of the body as*

TABLE A.12   CONTINUED

1.1   *to be sicke,*
1.2   *to be weake,*
1.3   *to be feeble.*
2.   *Of the minde as*
2.1   *to be forgetfull,*
2.2   *to be vnapt to be taught.*

Source: Blundevil[l]e, 1599, 28. BL 8465 b. 9.

TABLE A.13   Samuel Smith, *'De Substantia'*, and John Wilkins, *'World'*

Smith

Substantia series	2.212 *mineralia*
1 *incorporea*	2.2121 *metalla ut aurum*
1.1 *intelligentia*	2.2122 *medium ut sulphur*
1.11–1.19 *['seraphim'—*	2.22 *animantium*
'angelus', hierarchy of angels]	2.221 *insensi[bi]le: planta*
1.2 *anima*	2.2211 *arbor*
1.21 *vegetativa*	2.2212 *frutex*
1.22 *sensitiva*	2.2213 *herba*
1.23 *rationalis*	2.222 *sensi[bi]le*
2 *corporea*	2.2221 *irrationale: bestia*
2.1 *incorruptibile*	2.22211 *volatilis ut avis*
2.11–2.1(11) *['coelum'—'luna',*	2.22212 *gradeus ut equus*
stars]	2.22213 *aquatilis ut holec*
2.2 *corruptibile*	2.22214 *reptilis ut vipera*
2.21 *inanimantium*	2.2222 *rationale: Socrates,*
2.211 *elementum*	*Plato, Cato, Caesar*
2.2111–2.2114 *[elements]*	

Source: Smith 1627, B2[r]. BL 527. a. 50. (spelling adapted).

Wilkins

World	2.2 *earth*
1. *Spiritual*	2.3 *water*[1]
1.1 . . . *doth not relate to the body*	2.4 *animate parts of the world*
(angel, etc.)	2.41 *vegetative*
1.2 *doth relate to the body: soul*	2.411 *mineral*
1.21 *vegetative*	2.412 *plant*
1.22 *sensitive*	2.413 *animal*
1.23 *rational*	2.414 *rational: man.*
2. *Corporeal substances*	
2.1 *heaven (stars, etc.)*	

See also genus VII: 'elements' (56–60):

1. *fire*
2. *air*
3. *water*
4. *earth*
5. *appearing meteors*
6. *weather*

---

[1] 'Earth' and 'water' are treated by Wilkins from the geographical point of view; for their treatment as elements see below.

Source: Wilkins 1968, 51–5.

TABLE A.14   John Ray, *Herbarum Tabula generalis, summa genera exhibens*

I follow Ray's italicization and capitalization, but replace his other typographical means of indicating taxonomic hierarchy by a number code. The words used are all taken from the original table, but the punctuation has been adapted.

Herbae sunt vel
1.   *Imperfectae*; ut FUNGI, ALGAE, et MUSCI species.[1] Liber II
2.   *Perfectiores*, quae flore & semine donantur, saltem semine. Hae vel sunt semine
2.1   *Minutissimo*; ut CAPILLARES herbae dictae. Liber III
2.2   *Majore*, quae vel sunt Plantula seminale
2.21   *Bifolia*. Sunt autem vel flore
2.211   *Imperfecto* seu stamineo. Liber IV
2.212   *Perfecto* seu petalode aut bracteato. Vel sunt
2.2121   *Composito*, seu ex pluribus flosculis in unum totalem florem coeuntibus aggregato:
2.21211   vel *Plantifolius*. Liber V
2.21212   *Discoides*, vel
2.212121   *Pappo innascente alato*, in PAPPOSIS inde dictis. Liber VI
2.212122   *Solido et papo destituto*, in CORYMBIFERIS. Liber VIII [!]
2.21213   *Fistularis*, quod genus herbae CAPITATAE dicuntur. Liber VII [!].
2.2122   *Simplici*, seu ex petalis tantum cum staminibus & stylo constantem. Hae vel sunt seminibus:
2.21221   *Nudis*, vel
2.212211   *Singulis*. Liber IX, pars I
2.212212   *Binis*, floribus, vel
2.2122121   *Pentepetalis*, inumbellae formam, UMBELLIFERAE. Liber IX, pars II
2.2122122   *Monopetalis*, in quatuor lacinias dissectis, STELLATAE. Liber X, pars I
2.212213   *Ternis*, cujus generis est *Nasturtium Indicum* dictum,
2.212214   *Quaternis*. Hae vel sunt foliis in cauli
2.2122141   *Ex adverso binis*, VERTICILLATAE. Liber XI[!]
2.2122142   *Alterno vel nullo ordine positis*, quae ob folia in plerisque speciebus aspera ASPE-RIOFOLIAE denominantur. Liber X, pars II
2.212215   *Pluribus quatuor*, nullo certo aut definito numero, quas *Gymnospermas polyspermas* vocamus. Liber XII.
2.21222   *Conceptaculis propriis & a perianthio diversis donatis*, quae constant vel *Pericarpio molli*, seu pulpa per fructus maturitatem humida semina ambiente. Hae vel sunt fructu

TABLE A.14   CONTINUED

2.212221   *Majore*, POMIFERAE dictae. Liber XIII, pars I

2.212222   *Minore*, BACCIFERAE. Liber XIII, pars II

2.21223   *Materia per maturitatem sicciore.* Hae autem vel in

2.212231   *Conceptaculis pluribus et distinctis*, quas MULTISILIQUAS dicimus. Liber XIV.

2.212232   *Conceptaculis solitariis et singulis*, quas florum respectu dividimus in

2.2122321   *Monopetalas*, flore vel

2.21223211   *Uniformi,*

2.21223212   *Difformi.*

2.2122322   *Tetrapetalas*, flore itidem

2.21223221   *Uniformi* seu

2.212232211   SILIQUOSAS, flori succedente vasculo oblongo,

2.212232212   SILICULOSAS, capsulatasqve, vasculo succedente curto.

2.21223222   *Difformi*, papilionem alis expansis quadantenus referente, quas idcirco PAPIL-IONACEAS vocant.

2.2122322   *Pentapetalas* seu

2.21223221   *Veras et genuinas*, quarum flos quinque petalis distinctis constat,

2.21223222   *Apparentes*, quarum flos revera monopetalos est.

2.22   *Unifolia* aut *aphyllo*, i.e. singulis aut nullis cotyledonibus donatata, ideoque soliis succedentibus similibus, e terra exit. Hae vel sunt

2.221   *Flore imperfecto* seu stamineo, seu

2.2211   CULMIFERAE, sunt vel grano

2.22111   *Majore*, FRUMENTA et CEREALIA dictae,

2.22112   *Minore*, GRAMINA.

2.2212   *Caule geniculis nodosis non intercepto,* vel non tereti.

2.222   *Flore perfecto*, seu petalode, quae vel sunt

2.2221   *Bulbosa,*

2.2222   Tuberosa.

---

[1] *Plantae imperfectae* have their own table which I do not quote.

Source: Ray, 1593, 59/–/60. BL 1505/117.

TABLE A.15   Johannes Murmellius, *Pappa*, macrostructure

---

[1]   *De deo & rebus celestibus. Ua[n] gode ende hemelschen dingen*

[2]   *De te[m]poribus. Uan den tijden*

[3]   *De quattuor elementis & eis que in aere generantur. Uan deen vier elemente[n] ende den dinghen welck in der lucht generyert worden*

[4]   *Terre aquaru[m] et locorum vocabula. der eerden wateren ende steden of playtsen vocabulen*

[5]   *Terrarum. gentium & ciuitatum nomina. Der landen. ende der natien. ende der steeden namen*

[6]   *De animaliu[m] generibus. Uan den specien der dyeren*

[7]   *De etatibus et partib[us] ho[min]is. Uan den olderen ende deylen des mynsschen*

[8]   *De auibus. Uan den voghelen*

[9] *De piscibus. Uan den visschen*
[10] *De serpe[n]tibus. Uan den serpente*
[11] *De vermibus. van den wormen*
[12] *De arboribus. van den bomen*
[13] *De fructib[us] arborum. Uan vruchten der bome[n]*
[14] *De fructibus. va[n] cleyne[n] bomkens of twygere[n]*
[15] *De herbis. van cruden*
[16] *De florib[us]. va[n] den blomen*
[17] *De aromatib[us]. va[n] wailruyckeden cruderen*
[18] *De frume[n]tis et leguminibus. Uan korne ende vruhte[n] die me[n] leest mit der ha[n]t.*
[19] *De lapidib[us] et gemmis. Uan steine[n] ende eedelen steinen.*
[20] *De metallis. van metalen.*
[21] *De ecclesia et rebus ecclesiasticis.* [no translation]
[22] *Sacramenta sancte ecclesie. Die sacramenten der hylliger kerken.*
[23] *De domo et ei[us] partibus. Uan den huse. ende syne deyle*
[24] *De varia supellectile. Van mennigerha[n]de huisrayt*
[25] *De vestibus.* [no translation]
[26] *De cibi generibus. van menigherha[n]de spyse*
[27] *De pot[ibus] generibus. Uan men[n]igerley dranc.*
[28] *Vocabula cognat[ion]is. Vocabulen der maichtail*
[29] *Coniugij et affinitatis nomina.* [no translation]
[30] *Nomina dignitatu[m] ecclesiasticaru[m]. vocabulen der geystlyken digniteiten.*
[31] *Dignitatu[m] seculariu[m] vocabula Uocablen der werretlyken digniteten.*
[32] *De bonar[um] artium pfessorib[us]. Uan den pfessores der guder konsten*
[33] *Artific[ior]u[m] et mechanicor[um] no[m]i[n]a. Constener ende handwerckerluyde vocabulen.*
[34] *De libiris. uan den boeken.*
[35] *De po[n]deribus et mensuris. Uan gewichten ende maten*
[36] *De pecunijs. van gelde.*
[37] *No[m]i[n]a numeralia cardinalia. principael nomina der getalen.*
[38] *Numeralia distributiua.* [no translation]
[39] *Ordinalia nomina.* [no translation]
[40] *Numeralia inarius multiplicato[n]em rerum.* [no translation]
[41] *Numeralia multiplicatiua.* [no translation]
[42] *Numeralia forme multiplicatiua.* [no translation]
[43] *Numeralia inanus.* [no translation]
[44] *Aduerbia numeralia.* [no translation]
[45] *Tres virtutes theologice. dry doechden van weleken die leeres der gotheyt van spreken*
[46] *Quattuor virtutes cardinales. veyr p[r]incipale doechden*
[47] *Septe[m] vitia capitalia. Seuen doitlike sunden*
[48] *Quattor nouissima. die veyr vterste dingen*
Pappe caput secundu[m]

Source: Ioa[n]nis Murmellij Ruremu[n]densis, cui titulus est Pappa . . . , 1513. WF Kg 369.

TABLE A.16   Adam of Rotweil, *Introito e porta*, macrostructure

Table A.16 presents the two overviews—the Italian and the German. They have been copied as faithfully as possible. Inconsistencies of spelling and punctuation have been retained.

The Italian overview

El .1. c. sie de dio e dela trinita e dela polencia e richeza.
El .2. c. deli sa[n]ti e deli nomi deli homini e dele femine.
El .3. el pater noster e el aue maria.
El .4. del diauolo e del inferno e in purgatorio.
El .5. de te[m]po anni setemani e deli zorni.
El .6. si sia del homo e de tutti soi parti interiori et exteriori.
El .7. del imperio e dela signoria.
El .8. dela imperadrixe e do[n]ne magnifice.
El .9. deli famegli.
Fl .10. del bisauo e dele tute parentade.
El .11. dele noze e tuti listadi.
El .12. dela citade e deli iudixi e deli ofici.
El .13. del numero sempio e composito cifero e denari.
El .14. del oro argento e tute le chose che sia smalto.
El .15. sie del peuere zen zero e tute le specie e marcadantie
El .16. c. dela marzeria e pa[n]no e tele e altre simile cose.
El .17. deli marcadanti e deli artexani e mestieri.
El .18. de le cholore.
El .19. dela massaria e deli vestimenti.
El .20. dele chaxamente
El .21. del pan e del vin e tute le chose che se mangia.
El .22. dele ordenge et instrumenti.
El .23. dele piere preciose e tute le piere e altre multe chose.
El .24. del meistro dele arme e de tute le arme.
El .25. d[e]la villa e deli villani.
El .26. del orto e deli sui fruti zardini et tuti li arbori.
El .27. del boscho e dele cose saluatiche.
El .28. deli animali.
El .29. dela formicha e d[e]li vermi et tuti li bestiani.
El .30. deli oseli e deli sui generationi.
El .31. deli pessi et deli soi generationi.
El .32. d[e]li naue e d[e]le galie
El .33. de aiere e deli ve[n]ti.
El .34. dele montange e valle.
El .35. d[e]le paexe e paexa[n]e
El .36. d[e]li citade e castele
El .37. dela christianita d[?] deli infideli.
El .38. dela bataia e dela guerra e deli zugadori.
El .39. deli sonatori e piferi.
El .40. dela infirmita et malatia.
El .41. dele septe peccate mortale.

El .42. deli cinque sentimenti.
El .43. dele sie opere de la mixericordia
El .44. dele diexe coma[n]damente de dio.
El .45. delo studio e dela schuola.
El .47 [!]. del oficio eclexiastico.
El .47. dele aque e dela humitade.
El .48. c. del fuogo e del caldo.
El .49. dela obidiencia.
El .50. deli mati.
El .51. deli palaci.
El .52. dela canaua e q[ue]le che la contiene.
El .53. d[e]la stua e dela chuxina e quel che la contiene.
El .54. dela chamera e quele che la contiene.
El .55. del granaro e deli grani.
Questo libro sie el segu[n]do libro che cu[n]tiene dele uerbe e dele parole segu[n]do tute suo muodo.
El primo .c. si sia dele verbe e dele parole.
El segundo cap. dela ambasada e ambasadori.
El .3. cap. deli nomi e p[ro]nomi.
El .4. ca. dela legreza e grameza.
El .5. c. dele comandamente e dele risposte.
El .6. c. del chaminare e del chaualchare e deli chauali e tuti loi pertine[n]cia e altre certe bele chose
El .7. c. come se domanda da vna cosa.
El .8. c. de le cuoge e soi instrumenti
El .9. c. del dormir e del sono

The German overview
dAs[!] erst capitl sagt von got vnd von der heiligen driualtikait von mechtikait vnd reichtum
Das ander capitel sagt von den heiligen vnd von alen nåmen der menschen.
Das drit ca. vom pater noster vnd der aue maria.
Das vierd von dem teufel vnd von der v[er]damnus.
Das finft capitel sag vo[n] der zeit iar wochen vnd vo[n] den tagen.
Das sexte capitel sag vo[n] den manen vo[n] alen geslechten der menschen vnd von aler irer czugehőrung.
Das sibe[n]t capitel sagt von kaiser vnd vo[n] der herschaft
Das achtet capitel sagt von der kaiserin vnd von den edeln frauen.
Das neund capitel sagt von knechte[n] vnd vo[n] diern.
Das zehent capitel von den enn vnd våtern freunte[n] vnd geslechten.
Das .11. capitel sagt vo[n] den hochczeiten.
Das .12. capitel sagt vo[n] stete[n] vnd von etleiche[n] rechte[n].
Das .13. c. sagt vo[n] czeln vnd czal vnd vo[n] der czifer.
Das .14. capitel sagt vo[n] gold silber vnd von ale[n] dingen die man smelczt.
Das .15. c. saget von pfefer ingber vnd vo[n] aler speczerei.
Daz .16. c. sagt von cråmerei tůchern leinbat vnd von solchen dingen.
Das .17. c. von kaufleuten vnd vo[n] ale[n] ha[n]tberche[n].
Das .18. sagt vo[n] alen farben.

TABLE A.16   CONTINUED

Das .19. c. sagt von ale[m] hausgerecht vnd klaidern.

Das .20. c. sagt von den håuseren.

Das .21. c. saget vo[n] prot vnd wein vnd allen dingen das man isst.

Das .22. c. sagt von ale[n] werchczeug.

Das .23. capi. sagt von edelm gestain.

Das .24. c. sagt vo[n] ale[n] harnasch.

Das .25. c. sagt von den pauern vnd von de[n] dörfern.

Das .26. c. sagt vo[n] den gårten vnd vo[n] den crautern.

Das .27. c. sagt von den wålden vnd von allen wilden dingen.

Das .28. c. sagt von den wilden tieren.

Das .29. c. sagt vo[n] der amås vnd vo[n] allen wůrmen vnd von allen vichern.

Das .30. c. sagt von den fogeln vnd vo[n] ire[n] geslechte[n]

Das .31. c. sagt von den fischen vnd vo[n] ire[n] geslechte[n]

Das .32. ca. ist von den schefen.

Das .33. c. sagt vo[m] wint vnd vom luft.

Das .34. c. sagt vo[n] perg vnd von tal.

Das .35. c. sagt von den lande[n] vnd vo[n] de[n] la[n]tsleute[n].

Das .36. c. sagt von den steten vnd geslössern.

Das .37. c. sagt von der cristenhaid vnd von de[n] vnglaubigen.

Das .38. capi. sagt von streit von crieg vund vo[n] spilern.

Das .39. c. sagt von ale[m] saitenspil.

Das .40. cap. sagt von krankhait.

Das .41. c. sagt von de[n] siben tod sůnden

Das .42. cap. sagt von den fůnf sinnen

Das .43. capitel ist von den sex werchen der parmherczikayt

Das .44. capitel ist vo[n] den czehen poten gotes

Das .45. capitel, sagt vo[n] der studi vnd von der hohe[n] schůl.

Das .46. cap. sagt von dem geistleichen ambt

Das .47. cap. sagt von den wasseren vnd von der fåuchtikayt.

Das .48. capitel sagt vo[n] dem feůr vnd von der hicz.

Das .49. capitel saget von der gehorsamikayt

Das .50. capitel sagt vo[n] den narren.

Daz .51. capitel sagt vo[n] den pålåsten.

Das .52. capitel sagt vo[n] dem keller vnd von seiner zůgehörung

Das .53. capitel sagt vo[n] stuben vnd ierer zůgehörung

Das .54. capitel sagt vo[n] den kåmern vnd irer zůehörung.

Das .55. capitel sagt vo[n] de[m] korn haus und vo[m] weicz vnd korn.

Diß ist das ander puch das haltet in di red vnd di wort ein ieczleiches nach seinem lauf.

Das erst capitel sagt vo[n] den wörtern vnd von der red.

Das ander cap. sagt vo[n] potschaft

Das .3. cap. sind di nåm vnd sprůch.

Das .4. cap. von fråud vnd laid.

Das .5. c. von piete[n] vnd schafen.

Das .6. c. sagt von geen vnd von reiten vnd sunst manigerlai dingen.

Das .7. c. wie ma[n] fodert oder fragt.

Das .8. c. von de[n] köchen vnd ierem hantwerch.
Das 9. c. sagt vo[m] slaf.

Source: *Questo[!] libro el duale silbi ama introito e porta . . .* , 1477. BSB Inc. C. a. 106 4° Rotweil.

TABLE A.17   Nicodemus Frischlin, *Nomenclator trilinguis*, macrostructure

INDEX CAPITVM
1. *De Deo & Angelis.*
2. *De Caelo & Astris.*
3. *De Natura & rebus naturalibus.*
4. *De Loco, eiusque differentiis.*
5. *De Tempore, eiusque differentiis.*
6. *De Elemento ignis & aeris, & his quae in utroque existunt.*
7. *De aqua & speciebus, seu differentiis aquae: item de ponte, fronte & puteo.*
8. *De praecipuis aliquot fluuiis.*
9. *De Mari, eiusque diuersis appellationibus.*
10. *De Terra eiusque differentiis secundum naturam: vbi etiam de montibus.*
11. *De praecipuis Regionibus.*
12. *De praecipuis Insulis.*
13. *De Metallis.*
14. *De Lapidibus & gemmis.*
15. *De Anima eiusque differentiis, & de rebus animatis.*
16. *De Facultate nutritiua & generetiua.*
17. *De Arboribus, earumque partibus.*
18. *De Arboribus hortensibus & satiuis.*
19. *De Arborum hortensium fructibus.*
20. *De Arboribus syluestribus.*
21. *De Arborum sylvestrum fructibus.*
22. *De Fructibus.*
23. *De Rosa & vite speciatim.*
24. *De Gummi & Lacrimis.*
25. *De Aromatis & condimentis.*
26. *De Fungis & tuberibus.*
27. *De Herbis, earumque differentiis & partibus.*
28. *De Herbis frumentaceis, siue de frumentis.*
29. *De Leguminibus.*
30. *De Oleribus.*
31. *De herbis coronariis & odoriferis.*
32. *De herbis Medicinalibus.*
33. *De sensu & sensili, rebusque sentientibus.*
34. *De facultate motiua, & secundum eam differentibus animalibus quadrupedibus.*
35. *De Volucribus, earumque partibus peculiaribus.*
36. *De Volucribus domesticis.*

TABLE A.17 CONTINUED

37. De Volucribus aeris minoribus.

38. De Auibus aeris maioribus.

39. De auibus terrestribus seu humiuolis.

40. De Auibus aquaticis.

41. De Auibus rapacibus.

42. De Piscibus, eorumque partibus peculiaribus.

43. De Piscibus fluuiatilibus & squamosis.

44. De Piscibus fluuiatilibus & mollibus.

45. De Piscibus marinis.

46. De Ostreis & Zoophytis.

47. De Vermibus & serpentibus seu reptilibus.

48. De Insectis volatilibus.

49. De Insectis reptilibus.

50. De Auibus speciatim.

51. De Animalibus quadrupedibus, & eorum partibus similaribus.

52. De partibus eorundem diſſimilaribus.

53. De partibus certo animalium genere peculiaribus, & de excrementis.

54. De animalibus quadrupedibus, mansuetis & cornutis.

55. De Quadrupedibus domesticis, mansuetis, non cornutis.

56. De Quadrupedibus feris & cornutis.

57. De Quadrupedibus feris, non cornutis.

58. De Vocibus diuersorum animalium.

59. De bonis & malis corporis, praesertim de morbis.

60. De Morbis certarum corporis partium.

61. De Morbis incertarum partium.

62. De Tumoribus.

63. De Vlceribus.

64. De Morbis totius corporis.

65. De vitiis corpori innatis.

66. De Anima RATIONALI, & de Homine.

67. De Hominum differentiis secundum sexum & aetatem.

68. De Affectibus.

69. De virtutibus moralibus & de virtute praeditis.

70. De vitiis moralibus, & de vitiosis.

71. De Iustitia commutatiua vniversali.

72. De Iustitia commutatiua particulari.

73. De iustitia distributiua vniversali.

74. De iustitia distributiua particulari.

75. De virtutibus intellectus, siue de scientiis & artibus.

76. De vitiis intellectus.

77. De Schola.

79 [*sic:* 78]. *De Arte Typographica.*

79. De re Libraria, & de scribtis atque tablino.

80. De Arithmetica.

126. De Molitore & mola.

127. De Pistore, eiusque instrumentis & operibus, quae nihil aliud sunt, quam diuersorum panum genera.

128. De Venatoribus, Aucupibus & Piscatoribus.

129. De Laniis & fartoribus.

130. De Coco et Culina.

131. De Penore.

132. De Cibis variis.

133. De Cella vinaria & potu.

[134. vacat]

135. De mensa rebusque ad mensam pertinentibus.

136. De Opificibus, qui versantur circa vestitum.

137. De Lanificio & fullonia.

138. De Textore & tinctore.

139. De Sartore.

140. De Vestibus virorum.

143 [*sic:* 141]. *De Vestibus mulierum.*

124 [*sic:* 142]. *De Coriario & Sutore.*

143. De Restione & Ephippiario.

144. De Opificibus, qui versantur circa lutum, lapides & ligna.

145. De Figulo & laterario.

146. De Lapicida & Caementario.

147. De Materiario & fabris lignariis.

148. De domo eiusque praecipuis partibus.

149. De Cubiculo speciatim.

150. De varia suppellectili domestica.

151. De Familia & cognatione.

152. De Matrimonio & affinitate.

153. De Puerperio.

154. De Domino & Seruitute.

155. De Vrbe eiusque partibus.

156. De praecipuis omnium fere regionum ciuitatibus.

157. De Templo, Ecclesia, rebusque Ecclesiasticis.

158. De muniis atque ordinibus Ecclesiasticis.

159. De Ecclesiaste & rebus quas praecipue tractat.

160. De praecipuis titulis & vocabulis Iuris Canonici.

161. De Republica, eiusque formis.

162. De Regio statu & aula.

163. De Ciuibus & statu ciuili.

164. De Curia & Senatu.

165. De Causa & iudicio.

166. De Inuriis & maleficiis.

167. De Carcere & poenis.

168. De Materiis Institutionum Iuris.

169. De titulis Pandectarum.

170. De Armamentario & armis.
171. De Nauali & re nautice.
172. De Muniis nauticis.
173. De pace & bello.
174. De Imperio & ordinibus militaribus.
175. De Castris & obsidione.
176. De Acie & pugnis.
177. De Ludis & rebus ludicris.
178. De Testamento, morte, & sepultura.

Source: Nicodemi Frischlini Nomenclator Trilinguis . . ., 1600. WF 53.4 Gram. 8ᶜ.

TABLE A.18 *Dictionarium Latino-Germanicum* .... *Ex Nomenclatore Iuniano* ..., macrostructure

I. [= liber primum]
SVBSTANTIA.

SVBSTANTIAE Naturales.
Deus
Substantia incorporea [angels, gods]
Substantia corporea simplex, incorruptibilis [sky, sphere]
    Stellae
    Sydera seu asterismi [stars, weather]
Simplicia corpora [elements]
    Meteora [fire]
    Aeria corpora [air, wind]
    De Aqva et speciebvs aquae
    Maria [names]
    Fluvvii [names]
    Terra et eivs species [valley, mountain, field]
    Insulae maris [names]
    Terrae partes et regiones [continents, countries]
    De montibus [names, alphabetical]
    Promontoria [names, alphabetical]
Corpus perfecte mixtum fossile
    Lapides
    Gemmae
Substantiae corporeae mixtae
    Metalla
    De re herbaria
    Herbarum species
    De frumentis et leguminibus
    De oleribus
    De aromatibus
    Frutices

TABLE A.18   CONTINUED

Vvarium species
  De arboribus et fructibus
  Fructus arborum
Substantia animata, sentiens, irrationalis
  Pisces
  Aves
  De animalibus quadrupedibus
  De vermibus et insectis
  Serpentes
  Homo, corporis humani partes
  De cibis
  De potu
  De obsoniis et fructibus
Substantiae artificialis
  Instrumenta typographica
  Instrumenta doctorum [writing utensils]
  Instrumenta et materiae pharmacopolae
  Instrumenta aurifabrorum
  Instrumenta vietorum
  Instrumenta vinitorum
  [Instrumenta] arcularii
  Instrumenta tornarii
  [Instrumenta] plaustrarii
  [Instrumenta] metallarii
  [Instrumenta] aquilegis
  [Instrumenta] monetarii
  Instrumenta fabrorum
  Instrumenta et supellex domestica [furniture, household goods]
  Instrumenta coquinaria
  Instrumenta cubicularia
  Instrumenta mulierum [spinning, jewellery]
  [Instrumenta] textoris
  [Instrumenta] sutoris
  [Instrumenta] pistoris
  [Instrumenta] molitoris
  [Instrumenta] piscatoris
  [Instrumenta] venatoris
  [Instrumenta] chirurgi
  Instrumenta fabri lignarii
  [Instrumenta] sartorum
  [Instrumenta] coriarii
  Instrumenta lanificii
  Instrumenta figuli
  Instrumenata lapicida
  Instrumenta cementarii

Instrumenta nautae
Instrumenta rustici
Instrumenta equorum
Instrumenta militaria
Instrumenta lusoris
Instrumenta architecti
Instrumenta ecclesiastica
Instrumenta musica
Instrumenta vinaria
Substantia composita aromatica, ad usum medicina
  [Fifteen sub-sections]

LIBER SECVNDVS continet seriem accidentium. Quae in 9. praedicamentis continentur.

QVANTITAS
Accidens inseparabile
Quantitatis continuae
  De dimensionibus, secundum longitudinem, latitudinem & profunditatem
  De mensuris liquidorum & aridorum
  De ponderibus.
Quantitatis discretae
  De numeris
  De nummeratione temporis
  De re nummeraria
  De oratio et eius partes, grammatica, ethymologia [debates, rhetoric, metres]

QVALITAS
Qualitatis
  De affectionibus animi, bonis et malis [adjectives]
  De virtutibus (Habitus animi, bonus) [nouns]
  De vitijs [nouns]
  De artibus et scientiis (Habitus intellectus)
  De opificijs [crafts]
  De affectionibus corporis, morbi
  De habitu corporis
  De potentijs animae (Potentiae naturales)
  De qualitatibus quae afficiunt visum
  De coloribus
  De qualitatibus quae afficiunt auditum [voices of animals]
  De qualitatibus quae afficiunt gustum
  De qualitatibus quae afficiunt olfactum
  De qualitatibus quae afficiunt tactum
  De qualitatibus quae animum afficiunt [moods]
  De corporis affectionibus [weeping, trembling]
  De figuris et formis [geometry]

RELATIONES (DE RELATIONE, quarto predicamento)
  De personis in dignitate aliqua vel munere quodam constitutis

TABLE A.18   CONTINUED

De personis militaribus
De personis publicis & civilibus
De personis sanguinitate & affinitate iunctis

CLASSIS RELATIONIVM I. ORDINIS
  De personis Ecclesiasticis
  De personis iure ordinatis
  De personis literatis & literatorum amantibus
  [ten more subsections on professions, craftsmen, offices]
II. CLASSIS RELATIONIVM
  Theologica [practical]
  Politica et iuridica (De legibus) [practical, penalties]
  Actiones legitimae [procedures in court]
[III. CLASSIS RELATIONIVM]
  De collationibus [whole and parts, numbers not in sequence]

ACTIO ET PASSIO
[actions, processes, happenings etc., clustered around subjects; in fact a large collection of
verbs, partly alphabetically arranged]
  Actiones elementorum, ignis, aeris, aqua, terrae
  Actiones stirpium & plantarum
  Actiones naturales animalium, absolutae & transitivae
  Actiones animalium propriae
  Actiones animalium absolutae & transitivae
  Actiones sensuum & affectum
  Actiones mentis absolutae & transitivae
  Actiones mentis & corporis ac ipsius vocis
  Actiones humanae voluntariae locomotiuae
  Actiones humanae voluntariae
  Actiones voluntariae politicae forenses
  Actiones humanae voluntariae vitiosae
  Actiones humanae voluntariae opificium
  Actiones voluntariae quae fiunt instrumentis et sensibilis sunt ac opus aliquod relinquunt
  Actiones oeconomicae
  Actiones oeconomicae rusticae
  Actiones politicae et polemicae
  Absoluta in [?]*definentia* [grow, become]
  Opera artificium

PRAEDICAMENTVM VBI
[Thirteen subsections on loci: hell, universe, earth, water, countries, ports, lakes [names],
woods [names], geographical formations, towns, houses, shops, gardens]
  Locum significantia sed indefinite [adverbs]
  Praecipuarum urbium nomina [names of towns, countries]

PRAEDICAMENTVM QVANDO
[Three subsections, seasons, parts of day, calendar; adverbs]

PRAEDICAMETVM SITUS
  De situ naturali perpetuo [sky, zones of earth]
  De variabili & uniformi [sun, moon, planets]
  De naturali & non perpetuo [forests, hills, gardens]
  De voluntarij situs generibus [verbs of movement]
  De situ mixto, durabili ac fortuito [houses]
  De situ casuali [island, mountain, column, statue, unrelated]

PRAEDICAMENTVM HABITUS
[Six subsections on clothes, garments, shoes]

Source: *Dictionarium* . . ., 1610 WF 87. Gram. 4°.

T A B L E   A.19   John Hig[g]ins, *The Nomenclator, or Remembrancer of Adrianus Junius*, macrostructure

The Contents of Nomenclators first Tome . . . .

1	*Of bookes, of writings, and all necessaries thereto belonging*
2	*Of man and woman, with the parts of their bodies*
3	*Of the lim[b]s and members*
4	*Of liuing creatures fourfooted*
5	*The names of beasts*
6	*The names of Dogs*
7	*Of birds or foules, with the parts of their bodies*
8	*The names of birds or fouls*
9	*Of fishes, their partes and kinds*
10	*The names of fishes*
11	*Of vermine and creeping things*
12	*The kinds of serpents or creepers*
13	*Of meats & vittels*
14	*Of wines, drinks, aand oyles*
15	*Of banketting dishes and fruites*
16	*Of Apothecarie ware, of spices, & the sorts of the[m]*
17	*Of corne, graine, and other pulse, as beans, pease, &c.*
18	*Of hearbs, their sundrie sorts and seuerall names*
19	*Of trees, shrubs, plants, &c.*
20	*Of faultes in plants, trees, and wood*
21	*The parts of a rose*
22	*The names of trees, plants, shrubs, &c.*
23	*Of apparel*
24	*Of priests apparell*
25	*Of mens apparell*
26	*Of womens apparell*
27	*Of furniture or attire for the head*
28	*Of furniture for the feet and the rest of the body*
29	*Of colours*

TABLE A.19   CONTINUED

30   *Of building with diuers sorts of houseroomes, & places of office*
31   *Of prisons and sundrie punishments*
32   *Of buildinges with many kinds of workmanship, & necessary appurtenances*
33   *Of ships and ship furniture*
34   *The parts of a ship, & things thereto belonging*
35   *The instruments or furniture of a ship*
36   *Houshold stuffe of sundrie sorts, and first of implements for a house*
37   *Of necessarie things for the table*
38   *Of implements for the kitchin*
39   *Of impleme[n]ts for the chamber*
40   *Of necessarie things for womens vse*
41   *Of weauers tooles*
42   *Of shoemakers tooles*
43   *Of bakers tooles*
44   *Of fishers or Anglers tooles*
45   *Of hunters tooles*
46   *Of surgions instruments or tooles*
47   *Of countrie tooles or implements*
48   *Of furniture for horses*
49   *Of furniture for warre and souldiers*
50   *Of termes in warre*
51   *Of games or playes with their appurtenances*
52   *Of instruments or tooles necessarily vsed in and aboute building*
53   *The Carpenters tooles and other occupations*
54   *Of instruments and necessarie furniture for the Churche*
55   *Of money and coynes with their value, their stamps, and stuffe*
56   *Of termes properly vsed in mony matters*
57   *Of mony*
58   *Of measures & weights*
59   *The measures of liquide things*
60   *The measures of dry things*
61   *The measures of lands spaces, of place and distaunces*
62   *The instruments of musick, with their appurtenances*
63   *The proportions of musicke, the words of art, the Gamma vt: also of tunes, noises, and sounds.*

The Contents of Nomenclators second Tome . . .
1   *Of the elementes & and their appurtenances*
2   *Of yeres, daies, times seasons and festiuals*
3   *The names of earthes or grounds, waters, and places both on water and land*
4   *Of mettals and minerals*
5   *Of stones*
6   *Of Pearles and pretious stones*
7   *The names of diseases, maladies, griefs, faults of nature, affections and passions*
8   *The state and disposition of the body good or ill*
9   *Of medicins, receits, ointments, plasters, and such like,*

10	*The kinds of tasts*
11	*Of God and of spirits*
12	*The names of ecclesiasticall preferments, dignities and offices*
13	*The names of ciuill preferments, dignities and offices*
14	*Officers and offices in warfare*
15	*Officers and offices in a shire citie or corporate towne*
16	*The names of arts, artists, and professors of learned sciences*
17	*Of handicrafts men, or men of occupation*
18	*The names of occupations belonging to the backe, and necessaries for wearing*
19	*Of trades seruing for [the] belly, as vittailing and such like*
20	*The names of cou[n]try trades and vocations*
21	*The names of officers belonging to sea and shipping*
22	*The names of trades that serue to make folke neat, trim and amiable*
23	*The names of seruants, drudges and slaues*
24	*The names of gamsters and vsers of diuers playes and exercises*
25	*The names of reprochfull persons, base trades and shifters*
26	*The names of consanguinity, affinitie, kinred, and aliaunce*

Finis.

Source: *The Nomenclator . . .* , 1585. BSB Microfilm 20822.

TABLE A.20   William Bathe, *Janua linguarum*, and Johannes Amos Comenius, *Janua linguarum reserata, tituli*

Bathe

CENTURIA PRIMA. SENTENTIARUM MORALIVM. De Virtute, & Vitio, in communi. Das erste Hundert. Der Moralischen oder Hoefflichen Sprüche. Von Tugend / und Laster ins gemein. The first Centurie. Of Morall Sentences. Concerning Vertue, and Vice, in generall. CENTURIA SECUNDA. DE PRUDENTIA, ET IMPRVDENTIA. Das ander Hundert. Von Fuersichtigkeit / und unfuersichtigkeit. The second Centurie. Of VVisedome, and Folly. CENTURIA TERTIA. DE TEMPERANTIA, ET INtemperantia. Das dritte Hundert. Von der Maessigkeit unnd Unmaessigkeit. The Third Centurie. Of Temperance, and Intemperance. CENTURIA QVARTA. DE IUSTITIA, ET INIUSTITIA. Das vierdte Hundert. Von der Gerechtigkeit und Ungerechtigkeit. The fourth Centurie. Of Iustice, and Iniustice. CENTURIA QUINTA. DE FORTITUDINE, ET IMbellicitate. Das fuenfte Hundert. Von der Staerke und Schwachheit. The fift Centurie. Of Fortitude, and Covvardice. CENTURIA SEX. DE ACTIONIBVS HVMAnis. Das sechste Hundert. Von den Menschlichen thaten. The sixt Centurie. Of humane actions. CENTURIA SEPTIMA. DE TURBUlentis, & Tranquillis. Das sibende Hundert. Von unruhigen/und ruhigen dingen. The seventh Centurie. Of things turbulent, and quiet.

TABLE A.20   CONTINUED

CENTURIA OCTAVA. DE ANIMAtis, & inanimatis.
Das Achte Hundert. Von lebendigen dingen/unnd denen so kein leben haben.
The Eight Centurie. Of things that have life and things vvithout life.
CENTURIA NONA. DE ARTIFIcialibus.
Das neunde Hundert. Von kuenstlichen dingen. The Ninth Centurie. Of Artificiall things.
CENTURIA DEC.MA. DE REBUS indistinctis.
Das zehende Hundert. Von allerhand dingen / ohn underscheid. The Tenth Centurie. Of Severall things vvithout distinction.
CENTURIA UNDECIMA. DE INDIstinctus. [from 1042] *APPENDIX DE AMBIGUIS*
Das Eilffte Hundert. Von ohn-underschiednen dingen. [from 1042] *Anhang Etlicher zweiffelhaftiger wo(e)rter. The eleuenth Centurie. Of seuerall things vvithout distinction.* [from 1042] *AN ADDITION Of vvords that haue diuers significations.*
CENTURIO DUODECIMA. SEQUITUR DIscursus, ex verbis post Sententias relictis compositus: in quo, neque ullum verbum bis repetitur; neque est ullum vocabulum, quod in mille & centum precedentibus sententiis reperitur. In Zoilum.
Das zwoelfte Hundert. Folget ein Discurs/auß den worten/so nach den Sententzen uberblieben/zusammen gesetzet: in welchem kein einig wort zweymahl widerholet wird: ist auch nicht einig Wort/daß in den Tausendt und einHundert vorhergehenden Spruechen zufinden. Wider den Schmaeher /oder Neidharten.The tvvelfth Centurie. Here follovveth a discourse, composed of the vvords remaining after the Se[n]tences vvere made: vvherein there is neither any vvord tvvice repeated; neither is there any that is found in the eleuen hundred precede[n]t Sentences. Against Zoilus, or the malicious Carper.
Peroravi. FINIS.
Ich hab außgeredt. ENDE. I haue finisht my speech. END.

Comenius

I. Introitus	*XX. De Homine*
II. De Orto Mundi	*XXI. De Corpore, Et Primum De Membris Externis*
III. De Elementis	
IV. De Firmamento	*XXII. De Membris Internis*
V. De Igne	*XXIII. De Accidentibus Corporis*
VI. De Meteoris	*XXIV. De Morbis*
VII. De Aquis	*XXV. De Ulceribus Et Volneribus*
VIII. De Terra	*XXVI. De Sensibus Externis*
IX. De Lapidibus	*XXVII. De Sensibus Internis*
X. De Metallis	*XXVIII. De Mente*
XI. De Arboribus Et Fructibus	*XXIX. De Voluntate Et Affectibus*
XII. De Herbis	*XXX. De Mechanicis In Genere*
XIII. De Fructibus	*XXXI. De Hortorum Cultura*
XIV. De Animalibus, Et Primo Avibus	*XXXII. De Agricultura*
XV. De Aquatilibus	*XXXIII. De Molitura*
XVI. De Jumentis	*XXXIV. De Panificio*
XVII. De Feris	*XXXV. De Pecuaria*
XVIII. De Amphibis Et Reptilibus	*XXXVI. De Lanionia*
XIX. De Insectis	*XXXVII. De Venatura*

XXXVIII. De Piscatione	*LXIX. De Musee*
XXXIX. De Aucupio	*LXX. De Grammatica*
XL. De Coquinaria	*LXXI. De Dialectica*
XLI. De Potulentorum Paratura	*LXXII. De Rhetorica Et Poesi*
XLII. De Aurigatione	*LXIII. De Arithmetica*
XLIII. De Navicularia	*LXXIV. De Geometria*
XLIV. De Itineribus	*LXXV. De Mensuris Et Ponderibus*
XLV. De Mercatura	*LXXVI. De Optica Et Pictura*
XLVI. De Vestiariis Opificiis	*LXXVII. De Musica*
XLVII. De Vestituum Generibus	*LXXVIII. De Astronomia*
XLVIII. De Fabrilibus Artificiis	*LXXIX. De Geographia*
XLIX. De Domo Ejusque Partibus	*LXXX. De Historia*
L. De Hypocausto	*LXXXI. De Medicina*
LI. De Coenaculo	*LXXXII. De Ethica In Genere*
LII. De Cubiculo	*LXXXIII. De Prudentia*
LIII. De Balneo Et Munditie	*LXXXIV. De Temperantia*
LIV. De Conjugio Et Affinitate	*LXXXV. De Castitate*
LV. De Puerperio	*LXXXVI. De Modestia*
LVI. De Cognatione	*LXXXVII. De Autarkeia*
LVII. De Oeconomia	*LXXXVIII. De Justitia, Primo*
LVIII. De Urbe	*Commutativa*
LIX. De Templo	*LXXXIX. De Justitia Distributiva*
LX. De Ecclesia	*XC. De Fortitudine*
LXI. De Ethnicorum	*XCI. De Patientia*
Judaeorumque	*XCII. De Constantia*
Superstitionibus	*XCIII. De Amicitia Et Humanitate*
LXII. De Curia	*XCIV. De Candore*
LXIII. De Judicii	*XCV. De Conversatione Erudita*
LXIV. De Maleficis Et Supplicis	*XCVI. De Ludicris*
LXV. De Statu Regio	*XCVII. De Morte Et Sepultura*
LXVI. De Regno Et Regione	*XCVIII. De Providentia Dei*
LXVII. De Pace Et Bello	*XCIX. De Angelis*
LXVIII. De Schola Et Institutione	*C. Clausula.*

Source: Bathe: Habrecht 1629, *passim*. German and English versions only. All irregularities of spelling in the original. BL 627.b.2. Comenius: *Opera Omnia*, vol. 15/I. 1986*b*, 269–301. All titles are printed here in capitals.

TABLE A.21   James Greenwood, *The London Vocabulary*, macrostructure

I. Of Things,	*VII. Of Birds,*
II. Of the Elements,	*VIII. Of Fishes,*
III. Of Minerals and Metals,	*IX. Of Beasts,*
IV. Of Plants,	*X. Of Man, respecting his Age, or Kindred,*
V. Of Trees and Shrubs,	*XI. Of the Parts of Man's Body,*
VI. Of Insects,	*XII. Of the Bones,*

XIII. *Of Diseases,*

XIV. *Of the Mind and its Affections,*

XV. *Of Meats and Drinks,*

XVI. *Of Apparel,*

XVII. *Of Buildings,*

XVIII. *Of Houshold Stuff,*

XIX. *Of the Country, and Country Affairs,*

XX. *Of Societies,*

XXI. *The School,*

XXII. *Of Church, or Ecclesiastical Affairs,*

XXIII. *Of Judicial Matters,*

XXIV. *Of Warfare, or Military Affairs,*

XXV. *Of Sea, or Naval Affiars,*

XXVI. *Of Time,*

XXVII. *Of Adjectives, or the Manner of Things,*

XXVIII. *Of Verbs,*

XXIX. *Of Pronouns,*

XXX. *Of Adverbs,*

XXXI. *Of the Prepositions,*

XXXII. *Of Conjunctions,*

XXXIII. *Of Interjections.*

Source: Grenwood 1713. BL 1568/4124. 12°.

TABLE A.22   Isidore of Seville, *Etymologiarum et Originum Libri XX, Index Librorum*

I. *De Grammatica et Partibus eius.*

II. *De Rhetorica et Dialectica.*

III. *De Mathematica, cuius partes sunt Arithmetica, Musica, Geometrica et Astronomia.*

IV. *De Medicina.*

V. *De Legibus vel Instrumentis Iudicium ac de Temporibus.*

VI. *De Ordine Scriptuarum, de Cyclis et Canonibus, de Festivitatibus et Oficiis.*

VII. *De Deo et Angelis, de Nominibus Praesagis, de Nominibus Sanctorum Patrum, de Martyribus, Clericis, Monachis, et ceteris Nominibus.*

VIII. *De Ecclesia et Synagoga, de Religione et Fide, der Haeresibus, de Philosophis, Poetis, Sibyllis, Magis, Paganis ac Dis Gentium.*

IX. *De Linguis Gentium, de Regum, Militum, Civiumque Vocabulis vel Affinitatibus.*

X. *Quaedam Nomina per Alphabetum Distincta.*

XI. *De Homine et Partibus eius, de Aetatibus Hominum, de Portentis et Transformatis.*

XII. *De Quadrupedibus, Reptilibus, Piscibus ac Volatilibus.*

XIII. *De Elementis, id est de Caelo et Aere, de Aquis, de Mare, [de] Fluminibus ac Diluviis.*

XIV. *De Terra et Paradiso et [de] Provinciis totius Orbis, de Insulis, Montibus ceterisque Locorum Vocabulis ac de Inferioribus Terrae.*

XV. *De Civitatibus, de Aedificiis Vrbanis et Rusticis, de Agris, de Finibus et Mensuris Agrorum, de Itineribus.*

XVI. *De Glebis ex Terra vel Aquis, de omni genere Gemmarum et Lapidum pretiosorum et vilium, de Ebore quoque inter Marmora notato, de Vitro, de Metallis omnibus, de Ponderibus et Mensuris.*

XVII. *De Culturis Agrorum, de Frugibus universi generis, de Vitibus et Arboribus omnis generis, de Herbis et Holeribus universis.*

XVIII. *De Bellis et Triumphis ac Instrumentis Bellicis, de Foro, de Spectaculis, Alea et Pila.*

XIX. *De Navibus, Funibus et Retibus, de Fabris Ferrariis et Fabricis Parietum et cunctis Instrumentis Aedificorum, de Lanificiis quoque, Ornamentis et Vestibus universis.*

XX. *De Mensis et Escis et Potibus et Vasculis eorum, de Vasis Vinariis, Aquariis et Oleariis, Cocorum, Pistorum, et Luminarorium, de Lectis, Sellis et vehiculis, Rusticis et Hortorum, sive de Instrumentis Equorum.*

Source: Isidore, ed. Lindsay 1911.

Bibliography

Primary sources

This section comprises original editions, reprints, and collected works.

[ADAM OF ROTWEIL, (1477)], *Questo libro el duale silbi ama introito e porta* . . . [Venice: s.n.].
—— (1971), '*Introito e Porta*', *vocabulario italiano = tedesco 'compiuto per Meistro Adamo de Roduila, 1477 adi 12 Auusto*'. Prefazione di A. Bart Rossebastiano. Reprint (Torino: Bottega d'Erasmo).
ANCHORAN, JOHN (1631), *Porta Lingvarvm Trilingvis Reserata Et Aperta* . . . . *The Gate of Tongves Vnlocked And Opened* . . . (London: Georgius Millerus for Michael Sparkes and Thomas Slater).
AUSTEN, RALPH (1653), *A Treatise of Fruit-Trees Shewing the manner of Grafting, Setting, Pruning, and Ordering of them in all respects* . . . (Oxford: Thomas Robinson).
BACON, FRANCIS (1859), *The Works of Francis Bacon*, coll. and ed. by J. Spedding, R. L. Ellis, and D. D. Heath. Vol III (London: Longman). Reprint (Stuttgart: Frommann / Holzboog 1963).
BARONUS, FRANCISCUS (1533), *Quinq[ue] linguaru[m] vtilissimus Vocabulista. Latine. Tusche. Gallice. Hyspanice. et Alemanice* . . . (Venice: s.n.).
BATHE, WILLIAM (1611), *Ianva Lingvarvm* . . . (Salamanca: Apud Franciscum De Cea Tesa).
—— (1615), *Ianua Linguarum* . . . [by William Bathe]: *cum indice vocabulorum, & translatione Anglicana eiusdem tractatus* [by William Welde]. (London: Matthaeus Lownes).
—— (1629), *Ianua Linguarum Silinguis, Latina, Germanica, Gallica, Italica, Hispanica, Anglica. . . . Auctore Isaaco Habrechto* . . . (Strasbourg: Eberhardus Zetznerus).
BERLAIMONT, NOEL DE (1536), *Vocabulare van nyens gheordineert. . . . . Vocabulaire de nouveau ordonne* . . . (Antwerp: Willem Vorstman).
[——] (1576), *Colloqvia Et Dictionariolvm Sex Lingvarvm: Teutonicae, Latinae, Germanicae, Gallicae, Hispanicae, & Italicae* . . . (Antwerp: Henricus Henricus).
[——] (1598), *Colloqvia Et Dictionariolvm Octo Lingvarvm, Latinae, Gallicae, Belgicae, Teutonicae, Hispanicae, Italicae, Anglicae, Et Portvgallicae* . . . (Delft: Brunonus Schinckelius).
[——] (1639), *New Dialogues or Colloqvies, And, A Little Dictionary of eight languages. Latine, French, Low-Dutch, Spanish, Italian, English, Portuguese.* . . . (London: E. G. for Michael Sparke jr.).
BIBBESWORTH, GAUTIER DE (1929), *Le traité de Walter de Bibbesworth sur la langage française: texte publié avec introduction et glossaire*, ed. by A. Owen. (Paris: Les Presses Universitaires). Reprint (Geneva: Slatkine 1977).
—— (1990), *Gautier de Bibbesworth: Le tretiz*, ed. by W. Rothwell (London: Anglo-Norman Text Society).

BIBBESWORTH, WALTER DE (1857), 'The Treatise of Walter de Bibbesworth', in T. Wright (1857), 142–74.

BISCHOFF, B., BUDNEY, M., HARLOW, G., PARKES, M. B., AND PHEIFER, J. D. (eds.) (1988), *The Épinal, Erfurt, Werden, and Corpus Glossaries.* Early Manuscripts in Facsimile XXII (Copenhagen: Rosenkilde and Bagger).

BLUNDEVIL[L]E, THOMAS (1599), *The Art of Logike* . . . (London: John Windet).

—— (1967), *The Art of Logicke 1599.* Reprint (Menston: Scolar).

BÖMER, A. (ed.) (1897), *Die lateinischen Schülergespräche der Humanisten.* Auszüge mit Einleitungen, Anmerkungen, Namen- und Sachregister. Vol. 1: 'Vom *Manuale scholarium* bis Hegendorffinus *c.*1480–1520.' Vol. 2: 'Von Barlandus bis Corderius 1524–1564.' (Berlin: Harwith Nachfolger). Reprint (Amsterdam: Schippers 1966).

BOSÁK Z VODŇAN, JAN (1511), *Ullis ferme vocabulis* . . . . *Tento wokabulař Lactifer* [= In a few words . . . This word-list Lactifer] (Pilzen: s.n.).

BOURNE, WILLIAM (1577), *A Regiment for the Sea: Conteynyng most profitable Rules, Mathematical experiences, and perfect knowledge of Nauigaton* . . . (London: Thomas Dawson and Thomas Gardiner for John Wight).

—— (1963), *A Regiment For The Sea and other writings on navigation by William Bourne of Gravesend, a gunner (c. 1535–82),* ed. E. G. R. Taylor (Cambridge: Cambridge University Press for the Hakluyt Society).

[BRACK, WENZESLAUS (1489)], *Vocabularius rerum* (Strasbourg: Schott).

BULWER, JOHN (1974), *Chirologia: or the natural language of the hand. And Choronomia: or the art of manual rhetoric,* ed. and with an introduction by J. W. Cleary (Carbondale and Edwardsville: Southern Illinois University Press).

CAXTON, WILLIAM (1900), *Dialogues in French and English,* ed. from Caxton's printed text with introduction, notes, and word-lists by H. Bradley. English Early Text Society Extra Series LXXIX (London: Kegan Paul, Trench, Trübner & Co.).

COMENIUS, JOHANNES AMOS (1667), *Janua Lingvarum Reserata Aurea: Sive Seminarium Lingvarum Et Scientiarum Omnium,* . . . . *Slatě Dwéře Jazykůw oteuřené / Aueb Plánjsté wssech Ržečj a Uměnj* . . . . *Aufgechlossene Güldene Sprachen-Thür: Oder Ein Pflanz-Garten aller Sprachen und Wissenschaften /* . . . (Prague, Typis Archi-Episcopalibus in Collegio S. Norberti excudebat Paulus Postrzibacz).

—— (1957), *Novissima Linguarum Methodus* . . . . *Anno 1648,* in *Opera Didactica Omnia. Editio anni 1657 lucis ope expressa.* Vol. I (parts I, II), Vol. II (parts III–IV). Sumptibus Academiae Scientiarum Bohemoslovenicae Pragae. In Aedibus Academia Scientiarum Bohemoslovenicae MCMLVII, vol. I, part 2: cols. 1–192 (Prague: Academia).

—— (1959), *Johannis A. Comenii Janua linguarum reserata. Editio synoptica et critica quinque authenticos textus Latinos necnon Janualem Comenii textum Bohemicum continens.* . . . , ed. by J. Červenka (Prague: Státní pedagogické nakladatelství [= State pedagogical publishing house]).

—— (1966a), *Iohannis Amos Comenii De Rerum Humanarum Emendatione Consultatio Catholica.* Editio princeps. Vols. I, II. Sumptibus Academiae Scientiarum Bohemoslovacae Pragae. In Aedibus Academiae Scientiarum Bohemoslovacae (Prague: Academia).

—— (1966b), *Liber Librorum ceu Bibliotheca portabilis, hoc est Lexicon Reale Pansophicum Rerum omnium quae sciri possunt ac debent. Definitiones veras (omnia qvae ad rei cujusqve constitutionem intimam spectant, explicantes) ordine Alphabetico proponens,* in Comenius 1966a, Vol. II: cols. 803–1275.

—— (1970–), *Opera Omnia Jan Amos Komensky* (DJAK = *Dílo Jana Amose Komenského*). In Aedibus Academiae scientiarum Bohemoslovacae (Prague: Academia).

—— (1970*a*), *Vestibuli Et Januae Lingvarum Lucidarium, hoc est Nomenclatura rerum ad autopsian deducta. Anno MDCLIII*, ed. by J. Červenka, in DJAK, vol. 17, 35–52.

—— (1970*b*), *Joh[annes] Amos Comenii Orbis Sensualium Pictus, hoc est Omnium fundamentalium in mundo rerum et in vita actionum pictura et nomenclatura. Editio secunda, multò emaculatior et emendatior. Die Sichtbare Welt, das ist Aller vornehmsten Weltdinge und aller Lebensverrichtungen Vorbildung und Benamung. Zum andernmal aufgelegt und an sehr vielen Orten geändert und verbessert. . . . Noribergae Typis et sumptibus Michaelis Endteri Anno Salutis MDCLIX*, ed. by J. Červenka and S. Králík, in DJAK vol. 17, 55–271, notes: 272–300.

—— (1970*c*), *Jan Amos Comenius: Porta Linguarum Trilinguis Reserata 1631*. Reprint (Menston: Scolar).

—— (1970*d*), *Orbis Sensualium Pictus 1659. Translated by Charles Hoole*. Reprint (Menston: Scolar).

—— (1974), *Sapientiae Primae Usus Triertium Catholicum Appellandus, hoc est Humanarum cogitationum, sermonum, operum scientiam, artem, usum aperiens. Clavis Triuna sive Amabile Logicae, Grammaticae, Pragmaticaeque cum Metaphysica osculum*, ed. by J. Borská and J. Nováková, in DJAK, vol. 18, 237–365.

—— (1986*a*), *Didactica Magna. Universale Omnes Omnia Docendi Artificium Exhibens, sive . . .*, ed. by V. Balík, M. Kyralová, and S. Sousedík in DJAK, vol. 15/I: 5–209, notes: 431–70.

—— (1986*b*), *J. A. Comenii Janua Lingvarum Reserata, sive Seminarium Lingvarum Et Scientiarvm Omnium. . . . . Primúmque anno 1631 edita*, ed. by M. Kyralová and M. Steiner, in DJAK, vol. 15/I: 257–301, notes: 482–509.

—— (1986*c*), *Januae Linguarum Reseratae Vestibulum . . .*, ed. by S. Sousedík, in DJAK, vol. 15/I: 306–22, notes: 509–13.

Corpus Glossariorvm Latinorvm (1882–1923). Started by Gustav Loewe. Seven vols; vol. III. *Hermenevmata Psevdodositheana.* Edidit Georgius Goetz (Lipsiae. In Aedibvs B.G. Tevbneri [vol. III] MDCCCLXXXXII). Reprint (Amsterdam: Hakkert 1965).

COTGRAVE, RANDLE (1650), *A French-English Dictionary . . . . With Another in English and French. Whereunto are newly added the Animadversions and Supplements, &c. of James Howell Esquire* (London: W. H. for Luke Fawne)

DALGARNO, GEORGE (1968), *Ars Signorum 1661*. Reprint (Menston: Scolar).

—— (2001), *Dalgarno on Universal Language. The Art of Signs (1661), The Deaf and Dumb Man's Tutor (1680), and the Unpublished Papers*. Edited with a translation, introduction, and commentary by D. Cram and J. Maat. Oxford: Oxford University Press.

DANIEL ADAM À WELESLAVINA (1586), *Nomenclator omnium rerum propria nomina tribus linguis, Latina, Boiemica et Germanica . . .* (Prague: Daniel Adam von Weleslavin).

—— (1598*a*), *Sylva Qvadrilingvis Vocabvlorvm Et Phrasium Bohemicae, Latinae, Graecae Et Germanicae Lingvae . . .* ([Prague]: Daniel Adam à Weleslavin).

DANIEL ADAM À WELESLAVINA (1598*b*), *Nomenclator Quadrilinguis Bohemicolatino Graecogermanicus . . .* ([Prague], Daniel Adam à Weleslavin).

Dictionarium Latino-Germanicum (1610), *Dictionarium Latino-Germanicum Omnivm Qvotquot Vbivis In Qvacvnqve facultate, tam liberali quam mechanica, vsurpantur nominum atque formularum.—Ordentliche Verzeichnuß und Außlegung aller und jeder Woerter . . .* (Frankfurt: Egenolphus Emmelius).

DOLETUS, STEPHANUS (1536–8), *Commentariorum linguae latinae tomus primus [and] secundus* (London: Sebastianus Gryphius).

DUEZ, NATHANAEL (1652), *Nova Nomenclatura Quatuor Linguarum, Gallico, Germanico, Italico, & Latino idiomate conscripta ... Postrema Editio, emendatissima* (Leyden: Elzevier).

DUGRES, GABRIEL (1660), *Dialogi Gallico-Anglico-Latini ...* (Oxford: A. Lichfield)

ELYOT, THOMAS (1970), *The Book Named The Governor 1531.* Reprint (Menston: Scolar).

EMMELIUS, HELFRICUS (1592), *Sylva Qvinqvelingvis Vocabulorum et Phrasivm Germanicae, Latinae, Graecae, Hebraicae, Gallicae linguae, in vsum studiosae iuuentutis ...* (Strasbourg: Theodosius Rihelius).

—— (1592), *Nomenclator Qvatrilingvis, Germanicolatinograecogallicus, In Classes IIII distinctus ...* (Strasbourg: Theodosius Rihelius).

[FAGE, ROBERT] (1632), *Peter Ramus ..., his Dialectica in two bookes ...* (London: W. J.).

FENNER, DUDLEY [1584], *The Artes Of Logike And Rethorike, plainly set forth in the English tongue ....* (s.l., s.d., s.n.).

[FITZHERBERT, JOHN (*c.*1523)], *[The boke of husbandrie].* [London: Richard Pynson).

FITZHERBERT, JOHN (1882), *Fitzherberts Booke Of Husbandrie. Devided Into foure seuerall Bookes, very necessary and profitable for all sorts of people ... At London, Printed by I. R. for Edward White, and are to be sold at his shoppe, at the little North doore of Paules Church, at the signe of the Gunne. Anno. Dom. 1598*, ed. with an introduction, notes, and glossarial index by W. W. Skeat (London: Trübner & Co.).

FLAJŠHANS, V. (ed.) (1926), *Klaret a jeho družina.* Sv. I: 'Slovníky veršované' [= Claretus and his companions. Vol. I: 'Dictionaries in verse'] (Prague: Nákladem české akademie věd umění [Prague: Czech Academy for the Sciences and Arts]).

FRISCHLIN, NICODEMUS (1600), *Nicodemi Frischlini Nomenclator Trilinguis, Graecolatinogermanicus ...* (Frankfurt: Wolffgangus Richter).

GARDINER, A. H. (1947), *Ancient Egyptian Onomastica.* Volumes 1 and 2: Text, [Volume 3:] Plates (London: Oxford University Press).

GARMONSWAY, G. N. (1953), *The Anglo-Saxon Chronicle* (London: Dent / New York: Dutton). Reprint (1977).

GESSLER, J. (ed.) (1931), *Les Livres des Metiers de Bruges et ses derivés. Quatre anciens manuels de conversation.* (Bruges: s.n.) [Le consortium des maitres imprimeurs Brugeois].

—— (ed.) (1934), *La Manière de Langage qui enseigne à bien parler et écrire le francais. Modèles de conversations composés en Angleterre à la fin du XIVe siècle.* Nouvelle édition—avec Introduction et Glossaire—publiée par ... (Brussels/Paris: L'Edition Universelle / Librairie Droz).

GIUSTINIANI, V. R. (1987), *Adam von Rottweil [!]. Deutsch-italienischer Sprachführer.* Tübingen: Narr.

GREENWOOD, JAMES (1713), *James Greenwood: The London Vocabulary, English and Latin ...* (London: A. Bettesworth).

HABRECHT, ISAAC (1629), *Ianua Linguarum Silinguis, Latina, Germanica, Gallica, Italica, Hispanica, Anglica [...].—Sechsfache spraachen-Thuer Lateinisch/Teutsch/ Frantzoesisch/ Italianisch/Spannisch/und Engellaendisch [...]* (Strasbourg: Eberhardus Zitznerus).

HESSELS, J. H. (ed.) (1890), *An Eighth-Century Latin–Anglo-Saxon Glossary Preserved in the Library of Corpus Christi College Cambridge* (Cambridge: Cambridge University Press).

—— (ed.) (1906), *A Late Eighth-Century Latin–Anglo-Saxon Glossary Preserved in the Library of the Leiden University* (Cambridge: University Press).

HIG[G]INS, JOHN (1585), *The Nomenclator, or Remembrancer of Adrianus Iunius . . .* (London: Ralph Newberie and Henry Denham).

HOLYBAND, CLAUDIUS (1607), *The French Littleton . . .* (London: Richard Field).

HOOKE, ROBERT (1705), *The Posthumous Works Of Robert Hooke . . . . Publish'd by Richard Waller, R. S . Secr.* (London: Sam Smith and Benjamin Walford).

HOOLE, CHARLES (1672), *Joh[annes] Amos Comenii Orbis Sensualium Pictus . . . .— Joh[annes] Amos Comenius's Visible World . . .* (London: T.S. for S. Mearne). Reprint, ed. by J. Brown (Sydney: Sydney University Press, 1967).

—— (1967), *Johannes Amos Comenii Orbis Sensualium Pictus [. . .] Johannes Amos Comenius's Visible World*, ed. by J. Brown (Sydney: Sydney University Press).

HOWELL, JAMES (1660), *Lexicon Tetraglotton, An English–French–Italian–Spanish Dictionary . . .* (London: J. G. for Cornelius Bee).

HUMBOLDT, WILHELM VON (1968), *Wilhelm von Humboldts Werke*, ed. by A. Leitzmann (Berlin: Behr 1906). Reprint (Berlin: de Gruyter).

HUNT, T. (ed.) (1991), *Teaching and learning Latin in thirteenth-century England*. Three vols. I: Texts, II: Glosses, III: Indexes (Cambridge: D. S. Brewer).

ISIDORE OF SEVILLE (1911), *Isidori Hispalensis Episcopi Etymologiarum Sive Originum Libri XX*. Two vols., ed. by W. M. Lindsay (Oxford: Clarendon).

JUNIUS, ADRIANUS (1567), *Nomenclator, Omnium Rerum Propria Nomina Variis Linguis Explicata Indicans . . .* (Antwerp: Christopherus Plantinus).

LEIBNIZ, GOTTFRIED WILHELM (1966), *Deutsche Schriften*, ed. by. G. E. Guhrauer. Two vols. (Hildesheim: Olms).

LINDHEIM, B. VON (ed.) (1941), *Das Durhamer Pflanzenglossar Lateinisch und Altenglisch*. Beiträge zur englischen Philologie 35 (Bochum Langendreer: Pöppinghaus).

LINDSAY, W. M. (ed.) [1921], *The Corpus, Épinal, Erfurt and Leyden Glossaries* (Oxford: Oxford University Press).

LOCKE, JOHN (1961), *Essay concerning human understanding*. ed. with an introduction by J. W. Yolton. Two vols. (London: Dent, Everyman's Library).

LODWICK, FRANCIS (1972), *The Works of Francis Lodwick. A study of his writing in the intellectual context of the seventeenth century* by V. Salmon (London: Longman).

MANWAYRING, SIR HENRY (1667), *The Sea-Man's Dictionary . . .* (London: W. Godbid for G. Hurlock). Reprint (Menston: Scolar, 1972).

—— (1972), *The Sea-Man's Dictionary [. . .]*. Reprint (Menston: Scolar).

MARKHAM, GARVIS (1613), *The English Husbandman . . .* (London: T. S. for John Browne).

—— (1615), *The English Hus-wife . . .* (London: John Beale for Roger Jackson).

MARTIN, BENJAMIN (1979), *An Introduction to the English Language and Learning. In Three Parts . . . . London: Printed for W. Owen, at Homer's Head, in Fleet-street. MDCCLIV.* Reprint (Ann Arbor: University Microfilms).

MAYRE, MARTEN LE (1606), *The Dvtch Schoole Master . . .* (London: George Elde for Simon Waterson).

MERRITT, H. D. (1945), *Old English Glosses. A collection* (New York: Modern Language Association).

MICHELANT, H. (ed.) (1875), *Le Livre des Mestiers: dialogues français-flamands composés au XIV siècle par un maitre d'école de la ville de Bruges* (Paris: Librairie Tross).

MIÈGE, GUY (1685), *Nouvelle Methode Pour Apprendre l'Anglois* . . . (London: Thomas Bassett).

MOLINAEUS, PETRUS (1645), *Opera Philosophica—Logica, Physica, Ethica* (Amsterdam: s.n.).

MÜLLER, J. (1882), *Quellenschriften und Geschichte des deutschsprachigen Unterrichts bis zur Mitte des 16. Jahrhunderts* (Gotha: s.n.).

MURMELLIUS, JOHANNES (1513), *Ioa[n]nis Murmellij Ruremu[n]densis. cui titulus Pappa* (Cologne: Quentell).

—— (1894), 'Des Münsterschen Humanisten Johannes Murmellius Pappa puerorum, mit Ausschluß des 1. Kapitels in einem Neudruck hg. von Dr. A. Bömer', in *Ausgewählte Werke des Münsterschen Humanisten Johannes Murmellius*, ed. by A. Bömer. Vol. 4 (Münster: Regensbergische Buchhandlung).

NAPIER, A. S. (ed.) (1900), *Old English Glosses*. Anecdota Oxoniensa. Texts, documents, and extracts chiefly from manuscripts in the Bodleian Library and other Oxford libraries. Medieval series part XI (Oxford: Clarendon).

NEEDHAM, PAUL (ed.) (1986), *The Printer and the pardoner. An unrecorded Indulgence printed by William Caxton for the Hospital of St. Mary Rounceval, Charing Cross* (Washington: Library of Congress).

NOVILIERS, GUILLEAUME ALEXANDRE DE (1629), *Nomenclatvra Italiana, Francese, E Spagnvola* . . . (Venice: Barezzo Barezzi).

OATES, J. C. T., and HARMER, L. C. (eds.) (1964), *Vocabulary in French and English. A facsimile of Caxton's edition ca. 1480*. With introductions by . . . (Cambridge: Cambridge University Press).

OFFELEN, HENRICUS (1687), *A double Grammar for Germans to learn English, and for Englishmen to learn the German tongue.—Zwey-fache Gründliche Sprach-Lehr, Für Hochteutsche, Englische, und für Engelländer Hochteutsch zu lernen* . . . (London: to buy from Nathaniel Thompson).

OLIPHANT, R. T. (ed.) (1966), *The Harley Latin–Old English Glossary edited from British Museum MS Harley 3376* . . . (The Hague: Mouton).

PALSGRAVE, JOHN (1969), *Lesclarcissement De La Langue Francoyse 1530*. Reprint (Menston: Scolar).

PAUSCH, O. (ed.) (1972), *Das älteste italienisch–deutsche Sprachbuch. Eine Überlieferung aus dem Jahre 1424 nach Georg von Nürnberg*. Veröffentlichung der historischen Kommission der österreichischen Akademie der Wissenschaften. (Vienna: Hermann Böhlau).

PHILLIPS, EDWARD (1969), *The New World Of English Words: Or, a General Dictionary:* . . . *London, Printed by E. Tyler, for Nath. Brooke at the Sign of the Angel in Cornhill, 1658.* Reprint (Hildesheim: Olms).

QUINN, K. J., and QUINN, K. P. (eds.) (1990), *A manual for Old English prose* (New York/London: Garland).

RAY, JOHN (1675), *Dictionariolum Trilingue: Secundum Locos Communes, Nominibus usitatoribus Anglicis, Latinis, Graecis* . . . (London: Andrea Clark for Thomas Burrel).

—— (1693), *Joannis Raii Societatis Regiae Socii Historia Plantarum Generalis* . . . (London: Samuel Smith and Benjamin Walford).

—— (1981), *Dictionariolum Trilingue. Editio prima 1675*. Facsimile with an introduction by W. T. Stearn (London: The Ray Society).

[RECORDE, ROBERT (1551)], *The pathway to Knowledg, Containing The First Principles of Geometrie* . . . (London: Reynold Wolfe).

—— (1974), *The pathway to Knowledg, Containing The First Principles of Geometrie, as they may moste aptly be applied vnto practice, bothe for vse of instrumentes Geometricall, and astronomicall and also for proiection of plattes in euerye kinde, and therfore much necessary for all sortes of men.* . . . . Facsimile edition (Norwood, NJ / Amsterdam: Walter Johnson, Inc. / Theatrum Orbis Terrarum, Ltd.).

REŠL, TOMÁŠ (1560), *Dictionarivm Latinobohemicvm* . . . (Olomuc: Johannes Gunterus).

—— (1562), *Dictionarivm Bohemicolatinum* . . . (Olomuc: Johannes Guntherus).

RIZZA, R., ABREU, M. H., DINI, E., GIACCHERINI, E., PAGANI, W., and WAENTIG, P. W. (eds.) (1996), *Colloquia, Et Dictionariolum Octo Linguarum Latinae, Gallicae, Belgicae, Teutonicae, Hispanicae, Italicae, Anglicae, Portugallicae.* A cura di . . . (Viareggio-Lucca: Mauro Baroni).

ROGET, PETER MARK (1852), *Thesaurus Of English Words and Phrases Classified And Arranged So As To Facilitate The Expression Of Ideas And Assist In Literary Composition* (London: Longman, Green, Longman, Roberts, & Green). 15th edn. 1863.

[ROSEMBACH, HANS (1991)], *Vocabulari molt profitos per aprendre Lo Catalan Alamany y Lo Alamany Catalan. Perpinya [Mdii].* Reprint ed. by T. D. Stegmann (1991), *Vocabulari Català–Alemany de l'any 1502. Katalanisch–Deutsches Vokabular aus dem Jahre 1502.* Reprint of a facsimile edition by P. B., 1916 (Frankfurt: Domus Editoria Europaea).

SACHS, HANS (1574), *Eygentliche Beschreibung Aller Stände auff Erden / Hoher und Nidriger/ Geistlicher und Weltlicher / Aller Künsten / Handwercken unnd Händeln / etc. vom größten biß zum kleinsten* . . . (Frankfurt: s.n.).

SANDERSON, ROB[ERT] (1618), *Logicae Et Physicae Compendivm. Authore Rob[ert] Sanderson* . . . (Oxford: Henricus Hall for Ricardus Davis). 8th edn. 1672.

SCHÄFER, J. (1989), *Early English lexicography.* Vol. 1: 'A survey of monolingual printed glossaries and dictionaries 1475–1660' (Oxford: Clarendon).

[SCHOBER, HULDREICH], (1684) *Nomenclator selectissimas Rerum Appellationes tribus Linguis, Latina, Germanica, Polonica, explicatas indicans: Septima editio sextae conformis. In usum scholarum Borussicarum & Polonicarum: maxime vero Gymnasii Thoruniensis. Nomenclator* . . . (Danzig: David Fridericus Rhetius for Augustinus Schultzen).

Sex linguarum (1570), *Sex Lingvarvm Latinae, Gallicae, Hispanicae, Italicae, Anglicae & Teutonicae, dilucidissimu[s] Dictionarium* . . . (Zurich: Froschauer).

[SHERRY, RYCHARD (1550)], *A treatise of Schemes & Tropes* . . . (London: s.n.).

—— (1961), *A Treatise Of Schemes And Tropes (1550). By Richard Sherry And His Translation Of The Education Of Children By Desiderius Erasmus.* A facsimile reproduction with an introduction and index by W. Hildebrand (University of Michigan: Scholars' Facsimiles & Reprints).

SINHA, AMERA (1808), *Côsha, Or Dictionary Of The Sanscrit Language. By* . . . . With an English interpretation, and annotations. By H. T. Colebrooke, Esq. (Printed at Serampoor).

SKEAT, W. W. (ed.) (1906), 'Nominale sive verbale', *Transactions of the Philological Society* 1*–50*.

SMITH, JOHN (1626), *An Accidence Or Path-way to Experience. Necessarie for all Young Seamen* . . . (London: Jonas Man and Benjamin Fisher).

—— (1627), *A Sea Grammar, With The Plaine Exposition of Smiths Accidence for young Seamen, enlarged* . . . (London: John Haviland). Reprint (Amsterdam/New York: Da Capo Press/Theatrum Orbis Terrarum Ltd., 1968).

SMITH, JOHN (1653), *The Sea-Mans Grammar: Containing Most plain and easie directions* . . . (London: Andrew Kemb).

—— (1691), *The Sea-Mans Grammar and Dictionary* . . . (London: Randal Taylor).

—— (1968), *A Sea Grammar. London 1627.* Reprint (Amsterdam/New York: Da Capo Press Theatrvm Orbis Terrarrum Ltd.).

—— (1970), *A Sea-Grammar. With The Plaine Exposition Of Smiths Accidence For Young Sea-Men, Enlarged. Written by Captaine John Smith, sometimes Gouvernor of Virginia, and Admirall of New-England. Original published in London, 1627.* Reprint, ed. by K. Goell (London: Michael Joseph).

SMITH, SAMUEL (1627), *Aditus Ad Logicam* . . . (London: William Stansby).

SPRAT, THOMAS (1966), *The History of the Royal Society of London, for the Improving of Natural Knowledge. By* . . . *London: Printed by T. R. for J. Matyn at the Bell without Temple-bar, and J. Allestry at the Rose and Crown in Duck-lane, Printers to the Royal Society. MDCLXVII.* Ed. Jackson, I. Cope, and Harold Whitmore Jones. Reprint, third printing (St. Louis MO: Washington University Press).

STEINMEYER, E., and SIEVERS, E. (eds.) (1879–1922), *Die althochdeutschen Glossen.* Five vols. (Berlin: Weidmannsche Buchhandlung). Reprint (Dublin and Zurich: Weidmann).

STEVENSON, W. H., and LINDSAY, W. M. (eds.) (1929), *Early Scholastic Colloquies.* Anecdota Oxoniensa. Medieval and Modern Series 15 (Oxford: Clarendon).

SWEET, HENRY (ed.) (1885), *The Oldest English Texts* (London: Early English Text Society).

VERDEYEN, R. (ed.) (1925–35), *Colloquia Et Dictionariolum Septem Linguarum. Gedrukt door Fickaert Te Antwerpen In 1616 Op Nieuw Uitgegeven Door Prof. Dr.* . . . . I. (Antwerp / 's Gravenhage: Nederlandsche Boekhandel / M. Nijhoff 1926); II (Id. 1925); III (Antwerp: Solvijnstraat, 70, 1935. Vereeniging Der Antwerpsche Bibliophilen, Uitgave Nos. 39, 40, 42).

Vocabularius (c.1474), *Vocabularius (rerum) Registrum vocabularii sequentis* (Augsburg: Günther Zainer).

WAENTIG, P. W. (2003), *Colloquia et Dictionariolum Octo Linguarum. Tedesco Protomoderno. Edizione e commento dell versione del 1656.* Bologna: CLUEB.

WARD, SETH (1970), *Vindiciae Academiarum Containing, Some briefe Animadversions upon Mr Webster's Book, Stiled, The Examination of Academies. Together with an Appendix concerning what M. Hobbs, and M. Dell have published on this Argument. Oxford, Printed by Leonard Lichfield Printer to the University, for Thomas Robinson. 1654,* ed. by A. G. Debus, *Science and Education in the Seventeenth Century. The Webster–Ward Debate* (London: Macdonald / New York: Elsevier).

WELDE, WILLIAM (1615), *Ianua Linguarum* . . . [by William Bathe] *Cum indice vocabulorum, & translatione Anglicana eiusdem tractatus* . . . [by William Welde] (London: H. L. for Mattaeus Lownes).

WELESLAVINA, see DANIEL ADAM À

WILKINS, JOHN (1968), *An Essay Towards a Real Character, and a Philosophical Language. By [. . .] D.D. Dean of Ripon, And Fellow of the Royal Society. London, Printed for Sa: Gellibrand, and for John Martin Printer to the Royal Society, 1668.* Bound together with: [William Lloyd], *An Alphabetical Dictionary, Wherein all English Words According to their Various Significations, Are either referred to their Places in the Philosophical Tables, Or explained by such Words as are in those Tables. London, Printed by J. M. for Samuel Gellibrand and John Martin, 1668.* Reprint (Menston: Scolar).

—— (1984), *Mercury; or, the secret messenger. Shewing how a Man may with Privacy and Speed communicate his Thoughts to a Friend at any distance (1707).* Reprinted from the third edition: *The Mathematical and Philosophical Works of the Right Reverend John*

Wilkins (1708). Together with an abstract of Dr. Wilkins's Essay *Towards A Real Character And A Philosophical Language* with an introductory essay by B. Asbach-Schnitker (Amsterdam: Benjamins).

WITHALS, JOHN (1553), *A shorte Dictionarie for yonge begynners* . . . (London: Lewis Evans).

—— (1556), *A shorte Dictionarie for yonge begynners* . . . (London: Thomas Bertheleth).

—— (1574), *A Shorte Dictionarie most profitable For Yong Beginners* . . . (London: s.n.).

—— (1586), *A Shorte Dictionarie in Latine and English, verie profitable for yong beginners* . . . (London: Thomas Purfoote).

—— (1602), *A Dictionarie In English And Latine for Children, and yong beginners* . . . (London: Thomas Purfoot).

WOTTON, ANTHONY (1626), *The Art of Logik, Gathered out of Aristotle, and set in due forme, according to his instructions, by Peter Ramus* . . . (London: I. D. for Nicholas Bourne).

WRIGHT, T. (ed.) (1857), *A Volume of Vocabularies, Illustrating the Condition and Manners of our Forefathers, as well as the History of the Forms of Elementary Education and of the Languages Spoken in this Island, from the Tenth Century to the Fifteenth. Edited from Mss. in Public and Private Collections by* . . . (s.l.: privately printed).

—— (1873), *A Second Volume Of Vocabularies, Illustrating The Condition And Manners Of Our Forefathers, As Well As The History Of The Forms Of Elementary Education And Of the Languages Spoken In This Island, From The Tenth Century To The Fifteenth. Edited From Mss. In Public And Private Collections by* . . . (s.l.: privately printed).

—— and WÜLCKER, R. P. (eds.) (1884), *Anglo-Saxon and Old English Vocabularies*. Two vols. (London: Trübner). Reprint (Darmstadt: Wissenschaftliche Buchgesellschaft 1968).

WRIGHT, W. A. (ed.) (1909), *Femina. Now first printed from a unique MS. in the Library of Trinity College, Cambridge* (Cambridge: Cambridge University Press).

YOUNG, R. F. (1932), *Comenius in England. The visit of Jan Amos Komensky (Comenius), the Czech philosopher and educationist, to London in 1641–1642; its bearing on the origins of the Royal Society, on the development of the encyclopedia, and on plans for the higher education of the Indians of New England and Virginia. As described in contemporary documents, selected, translated and edited with an Introduction and Tables of Dates, by* . . . (London: Oxford University Press).

ZEUSS, I. C., and EBEL, H. (eds.) (1871), *Grammatica Celtica E Monumentis Vetustis Tam Hibernicae Linguae Quam Britannicarum Dialectorum Cambricae, Cornicae, Aremoricae Comparatis Gallicae Priscae Reliquis.* . . . (Berolini: apud Weidmannos / Paris: Maisonneuve).

ZUPITZA, J., and GNEUSS, H. (eds.) (1966): *Aelfrics Grammatik und Glossar*. 2nd edn. with an introduction by H. Gneuss (Berlin: Weidmannsche Buchhandlung).

Secondary sources

AARSLEFF, H. (1982), 'John Wilkins', in H. Aarsleff, *From Locke to Saussure. Essays on the study of language and intellectual history* (London: Athlone), 239–77.

—— (1994), 'Locke's influence', in Chappell (1994), 252–91.

ABEL, C. (1885), *Sprachwissenchaftliche Abhandlungen* (Leipzig: Wilhelm Friedrich).

ACHESON, R. (1997), 'Traces of Comenius in America', *Bulletin of the Canadian Society of ComenianStudies* 5, 2: 11–20.

ALSTON, R. C. (1974), *A bibliography of the English language from the invention of printing to the year 1800. A corrected reprint of volumes I–X* (Ilkley: Janus).

AMT, E. (ed.) (1993), *Women's lives in medieval Europe. A sourcebook* (New York: Routledge).

[ANONYMOUS (1956)], *Proceedings of the seventh International Congress of Linguists.* (London: [s.n, s.l., s.d.).

ARNDT, H. W. (1979), 'John Locke: Die Funktion der Sprache', in J. Speck (ed.), *Grundprobleme der großen Philosophen. Philosophie der Neuzeit 1* (Göttingen: Vandenhoek & Rupprecht), 176–210.

ASBACH-SCHNITKER, B. (1984), 'Introduction' to John Wilkins, *Mercury*, IX–CIX.

BAKER, J. H. (1989), 'A French vocabulary and conversation guide in a fifteenth century legal notebook', *Medium Aevum* 58: 80–192.

BALDINGER, K. (1952), 'Die Gestaltung des wissenschaftlichen Wörterbuchs', *Romanistisches Jahrbuch* 5: 65–94.

—— (1956), 'Grundsätzliches zur Gestaltung des wissenschaftlichen Wörterbuchs', in Deutsche Akademie der Wissenschaften zu Berlin (ed.), *Deutsche Akademie der Wissenschaften zu Berlin 1946–1956* (Berlin: Akademie Verlag), 379–88.

—— (1960a), 'Alphabetisch oder begrifflich gegliedertes Wörterbuch?', *Zeitschrift für Romanische Philologie* 76: 521–36.

—— (1960b), 'Semasiologie und Onomasiologie in zweisprachigen Wörterbüchern', in K. R. Bausch and H. M. Gauger (eds.), *Interlinguistica. Sprachvergleich und Übersetzung. Festschrift zum 60. Geburtstag von Mario Wandruszka* (Tübingen: Niemeyer), 136–49.

BARON, D. (1986), *Grammar and gender* (New Haven: Yale University Press).

BART ROSSEBASTIANO, A. (1971), 'Introduzione' to [Adam of Rotweil] *Introito e porta*, Reprint, V–X.

—— (1984), *Antichi vocabulari plurilingui d'uso popolare: la tradizione del 'Solenissimo Vochabulista* (Alessandria: Edizioni dell'Orso).

BEAUGRANDE, R. DE, and DRESSLER, W. (1981), *Introduction to text linguistics* (London: Longman).

BÉJOINT, H. (1994), *Tradition and innovation in modern English dictionaries* (Oxford: Clarendon).

BENEŠ, J., and STEINER, M. (1985), 'Die Janva lingvarum reserata 1631–1657', *Acta Comeniana* 6 (XXX): 185–99.

BENNETT, H. S. (1970), *English books and readers, 1475 to 1557* (Cambridge: Cambridge University Press). 2nd edn.

BERLIN, B., and KAY, P. (1969), *Basic color terms. Their universality and evolution* (Berkeley: University of California Press).

BIERBAUMER, P. (1979), *Der botanische Wortschatz des Altenglischen. III: Der botanische Wortschatz in altenglischen Glossen* (Bern: Francke).

BISCHOFF, B. (1966), 'The study of foreign languages in the Middle Ages', in B. Bischoff (ed.), *Mittelalterliche Studien 1* [and] 2 (Stuttgart: Hiersemann), 2: 227–45.

BLAICHER, G., and GLASER, B. (eds.) (1994), *Anglistentag 1993. Eichstätt. Proceedings* (Tübingen: Niemeyer).

BLAKE, N. F. (1965), 'The vocabulary in French and English printed by William Caxton', *English Language Notes* 3: 7–15.

—— (1969), *Caxton and his world* (London: André Deutsch).

BLAMIRES, D. (1990), 'British knowledge of German before "The High-Dutch Minerva"', *German life and letters* 43, 2: 103–12.

BLEKASTAD, M. (1969), *Comenius. Versuch eines Umrisses von Leben, Werk und Schicksal des Jan Amos Komenský* (Oslo / Prague: Universitetsforlaget / Academia).

BORST, A. (1983), *Alltagsleben im Mittelalter* (Frankfurt: Insel).

BRANDIS, T. (1984), 'Handschriften- und Buchproduktion im 15. und frühen 16. Jahrhundert', in Grenzmann and Stackmann (1984), 176–96.

BRANDT, R. (1988), '... John Locke', in J. P. Schobinger (ed.), *Die Philosophie des 17. Jahrhunderts*, vol. 3, *England* (Basle: Schwabe), 3/2: 607–713.

BRAUNER, H. (1939), *Die tschechische Lexikographie des 16. Jahrhunderts* (Breslau: Plischke).

BROWN, G., and YULE, G. (1983), *Discourse analysis* (Cambridge: Cambridge University Press).

BRTOVÁ, B., and VIDMÁNOVÁ, S. (1978), 'Seznam děl J. A. Komenského uchoraných pouze v zahraničí [= List of the writings of J. A. Comenius preserved abroad]', *Studia Comeniana et historica* XVIII: 123–228.

BUBLITZ, W. (1996), 'In the eye of the beholder: "The rather mystical notion of coherence"', in K. Carlon, K. Davidse, and B. Rudzka-Ostyn (eds.), *Perspectives on English. Studies in honour of Professor Emma Vorlat* (Leuven-Paris: Peeters), 213–30.

BURIDANT, C. (1986), 'Lexicographie et glossographie médiévales. Esquisse de bilan et perspectives de recherche', *Lexique* 4 ('La lexicographie au Moyen Age'): 9–46.

BURKHANOV, I. (1994), 'The requirements for ideographic dictionaries in the development of communicative competence of non-native spakers', in S. Gajda and J. Nocon (eds.), *Ksztatcenie poroznmiewania sie* [Learning how to communicate] (Opole: Opole University Press), 241–8.

—— (1995), 'On the theoretical foundations of ideography', in H. Kardela and G. Persson (eds.), *New trends in semantics and lexicography. Proceedings of the international conference at Kasimierz, December 13–15, 1993* (Umea: Swedish Science Press), 17–24.

—— (1996), 'On the ideographic description of stylistically and pragmatically relevant aspects of lexical meanings', *Stylistica* 5: 63–70.

—— (1998), *Lexicography. A dictionary of basic terminology* (Rzeszów: Wydawnictwo wyższcy szoly pedagogicznej (Press of the pedagogical university).

BURSILL-HALL, G. L. (1963), 'Medieval grammatical theories', *Canadian journal of linguistics* 9, 1: 40–54.

—— (1971), *Speculative grammar of the Middle Ages: The doctrine of 'artes orationis' of the Modistae* (The Hague: Mouton).

ČAPKOVÁ, D. (1968), *Předškolní výchova v díle J. A. Komenského, jeho předchů dcu a pokračovatelů* [= Pre-school education in the work of J. A. Comenius, his predecessors and followers] (Prague: Státní pedagogické nakladatelství [= State pedagogical publishing house]).

CAPLAN, H. (1970), *Of eloquence. Studies in ancient and medieval rhetoric*, ed. and with an introduction by A. King and H. North (Ithaca and London: Cornell University Press).

CARAVOLAS, J. (1984), *Le Gutenberg de la didacographie où Coménius et l'enseignement des langages* (Montréal: Guérin).

—— (1991), 'La "Janua" de Bathe et celle de Coménius', *Rassegna italiana di linguistica applicata* XXIII: 2, 1–27.

—— (1993), 'Comenius and the theory of language teaching', *Acta Comeniana* 10 (XXXIV): 141–62.

—— (1994), *La didactique des langues. Précis d'histoire I. 1450–1700.* And: *Anthologie I. A l'ombre de Quintilien* (Montreal / Tübingen: Les presses de l'université / Narr).

CARDONA, G. (1994), 'Indian linguistics', in Lepschy (1994), 25–60.

CARRUTHERS, M. (1990), *The book of memory. A study of memory in medieval culture* (Cambridge: Cambridge University Press).

CHAPPELL, V. (ed.) (1994), *The Cambridge companion to Locke* (Cambridge: Cambridge University Press).

CLAES, F. (1977), *Bibliographisches Verzeichnis der deutschen Vokabulare und Wörterbücher, gedruckt bis 1600* (Hildesheim: Olms).

—— (1982), 'Einführung' to *Matthias Schenckius Nomenclator Hadriania Junii Medici as scholarum usum accomodatus*. Reprint (Hildesheim: Olms).

COATES, J. (1986), *Women, men and language* (London: Longman).

COLLISON, R. L. (1955), *Dictionaries of foreign languages. A bibliographical guide to the general and technical dictionaries of the chief foreign languages, with historical explanatory notes and references* (New York and London: Hafner). 2nd edn. 1971.

—— (1964), *Encyclopedias. Their history throughout the ages. A bibliographical guide* (New York and London: Hafner).

COLÓN, G. (1983), 'Concerning the Catalan–German vocabulary of 1502: "Vocabolari molt profitós per apendre Lo Catalan Alemany y Lo Alemany Catalan"', *Quaderni di Semantica* IV, 2: 395–9.

Commission internationale pour une histoire du développement scientifique et culturel de l'humanité (1966), *Cahiers d'histoire mondiale. Journal of world history. Cuadernos de historia mundial.* [Topical issue] IX, 3: 'Encyclopédies et civilisations. Encyclopedias and civilisations. Enciclopedias y civilizaciones'.

CONNELL-GINET, S., BORKER, R., and FURMAN, N. (eds.) (1989), *Women and language in literature and society* (New York: Praeger).

COP, M. (1990), *Babel unravelled. An annotated world bibliography of dictionary bibliographies, 1658–1988* (Tübingen: Niemeyer).

CORCORAN, T. (1911), *Studies in the history of Classical teaching* (Dublin/Belfast: The Educational Company of Ireland).

COVINGTON, M. A. (1984), *Syntactic theory in the high Middle Ages* (Cambridge: Cambridge University Press).

CRAM, D. (1980), 'George Dalgarno on "Ars Signorum" and Wilkins' "Essay"', in E. F. Konrad Koerner (ed.), *Progress in linguistic historiography. Papers from the International Conference on the History of the Language Sciences, Ottowa . . .* (Amsterdam: Benjamins), 113–21.

—— (1989), 'J. A. Comenius and the universal language scheme in George Dalgarno', in Kyralová and Přívratská (1989), 181–7.

—— (1990), 'John Ray and Francis Willughby: Universal language schemes and the foundations of linguistic field research', in Hüllen (1990c), 229–40.

—— (1991a), 'Birds, beasts and fishes *versus* bats, mongrels and hybrids. The publication history of John Ray's *Dictionariolum*', *Paradigm* 6: 4–7.

—— (1991b), 'Nomenclators and classified vocabularies: A check-list of works relating to the seventeenth-century curriculum' (Unpublished).

—— (1994a), 'Universal language, specious arithmetic and the alphabet of Simple Notions', *Beiträge zur Geschichte der Sprachwissenschaft* 4, 2: 213–34.

—— (1994b), 'Collection and classification: Universal language schemes and the development of seventeenth-century lexicography', in Blaicher and Glaser (1994), 59–69.

—— (1996), 'Dalgarno, George', in Stammerjohann (1996), 216–19.

—— and MAAT, J. (1996),), 'Comenius, Dalgarno and the English translations of the *Janua Linguarum*', in 'J.A. Comenius and the intellectual paradigm of the Czech and the English societies in the early modern period', *Studia comeniana et historica* 26, 55/56, 148–60.

CRUSE, D. A. (1986), *Lexical semantics* (Cambridge: Cambridge University Press).

—— (1988), 'Word meaning and encyclopedic knowledge', in W. Hüllen and R. Schulze (eds.), *Understanding the lexicon. Meaning, sense and world-knowledge in lexical semantics* (Tübingen: Niemeyer), 73–84.

CRYSTAL, D. (1980), *A first dictionary of linguistics and phonetics* (London: André Deutsch).

DAVIES, A. M. (1998), 'Nineteenth-century linguistics' in G. Lepschy (ed.), *History of linguistics* Vol. IV (London: Longman).

DEBUT, J. (1983), 'De l'usage des listes de mots comme fondement de la pédagogie dans l'antiquité', *Revue des études anciennes. Annales de l'Université de Bordeaux III*. Tome LXXXV, 3–4: 261–74.

—— (1984), 'Les *Hermeneumata Pseudodositheana*. Une méthode d'apprentissage des langues pour grands débutants', KOINONIA 8, 1: 61–85.

DEELY, J. (1982), *Introducing semiotics. Its history and doctrine* (Bloomington: Indiana University Press).

DELBRÜCK, B. (1889), *Die indogermanischen Verwandtschaftsnamen. Ein Beitrag zur vergleichenden Alterthumskunde* (Leipzig: Teubner).

DEROLEZ, R. (1992), 'Anglo-Saxon glossography: A brief introduction', in R. Derolez (ed.), *Anglo-Saxon glossography. Papers read at the international conference held in the Koninklijke Academie voor Wetenschaapen, Letteren en Schone Kunsten van Belgie* (Brussels: Paleis der Academien), 9–42.

DESHPANDE, M. M. (1992), 'Sanskrit', in W. Bright (ed.), *International encyclopedia of linguistics*, Vol. 3 (New York / Oxford: Oxford University Press), 366–72.

Dictionary of national biography (1917–), ed. by Sir Leslie Stephen and Sir Sidney Lee, 'William Caxton'. Reprint (Oxford: Oxford University Press 1973), Vol. 3, 1290–8.

DIESNER, H.-J. (1976), 'Lexikographie und Enzyklopädie in der Antike', in Diesner and Gurst (1976), 11–60.

—— and GURST, G. (eds.) (1976), *Lexika gestern und heute* (Leipzig: VEB Bibliographisches Institut).

DIETZ, F. (1875), *Romanische Wortschöpfung* (Bonn: Weber).

DIJK, T. A. VAN (1980), *Textwissenschaft. Eine interdisziplinäre Einführung* (Munich: Deutscher Taschenbuchverlag).

DIONISOTTI, A. C. (1982), 'From Ausonius' schooldays? A schoolbook and its relatives', *The Journal of Roman Studies* LXXII: 83–125, three plates.

—— (1988), 'Greek grammars and dictionaries in Carolingian Europe', in M. W. Herren (ed.), *The sacred nectar of the Greeks: The study of Greek in the West in the early Middle-Ages* (London: King's College), 1–56.

—— (1996), 'On the nature and transmission of Latin glossaries', in J. Hamesse (ed.), *Les manuscripts des lexiques et glossaires de l'Antiquité tardive à la fin du Moyen Âge* (Louvain-La-Neuve: Fédération Internationale des Instituts d'Études Médiévales), 205–52.

DOLEZAL, F. T. (1983), 'The lexicographical and lexicological procedures and methods of John Wilkins', Diss., University of Illinois (Ann Arbor: University Microfilms International).

—— (1985), *Forgotten but important lexicographers: John Wilkins and William Lloyd. A modern approach to lexicography before Johnson* (Tübingen: Niemeyer).

—— (1986), 'John Wilkins and William Lloyd's "Alphabetical Dictionary" (1688): Towards a comprehensive, and a systematically defined, lexicon', *Papers in Linguistics* 19, 1: 111–30.

DOLEZAL, F. T. (1987), 'John Wilkins and the development of a structural semantics', in H. Aarsleff, L. G. Kelly, and H.-J. Niederehe (eds.), *Papers in the history of linguistics* (Amsterdam: Benjamins), 271–82.

DORNSEIFF, F. (1933), 'Wortschatzdarstellung und Bezeichnungslehre' [Introduction], in F. Dornseiff, *Der deutsche Wortschatz nach Sachgruppen* (Berlin: de Gruyter), 29–66.

DUBOIS, M. M. (1943), *Aelfric: sermonnaire, docteur et grammairien. Contribution à l'étude de la vie et de l'action bénédictines en Angleterre au xe siècle* (Paris: Droz). Reprint (1972).

DUBY, G., and PERROT, M. (eds.) (1992–4), *A history of women*. Five vols. (Cambridge MA: Belknap Press of Harvard University Press).

DVOŘÁK, J. (1985), 'Universalsprache, Enzyklopädie und die "Allgemeine Verbesserung der menschlichen Dinge" bei J. A. Comenius', in R. M. Chisholm *et al.* (eds.), *Philosophie des Geistes. / Philosophie der Psychologie. Akten des 9. Internationalen Wittgenstein Symposions* (Vienna: Hölder-Pichler-Tempski), 645–7.

ECO, U. (1995), *Search for the perfect language* (Oxford: Blackwell). Translation of: *La ricerca della lingua perfetta nella cultura europea* (Rome: Laterza 1993).

EISENSTEIN, E. L. (1983), *The printing revolution in early modern Europe* (Cambridge: Cambridge University Press).

EYBL, F. M., HARMS, W., KRUMMACHER, H. H., and WELZIG, W. (eds.) (1995), *Enzyklopädien der frühen Neuzeit. Beiträge zu ihrer Erforschung* (Tübingen: Niemeyer).

FORSTER, L. (1960), 'Comenius und die Emblematik', *Acta Comeniana* XIX: 218–20.

FULLER, G. H. (1942), *Foreign language–English dictionaries. A selected list* (New York: US Congress Library, general reference and biography division).

FUNKE, O. (1929), *Zum Weltsprachenproblem in England im 17. Jahrhundert* (Heidelberg: Winter).

GEISSLER, H. (1959), *Comenius und die Sprache* (Heidelberg: Quelle und Meyer).

GIESECKE, M. (1980), ' "Volkssprache" und "Verschriftlichung des Lebens" im Spätmittelalter—am Beispiel der Genese der gedruckten Fachprosa in Deutschland', in H.-U. Gumbrecht (ed.), *Literatur in der Gesellschaft des Spätmittelalters* (Heidelberg: Winter), 39–70.

GILL, W. J. C. (1968), *Captain John Smith and Virginia* (London: Longmans).

GNEUSS, H. (1989), 'Glossen, Glossare V', in *Lexikon des Mittelalters*, Vol. 4, 1513–14 (Munich and Zurich: Artemis).

—— (1996), *English language scholarship: A survey and bibliography from the beginnings to the end of the nineteenth century* (Binghampton NY: Medieval and Renaissance Texts and Studies).

GRADDOL, D., and SWANN, J. (1989), *Gender voices* (Oxford: Blackwell).

GREEN, J. (1997), *Chasing the sun. Dictionary makers and the dictionaries they made* (London: Pimlico).

GRENZMANN, L., and STACKMANN, K. (eds.) (1984), *Literatur und Laienbildung im Spätmittelalter und in der Reformationszeit*. Symposion Wolfenbüttel 1981 (Stuttgart: Metzeler).

GRICE, H. P. (1975), 'Logic and conversation', in P. Cole and J. L. Morgan (eds.), *Syntax and semantics*, Vol. 3 (New York: Academic Press), 41–58.

GRIERSON, PH. (1957), 'The dates of the "Livre des Metiers" and its derivatives', *Revue Belge de Philologie et d'Histoire* XXXV: 778–83.

HALLIDAY, M. A. K., and HASAN, R. (1976), *Cohesion in English* (London: Longman).

HALLIG, R., and VON WARTBURG, W. (1952), *Begriffssystem als Grundlage für die*

Lexikographie. Versuch eines Ordnungsschemas. Système raisonné des concepts pour servir de base à la lexicographie. Essai d'un schéma de classement (Berlin: Akademie Verlag). 2nd edn. 1963.

HARMS, W. (1970), 'Wörter, Sachen und emblematische "Res" im "Orbis sensualium pictus" des Comenius', in D. Hofmann (ed.), *Gedenkschrift für William Foerste* (Cologne/Vienna: Böhlau), 531–42.

HARRIS, R. (1980), *The language makers* (London: Duckworth).

HAUSMAN, F. J. (1990), 'Le dictionnaire analogique', in Hausmann *et al.* (1989–91), II: 1083–94.

—— REICHMANN, O., WIEGAND, H. E., and ZGUSTA, L. (eds.) (1989–91), *Wörterbücher. Dictionaries. Dictionnaires. Ein internationales Handbuch zur Lexikographie.* Three vols. (Berlin: de Gruyter).

HEGER, K. (1964), 'Die methodologischen Voraussetzungen von Onomasiologie und begrifflicher Gliederung', *Zeitschrift für Romanische Philologie* 80: 486–516.

HELLINGER, M. (1990), *Kontrastive feministische Linguistik—Mechanismen sprachlicher Diskriminierung im Englischen und im Deutschen* (Ismaning: Hueber).

—— (1995), 'Geschlechtsspezifischer Sprachgebrauch', in R. Ahrens, W.-D. Bald, and W. Hüllen (eds.), *Handbuch Englisch als Fremdsprache (HEF)* (Berlin: Erich Schmidt), 175–8.

HELMER, K. (1980), 'Lexikographie bei Comenius', *Pädagogische Rundschau* 34: 521–31.

HENNINGSEN, J. (1966), '"Enzyklopädie", zur Sprach- und Bedeutungsgeschichte eines pädagogischen Begriffs', *Archiv für Begriffsgeschichte* (Bonn: Bouvier), 10: 271–356.

HERBERMANN, C.-P. (1996), 'Felder und Wörter', in Hoinkes (1996), 263–91.

HILDEBRANDT, R., and KNOOP, U. (eds.) (1986), *Brüder-Grimm-Symposion zur Historischen Wortforschung. Beiträge zu der Marburger Tagung vom Juni 1985* (Berlin: de Gruyter).

HOFFMANN, L., KALVERKÄMPER, H., and WIEGAND, H. E., together with Galinski, C., and Hüllen, W. (1998–9), *Fachsprachen. Languages for Special Purposes.* Two vols. (Berlin: de Gruyter).

HOINKES, U. (ed.), *Panorama der lexikalischen Semantik. Thematische Festschrift aus Anlaß des 60. Geburtstags von Horst Geckeler* (Tübingen: Narr).

HÖLTGEN, K. J. (1986), *Aspects of the emblem. Studies in the English emblem tradition and the European context* (Kassel: Reichenberger).

HOOF, HENRI VAN (1994), *Petite histoire des dictionnaires* (Louvain-la-neuve: Peeters).

HOUSEHOLDER, F. W., and SAPORTA, S. (eds.) (1962), *Problems in lexicography* (Bloomington: Indiana University).

HOWATT, A. P. R. (1984), *A history of English language teaching* (Oxford: Oxford University Press).

HOWELL, W. S. (1961), *Logic and rhetoric in England, 1500–1700* (New York: Russell & Russell).

HUFTON, O. (1993), 'Women, work and family', in Duby and Perrot (1992–4), III: 15–45.

HUGHES, D. O. (1992), 'Regulating women's fashion', in Duby and Perrot (1992–4), II: 136–58.

HUIZINGA, J. (1965), *Herbst des Mittelalters. Studien über Lebens- und Geistesformen des 14. und 15. Jahrhunderts in Frankreich und in den Niederlanden*, ed. by K. Köster [Transl. of *Herfstij der middeleeuwen*, 5th edn. 1941] (Stuttgart: Kröner). 9th edn.

HULL, S. W. (1996), *Women according to men. The world of Tudor-Stuart women* (Walnut Creek: Alta Mira).

HÜLLEN, W. (1989), *'Their manner of discourse'. Nachdenken über Sprache im Umkreis der Royal Society* (Tübingen: Narr).

HÜLLEN, W. (1990*a*), 'Motives behind seventeenth century lexicography: A comparison between German and English dictionaries of that time', in T. Magay and J. Zigány (eds.), *BudaLEX '88 proceedings. Papers from the 3rd International EURALEX Congress* ... (Budapest: Akadémiai Kiadó), 189–96.

—— (1990*b*), 'Rudolf Hallig and Walther von Wartburg's "Begriffssystem" and its non-acceptance in German linguistics', in P. Schmitter (ed.), *Essays towards a history of semantics* (Münster: Nodus), 129–68.

—— (ed.) (1990*c*), *Understanding the historiography of linguistics. Problems and projects* (Münster: Nodus).

—— (1993), 'Picturae sunt totius mundi icones. Some deliberations on lexicography, ars memorativa and the "Orbis sensualium pictus"', *Acta Comeniana* 10 (XXXIV): 129–40.

—— (1994*a*), 'A great chain of words: The onomasiological tradition in English lexicography', in Blaicher and Glaser (1994), 32–46.

—— (1994*b*), 'Von Kopf bis Fuß. Das Vokabular zur Bezeichnung des menschlichen Körpers in zwei onomasiologischen Wörterbüchern des 16. und 17. Jahrhunderts', in Hüllen (1994*c*), 105–22.

—— (1994*c*), (ed.), *The World in a List of Words* (Tübingen: Niemeyer).

—— (1995*a*), 'Die semantische Komponente der Universalsprache von John Wilkins', in Hoinkes (1995), 329–46.

—— (1995*b*), 'Good language—bad language. Some case studies on the criteria of linguistic evaluation in three centuries', in K. D. Dutz and K.-A. Forsgren (eds.), *History and rationality. The Skövde papers in the historiography of linguistics* (Münster: Nodus), 315–34.

—— (1996*a*), 'Schemata der Historiographie. Ein Traktat', *Beiträge zur Geschichte der Sprachwissenschaft* 6, 1: 113–25. Transl. 'On the Method of Linguistic Historiography', in N. McLelland and A. R. Linn (eds.) (2005), *Flores Grammaticae. Essays in memory of Vivien Law* (Münster: Nodus), 9–10.

—— (1996*b*), 'Who wrote the first German grammar in English?', *Meesterwerk. Berichten van het Peeter Heynsgenootschap* 7: 2–10.

—— (1996*c*), 'Some yardsticks of language evaluation 1600–1800 (English and German)', in Law and Hüllen (1996), 275–306.

—— (1997), 'Onomasiological dictionaries 800–1700: Their tradition and their linguistic status', in K.-P. Konerding and A. Lehr (eds.), *Linguistische Theorie und lexikographische Praxis. Symposiumsvorträge, Heidelberg 1996* (Heidelberg: Niemeyer), 127–37.

—— (1998), 'Historiographie als Aufforderurg zum kritischen Anachronismus', in P. Schmitter and M. van der Wal (eds.), *Metahistoriography. Theoretical and Methodological Aspects of the Historiography of Linguistics* (Münster: Nodus), 171–81.

—— (2000), 'A Janua for Catholics', in *Unie Comenius Bulletin* č. 12 (Mimořádné čislo k žuvotnímu jubileu prof. PhDr. Dagmar Čapkové, DrSc., dr.h.c.), Prague, 36–41.

—— (2002), *Collected Papers on the History of Linguistic Ideas.* Ed. by Michael M. Isermann. Münster: Nodus.

—— (2004), *A History of Roget's Thesaurus. Origin, Development, and Design.* Oxford: Oxford University Press, Pb ed. 2005.

HUNT, R. W. (1984), *The schools and the cloister. The life and writings of Alexander Nequam (1157–1217)*, ed. and revised by M. Gibson (Oxford: Clarendon).

HUPKA, W. (1989), *Wort und Bild. Die Illustrationen in Wörterbüchern und Enzyklopädien.* With an English summary. Avec un résumé français (Tübingen: Niemeyer).

IVINS, JR., W. M. (1953), *Prints and visual communication* (London: Routledge & Kegan Paul).

JABERG, K. (1937), *Sprachwissenschaftliche Forschungen und Erlebnisse*, ed. by his pupils and friends (Paris / Zürich: Droz / Niehaus).

JOHNSON, J. H. (1994), 'Ancient Egyptian linguistics', in Lepschy (1994), 63–76.

KALTZ, B. (1995), 'L'enseignement des langues étrangères au XVIe siècle. Structure globale et typologie des textes destinés à l'apprentissage des vernaculaires', *Beiträge zur Geschichte der Sprachwissenschaft* 5, 1: 79–106.

KELLY, L. G. (1969), *Twenty-five centuries of language teaching* (Rowley MA: Newbury House).

KER, N. R. (1957), *Catalogue of manuscripts containing Anglo-Saxon* (Oxford: Clarendon).

—— R. (1975), 'A supplement to *Catalogue*', *Anglo-Saxon England* 5: 121–33.

KEY, M. R. (1975), *Male/Female language* (Metuchen NJ: Scarecrow Press).

KIBBEE, D. A. (1991), *For to speke Frenche trewely. The French language in England, 1000–1600: Its status, description and instruction* (Amsterdam: Benjamins).

KING, M. L. (1991), *Women of the Renaissance* (Chicago: University of Chicago Press).

KIPFER, B. A. (1986), 'Investigating an onomasiological approach to dictionary material', *Journal of the Dictionary Society of North America* 8: 55–64.

KNOWLSON, J. (1975), *Universal language schemes in England and France* (Toronto/Buffalo: University of Toronto Press).

KOCH, J.(1934), 'Der anglo-normannische Traktat des Walter von Bibbesworth in seiner Bedeutung für die Anglistik', *Anglia* 58: 30–77.

KRAEMER, G. B. (1977), *Sprache und Sprachbildung in der Sicht des Comenius*', Diss., Tübingen.

KRÁLÍK, S. (ed.) (1981), *Otázky současné komeniologie* [= Questions of contemporary Comeniology] (Prague: Academia).

KRETZMAN, N. (1972), 'Semantics, history of', in *The encyclopedia of philosophy* (London: Collier-Macmillan), vol. 7: 358–406.

KUSAKAWA, S. (1999), 'Petrus Ramus (1515–1572). Reform und Methode', in P. R. Blum (ed.), *Philosophen der Renaissance* (Darmstadt: Wissenschaftliche Buchgesellschaft), 130–6.

KYRALOVÁ, M., and PŘÍVRATSKÁ, J. (eds.) (1989), *Symposium Comenianum. J. A. Comenius's contribution to world science and culture. Liblice, June 16–20, 1986* (Prague: Academia).

LABARRE, A. (1975), *Bibliographie du dictionarium d'Ambrogio Calepino (1502–1779)* (Baden-Baden: Koerner).

LAKOFF, G., and JONSON, M. (1980), *Metaphors we live by* (Chicago: Chicago University Press).

LAKOFF, R. (1975), *Language and women's place* (New York: Harper & Row).

LAMBLEY, K. (1920), *The teaching and cultivation of the French language in England during Tudor and Stuart times* (Manchester/London: Manchester University Press/Longman, Green & Co.).

LANDAU, S. I. (1984), *Dictionaries. The art and craft of lexicography* (Cambridge: Cambridge University Press). 2nd edn (1993).

LAPIDGE, M. (1982), '. . . The evidence of Latin glosses', in N. Brooks (ed.), *Latin and the vernacular languages in early medieval Britain* (Leicester: University of Leicester Press), 99–140.

LARGE, J. A. (1985), *The artificial language movement* (Oxford: Blackwell).

LAW, V. (1982), *The insular Latin grammarians* (Woodbridge, Suffolk: The Boydell Press).

—— (1990), 'The history of morphology: Expression of a change of consciousness', in Hüllen (1990c), 61–74.

LAW, V. (1994), 'Glossaries and dictionaries, medieval. Latin based', in R. E. Asher and J. M. Y. Simpson (eds.), *The encyclopedia of language and linguistics*, vol. 3 (Oxford: Pergamon Press), 1437–9.

—— and HÜLLEN, W. (eds.) (1996), *Linguists and their diversions. A Festschrift for R. H. Robins on his 75th birthday* (Münster: Nodus).

—— and SLUITER, I. (eds.) (1995), *Dionysius Thrax and the 'Techné Grammatiké'* (Münster: Nodus).

LAZZARI, L., and MUCCIANTE, L. (1984), *Il 'Glossario' di Alfric: studio sulle concordanze* (Rome: Edizioni Dell'Ateneo).

LEARMOUTH, T., and MACWILLIAM, S. (1986), *Historic English dictionaries 1595–1899. A Union catalogue of holdings in Exeter libraries* (Exeter: Dictionary research centre).

LEHNERT, M. (1956), 'Das englische Wörterbuch in Vergangenheit und Gegenwart', *Zeitschrift für Anglistik und Amerikanistik* 4: 265–323.

LEPSCHY, G. (ed.) (1994), *History of linguistics*. vol. 1: 'The eastern traditions of linguistics' (London: Longman).

LEWANDOWSKI, TH. (1976), *Linguistisches Wörterbuch*. Three vols. (Heidelberg: Quelle und Meyer).

Lexikon des Mittelalters (1989), 'Glossen, Glossare', vol. 4, 1508–15 (Zurich: Artemis).

LINDEMANN, M. (1994), *Die französischen Wörterbücher von den Anfängen bis 1600. Entstehung und typologische Beschreibung* (Tübingen: Niemeyer).

Linguistics (1989) [topical issue], 'Prospects and problems of prototype theory'. 27, 4.

LIPKA, L. (1987), 'Prototype semantics or feature semantics: An alternative?', in W. Lörscher and R. Schulze (eds.), *Perspectives on language in performance. Studies in linguistics, literary criticism, and language teaching and learning. To honour Werner Hüllen on the occasion of his sixtieth birthday* (Tübingen: Narr), I: 282–98.

LOONEN, P. L. M. (1991), *For to learne to buye and sell. Learning English in the Low Dutch area between 1500 and 1800. A critical survey* (Amsterdam / Maarssen: ADA—Holland University Press).

—— (1994), 'The influence of Comenius on modern language teaching: the case of Nathanael Duez', *Paradigm* 15: 1–8.

LÖRSCHER, W. (1983), *Linguistische Beschreibung und Analyse von Fremdsprachenunterricht als Diskurs* (Tübingen: Narr).

LOSONSKY, M. (1994), 'Locke on meaning and signification', in G. A. J. Rogers (ed.), *Locke's philosophy. Content and context* (Oxford: Clarendon), 123–42.

LOWENTHAL, D. (1985), *The past is a foreign country* (Cambridge: Cambridge University Press).

LUDIN, F. (1898), *Adam Sibers Bearbeitung des 'Nomenclator H. Junii', Lexikalisch erläutert (Als Beitrag zur Localisierung des nhd. Wortbestandes)*, Diss., Freiburg (Karlsruhe: L. Gillardon'sche Druckerei).

LUTZEIER, P. R. (1981), *Wortsemantische Fragestellungen mit besonderer Berücksichtigung des Wortfeldbegriffs* (Tübingen: Niemeyer).

—— (ed.) (1993), *Studien zur Wortfeldtheorie / Studies in the lexical field theory* (Tübingen: Niemeyer).

LYONS, J. (1968), *Introduction to theoretical linguistics* (Cambridge: Cambridge University Press).

—— (1977), *Semantics 1* [and] 2. Two vols. (Cambridge: Cambridge University Press).

MCARTHUR, T. (1986a), 'Thematic lexicography', in R. R. K. Hartmann (ed.), *The History of*

Lexicography. Papers from the Dictionary Research Centre Seminar at Exeter, March 1986 (Amsterdam: Benjamins), 157–66.

—— (1986b), *Worlds of reference. Lexicography, learning and language from the clay tablet to the computer* (Cambridge: Cambridge University Press).

McCONCHIE, R. W. (1997), *Lexicography and physicke. The record of sixteenth-century English medical terminology* (Oxford: Clarendon).

MACKEY, W. F. (1971), *Language teaching analysis* (Bloomington: Indiana University Press).

MALKIEL, Y. (1962), 'A typological classification of dictionaries on the basis of distinctive features', in Householder and Saporta (1962), 3–24.

MALKIEL, I. (1993), *Etymology* (Cambridge: Cambridge University Press).

MALMQVIST, G. (1994), 'Chinese linguistics', in Lepschy (1994), 1–24.

MARELLO, C. (1990), 'The thesaurus', in Hausmann *et al.* (1989–91), II: 1083–94.

MARSDEN, W. (1796), *A catalogue of dictionaries, vocabularies, grammars, and alphabets* (London: privately printed).

MEHRINGER, R. (1909), 'Wörter und Sachen', *Germanisch-Romanische Monatsschrift* 1: 593–8.

—— (1912), 'Zur Aufgabe und zum Namen unserer Zeitschrift', *Wörter und Sachen* 3: 22–56.

MEYER, C. (1984), 'Grundzüge der mittelalterlichen Enzyklopädik. Zu Inhalten, Formen und Funktionen einer problematischen Gattung', in Grenzmann and Stackmann (1984), 467–503.

—— (1995), 'Der Wandel der Enzyklopädie des Mittelalters vom *Weltbuch* zum Thesaurus sozial gebundenen Kulturwissens', in Eybl *et al.* (1995), 19–42.

MEYER, P. (1903), 'Dialogues français composés en 1415', *Romania* 32: 47–58.

MICHAEL, I. (1970), *English grammatical categories and their tradition to 1800* (Cambridge: Cambridge University Press).

MICHATSH, F. J. (1917), 'Lexikalische Materialien zu Rosembachs "Vocabulari Català-Alemany 1502"', *Estudis romànics (Llengua i literatura)* IX, 2: 176–233.

MORRIS, C. W. (1938), *Foundations of the theory of the sign* (Chicago: Chicago University Press).

MÜLLER, P. O. (2001), *Deutsche Lexikographie des 16. Jahrhunderts. Konzeptionen und Funktionen frühneuzeitlicher Wörterbücher*. Tübingen: Niemeyer.

MURRAY, J. A. H. (1900), *The evolution of English lexicography* (Oxford: Clarendon).

NIEDEREHE, H.-J. (1995), *Bibliografía cronológica de la lingüística, la gramática y la lexi-cografía del español. (Bicres) Desde los comienzos hasta el año 1600* (Amsterdam: Benjamins).

NÜßLEIN, TH. (ed.) (1994), 'Einführung', to *Rhetorica Ad Herrennium Lateinisch-Deutsch*, ed. and translated by Theodor Nüßlein (Zürich: Artemis and Winkler), 322–56.

O'MATHÚNA, S. P. (1986), *William Bathe, S.J., 1564–1614. A pioneer in linguistics* (Amsterdam: Benjamins).

O'NEILL, R. K. (1988), *English language dictionaries, 1604–1900. The catalogue of the Warren N. and Suzanne B. Cordell Collection* (New York: Greenwood).

ONG, SJ, W. J. (1967), *The presence of the word. Some prolegomena for cultural and religious history* (New York: Simon & Schuster).

OPITZ, C. (1992), 'Life in the Middle Ages', in Duby and Perrot (1992), II: 267–317.

ORME, N. (1973), *English schools in the Middle Ages* (London: Methuen).

OSSELTON, N. E. (1999), 'English specialized lexicography in the late Middle Ages and in the Renaissance', in Hoffmann *et al.* (1998–9), vol.2, 2458–64.

PADLEY, G. A. (1976–88), *Grammatical theory in western Europe 1500–1700*. Vol 1: 'The Latin tradition', vol. 2: 'Trends in vernacular grammar I', vol. 3: 'Trends in vernacular grammar II' (Cambridge: Cambridge University Press).

PAGE, R. I. (1979), 'More Old English scratched glosses', *Anglia* 97: 27–45.

PILZ, K. (1967), *Johann Amos Comenius. Die Ausgaben des Orbis Sensualium Pictus. Eine Bibliographie* (Nuremberg: Selbstverlag der Stadtbibliothek).

PINAULT, G.-J. (1996), 'Amara . . .', in Stammerjohann (1996), 22–3.

PLETT, H. F. (1995), *English Renaissance, rhetoric and poetics. A systematic bibliography of primary and secondary sources* (Brill: Leyden).

POLLARD, A. W., and REDGRAVE, G. R. (1991), *Short-title catalogue of books printed in England, Scotland, and Ireland, and of English books printed abroad. 1475–1640* (London: Bibliographical Society).

POMBO, O. (1987), *Leibniz and the problem of a universal language* (Münster: Nodus).

POSNER, R., ROBERING, K., and SEBEOK, T. A. (eds.) (1997), *Semiotik. Semiotics. Ein Handbuch zu den zeichentheoretischen Grundlagen von Natur und Kultur. A handbook on the sign-theoretic foundations of nature and culture.* Vol. 1 (Berlin: de Gruyter).

PREISLER, B. (1986), *Linguistic sex roles in conversation* (Berlin: Mouton de Gruyter).

PŘÍVRATSKÁ, J. (1987), 'The methodological approach in the linguistic studies of Comenius', *Acta Comeniana* 7 (XXXI): 91–102.

—— (1989), 'On the function of language in the General Consultation of Comenius', in Kyralová and Přívratská, (1989), 175–9.

—— (1991), 'Grundzüge der sprachlichen Konzeption von Jan Amos Komenský', *Acta Comeniana* 9 (XXXIIII): 131–47.

—— (1994), 'Dictionary as a textbook—textbook as a dictionary: Comenius' contribution to Czech lexicography', in Hüllen (1994c), 151–8.

—— (1996), 'Panglottia—Comenius' model for language unification', in K. R. Jankowski (ed.), *Multiple perspectives on the historical dimensions of language* (Münster: Nodus), 75–80.

QUADRI, B. (1952), *Aufgaben und Methoden der onomasiologischen Forschung. Eine entwick-lungsgeschichtliche Darstellung* (Bern: Francke).

QUIRK, R. (1982), *Style and communication in the English language* (London: Longman).

REICHL, K. (1993), *Englische Sprachwissenschaft. Eine Bibliographie* (Berlin: Erich Schmidt).

REICHLING, D. (1880), *Johannes Murmellius. Sein Leben und seine Werke. Nebst einem ausführlichen Verzeichnis sämmtlicher Schriften und einer Auswahl von Gedichten* (Freiburg. Reprint [s.l.]: Nienkoop-de Graaf 1963).

REICHMANN, O. (1986), 'Historische Bedeutungswörterbücher als Forschungsinstrumente der Kulturgeschichtsschreibung', in Hildebrandt and Knoop (1986), 242–63.

—— (1990), 'Das onomasiologische Wörterbuch. Ein Überblick', in Hausmann *et al.* (1989–91), II: 1057–67.

REINSMA, L. M. (1987), *Aelfric: An annotated bibliography* (New York: Garland).

RISSE, W. (1964), *Die Logik der Neuzeit.* Two vols. (Stuttgart / Bad Cannstatt: Fromman/Holzboog).

ROBINS, R. H. (1990), *A short history of linguistics* (London: Longman). 3rd edn.

—— (1994), 'William Bullokar's "Bref Grammar for English": Text and context', in Blaicher and Glaser (1994), 19–31.

ROSCH, E. (1973), 'Natural categories', *Cognitive Psychology* 4: 328–50.

—— (1978), 'Principles of categorisation', in E. Rosch and B. B. Loyed (eds.), *Cognition and categorization* (Hillsdale NJ: Erlbaum), 27–48.

ROTHWELL, W. (1968), 'The teaching of French in medieval England', *The Modern Language Review* 63: 37–46.

—— (1976), 'The role of French in thirteenth-century England', *Bulletin of the John Rylands Library Manchester* 58: 445–66.

—— (1982), 'A mis-judged author and a mis-used text: Walter de Bibbesworth and his "Tretiz"', *Modern Language Review* 77: 282–93.

SADLER, J. E. (1966), *J. A. Comenius and the concept of universal education* (London: Allen & Unwin).

SALMON, V. (1979), *The study of language in seventeenth century England* (Amsterdam: Benjamins).

—— (1996), 'Tradition and innovation in the writings of Charles Butler (c. 1561–1647)', in Law and Hüllen (1996), 99–122.

SANDERS, W. (1992), 'Sprachglossen. Zur Metamorphose eines alten Fachbegriffs', in H. Burger, A. M. Haas, and P. von Matt (eds.), *Verborum Amor. Studien zur Geschichte und Kunst der deutschen Sprache. Festschrift für Stephan Sonderegger zum 65. Geburtstag* (Berlin: de Gruyter), 47–70.

SAUER, H. (1992), 'Towards a linguistic description and classification of the Old English plant names', in M. Korhammer (ed.), *Words, texts, and manuscripts. Studies in Anglo-Saxon culture presented to Helmut Gneuss on the occasion of his sixty-fifth birthday* (Cambridge: Brewer), 381–408.

—— (1991), 'Angelsächsische Glossen und Glossare und ihr Fachwortschatz', in Hoffmann *et al.* (1998-9), vol. 2, 2452-8.

SCHALLER, K. (1967), *Die Pädagogik des Johann Amos Comenius und die Anfänge des Pädagogischen Realismus im 17. Jahrhundert* (Heidelberg: Quelle und Meyer). 2nd edn.

SCHELLENBERG, G. (1933), *Bemerkungen zum Traité des Walter von Bibbesworth*. Diss., Berlin.

SCHLIEBEN-LANGE, B. (1983), *Traditionen des Sprechens. Elemente einer pragmatischen Sprachgeschichtsschreibung* (Stuttgart: Kohlhammer).

SCHMIDT-BIGGEMANN, W. (1995), 'Enzyklopädie und philosophia perennis', in W. Eybl *et al.* (1995), 1–18.

SCHMITTER, P. (1991), 'Vom "Mythos" zum "Logos": Erkenntniskritik und Sprachreflexion bei den Vorsokratikern', in P. Schmitter (ed.), *Sprachtheorien der abendländischen Antike. Geschichte der Sprachtheorie*. Vol. 2 (Tübingen: Narr), 57–86.

SCHNELL, B. (1986), 'Die Inkunabelfassung des *Vocabularius ex quo*. Zur Revision eines Wörterbuchs im 15. Jahrhundert', in Hildebrandt and Knoop (1986*)*, 179–92.

SCHULZE-STUBENRECHT, W. (1990), 'Das Bilderwörterbuch', in Hausmann *et al.* (1989–91), II: 1103–12.

SCHWARZ, A. (1977), 'Glossen als Texte', *Beiträge zur Geschichte der deutschen Sprache und Literatur* 99: 25–36.

SHAPIRO, B. J. (1969), *John Wilkins 1614–1672. An Intellectual Biography* (Berkeley: University of California Press).

SIDARUS, A. (1978), 'Coptic lexicography in the Middle Ages. The Coptic–Arabic "Scalae"', in R. Mcl. Wilson (ed.), *The future of Coptic studies* (Leiden: Brill), 125–42.

—— (1990*a*), 'Les lexiques onomasiologiques Gréco-copto-arabes du Moyen Âges et leurs origines anciennes', in R. Schulz and M. Görg (eds.), *Lingua Restituta Orientalis. Festgabe für Julius Arsfalg* (Wiesbaden: Harrassowitz), 348–59.

—— (1990*b*), 'Onomastica aegyptica: La tradition des lexiques thématiques en Égypte a travers les âges et les langues', *Histoires Épistémologie Langage* 12, 1: 7–19.

SIDARUS, A. (1990c), 'Bibliographical introduction to medieval Coptic linguistics', *Bulletin de la Société d'Archéologie Copte* XXIX: 83–5.

SINCLAIR, J. McH., and COULTHARD, R. M. (1975), *Towards an analysis of discourse* (London: Oxford University Press).

SLAUGHTER, M. M. (1982), *Universal language and scientific taxonomy in the seventeenth century* (Cambridge: Cambridge University Press).

SMET, G. DE (1968), 'Alte Lexikographie und moderne Wortgeographie', in W. Mitzka (ed.), *Wortgeographie und Gesellschaft* (Berlin: de Gruyter), 49–79.

—— (1979), 'Wörterbücher', in *Reallexikon der deutschen Literaturgeschichte*. Vol. 4 (Berlin: de Gruyter), 930–46.

—— (1986), 'Die frühneuhochdeutsche Lexikographie: Möglichkeit und Grenzen ihrer Interpretation', in Hildebrandt and Knoop (1986), 59–80.

SONDEREGGER, S. (1987), *Althochdeutsche Sprache und Literatur. Eine Einführung in das ältere Deutsch* (Berlin: de Gruyter).

STAMMERJOHANN, H. (ed.) (1996), *Lexicon grammaticorum. Who's who in the history of world linguistics* (Tübingen: Niemeyer).

STAMMLER, W. (ed.) (1933), *Die deutsche Literatur des Mittelalters. Verfasserlexikon*. Vol. 1 (Berlin: de Gruyter).

—— (1960), *Deutsche Philologie im Aufriß*. Vol. 2. (Berlin: Erich Schmidt).

STANKIEWICZ, E. (1984), *Grammars and dictionaries of the Slavik languages from the Middle Ages to 1875* (Berlin: Mouton).

STARNES, DeW. T. (1954), *Renaissance dictionaries. English–Latin and Latin–English* (Austin: University of Texas Press).

—— and NOYES, G. E. (1946), *The English Dictionary from Cawdrey to Johnson 1604–1755*. New edition with an introduction and a select bibliography by G. Stein (Amsterdam: Benjamins 1991).

STEGMANN, T. D. (ed.) (1991), 'Vorwort' to *Vocabulari Català–Alemany de l'any 1502. Katalanisch–Deutsches Vokabular aus dem Jahre 1502* (Frankfurt: Domus Editoria Europaea), 7–40.

STEIN, G. (1985), *The English dictionary before Cawdrey* (Tübingen: Niemeyer).

—— (1989a), 'The emerging role of English in the dictionaries of Renaissance Europe', *Folia Linguistica Historica* IX, 1: 29–138.

—— (1989b), 'Problems of affinity in early polyglot word lists', in U. Fries and M. Heusser (eds.), *Meaning and beyond. Ernst Leisi zum 70. Geburtstag* (Tübingen: Narr), 93–114.

—— (1991a), 'Introductory Materials', to DeW. T. Starnes and G. E. Noyes, *The English dictionary from Cawdry to Johnson* (Amsterdam: Benjamins), vii–cxi.

—— (1991b), 'Illustrations in dictionaries', *International journal of lexicography* 4, 2: 99–127.

—— (1997), *John Palsgrave as a Renaissance linguist. A pioneer in vernacular language description* (Oxford: Clarendon).

STEINBERG, S. H. (1961), *Five hundred years of printing* (Harmondsworth: Penguin).

ŠTĚPÁNEK, M. (1976), 'Die historische Entwicklung und das ideologische Profil der enzyklopädischen Literatur in den tschechischen Ländern', in Diesner and Gurst (1976), 297–318.

STRASSER, G. F. (1988), *Lingua Universalis. Kryptologie und Theorie der Universalsprachen im 16. und 17. Jahrhundert* (Wiesbaden: Harrassowitz).

SUBBIONDO, J. L. (1977), 'John Wilkins' theory of meaning and the development of a semantic model', *Cahiers linguistique Ottawa* 9: 41–61.

—— (ed.) (1992), *John Wilkins and seventeenth-century British linguistics* (Benjamins: Amsterdam).

—— (1996), 'Francis Bacon's "New Atlantis" and John Wilkins' "Essay": Educational reform and philosophical language in seventeenth-century England', in Law and Hüllen (1996), 123–40.

SWIGGERS, P. (1997), 'Language contact, language history and history of linguistics: John Palsgrave's "Anglo-French" grammar (1530)', in R. Hickey and S. Puppel (eds.), *Language history and linguistic modelling. A Festschrift for Jacek Fisiak on his 60th birthday*. Two vols (Berlin: de Gruyter), 929–40.

TANNEN, D. (1990), *You just don't understand: Women and men in conversation* (New York: Ballentine).

TAYLOR, J. R. (1989), *Linguistic categorization. Prototypes in linguistic theory* (Oxford: Clarendon).

THORNE, B., and HENLEY, N. (1975), *Language and sex: Difference and dominance* (Rowley MA: Newbury House).

—— KRAMARAE, K., and HENLEY, N. (1983), *Language, gender, and society* (Rowley MA: Newbury House).

TITKIN, H. (1910), 'Wörterbücher der Zukunft', *Germanisch-Romanische Monatsschrift* 2: 243–53.

TOLLENAERE, F. DE (1960a), *Alfabetische of ideologische lexicografie?* (Leiden: Brill).

—— (1960b), 'Lexicographie alphabétique ou idéologique', *Cahiers de lexicologie* 2: 19–29.

TOTOK, W. (1981), *Handbuch der Geschichte der Philosophie IV: Frühe Neuzeit 17. Jahrhundert* (Frankfurt: Klostermann).

TRIER, J. (1931), *Der deutsche Wortschatz im Sinnbezirk des Verstandes. Von den Anfängen bis zum Beginn des 13. Jahrhunderts* (Heidelberg: Winter). 2nd edn. (1973).

ULLMANN, S. (1962), *Semantics: An introduction to the science of meaning* (Oxford: Blackwell). Reprint (1972).

—— (1967), *The Principles of Semantics* (Oxford: Blackwell).

URBANKOVÁ, E. (1959), *Soupis děl J. A. Komenského v československých knihovnach, archiveh a muséich* [= List of the writings of J. A. Comenius in the Czechoslovak libraries, archives, and museums].(Prague: Státní pedagogické nakladatelstvi (= State pedagogical publishing house)).

VANN, W. H. [1924], *Notes on the writings of James Howell* (Waco, TX: Baylor University Press).

VATER, J. S. (1815), *Linguarum totius orbis index alphabeticus . . . . Litteratur der Grammatiken, Lexika und Wörtersammlungen aller Sprachen der Erde* (Berlin: s.n.). 2nd edn. 1847.

VINEIS, E. (1994), '[Medieval] linguistics and grammar', in G. Lepschy (ed.), *History*, vol. II: 'Classical and medieval linguistics' (London and New York: Longman), 136–96.

VOLKMANN, L. (1929), 'Ars memorativa', *Jahrbuch der kunsthistorischen Sammlungen*, Vienna, 30: 111–203.

WARNICKE, R. M. (1989), *The rise and fall of Anne Boleyn. Familiy politics at the court of Henry VIII* (Cambridge: Cambridge University Press).

WASWO, R. (1987), *Language and meaning in the Renaissance* (Princeton: Princeton University Press).

WATSON, F. (1909), *The beginnings of the teaching of modern subjects in England* (London: Pitman). Reprint (Menston: Scolar 1971).

WATSON, F. (1968), *The English grammar schools to 1660. Their curriculum and practice* (London: Cass).

WEBSTER, C. (1975), *The great instauration. Science, medicine and reform 1626–1660* (London: Duckworth).

WEISGERBER, L. (1927), 'Die Bedeutungslehre—ein Irrweg der Sprachwissenschaft', *Germanisch-Romanische Monatsschrift* 15: 161–83.

WENINGER, S. (1994), 'Das "Übersetzerbuch" des Elias von Nisibis (10./11. Jh.) im Zusammenhang der syrischen und arabischen Lexikographie', in Hüllen (1994c), 55–66.

WHEATLEY, H. B. (1865), 'Chronological notices of the dictionaries of the English language', *Transactions of the Philological Society* (London/Berlin: Asher & Co for the Philological Society), 218–93.

WHITNEY, E. (1990), 'Paradise restored. The mechanical arts from antiquity through the thirteenth century', *Transactions of the American Philosophical Society*, 80, 1.

WIEGAND, H. E. (1969–70), 'Synchronische Onomasiologie und Semasiologie. Kombinierte Methoden zur Strukturierung der Lexik', *Germanistische Linguistik* 1: 243–384.

—— (1996), 'Über usuelle und nichtusuelle Benennungskontexte in Alltag und Wissenschaft', in C. Knobloch and B. Schaeder (eds.), *Nomination—fachsprachlich und gemeinsprachlich* (Opladen: Westdeutscher Verlag), 55–103.

—— (1998), 'Historische Lexicographie', in W. Besch, A. Betten, O. Reichmann, and S. Sonderegger (eds.), *Sprachgeschichte. Ein Handbuch zur Geschichte der deutschen Sprache und ihrer Erforschung.* 2nd edn. (Berlin: de Gruyter), vol. 1, 643–715.

WILSON, R. M. (1958), 'The contents of the medieval library', in F. Wormald and C. E. Wright (eds.), *The English library before 1700. Studies in its history* (London: Athlone Press), 85–111.

WING, D. (1994), *Short-title catalogue of books printed in England, Scotland, Ireland, Wales and British America and of English books printed in other countries 1641–1700* . . . Revised by J. Morrison, C. W. Nelson, and M. Seccombe (New York: Modern Language Association).

WOOLHOUSE, R. S. (1971), *Locke's philosophy of science and knowledge* (Oxford: Oxford University Press).

YATES, F. A. (1966), *The art of memory* (London: Routledge & Kegan Paul).

YOUNG, R. F. (1932), *Comenius and the Indians of New England* (London: Hodgson).

ZAUNMÜLLER, W. (1958), *Bibliographisches Handbuch der Sprachwörterbücher. Ein internationales Verzeichnis von 5600 Wörterbüchern der Jahre 1460–1958 für mehr als 500 Sprachen und Dialekte. An annotated bibliography of language dictionaries. Bibliographie critique des dictionnaires linguistiques* (Stuttgart: Hiersemann).

ZGUSTA, L. (1971), *Manual of lexicography* (Prague / The Hague: Academia / Mouton).

—— with FARINA M. T. CR. (1988), *Lexicography today. An annotated bibliography of the theory of lexicography* (Tübingen: Niemeyer).

ZISCHKA, G. A. (1959), *Index lexicorum. Bibliographie der lexikalischen Nachschlagewerke* (New York: Hafner and Vienna: Hollinek).

ZÖLLNER, W. (1976), 'Mittelalterliche Enzyklopädien', in Diesner and Gurst (1976), 61–94.

Index

*Page references in **bold** type indicate primary treatment of the subject.*

William the Conqueror 236
Willughby, F. 254, 292, 294
Wilson, R. M. 59, 151
Windet, J. 289
Wing, D. 384
Winthrop the Elder, J. 385
Winthrop the Younger, J. 385
Withals, J. 168–77, 178, 181–2, 184, 189, 201, 298,
    420
Wolfe, R. 155
Woolhouse, R. S. 445
wordbook 66, **78**, 81, 88, 90, 97
word-field 13, 18
word-list 4, 18, 21, 23, 26, 30, 33–5, 46, 47,
    51–3, 66, 69, 78, 79, 81, 88, 97, 99, 102,
    104, 105, 117, 118, 122, 130, 132, 143–7,
    151, 154, 161, 162, 201, 230, 246, 247,
    250, 252, 261, 265, 285, 290, 299, 305,
    316, 319, 329, 330, 332, 338, 356, 378,
    380, 381, 386, 439, 444
Wortfeld 213, 214, 220
Wotton, A. 286
Wright, C. E. 81, 83
Wright. T. 55, 63, 66, 67, 68, 79, 133
Wright, W. A. 90

Wülcker, R. P. 55, 63, 66, 67, 68, 79, 133
Wüst, W. 18
Wyatt, Sir Thomas 150
Wyght, J. 157
Wykes, H. 169

Xiong, Yang 31

Yates, F. 50
Young, R. F. 385
Yūhannā 'l-Sammanūdi 33
Yule, G. 23

Zainer, G. 320
Zauner, A. 16
Zaunmüller, W. 38
Zedler, J. H. 447
Zetznerus, E. 380
Zeus, I. C. 65
Zgusta, L. 4, 5, 20
Zischka, G. A. 38
Zöllner, W. 436
Zupitza, J. 63, 65
Zwey-fache Gründliche Sprach-Lehr 129